# The Courts in Our Criminal Justice System

❖

## JON'A F. MEYER, Ph.D

Rutgers University

## DIANA R. GRANT, Ph.D

Sonoma State University

Upper Saddle River, New Jersey 07458

**Library of Congress Cataloging-in-Publication Data**

Meyer, Jon'a
    The courts in our criminal justice system / Jon'a F. Meyer, Diana R. Grant.
      p.  cm.
    Includes bibliographical references.
    ISBN 0-13-525957-6
    1. Criminal courts—United States.    I. Grant, Diana Ruth.    II. Title.
KF9223.M49 2002
345.73'01—dc21                      2002066342


**Publisher:** Jeff Johnston
**Executive Editor:** Kim Davies
**Assistant Editor:** Sarah Holle
**Production Editor:** Kathleen Glidden, Stratford Publishing Services
**Production Liaison:** Barbara Marttine Cappuccio
**Director of Production and Manufacturing:** Bruce Johnson
**Managing Editor:** Mary Carnis
**Manufacturing Buyer:** Cathleen Petersen
**Creative Director:** Cheryl Asherman
**Cover Design Coordinator:** Miguel Ortiz
**Cover Design:** Marianne Frasco
**Cover Image:** Steve Dunwell/The Image Bank
**Formatting and Interior Design:** Stratford Publishing Services
**Printing and Binding:** Phoenix Book Tech Park


Pearson Education LTD, *London*
Pearson Education Australia PTY, Limited, *Sydney*
Pearson Education Singapore, Pte. Ltd.
Pearson Education North Asia Ltd., *Hong Kong*
Pearson Education Canada, Ltd., *Toronto*
Pearson Educación de Mexico, S.A. de C.V.
Pearson Education—Japan, *Tokyo*
Pearson Education Malaysia, Pte. Ltd.

10  9  8  7  6  5

ISBN 0-13-525957-6

# Dedication

For our parents, Jon and Faye, and Karlyn and Quinton;
for Paul Jesilow, for his valued mentorship;
and for Humayun, for his patience and support during this writing process

*Malama pono, Malama i na kupuna*
Be righteous and cherish the heritage of our ancestors

# Contents

❖

# Preface

❖

*The Courts in Our Criminal Justice System* looks at the role of American criminal courts in the broader context of the American legal system. We designed this text and the Instructor's Manual with the goal of helping students understand and appreciate the complexities of the court system; for example, by comparing the functioning of the court system in theory and in practice. We have also provided students with a rich picture of the history of the American court system in order to show how the roles and functions of our courts have developed in response to societal changes. We believe this historical perspective, in conjunction with the text's focus on how our courts grapple with current legal and societal issues, will help students understand the broader context of the American court system.

Throughout the text, we consistently provide examples designed to help students appreciate the relevance and impact of the courts on the daily lives of people living in the United States; whether they are ordinary people who have little contact with the courts but whose lives are influenced by court decisions on civil liberties questions; or people who have direct contact with the court system, such as defendants, victims, jurors, or witnesses; or people who work within the legal system itself.

One of our purposes in writing this text was to combine our individual strengths to paint an accurate and engaging portrait of American courts and processes over time and in the modern era. Throughout the text are boxes, designed to provide you with additional material and to bring the subject of courts alive. We hope you complete this text and course with both interest in and passion for our legal system. As you read and learn more about our justice system, think about the importance the courts—and the individual criminal justice agencies with which they interact—have for you as a private citizen. Even if you do not have direct contact with the courts, they are important for you to understand.

While we were in the process of writing this book, the events of September 11, 2001, occurred. These events and the domestic and worldwide reactions to them have made it even clearer how the rule of law, embodied by the activities of the legislative, judicial, and executive branches of our government, reflects and shapes current political, social, and cultural concerns. As a democratic society founded on the premise of respect for freedom, individuality, and a commitment to the rule of law, America faces the challenge of responding in a way that exemplifies such ideals. As we work on this task, it will undoubtedly highlight the critical—and often underappreciated—role that our court system plays in not simply legal change, but societal change as well.

We kindly solicit your input concerning any facet of this text. Feel free to contact either of us if you have ideas for improving it.

Jon'a F. Meyer, Ph.D
Department of Sociology, Anthropology, and Criminal Justice
Rutgers University
311 N. Fifth Street
Camden, NJ 08102
meyerj@camden.rutgers.edu

Diana R. Grant, Ph.D
Criminal Justice Administration
Sonoma State University
1801 East Cotati Avenue
Rohnert Park, CA 94928
diana.grant@sonoma.edu

# Acknowledgments

❖

We owe special thanks to the many research assistants and others who helped us at all stages of the writing. The project may not have taken place without the assistance of many people, including Michael Cerkez, Gemma Espiritu, Christine Hastings, Mary Lou Franco, Angela Mayes, and Suzanne Williams.

We would also like to thank Evelyn Dormekpor, Faye Hart, and Sarah Holle, and the Prentice Hall reviewers listed below for their comments on earlier versions. Without the assistance provided by Prentice Hall staffers through the editing, copy editing, and final production stages, this book would never have come out.

We also wish to thank the judges and courtroom staff whose interview segments appear in this text. Their insight and comments add a valuable context to this work and we thank them for that. We extend hearty thanks to Phyllis B. Gerstenfeld, an expert in juvenile justice, who contributed the chapter on juvenile courts. Also important are the many students (and others) who contributed their own writings for inclusion in the text. While they are named near their own selections, they deserve a sincere thank you for allowing us to use their materials. And thanks to our secretaries, who put up with last-minute requests for copies and mailing: June Chaffin, Thea Dugan, and Jean Langevin.

We wish to thank the following reviewers: Judith Hails Kaci, California State University, Long Beach, California; Robert Lockwood, Portland State University, Portland, Oregon; Louis Holscher, San Jose State University, San Jose, California; Gayle Fisher-Stewart, University of Maryland, College Park, Maryland; William Kelly, Auburn University, Auburn, Alabama; Marty Gruher, Rogue Community College, Grants Pass, Oregon; Barbara Belbot, University of Houston-Downtown, Houston, Texas; Carolyn Brown-Dennis, Fayetteville Technical Community College, Fayetteville, North Carolina; and G. G. Hunt, Wharton County Junior College, Wharton, Texas.

Lastly, we thank our friends and family, who have been tremendous sources of happiness and support for us when times were difficult. When we needed ideas and suggestions, these were the people we turned to first. We thank them all, but foremost among them are Gloria and Tom Bogdan, Humayun Deura, Paul Jesilow, and James Zion.

# PART I

# Introduction to the Courts

# Step 1
## A Society Designs Laws

---------------------------------- ❖ ----------------------------------

The judge's powerful shouts of "Order in the court!" combine with the pounding of his gavel, but these sounds are easily overpowered by the clamor of the courtroom spectators, many of whom are eyewitnesses in the murder trial. As usual, the courtroom is packed with people of all ages, shapes, and sizes. The prosecutor and defense attorney, both well-prepared adversaries, have butted heads throughout the trial, but now defense attorney Perry Mason has gained the upper hand by skillfully maneuvering the prosecution's star witness into confessing on the stand. The courtroom murmur is slow to subside as the poor fool continues to provide all the sordid details of the infamous crime, while the court stenographer records every word he says and all the other eyewitnesses and the prosecution look on in utter disbelief. Justice triumphs again as the former witness trades places with the innocent accused as the focus of inquiry.

This courtroom scene is familiar to most Americans and may form the basis of their information about the courts. Unfortunately, legal docudramas like *Perry Mason* are best viewed as entertainment rather than education. This is not to downplay the value of Perry Mason and his fellow television attorneys. Together, they generate and maintain interest in the courts, and it may be shows like *Law & Order,* or *The Practice,* or *Judge Judy* that sparked your interest in knowing more about the courts. However, these programs should not be seen as examples of real courtroom activity.

This book will take you on a tour of America's courts from the design of laws to the trial and beyond. You will learn about those who make the courts work, from the judges and attorneys to the citizens who might serve as witnesses, jurors, victims, or defendants. When you have completed this book, you will be familiar with numerous court processes and will be able to point out the factual errors in your favorite (or least favorite) legal docudrama. Let the tour begin!

This first step will introduce you to the courts and the role they play in society. It will also present a brief discussion of our legal heritage and the nature of criminal law. We will also discuss some case studies that help explain courts and the law, then finish up with some justice themes for you to consider.

## THE CREATION OF LAWS

Any welcome to the courts would have to begin with how laws come to be and the rules for lawmaking. In democracies like ours, laws are bodies of rules enacted by public officials. The legislative branch of government (state or federal legislators) enacts laws. Once enacted, laws are then enforced by the executive branch, which controls law enforcement agencies. The judicial branch acts as more of a referee by applying laws and making sure laws are valid when compared to the principles in the United States Constitution and other important American legal documents, including prior court decisions. Because we have a system of checks and balances, no single branch is free to act without some oversight from the other two branches.

The Capitol in Washington, D.C., is the premier site of federal lawmaking in this country. The building houses the meeting chambers for Congress, which includes the Senate and House of Representatives. Citizens (such as the group on the steps holding banners) sometimes try to drum up support for laws in order to get them sponsored by a legislative representative. Though most of Congress's work is done in committees, the public is invited to observe them at work in the chambers. After discussions, sometimes brief, but often protracted, votes are cast by the lawmakers. If you want to see lawmaking in progress, you could also visit your local town or city hall, or travel to your state's capital and view the state legislature, which is empowered to create laws that apply to a whole state rather than one jurisdiction. Federal laws are the purview of Congress in Washington, D.C., and federal executive agencies such as the Environmental Protection Agency.   SOURCE: Courtesy of Jon'a Meyer.

## Neonaticide As a Case Study

Let us consider neonaticide as a case study to illustrate how laws come to be. Neonaticide, the killing of a newborn within the first twenty-four hours of life, has become a common topic of discussion in the past few years, in part because of the intense media coverage of Amy Grossberg and Brian Peterson, whose newborn son was discovered in a garbage bin in Delaware in November 1996. Because of this coverage, the public became immediately convinced that the incidence of neonaticide is increasing and demanded penalties to deter the crime in the future.

Actually, neonaticide has been around since ancient times. The early Greeks left unwanted newborns on hillsides to die of exposure. Tribal societies around the world practiced neonaticide to regulate births when resources were scarce or the number of children grew too large for the community to support. These early societies considered neonaticide to be an acceptable form of postpartum birth control.[1]

Neonaticide was tolerated in early and medieval England, but it began to attract the public's attention and condemnation during the sixteenth and seventeenth centuries in Europe. Citizens began to question the morals of young women who engaged in extramarital sexual intercourse and, after skillfully concealing their pregnancies, disposed of the evidence of the disgraceful liaisons. To complicate matters, women who were formally charged with murdering their illegitimate newborns often claimed that the children had been born dead and then disposed of by the distraught mothers. The lack of available medical knowledge made it difficult to prove otherwise.

The topic continued to gather more and more interest and generated increasing concern about the actions until finally Britain's parliament passed the 1624 Act to Prevent the Destroying and Murdering of Bastard Children, which doomed any woman who concealed the death of her illegitimate child. The 1624 Act held that mothers who could not produce at least one witness to corroborate their claims of stillborn children would be put to death as in other murder cases. As a side note, one way to escape the death penalty was to claim the "benefit of linen." Women who had taken concrete steps to prepare for the birth of their children, including the manufacture of the child's linen birth goods (blankets, clothing, etc.), were considered to have planned for a live birth and were eligible for acquittal.

Curiously, the Act applied only to illegitimate children born to unmarried women (Ledwon, 1996, p. 5). The first part of the 1680 version of the Act is presented in Box 1.1. *(NOTE: Numbered boxes appear throughout the text to provide you with additional material to help you understand how courts and law operate; they contain in-depth quotes or excerpts from court cases, summaries of actual cases, tables, graphs, and other important material.)* As you read the Act, consider the motivations behind the law (i.e., what the lawmakers envisioned was causing neonaticides). What can we say about the society in which this law was written?

The disapproval of neonaticide was by no means limited to England, as Scotland passed similar legislation in 1690. Once the laws were in place, women could

---

**BOX 1.1**

## The Text of the 1680 Act to Prevent the
## Destroying and Murdering of Bastard Children

Whereas many Lewd Women that have been delivered of Bastard Children, to avoid their shame and to escape punishment do secretly bury or conceal the Death of their Children; and after, if the Child be found dead, the said Women do alledge that the said Child was born dead, whereas it falleth out some times (although hardly it is to be proved), that the said Child or Children were Murthered by the said Women, their lewd Mothers, or by their assent or procurement.

For the preventing therefore of this great mischief, Be it Enacted by the Authority of this present Parliament, that if any Women after one month next ensuing the end of this next Session of Parliament, be delivered of any Issue of her body, Male or Female, which being born alive, should by the Laws of this Realm be a bastard, and that the endeavour privately either by drowning or secret burying thereof, or any other way, either by her self or the procuring of others, so to conceal the death thereof, as that it may not come to light, whether it were born alive or not, but be concealed; In every such case, the said Mother so offending shall suffer Death, as in case of murther, except such Mother can make proof by one Witness at the least, that the Child (whose death by her so intended to be concealed) was born dead (Vvagstaffe, 1680).

---

be, and were, hung for the deaths of their newborns, regardless of whether they had actually killed the children. Deterrence was definitely in the air, as judges handed down harsh penalties. One midwife who had allowed pregnant girls to live in her house and had then helped them kill and dispose of their unwanted infants was roasted alive in a cage with sixteen wildcats for her crimes (Unknown, 1673).

Reading the Act illuminates a great deal about lawmaking. First, the Act describes the problem at hand. Policymakers perceived an increase in sexually active unmarried women (i.e., "lewd women") killing their newborns following concealed pregnancies. The policymakers attribute this to the shame associated with illegitimate children and also to a fear of punishment (it is important for us to remember that nonmarital sexual relations and illegitimate births at that time in history subjected women to whippings, incarceration, and other punishments [Hoffer and Hull, 1981, pp. 13–14]). Community leaders also saw this law as a way to get around the difficulty of establishing proof in cases that might be otherwise impossible to prove (absent marks of violence on the victim's body, scholars in the early 1600s had no forensic tests to ascertain whether a child had been born alive). Indeed, it was hoped that this law would eliminate, through deterrence, the problem of discarded newborns, especially as denouncing the crime in church had not achieved that goal.

One of the most interesting features of this law is that it departs from the Anglo-Saxon legal maxim "innocent until proven guilty." The Act was atypical in this regard. The rationale for England's Parliament to eliminate the burden of proof for neonaticide lies in the pressure on legislators to reduce the incidence of new-born murders, which were attributed to poor servants whose sexual liaisons had been condemned by policymakers for some time. What was society to do when prosecutors could not prove that newborn after newborn was being delivered alive and then murdered? The Act against neonaticide shows how desperate the courts and legal system must have been. Of interest, it was not until 1803 that the law was changed to require the prosecution to prove the victim was born alive, making the burden of proof similar to other murder cases (Rose, 1986, p. 70).

Note also that the law spells out clearly the evidence required for a woman to avoid conviction and execution if her newborn was found dead after a concealed pregnancy (i.e., having "one Witness at the least" who could testify that the child was stillborn). Although most modern laws are the opposite because they provide the requirements for conviction (e.g., a person who "threatens another with" bodily harm during the course of a theft is guilty of robbery in New Jersey, Penal Code 2C:15–1), some do provide circumstances that point to a defendant's innocence. Married individuals who marry a second spouse can be convicted of bigamy in New Jersey, for example, "unless at the time of the subsequent marriage" one of four special circumstances is present, such as believing one's first spouse is dead or "reasonably" believing one is "legally eligible to remarry" (NJ Penal Code 2C:24–1). Still, the law against neonaticide is unique in that it automatically promoted to capital murder the concealment of any dead newborn's body, making it an early example of a felony murder law (you will learn about felony murder laws in Step 2).

Another very important concept is illustrated by the Act against neonaticide. Note that the law applied only to births that occurred after a future date (i.e., those occurring "after one month next ensuing the end of this next Session of Parliament"). This meant that women who had concealed the births of bastard newborns before that time could not be prosecuted under this law. It appears that long before the United States and our Constitution, the idea of *ex post facto* laws was already considered repugnant. You will learn more about *ex post facto* laws later in this chapter.

Unfortunately for the legal system, the Act did not eliminate neonaticide and the law fell out of favor with the public, who felt it was too harsh. During periods of economic difficulties, juries began to acquit maids and household servants whose homicidal actions appeared to be based on desperation rather than depravity. During the height of the Victorian era and the Industrial Revolution, deaths of children rose. During 1863–1887, infanticides comprised more than 60 percent of all recorded homicides in England (Rose, 1986). Child deaths were also common in nineteenth-century Ireland where, between 1866 and 1892, women killed their infants nearly 100 times more often than they killed older children or husbands (Conley, 1995). Despite the fact that the rate of infanticides remained high (Langer, 1974, p. 359), the rate of convictions by jury declined (Conley, 1995, p. 801; Jones, 1980, p. 62). Neonaticide, although still illegal and still occurring at high rates, seemed to go unpunished.

Some questions for you to consider are:

- What was going on that first attracted attention from the public and from lawmakers?
- Why were the laws written the way they were?
- Why did juries begin acquitting women, even after clamoring for harsher sentences?
- Why did the sentences return to being harsh?
- What lessons can we learn from this case study that could help contemporary lawmakers, who have recently been asked to craft new legislation to deal with the problem of women who kill their newborns?

## Lessons Learned from the Neonaticide Case Study

The preceding case study illustrates several points about lawmaking. First, an action must attract condemnation before laws are designed to eliminate it. In the case of neonaticide, the killing of newborns progressed from being socially accepted to socially condemned (although different segments of society reacted differently to the problem). If you look at the history of other laws, you will often see a similar pattern. Megan's Law (which requires sexual offenders to register with authorities so their neighbors will know there is a sex offender living in their communities), for example, followed public outcry during the 1990s about pedophiles who continued to victimize children even after treatment and/or punishment in the criminal justice system. The law was named for Megan Kanka, a seven-year-old who in 1994 was murdered in New Jersey by a twice-convicted child sex offender. All fifty states now have some version of Megan's Law, and federal law mandates that states create and maintain Megan's Law databases, or they lose part of their federal funding for law enforcement (Koenig, 1998, pp. 725, 729).

The neonaticide case study also illustrates the flexibility of the law in terms of reducing an individual's ability to avoid prosecution through creative excuses or defenses. In the case of neonaticide, public disapproval became so high that lawmakers made any woman who concealed her pregnancy liable for the death penalty if her child was found dead, even if she claimed the child had been stillborn. In many respects, contemporary mandatory sentences reflect the ability of the law to ensure that criminals receive the punishments that the public (through their legislators) feel are appropriate for their crimes.

The third point illustrated by this case study is that jurors who feel the penalties for a given crime are too harsh may ignore the law. When jurors began acquitting women in large numbers for committing neonaticide, the laws were, in fact, rewritten. In 1866, England's legislative body reacted to the softened public sentiment by considering a bill that would regard infanticide as a less serious form of homicide than other killings; the bill did not get enough support to make it law but demonstrates that the legislature was aware of the change in attitude toward neonaticide. Then, in 1922, England's lawmaking body passed a new law that made those who committed infanticide eligible for treatment rather than punishment. Contemporary jurors continue to acquit those they feel may be guilty but undeserving of potentially harsh punishments called for by law, or guilty parties they feel were unfairly treated by the justice system (e.g., criminals who were discriminatorily selected for arrest or who were mistreated by police). In refusing to convict, the juries send a message to the justice system that the public does not agree with the laws as written or that they disapprove of actions taken by the justice system.

Finally, this case study shows how societal sentiments are reflected in the laws generated by that society. Apathy was originally followed by ire, which was followed by sympathy for the women who killed their newborns. Ironically, this situation is now being repeated. Public sentiment is now calling for renewed attention to the problem of neonaticide. Right after Amy Grossberg and Brian Peterson were charged, most people demanded increased penalties, but after a few years, some people began to prefer social programs such as places where women can leave unwanted newborns without fear of prosecution. As you can see, the issue of neonaticide illustrates how law reflects societal norms and how laws can change over time to reflect new social thought.

## THE COMMON LAW HERITAGE OF THE AMERICAN LEGAL SYSTEM

The American common law system derives from medieval England, when criminal and civil laws were defined by judges on the basis of the individual cases over which they presided. Laws were based on existing customs as interpreted by judges because there were few if any written statutes except for the most serious crimes (and those were typically copied from the Bible). Historical common laws are sometimes called "judge made" laws for this reason. Two concepts are very important in the development of our current legal system from its common law roots.

The first important concept is precedent, or **stare decisis**. Precedent means that a judge must decide a case by applying the rules of law found in earlier cases, provided that the facts in the current case are similar. If they did not rely on precedent, judges would have to decide each case as though it were totally new. By employing stare decisis (literally, "let the decision stand"), however, a certain consistency develops in law. The doctrine of stare decisis does not apply when compelling reasons exist to modify or overturn prior decisions, such as when the notions of justice and fairness necessitate change. In those rare cases, prior decisions may be overturned in total or in part. For example, although the U.S. Supreme Court upheld the idea of "separate but equal" facilities for blacks and whites in their 1896 *Plessy v. Ferguson* decision, that case was overturned by *Brown v. Board of Education* in 1954. That prior cases are sometimes overturned should not be viewed as a weakness in our legal system; instead, this phenomenon shows how the laws can change to fit new circumstances and social definitions of fairness.

The second important concept when discussing our common law roots is codification. **Common law** is uncodified; that is, it is not written down in any one central place like a legal register.[2] **Codified law**, on the other hand, is based on written codes (statutes) that are maintained by the government (e.g., the monarch or legislature). Many early codes, like those written by the Anglo–Saxons around 600 A.D., appear to be a simple "recording of pre-existing custom" (Kempin, 1990, pp. 109–110). Later codes were enacted in a process closer to that now used in this country, where statutes came out of meetings of those individuals who were empowered to create law (e.g., legislators).

However, the American legal system is based on laws originally developed as part of common law. During the first half of the 1800s, legislatures started codifying the offenses defined under common law (Kempin, 1990, p. 113). By the early 1900s, most state legislatures had their own set of codified laws. When crafting those laws, legislatures had to keep two important concepts in mind: a requirement of fair notice and a ban on *ex post facto* laws. However, just because codified law is based in common law does not mean that it is static or unchanging, as we will see below.

## Fair Notice and *Ex Post Facto* Laws

The first important concept that must be considered by lawmakers is that of fair notice. Even today, those who read constitutional cases will observe that the notion of fair notice is mentioned repeatedly. Basically, **fair notice** means citizens must be forewarned that actions they are planning will be treated as illegal and that individuals cannot be tried for acts that do not involve such warnings. Fair notice can be achieved through codification of laws against an activity or it can be derived from prior rulings by a state's supreme court that an activity is punishable. Either way, citizens are alerted to the potential punishment that might follow actions they are contemplating. In 1926, the U.S. Supreme Court ruled that the Fourteenth Amendment's guarantee to due process meant that individuals could not be prosecuted for statutes that were incomprehensible by the public due to being written in vague terms, because such laws did not provide fair notice (*Connally v. General Construction Company*, 1926), and several laws have been invalidated for violating this important ban. Even common law jurisdictions have to provide fair notice to their citizens that certain acts will be treated as crimes, but this may be achieved either through legislation or through state supreme court rulings that particular acts will be considered illegal if committed in the future.

The second important concept that legislators must consider is the ban on *ex post facto* laws (i.e., laws that are retroactively applied to actions that took place before the law was enacted). *Ex post facto* laws are forbidden by the U.S. Constitution (art. 1, secs. 9 and 10), and were defined comprehensively by the U.S. Supreme Court in 1798 to include the enactment of new laws, modifications to existing laws, changes to the punishments associated with existing laws, and changes to existing evidentiary concerns (*Calder v. Bull*, 1798, p. 390). Taken together, these bans prohibit legislatures from holding defendants accountable for actions for which they had no prior knowledge. Whereas it is permissible and proper to update legal codes, individuals cannot be held responsible for actions they did before the changes took effect. Box 1.2 presents excerpts from the U.S. Supreme Court cases on fair notice and *ex post facto* laws. As you read them, consider how the concepts are similar, how they differ, and how they are related to American concepts of justice and fairness.

---

## BOX 1.2

## Excerpts from U.S. Supreme Court Cases on Fair Notice and *Ex Post Facto* Laws

The excerpts below illustrate the U.S. Supreme Court's thinking in two cases that helped define the rules that must be followed by legislatures when writing statutes. As you read them, consider how the concepts discussed are similar and how they differ. What is the overarching goal of both concepts?

The U.S. Supreme Court defined and clarified *ex post facto* laws in the 1798 case, *Calder v. Bull* (p. 390):

> The prohibition, "that no state shall pass any *ex post facto* law," necessarily requires some explanation; for, naked and without explanation, it is unintelligible, and means nothing. Literally, it is only, that a law shall not be passed concerning, and after the fact, or thing done, or action committed. . . . I will state what laws I consider *ex post facto* laws, within the words and the intent of the prohibition.
>
> 1st.  Every law that makes an action, done before the passing of the law, and which was innocent when done, criminal; and punishes such action.
>
> 2nd.  Every law that aggravates a crime, or makes it greater than it was, when committed.
>
> 3rd.  Every law that changes the punishment, and inflicts a greater punishment, than the law annexed to the crime, when committed.
>
> 4th.  Every law that alters the legal rules of evidence, and receives less, or different, testimony, than the law required at the time of the commission of the offence, in order to convict the offender.

In 1926, the U.S. Supreme Court ruled in *Connally v. General Construction Company* (p. 391) that due process requires that laws must not be vague:

> That the terms of a penal statute creating a new offense must be sufficiently explicit to inform those who are subject to it what conduct on their part will render them liable to its penalties is a well-recognized requirement, consonant alike with ordinary notions of fair play and the settled rules of law; and a statute which either forbids or requires the doing of an act in terms so vague that men of common intelligence must necessarily guess at its meaning and differ as to its application violates the first essential of due process of law.

# THE CONSTANT METAMORPHOSIS OF AMERICAN LAW

The American legal system undergoes constant metamorphosis. Every year, new laws are enacted to deal with current situations, old laws are modified in order to keep them up-to-date, and a few laws are removed from the codes. Many of these changes are rather minor, such as updating the amounts that qualify for grand theft, as inflation makes existing values appear outdated. At times, however, a state supreme court or the U.S. Supreme Court invalidates a law, and so it must be removed from future editions of the penal code. Sometimes new laws that reflect public sentiment against crime (e.g., "three strikes and you're out" laws) are enacted and take their place in the penal codes.

Sometimes new crimes are defined as people find new ways to harm others or offend society's principles. New laws often result from unsuccessful attempts to utilize existing laws to prosecute new forms of questionable behavior. After its surge in popularity as a tool to incapacitate rape and robbery victims, for example, the sale and distribution of the powerful tranquilizer Rohypnol (aka "roofies") was outlawed in 1997 by the California legislature (Leiser, 1997). The same legislature also made it illegal to recruit members into a gang. Both of these examples show how new laws may be enacted when previously existing statutes are inadequate to prosecute new forms of deviance.

Developing new laws is not always easy. As criminals have infiltrated the technological world, for example, legislatures have had a difficult time defining laws relating to computer crime. At first, prosecutors attempted to use existing common theft statutes to prosecute computer crimes, but judges sometimes dismissed the charges, saying the alleged actions were not prohibited by statute (Meyer and Short, 1998). In response to those dismissals, legislatures have attempted to fashion usable computer laws that define computer crimes and make it clear that they will be punished (Nugent, 1991).

Laws are not simply the inventions of a few legislators who hope laws will be named after them. Someone, or some group, influences legislators to write and sponsor laws. Child advocacy groups, for example, have been successful in modifying the statute of limitations for prosecution of child abuse; in some jurisdictions, this important clock begins ticking only after the victim knows about the abuse, even if it is "discovered" through therapy many years after the abusive actions (e.g., the state of Washington's "special" statute of limitations allows victims to bring claims against alleged child molesters within three years of the abusive act or within three years of discovering that it happened). A Michigan appellate court recently allowed a civil suit by a woman whose flashbacks, which occurred forty-nine years after the abuse she endured as a child, alerted her to the injuries she had suffered at the hands of her family (Memory of Abuse, 1993). Similarly, tort reform groups have successfully lobbied to limit punitive damages in many states and anti-drunk-driving groups have fought for legislation favorable to their agendas. Even well-known laws such as Megan's Law (which allows notification of the public regarding the presence of sexual offenders in their neighborhoods) and the hotly debated "three strikes and you're out" laws were sponsored by citizen's groups who argued their cause, gathered support, and lobbied for the law's passage. Without the support of many citizens, most laws in our society would never make it to the books. In this way, the citizens in democratic legal systems have some influence on the laws by which they are governed.

Occasionally, laws are passed that have the support of a vocal minority, but not necessarily the population as a whole. Laws such as Prohibition (which outlawed the manufacture, sale, or distribution of alcoholic beverages in the United States from 1920 until it was repealed in 1933) and 55-miles-per-hour speed limit laws are but two examples of laws that somehow obtained enough support from

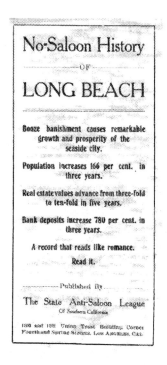

Though alcohol had been a concern for many years, the move toward Prohibition became national in the late 1800s when the Anti-Saloon League was founded. This pamphlet was created by the State Anti-Saloon League of Southern California and shows one way that groups wishing to outlaw the manufacture, distribution, and sales of alcohol gained support among the voting public. In 1918, due in part to the success of pamphlets like this one in attracting support, the Eighteenth Amendment was passed, which effectively outlawed alcohol in the United States. Due to public dissatisfaction with the law, the Eighteenth Amendment was finally repealed in 1933. Now, scholars use Prohibition as an example to show that laws cannot be successful without public support.   SOURCE: 1906 Prohibition pamphlet, personal collection of Jon'a Meyer.

lawmakers to get passed despite a lack of support from the majority of Americans. The process of lawmaking, then, is not purely democratic in the sense that only bills that are widely supported become laws. Sometimes, laws are imposed "from the top down," meaning that powerful elites pass laws that interest or benefit them, but do not appear to serve the rest of society. Many conflict theorists, for example, point to the weak enforcement and penalties attached to white-collar crimes, compared to low-level criminal offenses, as proof that laws can sometimes be imposed on the masses from those socially higher up. Consider the uproar over laws that mandate more severe penalties for possession of "crack" cocaine than for powder cocaine; many argue that these laws reflect the fact that inner-city blacks are more likely to be caught with crack whereas powder cocaine is more often used by upper-class whites (e.g., Mann, 1995). That the lawmaking process sometimes fails to reflect what the majority wants does not mean our system is irreparable. Instead, it points to an area where reform may be needed.

## ODDBALL CODES OF ANTIQUITY

In 1973, Federal judge Marvin Frankel decried the illogical hodgepodge of laws that existed in many states. He noted, for example, that a California statute punished breaking into a car to steal from its glove compartment with up to fifteen years in prison, whereas stealing the entire car carried a maximum of only ten years. Similarly, stealing a dog in Colorado could result in ten years in prison, whereas killing the same dog could result in only six months in jail and a fine. One compendium of humorous laws (Hyman, 1971) alerts readers that it is illegal to hunt camels in Arizona or to lasso fish in Knoxville, Tennessee. Similarly, those who tickle girls under the chin with a feather duster in Portland, Maine, face criminal prosecution. Obsolete codes sometimes remain on the books for years in a sort of legal limbo: not actively prosecuted, nor actually deleted. Most of these apparently bizarre codes would be stricken down by appellate courts as vague, discriminatory, or unrelated to public welfare. Until they are challenged, however, nothing prevents them from being reprinted each year as part of the codes.

These inconsistencies usually arise from knee-jerk reactions to a situation that attracts more than its fair share of media attention. California's specific attention to thefts from automobile glove compartments likely resulted from attempts to deter criminals from breaking into cars to rifle through their contents. When the legislature decided on a penalty, however, it forgot to scale it according to those of related crimes. In this manner, less serious offenses may be punished more harshly than more egregious acts.

Some of the ambiguities in law are discovered only after a statute has been enacted and the justice system has tried to apply it to an offense. The courts may discover that the ambiguities are so great that they prevent the statute from being used as law. This fate befell Jacksonville's municipal "prowling by auto" ordinance; it was held to be so vague that a reasonable person could not ascertain whether his or her intended activities would be illegal, so it had to be rejected as law by the court (*Papachristou v. City of Jacksonville,* 1972). Appellate courts may also rule that a statute is unacceptable as worded or "void for vagueness" (i.e., it did not provide "fair notice" about what actions were prohibited).

Sometimes there is an interesting interplay between legislators and judges as the judges attempt to circumvent the legislature's intent by employing "creative interpretation" of certain statutes, especially those requiring mandatory penalties (Meyer and Jesilow, 1997, pp. 54–57; Peyser and Foote, 1994, p. 53). In a few cases, legislatures intentionally leave the courts some discretion in interpreting statutes that are still undergoing what could be called a "fine-tuning process"; allowing judges to dismiss charges "in the interests of justice" is one way to acknowledge that statutes cannot be written to address every individual case.

At times the differences in statutes make plea bargains very attractive to defendants. If a similar criminal act could result in a much lower penalty, defense attorneys will try to establish bargains where their clients plea guilty to the related offense. In California, for example, attorneys for drunk drivers were successful at getting charges reduced to reckless driving and other lesser offenses for several years before the legislature took notice of the practice and passed a new law that forced prosecutors to justify such bargains in writing (CA Penal Code, sec. 23635).

If there is one thing history has clearly demonstrated, it is that merely drafting and enacting laws does not mean they will be logical. Nor must they be fair. Although the inconsistencies in laws can usually be traced to knee-jerk reactions, oddball codes still make for fascinating study. The next time you encounter a law you think is peculiar, stop and think about how it came to be. Think also about the historical time and situations under which the law might have been drafted and what the law meant to those who created it.

## THE EFFECTS OF CRIMINAL LAW ON THE COURTS

Criminal law affects the courts in several ways. First, it delineates the offenses that form the basis for criminal justice intervention. If no laws have been broken, there cannot be a criminal trial. When there are multiple elements to a crime, the courts must ensure that each element is proven; one cannot be convicted of grand theft, for example, unless she or he has been shown to have (1) stolen something that was (2) worth a certain amount. If one or more elements cannot be shown to be true in a particular case, the defendant is not guilty of that particular charge.

The penal codes also define the penalties that accompany each code violation, and courts then determine what penalty will apply in a particular case. Penal codes specify the types of punishment that may be imposed on offenders. Speeding, for

Laws are not actually "made" here, but the U.S. Supreme Court still has a strong influence on law-making because it serves as the final authority on whether laws are constitutional. Even if a law was enacted with huge public support, it could be ruled invalid by the U.S. Supreme Court. SOURCE: Courtesy of Jon'a Meyer.

example, is usually punished by a fine or community service term. Theft can be punished by fines, community service, or other sanctions, including jail time. Penal codes also specify the severity of the penalties allowed under law. For example, those convicted of first degree murder may be executed in jurisdictions that allow that penalty, but petty thieves cannot. Some statutes specify mandatory penalties that judges must impose on those found guilty of certain offenses. This is especially true of drunk drivers; many states now have mandatory penalties for those convicted of driving under the influence of alcohol.

Finally, criminal law affects the courts by specifying the processes by which trials are conducted. Appellate courts, including the U.S. Supreme Court, hand down rulings about what is and what is not acceptable criminal court procedure. Rulings based on the constitutionality of certain statutory provisions, for example, can have profound effects on final trial outcomes.

## TWO MODELS FOR HOW CASES PROGRESS THROUGH THE COURTS

In 1968, noted scholar Herbert Packer argued that the effects of criminal law on the courts are mediated somewhat by whether emphasis is placed on defendants' due process rights or whether the primary goal of a legal system is to curb crime.

Packer created two primary models to explain how the criminal justice system operates: the Crime Control Model and the Due Process Model. He did not intend for people to use his models as "rigid" categories (meaning that every element of the model must be satisfied to earn a classification as Crime Control versus Due Process); instead, he felt that the models represent extreme values between which the criminal justice system and its workers may lie (1968, pp. 153–54). With this in mind, let us discuss the differences between the two models. The following summary presents only some of the differences between Packer's two models; the interested student is referred to his book to learn more about his models and how they work.

The first approach is the **Crime Control Model**, which views the purpose of the court as punishing guilty parties promptly and efficiently in an attempt to reduce crime. Under this model, trained law enforcement officials and prosecutors are entrusted with protecting society. There are, of course, some trade-offs for a safe society, one of which is the relinquishment by members of society of some of their rights.

Those who support the Crime Control Model feel that the vast majority of defendants are guilty of some crime or they would not have been arrested in the first place. Because of this belief, the Crime Control Model sometimes tolerates punishment of otherwise "innocent" defendants. In the end, truly innocent parties need not fear punishment because diligent work by police and prosecutors will eliminate their cases from the court docket prior to trial. Legal safeguards such as strict search and seizure rules are used by guilty defendants to circumvent justice and escape punishment, so they should be abolished or minimized. Plea bargains are desirable because they provide punishment to guilty parties while simultaneously ensuring that the system is not bogged down in cases. Crime Control Model advocates favor punishment that deters offenders and others from committing crimes because deterrence reduces the incidence of crime.

The second approach discussed by Packer is the **Due Process Model**, which views the purpose of courts as more of a forum in which judges and other justice workers must protect defendants' rights to due process from overzealous police and/or prosecutors. With this model, the police and prosecutors cannot be trusted to select only guilty parties for criminal justice processing, because, for example, science is not yet advanced enough to guarantee accurate classification in every case.

The Due Process Model considers all defendants to be innocent until proven guilty, so many safeguards (e.g., strict search and seizure rules and the absolute right to legal counsel) are necessary to protect defendants at all stages of the justice system. Plea bargains must be eschewed as cheap imitations of justice that encourage innocent parties to relinquish their rights to a full trial during which mistakes by police and prosecutors could be uncovered. Due Process Model advocates favor treatment programs that effectively help offenders avoid future criminality, thus reducing the incidence of crime.

As should be evident by now, the Crime Control Model "de-emphasizes [the] adversary aspect of the process; the Due Process Model tends to make it central" (Packer, 1968, p. 157). Stop and think for a moment about which model you most support. You may identify strongly with one of the models or you may simply support one more than the other. Either position is fine, because very few people completely assign themselves to one of the two models. Write down your rationale for why you identify with the model you selected, because you may wish to compare your current beliefs to the ones you will have after reading this book or when you graduate from college. Packer noted that people move back and forth on his continuum over time, so you may find yourself moving away from your current beliefs, or you may move closer to the extreme to which you now ascribe.

The importance of Packer's two models for the courts is that they help explain how individual workers and agencies in the criminal justice system interact. It should come as no surprise, for example, that judges who lean toward the Due Process Model are more likely to throw out evidence obtained by the police under questionable circumstances (e.g., without a warrant), whereas judges who lean toward the Crime Control Model may be more likely to view certain evidence as important in showing whether a given defendant is guilty (Packer, 1968, pp. 198–201). Of course, the labels we place on those judges (as leaning toward one of the models), or even the labels they use to describe themselves, cannot predict their behavior on every decision they make because we must acknowledge that the models are but general classification schemes and do not apply to individual decisions. In fact, a person may lean toward the Due Process Model on some issues (e.g., she or he might insist that all defendants have access to free, quality attorneys at all stages of the system) and yet support the Crime Control Model for other issues (e.g., the same person may feel that search and seizure rules are too restrictive to allow the police to effectively investigate crimes). As you read this book, consider which models the players in the system seem to support and how their beliefs may affect justice outcomes.

## SOME IMPORTANT THEMES TO CONSIDER WHEN READING THIS BOOK

No examination of American courts would be complete without some important social considerations. First is the expectation that courts dispense justice fairly. When the public expects fairness but instead sees corruption and discrimination, people might lose their faith in the courts. Unfortunately, corruption and discrimination sometimes do occur in our court system, despite the presence of safeguards against these negative outcomes. Although it may be argued that racial biases are less prevalent than before the civil rights movement, for example, such biases continue to be alleged on a regular basis. One goal of the courts is to dispense justice whenever it is needed, but some critics have noted that access to the courts is curtailed for the poor and/or uneducated. As you are reading this text, consider the situations under which corruption and discrimination have occurred in the past and how those two issues are relevant in today's courts. Also consider how the identity of the groups that most feel the brunt of discrimination have changed over time.

The second important consideration is the difference between "law on the books" and "law in action." Just because a law is written (i.e., "on the books") does not mean it is enforced as it was intended. Instead, how the law is enforced may depend on the characteristics of those who enforce it or those against whom it is enforced. While we all agree that violent crimes should be illegal, we also acknowledge that all violence is not treated as equal by the courts. Consider, for example, the difference in priority assigned to violent acts committed by strangers versus those that occur between intimates or acquaintances. Similarly, are there differences in priority assigned to embezzlement perpetuated by white-collar criminals versus thefts committed by burglars?

A third issue you should watch for are examples of how the law is both a catalyst for and a reflection of social change. In some cases, a law creates social change (e.g., affirmative actions laws attempt to create a workplace that is race- and gender-neutral). At the same time, however, laws may reflect social changes (e.g., extending pornography laws into the cyber-realm through laws against cyberporn). In many cases, a law can serve both functions, reflecting the social values held by a majority who hope that the law will produce a value change in those who do not yet share their views (e.g., laws against hate crimes attempt to educate the public that hateful actions are undesirable and may be punished). The role of law as a catalyst for and reflection of social change is an important one, and recognizing this role will help you understand how American courts and law function.

Finally, there is the reality of the courts and how it differs from how the courts "are supposed to" operate. Pay attention to the theoretical goals of the courts, how the courts theoretically function, and how the laws are theoretically carried out. How do the theoretical workings differ from what really happens in the courts? Theoretically, the courts devote as much time to a case as is necessary to fully explore the legal issues involved, but the reality is that courtroom workers are more likely to be hurried through much of the work they do. Theoretically, only legal factors, such as offense severity, play a role in sentencing, but the reality is that many extra-legal factors, such as whether one pleads guilty, play a large role in sentencing. The examples are endless, as you will see as you read and reflect on the text.

## CONCLUSION

In this chapter, we did a lot of things. First, we looked at how laws are created, and studied some historical laws against neonaticide as a case study to understand how laws come to exist. Then, we looked at how American law is always changing and will continue to change. We also explored how criminal law affects the courts and learned about Packer's models as to how the courts operate. Finally, we considered some themes that are important in criminal justice and that you should be on the lookout for as you read this text. This introductory chapter served to alert you to a number of issues and to set the stage for the rest of this book.

In the next chapter, we will get into the study of courts themselves. We will learn about the three elements of every crime and about some of the defenses raised by defendants in court to excuse their actions. We will also learn what happens after a crime has been committed, but before a trial takes place. Do not worry, we will learn about trial processes, too, but that topic is saved for a future chapter.

Future chapters in this section of the book discuss defendants' rights in the criminal justice system, how the adversarial system works (or is supposed to work), the history of federal and state courts, and how the courts operate. The next section of the book is devoted to the players in the justice drama, including the "big three" (i.e., prosecutors, defense attorneys, and judges), and other important people in the system such as victims, defendants, jurors, witnesses, and others who interact with the courts. The third section of the book will expose you to courtroom processes, including pre-trial screening by prosecutors and other justice decision-makers, how the bail system works, pre-trial motions, plea bargaining, and the trial

---

## BOX 1.3

## Accounts Written by Three Students About Their First Encounter with American Courts

Shannon L. Williams was amazed at how "calm" everyone was:

> The defendant, the plaintiff, the prosecution, the defense, the jury, and the audience for both sides were in a calm and very cool manner throughout the entire case. I guess I'm used to seeing a little tension between the people involved in the case like one would normally see in television shows like *Judge Judy* or *Matlock*. That was practically my first time ever being in a courtroom and I guess I was expecting to see some clashing in the courtroom and the judge ordering the bailiff to remove somebody from the courtroom. As stated before, it was a little different than what I had expected.

Kathleen Garrity noticed that lower courts were very busy:

> I found the whole court scene very disruptive and was waiting for the judge to call out, "ORDER IN THE COURT," however, he never did.

Shauna Y. Creek noted the same about another city court:

> The courtroom waiting area was chaotic, crowded, and tension filled. Observing the waiting area was very emotional. There were mothers who wept for their sons' freedom, victims who were leaving the courtroom with complacent smiles, and counselor/accused interactions all going on as court was in session.

itself. The final section will expose you to post-conviction processes, such as how punishment is decided and how appeals work, and will discuss the special court processes used when the accused is a juvenile.

Do not worry if all you know about courts is from television and media accounts, because you are not alone. This book will help you learn about courts and their inner workings. Box 1.3 contains excerpts written by students like you about their first experience with the courts, and you will notice that all three were surprised at what they saw. You will hear from these and other students later in the book wherever their observations are pertinent. Now, let us begin our journey through the American courts system!

## DISCUSSION QUESTIONS

1. Laws are everywhere I look and I haven't gotten out of bed yet! Laws regulate the manufacture of the mattress on which I sleep and the packaging of the milk I drink with my breakfast. Think of all the laws that have affected you in the last twenty-four hours (e.g., manufacturing/packaging laws, road laws, criminal laws, etc.). Why were these laws passed? How are they enforced? Do you feel they are a good idea?

2. Think of a social problem that interests you (e.g., racial discrimination). How have laws dealt with that problem in the past (this might require some library research)? What laws do you feel are necessary to alleviate the social problem? Do you feel that new laws are the best solution, or would another plan of action be better? Why do you feel this way?

3. Think of your favorite character in a courtroom docudrama. To which of Packer's models does she or he lean? What about the character you dislike most? How close are these two characters to your own leanings? Are you closest to your favorite or least favorite character's leanings?

4. What is a new form of deviance that is attracting attention and against which the public (or certain interest groups) wants a law to be enacted? Why haven't existing laws been adequate?

5. Think of five court-related questions that you want answers to this term. During the course of the term, try to find the answers (e.g., in the class text or a library resource or by asking your instructor). At the end of this term, you will re-read your list to see if you have learned the answers.

## NOTES

1. And, anthropological data suggests that some societies still believe that neonaticide is an acceptable practice (e.g., Jones, 1980).

2. Note that contemporary jurisdictions that use common law rely on both codification and rulings by their state's supreme court to arrive at an enforceable body of law. This stands in contrast to historical common law, which was not typically written down and kept in a central location.

## REFERENCES

*Brown v. Board of Education*, 347 U.S. 483 (1954).

*Calder v. Bull*, 3 U.S. 386 (1798).

California Penal Code. (2001). *West's California Codes: Penal Code*. St. Paul, MN: West.

*Connally v. General Construction Company*, 269 U.S. 385 (1926).

Conley, C. (1995). No pedestals: Women and violence in late nineteenth-century Ireland. *Journal of Social History*, 28: 801–819.

Frankel, M. (1973). *Criminal Sentences: Law without Order*. New York: Hill and Wang.

Hoffer, P.C., and Hull, N.E.H. (1981). *Murdering Mothers: Infanticide in England and New England, 1558–1803*. New York: New York University Press.

Hyman, D. (1971). *It's Against the Law*. Pleasantville, NY: Reader's Digest Association.

Jones, A. (1980). *Women Who Kill*. New York: Holt, Rinehart and Winston.

Kempin, F.G. (1990). *Historical Introduction to Anglo-American Law* (3rd ed.). St. Paul, MN: West.

Koenig, W. P. (1998). Does Congress abuse its spending clause power by attaching conditions on the receipt of federal law enforcement funds to a state's compliance with "Megan's Law"? *Journal of Criminal Law and Criminology, 88*, 721–765.

Langer, W.L. (1974). Infanticide: A historical survey. *History of Childhood Quarterly*, 1: 353–365.

Ledwon, L. (1996). Maternity as a legal fiction: Infanticide and Sir Walter Scott's *The Heart of Midlothian*. *Women's Rights Law Reporter*, 18: 1–16.

Leiser, K. (1997, Jan. 1). New year, new California laws: Here's a look at laws taking effect this year. *San Diego Union–Tribune*, p. A3.

Mann, C.R. (1995). The contribution of institutionalized racism to minority crime. In D.F. Hawkins (Ed.), *Ethnicity, Race and Crime: Perspectives Across Time and Place*. New York: State University of New York Press.

Memory of abuse: OK to sue 50 years later. (1993, December). *ABA Journal, 78*.

Meyer, J.F., and Jesilow, P. (1997). *"Doing Justice" in the People's Court: Sentencing by Municipal Court Judges*. New York: State University of New York Press.

Meyer, J., and Short, C. (1998). Investigating computer crime: Concerns voiced by local law enforcement agencies. *Police Chief*, 65(5): 28–35.

New Jersey Statutes Annotated § 2C. (2001). St. Paul, MN: West Group.

Nugent, H. (1991). *State Computer Crime Statutes*. Washington, DC: National Institute of Justice.

Packer, H. (1968). *The Limits of Criminal Sanction*. Stanford, CA: Stanford University Press.

*Papachristou v. City of Jacksonville*, 405 U.S. 156 (1972).

Peyser, M., and Foote, D. (1994, August 29). Strike three, you're not out. *Newsweek*, p. 53.

*Plessy v. Ferguson*, 163 U.S. 537 (1896).

Rose, L. (1986). *Massacre of the Innocents: Infanticide in Great Britain 1800–1939*. London: Routledge and Kegan Paul.

Unknown. (1673). *The Murderous Midwife, with her Roasted Punishment: Being a True and Full Relation of a Midwife that was Put into an Iron Cage with Sixteen Wild-cats, and so Roasted to Death, by Hanging over a Fire, for Having Found in her House-of-Office no Less than Sixty Two Children, at Paris in France*. London, England: Private printing.

Vvagstaffe, V. (1680). *An Act to Prevent the Deftroying and Murthering of Baftard Children*. London, England: Samual Roycroft.

# Step 2

# A Crime Is Committed

❖

Before the courts can get involved in any criminal matter, a law must be broken. As discussed in the first chapter, many rules for lawmaking have come to be designed over time. Here, we will discuss the elements of crimes and some defenses raised by defendants in court. We will also present a brief discussion of the criminal justice process that occurs after a crime is committed. By the end of this chapter, you will be able to recognize a crime and its corresponding law and break laws down into their important parts. You will also be able to identify nine common defenses used by those accused of committing crimes, and will be able to briefly outline how crimes get to the courts and how the courts are involved in cases prior to the arrest of defendants.

Remembering that laws are enforceable bodies of rules enacted by public officials, let us now define what a crime is. A standard dictionary entry for **crime** is: "An act that subjects the doer to legal punishment; the commission or omission of an act specifically forbidden or enjoined by public law" (Funk and Wagnalls, 1987, p. 306).

The first thing you will notice about this definition is that crimes "subject" the perpetrator to legal punishment. This means that the acts have already been labeled as criminal, and possible punishments for such acts have already been laid out in official documents, usually state or federal penal codes or local ordinances. If an act is not legislatively prohibited, then it is not a crime, no matter how loathsome the act. To illustrate, consider the following California case. An imaginative fellow contacted a number of women who had previously visited a health clinic and convinced them that they had a rare disease that could easily be treated by having intercourse with a specially treated donor male. When the women agreed to the treatment, the man showed up at their homes and had intercourse with them. When the women later found out that they had been deceived, they wanted to press criminal charges. Nothing in the California Penal Code, however, addressed this specific type of act. The women had technically consented to the sex, ruling out rape or sexual assault. In response, the state legislature enacted a law that defined a new crime, seduction by trick or deceit. Ironically, the man continued his ruse after the law was enacted and was ultimately prosecuted for these acts.[1] Had the innovative criminal discontinued his practices after the law prohibiting them was enacted, he could not have been prosecuted. In the end, we need to remember that acts are not crimes unless they have been legislatively prohibited.

Another case illustrating this principle is the 1982 case *People v. Weg*. Theodore Weg, a computer programmer for the New York City Board of Education, used his employer's computer system to maintain his own private business. Since the employer did not consent to this conduct, Weg was charged with theft of services (because the computer's resources were used for Weg's personal benefit). It is important to recognize that this was not a personal computer; it was a big system that was expensive to operate. The theft of service law was written to prevent people from stealing labor from commercial enterprises (e.g., getting a haircut with no intentions of paying the hairdresser) or using others' "business, commercial, or industrial equipment" for their own benefit. The prosecutor accused Weg of diverting the use of the computer to his own projects. Weg countered the charges by stating that his conduct did not violate any existing statute. The New York Supreme Court accepted Weg's argument. Because the Board of Education was not a business whose services were sold, its computers were not commercial equipment, so Weg could not be convicted of theft of service. The court then went on to state that if the State of New York wanted to sanction actions like Weg's, it would have to enact a law that did so (see Box 2.1 for the court's admonishment to the state; the court first acknowledged that Weg's actions were deplorable, then it pointed out that other states had already enacted laws to address the issue and encouraged the State of New York to do the same if it wanted to be able to prosecute similar acts in the future). Weg's actions, then, however objectionable, could not subject him to punishment because they had not yet been prohibited by law.

So, the next time you want to do something to get even with your ex-boss, you simply need to make sure there are no laws against it, right? Sure, but this is no easy task. You have to make sure it does not violate any laws governing the jurisdiction you are in. That includes federal laws, state laws, county laws, city ordinances, and even neighborhood ordinances.

Then, to complicate matters, there might be some administrative law that prohibits what you want to do. **Administrative regulations** are rules enacted by regulatory agencies to govern certain activities because those agencies have been assigned the duty of ensuring that the activities they oversee are safe, reasonable, just, or otherwise carried out in an appropriate fashion. Those who want to fly airplanes, for example, must comply with Federal Aviation Association (FAA) regulations, which were designed to ensure the safety of passengers, crews, and anyone else whose life could be affected by airplanes. Another set of administrative laws/rules, those enacted by the Federal Drug Administration (FDA), control which drugs can be sold to the public, what type of research is necessary to show they are

---

### BOX 2.1
### The Court's Admonishment in *People v. Weg* (1982)

In 1982, the Legislature of the State of New York could reasonably find a need to regulate, even by penal sanction, conduct of the type alleged in this [case]. Perhaps computers are a special type of expensive, commonly owned equipment so subject to misuse that the Legislature might wish to give their owners special protection.

Extensive literature in the field of computers describes the widespread unauthorized use of this type of equipment. . . . Other Legislatures have recently addressed this problem. Illinois created the offense of "[unlawful] use of a computer," which includes any use of a computer without consent, whether or not the computer service is for hire. . . . This court, however, may not create an offense. Unless . . . the Penal Law is amended, it will apply only to unauthorized tapping into a computer whose service is for hire (*People v. Weg*, 1982, pp. 1023–1024).

---

safe, and how that research must be conducted. Even drivers' licenses are overseen by a regulatory agency, the Department (or Division) of Motor Vehicles (DMV). The Occupational Health and Safety Administration (OSHA) is an example of an administrative agency that issues regulations that address workplace safety across the nation, whether you work in a factory, an office, or the fields. There are many regulatory agencies that have been given the authority to protect us from a host of possible dangers or to fulfill other needs established by the government. You may not have realized, for example, that those little signs in restaurant washrooms that say "employees must wash hands before returning to work" are an enforceable administrative regulation.

Even if you spend a lot of time researching your intended activity and find out that it is not against any law, if you commit a **tort**—a legal wrong defined under tort law—you could still get dragged through the **civil courts** if your boss or anyone else harmed by your actions sues you for injury of self or property. Tort law is part of civil law, and thus civil courts are fora in which citizens can bring lawsuits against others for harming them or their property, or breaking contracts. Box 2.2 presents some additional information on criminal, administrative, and civil law.

Looking again at our definition of crime, notice that the punishment that occurs for crimes must be "legal." This means that the possible penalties are defined in advance and imposed by the criminal justice system after a fair hearing in the courts. When family members, ecclesiastical (church) officials, or other parties impose sanctions, such as grounding or disfellowship, these are not "legal" punishments because they do not follow a court hearing and because those doing the sanctioning are not empowered by the criminal justice system to do so. An example of a penalty imposed by ecclesiastical officials is the excommunication of a Nebraska woman because she would not leave a pro-choice group to which she belonged (Ruff, 1997); her penalty was imposed by the Catholic church, not the criminal justice system. It will not show up on her criminal record (if she has one), nor can it be used in a court of law to increase her sentence under a repeat offender law. She cannot be sent to jail or punished in any other way by the criminal justice system because the offense was against her church, not society at large. In order to be "legal," penalties must be within any guidelines established by law.

Finally, we must note that crimes can be either commissions or omissions. Most crimes are commissions; that is, they result when people do things that have been defined as criminal. Speeding, for example, is the commission of an act that is forbidden by law. Sometimes, however, omissions can be crimes. Failing to pay one's taxes or properly care for one's children, for example, are omissions that can be punished in the legal system.

---

## BOX 2.2
## Some Differences Between Types of Law

| | Criminal Law | Administrative Law | Civil Law |
|---|---|---|---|
| Types of actions governed | Violations of criminal or penal codes | Violations of rules established by regulatory agencies that are typically known by their acronyms (e.g., FDA and IRS) | Behavior that harms another or breaks a contract |
| Goals of the systems | Prevent and control crime (e.g., laws against robbery) | Ensure safety etc. of activities under agencies' authority and remedy dangerous conditions (e.g., OSHA regulations) | Compensate individuals for harms they have suffered at the hands of others |
| Who has been harmed | The specific victims(s) and the rest of society as well | There is no harm necessary as administrative law proceedings may be initiated against anyone who violates a regulation, even if no one was harmed by the specific act (e.g., failure to maintain proper records can result in proceedings). | A private individual (this person may also be the victim of a crime as crime victims are entitled to sue civilly for damages); could also include a group of individuals (i.e. class action lawsuits). |

|  | Criminal Law | Administrative Law | Civil Law |
|---|---|---|---|
| Who "prosecutes" the actions | A prosecutor who represents the state or federal government | Regulatory agencies have their own attorneys who present the agency's side of cases filed against suspected rule violators. | The plaintiff who has been harmed (or an attorney hired by the plaintiff) |
| Possible sanctions | Punishments imposed by criminal justice system (e.g., fines, probation, community-based corrections, incarceration, death penalty, etc.) | Loss of any licenses granted by the regulatory agency, civil penalties (e.g., civil fines or orders to stop engaging in a prohibited behavior), and penalties imposed in criminal courts if the violations of the rules also violate criminal laws (note: regulatory agencies cannot enact criminal statutes themselves, but legislatures may pass laws outlawing behaviors prohibited by regulatory agencies) | Financial sanctions to compensate plaintiffs for harms they suffered, punitive damages awarded to plaintiffs, orders to stop a noxious behavior (e.g., manufacturing a product whose patent is owned by another person or playing loud music every night) |

As you can see from the preceding discussion, laws must be written in rather specific terms. Laws must define the prohibited (or mandated) activity, and must present the penalty that may be imposed on those who break the law. Even if a law is written in legalese, you should always be able to identify the crime and punishment issues. A hastily written law may sound like gobbledygook and may be useless. In 1994, the Missouri legislature decided to "update" its sex laws and nearly outlawed consensual sex (Lambe, 1994). See if you can find the prohibited actions in the following law:

A person commits the crime of sexual misconduct in the first degree if he has deviate sexual intercourse with another person of the same sex, or he purposely subjects another person to sexual contact or engages in conduct which would constitute sexual contact except that the touching occurs through the clothing without that person's consent.

Despite the obtuse wording that seems to outlaw any intentional sex and implies that touching of nude persons is more legal than touching those who are clothed, the law was intended only to outlaw all homosexual sexual contact and all forms of nonconsensual sex, even sexualized touching of a fully clothed person. Fortunately, the legislature agreed to rewrite the law. Presumably, as all laws must, later sections of the law prescribed the penalties for those engaging in the prohibited activities.

## THE ELEMENTS OF A CRIME

To be a crime, an act requires three important elements: *actus reus, mens rea,* and concordance between the two. We will discuss them one at a time.

### Actus Reus

First, the act must be a "guilty" act or omission (e.g., failing to pay one's taxes). This is called the ***actus reus*** of a criminal offense. In order to qualify as a "guilty" act, the action must be voluntary in addition to breaking an existing criminal statute. If I were to have a seizure or touch an electrical wire that made me jerk involuntarily and I unintentionally hit you while jerking, the act would not be considered voluntary. In addition, it is not enough that a person merely thought about burglarizing a store, but then never even went to the store to do so. To be considered a criminal, the individual must have at least attempted to burglarize the store.[2]

But, do not let this paragraph delude you into thinking that *actus reus* is an overly easy concept. Sometimes, it is difficult to differentiate between a "guilty" act and a noncriminal one. Whereas fighting in the boxing ring is considered sport, fighting on the streets is a crime. Selling pornographic pictures might be distasteful but legal, but selling nude pictures of teenaged children is illegal, as is the selling or even showing of any pornography to children. Although keeping prices low may seem like a good business practice, reducing them too low might be considered a violation of pricing laws. Traveling at 55 miles per hour might be fine on the freeway, but may constitute a traffic violation in town. In the end, it is important to know which acts have been criminalized and the circumstances under which they are criminalized so that you can know an *actus reus* when you see it. Guilty acts are those that have been forbidden by law.

It is also important to recognize the difference between an act and the harm resulting from that act. It is not necessary that harm result from individuals' actions before they can be considered criminal. Whereas most people would agree that it is criminal to deliver poisoned chocolates that are thrown in the trash by the intended victim before anyone eats any, there are individuals who argue that consensual prostitution harms no one and who question why it is still illegal in most jurisdictions. Similarly, failing to stop at a stop sign is still a traffic violation, even when there is no one else nearby who could be endangered. And, in many cases, attempting to commit a crime is a crime, and planning a crime with others is a special category of crime called **conspiracy**. In the end, there is no requirement that the alleged actions harmed anyone.

## Mens Rea

Second, all crimes need a "guilty" state of mind, or a *mens rea*. Our laws are based on the idea that blameless people should not be punished for their actions. Travelers who accidentally switch briefcases with those in line with them at the airport, for example, should not be punished as thieves, because they lack a "guilty" state of mind. Sometimes, the idea of the *mens rea* causes the courts a great deal of trouble. How can we as mere mortals know for certain when a person intended to break a law? Some statutes declare that certain crimes must be "knowingly" committed, that is that perpetrators have knowledge of what they are doing. In California, for example, it is a crime to "knowingly" develop photos of minors under the age of fourteen engaged in sexual conduct (CA Penal Code, sec. 311.3). This does not mean that perpetrators need to know that such activities are illegal, just that they know that they are developing photos of persons under fourteen engaged in sexual conduct. We will talk more about this type of mistake when we learn about defenses to crimes.

There are some special forms of the *mens rea* rule. First, one can be convicted of offenses such as vehicular homicide even if she or he did not intend to harm anyone (i.e., if the offender made a conscious decision to drive a car under unsafe or illegal conditions and in doing so was reckless). Reckless individuals do not stop and consider the consequences of their actions, even when it is reasonable to assume that harm could result from their actions. Driving too fast, for example, can be reckless if the weather is bad. Thus, the offender knew or should have known that harm could occur; this idea, **foreseeability**, can be important when determining whether an individual possessed *mens rea*. Thomas Richard Jones made history in 1996 when a North Carolina prosecutor sought the death penalty for his killing of two students while driving under the influence of alcohol and painkillers (Sack, 1997). Although they convicted the three-time drunk driver of murder, the jury spent just one hour deciding that he should get life without parole rather than the death penalty. The prosecutor had argued that Jones's habit of using painkillers and alcohol before driving substituted for an intent to kill; the jury clearly agreed that his actions were reckless.[3] In another case, a New Jersey teen set off a smoke bomb at a shopping mall, and a pedestrian was killed by a fireman responding to the call; the youth was convicted of reckless manslaughter because had it not been for his reckless use of the smoke bomb, the pedestrian would not have been killed (Calendar, 1998). In both cases, the defendants made conscious decisions to participate in dangerous behaviors. By engaging in certain dangerous behaviors (e.g., playing Russian roulette with friends or shooting cans off one's back fence in a residential area), one can be held criminally (in addition to civilly) responsible if harm results.

A second type of special case involves deaths due to culpable negligence, especially if the victim is someone for whom the defendant had a duty of care (e.g., a child or elderly parent). When people are **negligent**, they act in a careless manner. As we learned above, one way negligence can be culpable is when individuals are so negligent that their actions are actually reckless. When there is a duty to care for someone, however, negligence need not be reckless to be blameworthy because people must exercise the level of care that is expected of them by society. Along these lines, a number of people are tried each year in the deaths of children who die of exposure in overheated cars and some parents are charged with neglect for allowing others (e.g., irate boyfriends) to kill their children. Thus, one New York woman was convicted of murdering her newborn for allowing her husband to bury the infant alive because the child was fathered by another man (Associated Press, 1995). Even if she did not kill the child herself, she had a duty to protect her newborn from harm. Sometimes, caregivers are expected to look beyond their own personal beliefs and act in the best interests of their wards. Two parents who turned to faith healing rather than traditional medicine when their daughter became ill with diabetes were convicted of involuntary manslaughter when she died from a heart attack related to her illness (Combs, 1997). The court argued that her condition was treatable and that the parents should have sought proper care for their ill child. In these cases, although the perpetrators did not intend to harm their children, their negligence was the primary factor in the deaths. It is important to re-emphasize the special relationship between the victims and the perpetrators. Leaving a capable adult in a car, for example, would not be considered culpable negligence because the adult could easily exit the car if it became too hot. Negligence also requires foreseeability of harm; if a reasonable person would not imagine any harm resulting from an action, then engaging in the action would not be considered negligent.

Under a third type of special case, the **felony murder rule**, one can be convicted of a murder that occurs during certain serious felonies such as robbery or rape. A robber who uses an unloaded gun because she or he does not want to hurt anyone could still be convicted of murder if someone dies during the robbery (perhaps due to a heart attack or fall).[4] The reasoning behind the felony murder rule is that the intent to commit the first serious felony substitutes for the intent to commit murder. It was the felony murder rule that allowed a California man to be convicted of murder in the death of a female bystander who was accidentally shot by police (Ex-con gets 32 years. . . , 1995). Because her death resulted from police attempts to subdue the man as he fired at them, he was held responsible for her death. Similarly, a New Jersey purse-snatcher was convicted of murder when the elderly victim whose handbag he had just taken died of a heart attack (Purse thief sentenced. . . , 1998). In another case, a robbery victim died after scrambling out of a fifth-story

window to escape from three gun-toting robbers (Man fle
His atypical death could qualify as murder because it happ
robbery. Box 2.3 contains some real and hypothetical case.
whether the actors possessed *mens rea.*

32

## Concordance between *Actus Reus* and *Mens Rea* and ...er Issues

Finally, before an act can be defined as a crime, there must exist a concordance
between the *actus reus* and the *mens rea.* If two people independently shoot at
a victim, both cannot be convicted of murder unless they were acting together as

---

# BOX 2.3

## Some Cases for You to Consider

Do the individuals in the following real and hypothetical cases possess *mens rea?* If it is a special
kind, which type is it (i.e., reckless negligence, culpable negligence, or felony-murder rule)?

- A man picked up his friend at the police station three hours after he had been arrested for
drunk driving. Although his friend was still drunk, the man let him drive home. On the way
home, the friend was involved in a fatal crash that killed himself and the driver of the other car
(Man charged in friend's fatal crash, 2000).
- A twenty-one-year-old man was playing "cops and robbers" with his fourteen-year-old
cousin, with whom he was a very close friend. During the game, the gun accidentally dis-
charged, killing the cousin (Racher, 1998).
- A woman leaves her severely intoxicated friend in her car while she goes to work, so the
friend can "sleep it off." The interior of the car becomes too hot, killing the friend.
- A man involved in a fight was brandishing a firearm outside a restaurant, when a plainclothes
police officer approached the scene to assist the two uniformed police officers who were
already there. The uniformed police officers did not recognize the other officer and ordered
both men to drop their guns. The brandisher complied and dropped his gun, but the plainclothes officer did not respond to commands to drop his firearm. Fearing him to be an involved
party, the uniformed officers shot and killed the plainclothes officer (Police officers kill off-
duty cop, 2000).
- A man jumped into the water to save a friend's seven-year-old daughter but was caught in the
currents and panicked. He then took the girl's life preserver and saved himself, so the girl
drowned (Hardwell-Byrd, 2000).
- A drug dealer killed an eight-year-old boy and his mother to prevent the boy from testifying in
an upcoming murder trial (Lavoie, 2000).
- A man and woman get into a verbal disagreement in the man's car and she demands to be let
out of the car. The man immediately stops and lets her out. After the man drives away, the
woman is killed during a botched robbery.

o-offenders.[5] Only one person's bullet killed the victim (unless the victim died from the combined trauma of the two injuries rather than from the injuries caused by one of the shooters). The other shooter may be guilty of attempted murder because she or he intended to kill the victim, but not murder, because there is no merging of *mens rea* and *actus reus*. Similarly, if a man intends to break into a neighbor's garage but mistakenly enters his own garage because of extreme darkness, there is no merging of guilty act and guilty state of mind. In both cases, the intent to cause harm is there, but the actual harm is missing.

Some offenses require that "attendant circumstances" be fulfilled. Attendant circumstances are conditions that must be present (or absent) in order for a crime to take place. In some states, for example, it is necessary for potential assaulters to have the "present ability" to carry out their threats before they can be convicted of assault. Using this logic, a man in California was granted a new trial by the California Supreme Court nearly a century ago when it felt he could not be convicted of assault of his neighbor because the gun he carried was not loaded (*People v. Sylva*, 1904).[6] Similarly, most states have cutoff dollar values for theft; larceny of less than a certain amount is a misdemeanor (i.e., petty theft), while stealing more than that amount is a felony (i.e., grand theft). Stealing more than the threshold value is an attendant circumstance for felony theft. When a Vermont woman successfully argued that she should be given credit for the sales discounts on the merchandise she had shoplifted from a supermarket, she was hoping to show that she did not meet the attendant circumstance for felony theft. The stolen merchandise added up to $101.49, just over the felony cutoff value of $100; if one used the sales prices in effect that day, however, the amount taken was only $97.37 (Associated Press, 1997). Her purpose was not purely academic; the felony charge carried a maximum sentence of ten years in prison, whereas the misdemeanor charge could result in only six months in jail and a fine.

These three (sometimes four) elements are referred to collectively as the corpus delicti (Latin for "body of a crime"). There can be no crime unless a guilty act follows a guilty intent, and the two combine to produce criminal harm. Certain attendant circumstances may also be necessary.

At this point, it is important to mention two other special categories of offenses: those that involve strict or vicarious liability. **Strict liability** offenses are those for which one can incur liability without *mens rea*. One can be ticketed for speeding, for example, whether or not one knew one was speeding even if the speedometer was faulty and one did not know this. In **vicarious liability** cases, one is held responsible for the conduct of another person if a particular type of legal relationship exists between the two. Employers, then, can be charged criminally if their employees sell alcohol to minors even if they claim they were unaware that the sales took place. The employer can be punished under the doctrine of vicarious liability, although some state's courts (e.g., Pennsylvania's) have ruled that employers cannot be incarcerated for their employees' actions because it would be a violation of due process to deny a person freedom on the basis of criminal actions of others (e.g., *Commonwealth v. Koczwara*, 1959). In such cases, perpetrators face other penalties.

## LEGAL DEFENSES

Remember from above that, except for strict and vicarious liability offenses, criminal acts must be committed with a guilty state of mind. Sometimes, people commit acts for which they should not be punished because their actions lacked *mens rea*. Under the law, people may be innocent of a crime due to the presence of legally recognized justifications for their actions or because they were not legally responsible for their actions. There are ten general legal defenses, discussed in greater detail in this section and summarized briefly in Box 2.4 for your reference.

---

### BOX 2.4

### A Summary of Ten General Legal Defenses Used by Defendants in Court to Excuse Their Behavior

The defendant should not be held accountable for his/her criminal actions because:

1. Infancy—she or he is too young (typically younger than seven years of age) to be able to form the *mens rea* necessary to commit a criminal act.
2. Insanity—his or her insanity at the time of a crime meant he or she could not rationally form *mens rea* to commit a criminal act.
3. Intoxication—his or her involuntary intoxication made it impossible for him/her to rationally form *mens rea* to commit a criminal act.
4. Self-defense—his or her actions were meant to protect him- or herself from death or serious bodily harm.
5. Prevention of a violent felony—she or he was protecting others or preventing a violent felony.
6. Coercion/duress—his or her actions were in response to a rational fear of immediate death or serious bodily injury.
7. Necessity—his or her actions were necessary to prevent a larger evil.
8. Entrapment—the idea and motivations for committing the crime were planted by a government agent.
9. Syndromes—the defendant was significantly affected by a psychological syndrome that diminished his or her ability to rationally form *mens rea* to commit a criminal act.
10. Mistake of fact—the acts arose from an honest and reasonable mistake, such as accidentally picking up someone else's umbrella instead of one's own.

---

## Infancy

Under common law, children younger than seven were considered incapable of forming the *mens rea* required for criminal acts because they did not know right from wrong. Young children, then, could not be prosecuted for their acts, no matter how extreme. This defense was rebuttable for children between the ages of seven and fourteen (meaning prosecutors could oppose the assumption as long they had evidence to support their claims); the courts would decide on a case-by-case basis if a particular child knew right from wrong. Today, the courts still rely on a similar standard. Adolescents above a statutorily defined age who commit certain serious acts (e.g., murder) can be **certified** for trial in adult courts if the prosecuting attorney can show that they are "unsuitable" for juvenile court proceedings. Those who are "certified" are tried in the adult courts rather than in the juvenile courts, as you will learn in Step 16 on juvenile courts.

The defenses raised in this colonial Pennsylvania courtroom certainly differed from those used today. While infancy, as a defense, was established in common law, and many of the other defenses were offered from time to time, the syndromes that are now presented in court (e.g., postpartum depression, post-traumatic stress disorder, etc.) are relatively new ways of explaining away responsibility for criminality. This particular courtroom, in Philadelphia, is similar in physical setup to others of its day: the elevated area behind the tables where the judges sat, the witness stand off to the left of the picture, the wooden jury box (not visible in this picture; it is to the right of the elevated platform), the tables where counsel and other court personnel sat, and the central location of the cagelike prisoner's dock where all prisoners stood throughout their trials. Courts in Pennsylvania, however, differed from their colonial counterparts due to the philosophy of the colony's founder, William Penn. Pennsylvania courts offered protections similar to those in the Bill of Rights long before that document was created, sentences were not as harsh as in neighboring colonies, and mixed-race juries (six whites and six Native Americans) heard disputes between whites and Indians to ensure that "wee may Live friendly together" (Hoffer, 1992, pp. 30–32).   SOURCE: Courtesy of Jon'a Meyer.

Infancy is rapidly losing ground as a defense as more and more juveniles commit serious crimes. The recent episodes of schoolyard shootings, in particular the ambush-like attack by two boys, aged eleven and thirteen, in Jonesboro, Arkansas (Breed, 1998), has refocused the public on increasing the punitiveness with which we deal with juveniles. And, the apparently senseless killings by even younger children, including the six-year-old boy who was charged with nearly beating a one-month-old infant to death after breaking into a house to steal a tricycle (Locke, 1996), serve to fuel the fire of anger toward "killer kids." Even cases where children are young enough to be completely excused under the infancy defense, like the five-year-old and six-year-olds whose cases are presented in Box 2.5, are leading legislators to author and support get-tough-on-juvenile-crime bills. Indeed, it is events like these that led one Texas legislator to propose a bill to lower his state's minimum execution age so that eleven-year-olds could be put to death (Walt, 1998). One thing is certain: The attitude toward juveniles is changing, and new laws are slowly eroding this defense.

---

## BOX 2.5

## Should Infancy Protect a Child from Prosecution?

Consider the three cases below. If you had to decide how to act in the following cases, what would you do? What factors would you consider important? Should laws be changed because of these relatively isolated incidents? Is new legislation appropriate? If new laws are the answer, what type of legislation would you call for?

Case #1: Memphis, TN—A five-year-old kindergartner was arrested after bringing a loaded gun to school to kill his teacher because she had punished him with a "timeout" (timeouts are commonly used with young children and typically involve having the child sit still in a chair for a few minutes for misbehaving). "He said he wanted to shoot and kill several pupils, as well as a teacher . . . He stated that he was going to shoot Ms. Foster for putting him in timeout." Said one juvenile court judge about the case: "A five-year-old is not capable of forming criminal intent." (Police: 5-year-old targeted teacher, 1998)

Case #2: Flint, MI—A six-year-old boy was angry with a female classmate, and he brought a gun to school the next day and shot her in their first-grade classroom. Although he originally tried to blame the shooting on another boy in the classroom, he later said he was only trying to scare the girl when the gun accidentally went off. Michigan law considers youths younger than seven to be incapable of forming criminal intent. (Deal reached. . . , 2000)

Case #3: Blythe, CA—Two girls, aged five and six, smothered a three-year-old toddler with a pillow. First, the girls had pushed him into a mud puddle, but he escaped from them. Then, they tripped him and he fell on a board. Then, one girl sat on his legs so he could not get away while another put a pillow over his head and sat on it until he stopped moving. Police interviews show that the girls intended to kill the boy, but they were not charged because California law does not recognize children that young as capable of committing crimes. (Kids smothered little boy, 2000)

## Insanity

Being insane at the time of one's crime is a complete defense to crime. The idea is that the system should not punish people who do not possess mens rea. There are several insanity tests in use around the country. The most common is the M'Naghten Rule, which holds that a person is insane if he or she was "laboring under such a defect of reason, from disease of the mind as not to know the nature and quality of the act he was doing, or, if he did know it, that he did not know he was doing what was wrong." In other words, the defendant either did not know what she or he was doing, or literally did not know it was wrong (e.g., believed that his or her actions were truly in self-defense).

The rule was named for Daniel M'Naghten, whose paranoid delusions led him to believe that Sir Robert Peel, then prime minister of Britain, was part of an imagined conspiracy to kill him. After various attempts to hide from Peel's supposed influences, M'Naghten lay in ambush at Peel's residence, hoping to permanently eliminate the cause of his suffering. M'Naghten fired into Peel's carriage, but, in a twist of fate, instead killed Peel's secretary. M'Naghten's attorneys argued that he was insane, and the jury reportedly rendered a verdict of not guilty by reason of insanity before even leaving the jury box to deliberate (Wrightsman, 1987, p. 264). Queen Victoria was outraged by the outcome of the assassination attempt and demanded further examination of Britain's insanity rule. After great debate, the House of Lords issued their new standard, now known as the M'Naghten Rule. Ironically, because M'Naghten knew that firing into Peel's carriage was wrong, he would not have met the requirements of insanity under his own test. The rule was created in 1843 and still survives to this day, despite criticism from those who complain that it has not kept up with improvements in the psychiatric field (e.g., Cardozo, 1931).

An example of a case that a court felt did not meet the M'Naghten criteria occurred when an Indianapolis man thought his father was the devil; he stabbed his father more than 200 times to release the evil spirits from his body, then ate part of his brain (Police: Man ate father's brain, 1997). Acknowledging his profound mental illness, the man was found "guilty but mentally ill" because he knew right from wrong and knew what he was doing at the time of the killing. Had he felt that he was protecting himself from deadly attack by his father (as the devil), he might have met the demanding criteria of the M'Naghten test. This case illustrates a crucial element of the insanity defense. To be a valid defense, the defendant must have been legally insane at the time of the crime, and insanity differs from the medical definition of mental illness in that insanity cannot apply when defendants understand what they are doing and know what they were doing is wrong. So, it is possible for defendants who suffer from serious mental illnesses to be tried and convicted for committing crimes, even crimes committed during episodes of their mental illnesses. This illustrates the fact that "insanity" is a legal concept, not a psychological/medical one.

Another insanity test is the American Law Institute (ALI) test, which holds that defendants are not responsible for their acts if they "lacked substantial capacity either to appreciate the criminality of their conduct or to conform their conduct to the requirements of law." A third test is the "Irresistible Impulse" rule, which recognizes that defendants may know right from wrong, but still be "irresistibly compelled" to commit crimes (e.g., kleptomaniacs may be compelled to commit thefts they know are wrong). All these tests have one thing in common: They require that offenders' reasoning abilities be diminished so that their acts cannot be considered truly voluntary.

A few states, including Idaho, Montana, and Utah, have abolished the use of the insanity defense altogether. Because of the public uproar over the perception that some defendants are "getting off" by claiming insanity, there is a move in some jurisdictions to create "guilty, but insane" and "guilty, but mentally ill" verdicts. After such offenders are treated for their mental illness, they are moved from a psychiatric facility to prison to complete their terms of incarceration. As for fear of individuals misusing the insanity plea, it is employed in fewer than 1 percent of felony cases and is successful in approximately one-fourth of the cases in which it is attempted (Callahan, Steadman, McGreevy, and Robbins, 1991).[7] And, those who successfully argue that they were insane at the time of their crimes are seldom released; instead, they are sent to a psychiatric facility until they are found to be sane, even if the time that takes amounts to a life sentence. It is also important to remember that offenders must be insane at the time of their crimes in order to mount an insanity defense. Those who become insane after their crimes must be treated for their illness until they are considered competent to stand trial. In some cases, defendants are never considered competent so they remain in a treatment facility.

## Involuntary Intoxication

Involuntary intoxication is another defense to crime. Those who were "slipped a Mickey" (i.e., had a drug slipped into their beverages about which they were unaware), for example, may claim that their intoxication was involuntary and that they should be excused for their criminal actions while under the influence. This appears logical when viewed against the requirements of *mens rea* because there was no intent to commit a crime.

In contrast, voluntary intoxication is not a good defense to crime. It may, however, mitigate the degree of the crime if the offense is one that requires specific intent.[8] Such a defendant could claim that she or he could not premeditate while drunk, for example, to reduce first degree murder to a lesser crime. Although some defendants have tried to argue otherwise, voluntary intoxication is not a defense to drunk driving. Whereas being drunk indeed may impair their driving judgement, they chose voluntarily to drink and then drive.

## Self-Defense

The victim of an actual or apparent deadly attack may kill another person if it is reasonably necessary to use such force to protect oneself from death or serious bodily harm. So, if an attacker tries to kill you, and you cannot get away, you are generally allowed to engage in whatever self-defense is necessary. Under this line of reasoning, a woman could be allowed to kill her assailant to prevent a forcible rape. Most states, especially in the East, recognize a **duty to retreat**, however, so private citizens must be very careful in their use of force. One California man was arrested after he discovered a burglar in his home and fractured the intruder's skull with a baseball bat; police felt he had hit the burglar too many times and had beat him after he tried to leave (Locke, 1997). Fortunately for the man, the prosecutor's office declined to press charges because, under California law, he was allowed to try to apprehend the burglar (No trial in clubbing. . . , 1997). The key to understanding self-defense is the idea of proportionate force. One must not overreact to the threat of harm.

Lesser levels of force may be used to protect oneself from less serious harm, such as being hit by someone or having something nonlethal thrown at one. Deadly force to protect property is not a good defense; one cannot use deadly force to protect property. Shopkeepers who rig guns to go off when individuals break into their stores, for example, may be prosecuted because they are employing too much force. Besides, what if someone had a valid reason for entering through the window, such as a fireman or the shopkeeper's son who had lost his key? Would the gun be able to tell the difference between a real threat and an authorized individual?

One exception to this rule is Colorado's 1985 "make my day" law, which specifically gives residents the right to use deadly force against intruders in their homes if they reasonably believe the intruder: (1) has committed or plans to commit a crime in addition to the unlawful entry (e.g., theft or rape) and (2) will use physical force against an occupant of the dwelling (Furman, 1995). Even the 1997 Louisiana law that gives victims of carjackings the right to protect themselves using deadly force is not an invitation for people to protect their property with violence; instead, the law addresses one particular crime during which the victims are in considerable danger of injury. It is important to note that both of these exceptions involve some level of actual or perceived physical danger to the victims.

Private citizens should always be careful not to go too far. When a New York father saw a man stealing one of his children's bicycles, he chased the thief then shot him in the foot (McQuiston, 1997). Noting that neither the man nor any other person was in danger of being harmed by the thief, police arrested both parties, and they faced the same seven-year term if convicted. Had the wound been fatal, the father may have found himself charged with murder because of the unreasonableness of his actions.

Self-defense differs from other defenses to crime in that the defendant who claims self-defense is actually asserting that she or he acted appropriately. The defendant who claims infancy, insanity, or intoxication, for example, seeks to be held to a different (lower) standard of behavior because his or her age, mental status, or inebriation affected his or her ability to think and act rationally. Those who claim self-defense, on the other hand, are claiming that they acted properly under the circumstances because they were in serious danger, and failing to act as they did would have resulted in their being killed or seriously injured.

## Prevention of a Violent Felony

Coming to the defense of others is permissible if the defendant believes that force is necessary to protect others or to prevent a violent felony. This defense is also known as **defense of others**. Stories about off-duty policemen and others interrupting store robberies illustrate this defense, as do accounts of people who intervene in fights to protect victims from being harmed. Even if the perpetrator of the original crime is injured by the person who sought to prevent the violent felony, this defense can still protect the good Samaritans from prosecution.

Some jurisdictions require that the would-be victims actually need assistance. To illustrate this possibility, consider a person who overhears a woman in a parking lot who is screaming, "Help, he's attacking me!" In a jurisdiction that requires would-be victims to be in actual need of assistance, a potential good Samaritan must first ensure that the woman is really in danger of being attacked before interfering in the situation, which of course may be impossible to determine. It is possible that she is simply angry with the other person and hopes that her false distress cry will lead him to leave her alone. She might also be in little danger, but fear someone who has approached her for legitimate reasons (e.g., to ask for donations or seek directions).

## Coercion/Duress

Coercion or duress is usually a defense to a crime because it is presumed that the defendant's crimes resulted from fear of death or serious bodily injury. In order to be a valid defense, the defendant must have faced immediate threat of death or serious bodily injury. This defense also covers acts to protect one's immediate family. The common plot in old movies wherein a crook calls a bank official and says he will kill the official's kidnapped daughter if he does not receive a certain sum of embezzled funds, then, is a valid example of coercion/duress to justify embezzlement if the official felt his daughter's life was in danger.

Coercion/duress is not a good defense for killing, however, because the law maintains that one innocent life is no more valuable than another. You cannot kill a blameless individual even if doing so is necessary to save your own life, as we will learn in the next defense, necessity.

## Necessity

Necessity is a justification when a crime is committed to prevent a greater evil. Those who break into homes only to get out of freezing weather, for example, may claim that they were trying to avoid serious injury or death. In at least one case, a defense of necessity was considered "a viable defense" when an inmate justified her escape from prison because of her fear of being sexually assaulted by other inmates; the inmate had been attacked and beaten before, and fled to avoid a sexual attack (*People v. Lovercamp*, 1974). The California Court of Appeals held that such an escape was permissible, but that escapees are under an obligation to return themselves to custody as soon as safely possible (e.g., the escape may only be used to avoid an immediate threat, not to achieve permanent or long-term liberty):

> However, before Lovercamp becomes a household word in prison circles and we are exposed to the spectacle of hordes of prisoners leaping over the walls screaming "rape," we hasten to add that the defense of necessity to an escape charge is extremely limited in its application. This is because of the rule that upon attaining a position of safety from the immediate threat, the prisoner must promptly report to the proper authorities. (Lovercamp, 1974, p. 831)

Now, let us consider another case. California engineer Douglas Chin, who had been battling prostitution in his neighborhood, finally began throwing pipes at cars driven by people who stopped to solicit prostitutes (Hartlaub, 2000). At trial, Chin attempted to mount a necessity defense, claiming that his actions were necessary because repeated calls for police assistance over a ten-year period did no good. Instead of harming others, Chin claimed he only sought to scare the drivers or draw attention to the problem and that he used his knowledge of physics to ensure that no one was hurt. Although the jury did not buy Chin's defense completely, they did vote to reduce his charges from felonies to misdemeanors. Was Chin's defense valid? Let us find out.

This seldom-used defense requires four elements to be effective. First, the crime must be committed in order to prevent a significant and imminent evil (e.g., one's own death). Second, the defendant must not have available to him or her a reasonable legal alternative (e.g., there is no other shelter nearby). Third, the criminal act must not be disproportionate to the evil it sought to prevent (e.g., merely breaking into a home seems justifiable if it is done to save one's life). Finally, the defendant must have acted with good faith, believing that the act was necessary to prevent the evil (e.g., there was no sign of the snowstorm letting up). Using these four criteria, what was wrong with Chin's attempt to use necessity?

Sometimes, environmentalists or other interest groups feel there are few options available to them in their quest for justice, so they employ direct interventions to sabotage efforts by their adversaries to engage in noxious behavior. Some individuals, for example, have tried to use the necessity defense to justify actions taken against harpooning boats that harvest seals. Let us see how the idea to sink boats operated by seal hunters stacks up under the four criteria needed for necessity. One could argue that the slaughter of seals is a significant and imminent evil, but one also has other reasonable legal alternatives, including the use of civil and criminal courts. Also, sinking a boat to prevent harpooning of seals would be disproportionate because of the possible harm to the people on board the craft, not to mention the damage to the boat itself. Even though their goals are laudable, it looks as though would-be boat sinkers must find another, more acceptable way to end harpooning.

Necessity has also been tried by custodial parents who refuse to surrender their children to honor court-ordered visitation with the other parent. Unable to show that her actions were necessary to protect her child, one custodial mother was jailed for more than two years because she refused to disclose the whereabouts of her child so her husband could exercise his visitation rights (*Morgan v. Foretich*, 1988; Custody dispute resurfaces . . . , 1997).

Necessity is not a good defense for murder, and this failure is possibly best explained through a brief discussion of a famous British case, *Regina v. Dudley and Stephens* (1884), in which four survivors from a sunken sea vessel were cast adrift in a lifeboat without water and with only two pounds of canned turnips for twenty-four days. After twenty days of drinking only the small quantities of rainwater they could capture in their boat and eating one small turtle they managed to catch, two of the men killed the vessel's cabin boy, who was near death from starvation and had been further weakened from drinking sea water. They were rescued four days after the homicide, and were later charged with murdering the cabin boy. The jury in the case refused to determine whether the men were guilty, and instead referred the case to the justices for the Queen's Bench (i.e., the highest British court of common law). Whereas the justices of the Queen's Bench recognized that the men "would probably not have survived" had they not consumed the boy's flesh and blood, they also noted that the victim was "a weak and unoffending boy" who was "incapable of resistance," and convicted the men of murder and sentenced them to death.[9] Although this example is from another country, it illustrates the reality that no amount of necessity justifies the taking of an innocent life. Had the cabin boy become delirious and attacked the other survivors, they may have been able to satisfactorily mount a self-defense case. Absent any such actions from the youth, however, the others were wrong to take his life to preserve their own.

## Entrapment

Entrapment is a situation in which the government takes actions that lead to or "create an opportunity" for crime to happen. In other words, someone who would not normally commit a crime is induced by the government or its agents (e.g., the police) to do so. Entrapment should not be confused with good undercover work that simply facilitates the mens rea that already exists in some people. Law enforcement agents who pose as drug users, for example, do not persuade noncriminals to break the law by selling drugs to them. Presumably, only those who are already predisposed to participating in drug sales sell to undercover agents. Posing as drug users (or the elderly or homeless people or tourists in attempts to arrest those who commit crimes against those populations) is considered good police work. One nationwide sting involves a number of police investigators (and other adults) posing as children on the Internet to attract and arrest would-be child molesters. Posing as children aged thirteen and younger, the investigators participate in online chat rooms and set up liaisons with individuals who seek children as sex partners. In one case, a thirty-one-year-old kindergarten teacher was arrested after he traveled to another state for a rendezvous with what he thought was an eleven-year-old boy (Hanley, 1997). These stings are designed to capture only those who initiate criminal activity and are not considered entrapment.

In contrast, if a government agent convinces an otherwise innocent person (i.e., someone who would not otherwise have committed the crime) to commit a crime, that would be entrapment. Entrapment is alleged by many, but is rarely successful as a defense. The entrapment test is whether a reasonable person would commit the crime under the same circumstances. One case in which entrapment was successfully argued was *Jacobson v. United States* (1992). In that case, Keith Jacobson ordered two magazines depicting nude boys before they were outlawed. After a new law in 1984 outlawed that type of child pornography, government investigators sent him mailings from five different fictitious groups and an investigator who posed as his pen pal. Many of the mailings were political in nature, decrying the new law, arguing for sexual freedom, and soliciting him to order additional magazines. After receiving twenty-six months of mailings, Jacobson finally ordered a magazine that depicted child pornography and was promptly arrested. At his trial, he raised an entrapment defense, and the U.S. Supreme Court agreed, noting that a search of Jacobson's home had turned up only the two magazines purchased before the 1984 law and the many materials sent to him over the more than two-and-a-half years he was on the government sting mailing list. The Supreme Court noted with displeasure that it took twenty-six months for the government to persuade Jacobson to order a magazine to support the cause. Some excerpts from the case are presented in Box 2.6.

Entrapment is not a valid defense unless it was a government agent who planted the idea in someone's mind; being persuaded by other private citizens to commit an illegal act is not a legal defense. It is irrelevant how hard I persuaded you to steal paintings from your local museum, even if you did not have one iota of intent to do so before encountering me and my high-pressure tactics. Since I am not an agent of the government, you would be guilty of theft, most likely grand theft. Depending on the circumstances, I may also be charged in the scheme, but you are not getting off scot-free. Entrapment is only valid if the ideas are planted by an agent of the government.

---

**BOX 2.6**

## Excerpts from the U.S. Supreme Court's Arguments in a Valid Entrapment Defense

The following excerpts are from *Jacobson v. United States* (1992), discussed in the text. As you read them, notice the issues raised by the Supreme Court and what differentiated this case from one that merely involved good undercover work by the government to uncover those who possess the *mens rea* to break the law:

> . . . Jacobson was not simply offered the opportunity to order pornography, after which he promptly availed himself of that opportunity. He was the target of twenty-six months of repeated Government mailings and communications, and the Government has failed to carry its burden of proving predisposition independent of its attention. (pp. 540–541)

> . . . the strong arguable inference is that, by waving the banner of individual rights and disparaging the legitimacy and constitutionality of efforts to restrict the availability of sexually explicit materials, the Government not only excited Jacobson's interest in material banned by law but also exerted substantial pressure on him to obtain and read such material as part of the fight against censorship and the infringement of individual rights. Thus, rational jurors could not find beyond a reasonable doubt that Jacobson possessed the requisite predisposition before the Government's investigation, and that it existed independent of the Government's many and varied approaches to him. (p. 541)

---

## Psychological Syndromes

Recently, a number of psychological syndromes have been introduced at trial as legal defenses. Battered woman's syndrome is only one of the better-known syndromes that have been used to explain why people engage in violent actions toward others. Other syndromes include battered child syndrome, post-partum depression, and post-traumatic stress disorder. It is important to recognize that these syndromes were created by psychologists, researchers, physicians, and other nonlegal personnel, but they have been employed by defendants and attorneys to try to excuse criminal behavior. Because of this distinction, syndromes are not invalidated just because they were used unsuccessfully in court to excuse crimes; in fact, they may still be very effective in a treatment setting or other context.

Sometimes, syndromes are unsuccessfully introduced in court, including "involuntary subliminal television intoxication," where the defense tried to justify the defendant's murder as the outgrowth of his exposure to violence on television (*Florida v. Zamora,* 1978). In another unsuccessful case, the defense tried to argue that the defendant's "rotten social background" (i.e., his unsavory childhood) led him to react violently when he was called a racial slur (*United States v. Alexander and Murdock*, 1973).

Even when syndromes are not successful in excusing crime, they are sometimes used to mitigate sentences. A court could find, for example, that the domestic violence endured by a woman may not excuse the murder of her husband, but justifies giving her a lighter prison term than a woman who had not endured any abuse from her victim. In fact, the use of battered woman's syndrome and related justifications may partially explain why men are sentenced more harshly than women for spousal murders (15 percent of men receive a life sentence versus 8 percent of women, 16 percent of women receive probation versus 5 percent of men, and the average prison term for men is 17.5 years versus 6.2 years for women [Bureau of Justice Statistics, 1994]).

## Mistake of Fact

Mistake of fact is possibly the most elementary defense to negate *mens rea*. Those who plead mistake of fact argue that they committed an act based on an honest and reasonable misunderstanding of the facts surrounding an offense. Consider, for example, a woman who left a store and mistakenly got into the wrong vehicle because the car was the same color and model as her own and her key unlocked the door.[10] After locking her purchases into the car, she realized with surprise that she did not have faux fur seat covers, extracted her purchases and transferred them to her own vehicle. If she were to be charged with auto burglary (or theft if she drove away in the car), she could argue mistake of fact. There was no *mens rea*, and a reasonable person could easily make the same error. Note that mistake of fact is different from defendants claiming that they were unaware of a law (i.e., "ignorance of the law"). Being unaware of or misunderstanding a law is a valid defense only under limited circumstances such as violations of confusing or complicated laws such as the tax code (e.g., *Cheek v. United States*, 1991). Mistake of fact is more akin to innocently switching briefcases at the airport because of being rushed. Of course, the mistake must be reasonable, so "accidentally" driving off in someone's new Jaguar instead of on one's own late-model Schwinn bicycle may not qualify.

It is relatively common for laws to state that defendants must have "knowingly" committed an offense. For example, one who enters a New Jersey building "knowing that he is not licensed or privileged to do so" is guilty of "unlicensed entry of structures," a form of trespass under New Jersey Penal Code 2C:18–3. That defendants must "know" they are not allowed to enter a building means that defendants could argue they did not realize they were breaking a law because they were mistaken about the circumstances that led up to the entry. Just-fired employees who have not yet received their letters of termination, for example, may have no reason to think their entry is prohibited. Similarly, those who write bad checks

Mistake of fact or mistake of luck? If the owners of these two suitcases accidently picked up the other's luggage, they might be able to claim mistake of fact due to the similarities: both are the same color and size and could be confused. If this happened, neither individual would have the required *mens rea* to combine with the actus reus of taking the suitcase, so society agrees the behavior is blameless and should not be punished. Once the mistake is discovered, however, both would be expected to report the mixup and return the mistaken property to its true owner. If the switch was not accidental, on the other hand, a crime was committed by the individual who knowingly took the other's suitcase.    Source: Courtesy of Jon'a Meyer.

in New Jersey are guilty of violating section 2C:21–5 (bad checks) if they do so "knowing it will not be honored by the drawee." Those who honestly believe they have funds to cover purchases by check, then, are given time to satisfy the debts rather than face prosecution. To criminally charge every person who writes a singular bad check would essentially criminalize large numbers of people who lacked *mens rea.*

In conclusion, it is important to recognize that all ten defenses to crime address the issue of *mens rea.* Successful cases demonstrate that the defendants would not normally have committed the crimes with which they are charged. Instead, they were insane or laboring under the psychological difficulties explained by a syndrome, involuntarily intoxicated, defending or protecting themselves or others, entrapped by government officials, or they made an honest mistake. Instead of being the kind of people society wishes to punish, most people would agree that these offenders deserve treatment or absolution for their acts.

## THE PROCESS AFTER A CRIME HAS BEEN COMMITTED

Once a law has been enacted and broken, the wheels of the justice system begin to turn. Crimes may come to the attention of the criminal justice system either through reporting by a citizen (e.g., a victim or witness) or through observation by a criminal justice official. When someone is physically injured or has his or her property damaged, he or she may call the police to report the harm. Sometimes, uninvolved witnesses call the police on behalf of others, such as when neighbors report domestic violence situations or when people call to say they have heard gunshots fired in their neighborhood. Other crimes are directly observed by the police, much to the chagrin of many speeders. Finally, some crimes may be discovered by private citizens who report unusual or suspicious events (e.g., the Philadelphia man who found unidentified bones buried in the basement of his new home; Jennings, 1998) or by persons who are acting in a criminal justice capacity (e.g., investigators who uncover dubious bank transactions)—these individuals do not observe the crime in progress but stumble on evidence that a crime has taken, is taking, or will take place in the future. That offenses come to the attention of authorities may affect the likelihood of prosecution, as discussed in Step 9.

For a variety of reasons, not all victims report crimes they have experienced. Estimates are that only 35 percent of all crimes and fewer than half of felonies (serious crimes, discussed in more detail in Step 4) are reported to authorities (Harlow, 1985; Bureau of Justice Statistics, 2000, p. 94). Sometimes, victims are afraid of retaliation by the offender, such as children who have been threatened with injury if they report the sexual abuse they are enduring. Other victims are afraid of embarrassment, including both male and female victims of sexual assault. A few victims might not want to become entangled in the criminal justice web because of their own dubious actions. Consider, for example, the Florida woman who probably should have let the fraud she felt she suffered go unreported; she was arrested for drug possession after she called police to report that she had been "ripped off" in a bad drug deal (Woman calls cops. . . , 1997). Others may be afraid of attracting attention to themselves, including undocumented citizens and homosexuals in jurisdictions that still prosecute consensual sex between same-sex partners. Sometimes, victims do not even know they have been victimized (e.g., theft of small items from one's yard or desk at work). A few victims might not realize a crime has been committed, so they do not report it to anyone; examples include women who do not realize that marital rape is a crime in their jurisdictions, elderly people who are victimized by telephone scams, and couples who are illegally denied housing on the basis of their race or for having children.

The majority of victims, however, feel the crime they have experienced is not worth reporting or view it as a "private matter" (e.g., Gove, Hughes, and Geerken, 1985). These victims often believe that they will not get their property returned to them, and they do not want the hassle of reporting the crime and possibly having to take a day off from work to testify. If you feel this low reporting rate is hard to believe, think for a moment whether you would report to police the theft of a highlighter pen from your backpack or a deliberate scratch on your car. Many individuals would feel the events are too trivial to justify reporting them, unless the highlighter pen was somehow very special or the car was a new Ferrari. It is only those offenses that invoke our ire or otherwise attract our attention that get reported. The nature of the offense, then, is the first screening criterion that determines whether an offense ever makes it to the courts. Only offenses that meet whatever threshold individuals have established for themselves have a chance of becoming part of any court's caseload.

If the crime is reported, a law enforcement official may be dispatched to take a crime report, or the complainant may be asked to go to a police station or prosecutor's office to file a crime report. The crime report documents what is alleged to have happened and any information about the identity of any parties that may have been involved (and if property was involved, its description). As criminal justice officials, law enforcement officers serve as the second screening tier. If the offense appears to be too trivial (e.g., a person calling a neighbor an "idiotic jerk" or other inane names), the officer (in his or her role as system gatekeeper) may refer the complainant to more appropriate agencies (e.g., a neighborhood dispute resolution center).

If the crime is in progress when the law enforcement officer arrives at the scene, the offender may be immediately arrested and the crime report taken afterward. If the police officer believes that a crime has taken place (this concept, **probable cause**, will be discussed in more detail in Step 3), she or he may arrest the offender if that person is known to the victim, or is described in such a way that the police officer recognizes her or him. Otherwise, the case becomes part of the police investigative caseload. In most jurisdictions, someone other than the officer who filled out the crime report does the actual investigation.

Although it may seem like the courts have little to do with the handling of the case by law enforcement personnel, they serve to regulate the actions taken by the police. Whether the officer makes an arrest is governed by court decisions regarding probable cause. Which offenses are considered for the crime report may also be governed by court decisions (e.g., laws that have been declared unconstitutional may not be enforced). Even the methods used by police officers when interviewing witnesses are regulated by the courts (e.g., those that produce biased information are prohibited). The major way the courts regulate the police is through excluding evidence that was gathered improperly or excluding charges that appear inappropriate. In essence, even though they appear to be the end result in a criminal case, the courts are involved at every stage in the criminal justice system. For example, the U.S. Supreme Court recently decided that a police officer's arrest of Texas resident Gail Atwater for driving with her two children without seatbelts was constitutional. Atwater, who was stopped while picking up her kids from soccer practice, had challenged her arrest as an "unreasonable" seizure in violation of the Fourth Amendment because the offense is typically punished in Texas by a $50 fine. This decision could have a significant impact on police practices in many states (Yi, 2001).

After an individual is arrested, the courts become more visible to the casual observer. First, the individual, now called a **defendant**, must be brought before a judge who ensures that the accused knows what charges he or she faces and his or her rights. Even if the defendant has an attorney to help him or her, a judge will read the charges and explain the defendant's rights. At some point, bail may be set, usually by a judge. In some cases, judges conduct hearings to determine if enough evidence exists to justify holding the defendant for a trial. These post-arrest processes have become the fodder for many television shows, including the popular series *Law and Order* and *The Practice.*

## SUMMARY

In this chapter, we learned that in order to be considered a crime, an act must first be prohibited (or mandated, as in the case of paying taxes) by law, and then must be such that it results in legal punishment to those who break the law. We learned that every crime has at least three elements: a guilty act, a guilty intent, and the concordance of the two. We also learned that some crimes require certain attendant circumstances.

We then looked at ten legal defenses that may excuse crimes due to the lack of *mens rea:* infancy, insanity, involuntary intoxication, self-defense, prevention of a violent felony, coercion/duress, necessity, entrapment, psychological syndromes, and mistake of fact. Defendants who successfully present one of these defenses are found not guilty. Even defenses that are unsuccessful, however, may mitigate the penalty that is imposed by the court for the crime. Finally, we looked briefly at how differential reporting of offenses can affect the court caseload and how the courts are involved in an investigation even before anyone is arrested for a crime.

The next chapter will examine how laws govern what happens in the courts after an arrest. Particular attention will be paid to the defendant's rights, including the history and importance of those rights. The adversarial system will be defined and explained, as will some important court processes. We are halfway through our introduction to the courts.

## DISCUSSION QUESTIONS

1. Pick a partner and see which of you can come up with the most ways that regulatory agencies affect our lives. Include the regulated actions and how that regulation affects you in your daily activities or in other ways. For example, the bacon you ate for breakfast was overseen by multiple regulatory agencies: the quality of the bacon itself is regulated; OSHA regulates the conditions at the plants where the bacon was packaged or prepared; and other agencies regulate the conditions under which the pigs who provide the bacon are kept, the packaging materials and use of preservatives, the claims made by the company in advertisements, and so on. Even the stores that sell the bacon are regulated with respect to what they may sell and how they must store the goods they sell.

2. Can you think of an action that violates criminal, civil, and administrative laws? Why would processing such an act through three separate tribunals not be a violation of laws against double jeopardy? Double jeopardy, discussed at greater length in Step 3, occurs when someone is prose-

cuted after she or he has been convicted or acquitted at trial, or when she or he is punished more than once for the same crime.

3. What are some examples of crimes of commission and omission?

4. Think of four crimes, then identify the elements of each. For example, the *actus reus* for shoplifting is the actual theft of goods, the *mens rea* includes the intent to take the goods without paying for them, and the concordance occurs when the intent to steal results in the actual theft. In this case, the attendant circumstances would involve the degree of the theft; for example, a charge of grand theft would likely follow the theft of a diamond bracelet but the charge would be petty theft if the bracelet were simply a dimestore trinket.

5. Look over the real and hypothetical cases presented in Box 2.3. Do the individuals possess *mens rea*? If it is a special kind, which type is it (i.e., reckless negligence, culpable negligence, or felony-murder rule)?

6. Consider the three cases presented in Box 2.4. If you had to decide how to act in those cases, what would you do? What factors would you consider important? Should laws be changed because of these relatively isolated incidents? Is new legislation appropriate? If new laws are the answer, what type of legislation would you call for?

7. Why does voluntarily becoming incapacitated by alcohol or drugs not make one's uninhibited behavior involuntary, as in the defense of involuntary intoxication?

8. Scan your local news or the major newswires (such as the Associated Press or Reuters) for stories that discuss defenses to crime. Which defenses are used and for what type of cases? For each case you found, what do you feel about the validity of the defense and why do you feel this way? Design some hypothetical cases to illustrate the defenses for which you were unable to locate stories.

9. In addition to those mentioned in the text, what are some reasons victims have for not reporting crimes? How could the criminal justice system improve reporting rates for crimes? Is the criminal justice system interested in having all crime reported, no matter how trivial? What would be some of the ramifications to the system as a whole if every crime were reported?

## NOTES

1. Thanks to William Thompson for bringing this case to our attention.

2. Or planned the offense with others, making it a "conspiracy."

3. Another North Carolina drunk driver, Timothy Blackwell, received life in prison without parole after he struck and killed a four-year-old (Miller, 1998).

4. The robber could also be charged under felony murder if a fellow robber was shot by someone else, including the police.

5. This phenomenon is not to be confused with cases where multiple offenders are charged with the same harm, such as the bizarre California case in which a prosecutor successfully argued that two robbers fired the same fatal bullet. The prosecutor told the first jury that John Winkelman was the triggerman, but told a second jury that the evidence was "100 percent consistent with Stephen Davis firing that fatal round" (Canto, 1997). Obviously, the victim could only have been shot by one of the robbers, but the prosecutor defended his actions by stating that both were equally culpable under felony murder rules anyway.

6. Notice that this case dealt with assault and not with robbery. The court's rationale was that Sylva could not have assaulted his victim because he did not have the "present ability" to carry out the threat. If the victim died or was injured during the act, a crime may have indeed been committed. Also, newer laws in California outlaw the mere display of weapons around others.

7. Of interest, one survey found that the public believes that insanity defenses are attempted in 37 percent of felony cases (Silver, Cirincione, and Steadman, 1994).

8. Not all states allow defendants to use voluntary intoxication to show that they could not form intent. Ruling on a Montana case, the U.S. Supreme Court recently held that such a bar (on the use of this possible defense) is not unconstitutional (*Egelhoff v. Montana*, 1996).

9. After the sentence was pronounced, the Crown intervened and commuted the men's sentence to six months' imprisonment. Regardless of the commutation, this example demonstrates the legal view of the men's actions as murder.

10. This is an actual event experienced by one of the authors. The "twin" vehicles were parked three spaces apart and were identical except that one had faux fur seat covers. No charges were considered. In fact, the owners of both cars were amazed that their keys were interchangeable.

# REFERENCES

Associated Press. (1995, June 18). Mom who stood by convicted of murder. *San Diego Union-Tribune Wire.*

Associated Press. (1997, December 25). Woman gets deal on theft charge. *San Diego Union-Tribune Wire.*

Breed, A.G. (1998, March 28). Ark. Citizens not quick to forgive. *Associated Press Wire.*

Bureau of Justice Statistics. (1994). *Violence Between Intimates.* Washington, DC: U.S. Department of Justice.

Bureau of Justice Statistics. (2000). *Criminal Victimization in the United States, 1995.* Washington, DC: U.S. Department of Justice.

Calendar, B. (1998, April 22). South Brunswick boy gets probation after smoke bomb prank led to death. *Home News Tribune Wire.*

Callahan, L.A., Steadman, H.J., McGreevy, M.A., and Robbins, P.C. (1991). The volume and characteristics of insanity pleas: An eight-state study. *Bulletin of the American Academy of Psychiatry and Law, 19:* 331–338.

Canto, M. (1997, June 12). Lawyer: Two triggermen, one bullet. *Associated Press Wire.*

Cardozo, B. (1931). What medicine can do for law. In *Law and Literature and Other Essays and Addresses.* New York: Harcourt, Brace and Company.

*Cheek v. United States,* 498 U.S. 192 (1991).

Combs, C. (1997, June 11). Sentence in faith healing death. *Associated Press Wire.*

*Commonwealth v. Koczwara,* 397 Pa. 575, 155 A.2d 825 (1959).

Custody dispute resurfaces in U.S. (1997, May 20). *Associated Press Wire.*

Deal reached in school shooting case. (2000, August 22). *Associated Press Wire.*

*Egelhoff v. Montana,* 116 S.Ct 2013 (1996).

Ex-con gets 32 years to life for causing death. (1995, September 16). *San Diego Union-Tribune Wire.*

*Florida v. Zamora,* 361 So.2d 776 (1978).

Funk and Wagnalls. (1987). *New International Dictionary of the English Language: Comprehensive Edition.* Chicago: J.G. Ferguson Publishing.

Furman, P. (1995, December). Self-defense in Colorado. *The Colorado Lawyer.*

Gove, W.R., Hughes, M., and Geerken, M. (1985). Are uniform crime reports a valid indicator of index crime? *Criminology, 23:* 451–501.

Hanley, R. (1997, April 1). Teacher is arrested in Internet child pornography case. *New York Times Wire.*

Hardwell-Byrd, S. (2000, May 21). Cops: Man took kid's life preserver. *Associated Press Wire.*

Harlow, C.W. (1985). *Reporting Crimes to the Police.* Washington, DC: U.S. Department of Justice.

Hartlaub, P. (2000, July 11). Capp St. vigilante convicted, sent home. *San Francisco Examiner Wire.*

Hoffer, P.C. (1992). *Law and People in Colonial America.* Baltimore: Johns Hopkins University Press.

*Jacobson v. United States,* 503 U.S. 540 (1992).

Jennings, J.W. (1998, July 1). Man charged after skeleton found buried in basement. *Philadelphia Inquirer Wire.*

Kids smothered little boy. (2000, August 18). *Associated Press Wire.*

Lambe, J. (1994, November 10). Sex in Missouri carries with it tough sentence: Poor syntax means law may forbid intercourse. *Kansas City Star Wire.*

Lavoie, D. (2000, June 8). Conviction in death of 8-year-old. *Associated Press Wire.*

Locke, M. (1996, July 13). Six-year-old ruled unfit to face trial. *San Diego Union-Tribune,* A5.

————. (1997, May 10). Self-defense case sparks debate. *Associated Press Wire.*

Man charged in friend's fatal crash. (2000, October 26). *Associated Press Wire.*

Man fleeing thieves plunges to his death. (1997, January 20). *New York Times Wire.*

McQuiston, J.T. (1997, April 15). Man arrested for shooting bike thief. *New York Times Wire.*

Miller, B. (1998, April 17). N.C. drunk driver sentenced to life. *Associated Press Wire.*

*Morgan v. Foretich,* 846 F.2d 941 (4th Cir., 1988).

No trial in clubbing of intruder. (1997, May 15). *San Diego Union-Tribune Wire.*

*People v. Lovercamp,* 43 Cal. App. 3d 823 (1974).

*People v. Sylva,* 143 Cal. 62; 76 P. 814 (1904).

*People v. Weg,* 113 Misc. 2d 1017; 450 N.Y.S.2d 957 (1982).

Police: 5-year-old targeted teacher. (1998, May 9). *Associated Press Wire.*

Police: Man ate father's brain. (1997, March 24). *Associated Press Wire.*

Police officers kill off-duty copy. (2000, January 29). *Philadelphia Daily News Wire.*

Purse thief sentenced for murder. (1998, September 5, 1998). *Associated Press Wire.*

Racher, D. (1998, July 13). Fatal play with gun gets him 5 years. *Philadelphia Inquirer Wire.*

*Regina v. Dudley and Stephens,* 14 Q.B.D. [Queen's Bench Division] 173 (1884).

Ruff, J. (1997, March 21). Excommunication order ignored. *Associated Press Wire.*

Sack, K. (1997, May 7). Drunken driver is spared the death penalty. *New York Times Wire.*

Silver, E., Cirincione, C., and Steadman, H.J. (1994). Demythologizing inaccurate perceptions of the insanity defense. *Law and Human Behavior, 18:* 63–70.

*United States v. Alexander and Murdock,* 471 f.2D 923 (1973).

Walt, K. (1998, April 6). Lawmaker seeks to lower age on death penalty to 11. *Houston Chronicle Wire.*

Woman calls cops over fake crack. (1997, March 4). *Associated Press Wire.*

Wrightsman, L.S. (1987). *Psychology and the Legal System.* Pacific Grove, CA: Brooks/Cole.

Yi, M. (2001, April 25). Justices OK jail for minor infractions. *San Francisco Chronicle,* A11.

# Step 3

# After Arrest: Law, the Court, and Post-Arrest Procedures

❖

In the previous chapter, we learned how crimes are defined and about some defenses used by those accused of breaking the law. This chapter will look at the important stages that happen after an allegation has been made that a crime has occurred and the rights afforded to those against whom the accusations are made. Imagine that it's 3:00 A.M. and you've just been arrested by a member of your local police department. What in the world happened, you wonder? How did I get into this situation? What happens next? This chapter will provide some of the answers.

## WHAT HAPPENS AFTER ARREST?

After a suspect is arrested, the next step in the legal process is the initial appearance before a judge. During this proceeding, called a **preliminary** (or **probable cause**) **hearing**, the police must demonstrate that probable cause existed to arrest the suspect, and the prosecutor must demonstrate that there is sufficient evidence against the accused to proceed with the case. If so, the case will be "bound over" for trial, meaning that a trial date is set. If not, the judge will dismiss the case. The judge may also set bail for the accused at the preliminary hearing.

In most jurisdictions, the next step is the **arraignment**. Although the procedural issues addressed at arraignment and the timing of the arraignment before trial vary quite a bit between jurisdictions, typically the following occur: Charges against the accused will be formally read in court, and the accused will have the opportunity to enter a plea of guilty, not guilty, or **nolo contendere** ("no contest"). Unlike what was true throughout much of Anglo–Saxon legal history (which will be discussed in the next chapter), defendants are no longer forced to enter a plea and may instead "stand mute." If the defendant refuses to enter a plea, the court will enter a plea of "not guilty" on behalf of the accused. The judge may question the accused to ensure that he or she understands the charges, and the judge will inform the accused of his or her legal rights. These include the right to have legal counsel and to have the court appoint counsel if the defendant is unable to afford it. The judge will also address the matter of bail.

At each of these steps, the proceedings are structured according to laws and rules of procedure intended to ensure that the accused person moves through the criminal justice system with adequate legal safeguards against erroneous conviction. However, each step in the proceedings also takes place in the context of complex organizational arrangements and customs characterizing courtroom work and linking key courtroom players. A thorough understanding of court processes entails examining both the formal and informal organizational arrangements influencing court processes.

## THE ADVERSARIAL SYSTEM: COMPETITION IN THE COURTROOM

The U.S. legal system is an **adversarial** system, reflecting the theory that truth and justice can best be found when opposing legal teams battle in court to try to determine the facts of the case and find the best resolution. One of the guiding principles underlying the adversarial system is the idea that an accused person must be considered "innocent until proven guilty." In contrast, many countries have an **inquisitorial system** of justice, where the accused is presumed guilty and may be required in court to prove his or her innocence.

In an adversarial courtroom competition, the state (represented by the prosecution) and the defense are adversaries who each try to advance their case, with the court (the judge) as the neutral arbiter who enforces the rules by which the "contest" is conducted. The idea is that when the parties contest each others' versions of events, they serve as a check-and-balance system, thus maximizing the likelihood that the truth will be found.

The adversarial system has often been compared to a sporting event, where two teams compete against each other and a referee oversees the process. Whether the "playing field" in the courtroom is truly level, however, is an important question to consider; when one side has more resources than the other, is this a fair competition?

Although the sports analogy can be useful, it fails in an important respect; whereas sports competitions are oriented toward the present and future, as teams actively compete to win, opposing legal teams are oriented toward the past as much as the present and the future. The prosecution and defense are actively engaged in the search to uncover past actions, events, and states of mind, to interpret these prior happenings in their narratives to the judge and jury, and to argue for a particular verdict.

The adversarial system's competitive focus is seen by some legal scholars as reflective of the wider American free market ethos, which views competition as an

Brooklyn felony court judge J. Roland Sala, speaking from the bench. Our legal system depends on an adversarial model, which encourages a spirited competition between the defense attorney (representing the defendant) and the prosecutor (representing the state). The competition is overseen by a judge, who is responsible for ensuring that the rules of trial are properly followed. The adversarial model contrasts with the inquisitorial model of justice, which assumes that defendants are guilty until they prove themselves, or are otherwise shown to be, innocent. SOURCE: Library of Congress, Prints and Photographs Division, FSA-OWI Collection, LC-USW3-013545-D DLC, Marjory Collins, photographer.

essential force for allowing the best products and services to emerge. Some observers argue that the adversarial system's competitiveness does a disservice to the cause of justice because both parties in a case may become too intent on advancing their particular position in a case (e.g., Lind, 1982). However, research suggests that the adversarial system's procedures are perceived as more fair in comparison to the inquisitorial system by both litigants themselves and observers (Thibaut and Walker, 1975; Lind, Erickson, Friedland, and Dickenberger, 1978).

But how competitive is the adversarial system in actual practice? Could the adversarial system actually be more cooperative than competitive in some respects? Research on how judges, defense attorneys, and prosecutors work together to handle cases demonstrates that a highly developed system of cooperation is often evident. Members of the courtroom work group develop shared norms about how certain types of crimes should be handled: what sort of plea bargain is acceptable given the circumstances of the offense, the offender's history, and the relationship between victim and offender (Walker, 2001). Such cooperative effort makes sense, because the members of the courtroom work group share in common the need to handle cases as expediently as possible, and they interact with each frequently as they work on moving the crowded court docket.

## The Law and Due Process

*No person . . . shall be deprived of life, liberty, or property without due process of law.*

This succinct yet eloquent statement, one of the protections provided by the Fifth Amendment (1791), is one of the most powerful provisions of the U.S. Constitution. But just what is "due process of law"? Therein lies a continuing debate and the source of much work for the courts. There is no universally agreed-upon formal definition of due process (Cecil, 1983).

But despite the seemingly straightforward wording of the due process clause, many years and many court decisions would be required for the concept to achieve the legal reach that it has in modern American law. The evolution of due process doctrine illustrates the distinction between law on the books and law "in action," and the importance of considering how courts interpret and apply legal principles. At one time, for example, the institution of slavery was not considered legally incompatible with the concept of due process. Why not? A complete answer would require consideration of the complex constellation of political, legal, and social factors that sustained the practice of keeping humans in bondage until slavery was abolished in 1863. Such a complete consideration is beyond the scope of this chapter, but partial answers can be found in the decisions and debates of legislators and courts concerning issues such as citizenship, personhood, and federalism.

Another illustration of the importance of how courts interpret and apply the law is illustrated by the fact that it took another constitutional amendment for the powerful concept of due process embodied in the Fifth Amendment to be extended throughout the nation. This was necessary because the Bill of Rights had originally been interpreted as protecting citizens only from infringements of their basic civil rights by agents of the *federal* government, but not agents of state governments. This meant that states could violate the civil rights of citizens with relative legal impunity.

Congress responded to this situation by enacting the Fourteenth Amendment in 1868 to protect the rights of newly freed slaves after the Civil War. Congress's intent in creating the Fourteenth Amendment was to provide a federal legal mechanism for enforcing state violations of civil rights. For example, the right to vote, a defining characteristic of citizenship in a democracy, was thwarted in many places by ordinances that allowed election officials to require literacy tests of potential voters. Such practices disproportionately affected African Americans, in essence disenfranchising many people from their right to vote.[1]

The language of the due process clause of the Fourteenth Amendment is nearly identical to that of the Fifth Amendment; the critical difference is that the Fourteenth Amendment explicitly refers to restraints on state government actions: ". . . nor shall any State deprive any person of life, liberty, or property, without due process of law . . ." (1868).

In the 1960s, some of the most significant legal developments in the area of due process and individual rights occurred in what has been called "the due process revolution." In a series of decisions, the U.S. Supreme Court held that most of the guarantees of the Bill of Rights applied to state governments as well as the federal government, through the due process clause of the Fourteenth Amendment. That is, because the Fourteenth Amendment applies to state governments, incorporating the legal protections provided by the Bill of Rights as part of the concept of due process enables them to be applied to the states as well. Because the Supreme Court decided that most, but not all, of the guarantees provided by the Bill of Rights are incorporated within the meaning of due process, the process is often referred to as **selective incorporation**.

The concept of due process of law embodies the idea of fairness and protection of the individual against the power of the state. Due process emphasizes the public nature of our legal system, the idea that our government is accountable to us (rather than the other way around), and that public scrutiny of the legal process is not only desirable but necessary to help ensure equality and justice. Due process is also important in the sense that the perceived legitimacy of the law, the courts, and legal actors depends upon public perceptions that the system is fair. In turn, perceptions of fairness—or unfairness—reflect concern with the process of justice as well as the outcome.

Due process is intended to provide us with protection from government infringement on our civil (legal) rights to life, liberty, and property without due process of law. These three categories encompass a very broad spectrum of our legal rights, reflecting the broad scope of impact that due process has on our lives. Let's look at some examples.

## Life, Liberty, and Property Rights

### Due Process and Life

The government cannot deprive a defendant convicted of a capital crime of his or her life before the appeals process has been exhausted. In theory, although not always in reality, this provides sufficient safeguards for those sentenced to death. In 1999, Republican Governor George H. Ryan imposed a temporary halt to executions in Illinois because of concerns about the possibility of executing innocent people. The governor noted that since the death penalty had been reinstated in Illinois, twelve people had been executed, but thirteen inmates on death row had been released when evidence showed they were innocent (Cawthon, 2000). Research on the death penalty has identified 300 cases in the United States where the person sentenced to death was arguably innocent, based on the evidence. In twenty-nine of these cases, the person was executed (Radelet and Bedau, 1998).

The question of what this constitutional protection means in practice is a subject of continuing debate; for example, even if new evidence that could potentially exonerate an inmate on death row is discovered, the inmate has no automatic legal right to have this evidence reviewed. Instead, the inmate must petition the court for a hearing, and the court may or may not grant such a petition. If the inmate is nearing the date of execution, then the governor of the state where the inmate is imprisoned may be petitioned for a stay of execution so that the new evidence can be considered. The governor has the discretion to grant or deny the request, after reviewing the case.

### Due Process and Liberty

All of us, from schoolchildren to senior citizens, from prison inmates to everyone in the free population, are affected by the "liberty" aspect of the due process clause. That is, all of us have various "liberty interests" that the government cannot take from us without due process of law.

If you are a defendant facing a possible loss of freedom via incarceration, you have a clearly defined liberty interest. Legal protections such as the right to counsel, the right to trial by jury, and others are intended to help provide due process of law to ensure that you are not unfairly deprived of your liberty. Even while incarcerated, prison inmates have the right to be afforded minimal due process protections if they are subjected to disciplinary actions, which could represent an infringement on a potential liberty interest, such as revocation of "good time" credits, being placed in solitary confinement, or losing the opportunity to attend prison programs and services (*Wolff v. McDonnell,* 1974; *Sandin v. Connor,* 1995).

The police cannot legally stop us while we are walking or driving without legal cause; and if they search us, or arrest us, they must have specific, legally supportable reasons amounting to probable cause (or in some cases, reasonable suspicion) for doing so. Such restrictions on police action are intended to preserve individual liberty, and perceived failures of police to adhere to such restrictions often form the basis of lawsuits against police alleging deprivation of civil rights.

Sometimes, the concept of what constitutes a "liberty interest" is less clear. In *Goss v. Lopez* (1975), public high school students were found to have a liberty interest in the right to remain in school; thus, students have the right to an informal hearing before being subject to disciplinary action resulting in their suspension.

Policies providing for preventive detention of criminals designated as "sexually violent predators" and sex offender registration requirements have raised questions about whether such practices may unconstitutionally restrict potential liberty interests of offenders. For example, does the requirement that sex offenders provide personal information for dissemination in community notification databases raise a liberty interest that would require due process protection? Courts have come to differing answers on the question of whether a liberty interest exists in sex offender notification cases (Logan, 1999).

### Due Process and Property

Due process is also intended to protect our property, whether we own substantial acreage or merely a small bundle of personal possessions. Therefore, appropriate legal procedures must be followed if the government attempts to deprive a person of property. For example, a local government might attempt to seize your land through the exercise of the government's power of eminent domain in order to build a new highway. What does due process with respect to government seizures of property mean in practice? This is a controversial legal issue, as the practice of asset forfeiture described in Box 3.1 illustrates.

---

## BOX 3.1

## Due Process, Property, and Asset Forfeiture

As you read this, consider some cases where asset forfeiture is a good idea and seems fair, and also cases that illustrate its unfairness. Can you suggest modifications that would make sure the process was implemented fairly?

One woman discovered that her husband's illegal activity would cost her in more ways than one. Unbeknownst to the woman, her husband used their car to solicit sex from a prostitute. The police caught her husband and confiscated the car under a legal provision referred to as "asset forfeiture," which allows persons suspected of criminal activity to have their assets seized by law enforcement agents. In this case, the woman challenged the constitutionality of asset forfeiture provisions, arguing that seizing the family car deprived her of transportation and penalized her unfairly for her husband's crime. The U.S. Supreme Court rejected her challenge to the law and upheld the legality of asset forfeiture provisions in *United States v. Bennis* (1996).

In another case, a family's house and forty-nine acres of land were nearly seized by the government after a man was found guilty of growing six marijuana plants without his family's knowledge. Public protests made the government reconsider the seizure (Palmer, 2000).

Increasing public outcry over asset forfeiture cases, such as this and others (mostly related to drug enforcement cases), has been the catalyst for attempts to reform the legal provisions allowing seizures such as this. In 2000, Congress approved the Civil Asset Forfeiture Reform Act. Previously, property could be seized by law enforcement agents under civil asset forfeiture provisions if there was ". . . mere probable cause to believe that it either facilitated illegal drug activity or represents the proceeds of such activity" (21 U.S. Section 881(b)(4)). The new civil asset forfeiture legislation provides property owners with several significant legal protections, including shifting the burden of proving the linkage between the seized property and a crime to the government, rather than the property owner, and raising the standard of proof from probable cause to the much higher standard of "clear and convincing evidence."

---

# DUE PROCESS AND THE RIGHTS OF
# THE ACCUSED: MAJOR CASES

Now that we've done an overview of the concept of due process, let's look at some of the specific due process protections of the accused. The prosecutor has the legal burden of proving the state's case against the accused beyond a **reasonable doubt**.

There is no legal requirement that the defendant even present a defense. This focus on protecting the accused against the power of the state is embodied in the concept of "due process" and legal protections for the rights of the accused. Some of these protections date from the inception of America as an independent country, and some are quite recent.

Think back to our hypothetical situation in which you have been arrested by the police. "That would never happen!," you may be thinking. "I'm not a criminal!" Indeed, let's assume you're innocent; after all, the presumption of innocence is the theoretical foundation of American criminal justice and the legal principle upon which due process is built. In the following section, you'll learn about some of the most significant cases dealing with the key constitutional rights of the accused. These cases have an enormous amount of relevance for you as a person accused of a crime, because they specify many of your most important rights and what procedures the state must take to safeguard those rights consistent with the requirements of due process.

## The Fourth Amendment

The Fourth Amendment to the Constitution gives us the right to be secure against "unreasonable searches and seizures" by the government (i.e., it does not apply to private individuals such as bounty hunters). The Fourth Amendment provides:

> The right of the people to be secure in their persons, houses, papers, and effects, against unreasonable searches and seizures, shall not be violated, and no Warrants shall issue, but upon probable cause, supported by Oath or affirmation, and particularly describing the place to be searched, and the persons or things to be seized.

---

## BOX 3.2
## Just What *Is* "Reasonable Doubt"?

One of the most difficult concepts for some students of the law is to recognize reasonable doubt when they see it, and to be able to clearly define it. The following jury instructions are more than 150 years old; they were first used in *Commonwealth v. Webster* (1850).

> Reasonable doubt is defined as follows: It is not a mere possible doubt; because everything relating to human affairs, and depending on moral evidence, is open to some possible or imaginary doubt. It is that state of the case which, after the entire comparison and consideration of all the evidence, leaves the minds of the jurors in that condition that they cannot say they feel an abiding conviction, to a moral certainty, of the truth of the charge.

This provides the substantive framework of criminal procedure describing how search and seizures must legally be conducted by agents of the government such as the police. The Fourth Amendment was intended to prevent the government from intimidating citizens who might oppose government policies. The Fourth Amendment thus provides that searches and seizures must be done after the police obtain a warrant from a judge. The warrant must state the reason the police want to search a particular location, specify the exact location, and describe what the police expect to find there (for example, drugs or weapons). Let's look at the case of Ms. Dolree Mapp, because it is one of the landmark cases that fundamentally influenced due process protections of the accused.

### *Mapp v. Ohio,* 1961

The Mapp case began when police felt that Dolree Mapp was harboring a fugitive and/or gambling materials in her home. When they sought her consent for a search, she sent them away on the advice of her lawyer because they did not have a search warrant. Three hours later, the officers attempted once again to gain entrance to her home. When she did not "immediately" answer her door, the officers forced their way into her home (although she had been under surveillance so they knew she had not left). During this time, Mapp's attorney arrived at her home but was prevented from entering the house or communicating with her. When Ms. Mapp came to the door, she demanded to see the search warrant, and one of the officers waved a piece of paper in front of her, which she snatched in the belief that it was a search warrant (it wasn't). The officers found some magazines in a trunk in her basement, and she was convicted of possession of obscene materials. She appealed on the grounds that the evidence was the product of an illegal search and seizure by police, because they had no warrant. Thus, Ms. Mapp's appeal argued that the illegally obtained evidence should not have been admitted to court in the case against her.

The U.S. Supreme Court agreed that illegally obtained evidence should be excluded from court according to the provisions of the **Exclusionary Rule**, which had been adopted by the Supreme Court in 1914 *(Weeks v. United States)* as a **remedial** measure; if police obtained evidence illegally, the remedy was to make such evidence inadmissible in court. This was also thought to help deter police from obtaining evidence illegally, as it would be fruitless. Prior to the Mapp case, however, the Exclusionary Rule was binding only in federal court (and those states that chose to adopt it).

The Mapp case made the Exclusionary Rule binding in all states, thus providing this remedial measure to every suspect whose case involved evidence obtained in an illegal search and seizure by police. Since most criminal cases arise at the state rather than the federal level, the effect of *Mapp* was to extend this key protection to the majority of criminal defendants, and to serve as an influence on police practices in all fifty states.

To understand exactly how the Fourth Amendment's Exclusionary Rule provision was made binding in every state by this Supreme Court decision, we must return to the Fourteenth Amendment. In the Mapp case, the Supreme Court applied the Fourth Amendment's prohibitions against unreasonable search and seizure to all the states, reasoning that the due process phrase of the Fourteenth Amendment, which by definition applies to all states, incorporated the Fourth Amendment's provisions.

The assumption illustrated by the Supreme Court's decision in the Mapp case is that the Exclusionary Rule will deter police misconduct in the form of improperly obtaining evidence. However, it is unclear to what degree this assumption is well-founded. Now that exceptions such as "good faith" exist, are police still adequately deterred from illegally obtaining evidence? (See Box 3.3 for more on the good faith exception to the Exclusionary Rule.) In theory, "good faith" excuses only honest law enforcement mistakes. Yet questions remain about the extent to which the Exclusionary Rule effectively deters police, given that illegally obtained evidence may still be admissible in court under "good faith" and other exceptions to the rule.

There are other exceptions to the Fourth Amendment that allow searches and seizures that occur without a warrant to be legal in certain circumstances, such as when suspects give their free consent to the search/seizure, when evidence that was not described in the warrant is nonetheless in "plain view," and when the search/ seizure takes place during "hot pursuit" (e.g., there is no time to stop and get a warrant).

For you, as a person accused of a crime, the Fourth Amendment provides the framework for evaluating whether your seizure (arrest) and any searches associated with your case were constitutionally acceptable, or flawed.

The two major questions that arise in challenges to the constitutionality of searches and/or seizures under the Fourth Amendment are (1) whether actions that would legally constitute a "search" were conducted; and (2) whether the search was reasonable. Recall that the Fourth Amendment provides protection against searches only if they are *unreasonable.* In the eyes of the law, the reasonableness of

---

## BOX 3.3
## The Good Faith Exception

Another exception to the Fourth Amendment's restrictions on evidence gathering relates to the state of mind of the officers involved. If police officers gather the evidence in "good faith" that a warrant obtained for the purpose of gathering that evidence is legally proper, then the evidence is admissible even if it is later found that the warrant was inaccurate (such as when the warrant lists an incorrect address, but police went to the correct, intended address instead). The rationale here is that if the police *believe* they are acting legally when searching and seizing evidence, there is no point in excluding this evidence from court since the goal of the Exclusionary Rule is to deter *intentional* misconduct by police.

the search hinges on whether the person searched had a "reasonable" expectation of privacy. This depends on the location and circumstances surrounding the search.

For example, suppose you're a passenger on a bus traveling across the country. When you boarded, you tossed your soft-sided suitcase in the overhead luggage rack. When the bus stops at a border checkpoint, federal agents board the bus and begin searching for evidence of drug smuggling. The agents roam the aisles looking at the luggage and giving all the soft bags a good squeeze. Is this a constitutionally acceptable search? Do you and other bus passengers have a reasonable expectation of privacy for your luggage in this circumstance? What do you think? (See Mauro, 2000.)[2]

## The Fifth Amendment

### *Escobedo v. Illinois,* 1964

Danny Escobedo appealed his murder conviction on grounds that he was not informed of his right to remain silent, as provided by the Fifth Amendment, and that he had been prevented from having an attorney present during his interrogation, in violation of the Sixth Amendment. The Supreme Court agreed with Escobedo's contention that his confession should thus be considered inadmissible. In a crucial ruling, the court established that once a suspect is the "focus of investigation," she or he is entitled to an attorney. This decision thus gave suspects the right to an attorney at earlier stages of the criminal justice process. Subsequent cases have wrestled with the issue of when and under what circumstances this legal protection is triggered—in other words, how to determine when someone is the "focus" of police investigation.

### *Miranda v. Arizona,* 1966

This case, arising from the Fifth Amendment protection against self-incrimination, brought massive procedural change to the criminal justice system. The Fifth Amendment provides:

> No person shall be held to answer for a capital, or otherwise infamous crime, unless on a presentment or indictment of a Grand Jury, except in cases arising in the land or naval forces, or in the Militia, when in actual service in time of War or public danger; nor shall any person be subject for the same offence to be twice put in jeopardy of life or limb; nor shall be compelled in any criminal case to be a witness against himself, nor be deprived of life, liberty, or property, without due process of law; nor shall private property be taken for public use, without just compensation.

Ernesto Miranda claimed his confession to rape was not voluntary, and the Supreme Court found that he had not been warned of his Fifth Amendment right to avoid self-incrimination. The court ruled that suspects must be warned of the following rights:

- You have the right to remain silent.
- Anything you say can and will be used against you in a court of law.
- You have the right to talk to a lawyer and have him or her present with you while you are being questioned.
- If you cannot afford to hire a lawyer, one will be appointed to represent you before any questioning, if you wish one.

There are numerous exceptions to this ruling. Police officers, for example, may question a suspect before informing him or her of these rights if there is an issue of public safety. Questioning is also allowed during traffic stops without Miranda warnings. Other exceptions exist as well, and some scholars argue that the existence of so many exceptions makes Miranda rights subject to misunderstanding and misuse by police (Steinberg, 2000).

Through these rulings, the Supreme Court implicitly recognized the potential for coercion taking place when someone is in police custody. Further, there is recognition that this coercion, whether physical or psychological, can result in a false confession (Leo, 1996; Leo, Ofshe, and Cassell, 1998). The rulings provide for the presence of an attorney for the suspect on the assumption that this will prevent possible coercion. Thus, Miranda, in combination with subsequent legal cases dealing with its applicability, is relevant to every criminal defendant. When you were informed of your rights under Miranda, you were learning about some of your most important legal rights, and you may have chosen to exercise them, for example, by requesting an attorney and by choosing to remain silent during police questioning. However, if you are like a significant proportion of defendants, you may have waived your rights during questioning by police.

## The Sixth Amendment

The Sixth Amendment provides, in part:

> In all criminal prosecutions, the accused shall enjoy the right to a speedy and public trial, by an impartial jury of the State and district wherein the crime shall have been committed, which district shall have been previously ascertained by law, and to be informed of the nature and cause of the accusation; to be confronted with the witnesses against him; to have compulsory process for obtaining witnesses in his favor, and to have the Assistance of Counsel for his defense.

### Gideon v. Wainwright, 1963

Gideon was a man with a string of petty crimes to his name. One day he was arrested for breaking and entering a pool hall and ransacking the cigarette vending machine. Unable to afford counsel, he asked the court to provide him with an attorney to help him mount his defense. The court refused, and Gideon represented himself at his trial as best he could. The jury convicted him and he was sentenced to five years in prison.

While in prison, Gideon petitioned to appeal his case. His handwritten petition provided the opportunity for the Supreme Court to re-examine relevant precedents and long-standing controversies surrounding the question of whether the right to counsel was a "fundamental" constitutional right. The Gideon case created one of our most significant due process rights, requiring a large-scale procedural change in the criminal justice system by providing indigent suspects with the right to have counsel appointed for them. The basis for this right was the Supreme Court's application of the Sixth Amendment right to assistance of counsel to state trials. Prior to Gideon, this right had been held applicable only to federal criminal trials, and in special circumstances such as when the defendant faced a capital charge or was illiterate, mentally ill, or very young.

In Gideon, the Sixth Amendment right to counsel was held to be incorporated by the due process clause of the Fourteenth Amendment, and thus to be binding for all states. Gideon extended the right to counsel in felony trials; in *Argersinger v. Hamlin* (1972), the right to counsel was applied to misdemeanor trials where the defendant could receive a sentence of incarceration, even if only for one day.

As a result of Gideon, the majority of criminal defendants, most of whom are indigent, are provided with an attorney by the state. If the charges against you carry a penalty of possible incarceration, you will be provided with an attorney (unless you hire one on your own). You may choose to represent yourself at trial. However, unless you are skilled in the ways of the law, this is unlikely to be a wise idea.

## A GOVERNMENT OF LAWS, NOT MEN

"A government of laws, and not of men." This philosophy of governance, stated in the original draft of the Massachusetts Constitution (1779), emphasizes the **Classicalist** belief that the law should apply equally to all people regardless of who they are.

What does this idea mean to you, and why should we care about it? The idea that legal decisions should be governed strictly by the law, rather than being influenced by subjective factors such as political considerations or individual whim or caprice, is part of the broader concept of egalitarianism underlying our system of government. It reflects a fundamental concern with fairness, and the ideal that the law (and its agents, such as judges) should treat everyone equally. Variations in treatment should reflect only legally relevant factors, such as the seriousness of the crime, and should not reflect irrelevant factors, such as the social status or ethnicity of the defendant (or the victim).

The goal of equal treatment under the law raises challenging questions for us and our society, because it requires us to define what we mean by equal treatment. Does equal treatment consist of treating everyone identically? Think about the implications of this. If equal treatment simply meant applying the same legal yardstick to everyone in the exact same manner, that would mean that variations between people would never be taken into account. For example, all criminal defendants would be treated identically, regardless of their mental capabilities, motives, characteristics, or the circumstances of the offense. It would not matter whether the offender was six years old or sixty; whether she or he was insane at the time of the crime, acting in self-defense, or committing a calculated crime for financial gain; nor would it matter whether a thief who stole $25 took it in the form of compact disks or food to feed a hungry family.

Yet these types of distinctions are the very stuff of which many court cases are made, and our criminal law historically makes important distinctions between offenders on the basis of their motives, their age, and their mental state at the time of the crime. It can therefore be argued that treating people equally is certainly not the same thing as treating them identically; and that, in fact, equality of treatment often requires recognizing relevant differences between people. Thus, our legal system distinguishes between people who kill in the heat of passion, in self-defense, and in the course of committing another crime such as robbery. We allow mitigating and aggravating factors to be taken into account at sentencing; we also distinguish (although increasingly to a lesser degree) between juveniles and adults who commit crimes.

But if equal treatment requires differential treatment, how should we proceed? How do we decide, for example, which characteristics are relevant for distinguishing among people? How do we decide whether such distinguishing factors are applicable in a particular case? Finally, after taking legally relevant differences into account, how do we decide what this means in terms of equal (fair) treatment? This is where the exercise of discretion by criminal justice decision makers, such as police officers and prosecutors, plays a central role. We will examine discretion in different contexts as we travel throughout the steps of the criminal justice process.

Many people scoff at the notion that the law applies equally to all, pointing out that, in reality, unequal treatment occurs. Yet defenders of this ideal argue that rather than abandoning the ideal of equal treatment under the law, society must simply continue to struggle to make reality as consistent with the ideal as possible.

## LAW ON THE BOOKS VERSUS LAW IN ACTION

Theoretically, only legally relevant factors, such as applicable laws and admissible evidence, influence cases as they are processed by the legal system. However, a large body of research demonstrates that what happens in the courtroom is often also influenced by an array of extra-legal factors. These range from broad influences such as the political zeitgeist (mood) of the times to very specific factors like the nonverbal behavior of judges.

Because of this, there are often inconsistencies or gaps between **law on the books**—that is, official rules and procedures specifying what should occur at any given step in the legal process—and **law in action**—how procedures are actually implemented.

Examples illustrating how a significant gap can exist abound. For example, research demonstrates that a disturbing number of Americans apparently do not subscribe to the key legal premise of the American justice system: that an accused person is innocent until proven guilty beyond a reasonable doubt (Willis, 1992). Instead, for some people the very fact that a person has been accused of a crime suggests that the accused is guilty, that "where there's smoke, there's fire." If this belief significantly influences key courtroom participants, such as jurors or judges, it could potentially prejudice their legal decisions (see Box 3.4).

Research and news from current events provide cases where innocent defendants were erroneously convicted of a crime, despite the safeguards that our legal system provides for the very purpose of preventing this. In 1980, Clarence Lee Brandley, an African American janitor at a high school, was convicted of raping and murdering student Cheryl Ferguson, whose body was found concealed on campus. On appeal, he was granted another trial, and was convicted and sentenced to death in 1985. But the questions posed by observers who doubted the evidence against Brandley finally succeeded in demonstrating a chilling fact: Brandley had been sentenced to die for a crime he did not commit, a conclusion supported by physical (DNA) evidence, the testimony of a member of the prosecutor's office detailing prosecutorial and law enforcement misconduct, and finally, the video-taped confessions of the actual killer, a white janitor at the high school, as well as of another janitor who helped the killer conceal the truth. Clarence Brandley was finally freed in 1989 after serving ten years in prison, most of them on death row (*Texas v. Brandley,* 1990; Abramson, 1994).

The Innocence Project, discussed in Box 3.5, has successfully investigated a number of wrongful convictions, demonstrating that innocent individuals are sometimes convicted of serious offenses and that DNA evidence, most often used to link individuals to crimes, can sometimes be a defendant's most valuable ally.

---

## BOX 3.4
## Probably Guilty—Until Trial?

According to Harold Rothwax, a criminal court trial judge in New York City for over two decades, the criminal justice system should recognize the legal distinctions between the investigative and trial phases of a case. Why? Rothwax states that most criminal defendants are "probably guilty," and that the presumption of innocence applies only to the trial phase of a case. In contrast, Rothwax says, "When a person is arrested, indicted by a grand jury, held in detention, or released on bail, it is all based on probable guilt" (Gavzer, 1996, p. 4).

---

## BOX 3.5

## The Innocence Project

The incredible potential of DNA technology as a crime-fighting tool is matched by its value as a tool for fighting unjust convictions. As new applications of DNA technology emerge and older applications are refined in the laboratory, some criminal defense attorneys are looking into old murder convictions that merit attention. In 1992, attorneys Peter Neufeld and Barry Scheck started The Innocence Project, which is part of the Benjamin N. Cardozo School of Law at Yeshiva University. By early 2002, the project had been instrumental in using DNA technology to exonerate 102 people who were erroneously convicted, and in some cases sentenced to death (Innocence Project, 2002).

---

Of course, it is also true that an unknown number of guilty defendants have been mistakenly acquitted, sometimes partly due to the legal safeguards described in this chapter. Available evidence, however, suggests that protections, such as the Exclusionary Rule (Fyfe, 1983; Davies, 1983) and Miranda warnings, are not costly in terms of lost convictions against defendants (Leo and Thomas, 1998). On the other hand, the costs of mistaken convictions include both the harm experienced by the innocent defendant and the harm done to society because the actual perpetrator remains undetected.

To develop a more realistic understanding of the legal system and the courts, it is useful to evaluate the degree to which the system deviates from the ideal in actual practice. Thus, our examination of the court system includes discussions on how a variety of legal and **extra-legal factors** (that is, factors that legally should not influence the case) can influence the process of seeking justice.

## THE "OBJECTIVITY" OF LAW: THEORY AND REALITY

In the words of Benjamin N. Cardozo, who served as a U.S. Supreme Court Justice from 1932 to 1938:

> There is in each of us a stream of tendency, whether you choose to call it philosophy or not, which gives coherence and direction to thought and action. Judges cannot escape that current any more than other mortals. All their lives, forces which they do not recognize and cannot name, have been tugging at them—inherited instincts, traditional beliefs, acquired convictions; and the resultant is an outlook on life, a conception of social needs, a sense in (William) James's phrase of "the total push and pressure of the cosmos," which, when reasons are nicely balanced, must determine where choice shall fall. In this mental background every problem finds its setting. We may try to see things as objectively as we please. None the less, we can never see them with any eyes except our own. (Cardozo, 1921, p. 12). (Reprinted by permission of the publisher from B.N. Cardozo, *The Nature of the Judicial Process.* Yale University Press, 1921.)

As we learned in Step 1, the American legal system is based on common law, meaning that much of our law is the result of individual court decisions. This is often referred to as "judge-made" law, and it is a crucial source of law in the American system, although the source of most law is statutes enacted by a governing body such as a federal or state legislature. Thus, although *laws* govern what happens in court in theory, in reality a judge (and sometimes a jury) must interpret and apply the law given a particular set of facts in a case, and this means that human discretion must enter the picture. Stop and consider the potential advantages and disadvantages of discretion in legal decision-making. What are some of the possible *benefits* of discretion? What are some of the possible *costs*?

## THE FUNCTIONS OF JUDICIAL DECISIONS

Judicial decisions often serve dual purposes: to settle a dispute among the parties in a particular case, and frequently (but not always) to serve as a precedent for future cases. Why is this significant? Our legal system accords great respect to continuity in legal reasoning, in the form of precedents. The legal system is geared toward generating judicial decisions that are consistent with previous court decisions germane to the legal issue at hand. Recall from Step 1 that this principle of respect for precedent is embodied in the term **stare decisis**, which translated from the Latin means "let the decision stand."

In a sense, then, judicial decisions are akin to a recipe that provides a meal now, and a guideline for future meals, some of which will begin with the recipe but end up substantially departing from it. Similarly, a case decision can serve as a key influence on legal reasoning in a long line of subsequent cases, a number of which will result in a decision substantially different from that of the precedent. This is particularly true of appellate (appealed) decisions.

## LAW AS A "LIVING BODY"

Legal and popular perceptions of the Anglo-American legal system have changed radically over the last century. The historical view of law and the courts conceived of legal reasoning as the means to discovering a hidden "truth," a "correct result" that could be found for all cases. In its barest form, this view emphasized that if the correct legal principles were selected and applied to the facts of a case, then inevitably a correct result would be reached, because these principles would unearth the correct decision waiting to be found. This perception of the legal process could be compared to an archaeological dig, with researchers carefully excavating to find the "truth" about ancient cultures.

This historical conception of the legal process allowed little room for notions of judicial subjectivity and other extra-legal influences on the law. It rejected the idea of judge-made law, instead envisioning judges as those who would merely apply the law: regardless of the judge, the same result should occur in a case if the correct legal principles were applied to the facts.

This idea of "found law" contrasts sharply with modern conceptions of the Anglo-American legal system, which emphasize the changing, dynamic nature of law and the importance of recognizing extra-legal influences on legal outcomes.

Given the central role stare decisis plays in American law, how can the law be changing? The answer is that the law is a growing body of knowledge evolving in a somewhat patchwork fashion—with different areas of law growing at different rates and sometimes in different directions.

Cases raising similar legal issues but arising in different jurisdictions (e.g., different states or counties) can produce conflicting precedents, and sometimes even cases in the same jurisdiction will do the same. Laws produced at the ballot box through the initiative process can conflict with federal or state statutes or constitutional provisions; California provides an illustrative example. In 1998, Californians voted approval of Proposition 215, the "Medical Marijuana" initiative, which specified that seriously ill individuals could use marijuana for therapeutic purposes (such as easing pain or stimulating appetite) if prescribed by a health care provider (California Attorney General's Office).

The proposal to allow use of medical marijuana has become mired in controversy for several reasons, however, not least of which is that federal drug laws have no provisions allowing marijuana use for therapeutic purposes. Thus federal and state laws on this issue stand in direct contradiction, with federal law taking precedence. Because of this clash between the "will of the people" and federal law, some law enforcement agencies have shifted their priorities away from enforcement of drug laws in cases involving actual or suspected use of medical marijuana. For example, the sheriff of the little town of Arcata, California, issued laminated identification cards for medical marijuana users to help law enforcement officers distinguish them from "regular" users (Hornblower, 1999).

Another illustration of the dynamic, changing nature of the law occurs when different areas of law that are germane to a particular legal issue appear to provide contradictory precedents. This may create a legal "gray area" of ambiguity, and the need to reconcile these inconsistent elements can be a catalyst for legal change (see Box 3.6).

*Why* is law dynamic? There are several reasons. New statutes can be created that change the nature or scope of the law with respect to a particular issue; new appellate decisions can have the same effect. A classic example of new statutory provisions arising in many states that have had significant ripple effects on the operation of courts are "three strikes" laws mandating or authorizing harsher sentencing for persons previously convicted of certain offenses.

The Supreme Court provides a good example of how changes at the level of appellate courts contribute to the dynamic nature of the law. As the ultimate appellate court, the United States Supreme Court's decisions on legal issues have

## BOX 3.6

## Fetuses, Personhood, and the Law

What is a legal "person?" The U.S. Supreme Court has affirmed that a "person," in the constitutional sense, refers to someone who has been born (although corporations are legally defined as persons).

Fetuses are thus not persons in the constitutional sense (*Roe v. Wade,* 1973). Therefore, if a pregnant woman is attacked and the fetus she is carrying is injured or killed, the perpetrator is usually criminally charged only in connection with the injuries to the woman herself, not the injuries sustained by her fetus.

Similarly, attempts to prosecute pregnant women who use drugs or alcohol under the provisions of child abuse or endangerment statutes have usually—although not always—been unsuccessful, because such statutes were legally intended to apply to people who were already born, not fetuses (Humphries et al., 1994). However, under the provisions of tort (civil) law, drivers whose negligence resulted in injuries to a fetus have been successfully sued for the injuries to both mother and fetus.

Thus, in recent years, more states have begun to examine their statutory definitions of "personhood" and to question whether legal personhood requires being born, or whether it should be conditioned upon scientific evidence demonstrating that a fetus at a certain stage is probably viable (that is, could survive outside the womb). As a result, successful criminal prosecutions of individuals (whether the mother or another person) for injuries to a fetus while *in utero* are increasing (Donnelly, 1997; Pasternak, 1997).

far-reaching consequences for courts across the nation. Occasionally, the Supreme Court will reverse one of its earlier decisions, as occurred with the question of whether victim impact statements should be admissible in court during the sentencing phase. In *South Carolina v. Gathers* (1989) and *Booth v. Maryland* (1987), the Supreme Court held that victim impact statements were not evidence, and as such should not enter into a judge's or jury's sentencing considerations. Just a few years later, however, the court rethought this position in *Payne v. Tennessee* (1991), ruling that victims' families and friends could testify in capital cases about the effect of the crime on their lives.

New legal issues that have not previously appeared in court (referred to as **cases of first impression**) arise with increasing frequency these days, leading to the development of whole new areas of law (or new areas of application for old principles of law). Rapid societal and technological changes in the world today are opening up new legal questions faster than ever before. For example, the advent of computer technology and the Internet brings with it a host of legal questions: How can computer crimes be prevented? Which jurisdiction should handle a computer-crimes case when the accused and the victim(s) live in different states, or nations?

Developments in biotechnology, especially reproductive technology, have recently raised ethical and legal questions related to parenthood. For example, what are the legal rights of a surrogate mother who claims custody of a child that she has carried to term, yet who is not genetically a relative? Can relatives of a deceased person harvest the person's sperm or eggs in order to have the deceased's child?

Changes in other areas of technology have brought many legal questions related to the protections provided us by the Bill of Rights. For example, how does the Second Amendment's provision of the right to bear arms, which was created two centuries before the invention of automatic weapons, apply to modern proposals to regulate such firearms? Do the provisions of the Fourth Amendment against unreasonable search and seizure apply when law enforcement agents use newly developed infrared, heat-sensing technology to "peer through" the walls of a suspected drug dealer's house and track movements? Can parents require their minor children to submit to regular drug testing?

As we saw in Step 1, changes in social customs, attitudes, and political and public opinions can cause some laws to fall into unenforced obscurity or be stricken from the books. For example, many states have laws against adultery remaining on the books, but these are almost never enforced. Conversely, sometimes issues that received relatively little legal attention come into the spotlight as a result of increasing public awareness of the problem (e.g., marital rape, sexual harassment), and the law changes to reflect this. Another form of legal change occurs when existing legal principles are applied in new ways, such as the Southern Poverty Law Center's innovative use of civil suits to bankrupt white supremacist groups (Southern Poverty Law Center, 2002). The increasing use of wrongful death actions by families of murder victims, such as occurred in the civil case finding O.J. Simpson liable in the deaths of Ron Goldman and Nicole Brown, is another example. Traditionally, wrongful death suits occurred almost exclusively in the context of deaths from occupational accidents or defective products.

A good illustration of how legal change is intertwined with societal changes concerns the Sixth Amendment's right to trial by a jury of your peers. Whereas the language of the Amendment remains unchanged, the way it has been interpreted has changed radically in the last two centuries. Only in relatively modern times has the right to a jury trial been interpreted to mean that women, members of ethnic minorities, and the poor (including poor white men) must have the opportunity to be in the jury panel from which members of the jury are selected (Abramson, 1994). As a result, a rather sizable body of law on jury selection has developed.

Supreme Court cases dealing with the rights of the accused further illustrate the changing nature of the law, in what they teach us about the court's response to the individual–societal rights dilemma: the right of a suspect, innocent until proven guilty, to procedural fairness versus the right of society to protect itself from guilty persons through vigorous law enforcement. These rulings illustrate how the law attempts to address the contradictory tensions inherent in simultaneously trying to protect the rights of suspects to procedural fairness and the rights of society to protect itself from guilty persons through vigorous law enforcement.

Wrightsman, Nietzel, and Fortune (1994) conceptualize this process as if the law were a pendulum, swinging back and forth between protecting the accused and then repealing or diluting some of those protections. Supreme Court rulings on the admissibility of evidence are an example. The Mapp case, discussed earlier, sets the substantive standard for all the states firmly on the side of individual rights; good faith and other exceptions represent shifts toward the societal rights end of the dilemma.

The fact that Supreme Court decisions usually follow political lines illustrates another key factor shaping the development of different areas of law in various directions. Law is shaped by the political climate of the times, and the subjective perspectives of key participants in the courtroom drama. It is a myth that legal decisions are made solely on the basis of objective case factors. Quite often extra-legal factors, such as the personal perspective of the judge and jurors, are also part of legal decisions, an element that is now widely acknowledged (Hogarth, 1971).

# CONCLUSION

Law is a changing body of knowledge that both reflects and shapes larger social, political, and economic processes. What does this mean for you and your 3:00 A.M. arrest? We will see in the next chapters how these processes play out as we look at the next step in the legal system's handling of your case.

## DISCUSSION QUESTIONS

1. How does the practice of asset forfeiture illustrate the complexity of applying legal concepts such as due process in specific situations?

2. Consider the practice of allowing asset forfeiture in cases where the suspect has not yet been tried. What are the goals of this asset forfeiture policy? What due process issues does this policy raise? What about the consequences of asset forfeiture for innocent third parties? Might there be constitutional issues here?

3. What did you think of Judge Rothwax's assertion (in Box 3.4) that defendants should be presumed innocent only during the *trial* phase of the case? What are the implications of assuming the defendant is "probably guilty" during the investigative phase of a case? Does Judge Rothwax appear to be an objective judge? Why or why not?

4. What are some of the changes in society that will require new laws or changes in existing laws in order to deal with legal dilemmas raised by these changes? For example, think about current events that illustrate changes in technology, changes in societal attitudes, or other kinds of changes that the law will have to address.

5. What does "reasonable doubt" mean to you? How might you change the jury instructions on reasonable doubt in order to make it very clear to jurors what this means?

# NOTES

1. In response to the widespread problem of states' disenfranchisment of African American citizens, in 1870 Congress ratified the Fifteenth Amendment, providing that voting rights ". . . shall not be denied or abridged by the United States or any State on account of race, color, or previous condition of servitude." Native Americans were not given the right to vote until Congress passed the Indian Citizenship Act in 1924. Despite this, Native Americans in Arizona were not allowed to vote until 1948, when the Arizona Supreme Court overturned a state law prohibiting Native Americans from voting. Native Americans could not vote under New Mexico state law until 1962, when the state supreme court overturned the law.

# REFERENCES

Abramson, J. (1994). *We, The Jury: The Jury System and the Ideal of Democracy.* New York: Basic Books.

*Argersinger v. Hamlin,* 407 U.S. 25 (1972).

*Booth v. Maryland,* 482 U.S. 496 (1987).

California Attorney General's Office web document. Available at vote96.ss.ca.gov/Vote96/html/BP/215.htm.

Cardozo, B.N. (1921). *The Nature of the Judicial Process.* New Haven, CT: Yale University Press.

Cawthon, R. (2000, February 1). Illinois governor puts death penalty on hold. *Pittsburgh Post-Gazette,* p. A6.

Cecil, A.R. (1983). *The Foundations of a Free Society.* Austin: University of Texas Press.

*Commonwealth v. Webster* (No number in original), Supreme Court of Massachusetts, Suffolk and Nantucket, 59 Mass. 386 (March 1850).

Davies, T. (1983, Summer). A hard look at what we know (and still need to learn) about the "costs" of the Exclusionary Rule: The NIJ study and other studies of 'lost' arrests. *American Bar Foundation Research Journal,* pp. 611–690.

Donnelly, S.B. (1997, December 15). The postpartum prosecutor. *Time,* p. 4.

*Escobedo v. Illinois,* 378 U.S. 478 (1964).

Fyfe, J. (1983, Summer). The NIJ study of the Exclusionary Rule. *American Bar Foundation Research Journal,* pp. 611–690.

Gavzer, B. (1996, July 28). We're in the fight of our lives. *Parade Magazine,* pp. 4–6.

*Gideon v. Wainwright,* 372 U.S. 335 (1963).

*Goss v. Lopez,* 419 U.S. 565 (1975).

Hogarth, J. (1971). *Sentencing As a Human Process.* Toronto, Canada: University of Toronto Press.

Hornblower, M. (1999, May 3). Here's my marijuana card, officer. *Time,* p. 7.

Humphries, D., Dawson, J., Cronin, V., Keating, P., Wisniewski, C., and Eichfeld, J. (1994). Mothers and children, drugs and crack: Reactions to maternal drug dependency. In B. Price and N. Sokoloff (eds.), *The Criminal Justice System and Women: Offenders, Victims, and Workers.* New York: McGraw-Hill, pp. 167–180.

Innocence Project at the Cardozo School of Law. (1999). Available at www.yu.educ/cardozo/law/innocent/html.

Leo, R. (1996). Inside the interrogation room. *Journal of Criminal Law & Criminology.* 86 (2): 266–303.

Leo, R., Ofshe, R., and Cassell, P. (1998). The consequences of false confessions: Deprivations of liberty and miscarriages of justice in the age of psychological interrogation. *Journal of Criminal Law & Criminology*. 88(2): 429–496.

Leo, R., and Thomas, G.C., III, (eds.) (1998). *The Miranda Debate: Law, Justice, and Policing.* Boston: Northeastern University Press.

Lind, E.A. (1982). The psychology of courtroom procedure. In N. Kerr and R. Bray (eds.), *Psychology in the Courtroom.* Orlando, FL: Academic Press.

Lind, E.A., Erickson, B.E., Friedland, N., and Dickenberger, M. (1978). Reactions to procedural models for adjudicative conflict resolutions. *Journal of Conflict Resolution,* 22: 318–341.

Logan, W.A. (1999). Liberty interests in the preventive state: Procedural due process and sex offender community notification laws. *Journal of Criminal Law & Criminology,* 89 (4): 1167–1231.

*Mapp v. Ohio,* 367 U.S. 643 (1961).

Mauro, T. (2000, April 18). Court favors privacy in another Fourth Amendment case. *The Legal Intelligencer,* p. 5.

*Miranda v. Arizona,* 384 U.S. 486 (1966).

Palmer, E. (2000, April 1). Senate passes asset seizure overhaul bill. *CQ Weekly,* 58 (14): 773.

Pasternak, J. (1997, February 2). Legal cases test if states act properly in seizing addicts whose behavior endangers fetuses. *San Francisco Examiner.*

*Payne v. Tennessee,* 501 U.S. 808 (1991).

Radelet, M., and Bedau, H. (1998). The execution of the innocent. *Law and Contemporary Problems,* 61, (4): 105–124.

*Roe v. Wade,* 410 U.S. 113 (1973).

*Sandin v. Connor,* 115 S. Ct. 2293 (1995).

*South Carolina v. Gathers,* 490 U.S. 805 (1989).

Southern Poverty Law Center. (2002). Available at www.sp/center.org/legalaction/la-index.html.

Steinberg, D. (2000, August 14). Miranda no longer works. *The National Law Journal,* p. A18.

*Texas v. Brandley,* 498 U.S. 817 (1990).

Thibaut, J., and Walker, L. (1975). *Procedural Justice: A Psychological Analysis.* Hillsdale, NJ: Erlbaum.

*United States v. Bennis,* 516 U.S. 442 (1996).

Walker, S. (2001). *Sense and Nonsense About Drugs and Crime: A Policy Guide.* Belmont, CA: Wadsworth.

*Weeks v. United States,* 232 U.S. 383 (1914).

Willis, C.E. (1992). The biasing of culpability judgments with evidence of prior bad acts. Paper presented at the 1992 meeting of the American Psychology-Law Society, San Diego, CA.

*Wolff v. McDonnell,* 418 U.S. 539 (1974).

Wrightsman, L., Nietzel, M., and Fortune, W. (1994). *Psychology and the Legal System* (3rd ed.). Belmont, CA: Wadsworth.

# Step 4

## The Courts Get Involved: The History of Courts and the Arrangement of Modern Courts

❖

In the previous chapter, we learned about the basis of our adversarial system. We learned about our fundamental rights and how they developed over time from our legal system's British roots. Then, we looked at some important cases that have shaped modern criminal courts. Ours is a government of laws, not men, and the law is constantly being refined over time.

Here, we will step back a bit from the law and look at the history of the courts themselves. American courts have a fascinating legacy; originally borrowed from England, they now have only casual similarities to their early roots.[1] Before we can look at the modern American courts, however, we need to examine their heritage.

## THE HISTORY OF COURTS

Anglo-Saxon courts were based on the adversarial system discussed in the previous chapter, and it is true that we derived that critical part of our system from England. An accused person had to be proven guilty before she or he could be held accountable for the crimes with which she or he had been charged. Of course, what constituted proof of guilt was very different then; and, defendants had no right to counsel and were not allowed to present witnesses on their behalf, although the government was entitled to call as many witnesses as it felt were necessary to prove its case (Moore, 1973, p. 57). Early Anglo-Saxon defendants had no Bill of Rights to protect them, but the *Magna Charta* (Latin for "The Great Charter") offered a number of protections.

The *Magna Charta*, signed by King John in 1215, has an interesting past. English barons, angered by the king's unfettered discretion over them and his widespread seizures of land and property, demanded under the threat of war that the king acknowledge basic rights such as rights to property and due process (Spooner, 1852,

p. 192). This was an historic event because no ruler before King John had accorded such common law rights in writing.[2] Like our Constitution, the *Magna Charta* was intended to serve as an important limit on the government's powers. See Box 4.1 for a few sections from the *Magna Charta* that relate to criminal justice.

When the English came to colonize what would later become the United States of America, they brought basic justice principles like the *Magna Charta* with them. These fundamental principles are reiterated over and over in our historical and contemporary court system. To understand our courts, then, we must know a little about the Anglo-Saxon courts on which they are based.

Very early Anglo-Saxon justice appears to have been the purview of the lords who owned the lands occupied by servants and others who provided some service in exchange for the right to use the lords' land. This system essentially meant that a

---

## BOX 4.1

## A Few Provisions from the *Magna Charta*

Know ye, that We, in the presence of God, and for the salvation of our own soul, and of the souls of all our ancestors, and of our heirs . . . have in the First place granted to God, and by this our present Charter, have confirmed, for us and our heirs for ever:

(20) A free-man shall not be fined for a small offence, but only according to the degree of the offence; and for a great delinquency, according to the magnitude of the delinquency, saving his contenement: a Merchant shall be fined in the same manner, saving his merchandise, and a villain shall be fined after the same manner, saving to him his Wainage, if he shall fall into our mercy; and none of the aforesaid fines shall be assessed, but by the oath of honest men of the vicinage.

(21) Earls and Barons shall not be fined but by their Peers, and that only according to the degree of their delinquency.

(39) No freeman shall be seized, or imprisoned, or dispossessed, or outlawed, or in any way destroyed; nor will we condemn him, nor will we commit him to prison, excepting by the legal judgement of his peers, or by the laws of the land.

(56) If we have disseised or dispossessed any Welshmen of their lands, or liberties, or other things, without a legal verdict of their peers, in England or in Wales, they shall be immediately restored to them.

(63) Wherefore, our will is and we firmly command that the Church of England be free, and that the men in our kingdom have and hold the aforesaid liberties, rights, and concessions, well and in peace, freely and quietly, fully and entirely, to them and their heirs, of us and our heirs, in all things and places, for ever as is aforesaid. (*Magna Charta*, 1215/1997, prepared by The American Revolution HTML project.)

The *Magna Charta*, signed by King John in 1215, acknowledged basic rights such as rights to property and due process. Like the U.S. Constitution, the *Magna Charta* was intended to serve as an important limit on the government's powers. When the English came to America, they brought basic justice principles like the *Magna Charta* with them.   SOURCE: Courtesy of the Granger Collection.

lord had the right to define and enforce the law in his manor in whatever manner he saw fit. These courts were characterized by inconsistency and, at times, capriciousness. Legal procedures and laws differed from manor to manor, and some lords were more liberal than others (Maitland, 1897).

After that time, the beginnings of what can be clearly labeled English law began to develop. At first, the king himself sat as judge in cases, but later a network of judges who traveled from area to area to hear both criminal and civil cases was established (Holten and Lamar, 1991, pp. 42–43). These judges were representatives of the king and represented his interests. Trials during this era, beginning in roughly the twelfth century, typically fell under three varieties: trial by ordeal, trial by battle, or trial by compurgation (or oath).

**Trial by ordeal** is an ancient form of justice in which the defendant in a civil or criminal case was ordered to undergo some ordeal to prove his or her innocence. The belief was that God would intervene on the defendant's behalf if she or he were blameless. It is important to recognize the enormous value assigned to God and religion by traditional European legal proceedings. In fact, during the Middle Ages, ecclesiastical law (i.e., laws governing the church) was indistinguishable from other laws due to the blending of religious and other rules together into one law (Maine, 1861). Given their lack of other methods to ascertain the truth (e.g., even rudimentary forensic techniques), an undying faith in the ability and willingness of God to help mere mortals uncover the guilty among them makes even more sense. England was like many other ancient societies in this regard.

Individuals were typically subjected to one of three ordeals (Lea, 1870/1996, pp. 4–5, 222). The first was the trial by fire, in which the suspected party walked barefoot across red-hot ploughshares or carried red-hot iron for a specified distance. Following the ordeal, the party's hands or feet were wrapped in bandages. Three days later, the bandages were unwrapped. If the party suffered no injury by the third day, she or he was declared innocent. In trial by hot water, an accused person plunged his or her hand into a cauldron of water brought to the boiling point to extract a pebble or ring from the bottom. If she or he evidenced no burns three days after the task, she or he was proclaimed innocent. The final ordeal, that of cold water, is best known because it was often used to ascertain the guilt of those suspected of being witches. The accused was bound hand and foot, then thrown into a lake or other body of water. Those who floated were declared guilty and executed; those who drowned were presumed to have died innocent individuals.[3] One defendant in 1083 may have thought he was being crafty when he had himself bound and lowered into a tub of water while awaiting trial to see if he would sink or float; when he sank, he agreed to be tried, but later floated much to his dismay (Lea, 1870/1996, pp. 252–53). Trial by ordeal was discontinued after Pope Innocent III banned its use by the church in 1215, the same year the *Magna Charta* was signed (Devlin, 1966, p. 9). As discussed below, this ban hastened the move toward jury trials (Cornish, 1968, p. 11; Stephen, 1883:i, p. 254).

**Trial by battle** is a curious form of fact-finding. Defendants in civil cases or those who had been accused by one person of committing a crime could either fight with their accusers themselves or choose champions to perform that service for them. The battles were not common duels; like ordeals, they were expected to be influenced by God, who would take a hand in determining the victor. In civil trials by battle, the victor at battle was the victor in court. In criminal trials by battle, if the defendant lost, he was executed and his estate defaulted to the Crown; if the accuser lost, he was incarcerated and fined as a false accuser (Bracton, 1250/1968:ii, p. 386). Regardless of the outcome, then, the Crown received funds and/or property from one of the parties. Trials by battle, though declining in number by the end of the thirteenth century, continued at least until 1638 and quite possibly into the middle 1700s (Moore, 1973, p. 84). In a 1422 case, for example, a plaintiff sued a tenant to recover some land (Moore, 1973, p. 84). The defendant chose trial by battle over a jury trial and chose a champion to represent his interests in the upcoming fight. The plaintiff then chose his own champion, and both defenders went to separate churches to pray for a fair outcome. Of interest, and pointing out one of the method's weaknesses, the defendant defaulted because his defender did not show up on the day of the scheduled battle. There is evidence that trial by battle was employed in America in Massachusetts Bay, New Hampshire, and North Carolina (Lea, 1870/1996, p. 199). Some writers have linked our present-day attorney system to the trial by battle, except that contemporary defenders are armed only with legal knowledge and no longer engage in physical fights (except in those rare cases in which verbal altercations between the two sides escalate into fistfights!).

**Trial by compurgation** (also called "trial by the swearing of oaths") was rather common in civil cases and required the parties to locate a required number of compurgators (i.e., neighbors who would vouch for the truthfulness of the party's oath that she or he was a guiltless party). Typically, the defendant would gather twelve compurgators who would state that the defendant's case was more worthy than the accuser's. In cases of theft, for example, the compurgators sometimes included the person who had sold or witnessed the sale of a disputed item to the defendant, thus demonstrating innocence (Holmes, 1881, p. 256). Compurgation was allowed in cases of nondocumented debts until 1752; all the defendant had to do was testify that he owed no debt and find eleven neighbors who would vouch for his honesty (Moore, 1973, p. 84). Our current jury system has its roots in trial by compurgation. The mysterious number twelve and the requirement for unanimity, for example, stem from the fact that before juries came into use, one needed twelve compurgators to clear one's name (Stephen, 1883:i, p. 304).[4]

Following the Norman invasion and conquest of England in 1066, English courts began to use juries. There is some disagreement among scholars as to whether the Normans brought the concept of juries to England (e.g., Moore, 1973, p. 18; Pollock and Maitland, 1895/1952, p. 140) or whether juries were an English invention (e.g., Cornish, 1968, p. 11). In any case, it appears that juries arose in England at about the time of the Norman Conquest. Although they do not specifically mention juries, see Box 4.2 for a few sections from the Laws of William the Conqueror that pertain to criminal justice issues.

The first juries were used to settle land disputes, which were quite common (Stephen, 1883:i, p. 255). From there, the use of juries expanded into other civil disputes and criminal trials. This incorporation process did not occur overnight; it took centuries for jury trials to gain recognition as a viable alternative to trial by ordeal, battle, or compurgation.

Juries were originally very different from those empaneled today (see Step 8 for information on modern juries). Like their contemporary counterparts, early English juries were "a body of neighbors . . . summoned by some public officer to give upon oath a true answer to some question" (Pollock and Maitland, 1895/1952, p. 138), but the similarities ended there. Instead of serving as a tool to protect citizens from the government, juries were themselves victimized by the power of the crown and in some respects actually contributed to the problem because of their lack of independence; jurors who failed to convict criminal defendants were often punished because the government could not seize a defendant's property if she or he was acquitted by a jury and the Crown took it out on the jurors. For this reason, serving on a jury could be a dangerous task that could easily cause a juror to lose all his property and land him in prison as well, as we will see later in this chapter.

Another key difference between contemporary and historic juries was how they functioned. Instead of rendering a verdict based on the evidence they heard during trial, early jurors were selected because they both knew the parties involved and could shed some light on whether the breach of contract or peace had happened

---

## BOX 4.2

## A Few Provisions from the Laws of William the Conqueror (1066)

The following excerpts are from the laws established by English King William after the Norman Conquest of England. In them, one can see references to trial methods of the day, oaths, sureties (a predecessor of the bail system), and the ever-so-popular fines that fed the royal treasury:

3. I will, moreover, that all the men whom I have brought with me, or who have come after me, shall be in my peace and quiet. And if one of them shall be slain, the lord of his murderer shall seize him within five days, if he can; but if not, he shall begin to pay to me forty six marks of silver as long as his possessions shall hold out. But when the possessions of the lord of that man are at an end the whole hundred [i.e., a local level of government] in which the slaying took place shall pay in common what remains.

6. It was also decreed there that if a Frenchman summon an Englishman for perjury or murder, theft, homicide, or "ran"—as the English call evident rape which can not be denied—the Englishman shall defend himself as he prefers, either through the ordeal of iron, or through wager of battle. But if the Englishman be infirm he shall find another who will do it for him. If one of them shall be vanquished he shall pay a fine of forty shillings to the king. If an Englishman summon a Frenchman, and be unwilling to prove his charge by judgment or by wager of battle, I will, nevertheless, that the Frenchman purge himself by an informal oath.

8. Every man who wishes to be considered a freeman shall have a surety, that his surety may hold him and hand him over to justice if he offend in any way. And if any such one escape, his sureties shall see to it that, without making difficulties, they pay what is charged against him, and that they clear themselves of having known of any fraud in the matter of his escape. The hundred and county shall be made to answer as our predecessors decreed. And those that ought of right to come, and are unwilling to appear, shall be summoned once; and if a second time they are unwilling to appear, one ox shall be taken from them and they shall be summoned a third time. And if they do not come the third time, another ox shall be taken: but if they do not come the fourth time there shall be forfeited from the goods of that man who was unwilling to come, the extent of the charge against him—"ceapgeld" as it is called—and besides this a fine to the king.

10. I forbid that any one be killed or hung for any fault but his eyes shall be torn out or his testicles cut off. And this command shall not be violated under penalty of a fine in full to me (Henderson, 1896).

---

(Devlin, 1979, p. 117). As amazing as it sounds, early jurors were more like witnesses who after disclosing what they knew about a case, then rendered a verdict on the basis of their individual and communal knowledge. In fact, the first juries heard no witnesses and had to rely exclusively on their own knowledge of a case (Blackstone, 1765/1897:iii, p. 374). Those who had no knowledge of a case could not serve on the jury (Stephen, 1883:i, p. 256). This is indeed a very different concept of "impartiality" than that which we associate with jurors today.

Police, as we know them, did not appear until 1829 (for example, Sir Robert Peel's "Peelers" in London [Greenberg, 1984, p. 22]), and early England had no prosecutors (Friedman, 1993, p. 21), meaning that judges had to conduct their own investigations into fact and used juries to achieve this function. Judges traveled from jurisdiction to jurisdiction, holding court sessions as needed. Before a judge arrived in town, a parish officer would assemble a jury for the judge's use during his visit (Cornish, 1968, p. 26).

Historically, it appears that there were two types of juries employed by the courts: accusing juries and trial juries.[5] Both were panels of citizens drawn from the local communities and both were used as investigatory tools. Accusing juries were panels of citizens used to ferret out crimes, and would be asked questions such as "Name all the persons in your district whom you suspect of murder, robbery or rape" (Pollock and Maitland, 1895/1952, p. 139). Those named by an accusing jury were then seized and brought to trial (Stephen, 1883:i, p. 257) or ordered to undergo trial by ordeal (Devlin, 1966, p. 9). The idea behind the accusing jury has survived to this day, and is the basis for the modern grand jury (Devlin, 1966, p. 9). You will learn more about grand juries in Step 5, which will discuss the role of grand juries in investigating and detecting crimes.

Trial juries, on the other hand, dealt with specific cases, although members of accusing juries sometimes sat on trial juries (Moore, 1973, p. 56), raising additional questions about fairness. The questions posed to the trial jury would be of the type: "Is Roger guilty of having murdered Ralph?" or "Whether of the two has the greater right to Blackacre, William or Hugh?" (Pollock and Maitland, 1895/1952, p. 139). The trial jurors made oaths stating that what they had heard or knew about a dispute or local custom was correct. Because of the lack of official record-keeping regarding births, some juries were assembled and asked to use their expertise (e.g., as parents of teenagers) to determine whether certain individuals were minors, because minors could not be fined or incur debt (Moore, 1973, p. 83).[6] Another type of jury, the only kind on which women were allowed to serve, was the "jury of matrons," whose sole duty was to use their own experiences as mothers to determine whether a given woman who claimed to be pregnant, usually to avoid execution, was indeed with child (Oldham, 1983, p. 171–72). In all these cases, the jurors were asked to use their own knowledge to arrive at their verdict rather than base their decision on any evidence.

If the trial jurors could not agree in a civil suit (i.e., the jurors were deadlocked), the case had to be settled through trial by battle (Stephen, 1883:i, p. 256), or the jurors could be taken by cart with the judge to his next destination (Blackstone, 1765/1897:iii, p. 376). If they could not agree in a criminal trial, or one in which the Crown was a party, the jurors could be confined without food, drink, or fire (used as a source of both heat and light in those days) until they rendered a unanimous verdict (Blackstone, 1765/1897:iii, p. 375; Stephen, 1883:i, p. 305). Sometimes, other steps were taken; for example, a holdout juror in a 1367 case was jailed when he would not agree with the other eleven jurors, whose verdicts were ultimately accepted (Moore, 1973, p. 56).

Jurors' decisions were closely monitored by the Crown. As a criminal offense, perjury could only be committed by jurors (Stephen, 1883:i, p. 241, iii, p. 255) and was considered a serious crime. Jurors whose verdicts were questioned were often fined and imprisoned (Stephen, 1883:iii, p. 242). One thirteenth-century legal scholar, Henry de Bracton (1250/1968:iii, p. 346), wrote that perjurers were to be treated severely:

> First of all, let them be arrested and cast into prison, and let all their lands and chattels be seized into the king's hand until they are redeemed at the king's will, so that nothing remains to them except their vacant tenements. They incur perpetual infamy and lose the *lex terrae*, so that they will never afterwards be admitted to an oath, for they will not henceforth be oathworthy, nor be received as witnesses, because it is presumed that he who is once convicted of perjury will perjure himself again.

Bracton (1250/1968:iii, p. 346) also discussed how perjurious jurors could mitigate their punishments by recanting their verdicts and throwing themselves on the mercy of the king, who would then only fine them heavily. It appears that the judge, a representative of the Crown, was the one who made the determination whether the jurors had perjured themselves.

Unfortunately, acquittals were often considered to be proof of lies by jurors; verdicts handed down by trial juries had to conform to the Crown's wishes or the jurors could be penalized. The judge had the right to separate the jurors and cross-examine them to determine if they somehow tried to "conceal the truth" (Stephen, 1883:i, p. 248). In fact, the now common oath taken by witnesses to tell "the whole truth" at one time meant that jurors could not conceal any facts in a case, whether or not they were directly asked questions about those facts (Blackstone, 1765/1887:iii, p. 372). Acquittals made it difficult for the Crown to seize a defendant's property, so it appears that the Crown instead recouped some of its losses by fining the jurors. Either way, the Crown received a payment.

The (correct) perception that juries were tools of the Crown made them an unpopular choice among defendants of the time. Defendants preferred even trial by battle to jury trials, leading the Crown to institute progressively more peculiar methods of persuasion to discourage people from resorting to other methods of trial. A 1275 statute provided for the incarceration of anyone who refused to be tried by jury until they agreed to do so; a 1291 law added that such individuals were to be kept "in the worst place in the prison" and fed only bread one day, then water the next, until they consented to be tried by jury; and by 1302 such individuals were to be pressed in addition to receiving only "three morsels of barley bread" on one day and stagnant water on the next until consent was given (Andrews, 1890/1991, p. 205;

Moore, 1973, p. 54–55). Pressing, an often fatal intervention, involved piling stones or irons on the accused as she or he lay prone on the floor until she or he agreed to enter a plea and be tried. One defendant, in 1741, endured 400 pounds of weights for several hours before he finally consented to plead not guilty to robbery (Andrews, 1890/1991, p. 207). Those who could endure the weight still faced starvation on the meager diet provided to those who would not plead.

The reasoning behind pressing was that the Crown could not seize assets of anyone who had not been found guilty at trial, so many defendants refused to even enter a plea (Andrews, 1890/1991, p. 205). Those who were killed during pressing (and everyone either perished or finally agreed to be tried) died knowing that their estates went to their spouses and children rather than to the Crown.[7] There were cases where the family and friends of defendants mercifully hastened their death by adding their own weight to the burdens (by standing on top of or jumping on the weights) to end the cruel torture of slowly being crushed (e.g., Andrews, 1890/1991, p. 210). The existence of this practice helped ensure that our Constitution specifically mentioned a person's right to remain silent when accused of committing a crime. Ironically, pressing was used in this country during the Salem witch trials to induce Giles Corey to enter a plea; wanting his estate to go to his children rather than the government, he chose being pressed to death rather than entering a plea (Hill, 1995, pp. 184–185).

Toward the end of the Middle Ages (i.e., around the fourteenth and fifteenth centuries), population growth and other societal changes made it difficult to find twelve individuals who knew about a given case, so judges began to allow those who knew about a case to testify as witnesses while the remaining jurors heard the evidence (Cornish, 1968, p. 11). Toward the end of the fifteenth century, the composition of juries further reflected this difficulty, as fewer and fewer individuals who were familiar with a case were included on juries (Waechter, 1997). By the sixteenth and seventeenth centuries, juries relied on outside witnesses to augment their own personal knowledge (Devlin, 1979, p. 117).

It was not until the eighteenth century that English juries no longer included individuals with prior knowledge of the case (Cornish, 1968, p. 12). By this time, juries had been completely transformed from groups of individuals who were assembled because of their knowledge of a case and whose oaths were based on that knowledge to a system in which jurors decide which of two scenarios (the first offered by the plaintiff/prosecution and the second by the defense) appeared to be the truth (Moore, 1973, p. 14).

Because of its importance in shaping American justice, the 1670 trial of William Penn and William Mead deserves special mention. Penn and Mead were on trial in England for unlawful assembly (for preaching to a group of Quakers) because the Crown had no law against being a "religious nonconformist" (O'Connor, 1995). The twelve-man jury was simultaneously sympathetic and savvy, however, and refused to convict either man, leading the judges (there were ten of them presiding over the trial) to first isolate the jurors without "food, drink, fire, and tobacco" until they had "a verdict that the court would accept . . . or you shall starve for it" (Moore, 1973, p. 87; Penn and Mead's Case, 1670). Despite being deprived of food and water for at least two days and being brought back into court several times to allow them to change their verdict, the jurors continued their refusal to grant the Crown the conviction it sought. The irate judges then fined each of the jurors forty marks (roughly two years' salary) for contempt of court and committed them to Newgate prison until the fines were paid. The leader of the jurors, Edward Bushell, and three others refused to pay the fines and filed a writ of **habeas corpus** (i.e., an official document ordering the government to show that the incarceration of a certain person is legal). After the four former jurors had spent nine difficult weeks in prison (often without food, water, or toilet facilities), a new judge granted the writ of habeas corpus and ruled that future juries could not be disciplined for their verdicts (Bushell's Case, 1670). After that time, judges could set aside verdicts (which they sometimes do to this day),[8] but jurors could no longer be penalized for refusing to cooperate with the government (Devlin, 1979, p. 118).

William Penn, of course, later moved to the New World, founded the Commonwealth of Pennsylvania, and played a role in the development of the American criminal justice system. His experiences during the trial helped shape the Founding Fathers' desire for an independent jury (Lehman, 1988), making trial by jury another key English development that was transported to the New World. Juries are now an important limitation on the government's power to prosecute or punish citizens because a panel of citizens must be convinced beyond a reasonable doubt by the state's attorney that an individual broke the law. Juries have been praised by several legal scholars and reformers. The famous legal scholar Sir William Blackstone (1765/1897:iii), for example, referred to trial juries as the "glory of the English law" and praised their immense value in systems in which oppression has been the norm:

> [I]t is the most transcendent privilege which any subject can enjoy, or wish for, that he cannot be affected in his property, his liberty, or his person, but by the unanimous consent of twelve of his neighbors and equals. (p. 379)

## COLONIAL AND EARLY AMERICAN COURTS

It is important to remember that the first American courts were actually English institutions, because this country existed as a colony of England until the Revolutionary War. For this reason, many legal elements were directly imported from England. A few courts remained under complete control of the Crown, such as the Vice Admiralty Courts, which "co-existed" with other colonial court structures but "not always on the best of terms" (Owen and Tolley, 1995, p. 19). Established in America because the Crown felt the colonists were evading the payment of duties on shipments to and from the New World (Owen and Tolley, 1995, p. 5), the Vice Admiralty Courts were authorized to dispatch officers to board ships and search for contraband for which duties had not been paid. Many New World ships and goods were seized, but the colonists' greatest concern was the courts' disturbing ban on jury trials (Owen and Tolley, 1995, p. 16). Without juries, the colonists felt they were not protected from overzealous prosecution by the Crown.

Even where the colonies operated their own courts, they were technically overseen by the Crown. Rulings by colonial courts were expected to conform to English law, but this requirement created problems because the social and economic situation in the colonies differed somewhat from that left behind in England (Labaree, 1972, p. 70). Individuals who did not perform their fair share of planting and other work, for example, could mean disaster for the remaining settlers in their villages, meaning that laziness and idleness were grounds for severe punishment. The colonies adapted by incorporating those legal procedures and laws from England that seemed most appropriate for their particular needs (Langdon, 1966, p. 93) and then supplementing that body of law with their own laws to address such concerns as slavery and dealing with Native Americans (Friedman, 1993, p. 22). In the end, colonial law's English roots were clearly visible, but so too were the innovations added by America's settlers.

Judicial functions were typically fulfilled by the governor and his assistants sitting as a panel (Langdon, 1966, p. 92; Wall, 1972, p. 5), and these individuals were often appointed by England's monarch. Further demonstrating the influence of the Crown on the colonial legal system, some accused criminals were to be returned to England for trial; in 1660, for example, the king ordered that all Quakers be tried in England for holding their nonconforming religious beliefs (Langdon, 1966, p. 76). In addition, some cases could be appealed from colonial courts to the Crown's courts in England (Friedman, 1993, p. 24). Most of the Crown's oversight was less direct, however, as illustrated by a 1703 letter addressed to the "Governors of all her Majesty's Plantations in America." After acknowledging that some citizens have complained about delays in justice, the letter reminds the governors "to take care that Justice be impartially administered," then asks them to enable legislation to create special courts "for determining of Small Causes" (Whitehead, 1881, p. 539). Of course, England was much more than an Internet connection away, so the day-to-day concerns of the colonial courts were left up to the colonists.

In general, colonial courts were far less complex than their English counterparts. First, the early courts served very small groupings of rather homogeneous citizens. For the first five years of New Plymouth's existence, for example, the only formal government was a governor, who served as governor, treasurer, secretary of state, and judge, and one assistant (Usher, 1984, p. 212). Similarly, the population of early Massachusetts was too small to necessitate the use of an accusing jury, so none was established (Friedman, 1993, p. 24). The demand for legal interventions was so infrequent in the New World that court sessions were held only three or four times a year in many colonies (e.g., Langdon, 1966, p. 94).

Second, the small number of legally trained individuals in the colonies meant that only the most familiar aspects of the courts could be replicated (e.g., Usher, 1984, p. 214; Walker, 1980, p. 22). Instead of lawyers, the New World was filled with religious leaders and devotees who had fled from England, and this is reflected in the early legal systems. Religion had a more "powerful influence in New England" than in the Mother Country (Friedman, 1993, p. 23), as was readily apparent from some of their early legal codes and procedures. The Puritans sought to establish "a godly society" in the New World (Friedman, 1993, p. 24) and seemed to believe that such a utopia could be legislated into existence. Failure to attend religious services in the early Jamestown settlement, for example, resulted in the loss of a week's rations; a second offense added a whipping to the loss of rations and the third offense merited the death penalty (Johnson, 1988, p. 99).[9] Similarly, New Plymouth's 1685 legal codes included a number of capital crimes inspired by the Bible: idolatry, blasphemy, and rebellion by a child who was aged sixteen or older (Langdon, 1966, p. 209).

In the absence of legal training, the Bible became the predominant source of law. When a teenaged servant was executed for sodomizing some of his master's livestock, for example, the court was very interested in identifying each of the animals he had abused so that it could be destroyed as mandated by the Bible in Leviticus 20:15 (Bradford, 1646/1952, p. 320). The 1648 laws for Massachusetts may have been the most biblically informed legal codes, as a quick perusal of Box 4.3 will demonstrate.

---

## BOX 4.3

## Biblically Based Capital Crimes for Massachusetts in 1648

1. IF any man after legal conviction shall HAVE OR WORSHIP any other God, but the LORD GOD: he shall be put to death. Exod. 22:20. Deut. 13:6, 10. Deut. 17:2, 6.

2. If any man or woman be a WITCH, that is, hath or consulteth with a familiar spirit, they shall be put to death. Exod. 22:18. Lev. 20:27. Deut. 18:10, 11.

3. If any person within this Jurisdiction whether Christian or Pagan shall wittingly and willingly presume to BLASPHEME the holy Name of God, Father, Son or Holy-Ghost, with direct, expresse, presumptuous, or high-handed blasphemy, either by wilfull or obstinate denying the true God, or his Creation, or Government of the world: or shall curse God in like manner, or reproach the holy Religion of God as if it were but a politick device to keep ignorant men in awe; or shal utter any other kinde of Blasphemy of the like nature and degree they shall be put to death. Lev. 24:15, 16.

4. If any person shall commit any wilfull MURTHER, which is Man slaughter, committed upon premeditate malice, hatred, or crueltie not in a man's necessary and just defence, nor by meer casualty against his will, he shall be put to death. Exod. 21:12, 13. Num. 35:31.

5. If any person slayeth another suddenly in his anger, or cruelty of passion, he shall be put to death. Lev. 24:17. Num. 35:20, 21.

6. If any person shall slay another through guile, either by POYSONING, or other such develish practice, he shall be put to death. Exod. 21:14.

7. If any man or woman shall LYE WITH ANY BEAST, or bruit creature, by carnall copulation; they shall surely be put to death: and the beast shall be slain, and buried, and not eaten. Lev. 20:15, 16.

8. If any man LYETH WITH MAN-KINDE as he lieth with a woman, both of them have committed abomination, they both shal surely be put to death: unless the one partie were forced (or be under fourteen years of age in which case he shall be seveerly punished) Lev. 20:13.

9. If any person commit ADULTERIE with a married, or espoused wife; the Adulterer and Adulteresse shal surely be put to death. Lev. 20:19. and 18:20. Deut. 22:23, 27.

10. If any man STEALETH A MAN, or Man-kinde, he shall surely be put to death. Exod. 21:16.

11. If any man rise up by FALSE-WITNES wittingly, and of purpose to take away any mans life: he shal be put to death. Deut. 19:16, 18, 16.

12. If any man shall CONSPIRE, and attempt any Invasion, Insurrection, or publick Rebellion against our Common-Wealth: or shall indeavour to surprize any Town, or Townes, Fort, or Forts therin; or shall treacherously, and persidiously attempt the Alteration and Subversion of our frame of Politie, or Government fundamentally he shall be put to death. Num. 16. 2 Sam. 3. 2 Sam. 18. 2 Sam. 20.

13. If any child, or children, above sixteen years old, and of sufficient understanding, shall CURSE, or SMITE their natural FATHER, or MOTHER; he or they shall be put to death: unles it can be sufficiently testified that the Parents have been very unchristianly negligent in the eduction of such children; or so provoked them by extream, and cruel correction; that they have been forced therunto to preserve themselves from death or maiming. Exod. 21:17. Lev. 20:9. Exod. 21:15.

14. If a man have a stubborn or REBELLIOUS SON, of sufficient years and uderstanding (viz) sixteen years of age, which will not obey the voice of his Father, or the voice of his Mother, and that when they have chastened him will not harken unto them: then shal his Father & Mother being his natural parets, lay hold on him, and bring him to the Magistrates assembled in Court & testifie unto them that their Son is stubborn & rebellious & will not obey their voice and chastisement, but lives in sundry notorious crimes, such a son shal be put to death. Deut. 21:20, 21.

15. If any man shal RAVISH any maid or single woman, comitting carnal copulation with her by force, against her own will; that is above the age of ten years he shal be punished either with death, or with some other greivous punishmet according to circumstances as the Judges, or General court shal determin (Farrand, 1648/1929).

The third reason for the simplicity of the colonial legal system was that America's first courts served multiple functions, including executive and legislative duties. This meant that the executive, legislative, and judicial functions were sometimes blended together or somewhat distorted. The governor of New Plymouth, for example, could and did "personally arrest and imprison at discretion any citizen or stranger, and . . . examine all persons whom he felt to be suspicious" (Usher, 1984, p. 213). The Plymouth "General Court" was quite general indeed; in addition to its judicial duties, it served as the legislative body, land bureau, tax board, and department of war (Langdon, 1966, p. 93). Having members of the executive branch fulfill judicial functions sometimes created difficulties for the settlers when the governor/judge used his position as judge to penalize and drive away those whose beliefs he found undesirable or dangerous. Quakers, for example, were unwelcome in most New England colonies (Langdon, 1966, pp. 74–75), and were typically viewed as "opposers of the good and wholesome laws" of the colonies (Usher, 1984, p. 262).

Despite their lack of complexity, early American courts served important functions for the colonists, and they expanded to fill the needs created by an increasingly complex and diverse society. The earliest American courts were presided over by colonial governors rather than independent judges, and the laws they enforced were not always known to the public. As time progressed, however, more and more jurisdictions began documenting their laws and the rights that criminal defendants and civil litigants could expect to have at trial. The right to trial by jury, for example, was extended only to defendants in capital cases in the earliest years of the Puritan colonies but soon even they incorporated juries for all cases (Friedman, 1993, pp. 24–26).

As the colonies' governments became more stable and cities began to develop, the justice system had to adapt to new needs. The earliest courts remained, but justices of the peace (JPs) were established to handle minor crimes and disputes in their neighborhoods, requiring only more serious cases to be sent to the county seats for trial (Friedman, 1993, p. 24; Walker, 1980, pp. 21–22). JPs, an idea brought over from England, were individuals without legal training who nonetheless fulfilled local justice needs by presiding over nonserious cases. In addition to localizing justice, the JPs could act individually, that is, they did not have to sit in panels like the judges in the earliest courts (Langdon, 1966, p. 204).[10]

By the end of the seventeenth century, many jurisdictions had set up county courts to handle criminal and civil cases, requiring only the most serious cases (e.g., capital trials) to be heard in the centrally located court (Johnson, 1988, p. 100; Langdon, 1966, pp. 204–206). Specialized courts were beginning to develop, including specific courts to deal with crimes committed by slaves. These courts offered fewer procedural protections to defendants and issued harsher sentences (Johnson, 1988, p. 107). As the courts expanded and changed, the right to appeals also became a regular feature of the courts (e.g., Langdon, 1966, p. 206;

Whitehead, 1881, p. 407). It was rather difficult to appeal decisions when there was only one court and it was presided over by the colony's governor!

The rights accorded to defendants also changed with time. In 1636, the New Plymouth laws afforded only one protection to defendants, that of trial by jury. By 1685, however, a host of rights was guaranteed, including the right to post bail (except for capital and contempt of court cases), the right to counsel in civil cases, the right to twenty peremptory challenges to jurors in capital cases, the right to unlimited challenges for cause in all cases, and a requirement that convictions be based on the testimony of two witnesses "or other sufficient evidence" (Langdon, 1966, p. 209). The law even provided for a one-year statute of limitations for petty crimes. In many ways, the American system of justice was beginning to look more and more like the system we have today.

Some of these departures from tradition were attributable more to changing views of the law than simple population increases. By 1695, the Crown was well aware of the penchant by colonial juries to acquit criminal defendants (Owen and Tolley, 1995, p. 32). The great respect accorded by the English to the law was also lacking in this country. In contrast to their English ancestors, who thought of law as a social phenomenon that was constant and unquestionable, nineteenth-century Americans viewed the law as a way to get things done and achieve change (Walker, 1980, p. 115). In the wake of the Revolutionary War, most Crown judges feared traveling to remote areas of the colonies because of the public's dissatisfaction with their legal system (Johnson, 1988, p. 135). Clearly, the American obsession with avoiding oppression began long ago and likely will remain with us far into the future.

Some similarities to earlier courts remained well into the nineteenth century. American courts still did much more than administer justice. Local county courts in Kentucky, for example, collected taxes and operated river ferries (Walker, 1980, p. 114). Traveling judges still "rode the circuit" and conducted many trials in circuit courts at both the federal and state level, dispensing justice in a town by day, staying in the local inn or taverns at night, then pushing on to the next jurisdiction (e.g., Caton, 1893). Lawyers traveled those same circuits, sometimes commuting with the judges. See Box 4.4 for an advertisement and a few details about one of America's most famous nineteenth-century circuit attorneys, Abraham Lincoln. The phenomenon of traveling judges is rare now, occurring only in remote areas. Some small towns in New Mexico, for example, are still served by judges who travel in from larger districts once a week to hear the towns' cases.

Remnants of our legal heritage continue even to this day. The structure of our courts, for example, is quite similar to that developed to serve American justice needs after the Revolutionary War (Walker, 1980, p. 114). Local courts exist for minor offenses and small claims lawsuits, supplemented by county courts for felonies and lawsuits involving more substantial amounts of money. Appellate courts still hear appeals from the lower courts. All that has really changed is the level of specialization and the number of courts because as new tribunals were

## BOX 4.4

## Abraham Lincoln, a Famous Attorney Who Rode the Circuit

Most people know that Abraham Lincoln (1809–1865) was a lawyer before he was elected as our sixteenth president, but know little beyond that. Lincoln practiced law for twenty-four years in both state and federal courts in Illinois and surrounding states and spent a great deal of time practicing in the Illinois state Eight Judicial Circuit [Note: this was a state circuit and is not to be confused with the federal Eighth Circuit Court] (Lueckenhoff, 1996, pp. 397–98). Like most attorneys of his day, he rode the circuit twice a year, between mid-March to mid-June, then again from early September to late December, spending at least half of every year on the road practicing in courts outside his hometown of Springfield, Illinois. His cases were varied, ranging from civil business to personal injury to divorces to criminal law (Luthin, 1960, p. 61). Sometimes, he was hired ahead of time, but circuit attorneys in many cases were hired when they arrived in town, which gave them only one day to prepare their cases (Lueckenhoff, 1996, p. 398). This lack of time to prepare one's cases was not as problematic for Lincoln as one would assume because lawyers in the 1850s tried "even the pettiest of cases" before a jury, and Lincoln's performance in the courtroom was noteworthy (Thomas, 1968, p. 92). In fact, Lincoln was one of the most sought-after attorneys of his day (Carrington, 1997, p. 624).

Life on the circuit was not easy. As was customary for early- to mid-nineteenth-century attorneys, Lincoln followed the circuit judges on horseback, which made for slow traveling, and shared tight living quarters with other attorneys, sometimes sleeping four to a bed (Carrington, 1997, p. 624). Of interest, Lincoln was the only one of his contemporaries who practiced in courts in every county seat (Beveridge, 1928, p. 215). Although no one really knows how many cases Lincoln handled, more than 5,000 cases have been found bearing his signature or his handwriting (Babwin, 1998, pp. 132–33).[11]

Lincoln had three law partners during his lawyering days, and took out advertisements in local newspapers to generate clients. One of those advertisements, which appeared in the Sangamo (IL) Journal, appears below. The advertisement mentions that he and his first legal partner, John Todd Stuart, would take cases anywhere in the First Judicial Circuit (it was not until 1839 that Lincoln began to ride the Eighth Judicial Circuit). Because the print is hard to read, the text is reprinted here:

J.T. Stuart and A. Lincoln,
Attorneys and Counsellors at Law, will practice,
conjointly, in the Courts of this Judicial Circuit, —
Office No. 4, Hoffman's Row, upstairs,
Springfield, April 12, 1837.

Advertisement courtesy of The Lincoln Legal Papers, Springfield, Illinois.

The famous Judge Roy Bean trying an accused horse-thief in Langtry, Texas, around 1900. To the left of the courthouse, under guard, are two men who were accused of being the defendant's accomplices awaiting their own trials. As in other frontier courts, the justice dispensed by Roy Bean was quick and sometimes without precedent. After searching a drowning victim's pockets and finding a pistol and $40, he quickly pocketed the cash, proclaiming, "I hereby fine this corpse $40 for carrying a concealed weapon." When friends of a white defendant accused of murder threatened to destroy Bean's saloon if the defendant wasn't released, Bean allowed the victim's race to play a powerful role in the case. He flipped through his law books for a while before announcing, "Gentlemen, I find the law very explicit on murdering your fellow man, but there's nothing here about killing a Chinaman. Case dismissed" (Watson, 1998).    SOURCE: Historic American Buildings Survey or Historic American Engineering Record, Reproduction Number HABS, TEX, 233-LANG, 1-1.

needed, they were usually just added on to the existing structure. It is why the state courts are such a puzzle, as we will soon learn. The states developed at different rates, and so their court systems sometimes bear little resemblance to one another. Another factor that cannot be overlooked is the influence of "foreign" legal systems on individual states' laws. Louisiana's rich heritage, for example, includes strong French legal influences, making Louisiana the only state governed by Napoleonic Law. Similarly, the influences of Spanish and Mexican law can be seen in legal codes throughout the Southwest.

Before looking at the modern courts, we must take a moment to acknowledge the legal systems already in place when the European settlers first arrived on this continent. The many Native American tribes had criminal justice systems that served their needs (Meyer, 1998). In place of any schemes to enrich the Crown's treasury, Native American systems typically had as their focus reparations made to the victims of crime (Deloria and Lytle, 1983, pp. 111–113). Among the Iroquois, for example, a killer's family first convinced him or her to admit the crime, then expressed their willingness to make reparations to the victim's family (Dickson-Gilmore, 1992, p. 484). Among the Karok of California, crimes had specific payments that were expected by crime victims (Kroeber and Gifford, 1980, pp. 99–100). The Navajo system of peacemaking neatly addressed both criminal and civil wrongs; respected elders met with parties in conflict to help them restore harmony between themselves through apologies and restitution for wrongs suffered by victims (Yazzie, 1994). Although these courts had little influence on the mainstream American courts—and, in fact, tribal justice mechanisms were outlawed and replaced by European-style courts (Meyer, 1998)—it is still important to recognize their existence. See Box 4.5 for some definitions that show how Navajos viewed the adversarial justice system that was forced on them and a brief description of the traditional Navajo justice process, peacemaking.

---

## BOX 4.5

## Adversarial As Foreign: American Courts Through Navajo Eyes

After four years of captivity as prisoners of war, the Navajo Indians signed a treaty with the U.S. government and were allowed to return to their homeland in 1868. Their lives were forever changed, however, especially their methods of governance. One of the most significant changes was the imposition by the federal government of a foreign system of justice. Traditional Navajo methods of justice were more like mediation than a formal system of courts and trials and punishment. With the American-style courts came a whole new vocabulary, so words had to be created to describe the processes and actors in this form of justice. The following literal translations of legal words show a great deal about Navajo views of the adversarial system. They also show how truly foreign and unwanted this type of system was, as the literal translations seem to focus on only the negative parts of the justice ideas.

- police officer — "soldier" (Vicenti et al., 1972, p. 157): This may be based in their four years spent as prisoners of war, during which the military served as police officers.
- judge — "one who issues punishment" (Vicenti et al., 1972, p. 157): Note that there is no mention of the judge as arbitrator or purveyor of justice. Navajos repeatedly saw punishments handed down in the imposed courts and labeled judges based on their experiences.
- prosecutor — "one who places people in jail" (Vicenti et al., 1972, p. 161): Note that there is no mention of the prosecutor's role in seeking justice.
- defense attorney — "someone who pushes out with words" (Yazzie and Zion, 1996, p. 161): To this day, lawyers are viewed as pushy.
- defendant — "one who has a paper placed against him" (Vicenti et al., 1972, p. 158): This definition focuses on but one aspect of being a defendant, that of being a powerless individual.
- jury — "six people sitting in authority" (Vicenti et al., 1972, p. 162): Navajos felt that American juries were similar to their early British counterparts and existed only to help the judge. No one really believed juries could be independent.
- trial — "where a person is talked about" (Vicenti et al., 1972, p. 160): This translation may focus on the fear of rumors.

- beyond a reasonable doubt—"that which is explained without giving the appearance of two things" (Vicenti et al., 1972, p. 161): This is one of my favorite definitions and could be used in law books around the world because cases that meet this standard of proof should not have other plausible explanations.

- it carries a jail sentence — "it is equivalent to jail" (Young and Morgan, 1951, pp. 41–42): In the Navajo experience, maximum sentences were often handed down so possible penalties became actual penalties.

- he was charged with assault with a deadly weapon — "a paper was set down with the fact that he harmed a person with things that kill and frightful things" (Young and Morgan, 1951/1984, p. 47): Charges were always upheld, so merely being charged with a crime meant you must have committed it, hence the use of the phrase, "the fact that he harmed," rather than "the accusation that he harmed."

## Blessed Are the Peacemakers

As you read the following description of the traditional Navajo justice process, think how it relates to their inability to understand and support the Anglo-Saxon system, which was forced upon them by European Americans.

The Navajo Nation, like many other Native American peoples, had a functional justice system long before the arrival of Europeans and their Anglo-Saxon ideals; many tribal justice systems were rooted in the concept of restorative justice (e.g., Meyer, 1998). The traditional form of justice employed by Navajos combined three core elements: restoration (of victims, offenders, and community), healing, and protection of the public. The traditional Navajo method of justice and conflict resolution is called "peacemaking," and while it was developed from the rich Navajo cosmology, some of its core concepts may be transferrable to other cultures. The premise behind peacemaking is simple: Once you heal the parties involved in offenses, everyone can go on living without fear of future victimization. Of course, the process is far more complex than that.

First, the parties in dispute (or concerned family and friends) seek out a peacemaker (an elder or leader who is respected for his/her skills in helping parties end disputes) who will sit with them and help them fashion a response to the crime. Then, the disputing parties and their circles of support (e.g., family and friends) come together to talk about the offense and the harm to the victim. During the talking stage, individuals are allowed to speak until they have nothing more to say. After all parties in the dispute have spoken, attention is turned to undoing the offense through *nalyeeh,* which includes both tangible and intangible restitution. If I have harmed you, for example, I might make a public apology and pay you a certain amount of money or perform service for you or an individual or group you designate—whatever is necessary to ensure that there "are no hard feelings" between us and so that you feel that I will not repeat the offense in the future. Due to its often financial nature, *nalyeeh* has both punitive and restorative components.

Peacemaking has been used in thousands of cases, and individuals who choose to go through peacemaking are *more* satisfied with the courts and *less* likely to report future victimization by the offender than those who went through the contemporary courts (Gross, 1999, pp. 32–36). Other jurisdictions might learn a lot from a visit to observe the peacemaking courts in action.

## THE PUZZLE OF MODERN COURTS

Casual observers of the courts may find them puzzling because of the different types of cases they hear and the terminology used to describe them. Students, for example, sometimes wonder why trials in the television docudrama *Law & Order* take place in the New York Supreme Court when they know that state supreme courts do not typically hear trials. The reason is that some of the felony trial courts in New York are called supreme courts. The state's highest court (i.e., what most people would label as a supreme court), on the other hand, is called the Court of Appeals. So, in reality, trials in New York are not heard in the state's highest court, rather they are heard in the trial courts where we expect them to be heard.

To understand the modern courts puzzle, we need to examine them piece by piece. The first important concept is that of a dual system of federal and state courts, which work side by side. Usually, they work independently of one another, but frequently state cases are appealed to the federal courts. This is how landmark cases such as *Miranda v. Arizona* (1966) made it to the Supreme Court docket.

The second important concept is the difference between trial courts and appellate courts. **Trial courts** conduct trials whereas **appellate courts** only hear appeals from cases that have already been tried, but either the defense or prosecution said the trial was not conducted properly. These two levels of courts form **hierarchical jurisdiction** because a case can proceed from trial to appellate courts. Below is a simple diagram to get us started on our journey toward understanding the courts puzzle.

Because trials originate in them, trial courts are called **courts of original jurisdiction**. Courts of original jurisdiction can hear trials, witnesses and evidence can be presented there, and determinations of guilt and sentences are made there. There are two subdivisions of original jurisdiction: limited jurisdiction and general jurisdiction.

|  | **State Courts** | **Federal Courts** |
|---|---|---|
| Basic court structure | State appellate courts<br>↓<br>State trial courts | Federal appellate courts<br>↓<br>Federal trial courts |
| Source of laws | State constitutions, state penal codes and local ordinances, laws enacted by state and local governments | U.S. Constitution, Code of Federal Regulations, United States Code, laws enacted by Congress or executive agencies |

**Courts of limited jurisdiction** are able to hear **misdemeanor** cases (which are less serious crimes, such as shoplifting, that can typically result in jail terms of up to one year) and small claims cases (i.e., civil lawsuits for a small amount of money, usually less than $3,000). Traffic tickets also fall under the courts of limited jurisdiction and are often heard in special traffic courts set aside to process traffic cases. Courts of limited jurisdiction are typically not **courts of record**, that is, no official transcripts are made during the proceedings.

**Courts of general jurisdiction** can try both misdemeanors and felonies (i.e., serious crimes for which more than a year in jail can be imposed). They also serve as the forum for larger civil lawsuits. General jurisdiction courts are usually courts of record (there is more concern for due process because of the possibility of appeals), although an official transcript may not be made for misdemeanor cases. Finally, courts of general jurisdiction sometimes serve as appellate courts because they are able to hear appeals from the courts of limited jurisdiction; in some states, these appeals are called **trials de novo** because if there is no record, the trial must be conducted again as though it had never taken place.

Appellate courts are very different from courts of general jurisdiction. They hear appeals from the trial courts rather than conducting trials of their own. There are no witnesses or evidence presented at an appellate court hearing. Instead, appellate court outcomes are based on briefs submitted by both sides that contain their arguments and legal reasoning. The appeal may be argued orally by the attorneys, but the attorneys argue points of law rather than presenting any evidence in the case.

Appeals are not automatic, although nearly all jurisdictions mandate reviews of all imposed death penalty sentences. Instead, the attorneys for both sides must raise objections during the trial to preserve their right to appeal. Convicted defendants are also able to appeal, on the basis of ineffectual assistance of counsel if their attorneys were incapable of properly presenting a case, and on rare occasions, appeals are filed when substantial new evidence is found that exonerates a defendant who has already been convicted. You will learn more about appeals in Step 15, but it is important to mention that if appellate courts believe the appeal is legally valid, they typically **reverse and remand** the case back to the trial court, providing directions for the trial court to follow (e.g., forbidding the judge to allow an illegally obtained confession that was introduced during the first trial). The trial then begins anew, with the same defendant, same case, roughly the same evidence, but with a new jury. Now that we know the difference between courts of original jurisdiction and appellate courts, let us take a quick look at the federal, then state, court systems.

## The Federal Courts

The federal trial courts conduct trials for federal crimes, such as treason and mail fraud. The crimes for which one can be tried in federal courts are listed in several sources of federal penal codes, including the Code of Federal Regulations (CFR) and the United States Code (USC). The laws in the USC were enacted by Congress, whereas the laws in the CFR were enacted by executive agencies, such as the Federal Trade Commission or the Environmental Protection Agency. A few federal crimes, such as counterfeiting and treason, are specifically mentioned in the U.S. Constitution. The federal trial courts also hear felonies committed on Native American reservations because an 1885 federal law deprived tribes of their right to try their own felonies (Major Crimes Act, 18 USC sec. 1153). The federal courts hear cases in which the United States is a party (e.g., when someone sues the federal government). When the state courts may not be impartial (e.g., when citizens from different states sue each other or when states are suing each other), the federal courts provide a neutral forum for justice. Finally, the federal trial courts have jurisdiction over laws relating to navigable waterways.

The federal courts did not exist until after the colonies had achieved independence from England, at which time they were developed to complement the already existing state-level courts. A major conflict in political philosophy that was debated by the founding fathers was whether the United States should have a strong central government or whether the bulk of legislative power should reside with the states. The Federalists favored a strong federal government and advocated signing the Constitution. The Anti-Federalists opposed the Constitution entirely at first, and continued to advocate for states' rights after it was signed.

The Federalists wanted both a federal supreme court and federal district courts to complement the state courts, believing this approach would prevent states from acting prejudicially toward out-of-state litigants, including the merchants and business owners who supported the party (e.g., Freedman, 1996, p. 467). The Anti-Federalists, on the other hand, wanted only one federal court, the U.S. Supreme Court, with all other courts falling under the absolute control of the states. This approach was believed to prevent the federal government from usurping the states' sovereignty and citizens' individual rights (e.g., Freedman, 1996, pp. 467–68).

In the end, the two parties agreed to compromise. Both a U.S. Supreme Court and federal district courts were established, but the federal courts were organized along state lines, with judges coming from the respective states (thus bolstering state control), and the district courts were to enjoy a great deal of independence (Wheeler and Harrison, 1994, pp. 6–7). To this day, decisions that are binding on one federal **circuit** (i.e., one of the multistate jurisdictions into which the federal courts have been divided) need not be followed by the other circuits (see Box 4.6 for a map showing the current circuits). In the Second Circuit (New York, Connecticut, and Vermont), for example, evidence that is ruled inadmissible at a defendant's trial, due to it being seized illegally, may still be used to increase his or her sentence after conviction (*United States v. Tejada*, 2nd Cir, 1992). Because the U.S. Supreme Court refused to hear the appeal, this situation only applies to the federal courts in the Second Circuit and other circuits that have similar rulings. A later case (*United States v. Tauil-Hernandez and Mordan*, 1996, p. 581) acknowledged the lack of consistency before ruling that such evidence would be admissible in the Eighth Circuit as well:

> Most of our sister circuits have concluded that the Fourth Amendment's exclusionary rule does not apply in federal sentencing proceedings,[12] though two separate opinions have urged the contrary rule.[13]

The reason the Tejada case does not apply to other circuits is because the U.S. Supreme Court did not agree to hear the case, forcing the thirteen circuits to rely on their own internal appellate rulings. In a sense, the circuits may be compared to states. Decisions made by the Minnesota Supreme Court, for example, do not apply to any other state, although the courts in other states may cite the Minnesota decisions to support their own rulings. Decisions by the U.S. Supreme Court, on the other hand, must be followed by all of the circuits' courts and all of the state courts, too.

---

## BOX 4.6

## A Map Showing the Thirteen Federal Court Circuits

This map shows the thirteen federal court circuits. In which circuit do you live? Which other states are in your circuit, if any? If you have family members who live in other states, do they live in a circuit other than yours?

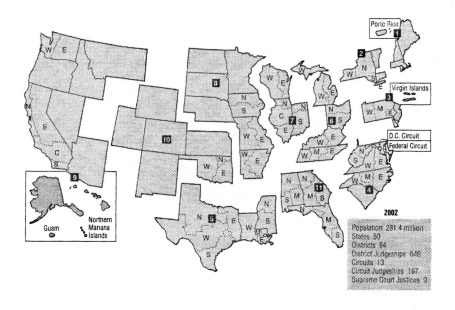

*Source:* Wheeler and Harrison, 1994, p. 26.

The federal trial courts have undergone a number of changes before reaching their current status. The federal court scheme created by the Judiciary Act of 1789 had a Supreme Court with six Supreme Court justices and thirteen district courts, each presided over by one district judge (Judiciary Act, 1789, sec. 1–3). The current portrait of federal courts differs substantially from its early-American form. For example, an intermediate level of appellate courts was created in 1891 to take some of the caseload pressure off the Supreme Court; this step served to "complete the modern federal courts system" (Walker, 1980, p. 114).

The current federal court setup includes three basic levels of courts. The **district courts** are the federal courts of original jurisdiction. The judges are appointed for life by the President of the United States with advice and consent of the U.S. Senate.[14] In 1995, charges were filed against 63,547 defendants in U.S. district courts (Chaiken, 1998, p. 39). The largest categories of offenses were drug charges, accounting for one-third of the cases, and fraud charges, which were 17 percent of the caseload (Chaiken, 1998, p. 41). Similar to the process in the state level courts, cases heard in the district courts are presided over by one judge.

The U.S. Court of Appeals (also called the Circuit Court of Appeals) is the intermediary appellate court level. Cases are typically heard by three judges cho-

The Mitchell H. Cohen Federal Building and U.S. Courthouse. This federal courthouse is one of the ninety-four federal courts of original jurisdiction, meaning that trials are conducted here. Like many of its federal district court counterparts, many of the cases heard in this building are drug related. Similar to other federal judges, the judges who preside over cases in this building are appointed for life by the president with advice and consent of the Senate. Because this is a high-volume district court, some of the cases are presided over by federal magistrate judges, who are appointed for eight-year terms to process preliminary hearings, pre-trial motions, misdemeanor trials, and some civil cases.  SOURCE: Courtesy of Images by Grice.

sen at random, but some significant questions are heard **en banc** (i.e., all of the judges in the court hear the case together). In 1995, 10,162 criminal appeals were filed, nearly half of which (n = 4,499) resulted from drug cases (Chaiken, 1998, p. 63). Nearly all (96 percent) of the criminal appeals in 1995 were filed by defendants,[15] and only 9 percent of the cases were remanded or reversed (i.e., sent back to the trial courts for retrial, Chaiken, 1998, p. 61). Created by the 1891 Circuit Court of Appeals Act, these courts cannot turn away appeals without first considering them (Wheeler and Harrison, 1994, p. 18).

The highest federal court is the **United States Supreme Court**. There is no higher appeal available in this country. The role of the U.S. Supreme Court is to ensure that the lower federal courts (and the state level courts) have correctly interpreted and applied the law. The Supreme Court can rule state or federal laws unconstitutional. It can also order acquittals or new trials on the basis of violations of the U.S. Constitution or federal statutes.

In addition to its appellate functions, the U.S. Supreme Court sometimes serves as a court of original jurisdiction. According to the U.S. Constitution, the Supreme Court has original jurisdiction over cases involving "ambassadors, other public ministers and consuls, and those in which a state shall be a party." It also has original jurisdiction in admiralty (navigation) cases.[16] Although it considers about one hundred petitions[17] each week (*New York v. Uplinger,* 1984, p. 250), the Supreme Court limits itself to hearing 100–200 cases per year. The justices do not initially consider the petitions in group meetings. Instead, the justices review the petitions on their own (or with substantial assistance from their law clerks who summarize the cases for them) and include on a discussion list only those they feel are worthwhile for the justices to discuss as a group.

The majority of cases that reach the Supreme Court do so under its appellate jurisdiction, as you will learn in the chapter on appeals. For now, you should know that the Supreme Court hears only cases that present a substantial federal question. Appeals based on concerns over the constitutionality of a law or procedure have a better chance of being heard by the Supreme Court. Some appeals seek clarification of laws; for example, the Supreme Court may be asked to clarify a law when lower court rulings have conflicted with one another (e.g., when jurisdictions differ in their interpretation of sentencing guidelines). In addition, a case cannot be appealed to the Supreme Court until it has exhausted all other possible remedies, including lower courts and any applicable state courts.

Although it can declare laws unconstitutional, the U.S. Supreme Court cannot enforce its own decisions. Instead, it must depend on others (e.g., Congress or the president) to enforce the rulings it hands down. Following the Supreme Court's order to desegregate public schools in *Brown v. Board of Education of Topeka, Kansas* (1954), for example, the governor of Arkansas ordered his state's militia to prevent black students from attending Central High School in Little Rock. Because the Supreme Court was powerless to act, President Eisenhower sent federal troops to ensure that the students were able to attend the school, ending segregation in Little Rock.

Currently, there are nine members of the Supreme Court, one chief justice and eight associate justices.[18] Like other federal judges, Supreme Court justices sit for life and are appointed by the president with the advice and consent of the Senate. The justices sit *en banc* during hearings, and at least six must be present when a case is argued. During arguments, each side is allocated thirty minutes in which to present all their points and field questions from the justices.[19] Afterward, the judges retire to consider the case and the final vote on a case is by simple majority. Individual justices may agree with the majority, concur (i.e., reach the same final decision as the majority but based on different legal reasoning),[20] or dissent (i.e., disagree with the majority). For each case heard, the justices write an opinion that is made public and becomes part of the Supreme Court's records.

Now that we have learned about the federal courts, let us turn our attention to the state courts. The state system shares a number of similarities with the federal system. It has trial and appellate courts, and the court processes are similar, as we will soon see.

## The State Courts

There is only one federal system, but there are fifty separate and independent state systems and an additional court system for the District of Columbia. Because each state developed its own court system, there are many differences among the states' courts. At times confusing, the seemingly hodgepodge state court system actually has an underlying structure, which will help you understand it and how it works. Understanding the state courts is important because the majority of criminal and civil cases in this country are heard there. Whereas 49,624 criminal defendants were convicted of felonies in federal courts in 1994, a whopping 872,218 were convicted in the state level courts, meaning that 96 percent of felony convictions took place in the state courts (Langan and Brown, 1994, p. 1). And, then there are the ubiquitous misdemeanor cases that fill the state-level dockets. In California alone, nearly nine million cases (not counting parking offenses) were disposed of by municipal court judges in 1990, for an average of more than 11,000 cases per judge (Judicial Council of California, 1992, p. 78). The state courts, then, handle an immense number of cases when compared to the federal courts. Those who have contact with the courts are much more likely to do so in the state courts.

State trial courts hear crimes that are state offenses rather than federal ones. A few crimes are mentioned in state constitutions (e.g., a few state constitutions mention that gambling on bingo is outlawed, or that such games may be conducted by only certain organizations such as charities). State level offenses also include violations of both state and local laws (e.g., county or city ordinances), including crimes against persons, property, and public order. The state courts also hear civil cases between citizens in the same state. Some state trial courts fulfill special roles like family courts (which deal with divorces and other family issues) and juvenile courts (which process crimes committed by minors). In states that do not have special courts for family and juvenile matters, those cases are heard in the standard trial courts.

We will begin our discussion of state courts by comparing three very dissimilar court systems: Alaska, New York, and South Dakota. These three states were selected because of their varying levels of complexity. See Box 4.7 for visual depictions of each of the three systems.

# BOX 4.7

## Three Sample State Court Systems
## (Alaska, New York, and South Dakota)

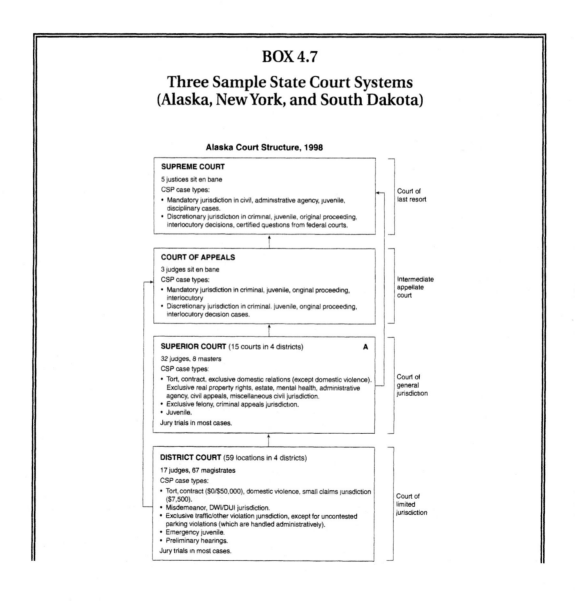

**Alaska Court Structure, 1998**

**SUPREME COURT**

5 justices sit en banc

CSP case types:
- Mandatory jurisdiction in civil, administrative agency, juvenile, disciplinary cases.
- Discretionary jurisdiction in criminal, juvenile, original proceeding, interlocutory decisions, certified questions from federal courts.

Court of last resort

**COURT OF APPEALS**

3 judges sit en banc

CSP case types:
- Mandatory jurisdiction in criminal, juvenile, original proceeding, interlocutory
- Discretionary jurisdiction in criminal. juvenile, original proceeding, interlocutory decision cases.

Intermediate appellate court

**SUPERIOR COURT** (15 courts in 4 districts)                 **A**

32 judges, 8 masters

CSP case types:
- Tort, contract, exclusive domestic relations (except domestic violence). Exclusive real property rights, estate, mental health, administrative agency, civil appeals, miscellaneous civil jurisdiction.
- Exclusive felony, criminal appeals jurisdiction.
- Juvenile.

Jury trials in most cases.

Court of general jurisdiction

**DISTRICT COURT** (59 locations in 4 districts)

17 judges, 67 magistrates

CSP case types:
- Tort, contract ($0/$50,000), domestic violence, small claims jurisdiction ($7,500).
- Misdemeanor, DWI/DUI jurisdiction.
- Exclusive traffic/other violation jurisdiction, except for uncontested parking violations (which are handled administratively).
- Emergency juvenile.
- Preliminary hearings.

Jury trials in most cases.

Court of limited jurisdiction

# BOX 4.7 *(continued)*

### New York Court Structure, 1998*

---

**COURT OF APPEALS**

7 judges

CSP case types:
- Mandatory jurisdiction in civil, capital criminal, criminal, administrative agency, juvenile, original proceeding case.
- Discretionary jurisdiction in civil, criminal, administrative agency, juvenile, disciplinary, original proceeding case.

Court of last resort

---

**APPELLATE DIVISIONS OF SUPREME COURT**

(4 courts/divisions)

56 justices sit in panels in four departments

CSP case types:
- Mandatory jurisdiction in civil, criminal, administrative agency juvenile, lawyer disciplinary, original proceeding, interlocutory decision cases.
- Discretionary jurisdiction in civil, criminal, juvenile original proceeding, interlocutory decision cases.

1st & 2nd departments

3rd & 4th departments

**APPELLATE TERMS OF SUPREME COURT**

(3 terms/1st and 2nd departments)

15 justices sit in panels in three terms

CSP case types:
- Mandatory jurisdiction in civil, criminal, juvenile, interlocutory decision cases.
- Discretionary jurisdiction in criminal, juvenile, interlocutory decision cases.

Intermediate appellate court

---

**SUPREME COURT**

(12 districts)

369 supreme court judges (plus 50 "acting" supreme court judges and 12 quasi-judicial staff)

CSP case types:
- Tort, contract, real property rights, miscellaneous civil. Exclusive marriage dissolution jurisdiction
- Felony, DWI/DUI, miscellaneous criminal.

Jury trials.

**COUNTY COURT**

(57 counties outside NYC)

127 county court judges

CSP case types:
- Tort, contract, real property rights ($0/$25,000) miscellaneous civil. · Trial court appeals jurisdiction.
- Felony, DWI/DUI, miscellaneous criminal, criminal appeals.

Jury trials

Court of general jurisdiction

---

**COURT OF CLAIMS**

(1 court)

72 judges (of which 50 act as supreme court judges)

CSP case types:
- Tort, contract, real property rights involving the state.

Jury trials

**SURROGATES' COURT**

(62 counties)

80 surrogates

CSP case types:
- Adoption, estate.

Jury trials in estate.

1st & 2nd departments

3rd & 4th departments

---

**FAMILY COURT**

(62 counties—includes NYC Family Court)

124 judges (plus 81 quasi-judicial staff)

CSP case types
- Domestic relations (except marriage dissolution), guardianship.
- Exclusive domestic violence jurisdiction.
- Exclusive juvenile jurisdiction.

No jury trials.

**DISTRICT COURT**

(Nassau and Suffolk Counties)

50 judges

CSP case types:
- Tort, contract, real property rights ($0/$15,000), small claims ($3,000), administrative agency appeals.
- Felony, misdemeanor, DWI/DUI.
- Moving traffic, miscellaneous traffic, ordinance violation.
- Preliminary hearings.

Jury trials except in traffic.

**CITY COURT** (79 courts in 61 cities)

158 judges

CSP case types:
- Tort, contract, real property rights small claims ($3,000),
- Felony, misdemeanor, DWI/DUI.
- Moving traffic, miscellaneous traffic, ordinance violation.
- Preliminary hearings.

Jury trials for highest level misdemeanor.

Court of limited jurisdiction

---

**CIVIL COURT OF THE CITY OF NEW YORK**

(1 court)

120 judges

CSP case types:
- Tort, contract, real property rights ($0/$25,00) small claims($3,000), miscellaneous civil, administrative agency appeals.

Jury trials

**CRIMINAL COURT OF THE CITY OF NEW YORK**

(1 court)

107 judges

CSP case types:
- Misdemeanor, DWI/DUI.
- Moving traffic, ordinance violation, miscellaneous traffic.
- Preliminary hearings.

Jury trials for highest level misdemeanor.

**TOWN AND VILLAGE JUSTICE COURT**

(1,487 courts)

2,300 justices

CSP case types:
- Tort, contract real property rights ($0/$3,000) small claims ($3,000).
- Misdemeanor, DWI/DUI, miscellaneous criminal.
- Traffic/other violations.
- Preliminary hearings.

Jury trials in most cases.

---

* Unless otherwise noted, numbers reflect statutory authorization. Many judges sit in more then one court so the number of judgeships indicated in this chart does not reflect the actual number of judges in the system.

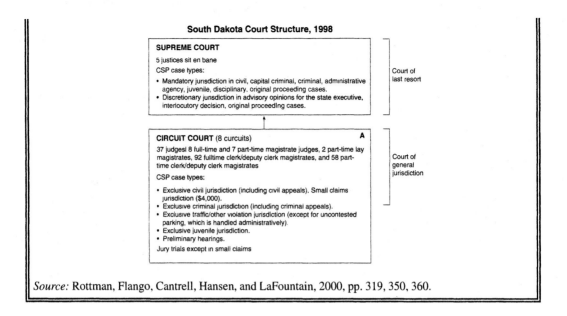

**South Dakota Court Structure, 1998**

**SUPREME COURT**

5 justices sit en banc

CSP case types:

• Mandatory jurisdiction in civil, capital criminal, criminal, administrative
  agency, juvenile, disciplinary, original proceeding cases.
• Discretionary jurisdiction in advisory opinions for the state executive,
  interlocutory decision, original proceeding cases.

Court of
last resort

**CIRCUIT COURT** (8 curcuits)                                              **A**

37 judges| 8 full-time and 7 part-time magistrate judges, 2 part-time lay
magistrates, 92 fulltime clerk/deputy clerk magistrates, and 58 part-
time clerk/deputy clerk magistrates

CSP case types:

• Exclusive civil jurisdiction (including civil appeals). Small claims
  jurisdiction ($4,000).
• Exclusive criminal jurisdiction (including criminal appeals).
• Exclusive traffic/other violation jurisdiction (except for uncontested
  parking, which is handled administratively).
• Exclusive juvenile jurisdiction.
• Preliminary hearings.

Jury trials except in small claims

Court of
general
jurisdiction

*Source:* Rottman, Flango, Cantrell, Hansen, and LaFountain, 2000, pp. 319, 350, 360.

Alaska's court system most closely resembles the four-tier state court proto-type. At the bottom tier are the courts of limited jurisdiction, called district courts in Alaska. The district courts hear misdemeanor, traffic, and small claims cases, and also conduct preliminary hearings. The second tier is formed by the courts of general jurisdiction, called superior courts in Alaska. The superior courts hear felony, juvenile, and non-small-claims civil cases. The third tier is the intermediate appellate courts, called courts of appeals in Alaska. The court of appeals hears the majority of the state's appeals. The fourth tier is the state's highest court, the Supreme Court of Alaska. Because there is an intermediate appellate court, the supreme court has discretion to turn some cases away without review.

South Dakota's court system is the simplest in the nation (the only other two-tier system is the District of Columbia). Because there is no court of limited juris-diction, South Dakota's circuit courts must process all criminal, civil, and traffic cases. Both felonies and misdemeanors must be heard by the circuit courts as well as all preliminary hearings. Because there is no intermediate appellate court, the South Dakota Supreme Court must hear all appeals. Had there been an intermediate court of appeals, the supreme court would have discretion to turn away some cases.

At first glance, the New York system appears to be a literal maze of jurisdic-tions and courts. On closer examination, however, one can see the familiar four-tier system. Eight of the courts (Court of Claims, Family Court, Civil Court of the City of New York, Criminal Court of the City of New York, District Court, Surrogate's Court, Town and Village Justice Court, and City Court) form the lowest tier of courts of limited jurisdiction. There are multiple types of courts due to county differences (e.g., the two City of New York courts serve only New York City) and jurisdictional differences (e.g., the Surrogate's Court handles only adoptions and estate cases). The second tier of courts, called the supreme courts and county courts in New York, handle felonies and non-small-claims civil cases. The third tier is made up of two appellate courts, the Appellate Divisions of Supreme Court and the Appellate Terms of Supreme Court, both of which hear appeals from different courts of original jurisdiction. New York's highest court is the court of appeals, and it functions like other state supreme courts.

A few of the differences between state courts become evident during an examination of the three sample court systems. First, and probably most aggravating for most people, is the wide variation in names for the courts. Even state supreme courts have differing names (e.g., New York's Court of Appeals), making it difficult to sort out which court does what. Another key difference is in the types of cases heard and the procedures used by each tier; jury trials, for example, are conducted in some states' courts of limited jurisdiction, but not in other states' lower courts. A third difference is the amounts used to define small-claims cases. In 1993, Montana capped small claims cases at $500, whereas Tennessee's small claims case cap was $15,000 (a typical small-claims cap is $2,000–$5,000). There are other differences, including the types of records kept by the court for hearings and the source of the court's funding (i.e., whether the court is supported by local or state funds), but these differences should not interfere with your ability to understand the operations of a given court.

From the puzzle of modern courts, one can deduce an underlying structure. Before moving on to Step 5, Box 4.8 presents a brief examination of the local, state, and federal courts in one state. As illustrated by the variety of courts in New Mexico, one can see how individual court systems may share geographical proximity, but fulfill very different functions.

In the next section of chapters, we will look at the participants in the courtroom drama, including chapters on the prosecutor, defense attorney, and judge. We will examine the role each plays in the courts and how they interact with one another. Then, we will turn our attention to others who play less visible roles in the courtroom drama, but without whom the courts would come to a standstill. There could be no trials without defendants, victims, and witnesses. Without bail bonds agents, the jails would be full of people awaiting trial. Then, there are court employees who make the system function properly: bailiffs, clerks, translators, and victim-witness assistants. Everyday citizens also play roles as jurors, spectators (often friends and family of defendants or victims), and court-watchers who observe the courts in action.

## BOX 4.8

## Frontier Justice: Courts in New Mexico As a Case Study

In one typical New Mexico county, there are four courts: three state courthouses and one federal court. The courts of original jurisdiction are the District Court (general jurisdiction), Magistrate Court (limited jurisdiction), and Municipal Court (limited jurisdiction).

The District Court hears both misdemeanor and felony cases and may impose prison and death sentences. District Court juries are made up of twelve individuals, and there are no lay (i.e., nonlegally trained) judges. As the court of general jurisdiction, the District Court is a court of record. The judges are elected.

The Magistrate Court hears only misdemeanor cases, and the maximum penalty is 364 days in jail. Magistrate Court juries are made up of six individuals, and lay judges are allowed. As a court of limited jurisdiction, the Magistrate Court is typically not a court of record but transcripts are made in some cases. The judges are elected.

The Municipal Court hears only misdemeanor cases, and the maximum penalty is three months in jail. There are no jury trials in the Municipal Court, and there are no lay judges. As a court of limited jurisdiction, the Municipal Court is typically not a court of record but transcripts are made in some cases. The judges are elected.

As with most counties, a federal court is accessible to the citizenry. The federal District Court hears trials for federal offenses (e.g., violations of laws enacted by Congress) and other federal cases.

Within a day's drive is a federal appellate court, the U.S. Court of Appeals. Accessible via airplane is the U.S. Supreme Court in Washington, D.C.

Also within a day's drive is the New Mexico Court of Appeals (which hears appeals from the state's district courts) and the New Mexico State Supreme Court (from which the only remaining appeal is to the U.S. Supreme Court). Like other judges in New Mexico, judges for both the appellate and supreme courts are elected via partisan election.

## DISCUSSION QUESTIONS

1. Why was the *Magna Charta* important to the Anglo-Saxons in 1215? Why is it important to our criminal justice system?

2. Why was trial by ordeal once accepted as valid by the criminal justice system? Can you think of some modern forms of justice in the United States or other countries that appear related to the concept of trial by ordeal?

3. How did the concept of trial by battle fit into the Anglo-Saxon ideals of justice? If cases were still settled this way, which types of cases do you feel would be most and least appropriate to be handled through this trial method? Would you prefer this method of trial or our contemporary methods? What is your reasoning?

4. Look over the provisions from the laws of William the Conqueror contained in Box 4.2. The eighth element discusses a bail situation that could be considered a "presumed guilty" model, which differs from today's "presumed innocent" model. What differences do you see between the model posed by William the Conqueror and today's model?

5. What are the benefits and drawbacks of seeking a trial by jury in modern America? How would your list of pros and cons differ during the Middle Ages? How have juries evolved over time into our modern concept of juries?

6. People today often try to avoid being put on a jury. How do modern complaints about jury service compare to the risks of being on a jury during the Middle Ages?

7. How did the structure of courts change with the developing United States (e.g., are there any societal reasons behind the changes American courts have seen over the years)?

8. Look over the laws in Box 4.3. How many of those laws still exist, even without the direct citations to the Bible? What can we say about the influence of religion on laws in general?

9. Go through your local newspaper and find at least two current or potential court actions (e.g., reports of crimes or lawsuits) that would be heard in the following courts:

   *State courts:*    • limited jurisdiction courts of original jurisdiction

                      • general jurisdiction courts of original jurisdiction

                      • appellate courts or state supreme court

   *Federal courts:*  • district courts

                      • U.S. Court of Appeals or U.S. Supreme Court

10. Look over the diagrams in Box 4.7. If you are not from one of these three states, use your school or community library to find out the structure of your state's courts. How do your courts compare with the four-tier state court prototype? Do you have any ideas for why your state's courts have developed or are organized the way they are?

## NOTES

1. England's courts have transformed immensely over the years, so that contemporary English courts have a number of similarities to American ones. In Britain, citizens do not have the exact same rights (e.g., Miranda rights and other rights that were developed through U.S. Supreme Court rulings), jury verdicts need not be unanimous (Devlin, 1979, p. 117), jurors had to own property until just recently (Cornish, 1968, p. 27; Oldham, 1983, p. 141), and other dissimilarities exist. Overall, however, the two court systems are very comparable.

2. See Step 1 for more about common law.

3. Some versions of trial by cold water involved lowering defendants into water bound by a rope, and using the rope to raise them up if they sank; however, "skillful manipulation" of the rope by the attendant could easily create an image of floating (Lea, 1870/1996, p. 246).

4. The required number of compurgators may result from an early British avoidance of the decimal system, such that there were twelve (rather than ten) pennies to a shilling (Devlin, 1966, p. 8).

5. The sparse writings about early English justice were sometimes confusing, leaving even nineteenth-century legal scholars puzzled about the exact nature of juries and their uses (e.g., Stephen, 1883:i, p. 258).

6. This use of juries was still in vogue in 1752 (Moore, 1973, p. 83).

7. In fact, convicted criminals' children could not even inherit from their grandparents due to a phenomenon known as "corruption of blood." Since the legal heirs could not inherit, the property defaulted to the Crown (Greek, 1991).

8. Although it is a rare occurrence, judges in states that allow them to do so sometimes set aside verdicts that they feel are unsupported by the evidence in the case. There is a great deal of controversy surrounding this form of judicial discretion.

9. This 1611 statute appears to be an example of an early "three strikes and you're out" law.

10. Before 1685, no judge in Plymouth could preside over a civil case alone; this was also true for England (Langdon, 1966, p. 204).

11. Lincoln sometimes helped other attorneys and signed their names to his work.

12. These included the D.C. Circuit (1991), Second Circuit (1992), Third Circuit (1991), Fifth Circuit (1993), Sixth Circuit (1993), Ninth Circuit (1994), and Eleventh Circuit (1991).

13. These were the Seventh Circuit (1991) and a dissenting opinion in the Ninth Circuit (1994).

14. District court judges in U.S. territories are appointed for ten-year terms rather than seated for life.

15. The remaining 4 percent of the appeals were filed by the government.

16. As we saw during the Senate trial following the impeachment of President Clinton, the chief justice of the Supreme Court also presides over those proceedings, but this process does not involve other members of the court.

17. In actuality, law clerks perform most of the initial screening of petitions.

18. This has not always been the number of judges. Initially, the Supreme Court had only six justices, and there have been other numbers of justices during the history of the Court.

19. Because the Supreme Court often schedules more cases than it can consider in a given term, some must be settled through summary dispositions that do not provide an opportunity for the parties to present oral arguments (Murphy and Pritchett, 1986, p. 566). Instead, the decisions are based on the legal briefs submitted with the petition. This is usually done when the issue is relatively minor or covered by prior Supreme Court cases.

20. An example of a concurring opinion would be when a justice agrees that a piece of evidence should have been excluded from trial, but not necessarily for the same reasons as the other justices.

## REFERENCES

American Revolution HTML Project. (1997). Text of the *Magna Charta*. Prepared and reprinted from the 1215 original. Available at odur.let.rug.nl/~usa/D/1400/magna.htm noot1.

Andrews, W. (1991). *Old Time Punishments*. New York: Dorset Press. (Originally published in 1890, London: Simpkin, Marshall, Hamilton and Kent.)

Babwin, D. (1998). Stealing history. *Chicago,* 47(10): 90–93, 132–123, 143.

Beveridge, A.J. (1928). *Abraham Lincoln 1809–1865* (vol. II). Boston: Houghton Mifflin.

Blackstone, W. (1897). *Commentaries on the Laws of England, in Four Books.* Philadelphia: Reese Welsh and Company. (Originally published in 1765 as *Commentaries on the laws of England,* Oxford: Clarendon Press.)

Bracton, H. de. (1968) *On the Laws and Customs of England.* Translated by S.E. Thorne from G.E. Woodbine's edition of the Latin text. Cambridge, MA: Harvard University Press. (Originally published as *De legibus et consuetudinibus Angliae,* c. 1250.)

Bradford, W. (1952). *Of Plymouth Plantation, 1620–1647* (new ed., annotated by S.E. Morison). New York: Alfred A. Knopf. (Written by Bradford in 1646).

*Brown v. Board of Education of Topeka, Kansas,* 347 U.S. 483 (1954).

Bushell's Case, 124 Eng. Rep. 1006 (C.P. 1670). Reprinted in I. Howell, *Cobbett's Complete Collection of State Trials,* Vol. VI, (1810): 999–1026.

Carrington, P.D. (1997). A tale of two lawyers. *Northwestern University Law Review,* 91: 615–635.

Caton, J.D. (1893). Early bench and bar of Illinois. Chicago: Chicago Legal News, pp. 241–242.

Chaiken, J.M. (1998). *Compendium of Federal Justice Statistics, 1995.* Washington, DC: Bureau of Justice Statistics.

Cornish, W.R. (1968). *The Jury.* London: Allen Lane.

Deloria, V., and Lytle, C.M. (1983). *American Indians, American Justice.* Austin: University of Texas Press.

Devlin, P. (1966). *Trial by Jury* (3rd ed.), London: Stevens and Sons.

Devlin, P. (1979). *The Judge.* Oxford: Oxford University Press.

Dickson-Gilmore, E.J. (1992). Finding the ways of the ancestors: Cultural change and the invention of tradition in the development of separate legal systems. *Canadian Journal of Criminology,* 34: 472–502.

Farrand, M. (1929). *The Book of the General Lawes and Liberties Concerning the Inhabitants of the Massachusetts* (facsimile edition). Cambridge: Harvard University Press. (Originally published in 1648.)

Freedman, E.M. (1996). The suspension clause in the ratification debates. *Buffalo Law Review,* 44: 451–468.

Friedman, L.M. (1993). *Crime and Punishment in American History.* New York: Basic Books.

Greek, C. (1991). Drug control and asset seizures: A review of the history of forfeiture in England and colonial America. In T. Mieczkowski (Ed.), *Drugs, Crime, and Social Policy.* Boston: Allyn and Bacon.

Greenberg, M.A. (1984). *Auxiliary Police: The Citizen's Approach to Public Safety.* Westport, CN: Greenwood Press.

Gross, E.K. (1999). *Preliminary Report to the National Institute of Justice Regarding Grant #97-IJ-CX-0039.*

Henderson, E.F. (1896). *Select Historical Documents of the Middle Ages.* London: George Bell and Sons.

Hill, F. (1995). *A Delusion of Satan: The Full Story of the Salem Witch Trials.* New York: Doubleday.

Holmes, O.W. (1881). *The Common Law.* Boston: Little, Brown.

Holten, N.G., and Lamar, L.L. (1991). *The Criminal Courts: Structures, Personnel, and Processes.* New York: McGraw-Hill.

Johnson, H.A. (1988). *History of Criminal Justice.* Cincinnati: Anderson.

Judicial Council of California. (1992). *1992 Annual Report.* Volume II: Judicial Statistics for Fiscal Year 1990–1991. Sacramento: Judicial Council of California.

Judiciary Act of 1789. Act of September 24, 1789, 1 Stat. 73.

Kroeber, A.L., and Gifford, E.W. (1980). *Karok Myths.* Berkeley: University of California Press.

Labaree, B.W. (1972). *America's Nation-Time: 1607–1789.* Boston: Allyn and Bacon.

Langan, P.A., and Brown, J.M. (1997). *Felony Sentences in the United States, 1994.* Washington, DC: Bureau of Justice Statistics.

Langdon, G.D. (1966). *Pilgrim Colony: A History of New Plymouth, 1620–1691.* New Haven, CT: Yale University Press.

Lea, H.C. (1996). *Superstition and Force: Torture, Ordeal, and Trial by Combat in Medieval Law.* New York: Barnes and Noble. (Originally published in 1870.)

Lehman, G.D. (1988). *The Ordeal of Edward Bushell.* San Francisco: Lexicon Publishing.

Lueckenhoff, S.K. (1996). A. Lincoln, a corporate attorney and the Illinois Central Railroad. *Missouri Law Review,* 61: 393–428.

Luthin, R.H. (1960). *The Real Abraham Lincoln: A Complete One Volume History of His Life and Times.* Englewood Cliffs, NJ: Prentice-Hall.

Maine, H. (1861). *Ancient Law: Its Connection with the Early History of Society and Its Relation to Modern Ideas.* London: J. Murray.

Maitland, F.W. (1897). *Domesday Book and Beyond: Three Essays in the Early History of England.* Cambridge: Cambridge University Press.

Major Crimes Act (18 U.S.C. sec. 1153).

Meyer, J.F. (1998). History repeats itself: Restorative justice in Native American communities. *Journal of Contemporary Criminal Justice,* 14: 42–57.

*Miranda v. Arizona,* 384 U.S. 436 (1966).

Moore L.E. (1973). *The Jury: Tool of Kings, Palladium of Liberty.* Cincinnati: W.H. Anderson.

Murphy, W.F., and Pritchett, C.H. (1986). *Courts, Judges, and Politics: An Introduction to the Judicial Process* (4th ed.). New York: McGraw-Hill.

*New York v. Uplinger,* 467 U.S. 246 (1984).

O'Connor, S.D. (1995). *Juries: They May Be Broke, But We Can Fix Them.* Paper presented at the First Worldwide Common Law Judiciary Conference, Washington, DC.

Oldham, J.C. (1983). The origins of the special jury. *University of Chicago Law Review,* 50: 137–214.

Owen, D.R., and Tolley, M.C. (1995). *Courts of Admiralty in Colonial America: The Maryland Experience, 1634–1776.* Durham, NC: Carolina Academic Press.

Penn and Mead's Case, 22 Charles II. (1670). Reprinted in I. Howell, *Cobbett's Complete Collection of State Trials* (Vol. VI). (1810): 951–999.

Pollock, F., and Maitland F.W. (1952). *History of English Law Before the Time of Edward I* (2nd ed.) (Vol. 1). London: Cambridge University Press. (Originally published in 1895.)

Rottman, D.B., Flango, C.R., Cantrell, M.T., Hansen, R., & LaFountain, N. (2000). *State Court Organization, 1998.* Washington, DC: U.S. Department of Justice.

Spooner, L. (1852). *An Essay on the Trial by Jury.* Boston: J.P. Jewett.

Stephen, J.F. (1883). *A History of the Criminal Law of England* (Vols. 1 and 3). London: MacMillan.

Thomas, B.P. (1968). *Abraham Lincoln: A Biography.* New York: The Modern Library.

*United States v. Tauil-Hernandez and Mordan,* 88 F.3d 576 (8th Cir. 1996).

*United States v. Tejada,* 956 F.2d 1256 (2d Cir., 1992). Certiorari denied.

Usher, R.G. (1984). *The Pilgrims and Their History.* Williamstown, MA: Corner House.

Vicenti, D., Jimson, L.B., Conn, S., and Kellogg, M.J.L. (1972). *Diné Bibee Haz'áanii: The Law of the People.* Ramah, NM: Ramah Navajo High School Press.

Waechter, R. (1997). Jurisprudential and historical aspects of jury service in Victoria. In *Jury Service in Victoria.* Melbourne, Australia: Victorian Law Review Committee.

Walker, S. (1980). *Popular Justice: A History of American Criminal Justice.* New York: Oxford University Press.

Wall, R.E. (1972). *Massachusetts Bay: The Crucial Decade, 1640–1650.* New Haven, CT: Yale University Press.

Watson, B. (1998). "Hang 'em first, try 'em later." *Smithsonian,* 29(3):96–107.

Wheeler, R.R., and Harrison, C. (1994). *Creating the Federal Judicial System* (2nd ed.). Washington, DC: Federal Judicial Center.

Whitehead, W.A. (1881). *Documents Relating to the Colonial History of the State of New Jersey* (Vol. II). Newark, NJ: Daily Advertiser Printing House.

Yazzie, R. (1994). "Life comes from it": Navajo justice concepts. *New Mexico Law Review,* 24: 175–190.

Yazzie, R., and Zion, J.W. (1996). Navajo restorative justice: The law of equality and justice. In B. Galaway and J. Hudson (Eds.), *Restorative Justice: International Perspectives.* Monsey, NY: Criminal Justice Press.

Young, R.W., and Morgan, W. (1951/1994). *Colloquial Navaho: A Dictionary.* New York: Hippocrene Books. (Originally published by Education Branch, United States Indian Service, Department of the Interior, 1951.)

# Participants in the Courtroom Drama

# Step 5

# A Prosecutor
# Considers the Charges

The first actor in the justice system that we will cover is the prosecutor. As you will learn, prosecutors are central to the justice drama. Let's get started with a few dialogues between prosecutors to introduce the varied roles fulfilled by them.

> "Really, it's a very marginal case," said the senior deputy district attorney to his colleague.
> The other D.A. reacted. "I'm reminded of the time [prior to three strikes] when these things came up, man, we never saw them because they'd be a misdemeanor. I mean, I don't care how bad his record is. His record is really not that bad. I've seen a lot worse. What are you gonna do with two bottles of cough syrup?" (Krikorian, 1996, p. B3)

These district attorneys are part of a group of prosecutors doing a weekly review of the cases that flood their urban jurisdiction. The question under discussion is whether the accused should be considered eligible to receive a sentence of twenty-five years to life, the mandated sentence for a defendant whose crime is a "third strike." In this case, the defendant's crime was stealing two bottles of cough syrup, worth a total of $52.41. He has already accumulated a long criminal record during the course of forty-two years, but does his current crime merit a third-strike sentence?

The next case the group considers is that of a man in his early twenties, a gang member with prior offenses who is charged with being an ex-felon in possession of a gun. Police arrested the defendant after seeing him with a handgun "hanging out in a driveway." Again, the issue is whether the defendant should be classified as eligible for a sentence of twenty-five years to life. The deputy district attorneys discuss some of the issues:

> "I'm not inclined to strike a strike [i.e., ignore a prior conviction]," said the deputy D.A.
> Another deputy D.A. adds, "He's had three robberies and he only did four years."
> "These were all recent. He's young. He's on the street. He doesn't have any skills, any trades, and it doesn't appear he has any inclination to go straight. Just hangin' around with a gun." (Krikorian, 1996, p. B3)

Later in this chapter, we'll consider the outcomes of these cases (Krikorian, 1996). But first, let's learn more about the people whose decisions have major

**113**

influence in the courtroom—prosecutors. Compared to other legal actors in the courtroom, the role of the prosecutor is perhaps the least understood by the public. Although prosecutors' decisions are often highly visible because of media and community attention, few people are well-informed about the nature, scope, and impact of the prosecutor's role. Part of this may be attributable to one-dimensional media depictions of prosecutors, which rarely go beyond showing the prosecution team briefly discussing the case or cross-examining a witness in court. Recall the last time you remember seeing a prosecutor shown on TV. What was the context? What was your impression of the prosecutor's function, daily work life, and dilemmas?

The modern prosecutor's legal role emerged gradually as society, and thus law and the legal system, became more complex and specialized. In the United States, the concept of prosecutors is part of the English common-law heritage of the American legal system. The Judiciary Act of 1789, passed by the U.S. Congress, created the federal judicial districts and the U.S. Attorney General's office. The U.S. Attorney General is the highest-ranking law enforcement person in the land, and is selected by presidential appointment. In turn, each federal district has its own attorney general, who is appointed to be the chief prosecuting attorney in that district. At the state level, voters in each state elect their attorney general.

## GETTING THE JOB: ELECTED PROSECUTORS AND POLITICS

At the state and county levels in many jurisdictions, the district attorney (the "D.A.") is an elected official, subject to the political pressures associated with holding elective office. Assistant D.A.s are hired staff. In some states, prosecutors are appointed. County prosecutors in New Jersey, for example, are appointed by the governor with the advice and consent of the state senate.

Elected prosecutors often use this highly visible public role to move up the career ladder. Therefore, prosecutorial election campaigns are often in the spotlight of public and media scrutiny. With this in mind, how might the need of prosecutors to be responsive to the voting public affect their decision-making, their priorities, and their goals? These questions are important to consider as we look at the prosecutor's role in detail.

## THE "MINISTER OF JUSTICE"

A prosecuting attorney represents society, rather than individual victims, and in that capacity is responsible for preparing and presenting the state's case against defendants in criminal and civil cases. Society is viewed as the injured party in prosecutions against those accused of crimes; a crime against one person is considered a crime against all. Because of this and the need for centralized power to

---

## BOX 5.1

## Prosecutorial Politics

As you sort through the following scenario, consider which characteristics voters would want to see in a prosecutor. What is the role of ethics, personality, and other personal traits? What characteristics do you feel are most valuable in a prosecutor? What accusations would you be willing to "overlook" in this election?

Put yourself in the shoes of a San Francisco resident observing the following rough-and-tumble election fight between an incumbent district attorney and his challenger, an experienced assistant D.A. According to the local news and information from the candidates, their backers, and their opponents, there are many things for you to consider as you decide how to cast your vote. On one hand, the incumbent apparently has the lowest conviction rate of any chief prosecutor in California (comparing rates between counties). Critics question his commitment to prosecuting domestic violence cases, and many of your fellow residents are reportedly incensed when this candidate publicly suggests that a convicted rapist/murderer may be a victim of professional misconduct on the part of the person who prosecuted his case (who happens to be the incumbent's challenger, of course). Furthermore, the incumbent has repeatedly been sanctioned by judges for courtroom outbursts, has been sued for sexual harassment, and has been accused of giving preferential treatment toward a murder defendant (Howe et al., 1999).

But what about the challenger in this election? He has twice been cited for prosecutorial misconduct, several of the murder convictions he obtained have been reversed on appeal, and critics question his possible involvement with a woman who is a convicted drug dealer. While you are digesting all this information, a vice squad raid on a massage parlor in the seedy part of the city turns up the challenger. When asked what he was doing in a tenderloin massage parlor at 11 P.M. on a Saturday night, the challenger explains that he was interviewing a nervous witness for a major upcoming murder trial, and that the witness picked the place and time (Matier and Ross, 1999).

Trying to decide on your vote, you have plenty of information to sort through, but which of it should you believe? Which of it is relevant to the question of which candidate would make a better prosecutor? You've got your work cut out for you.[1]

---

assess and prosecute cases, this function is vested in the state. In this sense, then, the prosecutor does not have a "client," because he or she is representing the interests of all members of society.

Despite the popular perception of prosecutors as the agents of the state who present the government's cases against the accused, few people realize that this is only a partial description of the prosecutor's function. In fact, the prosecutor is also responsible for ensuring both that the guilty are prosecuted and that legal safeguards protect the innocent from unwarranted prosecution. "The basic role of the prosecutor is to seek justice and not convictions" (Gifis, 1984). Thus, the prosecutor's role is that of a "minister of justice" (Flowers, 1996), a much broader function than the focus on prosecutions alone would suggest. Depending on the circumstances of a particular case, justice may be best served by pursuing a case against a suspect, or alternatively, by declining to prosecute a suspect even when there is suf-ficient evidence to support the charge that the suspect is guilty.

Although some might argue that the multiple functions of the prosecutor's role are conflicting, that need not be the case. If you think of the prosecutor's pri-mary function as acting in the interests of justice, then you can see how declining to prosecute in certain cases is both compatible with, and integral to, the prosecuto-rial role. Not only does justice require the prosecutor to "weed out" cases where evidence is weak, but the practical need to conserve scarce legal resources for only the most serious cases demands this. Indeed, the legal system loses credibility when defendants are convicted and then later found innocent. These are some of the main reasons why we must avoid thinking of prosecutors only in terms of their ability to win convictions (see Table 5.1).

Given that the role of the prosecutor can be conceptualized in terms of justice-seeking, how does this translate into everyday activities performed by pros-ecutors? The tasks that prosecutors perform fall into three broad categories: plan-ning and supervising the investigation phase of criminal and civil cases, case preparations, and responding to the issues related to appeals.

**TABLE 5.1    Criminal Cases Closed and Convictions by Prosecutors' Offices, 1996**

| | | Median | | | |
|---|---|---|---|---|---|
| | | Full-time offices (population served) | | | |
| Criminal cases closed | All offices | 1,000,000 or more | 250,000 to 999,999 | Under 250,000 | Part-time offices |
|---|---|---|---|---|---|
| All[a,b] | 900 | 39,445 | 13,334 | 900 | 221 |
| Percent convicted | 88% | 76% | 81% | 87% | 96% |
| Felony[c] | 250 | 11,197 | 2,928 | 260 | 57 |
| Percent convicted | 89% | 90% | 87% | 89% | 93% |
| Misdemeanor[d] | 825 | 30,167 | 11,435 | 825 | 200 |
| Percent convicted | 91% | 77% | 76% | 90% | 98% |
| Felony jury trial verdicts | 8 | 491 | 126 | 9 | 2 |

Note: Data on the total number of criminal cases closed were available for 991 offices; on felony cases closed, for 1,212 offices; and on misdemeanor cases closed, for 992. Conviction percentages for total criminal cases closed were available for 805 offices; for felony cases closed, 1,068 offices; and for misdemeanor cases closed, 830 offices. Data on felony trial verdicts were available for 1,345 offices.

[a]*Cases* refers to a defendant. A defendant with multiple charges was counted as one case.

[b]*Closed* case means any case with a judgment of conviction, acquittal, or dismissal with or without prejudice entered by the court.

[c]Each respondent categorized cases as felonies according to the State statute.

[d]Misdemeanor cases refer to cases in which criminal defendants had no felony charges against them.

*Source:* C. DeFrances and G. Steadman. (1998). *Prosecutors in State Courts, 1996.* Washington, DC: U.S. Department of Justice, Office of Justice Programs, p. 5.

The procecutor's office in Camden County, New Jersey, is shown above. Prosecutors are appointed by the governor for five-year terms and are responsible to the state attorney general. As their county's chief law enforcement officer, each prosecutor plays a prominent role in the detection and investigation of crime, as well as the arrest of suspects. Like many other prosecutors around the country, New Jersey prosecutors are responsible for bringing charges against accused individuals and for conducting trials.   SOURCE: Courtesy of Jon'a Meyer.

There is great variety in the daily responsibilities of prosecutors, depending on the jurisdiction, the type of prosecutor (federal, state, or county), and the particular job description of the individual. For example, in some jurisdictions, assistant D.A.'s are initially assigned to work exclusively on certain phases of case processing, such as pre-trial motions. Thus, as a case is processed through the court, different prosecutors work on the case as it proceeds through each legal stage. This is termed "**horizontal prosecution**." In contrast, other jurisdictions have a work style often called "**vertical prosecution**," where each case is followed through all stages by the same prosecutor(s). In some locales, particularly large urban areas, prosecutors may specialize in certain types of cases, such as domestic violence, or those involving abuse of the elderly, or cases involving juvenile defendants (or juvenile victims).

## PROSECUTORIAL DISCRETION

The prosecutor has a great deal of discretion—that is, the flexibility to choose among possible courses of action—when deciding what to do in a particular case. On the basis of an assessment of the evidence and other legal factors, the prosecutor can decide whether to file charges, and if so, what specific charges and how many counts (the number of charges). The prosecutor decides what offer to make to the defense as part of a possible plea bargain. The prosecutor can also ask the court to dismiss charges; conversely, the prosecutor has the discretion to refile charges against a defendant in certain circumstances, such as when a case ends in a mistrial.

Prosecutorial discretion is necessary to tailor the legal response to the circumstances of the case at hand. This reflects the fact that legal statutes, no matter how carefully crafted, cannot anticipate every conceivable set of circumstances. Thus, prosecutors must determine which statutes are applicable to the facts of a particular case, and consider whether prosecution is merited in light of that jurisdiction's legal and social norms. Indeed, part and parcel of the prosecutor's function is the exercise of good judgment as part of her or his discretion. "In addition, it is entirely proper—indeed, it is inevitable—that a significant factor in every prosecutor's discretion should be the prosecutor's own sense of morality" (Freedman, 1995, p. 24).

Prosecutors therefore have arguably more discretion than any other legal actor, including judges. How can this be? Although prosecutors certainly do not have unlimited discretion, in practice they operate with comparatively few legal constraints on their decision-making. For example, whereas judges' decisions are routinely reviewed by a higher court as part of the appellate process, prosecutors' decisions are rarely reviewed.

There is much evidence that prosecutors have even greater discretion today than before, as a result of changes in sentencing policy. Many legal observers believe that sentencing reforms designed to reduce judicial discretion and standardize sentencing have had the unintended consequence of simply shifting discretion away from judges and toward prosecutors. For example, in many states "Three Strikes" laws were passed with the goal of ensuring that a defendant who has two prior "serious" felony convictions would receive a mandatory prison sentence of a specified number of years (of course, the question of whether "Three Strikes" laws have achieved this is hotly debated).

Prior to mandatory sentencing policies, prosecutors negotiating a plea bargain with the defendant could offer to recommend that the judge impose a lesser sentence in exchange for the defendant's guilty plea. The understanding was that the judge would take the prosecutor's recommendation into consideration when sentencing. But with the advent of mandatory sentencing rules, judges' discretion in sentencing was sharply reduced; the judge was simply required to apply the specified sentence with little or no opportunity to tailor the sentence to reflect the circumstances of the case, including the prosecutor's sentencing suggestion.

Thus, prosecutors had to find new "carrots" to use as leverage for plea bargaining, such as agreeing to charge the defendant with a lesser charge, fewer charges, or fewer counts of a crime. The fact that the defendant accused of a crime carrying a mandatory sentence or sentence enhancement (e.g., for using a gun or committing a hate crime) faces a nonnegotiable sentence sometimes gives the prosecutor greater leverage during plea bargaining, because the prosecutor has discretion to decide the type and number of charges to file or drop. This illustrates how reducing judicial discretion has expanded the discretion already possessed by prosecutors during plea bargaining, because they are the only source of potential sentence reduction. In essence, negotiating charges is the "only game in town" for the accused person during plea bargaining.

The office of the prosecutor is often heavily scrutinized by the media, but the exercise of discretion is subject to few legal constraints and is largely unreviewed. Sanctions of prosecutors for their use or misuse of discretion are quite rare; in practice, this means that prosecutorial discretion is essentially unfettered (Pollock, 1998).

# PROSECUTORIAL CHARGING DECISIONS: LEGAL AND EXTRA-LEGAL FACTORS

If you were a prosecutor, how would you decide whether to file charges against a suspect? "That's not hard," you might say; "I'd just see whether the evidence supported the accusations against the suspect." Many prosecutors might wish that their decisions were so straightforward; not surprisingly, the reality is much more complex. Just as police cannot investigate all crime reports and the U.S. Supreme Court could not possibly hear every case submitted for review, prosecutors must be selective about which cases they pursue. This is true not only because limited prosecutorial and court resources require prioritizing, but because justice is sometimes better served by declining to prosecute.

What influences a prosecutor's decision to pursue a case? Research shows that a wide variety of factors influence this decision, including the quality of the evidence, merits of the case such as "winnability" and considerations of justice, the policies of the prosecutor's office, the availability of court resources, and public opinion. One chief prosecutor illustrated this when he discussed his office's policy on prosecuting prostitution cases:

> Prostitution itself is really a nuisance. Our office does not make it any kind of priority issue; the judges to be honest don't want those kinds of cases in their courts, they don't regard them as serious, and if we go to trial the juries very often refuse to convict. (Hallinan, 1999)

Before a prosecutor can charge a suspect, evidence must indicate that there is *at least* probable cause to believe that a crime has occurred and that the suspect is the perpetrator. In fact, some argue that prosecutors must believe that the evidence gives them more than probable cause: the National Association of District Attorneys asserts that a prosecutor "should file only those charges which he reasonably believes can be substantiated by admissible evidence at trial" (National District Attorneys Association, 1991).

Prosecutors may initiate charges against an individual by means of filing an **information**, a document which formally lists the charges against the defendant, or by presenting the evidence to a grand jury and seeking an **indictment**. An indictment is defined as "the formal charge issued by a grand jury stating that there is enough evidence that the defendant committed the crime to justify having a trial" (American Bar Association, 2001).

Depending on whether the matter is subject to federal or state prosecution, and the type of case and local jurisdictional practices, the prosecutor may present the evidence to a grand jury. Federal prosecutors, for example, present the state's evidence to the grand jury so that it can determine whether the evidence is sufficient to indict a suspect. State prosecutors may file charges via either method, depending upon whether their state customarily employs grand juries, or does not (many states do not). Given their importance, let's learn a little more about the role of grand juries and how they intersect with prosecutorial duties.

## THE GRAND JURY

There are two types of juries in the American legal system. The first type is the **petit jury**, which is what people typically think of when they hear the word "jury." In court cases that go to trial, whether criminal or civil, the defense and prosecution may select a group of people (traditionally twelve, but sometimes fewer) to hear the issues in that particular case.

In contrast, the second type of jury, called the **grand jury**, performs a quite distinct function in the legal system. Grand and petit jurors are selected from the same pool of jury-eligible citizens, but the grand jury is composed of twelve to twenty-three citizens who are impaneled to serve a specified term of service, ranging from less than one month to two years, depending on the state, but typically around one year (jurisdictions vary in the number of grand jurors and the term of service). During that time, grand jury members can consider several different legal matters arising in their geographic jurisdiction. What is the purpose of the grand jury? The Fifth Amendment to the Constitution provides:

> No person shall be held to answer for a capital, or otherwise infamous crime, unless on a presentment or indictment of a Grand Jury, except in cases arising in the land or naval forces, or in the Militia, when in actual service in time of War or public danger . . .

The Fifth Amendment's provision for indictments illustrates one of the major purposes grand juries were intended to serve: to help prevent unjust prosecutions, such as those motivated by political or personal grievances (*Hale v. Henkel*, 1906).

The grand jury is an **inquisitorial** body, meaning that it has broad legal power to investigate the matters before it: "The purpose of the body is to investigate and inform on crimes committed within its jurisdiction and to [indict persons for] crimes when it has discovered sufficient evidence to warrant holding a person for a trial" (Gifis, 1984, p. 205). Grand juries have considerable legal power and are characterized by a number of features that enhance their ability to investigate accusations. For example, grand jury hearings are held in secret, and members can consider types of evidence not usually admissible in court, such as hearsay testimony.

Despite the key role the Fifth Amendment outlines for grand juries in criminal prosecutions, in practice today grand juries are used only in certain types of cases and while federal crimes are prosecuted through means of a grand jury indictment, states are not required to use this mechanism for prosecuting state crimes; indeed, few do. Instead, grand juries are employed where they can be most useful, such as when a series of crimes may have been committed over the course of a long period of time (or in several different jurisdictions), or in cases involving alleged corruption of public officials. In the latter situation, the secrecy of grand jury hearings serves to protect both the reputation of the accused and the integrity of the state's case. If the grand jury decides that the prosecutor has not presented enough evidence to support the accusation, then the grand jury will not return an indictment, and the secrecy surrounding the proceedings will protect the accused official. On the other hand, secrecy also allows the prosecutor and the grand jury to conduct investigations with less likelihood of alerting potentially guilty parties who might try to hide or dispose of evidence or witnesses, or witnesses who might wish to flee to avoid testifying.

The role of the grand jury is controversial because of disagreement about the nature and scope of its powers. In theory, the prosecution presents the state's evidence to members of the grand jury so they can determine whether the evidence is sufficient to proceed with an indictment. Part of the controversy centers on the question of whether the grand jury is a legally autonomous body reviewing the evidence or is merely a "rubber stamp" for prosecutors. Skeptics of grand jury autonomy argue that grand jurors are likely to be unduly impressed by the arguments and evidence presented by the prosecutor.

## THE GOVERNMENT'S BURDEN OF PROOF

Central to the prosecutor's assessment of evidence when deciding whether to file charges is the fact that the prosecution bears the **burden of proof**; that is, they must convince a jury (or a judge in a bench trial) **beyond a reasonable doubt** that the accused is guilty (see Box 5.2). Although the vast majority of criminal cases are settled through plea bargaining rather than trial, the prosecutor's charging decision must consider the possibility that the matter will go to trial.

But will the jury convict? This is a key influence on the prosecutor's filing decision, but how does a prosecutor assess "case convictability"? Frohmann (1997) studied district attorneys in the sexual assault unit of a large urban area. She observed and interviewed these D.A.s as they evaluated potential cases and decided whether to accept them (by filing a case), reject them, or return them to police for further investigation. Frohmann documented the reasoning process used by D.A.s when they decided to reject cases where they felt the victim's allegations had merit, but that the cases lacked "convictability." For example, some D.A.s decided the circumstances surrounding the alleged assault would not persuade a jury to convict; their reasons included assumptions that the cultural expectations and understandings of the jurors would be so different from those of the victims and defendants that jurors would not be likely to convict. Frohmann interviewed an

---

**BOX 5.2**

**An Exercise on Standards of Proof**

Can you arrange these standards of proof in order from the highest (most difficult to meet) to the lowest (easiest to meet)?

- Preponderance of the evidence
- Articulable suspicion
- Beyond a reasonable doubt
- Clear and convincing evidence
- Probable cause

---

assistant district attorney who discussed the legal and ethical complexities of case convictability:

> What am I going to say? We are not going to file the case because we can't get twelve people to convict, that's our policy? Say we are down south, a white man rapes a black woman fifty years ago. There is strong evidence but we know twelve people aren't going to convict him. Would it be ethical to play along with biases and prejudices of community? Can I say, Sorry Ms. Victim, I know you were raped, but I know the chances of winning are slim to none? That is like saying I am going to perpetuate the biases and never going to know change because I am never going to test them. There are no evidentiary problems in the case. Do we measure evidence against the ruler of convincing twelve people, but the jurors' biases and prejudices are not on the ruler? The question is for the filing standard do you take these biases and prejudices into consideration during filing decisions . . . hopefully you don't . . . (Frohmann, 1997, p. 536).

On the other hand, the prosecutor may decide that the evidence does not provide probable cause to indicate the suspect is guilty of the crime charged, or that even with probable cause, the quantity and quality of evidence is insufficient. The prosecutor may decline to initiate a case in order to conserve scarce resources that could be used to prosecute cases that are more likely to result in conviction. To some people, the idea of prioritizing cases and selectively using legal system resources is unsettling. Critics argue that this is "rationing justice," which is neither fair nor just. But the reality is that it will always be necessary to allocate resources to the most deserving cases, because there could never be sufficient time, money, or personnel to pursue all cases.

In fact, this "cost-benefit" approach to prosecution characterizes decision-making throughout the justice system. Legal decision-makers must prioritize the demands on their resources and weigh the potential costs and benefits involved. For example, police departments and individual officers must determine which problems are most in need of their immediate attention; attorneys must decide which cases to pursue; judges and others, including correctional officials, must determine how to allocate scarce jail and prison slots when there are more inmates than space.

Selective application of legal system resources is essential to the goals of justice. All crimes for which a suspect could be prosecuted are not equally deserving of such attention from an ethical or public safety view, and selective prosecution distinguishes among cases in recognition of this. For example, the legal system routinely targets cases where the risk to public safety is judged greatest, which means other cases get less attention. As Pollock (1998, p. 237) notes, "The prosecutorial role is to seek justice, but justice doesn't mean the same thing to everyone and certainly does not mean prosecuting everyone to the fullest extent of the law." See Box 5.3 for two examples of cases illustrating prosecutorial dilemmas.

Prosecutors may also decline to file charges for a variety of other reasons. One of the classic D.A. "tools" is the use of information from informants. For example, prosecutors often plea bargain with a suspect who has valuable information about other criminals or crimes. By offering the suspect the opportunity to avoid being prosecuted or the chance to be prosecuted on lesser charges, the prosecutor is able to pursue "bigger fish." This common practice can be especially useful in the investigation and prosecution of criminal organizations or gangs, where information about illegal activities would be very difficult to obtain without "insider" information.

As one might imagine, the use of informants raises many thorny legal and ethical questions. How reliable are informants, especially jailhouse informants? Is it fair when suspects who are principals in a crime (and therefore have more information to trade) are offered a better deal than suspects who were less involved (and consequently have less information with which to bargain)? A nightmare scenario can arise for the prosecutorial team when an informant whose testimony was an important part of a successful prosecution is called into question.

A recent example illustrates this dilemma. Drug Enforcement Administration (DEA) informant Andrew Chambers provided information for almost two decades on a variety of cases across the country. Prosecutors nationwide pursued cases against suspected drug dealers, and used Chambers as a witness, without being aware that he had serious credibility (believability) problems. Among other things, he apparently failed to pay income taxes and lied about the numerous times he had been arrested. Although the DEA paid Chambers more than two million dollars in rewards, expenses, and fees for his information, the DEA's own internal investigation determined that Chambers' lying began early in his association with the DEA. To make matters worse, DEA agents were reputedly aware of the lies but did not inform prosecutors or defense attorneys.

As Chambers' checkered history came to light, defense attorneys across the country began requesting retrials for clients whose convictions were supported by information from Chambers. In addition, a number of prosecutors nationwide

## BOX 5.3

## You Are the Prosecutor: What Would You Do?

The decision whether or not to initiate charges against a suspect often involves complex considerations of what would best serve the goals of justice and fairness. Here, the prosecutor's power of discretion is fully apparent, as is the complexity of the charging decision. Consider what you would do if you were a prosecutor as you read about the following cases.

Case #1: A woman and her boyfriend go boating on the delta with her eight-year-old daughter and two other children. It's a very hot day, and the children don't want to wear life vests. The boat, which is towing Jet skis, is idling in the middle of the delta. The little girl is standing on the platform at the back of the boat, near the engine exhaust, when somehow she falls in the water and drowns. Her body is not recovered until the next day (Goodyear, 2000).

As a prosecutor, you must consider several issues. Why wasn't the child wearing a life vest, as required by boating regulations? Why was she standing at the back of the boat, near the engine exhaust (with the possibility of being overcome by exhaust fumes)? Were the adults negligent in their care for the little girl? The craft was being operated at a legal, responsible speed, and no alcohol or drugs were involved. You could charge one or both adults, who are stunned at the little girl's death, with child endangerment. Should you? Why or why not?

Case #2: On a country road one sunny afternoon, a car carrying four teenage girls is rear-ended at approximately 35 mph. The car's gas tank bursts into flames and the girls burn to death. The driver of the car that rear-ended the victims bent down to retrieve a cigarette that he had dropped; he survived the crash unscathed. The intense explosion, damage, and burn deaths that occur in this collision seem unusual for what appears to be an all-too-common, relatively low-speed rear-end collision. In researching the circumstances of this crash, you learn that the victims' car, a Ford Pinto, is unusually likely to suffer a ruptured fuel tank and explode when rear-ended, even at relatively slow speeds. In fact, the victims in this latest crash join dozens of others who were killed or severely disfigured after being burned in crashes involving Pintos.

Researching further, you learn that even before the Pinto was put on the market, Ford was aware of the problems with Pinto explosions. Ford's own crash tests had revealed that the gas tank on Pintos was located too close to the rear bumper, increasing the likelihood of an explosion in the event of a rear impact. In fact, you learn that cost projections on one of Ford's internal memos concluded that at $12.00 estimated cost per Pinto to retrofit the gas tanks and thus reduce the hazard, it would be more economical to set aside a lump sum for anticipated lawsuits by victims (Dowie, 1977).

As the prosecutor, what do you do with this information? Is this evidence of intentional wrongdoing on Ford's part? A search through the law library tells you that no one has ever tried to prosecute a company on criminal charges of negligent homicide. But could you be the first prosecutor to do so?

Consider your reactions to the cases above. Considering one of the cases which interests you most, discuss this question: Would you make the same decision in your role as "prosecutor"? Why or why not? Do you think the prosecutor was too harsh or lenient? Too concerned about "winnability"?

If you were given the chance to retry any of these cases, which would you choose? As a prosecutor, what charges, if any would you pursue in the case? Why?

have made the decision to drop cases that relied on information from Chambers (Scott, 2000).

## PURSUING A CASE: WHAT HAPPENS NEXT?

Once a district attorney has decided to file charges, there are several legal and ethical issues to consider. One of the first decisions to be made is *what* charges and *how many counts* of each charge are warranted by the case.

### Charging the Defendant with . . . What?

As the chapter on plea bargaining will describe, prosecutors take into account many factors in deciding the nature and number of charges against the accused. Depending on the case, the prosecutor may consider some or all of the following in determining the charges:

- The quality and quantity of the evidence supporting potential charging options
- The impact of the charges on the defense response during plea bargaining negotiations
- The potential reaction of jurors should the case go to trial
- The victim's wishes
- The defendant's prior criminal history (or lack thereof)
- Public reaction to the charges
- The amount of resources required to pursue the case
- The minimum and maximum possible sentence
- The seriousness of the crime alleged
- The possible deterrent effect on other potential offenders
- The impact on other cases (for example, if multiple offenders are charged in connection with the same offense)
- Possible mitigating factors in favor of a lesser charge

## THREE STRIKES CHARGING

A good example of how a wide variety of considerations can enter into the charging decision is provided by "three strikes" cases. Recall the two cases under consideration by a group of prosecutors that you read about at the beginning of the chapter. What do you think happened? In the case of the cough syrup thief, prosecutors declined to treat the case as a three strikes matter, and the defendant received a seven-year prison sentence. In contrast, the ex-felon charged with possessing a firearm was charged with a third strike, and the defendant opted to go to trial rather than plea bargain.

## THE PROSECUTOR AS PLEA-BARGAIN ENGINEER

As Step 11 describes, the process of plea bargaining is a critical component of the legal process, and the government's attorney is the central figure in this process. The prosecutor decides whether to offer a plea deal and determines its terms: Reduce the charges? Reduce the number of counts (of each charge) against the defendant? Drop some charges if the defendant will plead guilty to others? As the chapter on plea bargaining tells us, there are many factors influencing the plea-bargaining process and the prosecutor's decision-making with regard to it.

## DILEMMAS OF THE PROSECUTOR'S ROLE

As you can see, the role of the prosecutor has grown in complexity as societal and technological changes have led to the need for prosecution of sophisticated offenses

This legal paperwork results from one murder case in Pennsylvania and all of it was drafted or reviewed by the prosecutor. During the investigation and trial phases, the prosecutor is responsible for reading and understanding police and forensic reports, in addition to other documents. After deciding to pursue charges against a defendant, the prosecutor is responsible for drafting many of the important documents in the case, including the charging papers, search warrants, briefs regarding pre-trial motions and reactions to the defense attorneys' pre-trial motions, the paperwork necessary in preparation and during the trial, and briefs regarding post-trial motions for relief.   SOURCE: Courtesy of Jon'a Meyer.

such as computer crimes, corporate financial schemes, and organized crime. With this increasing complexity comes potential role conflicts and dilemmas, both large and small. This section discusses some of the issues that a district attorney must contend with.

A young assistant D.A. who was prosecuting his first domestic violence case encountered an all-too-common dilemma. On the day of the trial, the victim confronted him and accused him of pressuring her to lie about her injuries. Although the court established that this accusation had no basis in fact, the incident reflected the fact that victims are not always supportive of prosecutors, for many possible reasons (Garcia, personal communication, 1997).

A quite different dilemma helps illustrate the changing responsibilities of federal prosecutors. Increasingly, federal D.A.s are working on complex cases that require tracking the actions of many suspects over a long period of time. To pursue such cases, federal prosecutors must work closely with police investigators who are assembling evidence to ensure that all evidence-gathering techniques are legal; if they are not, evidence might be declared inadmissible. A classic example of this is the "sting" operation, where police set up an operation to catch suspects in the act; this can be seen when police officers go online and assume the identity of a minor to catch potential pedophiles in cyberspace.

Thus, prosecutors are increasingly involved in the construction of a potential case during the early stages of investigation, which leads us to the question of whether the prosecutor can effectively distinguish between the "fact-finding" role of a prosecutor during the investigative stages of a case and the "adversary" role he or she will take on if the assembled evidence develops into an indictable case. At the investigative stage, the prosecutor's role is to work with law enforcement to ensure that all relevant facts are gathered, in order to determine whether there is sufficient evidence against a particular suspect or suspects to proceed with the case—or not. Therefore, the investigative stage must focus on gathering not only facts that would tend to support the state's version of the case, but also those that would favor the defense in the event charges are filed. The prosecutor should function in a neutral, rather than adversarial, capacity during the investigative stage. In contrast, at the adversarial stage of the case, the prosecutor functions as an advocate of the state's case. This contrast illustrates how there can be tension between different facets of the prosecutor's role, especially for federal attorneys.

Another dilemma arises when prosecutors encounter situations where victims want charges dropped. This occurs frequently in domestic violence cases where the offender and victim know each other (Cardarelli, 1997). However, there are many other types of cases, such as when victims of robbery or assault by gang members fear retaliation by their attackers.

What should a prosecutor do when a victim wishes to drop charges? Although the victim's wishes are an important consideration, this fact alone is not sufficient to support a prosecutorial decision to drop charges. Because the prosecutor represents society as a whole, rather than simply the victim, prosecutors must consider whether their duties require them to protect the victim (and future potential victims) from harm by proceeding with the case despite the victim's wishes. Thus, many jurisdictions have "no drop" policies, whereby prosecutors can pursue cases against suspected perpetrators even where a victim refuses to file or maintain a complaint (see Box 5.4).

Prosecutors may be called upon to explain unpopular decisions to the public, whether this involves pursuing a case against a defendant who finds public sympathy or explaining the decision not to prosecute an unpopular suspect. In the latter situation, the district attorney can serve an important educational purpose in the process of explaining the legal reasons behind the decision not to prosecute. For example, in the case of Sherrice Iverson, a little girl who was sexually assaulted and killed in a Nevada casino, public outrage at the behavior of David Cash (a friend of the attacker, who witnessed part of the crime but did not intervene to stop the assault) led to repeated calls for his prosecution. However, there was no legal basis for prosecuting Cash; his failure to act was not an offense under the law at the time. Subsequently, a number of states have passed "Good Samaritan" laws providing criminal penalties for failure to report a crime. The laws' specific provisions, exceptions, and penalties vary from state to state.

---

## BOX 5.4

## Charging Decisions:
## How Much Should the Wishes
## of Victims Count?

In the noisy and often anguished public debate about capital punishment, much is said about the wishes of victims' families. A common question that appears in the debate is, "Should the wishes of the victims influence the prosecutor's decision to ask—or not to ask—for the death penalty in a capital case?" What do you think?

Would you want the prosecutor (and the jurors deciding whether to sentence the defendant to life or death) to take victims' wishes into account? Under what circumstances? Can you think of reasons why such wishes should *not* be formally considered by the prosecutor and/or the triers of fact (i.e., the jury or the judge)? Think about your answers to these questions.

Now consider: What if the situation were not at all what you might have imagined. What if, in fact, the families of the victim asked the prosecutor *not* to request the death sentence in a capital case? What if the *victim* himself or herself left written instructions for what to do if he or she became a murder victim—a "Declaration of Life"[2] requesting that the killer not be given the death penalty? Would your position on how to weigh victims' wishes change?

## THE PROSECUTOR AND THE COURTROOM WORK GROUP

Although the D.A.'s decision-making processes are highly discretionary, prosecutors certainly do not act in isolation from other parts of the court system. In fact, the prosecutor's office works closely with people representing all aspects of the legal system. It is critical for the prosecutor's office to have a good working relationship not only with other members of the courtroom work group, such as defense counsel, judges, and court staff, but also with local law enforcement agencies, including probation and parole units. At the federal level, the prosecutor's office must also be able to work effectively with federal agencies, such as the Federal Bureau of Investigation (FBI) and the U.S. Marshals. The relationships between prosecutors and other members of the legal system is an example of an "exchange system" because their decisions and actions are highly interdependent. For example, prosecutorial charging decisions influence police decisions on which crimes to prioritize; probation officers' pre-sentencing reports influence plea bargaining and sentencing decisions; judges' decisions reflect workload demands on attorneys (for example, granting or failing to grant continuances); and prison and jail overcrowding influences judges' sentencing decisions.

Let's look at the relationship between the prosecuting attorney and police as an example of the importance of prosecutorial relationships with other justice system actors. Good teamwork and communication between the D.A. and the police is essential for effective prosecution because the prosecutor must be able to rely on police for legally gathered and preserved evidence. The infamous O.J. Simpson case demonstrated the difficulties the prosecution can encounter when there are questions about the "chain of evidence"; specifically, how evidence was collected and preserved by police.

Conversely, the policies of the prosecutor's office influence how police prioritize which laws they should focus on enforcing. If police do not believe that a particular type of offense will be prosecuted, then they will be inclined to focus on other crimes they know are more likely to have the attention of prosecutors (Langworthy and Travis, 1994, p. 17).

For example, until recently in California, violations of the law against statutory rape (consensual sexual relations between a minor and an adult) were rarely pursued by police, and usually only in response to a specific complaint from the minor's parent. However, in response to new government attention to this crime and the resulting problem of teenage pregnancies, police are more likely to find that arresting a suspect for statutory rape will result in prosecution.

The need for cooperation between the prosecutor and the defense attorney is especially critical because of the due process rights of the defendant. This is quite evident when you consider the legal process called "discovery" (see Box 5.5 for more information on discovery).

---

**BOX 5.5**

**"Eureka!": The Process of Discovery**

While assembling the state's case, the prosecution team may encounter exculpatory evidence favoring the defendant. By law (*Brady v. Maryland,* 1963; *United States v. Bagley,* 1985), the prosecutor must disclose information favorable to the defense as part of the process of "discovery." The failure of the FBI to turn over several documents pertaining to the Oklahoma City bombing case is one of the most well-publicized recent examples of the importance of the discovery process. In this case, the fact that the documents had not been turned over to the McVeigh defense team was discovered only shortly before the convicted bomber was scheduled to become the first federal prisoner to be executed in over three decades. After court hearings determined that the documents in question did not call McVeigh's guilt into question, the execution proceeded a few weeks after the originally scheduled date (Romano, 2001).

The idea underlying this legal requirement is to attempt to balance the resources of each side; the prosecutor has the power of the state on its side, whereas the defense does not. Because it is the prosecutor who determines whether charges will be filed against an accused, based on evidence gathered by police, the prosecutor is in the best position to uncover exculpatory evidence while researching the case and deciding whether charges are merited, and when pursuing the state's case after charges against the accused are filed.

Given the ethical and legal incentives to avoid injustice, misused resources, and credibility damage, the idea of discovery makes sense because it is consistent with the prosecutorial role of pursuing justice. That is, while the district attorney's function in the adversarial system is often thought of mainly in terms of presenting the state's case in court for the triers of fact (judge or jury) to assess, prosecutors have an equally important obligation to provide exculpatory evidence to the defense for use at trial.

---

## THE AFTERMATH OF THE CASE: FURTHER PROSECUTORIAL ISSUES

The end of the trial phase of a case does not mean the end of the prosecutor's involvement. In a criminal case, a conviction often (in death penalty cases, automatically) results in an appeal to a higher court, and a prosecutor must defend the state's case in appellate court. Even when the defendant is acquitted, prosecutors often try to find reasons why they were unable to convince the jurors (or the judge, if it's a bench trial) of the defendant's guilt beyond a reasonable doubt. An **acquittal** does not mean the defendant has been proven innocent; it means that the prosecution failed to prove its case beyond a reasonable doubt. Thus, after an acquittal, prosecutors may ask departing jurors why the verdict turned out as it did. Sometimes jurors will respond and sometimes they will not. Prosecutors and defense attorneys are especially interested in talking to jurors when a case ends in a mistrial because the jury cannot reach consensus—known as a **hung jury**. In this instance, information about how jurors viewed the case can be very useful to both sides if the prosecutor decides to re-try the case.

## POST-TRIAL EVIDENCE

What happens when undeniable evidence of a defendant's culpability turns up *after* he or she has been acquitted of the crime? On rare occasions, this happens. See what you think about the prosecution team's attempts to deal with such a situation in the following case:

In 1991, Mel Ignatow stood trial on charges that he murdered his fiancée, Brenda Schaefer. At his trial, Ignatow's former girlfriend, Mary Ann Shore-Inlow, testified that she had watched while Ignatow tied his fiancée to a coffee table, sexually tortured her, and then killed her. Shore-Inlow testified that she had taken photographs of the crime in progress, but the pictures were nowhere to be found, and the jurors apparently did not find her credible. In the absence of physical evidence linking Ignatow to the death of Schaefer, the jury acquitted Ignatow (Wessel, 1999).

Ten months later, the new tenants in Ignatow's former residence found a roll of film in an air-conditioning duct. The developed pictures graphically documented what Ms. Shore-Inlow had described. Ignatow then admitted to his crimes against Schaefer, stating, "I did physically and sexually abuse her, and I did murder her."

Nonetheless, because of the "double jeopardy" provision of the Fifth Amendment, Ignatow could not be retried for the murder: once acquitted, always acquitted. However, prosecutors could take some comfort from the fact that Ignatow was already in prison serving a sentence of five years for committing perjury in an unrelated legal matter (Wessel, 1999).

Looking at the aftermath of cases also illustrates the very personal consequences that the work can have on prosecutors, from the ultimate nightmare of a defendant seeking revenge to the personal satisfaction of knowing one's work makes a meaningful difference to some people. See Box 5.6 on the hazards of a prosecutorial career, and Box 5.8 on prosecutors Buel and Darden.

## COMPARING DIFFERENT TYPES OF PROSECUTORS

The term "prosecutor" is used to refer to an attorney employed by the government who has prosecutorial responsibilities. The full name for such an attorney is a "public prosecutor." But unbeknownst to most, many jurisdictions allow a private person to function as a prosecutor to bring charges in a particular case. In theory, the private prosecutor acts under the supervision of the public prosecutor. However, whereas legally there is such a thing as a "private prosecution," in practice this is quite rare. See Box 5.7 for another type of prosecutor.

## BOX 5.6

## An Uncommon Occupational Hazard

The nature of the prosecuting attorney's work almost inevitably guarantees that prosecutors will encounter some people who are very unhappy with them. In addition to the obvious potential for defendants to feel animosity toward the prosecutor, a variety of other people with a stake in the outcome of a case may be dissatisfied with the prosecutor's decisions or trial strategies, or with the case outcome. Victims or their families may want the prosecutor to pursue a case more vigorously or to drop charges. Witnesses may resent the prosecutor's attempt to get them to testify, and even jurors may disagree with the prosecutor's presentation during trial. Such animosities rarely translate into violence against prosecuting attorneys in the United States, in contrast to the experiences of their counterparts in some countries. Nonetheless, work-related violence does sometimes strike prosecutors, as Joseph Warton (1995) describes:

- Malcolm Schlette waited more than thirty years to get his revenge against a prosecutor who had sent him to prison for twenty years on arson charges in 1955. Schelle, seventy-two, shot and killed former Marin County district attorney William Weissich in November 1986 and later turned the gun on himself.
- Florida assistant state's attorney Eugene Berry was gunned down in the doorway of his Fort Myers home in January, 1982. The wife of a drug defendant he helped convict was found guilty of his murder.

## BOX 5.7

## Special Prosecutors

Ken Starr is the best-known example of a special prosecutor, yet most people remain unaware of what a special prosecutor's function is supposed to be; what's "special" about this type of prosecutor? How does this differ from ordinary public prosecutors? The short answer is that a special prosecutor is an attorney appointed to independently investigate a specific case and determine whether charges should be pursued. The role of the special prosecutor took on special significance during the Watergate scandal, and most recently during the Clinton presidency.

## COMPARING FEDERAL AND STATE PROSECUTORS

There are interesting distinctions between prosecutors at the federal and state level, reflecting the different types of cases each handles. The bulk of routine criminal cases are prosecuted at the state level, but in recent years an increasing number of crimes have been designated as violations of federal law. Alternatively, in some cases existing federal statutes have been applied in new ways. Federal prosecutors (also called U.S. attorneys) now deal with an increasing range of offenses, including complex offenses, such as those identified during police and FBI "sting" operations, corruption cases involving public officials, "white collar" offenses, such as product liability issues, worker safety cases, organized crime rings, and cases involving the application of federal statutes, such as RICO (Racketeer Influenced and Corrupt Organizations Act) in drug cases.

Federal prosecutors are uniquely well-positioned to develop a "new strategic role" in long-range, broad-based crime prevention efforts. Because they have information from a variety of federal, state, and local agencies concerned with crime and social problems (e.g., social work agencies), U.S. attorneys can initiate efforts to consolidate and cross-reference information and help people from different agencies connect with each other. Exchanging information about suspects and offenses—for example, "mapping" the locations, times, and participants associated with violent offenses in a particular city—can serve as the foundation for a coordinated crime-prevention strategy carried out by all participants (Glazer, 1999).

---

## BOX 5.8

## The Personal Dimension of Prosecution Work

*The "working personality" of prosecutors is as varied as that of people in any other occupation, but for some prosecutors the issues they encounter become inextricably intertwined with their personal identities and beliefs. In some instances this reflects the attorney's conscious decision to meld the personal and the professional in their work as prosecutors; in other situations, prosecutors may find that their work has significant effects on their personal lives. The following excerpts, describing the lives of two prosecuting attorneys, illustrate this.*

**Excerpts from *Why They Stay: A Saga of Spouse Abuse*
by Hara Estroff Marano (1996):**

Whatever else American culture envisions of petite blondes, it doesn't expect them to end up as social revolutionaries. But just that turn of fate has brought Sarah Buel to Williamsburg, Virginia, from suburban Boston, where she is assistant district attorney of Norfolk County. To a gathering of judges, lawyers, probation and police officers, victim advocates, and others, she has come to explain why and, perhaps more importantly, precisely how domestic violence should be handled, namely as the serious crime that it is: an assault with devastating effects against individuals, families, and communities, now and for generations to come.

The judges and cops and court officers pay attention to Buel because domestic violence is a daily hassle that takes a lot out of them. And if there's one thing Buel knows, its how batterers manipulate the law enforcement system. They listen because Buel has that most unassailable credential, an honors degree from Harvard Law School. But mostly they listen because Buel has been on the receiving end of a fist. "Sometimes I hate talking about it," she confides. "I just want people to see me as the best trial lawyer."

## BOX 5.8 *(continued)*

Certainly Buel never had any intention of speaking publicly about her own abuse. It started accidentally when she was in a court hallway with some police officers on a domestic violence case. "See, a smart woman like you would never let this happen," the chief said, gesturing her way. And in an instant Buel made a decision that changed her life irrevocably, and the lives of many others. "Well, it did happen," she told him, challenging his blame-the-victim tone. He invited her to train his force on handling domestic violence. "It changed things completely. I decided I had an obligation to speak up. It's a powerful tool."

By speaking from her own experience, Buel reminds people that law can be a synonym for justice. In conferences and in courts, she has gotten even the most cynical judges to listen to battered women—instead of blaming them. "I am amazed at how often people are sympathetic as long as the victim closely resembles Betty Crocker. I worry about the woman who comes into court who doesn't look so pretty. Maybe she has a tattoo or dreadlocks. I want judges to stop wondering, 'What did she do to provoke him?'"

It's possible, she feels, to end domestic violence, although not by prosecution alone. Buel does not dwell on herself as victim but transmutes her own experience into an example for change, "so that any woman living in despair knows there's help." Not like she knew. She herself was clueless. By the time she was twenty-two, Buel was an abused woman. The verbal and psychological abuse proved more damaging than the physical abuse.

But no matter who she talks to or what she says about domestic violence, "it always comes down to one thing," says Buel. "They all ask the same question: Why do they [the women] stay." One of the biggest reasons women stay, says Buel, is that they are most vulnerable when they leave. That's when abusers desperately escalate tactics of control. More domestic abuse victims are killed when fleeing than at any other time.

Buel has a crystal-clear memory of a Saturday morning at the laundromat with her young son, in the small New Hampshire town where she had fled, safely, she thought, far from her abuser. "I saw my ex-partner, coming in the door. There were people over by the counter and I yelled to them to call the police, but my ex-partner said. 'No, this is my woman. We've just had a little fight and I've come to pick her up. Nobody needs to get involved.' I still had bruises on the side of my face, and I said, 'No, this is the person who did this to me, you need to call the police.' But he said. 'No, this is my woman. Nobody needs to get involved.' Nobody moved. And I thought, as long as I live I want to remember what it feels like to be terrified for my life while nobody even bothers to pick up the phone."

Toward the end of her undergraduate studies, her bosses asked her where she wanted to go to law school. "Harvard," she replied, "because they're rich and they'll give me money." The lawyers laughed and told her that wasn't how it worked: "They do the choosing, not you." They took pains to point out she just wasn't Harvard material. "You're a single mother. You've been on welfare. You're too old."

Angry and humiliated, Buel began a private campaign that typifies her fierce determination. In the dark after classes, she drove around the law school, shouting at it: "You're going to let me in." Soon she got braver and stopped the car to go inside and look around. Then she had to see what it was like to sit in a classroom. Harvard Law not only accepted Buel but gave her a full scholarship. Once there, she was surprised there was nothing in the criminal-law syllabus about family violence despite the fact that women are more likely to be the victim of a crime in their own home, at the hands of someone they know, than on the streets.

When Boston-area colleagues requested help on an advocacy program for battered women and she couldn't do it alone, Buel put an ad in the student newspaper; seventy-eight volunteers showed up for the first meeting. By year's end there were 215. The Battered Women's Advocacy Project is now the largest student program at Harvard Law; a quarter of the participants are men.

At first Buel thought it would be enough to become a prosecutor and make sure that batterers are held accountable for assaulting others. But she has come to see it differently. "That's not enough. My role is not just to make women safe but to see that they are financially empowered and that they have a life plan." So every morning, from 8:30 to 9:15, before court convenes, she sees that all women there on domestic issues are briefed, given a complete list of resources, training options, and more. "It's all about options."

What's more, Buel now sees domestic violence as just one arc of a much bigger cycle, intimately connected to all violence, and that it takes a whole coordinated community effort to stop it, requiring the participation of much more than attorneys and judges.

For her unusually diversified approach to domestic violence, Buel gives full credit to William Delahunt, her boss, the district attorney—"He has allowed me to challenge the conventional notion of what our job is."

There was the batterer who, despite divorce and remarriage, was thought to be the source of menacing gifts anonymously sent to his ex-wife—a gun box for Christmas, a bullet box for Valentine's Day, followed by the deeds to burial plots for her and her new husband. The woman repeatedly hauled her ex into court for violating a restraining order; one lawyer after another got him off. "Finally I got him for harassing her in the parking garage where she was going to college; of course he denied it. The lawyer contended she was making up all the stories. But a detective found a videotape from the garage, which corroborated her charge. In the appeals court, his lawyer, a big guy, leaned into my face and hissed, 'You may be a good little advocate for your cause, but you're a terrible lawyer.'"

She won the appeal. (Marano, 1996)

*Source:* Reprinted with permission from *Psychology Today,* copyright © 1996, Sussex Publishers, Inc.

## Excerpts from *The Trials of a Former Black Prosecutor* by Christopher Darden and Diane Weathers (1997):

*Christopher Darden, a prosecutor in the Los Angeles County D.A.'s office, was part of the prosecution team that attempted to convict O.J. Simpson in 1994.*

Just for a moment, put yourself in my shoes. You're a prosecutor in the district attorney's office, assigned to uphold the law in an unbiased manner. Then after fourteen years on the job, circumstances place you on what some people consider to be the wrong side of a very hot issue.

During the O.J. Simpson trial, I received a flood of faxes and mail attacking my role as prosecutor: "You're incompetent." "You're an Uncle Tom." "You're only on this case because you're Black." "You're ugly and have big lips." There were even threats made on my life. The Black press joined the fray, describing me as "brooding, inarticulate, a man without a country." One writer, in the pages of this magazine, likened me to Clarence Thomas. It was as if my efforts to search for truth in this case had made me an ultraconservative whose views on race were at odds with those of most of Black America.

One of the defense team's tactics was to vilify me, and it worked. They turned a case, at the heart of which was the issue of domestic violence, into a case about race. Somehow O.J. Simpson became a Blacker Black man than I.

## BOX 5.8 *(continued)*

Before I was a prosecutor, I was a Black man. It was always difficult to sit there and watch, on a daily basis, Black and other minority defendants being sentenced time and time again to long prison sentences. It was stressful. It could break your spirit. I've also seen the bad cops. I've seen instances in which they lied, planted dope on a suspect, used excessive force, or sexually abused an inmate.

But I've also seen the victims—I mean the real victims. When I've sent Black people to prison, it has been for a good reason. In most cases, it's because they have victimized another Black person. For years I have been on the board of a Los Angeles organization that counsels the survivors of people killed in violent crimes—such as the parents of a victim who suddenly find themselves raising their very young grandchildren. It is their plight that motivates me. How is it possible for us to celebrate the murderer over the murdered, the perpetrators of criminal acts over the people they have harmed? My most vocal critics complained that I was too sympathetic to the Goldmans and the Browns. But can you imagine the grief you would feel, losing your son or your daughter to such a violent act? Their tears were the same color as the tears I have seen so many times before in the eyes of Black survivors of violent crime. I cannot distinguish between the two.

Sometimes, in my darker moments, I would say to myself, 'To hell with all the critics.' A prosecutor's job is to search for the truth in a criminal case, and if people don't appreciate my efforts then let them go out and deal with the Crips and the Bloods and the crack dealing, raping, mugging, the child molestation, the drive-by shootings, the invasive home burglaries and the assorted crimes now plaguing our communities. Yes, I'm aware of the racism within the criminal-justice system. But I am also aware that in the neighborhood I grew up in, every other house has bars on the windows. On one hand, Black people are locking themselves in; on the other, they're locking out those who are preying on them, and most often those predators are Black.

You can't really right a wrong by sending somebody to prison. But you can help victims' survivors achieve some sense of justice. The survivors of a violent crime deal with a great amount of anger every day. Living with anger can be destructive. It can consume you. I believe that people who have lost their parents, their children or their siblings have a right to closure. If it means incarcerating the man or woman who took their loved one away, then they should be incarcerated.

But for now I've left that world. I was listening to a sermon one day, and the preacher was talking about how life can be broken into seasons. Time had passed, a season had passed, my time as a prosecutor had passed. When I went back to the D.A.'s office a year later, I had to ask myself how I'd existed in that environment before. The epiphany for me was to realize the conditions under which I'd worked. And I knew that from that moment on, it was probably better to leave it alone—to risk failing, to risk succeeding—than to go back again. It's in the past; it's over.

My anger and frustration are fading at last. Today I do not dwell on feelings about either the verdict or the trial participants. I realize that what doesn't kill us makes us stronger, and I've found an inner peace I could not have discovered but for the trials and challenges of these past three years. (Darden & Weathers, 1997)

*Source:* Reprinted with permission of *Essence.*

## PROSECUTIONS GONE WRONG: PROSECUTORIAL MISTAKES AND MISCONDUCT

What happens when a prosecutor makes a mistake, especially when that mistake results in the erroneous conviction of an innocent person? Can the victims of such mistakes sue the prosecutor? The answer is usually no. Prosecutors and judges possess "absolute immunity" from lawsuits related to certain aspects of their work, and "partial immunity" with respect to other aspects (such as the investigative function). The logic behind this is to protect prosecutors (and judges, who are also protected from lawsuits related to their judgments) from the legal threat of liability so that they can do their work without fear of retribution. In theory, at least, prosecutorial (and judicial) mistakes are minimized through due process protections, such as the adversarial system and the processes of discovery and appeals.

Far more disturbing is the fact that prosecutorial misconduct and mistakes have occurred. Clarence Brandley, whose case was mentioned briefly in Step 3, was convicted and served ten years in prison, most of it on death row, for a rape-murder that he did not commit. Evidence later demonstrated that in an overzealous attempt to hurriedly find and convict a likely suspect, the local prosecutor guided and staged the case in secret meetings with the judge. Exculpatory evidence was not only overlooked but actively suppressed, critical case files mysteriously disappeared, witness testimony suddenly changed, and inconsistencies in the evidence that should have been interpreted in the defendant's favor were conveniently ignored. It was only when a shocked court clerk told a defense attorney that something was amiss that the misconduct came to light.

In another series of cases, prosecutorial charging decisions played a crucial role in the mistaken convictions of innocent people. The article in Box 5.9 provides sobering reading.

## WHAT CONSTITUTES PROSECUTORIAL MISCONDUCT?

Prosecutorial actions that can be misconduct, raising legal and ethical concerns, include but are not limited to the following (Pollock, 1998):

- Communications with the defendant outside the presence of the defense attorney
- Failure to disclose evidence to the defense as part of discovery
- Communications with the judge about a particular case outside the presence of the defense attorney
- Conflicts of interest (especially applicable to part-time prosecutors who may also have a private law practice)
- Failure to correct false witness testimony

## BOX 5.9

## Excerpts from "Above the Law: When State Prosecutors Fail to Put Justice Before Winning, We All Lose," by J. Keedle, 1998

*This is a story of three men arrested and imprisoned for crimes they did not commit.*

Gilberto Rivera spent four months in jail after being wrongly charged with the murder of a gang member in Hartford's Pope Park during a crowded festival. Despite early evidence that Hartford police botched their investigation, despite federal agents' repeated claims that Rivera was the wrong guy and that they had the real killer in custody, the state's attorney still signed the arrest warrant.

Ultimately, Rivera wasn't prosecuted but he still lives in fear. To be charged is as good as a conviction on the street, and he's always on the lookout in case someone tries to exact revenge in the name of the gang member who died.

Murray Colton spent the past decade living with the threat of prison. He was tried three times for the same crime and served a total of three years in prison. After ten years of uncertainty, he breathed a sigh of relief two months ago, when the case against him was finally dismissed. Even so, he still runs into people who, because police have no other suspects, remain convinced that he was New Haven's notorious "dimes" murderer.

Larry Miller entered a Connecticut prison the father of two teenagers and came out a grandfather. He missed his son's high school graduation, his daughter's wedding, his twenty-fifth wedding anniversary, and countless birthdays and holidays. A former police officer and prison guard, he had no criminal record when he was arrested for the brutal beating and rape of two minors nearly the same age as his own children. At the age of fifty-one, he was released when the real rapist confessed—twelve years after Miller first went to prison.

At this point, there's nothing anyone can say or do to compensate for those lost years. Miller and Rivera have wrongful arrest lawsuits pending against the Danbury and the Hartford police departments, respectively, but how do you put a price on freedom? Still, when innocent people are wrongly convicted, someone should be held responsible. The question is, who?

People often blame inadequate or incompetent defense attorneys. But in the court system, there is only one person whose job description explicitly charges him to bring out the truth and serve justice. That is the prosecutor, the state's attorney who speaks for "the people" in the case against any defendant.

State's attorneys alone decide who to prosecute and how vigorously they should pursue the case. They base their decisions on what they believe can be proven beyond a reasonable doubt. Unlike defense attorneys, whose sole responsibility is to their client, state's attorneys represent us in that courtroom.

Referring to the 1992 Supreme Court case of *State v. Hammond,* former prosecutor and now state Supreme Court Chief Justice Robert Callahan described the job thus: "A state's attorney has a duty, not solely to obtain convictions, but to ensure that all evidence tending to aid in the ascertaining of the truth be laid before the court, whether it be consistent with the contention of the prosecution that the accused is guilty."

This is how the criminal justice system is supposed to work and most of the time, it does. "When I was a prosecutor in Hartford, every single day I would turn down warrants if I didn't feel it was a case where we could go before a jury and the elements of a crime were not there," says Chief State's Attorney John Bailey, who is the administrative head of Connecticut's thirteen state's attorneys. "A prosecutor is given products from the police. He doesn't usually do his own investigation."

And therein lies the problem. At the end of the day, the decision to prosecute rests not with Bailey, or with the judge, but with the state's attorney for a particular court district. Although Bailey is empowered by statute to take over a case if there is a suggestion of prosecutorial misconduct, he does so rarely. When weak cases, under-investigated by police, are vigorously prosecuted, the risk that an innocent person may be convicted increases.

Nevertheless, some believe wrongful convictions remain rare. "I have found, by and large, prosecutors and state's attorneys exercise their discretion fairly, so the wrongly convicted are, I think, few and far between," says Judge Aaron Ment, Connecticut's Chief Court Administrator since 1984 and a justice for over twenty-two years. "In nearly all those cases, a jury convicts. It's difficult for the prosecutor to say afterwards that the jury was wrong."

That said, should an overzealous prosecutor make a mistake, it's hard to prove intentional wrongdoing.

"I think these cases, where innocent people are prosecuted, highlight the problem. Prosecutors have enormous power and influence with judges and juries, and the prosecutor has nothing to lose no matter what he does," says Colton's attorney, Ken Rosenthal, of the New Haven law firm Brenner, Saltzman, and Wallman. "The risk is they will convict an innocent man."

That this does happen—and far more frequently than most people think—is truly horrifying. That charges against Rivera, Colton and Miller were ultimately dismissed is cold comfort considering they were all falsely imprisoned. When the justice system failed them, it failed all of us. (Keedle, 1998)

*Source:* Reprinted with permission of the *Hartford Advocate.*

Other examples of prosecutorial misconduct include inappropriate attempts to prejudice the jury against the defendant, such as by deliberately dropping hints about inadmissible evidence in front of jurors during trial, and other verbal and psychological tactics of "legal warfare" in court (Gershman, 1992).

Why does prosecutorial misconduct occur? The reasons are complex, and vary from case to case. In some instances, a prosecutor's individual bias plays a role. In many cases, however, misconduct probably reflects a combination of things, including structural features of the way the prosecutor's role is organized. For example, there may be powerful political pressures and incentives that help lead prosecutors to overemphasize winning without giving sufficient attention to other prosecutorial functions. In this situation, a prosecutor may fail to acknowledge exculpatory evidence while giving too much weight to weak or inconclusive evidence against the accused. Although pressures on prosecutors should never be considered justification for intentional misconduct, it is critical to acknowledge the influence they may have on prosecutors to better understand their actions.

Because there is no system of formal, regular review of prosecutorial decisions by other legal actors, how do prosecutorial misconduct or mistakes come to light? Only when a defense attorney requests a court review of the prosecutor's actions in a case. In this situation, the court may review the prosecutor's actions and determine that no misconduct occurred, that misconduct occurred that significantly influenced the case (potentially triggering a retrial), or that misconduct occurred but that it did not significantly influence the case's outcome. In the last scenario, called "harmless error," the court determines that the district attorney made a mistake, but finds it unlikely that the mistake would have made a material difference to the trial.

---

## BOX 5.10

## Pursuing the Guilty—At What Cost to the Innocent?

What happens when a witness for the prosecution suffers retaliation because of his or her cooperation? Does the prosecutor bear any legal or ethical responsibility for this?

In one case, sixteen-year-old Moises Torrez witnessed a killing by a gang member he knew. Torrez was tracked down by detectives and persuaded to name the killer on condition that his own identity would not be disclosed in court. However, despite the fact that detectives had agreed to this condition, Deputy District Attorney Dennis Ferris tried to get Torrez to testify at trial. When Torrez refused, Ferris read his statement to the police in open court, and jurors subsequently found the defendant guilty. A few days later, Torrez died after being stabbed more than forty times by a street attacker.

Torrez's family sued Ferris for wrongful death, alleging that his actions exposed Torrez to retaliation. Ruling on this case, the appellate court held that prosecutors have no legal duty to protect witnesses from possible retaliation, and thus cannot be held liable for actions taken in their official capacity as prosecutors.

One member of the appellate court, Judge Benjamin Aranda, supported the court's reasoning on prosecutor liability but nonetheless quite clearly expressed his view of the prosecutor's actions in a separate written opinion:

> In order to obtain a conviction, the life of a witness was deliberately put in jeopardy, if not outright sacrificed by the prosecution. (*Hernandez v. City of Pomona,* 1996).

Judge Aranda also noted that D.A. Ferris had previously been involved in a similar case, where a witness in a gang murder was killed right before trial.

Ferris defended his actions, stating that Torrez had refused an offer to be relocated, and questioning whether Torrez's murder was an example of retaliation. Ferris noted that Torrez's killer remained at large, leaving the motive for the killing unknown. While acknowledging that Torrez's testimony was required for the conviction, Ferris also noted, "He probably would have been killed even if the defendant was acquitted. Once they have proof of an informer, they usually retaliate in some manner."

Commenting on Judge Aranda, Ferris said: "I don't think this judge knows very much about street gang prosecutions. Either we go after these gang criminals with everything we have, or we let them walk away from their crimes unpunished." (Goldberg, 1996).

## CONCLUSION

The role, responsibilities, and discretionary power of a prosecuting attorney makes him or her one of the central legal actors in the courtroom work group. Using discretion to "seek justice," the prosecutor's decisions are shaped by a wide array of legal, organizational, ethical, and political considerations. The American prosecuting attorney's role is expanding as cases become more complex in legal and practical terms, requiring the prosecutor to participate in the investigatory stages to a greater degree, to work in cooperation with many different people and agencies in the legal system, and to coordinate the multiple "threads" of a potential case.

Now we turn to the next chapter to look at the prosecutor's adversary in court: the defense attorney. What is the role of the defense attorney in the criminal justice system? Turn to Step 6 and we'll take a look.

### DISCUSSION QUESTIONS

1. What did you think of the discussions by prosecutors about the cases at the beginning of this chapter? Did it surprise you that these conversations appeared to rely so much on the prosecutors' impressions of the defendant's character?

2. Discuss what types of factors lead to prosecutorial misconduct. Is it simply a matter of poor ethical values on the part of individual prosecutors? Or is it also linked to the way the legal system is organized (for example, the focus on case winnability)? Given the complex situations surrounding misconduct, what can be done to prevent it?

3. How do Christopher Darden's experiences as a prosecutor (see Box 5.8) illustrate the "double burden" that he carried as both a member of the legal establishment and a black person? Is it fair when members of minority communities are assumed to represent their communities?

4. What did you think of the Torrez case (see Box 5.10)? What are the potential consequences if we were to allow lawsuits against prosecutors for actions they took in their official capacity? How do you think this would influence prosecutors' decisions regarding cases?

5. What are the pros and cons of having elected versus appointed prosecutors?

6. Do you think that there is any tension between the different components of the prosecutor's role? If so, what sort of tensions exist, and why?

7. What are the pros and cons associated with increasing prosecutorial discretion at the cost of judicial discretion?

8. Compare prosecutorial discretion with that possessed by other members of the legal system. How does prosecutorial discretion compare with judicial discretion?

9. Given the circumstances in which plea bargaining occurs, should a defendant's guilty plea be considered truly voluntary? Why or why not?

10. Is the "probable cause" standard of proof for filing charges the appropriate standard, or should a higher—or lower—standard be used? Support your answer with examples.

11. One of the most noticeable characteristics about the U.S. court system is the openness of most court proceedings. With some exceptions, such as juvenile court, courtroom proceedings are open to the public. What do you think about the secrecy of grand jury hearings?

12. Should prosecutors be allowed to use the testimony of so-called "jailhouse informers" in exchange for extending leniency to them with respect to the charges against them? Why or why not? If yes,

under what circumstances and with what limits to the rewards? For example, would you allow prosecutors to rely only on the testimony of informants whose information could be corroborated by another person?

13. Consider the issue of case convictability. Given that prosecutors must prioritize which cases to pursue, do you believe it's always ethically acceptable for prosecutors to consider the "winnability" potential of a case? Or are there some circumstances under which prosecutors should pursue cases which they are unlikely to win? If you think there are, describe the circumstances and the reasons you think prosecutors should file charges in such cases.

14. Find a case in your local newspaper where the prosecutor's office declined to file charges. Discuss reactions to the prosecutor's decision: your reactions, the victim's reactions, the reactions of members of the public. The Ignatow case is an example of a rare phenomenon; in contrast, cases of people who are convicted and later found innocent are more numerous. Do you agree that "tis better ten guilty men should go free, rather than one innocent man suffer unjust conviction"? Why or why not?

15. What is the purpose of the double jeopardy provision of the Fifth Amendment to the Constitution? Why do you think the framers of the Constitution were so concerned about protecting those accused of a crime from repeat prosecutions?

16. Consider the provisions of the Fifth Amendment's double jeopardy protection. What are the possible benefits of this? What are the limits of the scope of double jeopardy—in other words, when is double jeopardy *not* applicable? Are there some situations, in your opinion, when double jeopardy should not be applicable?

17. In what ways is the courtroom work group an example of an "exchange system"? What are the implications for court functioning if there is tension or competition between different components of the system?

## NOTES

1. This was the situation in San Francisco in 1999, when incumbent district attorney Terence Hallinan battled challenger Bill Fazio, an assistant D.A., for re-election. Hallinan won.

2. A "Declaration of Life" is a standardized form that a living person signs indicating that if he or she should be murdered, the victim's wishes that the convicted killer not be given the death penalty should be respected. The document carries no legal weight, leaving the fascinating question of how much weight prosecutors should accord such wishes, if any, in a capital case. See the Logan article listed in the references section for further information.

## REFERENCES

American Bar Association. (2001). *How Courts Work: Steps in a Trial.* Available at www.abanet. org/publiced/courts/trialsteps.html.

*Brady v. Maryland,* 373 U.S. 83 (1963).

Cardarelli, A.P. (Ed.). (1997). *Violence Between Intimate Partners: Patterns, Causes, and Effects.* Boston: Allyn and Bacon.

Darden, C., and Weathers, D. (1997, November). The trials of a former black prosecutor. *Essence,* 28(7): 62.

DeFrances, C., and Steadman, G. (1998, July). *Prosecutors in State Courts, 1996.* Washington, DC: U.S. Department of Justice, Office of Justice Programs. NCJ 170092.

Dowie, M. (1977, September/October). Pinto Madness. *Mother Jones Magazine,* p. 20.

Flowers, R.K. (1996, September) A code of their own: Updating the ethics codes to include the non-adversarial roles of federal prosecutors. *Boston College Law Review.*

Freedman, M. (1995, October 16). A life or death decision for prosecutors. *The Connecticut Law Tribune,* p. 24.

Frohmann, L. (1997). Convictability and discordant locales: Reproducing race, class, and gender ideologies in prosecutorial decisionmaking. *Law & Society Review,* 31(3): 531–557.

Garcia, M., Merced County deputy district attorney. In personal communication with author Diana Giant, 1997.

Langworthy, R., and Travis, L.F. (1994). *Policing in America: A Balance of Forces.* New York: Macmillan.

Gifis, S. (1984). *Law Dictionary (2nd ed.).* Woodbury, New York: Barron's Educational Series.

Gershman, B.L. (1992, April). Tricks prosecutors play. *Trial,* 28(4): 46.

Glazer, E. (1999, Summer). New approaches to fighting crime: (III) How federal prosecutors can reduce crime. *Public Interest,* 136: 85–100.

Goldberg, D. (1996, October 8). Prosecutor has immunity, but is scolded by a jurist. *Daily Journal.*

Goodyear, C. (2000, July 11). Felony charges in girl's drowning. *San Francisco Chronicle,* p. A17.

*Hale v. Henkel,* 201 U.S. 43 (1906).

Hallinan, Terrence, D.A. for San Francisco, in an interview on A&E's "Inside Story." Video on San Francisco vice cops, 1999.

*Hernandez v. City of Pomona,* 49 Cal App. 4th 1492 (1996).

Howe, K., Van Derbeken, J., and Wallace, B. (1999, December 15). D.A. race goes down to the wire (incumbent Hallinan, Fazio neck-and-neck). *San Francisco Chronicle,* p. A1.

Keedle, J. (1998, November 19). Above the law: When state prosecutors fail to put justice before winning, we all lose. *Hartford Advocate,* pp. 14–15.

Krikorian, G. (1996, May 19). '3rd Strike' case arouses starkly different views. *Los Angeles Times,* p. B3.

Logan, W.A. (1999). Declaring life at the crossroads of death: Victims' anti-death penalty views and prosecutors' charging decisions. *Criminal Justice Ethics,* 18(2): 41.

Marano, H.E. (1996, May/June) Why they stay: A saga of spouse abuse. *Psychology Today,* 29(3): 56.

Matier, P., and Ross, A. (1999, December 3). A little mud gets kicked Fazio's way in D.A. Race. *San Francisco Chronicle,* p. A25.

National District Attorneys Association. (1991). National Prosecution Standards (2nd ed.). Alexandria, VA: National District Attorneys Association.

Pollock, J. (1998). *Ethics in Crime and Justice (Dilemmas and Decisions)* (3rd ed.). Belmont, CA: West/Wadsworth.

Romano, L. (2001, June 7). Judge refuses to delay execution of McVeigh. *The Washington Post,* p. A1.

Scott, D. (2000, July 12). Drug informant is caught lying; many cases are in jeopardy. *Des Moines Register,* p. 6.

*United States v. Bagley,* 473 U.S. 667 (1985).

Warton, J. (1995, December). Prosecutor murder raises gang fears. *American Bar Association Journal,* 81: 28.

Wessel, K. (1999, May 1). Ignatow may face another trial: Appeals court will not block perjury case. *The Courier-Journal,* p. B01.

# Step 6

# A Defense Lawyer Is Selected: The Defense Role

---

❖

---

As we saw in the previous chapter on prosecutors, the criminal court process is predicated on the assumption that justice is best achieved through the adversarial process. Yet to what extent is the adversarial ideal realized in practice? This chapter describes some aspects of the role defense counsel plays in the criminal court structure and process. As you'll see, the defense role, like the prosecution role, is complex and sometimes contradictory.

## THE DEFENSE ATTORNEY'S ROLE IN THE COURT SYSTEM

What role does defense counsel play in the court system? Some people might answer this question "To defend the defendant, of course" and think the question obvious. Yet the role of defense attorneys in courtroom proceedings is often misunderstood. Defense attorneys often face criticisms that their actions amount to condoning illegal behavior, letting guilty perpetrators go free, and stacking the justice system. Such comments reflect a lack of accurate and complete understanding of the role of defense attorneys. As Supreme Court Justice White noted, commenting on the defender's role: "Defense counsel has no comparable obligation to ascertain or present the truth. . . . Our interest in not convicting the innocent permits counsel to put the State to its proof, to put the State's case in the worst possible light, regardless of what he thinks or knows to be the truth" (*United States v. Wade*, 1967, p. 1174). A spirited defense makes sure that the defendant's side of the story is heard. This is done despite the fact that the majority of defendants are guilty. It is only by giving this spirited advocacy that the rights of those who are not guilty can be protected. A spirited defense also helps counteract overcharging by prosecutors. Thus, the defense attorney's role is to provide his or her client with the best defense possible, including:

- Providing legal counsel to client
- Arguing for legal innocence (not necessarily factual innocence)

- Searching out violations of the defendant's rights
- Arguing for reduced penalties in some cases

## ELEMENTS OF THE DEFENSE ROLE

Although the defendant is not required to present any defense because the prosecution has the legal burden of proving the accused's guilt beyond a reasonable doubt, typically a defense is mounted. The defendant and his or her attorney must search out potential violations of the defendant's legal rights and determine the best strategy for arguing on the defendant's behalf. This includes negotiating with the prosecutor for the best possible plea bargain, and deciding whether to take the case to trial. Either side may broach the topic of a plea bargain, but they are typically initiated by the defense. In some cases, the defense role includes arguing for reduced penalties. For example, in some cases where there is incontrovertible evidence that the defendant committed a killing, the defense attorney may focus on getting the jury to convict on lesser charges (such as manslaughter rather than murder). There are many key legal questions for the defense attorney to consider when he or she is developing a legal strategy, depending on the circumstances of the case:

- Does the case revolve around questions about the identity of the perpetrator, or other issues? For example, in some sexual assault cases the main issue is whether the defendant is the actual perpetrator of the crime. In other such cases, the issue is whether the act that occurred constituted rape or consensual sexual relations, but the defendant's identity is not an issue in the case.
- What evidence exists regarding the accused's mental state at the time of the crime? Recall from Step 2 that to be defined as a crime, an act (*actus reus*) must have been carried out with the requisite mental state (*mens rea*). Thus, the defense attorney must focus on how to handle the issue of the defendant's intent at the time of the alleged crime.
- Were there mitigating circumstances? Was the act committed in self-defense, or after extreme provocation, or in the heat of passion?
- What is the prosecutor's strategy likely to be? The defense will try to anticipate and prepare for the state's case to whatever degree possible.
- What would be an acceptable plea bargain? The defense attorney should be able to tell the defendant whether the prosecutor's plea offer is favorable when compared to the probable outcome of a jury trial.
- Are there questions about the reliability of any of the evidence in the case? For example, how did the police obtain and preserve the evidence in the case?

- Can the credibility of prosecution witnesses or expert witnesses be impeached? For example, how reliable is an eyewitness in the case? Can the testimony of the prosecution's expert witness be challenged during cross-examination?
- Should a change of venue be requested if the case seems likely to go to trial? If there is substantial pre-trial publicity, the defendant's right to a fair trial could be hampered because jurors are likely to have heard of and formed opinions about the case before trial.

The defense attorney may also serve as a source of guidance and psychological support for the defendant. This aspect of the defense role is an important function of defense attorneys, because it involves preparing the client for what lies ahead. This is particularly applicable to criminal defense attorneys in capital cases, where the attorney may serve not only as legal advisor but as social support for the defendant and the defendant's family as they contemplate the possibility that the accused will be convicted and possibly sentenced to death. This aspect of defense work can be particularly complex when a defendant in a capital case balks at plea bargaining, without considering the potential risks of going to trial. Although the decision about what course of action to take ultimately belongs to the defendant, whose future is at stake, the defense attorney needs to ensure that the accused's decision is grounded in knowledge of the realities of the legal process. For example, one attorney describes the complexities of getting some capital defendants to overcome their denial of the seriousness of their situation in order to appreciate the challenges they face:

> For many clients, the capital prosecution is a way to bask in societal attention. If they cannot be Bruce Willis or Michael Jordan, they will settle for being Gary Gilmore or Roger Coleman. Such romanticized, delusional thinking can kill your client. So defuse his sense of grandeur. Demonstrate that executions are already becoming old hat in many places. Talk about the paltry coverage they are given in states where people are routinely put to death. (Doyle, 1999)

This attorney goes on to describe strategies for negotiating a favorable plea bargain with the government and for convincing reluctant clients to consider the advantages of plea bargaining in order to avoid the risks of a trial and a possible capital sentence (see Box 6.1 for an example).

The American Bar Association (Monohan and Clark, 1995) notes that criminal defense work requires competence and skill at a variety of critical tasks, including but not limited to:

- Legal knowledge and skill
- Timeliness of representation
- Thoroughness and preparation

---

## BOX 6.1

## Helping Capital Clients Appreciate Risks

An experienced capital defense attorney describes one strategy he uses to persuade clients who are uninformed about the relative risks and benefits of accepting a plea bargain versus proceeding to a capital trial:

> Make the client explain his position. Make him tell you why, for instance, his professed moral innocence is a reason for him not to save his life. Have him detail how he will vindicate his name from the grave and what role he can play in his kids' lives once he is dead. Insist he tell you why he must self-destructively defy a system for which he has no respect. Identify who he is going to teach a lesson by going to the execution chamber and what he is going to prove. Let him defend his decision in light of the fact that straight murder is the best he can hope for and, under the habitual felon statute, that will mean life without parole in any event. Challenge senseless responses and then keep coming back to these questions. (Doyle, 1999)

*Source:* Reprinted with permission of *The Champion.*

---

- Client relationship and interviewing
- Communicating with and advising the accused
- Investigation
- Trial court representation
- Sentencing
- Appellate representation

How is the role of defense attorneys best described, then? Are defense attorneys strictly "legal tools" whose main purpose is to serve the legal interests of their clients? Or, are they also—or instead—"ethical agents"? What is the nature, scope, and extent of the defense attorney's potential as an agent of morality? Cohen (1991) uses the term "moral agent" in describing his view that an attorney must be concerned with the ultimate fairness and justice of the legal outcome, not simply the client's wishes. Cohen (1991) and Simon (1988) discuss the distinction between an attorney who functions primarily or solely as a legal agent for his or her client and an attorney who acts as a legal agent in the context of balancing broader ethical and social justice concerns. For example, in this conception of the defense role, the attorney must balance the legal interests of the client with the interests of society as a whole, other potential clients, and the interests of justice. As Simon (1988) notes, simply because you could win a case, does this mean you should?

## THE RIGHT TO COUNSEL: A BIT OF HISTORY

Under early English law, the accused was tried without the benefit of counsel, and therefore forced to face the awesome power of the state unaided. This increased the potential for government oppression of political dissenters tried by the Crown.

To provide greater protection of individual liberties against the power of the state, the framers of the Constitution crafted the Sixth Amendment (1791) to provide several key constitutional rights, including the right to ". . . have the assistance of counsel for his defence." A defendant's right to legal counsel has undergone quite an evolution since then. Until early in the twentieth century, the right to counsel meant simply that defendants had the right to hire their own counsel; those who could not afford to do so continued to face the prosecution alone.

The right to counsel took on new meaning in 1932, when the U.S. Supreme Court held in *Powell v. Alabama* that indigent defendants accused of a capital crime who would be unable to defend themselves must have counsel provided for them (see Box 6.2). The right of indigent defendants to have counsel provided for them was extended to all defendants charged in *federal* courts in 1938 *(Johnson v. Zerst).*

---

### BOX 6.2

### *Powell v. Alabama,* 1932

In 1931, eight young African American men were charged with raping two white women. The "Scottsboro Boys," as they were collectively referred to, ranged in age from thirteen to nineteen years old. The defendants and their accusers had been riding boxcars, a common method of transport for poor people in those days. During the arraignment, the judge noted that "all members of the bar" would serve to represent the defendants. In practice, this meant that the defendants were represented by two attorneys described by one commentator thus: "[The two defense attorneys] were no 'Dream Team.' Roddy was an unpaid and unprepared Chattanooga real estate attorney who, on the first day of trial, was 'so stewed he could hardly walk straight.' Moody was a forgetful seventy-year-old local attorney who hadn't tried a case in decades" (Linder, 1999, online).

The social and political climate of the deep South in the early twentieth century was characterized by deep racial tension, violence, and hostility; and no accusation was more controversial at the time than the charge that a black man had raped a white woman. Black men who were suspected of simply looking at or whistling at a white woman had very good reason to fear that angry white men, often members of the Ku Klux Klan, would retaliate violently. In such instances, the bodies of black men and boys were often found with their genitals mutilated. Newspaper accounts of the time regularly carried stories—sometimes with accompanying photos—of public lynchings and burnings of black men accused of rape who were summarily subjected to vigilante "justice" without benefit of ever seeing the inside of a courtroom.

This was the atmosphere in which the Scottsboro Boys, who were divided into subgroups in four separate trials, stood trial. The Scottsboro Boys might never have made it to trial, instead facing a lynch mob of townspeople, if the governor of Alabama had not ordered soldiers to keep the peace around the courthouse (Linder, 1999). At their trials, the defendants were charged and convicted of rape by all-white juries. One of the youngest defendants, tried by himself, was sentenced to life in prison after the jury deadlocked on the death penalty. The other defendants were sentenced to death (at the time, rape was punishable as a capital offense; that is no longer true).

The fate of the defendants might have gone unremarked but for the efforts of the International Labor Defense (ILD) group, a Communist Party organization dedicated to social justice. The ILD denounced the trial as an example of racism in the justice system, a claim which had rarely been publicly made before. With the assistance of volunteer attorneys, the defendants appealed; but the Alabama appellate court rejected the defendants' contention that the lack of counsel at their trial represented a denial of their Fourteenth Amendment right to due process. After a series of appeals from each of the four trials, the U.S. Supreme Court found in their favor and their convictions were reversed (*Powell v. Alabama*, 1932). The Court cited the lack of evidence, which was especially problematic after one of the women recanted her testimony, and proclaimed that due process required that capital defendants be represented by counsel at trial. The Court noted that the circumstances surrounding the representation of the defendants meant, essentially, that ". . . these defendants, that is to say, from the time of their arraignment until the beginning of their trial, when consultation, thoroughgoing investigation, and preparation were vitally important, the defendants did not have the aid of counsel in any real sense, although they were as much entitled to such aid during that period as at the trial itself" (*Powell v. Alabama*, 1932, p. 57).

This legal victory became a milestone in the right to counsel, but it was not without a high cost for the Scottsboro Boys themselves. Although they were eventually exonerated and released, several of the defendants spent years in prison before they were freed. (Linder, 1999).

The Powell and Johnson cases represented very important milestones in the right to counsel, but they did not apply to the vast majority of criminal defendants—people tried in state (versus federal) courts. Thus, most people accused of non-capital crimes still did not have the assistance of an attorney at their trial. This situation would not be changed until 1963, when as we saw in Step 3, the *Gideon v. Wainwright* decision provided indigent defendants in state felony cases with the right to have an attorney. In 1972, the right was finally extended to defendants accused of misdemeanors for which incarceration was a possible sentence (*Argersinger v. Hamlin*). Box 6.3 describes the Argersinger case in more detail.

When are defense attorneys most important? The Supreme Court has adopted a "critical stages" test, which means defendants are entitled to attorneys at every stage of prosecution "where substantial rights of the accused may be affected" (*United States v. Wade*, 1967). This includes, for example, pre-trial questioning and in-person (versus photo) line-ups in addition to the trial itself.

The history of the Sixth Amendment right to counsel is a good example of the differences that often exist between our constitutional rights in theory and in practice, and the critical role that the courts play in interpreting and implementing such rights.

# BOX 6.3

## Argersinger's Journey from Lower Court to U.S. Supreme Court

Jon Argersinger's problems started when he was charged with carrying a concealed weapon, a misdemeanor offense that could net him up to six months in jail. He opted for a bench trial (before a judge rather than a jury), was convicted, and was sentenced in a Florida lower court to ninety days in jail. Argersinger then began *habeas corpus* proceedings in the Florida Supreme Court because he had asked for and been denied the assistance of counsel at his trial. Had Argersinger lived in one of the nineteen states that provided counsel to indigents accused of misdemeanors, the outcome may have been very different.

In *State of Florida ex rel. Argersinger v. Hamlin* (1970), the Florida Supreme Court acknowledged that *Gideon v. Wainwright* (1963) required the courts to assign counsel to those charged with felonies, but noted that no such mandate existed for less serious charges. The panel of justices argued that even if the U.S. Supreme Court was later to extend the right to counsel to less serious charges, it would certainly be for those defendants who faced non-petty misdemeanors and could receive at least six months in jail:

> Assuming arguendo that that Court will eventually decide that Gideon should be extended to include misdemeanor trials, it is fair to presume that it would apply to the right-to-counsel rule the same principles applicable to a determination of the right to a jury trial, namely, that this right extends only to trials for non-petty offenses punishable by more than six months imprisonment. (*State of Florida ex rel. Argersinger v. Hamlin*, 1970, p. 443)

In the end, the Florida Supreme Court felt that providing counsel for all indigents, regardless of the amount of jail they face, could overextend local legal and judicial resources:

> Thus, the two classes of offenses [i.e., felonies vs. misdemeanors] are widely separated in type, kind, punishment and effect; and even though the basic and fundamental "due process" right guaranteed by the Fourteenth Amendment must be held to include the Sixth Amendment right-to-counsel in felony cases as was held in Gideon, it does not necessarily follow that this Sixth-Fourteenth tandem can reach down into the lowest echelons of petty offenders and hand out to them the free services of an elaborate and expensive public-defender system to defend them against charges of overparking or other petty offenses. In the words of Judge Mehrtens in Brinson [an earlier case in Florida], "The demands upon the bench and bar would be staggering and well-nigh impossible" (*State of Florida ex rel. Argersinger v. Hamlin*, 1970, p. 444).

Argersinger did not stop there. He filed an appeal with the U.S. Supreme Court, which ruled that counsel was important to justice in all cases where defendants face the prospect of jail:

We must conclude . . . that the problems associated with misdemeanor and petty offenses often require the presence of counsel to insure the accused a fair trial. (*Argersinger v. Hamlin,* 1972, pp. 36–37)

We reject . . . the premise that since prosecutions for crimes punishable by imprisonment for less than six months may be tried without a jury, they may also be tried without a lawyer. (*Argersinger v. Hamlin,* 1972, pp. 30–31)

---

## BOX 6.4
## Does Greater Diversity Equal More Justice?

Many people believe that justice should be colorblind, and some believe that it is. Many others believe that the reality is far different—that justice is too often color-conscious (and class- and gender-conscious as well). But are there circumstances where justice *should* be "color-conscious"? For example, suppose for a moment that you were accused of a crime. Would you prefer to be represented by someone from your own ethnic group? Why or why not? Would it matter to you whether the prosecutor in your case came from your ethnic group?

In some areas, legal observers are calling for greater ethnic diversity in the ranks of defense attorneys and DA's. These observers are concerned that there are few attorneys (whether prosecutors or defense counsel) from ethnic minority groups, but many minority defendants. But why should this matter? These critics of the legal system contend that attorneys and clients who share an ethnic background are better able to establish good communication, to understand cultural factors that may be important in the case, and to build trust.

"Minority defendants and victims often have cultural, social, economic and language issues that affect their cases," said Nicole Wong, regional governor of the National Asian Pacific American Bar Association. "You really want someone in the prosecutor's seat and in the defender's seat who understands those issues, who understands the person coming before the judicial system." Alameda County District Attorney Terry Wiley notes that "I've had many cases with African American witnesses who come in and are very intimidated with the whole criminal justice system . . . but upon them seeing me, I can just look in their eyes and see them become more at ease" (Richman, 1998, p. 1).

*Source:* Reprinted with permission of ANG Newspapers.

---

## DEFENSE ATTORNEYS AND THE COURTROOM WORK GROUP

In the courtroom, the interactions between defense counsel and the prosecution appear adversarial, but often these professional relationships have a different character outside the courtroom. Attorneys and other legal actors recognize the role that each plays in the courtroom "psychodrama" as part of an interdependent group.

## BOX 6.5

## International Association of Defense
## Counsel Tenets of Professionalism

1. We will conduct ourselves before the court in a manner which demonstrates respect for the law and preserves the decorum and integrity of the judicial process.

2. We recognize that professional courtesy is consistent with zealous advocacy. We will be civil and courteous to all with whom we come in contact and will endeavor to maintain a collegial relationship with our adversaries.

3. We will cooperate with opposing counsel when scheduling conflicts arise and calendar changes become necessary. We will also agree to opposing counsel's request for reasonable extensions of time when the legitimate interests of our clients will not be adversely affected.

4. We will keep our clients well informed and involved in making the decisions that affect their interests, while, at the same time, avoiding emotional attachment to our clients and their activities which might impair our ability to render objective and independent advice.

5. We will counsel our clients, in appropriate cases, that initiating or engaging in settlement discussions is consistent with zealous and effective representation.

6. We will attempt to resolve matters as expeditiously and economically as possible.

7. We will honor all promises or commitments, whether oral or in writing, and strive to build a reputation for dignity, honesty and integrity.

8. We will not make groundless accusations of impropriety or attribute bad motives to other attorneys without good cause.

9. We will not engage in discovery practices or any other course of conduct designed to harass the opposing party or cause needless delay.

10. We will seek sanctions against any other attorney only when fully justified by the circumstances and necessary to protect a client's lawful interests, and never for mere tactical advantage.

11. We will not permit business concerns to undermine or corrupt our professional obligations.

12. We will strive to expand our knowledge of the law and to achieve and maintain proficiency in our areas of practice.

13. We are aware of the need to preserve the image of the legal profession in the eyes of the public and will support programs and activities that educate the public about the law and the legal system.

*Source: Defense Counsel Journal, July, 1999.*

Recall that the courtroom work group is the center of the court system, and as such each member of the group acts in the context of group norms, customs, and expectations (Nardulli et al., 1988).

The place of defense counsel in the courtroom work group can be conceptualized as a "many-hatted" or multifaceted role. The defense attorney is both advocate for the client and officer of the court; a decision-maker with great discretion to significantly influence both the legal and ethical aspects of the case at hand and thus, ultimately, the legal system itself; and many defense attorneys have prior experience working as prosecutors. However, the complexity and richness of the defense attorney's occupational heritage carries with it inherent potential for tension between different aspects of the role. For example, in some instances the attorney's advocacy on behalf of a client may conflict with the expectations associated with being an officer of the court and a member of the courtroom work group.

This is amply illustrated by the situation faced by overloaded public defenders who must balance workload demands with the needs of the defendants they represent.

## DEFENSE COUNSEL: PRIVATELY RETAINED VERSUS GOVERNMENT-PROVIDED

Although some defendants have the resources to retain private attorneys, in criminal cases that is the exception. Most often, defendants are unable to pay for an attorney and thus rely on public defenders, members of legal aid groups, or private attorneys appointed by the court to represent them (see Table 6.1). Defendants facing homicide charges are most likely to hire their own defense attorneys, although the majority of such defendants still rely on government-provided counsel (Harlow, 2000, p. 7). There are two types of counsel provided by the state for defendants who cannot afford to hire counsel:

1. Assigned counsel—the court appoints a private attorney from a list of available lawyers. They are paid a flat fee for their work. Most have private and assigned clients.
2. Public defender (PD)—attorneys who work for state; PDs have no private clients.

Public defenders have a bad rap ("Did you have an attorney?" "No, man, I had a public defender."). The traditional "wisdom" concerning the relative merits of privately retained defense attorneys and government-provided counsel, from a defendant's viewpoint, is that private attorneys are preferable. Research illustrates differences between the two types of defense counsel in experience, caseload, type of cases/clients, and organizational constraints. For example, public defenders are often new attorneys with relatively little experience (Levin, 1977; Nardulli, 1988). In addition, public defenders often have very high caseloads, and are more likely to have cases of indigent defendants and those with prior criminal histories. A government report on public defender caseloads cited the situation of a public defender who was simultaneously handling seventy felony cases. The attorney had represented 418 defendants in a period of seven months (Spangenberg Group, 2001, p. 1). Assigned

## TABLE 6.1   Defense Counsel in Criminal Cases

**At felony case termination, court-appointed counsel represented 82 percent of state defendants in the seventy-five largest counties in 1996 and 66 percent of federal defendants in 1998.**

| | Percent of defendants | |
| --- | --- | --- |
| | Felons | Misdemeanants |
| **75 largest counties** | | |
| Public defender | 68.3% | — |
| Assigned counsel | 13.7 | — |
| Private attorney | 17.6 | — |
| Self (pro se)/other | 0.4 | — |
| | | |
| **U.S. district courts** | | |
| Federal Defender | | |
| Organization | 30.1% | 25.5% |
| Panel attorney | 36.3 | 17.4 |
| Private attorney | 33.4 | 18.7 |
| Self representation | 0.3 | 38.4 |

Note: These data reflect use of defense counsel at termination of the case.
—Not available.

• Over 80% of felony defendants charged with a violent crime in the country's largest counties and 66% in U.S. district courts had publicly financed attorneys.

• About half of large county felony defendants with a public defender or assigned counsel and three-quarters with a private lawyer were released from jail pending trial.

**Defendants with publicly financed or private attorneys had the same conviction rates.**

| Case disposition | Public counsel | Private counsel |
| --- | --- | --- |
| **75 largest counties** | | |
| Guilty by plea | 71.0% | 72.8% |
| Guilty by trial | 4.4 | 4.3 |
| Case dismissal | 23.0 | 21.2 |
| Acquittal | 1.3 | 1.6 |
| | | |
| **U.S. district courts** | | |
| Guilty by plea | 87.1% | 84.6% |
| Guilty by trial | 5.2 | 6.4 |
| Case dismissal | 6.7 | 7.4 |
| Acquittal | 1.0 | 1.6 |

• In state courts in the largest counties, 3 in 4 defendants with either court-appointed or private counsel were convicted; in federal courts 9 in 10 felony defendants with public or private attorneys were found guilty.

• In Federal court 88% of felony defendants with publicly financed attorneys and 77% with private lawyers received a prison sentence.

**Except for state drug offenders, federal and state inmates received about the same sentence on average with appointed or private legal counsel.**

| | State prison inmates | | Federal prison inmates | |
| --- | --- | --- | --- | --- |
| Offenses | Public counsel | Private counsel | Public counsel | Private counsel |
| Total | 155 mo | 179 mo | 126 mo | 126 mo |
| Violent | 223 | 231 | 164 | 162 |
| Property | 118 | 128 | 59 | 59 |
| Drug | 97 | 140 | 126 | 132 |
| Public-order | 80 | 98 | 103 | 119 |

• Three-fourths of state and federal inmates with an appointed counsel and two-thirds with a hired counsel had pleaded guilty.

*Source:* C.W. Harlow. (2000). Defense Counsel in Criminal Cases. Bureau of Justice Statistics Special Report (NCJ 179023). Washington, DC: U.S. Department of Justice, Office of Justice Programs.

to represent a man charged with several felonies including first-degree murder, the attorney filed a motion asserting that because of his workload and lack of resources (i.e., no investigative assistance), he would be unable to effectively represent his client (Spangenberg Group, 2001, p. 1). The case (*State v. Peart*, 1993) resulted in changes in Louisiana's workload allocation and funding efforts for public defenders (Spangenberg Group, 2001). Such working conditions are cited by public defenders themselves as significant influences on their case outcomes (Lippman and Wineberg, 1990). This situation is exacerbated by organizational constraints, such as a severe lack of resources available to public defenders and private attorneys assigned by the court to represent indigent defendants; for example, funds to pay for investigators or expert witnesses, such as experts to evaluate and interpret DNA evidence (Monohan, 1996).

Such organizational impediments to effective advocacy on behalf of clients can be exacerbated by policy changes, such as increased reliance on sentencing guidelines or the implementation of mandatory sentencing policies. For example, such policy changes may require more work by government-provided attorneys at the same time that they face decreasing resources, particularly in the case of public defenders (Hall, 1999). Other research has found that the war on drugs has put significantly more strain on public defenders' offices, because sharply increased drug caseloads have not been accompanied by commensurate increases in funding (Murphy, 1991). Legal and technological changes mean that for defense attorneys, "the complexity of criminal defense practice has increased dramatically" (Spangenberg Group, 2001, p. 3). The impact of differences in caseload and resources between government-provided and privately retained attorneys is reflected in research showing that defendants with government-provided attorneys saw them less frequently and later in their cases, compared to defendants with hired counsel (Harlow, 2000, p. 8).

Public defenders and private attorneys who work as assigned counsel also have fewer financial incentives to devote extra time to complex cases because they are not compensated for additional effort (Coyle et al., 1990). Interestingly, however, one study of attorneys appointed by the government to serve as appellate counsel found that rate and type of compensation had "no discernible influence" on the attorneys' efforts on behalf of their clients; all put forth the same efforts (Priehs, 1999).

In contrast, because privately retained attorneys generally have more manageable numbers of clients than public defenders, they can devote more time and resources to each case. Privately retained counsel in criminal cases also have a financial incentive to devote more time, because they are compensated according to the amount of time they spend on the case.

Thus, differences on these dimensions rather than legal skill per se must be considered when comparing the merits of private versus public defenders. Given such differences, is it indeed preferable from a defendant's perspective to have a private attorney?

This waiting room in the Camden County, New Jersey, Public Defender's office clearly demonstrates that many defendants who rely on this office's services have families. In fact, a number of parents who face criminal charges may be unable to secure alternative childcare to allow them to attend valuable legal meetings alone. Some even bring their young children to court hearings.   SOURCE: Courtesy of Jon'a Meyer.

## Non-Capital Cases

Earlier research on non-capital cases showed that public defenders are more likely to plea bargain and more likely to lose cases and that their clients are more likely to get longer sentences (Lizotte, 1978). More recently, a government report comparing case outcomes of defendants with government-provided versus privately retained defense counsel found no differences in conviction rates (see Table 6.1), but found notable differences in sentencing (see Table 6.2). At both the federal and state levels, defendants with government-provided attorneys were more likely to receive sentences of incarceration than defendants with privately retained counsel (Harlow, 2000, p. 1). However, this difference partially reflects differences in the types of cases each type of attorney handled: government-provided attorneys were more likely to represent defendants charged with violent or drug crimes, whereas privately retained attorneys were more likely to handle white-collar offenders (Harlow, 2000, p. 3).

Comparison of the effectiveness of the two types of defense attorney in terms of the average length of sentence received by defendants sentenced to incarceration reveals further interesting differences. Although both federal and state defendants were more likely to be incarcerated if represented by government-provided attorneys, their average sentence length was shorter than that of defendants represented by privately retained counsel (Harlow, 2000, pp. 4–6).

It is possible that public defenders may be preferable in some type of cases, because they are more likely to have well-developed relationships with other members of the courtroom work group than private attorneys. Indeed, a client may be better served when the defense attorney is familiar with and comfortable with the court system's key "players" and unwritten norms. For example, experienced public defenders often have well-established connections in the courthouse that allow them to better represent their clients.

However, others argue that this situation actually runs counter to the interests of the client, because attorneys who are part of the tight-knit courtroom work group are

**TABLE 6.2    Length of Prison Sentence Imposed on Felony Defendants Convicted in U.S. District Court, by Type of Counsel and Offense, Fiscal Year 1998**

| Offense and type of counsel | Number of Federal defendants | Sentence to prison | |
|---|---|---|---|
| | | Mean | Median |
| **Total** | | | |
| Public | 28,453 | 58 mo | 33 mo |
| Private | 12,563 | 62 | 37 |
| **Violent offenses** | | | |
| Public | 2,266 | 84 mo | 60 mo |
| Private | 471 | 74 | 41 |
| **Fraud offenses** | | | |
| Public | 3,413 | 22 mo | 15 mo |
| Private | 2,426 | 23 | 15 |
| **Other property offenses** | | | |
| Public | 862 | 38 mo | 18 mo |
| Private | 380 | 40 | 24 |
| **Drug offenses** | | | |
| Public | 12,297 | 75 mo | 51 mo |
| Private | 6,753 | 84 | 60 |
| **Regulatory offenses** | | | |
| Public | 261 | 33 mo | 17 mo |
| Private | 244 | 23 | 15 |
| **Other public-order offenses** | | | |
| Public | 9,329 | 46 mo | 27 mo |
| Private | 2,283 | 44 | 24 |

Note: Excludes 304 inmates sentenced to life or death, 2,803 with suspended or sealed sentences, 383 with missing offense data, and 445 with data missing on counsel type.

*Source:* Administrative Office of the U.S. Courts, Criminal Master File, FY 1998, from C.W. Harlow. (2000). Bureau of Justice Statistics Special Report (NCJ 179023). Washington, DC: U.S. Department of Justice, Office of Justice Programs.

ultimately bound by the norms, expectations and loyalties of the group (Blumberg, 1967). In this sense, the courtroom working relationships of public defenders may serve as another form of organizational constraint that may not work to the defendant's best interests. For example, public defenders may be more concerned than privately retained attorneys with the preferences and expectations of judges in whose courtrooms they appear (Levin, 1977). In a classic essay, Blumberg observes that criminal trials represent highly stylized, ritualistic performances by attorneys, judges, and other regular legal actors in the courtroom. In particular, Blumberg argues, criminal defense attorneys engage in very deliberate, conscious strategies of impression management in order to maintain the appropriate appearance in front of their clients; other officers of the court assist defense counsel with these strategies (Blumberg, 1967). Blumberg's characterization of criminal defense attorneys as "double agents" more interested in preserving their ties to the courtroom work group than in working for the best interests of their clients was examined in one study of court appointed attorneys in selected counties of two Midwest states (Uphoff, 1992). The research concluded that defense attorneys could better be characterized as "beleaguered dealers" coping with organizational constraints presented by large caseloads, inadequate resources, and prosecutorial demands (Uphoff, 1992).

Another study comparing the two types of attorneys concluded that public defenders and privately retained attorneys obtained similar results for their clients (Hanson and Ostrom, 1998). However, the methodology and conclusions of this study were severely criticized by the American Bar Association in a rebuttal report (Arango, 1993).

## Capital Cases

The distinction between privately retained and publicly appointed defense attorneys has much more significant implications in death penalty cases. In a recent reanalysis of data from a classic study of capital punishment in Georgia in the 1970s, the results showed that defendants in capital cases who were represented by assigned defense counsel were more likely to receive a death sentence than those represented by privately retained counsel. This result held even after controlling for relevant case variables such as the defendant's prior criminal history. However, the researchers concluded that the difference in case outcome reflected differential responses by prosecutors to cases defended by assigned counsel versus those defended by retained counsel (Beck and Shumsky, 1997). In some Southern states, recent research shows that capital defendants often are represented by the least competent defense attorneys, such as those with prior histories of professional ethics violations and those who have no experience with capital cases (Coyle et al., 1990). In a recent speech, Supreme Court Justice Sandra Day O'Connor highlighted the issue, discussing how ". . . defendants with more money received better legal defense," and pointing out that in Texas last year those represented by court-appointed lawyers were 28 percent more likely to be convicted than those who hired their lawyers. If convicted, defendants with court-appointed lawyers were 44 percent more likely to be sentenced to death. " 'Perhaps it's time to look at minimum standards for appointed counsel in death cases and adequate compensation for appointed counsel when they are used,' Ms. O'Connor said" (as quoted in Whitworth, 2001, online).

## DEFENDING INDIGENT CLIENTS: TOO LITTLE TIME AND MONEY

The problem is, the need for defense attorneys to represent indigent (i.e., impoverished) defendants far outpaces the supply of lawyers, and the problem has intensified in recent years as the so-called war on drugs has substantially increased the number of people facing criminal charges (Rohde, 2000). Critics charge that government resources for the defense are inadequate, citing very low fees paid to defense attorneys and slim or nonexistent budgets to pay for defense resources, such as investigators, expert witnesses, forensic tests, and the like (Blum, 1995). In 1992, Massachusetts defense attorneys appointed by the court to defend indigent clients were informed that they could not be paid because public funds had run out two months before the end of the fiscal year (Brelis, 1992). Recent government data indicates that caseloads for government-provided defense attorneys have increased but that funding allocations have not increased commensurately (Harlow, 2000, p. 2).

The problem of lack of defense resources has many roots: Tight government budgets mean that not only is there competition for scarce resources among different government sectors (healthcare, education, criminal justice), but that within the legal system different agencies compete with one another. Public demands for greater prosecution resources translate to media attention paid to the budget of the district attorney's office, whereas there is little public pressure to fund defense attorneys. Some attorneys argue that the constitutional right to assistance of counsel has little meaning in practice because of the chronic and severe shortage of defense resources. In the words of one defense attorney, "You have a lawyer in a sense, but a lawyer who can't work on your case. . . . There is virtually no difference between that and not having a lawyer at all" (Holdridge, quoted in Blum, 1995, p. 2). In one county that lacked an adequate supply of attorneys for indigent defendants, a man accused of murder remained in jail for five months before meeting his court-appointed attorney; several months later prosecutors determined that the man was not involved in the murder and all charges against him were dismissed (Blum, 1995). Reflecting on federal court rulings limiting the reach of the Sixth Amendment's right to counsel and the nationwide problem of lack of funding and resources for indigent defense, one author decries the erosion of the Sixth Amendment (Monohan, 1991). Clearly, government-provided attorneys working with too many clients and too few resources may sometimes fail to provide effective assistance of counsel.

Defense attorneys confronted with too many clients, too little time and other resources, and the inexorable pressure to move cases through the system must make hard choices. How much time can I spend with each client? Whose case requires my attention most? What, if anything, can be done to get the investigative work, expert testimony, and other resources that this case requires? Despite the efforts of the defendant's family and friends to help the defense in its investigative efforts, there remains a pressing need for professional investigative assistance in many cases. If the attorney fails to keep up with the pace of case processing that is expected by the judge, the district attorney, and other members of the court, this has a negative impact on the court overall and on the reputation (and ultimately, the effectiveness) of the defense attorney. On the other hand, the legal and ethical requirements of the defense role often dictate that more time and resources be devoted to clients than the attorney could possibly muster. This contributes to burnout among some public defenders (Lippman and Wineberg, 1990). New York State public defenders responding to a questionnaire on work-related stressors reported frequently having too much work; having conflicts related to upset defendants and family members and disagreements with prosecutors; worrying about whether and when a client's case might be called to trial, and if so, what defense to present; and stressors related to system constraints, such as inflexible sentences and judges who were displeased at the decision to hold out for trial rather than plea bargain (Lynch, 1997).

Thus, defense attorneys, especially (but not exclusively) those primarily serving indigent defendants, must attempt to reconcile these competing claims on their time, attention, and loyalty. In a few jurisdictions, however, there are encouraging signs that structural reorganization of public defender programs can improve outcomes for clients. For example, evaluation of the Neighborhood Defender Service (NDS), a team-oriented approach to defending indigent clients in Harlem showed promising results: NDS clients served significantly fewer days than a matched set of clients represented under the traditional public defender system (Anderson, 1997, p. 10). The NDS program differs from traditional public defender programs in several significant ways, most notably in its attempt to take a holistic approach to clients, including focusing on their social service needs as well as their legal needs.

## DEFENSE DILEMMAS

Defense attorneys can encounter a wide variety of legal, practical, and ethical dilemmas in the course of representing a client. For example, what if you are a defense attorney and your client adamantly disagrees with your proposed defense strategy? This was the situation faced by Theodore Kaczynski's attorneys as they defended him against charges that he was the notorious "Unabomber." They attempted to present an insanity defense on his behalf, but he refused to even allow them to mention the word "insanity" in court. He steadfastly rejected his attorneys' attempts to convince him that they should be allowed to present this defense, at one point attempting to fire his attorneys and represent himself (Gibbs and Jackson, 1998). Ultimately, the case was plea bargained and Kaczynski received a life sentence.

Douglas Allen Smith, a thirty-four-year-old man convicted of beating an elderly man to death and then stealing his car, sought the death sentence despite the fact that prosecutors had not charged him with a capital crime. The prosecutor said that Smith's case was not among the "worst of the worst" for which the death penalty would be requested by the state. Nonetheless, Smith asked his attorneys to request the death penalty at his sentencing hearing. This apparently unprecedented request by a defendant presented an ethical challenge for Jamie McAlister, one of the defense attorneys. "It was a difficult thing for me to do. . . . but when my client makes a careful, rational legal decision, I have an obligation to be a vigorous advocate on his behalf" (Hansen, 1998, p. 2). Smith's wish, however, was not granted; instead he was given a minimum sentence of sixty-two years (Hansen, 1998). Box 6.6 describes some of the issues that arise when a defendant chooses to represent himself or herself at trial.

---

## BOX 6.6
## The Case of Colin Ferguson

Does a defendant have the right to self-representation? Yes, if the trial judge determines that the defendant is competent, although defendants who are arguably seriously mentally ill can often meet this legal standard. In any event, people who represent themselves in court often make many mistakes. They may botch the evidence, contradict themselves, or fail to follow the proper legal procedures at trial. The stakes are quite high for defendants accused of a felony, especially if there are substantive reasons to believe that the defendant's mental state and lack of legal experience may make efforts at self-representation more harmful than helpful.

Can the defendant, then, represent himself or herself and then claim "ineffective assistance of counsel" later? The short answer is "no."

In 1993, Colin Ferguson was charged with murdering six people during a shooting spree on the Long Island subway. Ferguson rejected his defense attorneys' efforts to mount an insanity defense, choosing instead to represent himself at trial. This meant that Ferguson conducted the cross-examination of victims who were injured but survived, family members of dead victims, and other eyewitnesses at trial. During questioning, Ferguson would often refer to himself in the third person, adding to the bizarre character of the courtroom proceedings. Ferguson was convicted and sentenced to life in prison (Samuel, 1995; Milton, 1995).

---

## ATTORNEY-CLIENT CONFIDENTIALITY ISSUES

Communication between a lawyer and his or her client is legally "privileged," that is, protected from disclosure to third parties (Gifis, 1984). Privilege is essential for communication, trust, and confidentiality in the lawyer-client relationship that allows an attorney to effectively represent his client. The rationale is that if clients were not assured of the confidentiality of the information they share with their attorneys, then they would have an incentive to hide or distort facts necessary for their defense (Freedman, 1988; Pollock, 1998).

But this privilege is neither uncontroversial nor unlimited. How should an attorney respond when her client announces his intention to commit perjury when testifying in his own defense? What are an attorney's legal and ethical responsibilities in this situation? Should she withdraw from the case? Should she warn the client of the possible legal consequences if he is caught perjuring himself, but otherwise do nothing? Should she report the client's intention to the court, in her role as an officer of the court? Should she try to reason with the client to try and prevent him from lying, and report the perjury only if the client actually commits the crime?

The Supreme Court considered some of these questions in *Nix v. Whiteside* (1986), which addressed some of the constitutional issues raised when Whiteside's attorney reported to the trial court judge his belief that his client intended to commit perjury while testifying in court about events leading up to the death of the victim. Whiteside was convicted of murder, and the appeal raised the question of whether he was deprived of his Sixth Amendment right to assistance of counsel. The court decided that he was not, but this case raised—but did not settle—the issue of whether the attorney should have revealed this confidential information about his client to the court.

Freedman (1988) notes that the Whiteside case raises questions about the Fifth Amendment privilege against self-incrimination. To wit, if the accused cannot be required to give information that would tend to be incriminating, how can the accused's attorney be allowed to reveal such information?

Is this fair? Some legal commentators argued that this was a breach of the defense counsel's duty of loyalty to his client, a violation of the requirement of confidentiality. Other observers felt that as an officer of the court, the attorney was acting ethically and appropriately in reporting the defendant's supposed plans to lie to the court, in order to prevent the defendant from perpetuating a fraud upon the court.

Would it make a difference to your opinion on this issue if the client had already committed perjury, versus stating an intention to provide false information? What if the attorney believes his client intends to commit perjury, but the client has not yet done so? The reason defense attorneys may report perjury, despite attorney–client privilege, is to prevent perpetuation of a fraud against the court. But this raises another question: How certain must the attorney be before taking some action such as reporting the client to the court? In Whiteside, there was much discussion of what "standard of knowing" an attorney must use in making such a decision. For example, should the attorney believe beyond a reasonable doubt that the client has committed or intends to commit perjury? Or should the attorney merely be largely certain? Freedman notes that the Whiteside court did not settle these questions (1988).

What if a defendant charged with murder admits her guilt to her attorney? This is privileged information. But what if she admits to other crimes with which she has not been charged, including another murder? Her attorney is not legally obligated to disclose this, because of the confidentiality requirement. In fact, he or she is obligated *not* to disclose this information.

However, what if the defense counsel reasonably believes that the client intends to commit a crime? Because the issue here is a potentially avoidable future crime, confidentiality requirements change. In general, an attorney is not only legally permitted but is legally obligated to disclose this information to prevent future harm (Freedman, 1988). Of course, this raises further issues. How can an attorney distinguish between a client's idle threats and serious intentions? Even the most sophisticated methods currently available for attempting to predict future dangerousness are often unable to do so reliably.

## AN INADEQUATE DEFENSE: INCOMPETENCE AND MISCONDUCT

The role of the defense attorney carries weighty responsibilities, and the attorney's actions have life-altering consequences for the accused. What happens when a defense attorney fails to provide the best possible defense? Allegations of ineffective assistance of counsel can be difficult to substantiate, but if proven, can result in a defendant being granted a new trial. But if a defense attorney fails to provide effective assistance of counsel and this problem is not caught and corrected, a defendant may pay the ultimate price—death.

Ironically, defense attorneys provided for indigent defendants in death-penalty cases are typically given few resources, if any, to assist in preparing for the

---

### BOX 6.7

### With a Defense Like This, Who Needs the Prosecutor?

"I decided that Mr. Tucker deserved to die and I would not do anything to prevent his execution." These are the words of David B. Smith, one of the defense attorneys assigned to represent Russell Tucker at his trial for murdering a K-Mart security guard who had questioned him in the store parking lot. According to Smith, he decided after reading the trial transcript and meeting his client that "Mr. Tucker should be executed for his crimes." Smith thus decided to sabotage the case by allowing his co-counsel to unknowingly miss the critical deadline for filing an appeal. Smith, a former prosecutor who had switched to defense work, decided to come forward after the deadline passed and Tucker was scheduled for execution. Expressing remorse, Smith said he had to "tell the truth" and "disclose that I had failed him" (Nowell, 2000, p. A14).

*Source:* Reprinted with permission of The Associated Press.

case. Capital defense attorneys are often paid a flat fee per case, and courts rarely provide funds for defense investigators, expert witnesses, or other resources to assist in defense preparation. The problem appears to have grown worse in recent years (Dieter, 1999). Given this situation, even the most experienced, diligent, and motivated attorney would have difficulty providing a capital defendant with an adequate defense. However, the situation is complicated even further by the fact that many attorneys appointed by the court to defend individuals accused of a capital crime are inexperienced, overloaded with cases, and inadequately compensated. In Illinois, a judge appointed a tax attorney who had never tried a case to represent a defendant in a capital case; in another case, the lawyer appointed to represent a capital defendant had just been reinstated after being suspended for incompetence and dishonesty (Armstrong and Mills, 1999). But where should the line be drawn between incompetence due to inexperience with capital cases and misconduct? Consider the following examples of representation provided to defendants in death penalty cases:

- Death row inmate Leroy Orange won a new sentencing hearing after evidence showed his attorney failed to investigate his claims that his confession was coerced and failed to present any evidence or witnesses at his sentencing hearing. (Armstrong and Mills, 1999)

- Bernon Howery was sentenced to die by lethal injection, but won a new sentencing hearing after evidence showed his attorney failed to appear at some court dates, failed to investigate leads on other potential suspects, and failed to present evidence of mitigating factors at Howery's sentencing hearing. (Armstrong and Mills, 1999)

- In Illinois, an attorney with almost eighty disciplinary complaints on his record represented a defendant in a capital case; after his client was sentenced to death, the attorney was later disbarred. (Armstrong and Mills, 1999)

- Another attorney who was ultimately disbarred on two separate occasions represented four defendants in separate capital cases. All four received the death penalty. (Armstrong and Mills, 1999)

- A public defender who failed to present witnesses who could have helped the defendant's case gave a closing argument that a judge later noted ". . . may have actually strengthened the jury's resolve to impose the death sentence" (Armstrong and Mills, 1999, p. 5).

- A county public defender with more than 100 assigned cases was appointed to represent a capital defendant even though the lawyer had never tried a murder case (Bright, 2000).

- A defense attorney appointed by a Texas court to represent a gay defendant accused of capital murder repeatedly dozed off during his trial, and referred to his client and other gay men as "queers, fairies, and tush hogs" (Bright, 2000).

- In Texas, the state appellate court has refused to review the cases of defendants convicted and sentenced to death while their attorneys slept through parts of their trials (Shapiro, 1997)(see Box 6.8).

## HOW CAN YOU DEFEND THAT "MONSTER"?: PUBLIC PERCEPTIONS OF DEFENSE ATTORNEYS

"You fight against any impulse of being repulsed by the crime itself," said Chuck Sevilla, defense attorney for Robert Alton Harris, who killed two boys (Dolan, 1994, p. 4). Defense attorney Christie Warren found herself defending men accused of child molestation while she was expecting her own child. "You just have a little more baggage to get beyond," said Warren (Dolan, 1994, p. 5). One of the flash points of negative public opinion about defense attorneys, both public and private, is the idea that defense attorneys defend guilty clients and help them avoid justice. This idea is built upon several assumptions that bear questioning. First, it assumes that most defendants are guilty, glossing over the fact that an existing but unknowable percentage are not guilty of the instant crime. Second, it assumes that a guilty person does not need a defense, yet due process demands that everyone accused of

---

## BOX 6.8

### Lawyering in One's Sleep

Seated beside his client . . . defense attorney John Benn spent much of Thursday afternoon's trial in apparent deep sleep.

His mouth kept falling open and his head lolled back on his shoulders, and then he awakened just long enough to catch himself and sit upright. Then it happened again. And again. And again.

Every time he opened his eyes, a different prosecution witness was on the stand describing another aspect of the . . . arrest of George McFarland in the robbery-killing of grocer Kenneth Kwan.

When state District Judge Doug Shaver finally called a recess, Benn was asked if he truly had fallen asleep during a capital murder trial.

"It's boring," the seventy-two-year-old longtime Houston lawyer explained.

Court observers said Benn seems to have slept his way through virtually the entire trial.

"I customarily take a short nap in the afternoon," was his only explanation.

The co-counsel for the defense later said he thought Benn's sleeping might make the jury "feel sorry for us."

What was the judge's reaction? "The Constitution says that everyone's entitled to an attorney of their choice. But the Constitution does not say that the lawyer has to be awake."

*Source:* B. Shapiro. (1997, April 7). Sleeping Lawyer Syndrome. *The Nation.* Reprinted with permission.

a crime, whether guilty or not, receive a fair trial and if guilty, a fair sentence (Pollock, 1998). Third, the belief that defense attorneys merely "shield" wrongdoers from justice ignores the critical function played by defense counsel in our legal system. Focusing on the instances in which a legally guilty person may be acquitted, without examining this in context, overlooks the need for defense counsel to assist innocent people accused of a crime. As one scholar notes, "[D]ue process protects us all by making the criminal justice system prove wrongdoing fairly; the person who makes sure no shortcuts are taken is the defense attorney" (Pollock, 1998, p. 220).

Public perceptions of defense attorneys may reflect societal attitudes toward people accused of a crime, especially if the crime alleged is particularly heinous (see Box 6.9). And although the defense attorney's function is an indispensable part of due process, attorneys may disagree in how they interpret their role. For example, attorneys may vary greatly in their attitudes and willingness to defend certain types of cases—or clients.

---

## BOX 6.9

## "Guilt by Association"

While criminal defendants often face public suspicion that they "must have" done something wrong simply because they have been charged with a crime, even when the arrest results in a dismissal or a trial and acquittal (Willis, 1992), defense attorneys also may be tarnished in the eyes of the public because of their association with accused persons. Imagine the last time you saw a TV news byte featuring the defense attorney for someone accused of a violent crime, such as murder or rape, especially if the victim was a child. What did you think of the attorney?

Albert J. Krieger, an attorney who has represented some notorious defendants, described how he works hard to consciously combat suspicion, distrust, and distaste, especially on the part of jurors. His strategies include taking care to appear very professional in court (avoiding argumentativeness, for example), reminding jurors of his legal role as a defense attorney, using a proactive strategy of focusing on weaknesses in the prosecution's case, and raising doubts about the credibility of prosecution witnesses (Krieger, 1997).

Danny Davis defended Raymond Buckey, who was accused of sexually molesting preschoolers at his mother's daycare center in the notorious McMartin Preschool case. Raymond Buckey was ultimately acquitted of most of the charges against him. However, the jury deadlocked on twelve of the molestation charges against him, and he was retried on those charges. The second jury also deadlocked on those charges, resulting in a mistrial. During the trial, which lasted six years and was followed closely by the media, Davis learned just how strongly some members of the public felt about his role in the case. "Two of Davis' homes were firebombed, and men attacked him physically in the parking lot of the courthouse. 'I learned how to roll under my car, in my suit,' he said. 'That is the best defense'" (Dolan, 1994, p. A1).

Attorney David Baugh took on the challenge of defending Barry Black, an Imperial Wizard of the Ku Klux Klan (KKK) accused of violating state law when he held a Klan meeting that featured a cross-burning. The case raised First Amendment free speech issues, and Mr. Baugh volunteered to defend Mr. Black free of charge. Mr. Baugh has no illusions about the nature of the KKK, but he says the issue is freedom of speech. Mr. Baugh apparently believes that taking the case is a way of challenging perceptions of defense attorneys. Public reactions to his decision to represent this particular client have been strong, but few would doubt that Baugh dislikes the KKK and its beliefs: Mr. Baugh is African American. Boxes 6.9 and 6.10 illustrate some additional defense attorney experiences defending difficult cases.

Whether the public appreciates the role of defense counsel is questionable in the minds of some attorneys. As one defense attorney put it, "[T]alking to civilians about criminal defense work is like pushing an oyster into the coin slot of a parking meter. It can't be done, and it makes a mess" (Holding, 1999, p. 5). Nonetheless, in the courtroom itself the defense attorney must try to neutralize or reverse potentially negative impressions of the defense role in the eyes of the jury. Defense attorneys may attempt to establish credibility by discussing the role of the defense during jury questioning, by demonstrating professionalism and courteousness during court proceedings, and even by using humor to try to establish a sense of connection with the jury (Krieger, 1997).

---

## BOX 6.10

### A Defense Attorney's Nightmare

Criminal defense attorney Cristina Arguedas was representing a black man charged with raping a white woman. The police had picked him up as a registered sex offender—he previously served prison time for three rapes—and the victim tentatively identified him in a lineup. During the trial, Arguedas attacked the victim's identification of her client as not only weak but racist. She won an acquittal.

Four months later, she picked up her telephone and heard a public defender say that the man had just been arrested again for rape. "I went through this whole reflective, guilty thing that I had used my skills to injure another woman," she said. It was the ultimate criminal defense attorney's nightmare. For Arguedas, the nightmare proved short-lived. After a week of torment, the public defender called her back. Her former client had been in a bank at the time of rape and could not possibly have done it.

*Source:* Excerpted from Dolan, 1994. Reprinted by permission.

---

## BOX 6.11

## The Ungrateful Client

In 1998, twenty-year-old Jeremy Strohmeyer pled guilty to raping and murdering seven-year-old Sherrice Iverson in a Nevada casino. In exchange for his plea of guilty, Strohmeyer received a life sentence, avoiding the possibility of capital punishment if he had been tried and found guilty. The evidence in the case included Strohmeyer's confession, casino security videotape showing him following the girl into the restroom, and incriminating information provided by a friend of Strohmeyer's who saw him holding the little girl in the bathroom stall.

In 1999, Strohmeyer asked the court to throw out his guilty plea and allow him to stand trial. Strohmeyer claimed that his attorney, Leslie Abramson, coerced him into making the plea bargain so that she could reduce the time she spent on his case (A bid to withdraw plea, 1999).

---

## THE DECISION TO BECOME A DEFENDER

Despite the low pay, lack of resources, and low status associated with working as a criminal defense attorney, many criminal lawyers find deep satisfaction in their work. The commitment to social justice through legal action that draws many attorneys to defense work is apparent in the historical record of African American defense attorneys (see Box 6.12). The work is intriguing and intense, and one defense attorney speaking to colleagues at a conference described its attraction in these terms: "We will probably never persuade a majority of Americans that defending criminal defendants is heroic, and I don't even want to try. I know it is, you know it is, our clients and their families know it is. For us, that is enough" (Holding, 1999, p. 5).

It is not uncommon for an attorney to have work experience both as a prosecutor and as a defense attorney. Some attorneys adapt well to a switch from one side to the other; a former prosecutor turned defense attorney notes that: "That's what our roles are. . . . the best attorneys can [advocate for] either side." Another D.A. now doing defense work put it this way: "Most people who leave [prosecuting work] don't view defense as a force for evil. . . . they view it as a constitutional function testing the [government's] case. If, despite our best efforts, we lose, then the [government] has done its job" (Cohen, 2001, p. 1; reprinted by permission © 2001 NLPIP Company). In other cases, the switch is difficult. David Smith, the defense attorney who sabotaged his client's case (see Box 6.7), was a former prosecutor. Some attorneys who switch to defense work find they must work hard to reconcile their self-image with the fact of defending people accused of gruesome crimes, such as murders or sex crimes involving children. Psychiatrist Steven Ager describes the emotional turmoil that some attorneys who switched to the defense role experience:

Martin A. Martin of Danville, Virginia, became the first African American member of the Trial Bureau of the Department of Justice on May 31, 1943. Here he is shown being sworn in before becoming Special Assistant to then Attorney General Francis Biddle (who served under Franklin Roosevelt). Martin's appointment took place nearly a century after Macon Bolling Allen became the first African American admitted to the bar in this country in 1844. Times were often difficult for African American attorneys, due in part to perceptions by potential clients that they could not "prevail in American courts without a white lawyer" (Clemon and Fair, 2001, p. 1125). SOURCE: Library of Congress, Prints and Photographs Division, FSA-OWI Collection, LC-USW3-029899-C, Roger Smith, photographer.

> Sometimes we do the right thing for the wrong reason. And when you're a DA, you're one of the "good guys" putting the "bad guys" in jail. There's very little conflict. But when you switch to defending all of a sudden, you have to deal with the bad part of yourself you are in denial about. You go from this Roy Rogers–Tom Mix life to defending people you don't want to admit you are anything like. You don't have the same sense of accomplishment. These attorneys become more and more unhappy doing defense. (Cohen, 2001, p. 1)

Overall, defense attorneys, whether private or government appointed, show pride and satisfaction in their work. In contrast to negative public perceptions of criminal defense work, criminal defenders view their contributions to the legal system as important and meaningful (Kittel, 1990).

## CONCLUSION

Defense attorneys have many and varied functions in their role as client advocate and court officer. Their interactions with clients and other legal actors in the courtroom reflect legal requirements, ethical norms, courtroom work group expectations, and practical demands on their time and resources. Now that you have a

## BOX 6.12

## Historical Archives: African American Attorneys' Activism

Judith Kilpatrick describes how in Arkansas, beginning in the post–Civil-War era, a growing number of African Americans entered the practice of law and contributed to the community through their political activism and work in criminal and civil matters:

- In 1868, William H. Grey and Thomas P. Johnson were elected to the Arkansas constitutional convention, where they worked to shape the Arkansas constitution to provide greater legal rights to African Americans.
- In 1873, attorneys Lloyd G. Wheeler and Mifflin Gibbs successfully sued a barkeeper who violated state law by refusing to serve African Americans.
- Between 1874–1892, J. Pennoyer Jones served as a county sheriff, county clerk, and county judge.
- Between 1887–1890, J. Gray Lucas served several terms as an assistant county prosecutor.
- In 1895, J.D. Royce was appointed by the court to represent a white man charged with murder.
- In 1901, attorney Scipio Jones argued in two separate cases that the African American defendants had been deprived of their constitutional rights because of the fact that no African Americans had been allowed to serve on their juries. This legal strategy would later be employed by the NAACP in its efforts to address discrimination in jury selection. A few years later, Jones would be instrumental in appeals on behalf of several African American defendants accused of murder, ultimately winning their release from prison.

These men and other attorneys from the African American community also organized protests against segregationist laws, founded newspapers dedicated to educating the public on African American legal issues, formed a bar association, and worked to preserve due process on behalf of defendants accused of crimes.

*Source:* Adapted from Kilpatrick, 2001.

better understanding of the prosecutor and defense attorney, it's time to look at the judge's role in the courtroom. In the next chapter, you'll see how the judge serves to guide the courtroom proceedings and "referee" the contest between the state and the defense.

## DISCUSSION QUESTIONS

1. Why is the role of the defense attorney an indispensable part of our criminal justice process? For example, how do defense attorneys help preserve constitutional rights?

2. What are the major legal cases on the right to counsel? What were the issues in each case, and how was the case decided? How did these cases affect the right to counsel?

3. Compare the role of defense counsel with that of the prosecutor, which we learned about in the preceding chapter. In what ways are the defense and prosecution roles comparable, and in what ways are they significantly different?

4. In what ways is the defense role that of a "legal tool," and in what ways is a defense attorney a "moral agent"? How do these two conceptions of the defense role compare? Are these mutually exclusive perspectives on the defense role, or are they compatible visions?

5. What are some of the skills and abilities that a defense attorney needs to be effective in his or her work? Why are these qualities important?

6. How do organizational factors, such as resource limitations, influence the ability of attorneys handling the cases of indigent defenders?

7. What are some of the ethical dilemmas that defense attorneys may face in the course of their work?

8. According to research on indigent defense in capital cases, what are some of the main problems with providing quality defense representation for defendants facing capital charges? What could or should be done to deal with these problems?

9. What are some of the reasons that members of the public often have inaccurate or distorted perceptions of the role that defense attorneys play in the criminal justice system? What might help improve the accuracy of public perceptions of defense work?

## REFERENCES

A bid to withdraw plea in slaying of girl, 7. (1999, November 18). *San Francisco Chronicle*, p. A13.

Anderson, D.C. (1997). Public defenders in the neighborhood: A Harlem law office stresses teamwork, early investigation. Washington, DC: U.S. Department of Justice, National Institute of Justice, NCJ #163061.

Arango, J.B. (1993, Spring). Defense services for the poor: Criminal justice section's ad hoc Committee on Indigent Defense crisis challenges National Center for State Courts study. *Criminal Justice*, 8(1): 41–43.

*Argersinger v. Hamlin*, 407 U.S. 25 (1972).

Armstrong, K., and Mills, S. (1999, November 15). Inept defenses cloud verdict. *Chicago Tribune* Internet edition, accessed 2001: www.chicagotribune.com.

Beck, J.C., and Shumsky, R. (1997, October). Comparison of retained and appointed counsel in cases of capital murder. *Law and Human Behavior*, 21(5): 525–538.

Blum, A. (1995, May 15). Defense of indigents: Crisis spurs lawsuits. *The National Law Journal*, 17(37): A1.

Blumberg, A.S. (1967). The practice of law as confidence game: Organizational co-optation of a profession. *Law & Society Review*, 1: 15–39.

Brelis, M. (1992, July 22). U.S. courts out of funds for defense lawyers. *The Boston Globe*, p. 23.

Bright, S. (2000, December 4). Sleeping lawyer cases are a wake-up call; system that makes life and death decisions has gone awry. *Texas Lawyer*, p. 47.

Clemon, U.W., and Fair, B.K. (2001). Making bricks without straw: The NAACP legal defense fund and the development of civil rights law in Alabama 1940–1980. *Alabama Law Review*, 52: 1121–1152.

Cohen, E. (1991). Pure legal advocates and moral agents: Two concepts of a lawyer in an adversary system. In M. Braswell and B. McCarthy (Eds.), *Justice, Crime, and Ethics*, pp. 123–163. Cincinnati: Anderson.

Cohen, R.B. (2001, April 9). How they sleep at night: DAs turned defenders talk about their work. *The Legal Intelligencer*, p. 1.

Coyle, M., Strasser, F., and Lavelle, M. (1990, June 11). Fatal defense: Trial and error in the nation's death belt. *National Law Journal,* 12 (40): 30–44.

Dieter, R.C. (1999). With justice for few: The growing crisis in death penalty representation. Washington, DC: *Death Penalty Information Center.*

Dolan, M. (1994, June 1). Defense seldom rests on issues of ethics and duty. *Los Angeles Times,* p. A1.

Doyle, K. (1999, November). Capital cases. *The Champion* (National Association of Criminal Defense Lawyers). Available at www.criminaljustice.org/www.nacdl.org.

Freedman, M. (1988, June). Client confidences and client perjury: Some unanswered questions. *University of Pennsylvania Law Review,* 136: 1939–1956.

Gibbs, N., and Jackson, D. (1998, January 19). In fits and starts. *Time,* p. 24.

*Gideon v. Wainwright,* 372 U.S. 335 (1963).

Gifis, S.H. (1984). *Barron's Law Dictionary.* Woodbury, NY: Barron's Educational Series.

Hall, J. (1999, Fall). Guided to injustice? The effect of the sentencing guidelines on indigent defendants and public defense. *American Criminal Law Review,* 36(4): 1331–1370.

Hansen, M. (1998). Death's advocate: Defense lawyer seeks execution—at her client's request. *American Bar Association Journal,* 84: 22.

Hanson, R., and B.J. Ostrom. (1998). Indigent defenders get the job done and done well. In George Cole and Marc Gertz (eds.), *Criminal Justice System: Politics and Policies,* 7th ed., pp. 264–288. Belmont, CA: Wadsworth.

Harlow, C.W. (2000). Defense counsel in criminal cases. Special Report of the Bureau of Justice Statistics (NCJ 179023). Available at www.ojp.usdoj.gov/bjs/pub/pdf/dccc.pdf.

Holding, R. (1999, February 7). It's not a pretty job, but someone has to do it. *San Francisco Chronicle,* p. 5.

International Association of Defense Counsel Tenets of Professionalism. (1999, July) *Defense Counsel Journal,* 66 (3): 309.

*Johnson v. Zerst,* 304 U.S. 458 (1938).

Kilpatrick, J. (2001). Historical perspectives on pro bono lawyering: Race expectations: Arkansas African-American attorneys (1865–1950). *American University Journal of Gender, Social Policy & the Law,* 9: 63–79.

Kittel, G. (1990). Criminal defense attorneys: Bottom of the legal profession's class system? In Frank Schmalleger (Ed.), *Ethics in Criminal Justice,* pp. 42–61. Bristol, IN: Wyndham Hall Press.

Krieger, A.J. (1997, September 22). In drug defense, stress Constitution. *The National Law Journal,* 20(4): C6.

Levin, M.A. (1977). *Urban Politics and Criminal Courts.* Chicago: University of Chicago Press.

Linder, D.O. (1999). *A Trial Account.* Famous Trials Web site, available at www.law.umkc.edu/faculty/projects/ftrials/scottsboro/scottsb.htm.

Lippman, M., and Wineberg, R. (1990). In their own defense: A profile of Denver public defenders and their work. In Frank Schmalleger (Ed.), *Ethics in Criminal Justice,* pp. 8–41. Bristol, IN: Wyndham Hall Press.

Lizotte, A. (1978). Extra-legal factors in Chicago's criminal courts: Testing the conflict model of criminal justice. *Social Problems,* 25(5): 564–580.

Lynch, D.R.(1997). Nature of occupational stress among public defenders. *Justice System Journal,* 19(1): 17–35.

Milton, P. (1995, February 19). Jury foreman: Only God really knows motive. *The Record*, p. A12.

Monohan, E.C. (1991, Summer). Who is trying to kill the Sixth Amendment? *Criminal Justice*, 6(2): 24–28, 51–52.

Monohan, E.C. (1996, March). Funds for defense DNA experts required. *Advocate*, 18(2): 40–45.

Monohan, E.C., and Clark, J. (1995). Coping with excessive workload. In Rodney J. Uphoff (Ed.), *Ethical Problems Facing the Criminal Defense Lawyer: Practical Answers to Tough Questions*, p. 331. Chicago: American Bar Association.

Murphy, T.R. (1991, Fall). Indigent defense and the U.S. war on drugs: The public defender's losing battle. *Criminal Justice*, 6(3): 14–20.

Nardulli, P.F., Flemming, R.B., and Eisenstein, J. (1988). *The Tenor of Justice*. Urbana: University of Illinois Press.

*Nix v. Whiteside*, 475 U.S. 157 (1986).

Nowell, P. (2000, November 3). Lawyer admits sabotaging appeal of death row client he didn't like. *San Francisco Chronicle*, p. A14.

Pollock, J. (1998). *Ethics in Crime and Justice*. Belmont, CA: Wadsworth.

*Powell v. Alabama*, 287 U.S. 45 (1932).

Priehs, R. (1999). Appointed counsel for indigent criminal appellants: Does compensation influence effort? *Justice System Journal*, 21(1): 57–79.

Richman, J. (1998, August 2). Are the courts colorblind? *Tri-Valley Herald*, p. 1.

Rohde, D. (2000, February 17). Drug arrests overloading court system. *The New York Times*. Available at www.nytimes.com.

Samuel, T. (1995, February 17). Jury convicted Ferguson of N.Y. train shootings. *Philadelphia Inquirer,*(wire).

Shapiro, B. (1997, April 7). Sleeping lawyer syndrome. *The Nation*, 264(13): 27.

Simon, W.H. (1988, April). Ethical discretion in lawyering. *Harvard Law Review*, 101: 1083–1145.

Spangenberg Group. (2001, January). Keeping defender workloads manageable. Washington, DC: U.S. Department of Justice, Office of Justice Programs, Bureau of Justice Assistance Monograph. NCJ #185632.

*State of Florida ex rel. Argersinger v. Hamlin*, 236 So. 2d 442 (1970).

*State v. Peart*, 621 So. 2d 780, 791 (La. 1993).

*United States v. Wade*, 388 U.S. 218, 224 (1967).

Uphoff, R.J. (1992, September/October). Criminal defense lawyer: Zealous advocate, double agent, or beleaguered dealer? *Criminal Law Bulletin*, 28(5): 419–456.

Whitworth, D. (2001, July 4). Reagan-appointed judge says innocent are being executed. *The Times*. Available at www.thetimes.co.uk.

Willis, C. (1992). The biasing of culpability judgments with evidence of prior bad acts. Paper presented at the 1992 meeting of the American Psychology-Law Society, San Diego, CA.

Zuckoff, M. (1998, November 19). Black lawyer defending klansman in cross-burning. *San Francisco Chronicle*, p. A6.

# Step 7

# A Judge Is Assigned
# to Hear the Case

In the previous two chapters, we learned about the two attorneys in the courtroom drama, the prosecutor and the defense attorney. In this chapter, we turn our attention to the third member of the courtroom work group, the judge. We will learn what judges do and how they become judges. Then, we will look at judges' discretion and how it affects their relationships with others.

## INTRODUCTION

Judges are by far the most easily recognized member of the courtroom work group, both by their conspicuous robes and by their prominent position in the courtroom. They are also the subject of many stereotypes because the public wants to believe that judges combine patience, wisdom, and compassion to arrive at fair decisions, while they eschew the character flaws that sometimes form the basis of decisions by others, including prejudice, intolerance, favoritism, and hostility.

Unfortunately, judges are human and their decisions occasionally reflect such a reality. One West Virginia judge, for example, became so enraged at a defendant who began cursing at him in court that he jumped down from his bench, tore off his judicial robe, and bit the tip off the defendant's nose (Smith, 1998). He served five days in jail on state assault charges, and was then tried in federal court for violating the defendant's civil rights. Before he was acquitted of those charges, he acknowledged that his behavior was "bizarre and weird," and that he had reacted poorly in an emotionally charged situation. While this incident is isolated, it shows that judges are sometimes far from the ideals to which the public holds them. We will return to the subject of judicial misconduct later in the chapter. For now, let us look a little at what judges do and what they "look like."

## HERE COMES THE JUDGE: JUDICIAL RESPONSIBILITIES

Judges are responsible for many tasks in the courtroom. Most individuals are aware of their referee-like role during trials and that they serve as sentencing agents in criminal cases. These are but two of the many roles judges fulfill. Judges are involved in a myriad of significant decision points in the justice system, whenever decisions are made that can have important consequences for a person accused of committing a crime (in the criminal court system) or violating a civil contract or norm (in civil court processes). Judges oversee these justice decisions long before any trial and continue to do so throughout the appeals process. See Box 7.1 for a summary of the steps.

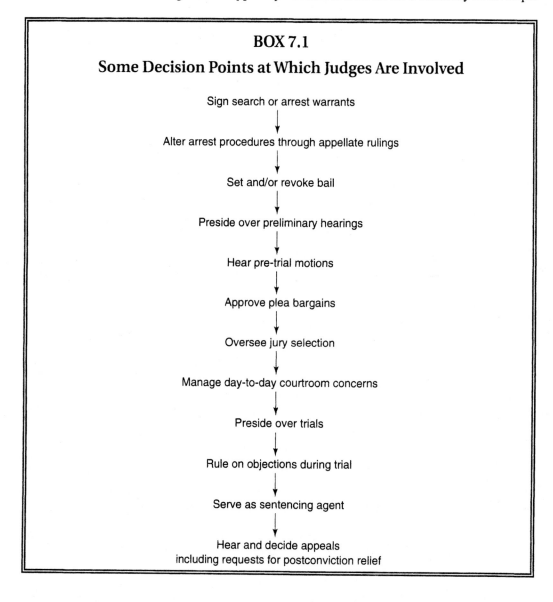

### BOX 7.1
### Some Decision Points at Which Judges Are Involved

Sign search or arrest warrants

Alter arrest procedures through appellate rulings

Set and/or revoke bail

Preside over preliminary hearings

Hear pre-trial motions

Approve plea bargains

Oversee jury selection

Manage day-to-day courtroom concerns

Preside over trials

Rule on objections during trial

Serve as sentencing agent

Hear and decide appeals
including requests for postconviction relief

## Judicial Involvement Prior to Arrest

Before an arrest, judges may be called upon to sign warrants authorizing either the search of some premises or the arrest of a person suspected of breaking a law. **Warrants** are essentially documents granting permission to conduct a search or make an arrest. Before either of these documents can be issued, a law enforcement official must convince a judge or **magistrate** (the term magistrate is typically used to describe judicial officials who have limited powers, such as justices of the peace or traffic magistrates, or who are authorized to conduct only certain functions, such as issue warrants and conduct preliminary or pre-trial hearings) that the search or arrest is necessary. Although a law enforcement official may make an arrest without a warrant (assuming he or she has probable cause), having one places the burden of proof on the defendant to show that no probable cause existed because a judicial official has already reviewed the facts presented by the officer and agreed that probable cause existed for an arrest. Without a warrant, the arrest may be declared invalid. Likewise, a search warrant may be issued when a judge is persuaded that someone has property that was stolen or is linked to an offense (i.e., it has been used or will be used to commit a crime). In both cases, an officer provides specific facts that demonstrate the need for a warrant. Whether a person is actually guilty of breaking a law is irrelevant when a judge considers whether a warrant may be issued, as are a police officer's hunches or suspicions. When deciding whether to sign warrants, judges may consider only those facts that would lead a reasonable person to believe that a search is appropriate or a person is guilty of the crimes he or she is suspected of committing. If that level of proof cannot be established, the judge cannot sign the warrant.

Through appellate court rulings, judges may affect the offenses for which, and the conditions under which, arrests are permissible. For example, the courts in many states have disallowed arrests for consensual homosexuality, and miscegenation laws (which prohibit whites from marrying other races) have been declared unconstitutional. Appellate judges may also alter the rights suspects have at the time of and following an arrest. Three landmark cases, which were discussed in detail in Step 3, occurred during the 1960s and clarified defendants' rights to an attorney (*Escobedo v. Illinois,* 1964; *Gideon v. Wainwright,* 1963) and the right to remain silent during questioning (*Miranda v. Arizona,* 1966). Although this type of ruling is made following appellate court hearings, they affect the pre-arrest decisions for future individuals accused of breaking the law. Civil court processes are also influenced by appellate court rulings.

## Judicial Involvement after Arrest, but Prior to Trial

After arrest, judges become more visible as decision-makers. As discussed in Step 10, judges are responsible for setting bail in most jurisdictions. In this role, judges must first determine whether to grant bail, then they must decide what amount is sufficient to guarantee that the individual will appear for future hearings. Like most decisions made by judges, the determination to grant bail involves input from other parties in the justice system, especially the defense attorney and prosecutor. After bail is set, it may be revoked by a judge (e.g., if a defendant breaks a condition of bail).

Judges have an important role at the time of the preliminary hearing. As discussed in Step 3, preliminary hearings are like bare-bones trials. The defense and prosecution are allowed to present their cases, and a judge determines if there is enough evidence to justify holding a trial. If the judge is persuaded that a crime was committed and that the accused was probably the perpetrator, he or she will order the accused to stand trial. If the evidence is insufficient, the accused must be released. Judges seldom find that the evidence is insufficient, however, because most prosecutors would rather wait until they have a solid case to present than risk being ruled against at this important step.

Judges also play a strong role during pre-trial motions. As discussed in Step 12 (on trials), judges hear arguments from the attorneys and issue rulings on pre-trial motions. Pre-trial motions are important because they shape the character and nature of the trial. For example, a confession may be ruled inadmissable during a pre-trial motion to exclude evidence, requiring the prosecution to rely on other evidence or develop another trial strategy. A ruling on a **change of venue** (i.e., a request to move a trial from the jurisdiction where a crime occurred to one where there is a better chance of securing an impartial jury) could have profound effects on the outcome of a trial. Rulings on pre-trial motions may form the basis of a future appeal, so judges' decisions must be consistent with existing laws and prior court decisions, especially U.S. Supreme Court rulings and those handed down by their state's supreme court.

If the defense and prosecution agree to plea-bargain, a judge must approve the arrangement. As discussed in Step 11, judges typically approve plea bargains, but they reserve the right to reject any agreement that does not meet their criteria for justice. In light of this possibility, the two attorneys must be careful that the bargains they craft are not too out of line with the ideals of fairness and local legal custom because judges have been known to throw out bargains that appear too lenient or too harsh given the circumstances of the offense. Judges, of course, vary in their level of involvement in plea bargaining. Some judges prefer to ratify deals brought to the table by the prosecution and defense attorney, while others take a more hands-on role and participate in the negotiations or actually negotiate with defendants themselves (especially in lower courts where defendants seldom have private counsel who can engage in plea bargaining for them and are not assigned publicly funded attorneys until their arraignment hearings, but many plea bargains are wrought during arraignments meaning that judges may participate in negotiations).

As discussed more fully in Step 12, judges oversee the jury selection process. In some states, such as New Jersey, they also conduct the questioning of potential jurors. Even where the attorneys do the questioning, the judge manages the procedure, determining whether potential jurors seem unable to be impartial and ruling on objections raised by the attorneys. Rulings during the jury selection process may form the basis of an appeal, so judges must be careful to follow acceptable policies.

## Judicial Involvement During and After Trial

Judges are responsible for managing the day-to-day concerns of their courtrooms. This is especially true for the courts of limited jurisdiction; in addition to maintaining their own paperwork, some lower court judges do their own typing and xeroxing (e.g., Ashman, 1975). It is in this management function that judges must decide what forms of media to allow during hearings; that is, whether photos or video footage will be allowed and the circumstances under which they may be used (e.g., some judges may disallow depictions of the victim or victim's family while allowing the defendant's image to be printed or broadcast). In rare situations, judges may exclude the public from a trial (e.g., during a juvenile victim's testimony in a trial, or during juvenile court or family court proceedings to protect the child).

In their most conspicuous role, judges preside over trials. During jury trials, judges fulfill a referee-like function and instruct the jury at the conclusion of the trial about their duties in determining guilt (or penalty, depending on the type of case and jurisdiction). Jurors are often called upon in capital cases to determine whether a convicted murderer should receive the death penalty or be sentenced to prison. During **bench trials** (i.e., those presided over by a judge with no jury), judges serve as referees and make determinations of guilt. While jury trials are more common than bench trials (roughly 3 percent of misdemeanor and felony cases filed by a prosecutor result in bench trials, compared to roughly 5 percent that involve juries [adapted from Boland and Sones, 1986, pp. 6, 26]), judges make almost as many determinations of guilt as jurors.[1] As discussed below, however, regular practice does not always mean that judges are comfortable deciding whether the defendants who appear before them are guilty.

During the trial, judges rule on objections raised by the attorneys and ensure that the decorum of the trial process is maintained. It is important to note that judges almost never initiate objections, even when an obvious error has been made by one of the attorneys. For example, if a defense attorney does not object to the inclusion of a piece of evidence that was illegally obtained by law enforcement personnel, the judge will allow it to be introduced because it is the attorneys' responsibility to recognize and raise objections. Judges sometimes object when the mistake negatively impacts the formality accorded to the courts (e.g., if an attorney berates a witness without objections from the other side or is engaging in questionable methods, such as questioning a witness to a crime about his or her sexual preferences when such information appears unrelated to the case). And even then, they typically call a **sidebar conference** (i.e., a conference between the attorneys and judge that the jury cannot hear) or quiz the offending attorney about the purpose to his or her actions. As discussed below, it is important that judges appear impartial in the cases before them.

Another well-known role played by judges is that of sentencing agent. In this capacity, judges must determine appropriate penalties. As discussed in detail in Steps 13 and 14, this function presents a dilemma for the sentencing judge. He or she must choose a penalty that fits both the offense and the offender, and this is no simple task. Although they get input from both attorneys and from probation staff, judges still complain that sentencing is a difficult art. Some judges complain about the difficulties of imposing mandatory penalties that they feel are unjust (e.g., Forer, 1994), and others lament that they cannot effectively address crime through the sentencing options that are available to them. Demonstrating the personal strain that sometimes accompanies having to impose harsh sentences on those in their courtrooms, one minority judge noted: "I am responsible for locking up [minorities] and breaking up families" (personal interview, 2000; also, see Box 13.2 for another judge's complaint that he cannot end the cycle of drug use by relying on jail and other nontreatment options that are available to him as a judge).

Even after the verdict is in and the sentence has been pronounced, judges continue to be involved in the case. As discussed in Step 15, appellate level judges hear the case if it is appealed. Some appeals are automatic, such as in jurisdictions that provide automatic reviews of all cases in which the death penalty is imposed. A few appeals are based on the discovery of exculpating evidence (e.g., the recent cases of men whose rape convictions have been overturned by the discovery of DNA evidence that shows they were not the rapists) or other courtroom mishaps (e.g., corrupt actions by prosecutors or mistakes made by jurors). The vast majority of appeals, however, are those that are based on legal errors attributed to the judge who presided over the trial. For example, the defense might argue that a trial court judge erroneously allowed a certain piece of evidence to be introduced during the trial, permitted a certain witness to testify, or gave incorrect jury instructions. Judges may have some difficulty applying the law when it is unclear how they should act, and the defense or prosecution may object even to decisions that are soundly based in accepted legal practice. Appellate court judges, then, often review decisions made by trial court judges.

It is important to note that different judges may be involved at different decision points. In fact, judges from a variety of levels may be involved in the same case as it progresses through the justice system. Even in felony cases, a lower court justice might set bail or preside over the preliminary hearing. After the preliminary hearing, the case would be transferred to the felony level courts, where a different judge may hear pre-trial motions and preside over the trial. Then, if the case is appealed, appellate level judges would become involved. If the appeal involves a constitutional issue, a federal appellate judge or panel of federal appellate judges may hear the appeal. It is a rare occurrence that a misdemeanor case makes it to the U.S. Supreme Court, but it is possible and has happened (e.g., the case of Jon Argersinger, discussed in Step 6, who, following his unsuccessful appeal to the Florida State Supreme Court in 1970, filed a famous appeal with the U.S. Supreme Court, which guaranteed counsel to misdemeanants who faced even brief jail [*Argersinger v. Hamlin*, 1972]).

## Two New Court Programs That Are Changing Judicial Involvement

There are two new court programs that deserve mention here as they have transformed the role of judges in substantial ways. The first are drug courts, which were created in the late 1980s in response to growing drug court dockets (Gebelein, 2000). These are offender-centered courts that seek to rehabilitate drug users through a combination of tough love and effective supervision. The programs typically pair drug treatment with programs designed to provide personal and family counseling, and job training and other skills. Not all drug defendants are offered the opportunity to participate in drug courts (e.g., many programs bar defendants

The nine best-known judges in the country are the justices of the U.S. Supreme Court. Wearing their judicial ascots are the first two women appointed to the nation's highest court: Ruth Bader Ginsburg and Sandra Day O'Connor. Justice Clarence Thomas is the second African American to sit on the court—Thurgood Marshall was the first. Front row (L-R): Antonin Scalia, John Paul Stevens, Chief Justice William Rehnquist, Sandra Day O'Connor, Anthony Kennedy. Back row (L-R): Ruth Bader Ginsburg, David Souter, Clarence Thomas, Steven Breyer. SOURCE: Photo by Richard Strass/ Smithsonian Institution, courtesy of Supreme Court Historical Society.

with a history of violent offenses); those who agree to complete the programs plead guilty or sign a contract with the court in order to participate.

In drug courts, the judge's role is not simply to oversee the work of lawyers in one or a sequence of impersonal hearings. Rather, the judge becomes more of a "parent," who regularly interacts with the offenders and the drug court team (not to be confused with the courtroom work group, **drug court teams** work together to ensure that offenders are provided appropriate services and supervision aimed at enforcing a drug-free lifestyle). The judge gets to know each participant well due to their regular courtroom appearances (sometimes more than once a week) and congratulates those who do well in the program while punishing those who break the rules with brief stints of incarceration or other sanctions. At this time, it is hard to ascertain the effectiveness of drug court, but a number of former drug addicts have credited the programs with turning their lives around. These court programs are among the few that feature treatment providers working side by side with other justice workers, being treated as equals.

The second innovative court program is the community court. Community courts were developed as a way to serve local neighborhoods that are faced with crime on a daily basis and may have become frustrated in their efforts to better their neighborhoods (Feinblatt and Berman, 2001). Whereas drug courts focus exclusively on drug (and sometimes alcohol) offenders, community courts focus on nonserious misdemeanor offenses that can better be described as quality of life issues. These are offenses that mainstream courts often refer to as junk cases, and may not take seriously. When processed through the mainstream courts, such offenses normally result in time-served sentences, minor fines that may not even be paid, or light community service sentences (Feinblatt and Berman, 2001, p. 2).

In community courts, these very cases define how the court operates. Like drug courts, there is a team feel to community courts. The members of the community court drama are in regular contact with one another, and social workers work alongside attorneys on a daily basis. Offenders sentenced in community courts are often ordered to improve their communities through working on sponsored work projects in addition to dealing with their own drug and health problems through a sophisticated network of social service providers. One court, the Midtown Community Court in New York City, reports that offenders complete $175,000 a year in community service work for their communities (Feinblatt and Berman, 2001, p. 2). The Midtown community court also reaches out and provides voluntary services to at-risk individuals who have not yet come to the attention of authorities for breaking any laws but who are likely to do so if they continue in their current lifestyles (e.g., suspected prostitutes and homeless individuals).

Both of these innovative court programs rely on a team approach and pair legal system personnel with social workers who are plugged into a vast network of services. Both programs rely on jail and other retributive sanctions only when other sanctions fail to work, and hold as their goal the treatment of the individual offender. When offenders seem unwilling or unable to focus on helping themselves, punishment is used to remind them of the court's power. These programs view justice as eliminating an individual offender's participation in future crime, thus reducing crime in the community. Viewed together, drug courts and community courts try to "make the court more than just a courtroom" by bringing together social services and legal personnel with the goal of eliminating future crime through helping offenders resolve their various problems (Feinblatt and Berman, 2001, p. 4).

## PUTTING A FACE ON JUSTICE

Now that we know what they do, we need to take a look at what judges "look like." One similarity among judges is their legal education. Most judges were born in the state in which they attended law school and serve their judicial post (Blumberg, 1967, p. 119; Emmert and Glick, 1987, p. 231; Glick and Emmert, 1986, p. 110; Myers and Talarico, 1988, p. 29; Vines, 1962, p. 105). Not surprisingly, most judges have at least some legal experience at the time of their appointment, although not necessarily in criminal law. In California, for example, candidates for lower court judgeships must be admitted to the state bar and have five years practice in law (California Constitution, art. VI, sec. 15). California is typical in requiring practical experience as a lawyer prior to their judgeships; forty-three states require that at least some levels of judges be admitted to their state bars before assuming their judgeships (Rottman et al., 2000, pp. 50–55).[2]

Although lay judges (i.e., those without law degrees) are becoming less common in the general jurisdiction courts, most states still allow non-lawyers to serve in the lower courts, especially as justices of the peace (JPs) who hear minor cases for which jail cannot be imposed.[3] If you appear before a newly appointed JP after you have completed this book, chances are that you will know more about American courts than he or she does, but I do not recommend trying to show off your knowledge. In a recent survey of lower courts across America, only 3 percent of magistrate court judges in New Mexico (who preside over misdemeanors and can impose up to 364 days in jail) were trained in the law and only 7 percent of Texas JPs had a legal education (Rottman, Flango, and Lockley, 1995, pp. 22–23). In West Virginia, only one of 154 magistrate court judges was educated in the law (Rottman, Flango, and Lockley, 1995, p. 24). This lack of legal education may result in problems when judges do not understand the rules of evidence or know the basis of the legal system they are representing. One rural Texas JP, for example, refused to evict strangers who had moved into one woman's home because she did not have a lease. The homeowner debated with the JP, showing him her home ownership papers, but the JP was adamant: no lease, no eviction. After the hearing, the woman called one of the authors of this text, who suggested that she go to the local stationary store, purchase a blank lease, and fill it out listing herself first as owner and then as leasee. When she returned to court, the JP promptly ordered the eviction because the woman was able to produce a lease. While this may sound like something from the nineteenth century, this case happened in the 1990s and it illustrates how JPs may not fully understand even basic legal issues. History is full of quaint tales about justices of the peace and their misadventures in American law.

Despite their similarities, judges are far from exact replicas of one another. Demographic similarities do not translate into similar backgrounds, beliefs, and philosophies, especially with regard to sentencing. Like others in the courtroom drama, judges represent every walk of life and every belief possible, and their personalities range from agreeable to caustic. Unfortunately, judges' personalities may have influences on perceptions of justice and fairness in their courts. See Box 7.2 for one student's observations regarding defendants' interactions with two different judges, one "friendly" and one not. While the public may consider distant or hostile judges to be less competent than their amiable counterparts, this is not always true.

## Women and Minority Judges

Demographically, judges tend to be cut from similar cloth. Judges, on the whole, tend to be white males (Feeley, 1979, p. 63; Flango and Ducat, 1979, p. 30; Myers and Talarico, 1988, p. 29), although increasing numbers of women and minorities are obtaining judgeships, especially at the lower court level (Emmert and Glick, 1987, p. 230; Glick and Emmert, 1986, p. 109; Graham, 1990, p. 30; Meyer and Jesilow, 1997, p. 49). This is not to say that the integration has been evenly applied throughout the country; black judges, for example, are much more likely to serve in predominately black communities, indicating their marginal acceptance in other districts (Cappell, 1990, p. 112). In fact, minority and women judges are much more likely to gain their positions through appointment rather than election (Graham, 1990, p. 32). The differential may be due, at least in part, to efforts by appointers to "bend over backward" to boost the numbers of underrepresented judges (e.g., Carbon, Houlden, and Berkson, 1982, p. 301), and to the advantage that incumbents often enjoy during elections. President Jimmy Carter, who appointed forty-one women to the federal bench, is credited with doing the most to integrate women into the judiciary (Martin, 1982, p. 307). Before that time, only eight women had served as federal judges. The most famous of his forty-one female appointees is probably Ruth Bader Ginsburg, who later joined the U.S. Supreme Court.

It has only been during the past twenty-five years that large numbers of women have gained entrance into the judiciary (Berkson, 1982; Carbon, 1982, p. 285). As with other careers, women's entry into the legal workplace was hindered by outdated ideas about women as incapable of being good lawyers. As late

## BOX 7.2

## Does a Friendly Judge Make a Difference?: One Student's Observations

Many people may think that the sole duties of a judge are to supervise court proceedings and sentence criminal defendants. . . . They probably would not imagine that the typical court case involves a lot of interaction between the judge and the defendant. . . . From [months of] observations, I have noticed that the defendants in one courtroom interacted more with their judge than did the defendants in the other courtroom. The courtroom, which involved more communication was led by the friendlier of the two judges, [Judge A, who] . . . speaks kindly to [his] courtroom and seems to be helpful and/or sympathetic. . . . The other judge [is] Judge B.

Judge A is a man of approximately fifty to fifty-five years of age. Upon entering the courtroom, he does not require everyone in the room to stand while he approaches the bench. Instead, he simply sits down and asks everyone how they are this morning. He then requests that people show, by a raise of hands, the offenses with which they have been charged. As people raise their hands for their respective offense, Judge A will inform the court what the minimum sentence is for the particular offense. He makes it very clear to the court that if at all possible, he will try to give the defendant the minimum sentence required if they choose to plead guilty.

Judge A calls up his cases one at a time, while joking with the court in between cases. Such joking includes talking about the game the other night or, if numerous names are called consecutively and all of the defendants obviously have failed to appear, Judge A will call Hannibal Lector to the bench just to see if everyone is listening for his or her name. After the defendant stands in front of the court, Judge A will ask the defendant if he or she wishes to say anything. This may account for the higher magnitude of interaction in [this courtroom].

Judge B is a forty-five- to fifty-year-old woman. Before entering the courtroom, she has the bailiff summarize the rules of her court. The bailiff then shows the court a video whereon Judge B appears to explain further rules and procedures. Upon entering the courtroom, everyone in the room is asked to stand and pledge allegiance to the flag. Judge B greets the court and then proceeds to call up cases. She will call seven to nine cases at one time and have all of the defendants stand before her. Judge B will then address each defendant independently until she is finished with the group, after which she will call up the next group. She does not make any small talk with the court; she simply states the charge, asks for a plea of guilty or not guilty, and then gives the sentence. . . .

The apparent friendliness of Judge A and Judge B seemed to affect the degree of communication between defendants and their respective judge. The defendants in Court A seemed to request community service in lieu of fines or jail sentences much more frequently than those defendants observed in Court B. . . . Although some defendants in Court B asked for community service, most did not request it unless it was offered to them. . . . Some defendants in Court A even went as far as to ask the judge for advice. . . . The defendants in Court A seemed much more relaxed, more talkative, and less scared than the defendants in Court B. . . . [Judge A] also told the court that he may suggest that certain defendants speak to the district attorney before entering a plea [and] asked the court to trust him and follow such a suggestion because it could be to their advantage. . . . Judge A also displayed fairness when interacting with individual defendants as they stood before the court. . . . Judge A usually asked if the defendants were able to pay their fines. If a defendant replied that he would be unable to fulfill such a responsibility,

Judge A would offer him community service or a payment plan. Such helpful and sympathetic behavior, as exhibited by Judge A, may be a partial explanation for why most defendants did not hesitate to ask for community service or for lighter fines. Judge A made the defendants feel like he was on their side and would be as fair to them as possible.

*Source:* Written by Sophie Kim (1993). Used with permission.

as 1869, the State of Illinois denied Myra Bradwell admission to their state bar because she was a woman. See Box 7.3 for a few excerpts from the U.S. Supreme Court when it upheld the state's decision. That same year, the State of Iowa admitted Arabelle Mansfield to their state bar, making her the country's first female attorney (Berkson, 1982).

The number of female judges increased at the time of the women's movement in the 1970s. At the beginning of that decade, about five percent of the judiciary were women (U.S. Bureau of the Census, 1973). By the 1990s, nearly one-fourth (23 percent) of judges were female (U.S. Bureau of the Census, 1992). Research comparing women judges to their male counterparts has shown that they are younger, probably due to their recent entry into judicial positions, and more likely to have attended private law schools (Carbon, Houlden, and Berkson, 1982). They also differ in other ways; women appointed by Jimmy Carter to the federal bench, for example, were more likely than his male appointments to assume primary responsibility for their households and to experience conflict between their judgeships and parental roles (Martin, 1990).

Women judges appear to have different philosophies regarding the law. Women appellate court judges in one study, for example, were more likely than their male counterparts to support claimants in employment discrimination cases and defendants in search and seizure matters (Davis, Haire, and Songer, 1993). A survey of state and federal women judges reported that they felt female justices brought "unique perspectives" to the bench and were "more sensitive" then male judges to claimants alleging sexual discrimination (Martin, 1993). Another study (Meyer and Jesilow, 1997, p. 120) found that women judges in lower courts were more likely to state that concern for crime victims played a role in their sentencing of offenders, whereas male judges focused on the crime itself and the offender when deciding sentences. The female judges were also more likely to mention entering the judiciary to help others. This is not to say that all women judges act in more nurturing ways; some may not do so as it would be politically unwise to abandon their status as "neutral decision-makers" in a profession that is still dominated by men (Davis, Haire, and Songer, 1993). Alternatively, some may feel expected to adopt a nurturing role.

Like female judges, minority judges may "inject new perspectives into the law" (Martin, 1993, p. 173). The increase in the number of minority judges parallels that of women. The first black judge, Robert Morris, sat on the Boston Magistrate

## BOX 7.3

### A Few Excerpts from *Bradwell v. Illinois* (1872)

From the U.S. Supreme Court's opinion to uphold the state of Illinois' decision to ban Myra Bradwell from the legal workplace because she was a woman:

> On Mrs. Bradwell's application first coming before the court, the license was refused, and it was stated as a sufficient reason that under the decisions of the Supreme Court of Illinois, the applicant—"as a married woman would be bound neither by her express contracts nor by those implied contracts which it is the policy of the law to create between attorney and client. . . ."
>
> [T]he civil law, as well as nature herself, has always recognized a wide difference in the respective spheres and destinies of man and woman. Man is, or should be, woman's protector and defender. The natural and proper timidity and delicacy which belongs to the female sex evidently unfits it for many of the occupations of civil life. The constitution of the family organization, which is founded in the divine ordinance, as well as in the nature of things, indicates the domestic sphere as that which properly belongs to the domain and functions of womanhood. The harmony, not to say identity, of interests and views which belong, or should belong, to the family institution is repugnant to the idea of a woman adopting a distinct and independent career from that of her husband. . . . [A] married woman is incapable, without her husband's consent, of making contracts which shall be binding on her or him. This very incapacity was one circumstance which the Supreme Court of Illinois deemed important in rendering a married woman incompetent fully to perform the duties and trusts that belong to the office of an attorney and counsellor (p. 141). . . .
>
> The paramount destiny and mission of woman are to fulfil the noble and benign offices of wife and mother. This is the law of the Creator. And the rules of civil society must be adapted to the general constitution of things, and cannot be based upon exceptional cases (pp. 141–142).

*Postscript:* Myra Bradwell continued to work as the publisher of the successful *Chicago Legal News,* a weekly legal newspaper, advocating for women's rights through her writings. As she was dying of cancer, her husband campaigned on her behalf and she was admitted to the Illinois state bar in 1890 and was admitted to practice before the U.S. Supreme Court in 1892. She died in 1894, before she was able to enjoy her new status as a recognized lawyer (Wheaton, 1997).

Court in 1852 (Spohn, 1990, p. 1197). From that humble beginning, minorities have made significant strides in becoming judges. In 1970, fewer than three percent of judges were minorities (U.S. Bureau of the Census, 1973). By 1990, however, four times as many (12 percent) were minorities (U.S. Bureau of the Census, 1992).

A new field of research has taken on the task of examining how justice is being transformed by the introduction of more minorities and women into judicial positions. The findings have been positive. Minority judges appear to be more blind to offender race (Holmes et al., 1993; Welch, Coombs, and Gruhl, 1988,

Justice Laverne Johnson of the Navajo Nation Judicial Branch is one of a growing number of women in the judiciary. Since the 1970s, the number of female judges has been on the increase. Some researchers suggest that women judges bring new perspectives to justice and that they may be more sensitive to some parties in their courtrooms. One prominent researcher, Carol Gilligan (1982), found that women "speak in a different voice"; that is, they answer moral dilemmas through empathy and compassion, whereas men focus on the rights of the individuals involved. Based on Gilligan's work, one would expect women judges to bring a nurturing, collaborative, and cooperative spirit to the practice of law.    SOURCE: Courtesy of Judge Laverne Johnson, Navajo Nation Judicial Branch.

p. 132), and female judges seem to be more blind to gender (Gruhl, Spohn, and Welch, 1981, p. 318). In other words, the historic favoritism shown to females and whites is less pronounced in cases presided over by minority and women judges than in cases managed by white male judges.

## THE PATH TO A JUDGESHIP: METHODS OF JUDICIAL SELECTION AND TRAINING

People do not become judges by simply waking up one morning and discovering a black robe in their bedroom closets. The paths individuals take to their judgeships are varied, differing both by level of court and geographic location. Judges are appointed or elected to their posts as discussed below.

### Methods for Selecting Federal Appellate Judges

Federal appellate judges are appointed by the President of the United States and are subject to Senate confirmation. As provided for in Article II of the U.S. Constitution, candidates for the Supreme Court are nominated and appointed for by the President with the advice and consent of the Senate. This means that the President's candidates must pass review by the Senate. While some candidates' applications are approved in an almost routine manner, appointments to the U.S. Supreme Court may generate a lot of controversy. The 1991 appointment of Clarence Thomas by President George Herbert Walker Bush, for example, was in danger when charges of sexual harassment were levied by one of his former employees, Anita Hill. The Senate conducted extensive hearings before allowing the appointment to take place. Sometimes, senators are accused of holding up the confirmation hearings to achieve political payback against a President who has submitted the candidate for a judgeship.

Federal appellate judges hold their positions for life, unless they are impeached or removed from office for an inability to perform their duties (e.g., due to illness). The guarantee of lifetime positions during good standing is intended to create judicial independence. If federal judges were accountable to anyone in particular (e.g., a political leader), their decisions might not reflect their true views based on the merits of the cases before them. Instead, decisions made by judges who do not enjoy lifetime appointments may reflect the wishes of those who control the selection process. While Circuit Judicial Councils were created to inquire into complaints of misconduct by federal judges, "their disciplinary powers are narrowly circumscribed" (Lubet, 1998, p. 59). We will return to a discussion of Circuit Judicial Councils later in this chapter.

## Methods for Selecting State Appellate Judges

State level appellate judges obtain their positions through a variety of ways, which are summarized briefly in Box 7.4 and are discussed here. A number of states (twenty of fifty) rely on the **merit system** (Rottman et al., 2000, pp. 21–24). This method is also called the **Missouri Plan** because Missouri was the first state to adopt the American Bar Association's 1937 proposal to transform judicial selection (Warrick, 1993, p. 5). Under the merit system, judges are appointed by the governor with input from a judicial nominating commission composed of judges, lawyers, and lay citizens. The commission evaluates potential judges and provides the governor with a list of three to five names from which he or she may appoint individuals (Warrick, 1993, p. 5). Although free to choose whichever candidate he or she prefers, the governor is limited to the names on the list. After their appointment, judges selected through the merit system are subject to a confirmation election in which the voters are asked whether the judge should be retained (Flango and Ducat, 1979, p. 26). In five of the twenty states, a modified merit system is used since the selected appellate judges are not required to stand for a confirmation election. The District of Columbia also follows a modified merit system, and because it has no governor, the president of the United States appoints the judges with confirmation by the Senate. See Box 7.4 for a table summarizing the selection methods used for state appellate court judges.

# BOX 7.4
## Methods of Selecting State Judges

The following table has been adapted from Rottman et al. (2000). How are judges in your state selected? How are judges in the states that border your state selected? As you compare the selection of appellate and trial court judges, which type is more likely to have been elected? Are there any patterns to the types of selection?

### Appellate Court Judges

| Merit System (n = 20 + Washington, D.C.) | Appointments (n=7) | | Elections (n=23) | | |
|---|---|---|---|---|---|
| | **Appointed by governor:** | **Legislature appoints:** | **Partisan election:** | **Nonpartisan election:** | **Elected by legislature:** |

**Merit System (n = 20 + Washington, D.C.)**

**Merit system:**
Alaska
Arizona
Colorado
Florida
Indiana
Iowa
Kansas
Maryland (also requires state senate approval)
Missouri
Nebraska
Oklahoma
South Dakota
Tennessee (non-partisan retention election)
Utah (also requires state senate approval)
Wyoming

**Modified form of merit system, requires third-party approval in addition to judicial nominating commission, but does not require retention election by voters:**
Delaware (state senate approval)
Hawaii (state senate approval)
Massachusetts (governor's council approval)
Rhode Island (does not required third-party approval and judges have life tenure)
Vermont (state senate approval, retention is through legislative election)

District of Columbia (President makes appointment with U.S. Senate consent)

**Appointments (n=7)**

**Appointed by governor:**
California (must then stand for unopposed retention election)
Maine
New Hampshire (requires approval of elected executive council)
New Jersey (for supreme court and requires approval of state senate, appellate judges appointed by chief justice of state supreme court)
New York

**Legislature appoints:**
Connecticut

**Elections (n=23)**

**Partisan election:**
Alabama
Arkansas
Illinois
New Mexico
North Carolina
Pennsylvania
Texas
West Virginia

**Nonpartisan election:**
Georgia
Idaho
Kentucky
Louisiana
Michigan
Minnesota
Mississippi
Montana
Nevada
North Dakota
Ohio
Oregon
Washington
Wisconsin

**Elected by legislature:**
South Carolina

# BOX 7.4 (continued)

## Trial Court Judges (general jurisdiction court):

| Merit System (n = 12 + Washington, D.C.) | | Appointments (n=6) | | Elections (n=32) | |
|---|---|---|---|---|---|
| **Merit system:**<br>Alaska<br>Colorado<br>Iowa<br>Kansas (partisan election in fewer than half the districts)<br>Nebraska<br>Utah<br>Wyoming | **Modified form of merit system, requires third-party approval in addition to judicial nominating commission, but does not require retention election by voters:**<br>Delaware (state senate approval)<br>Hawaii (state senate approval)<br>Maryland (state senate approval and participates in contested election one year later)<br>Massachusetts (governor's council approval, no retention process)<br>Vermont (state senate approval, retention is through legislative election)<br><br>District of Columbia (President makes appointment) | **Appointed by governor:**<br>Maine (requires approval of state senate)<br>New Hampshire (requires approval of elected executive council)<br>New Jersey (requires approval of state senate)<br>Rhode Island (requires approval of state senate) | **Legislature appoints:**<br>Connecticut<br>Virginia | **Partisan election:**<br>Alabama<br>Arkansas<br>Illinois<br>Indiana<br>Missouri (has merit system for one-ninth of circuits)<br>New Mexico<br>New York<br>Pennsylvania<br>Tennessee<br>Texas<br>West Virginia | **Nonpartisan election:**<br>Arizona (uses merit system in two counties)<br>California<br>Florida<br>Georgia<br>Idaho<br>Kentucky<br>Louisiana<br>Michigan<br>Minnesota<br>Mississippi<br>Montana (uses merit system for specialized courts)<br>Nevada<br>North Carolina (uses gubernatorial appointment for special courts)<br>North Dakota<br>Ohio<br>Oklahoma<br>Oregon<br>South Dakota<br>Washington<br>Wisconsin<br><br>**Elected by legislature:**<br>South Carolina |

In five states, appellate court judges are appointed by their respective governors without the input from a judicial nominating commission. In one of these states (California), appellate court judges are appointed by the governor, but then must stand for an unopposed retention election (this is not considered a merit system because there is no input from a judicial nominating commission). In two states (Connecticut and Virginia), the legislature appoints appellate court judges.

Elections, which began in 1812 when the State of Georgia moved to elections for lower court judges (Warrick, 1993, p. 3), are fairly modern methods of selecting judges. By 1832, Mississippi required all of its judges to be elected, in part due to concerns by the public that the judiciary was controlled by property owners who did not represent their interests (Warrick, 1993, p. 3).

Appellate court judges in twenty-three states are elected in popular elections. In eight states, this occurs through **partisan** elections (where the candidates are identified by political party), and in fourteen states through **nonpartisan** elections (where the candidates do not mention their party affiliation). In the remaining state (South Carolina), appellate court judges are elected by the legislature rather than in popular elections.

Unlike their federal colleagues who sit for life, state appellate court judge terms vary from five to fifteen years, except in Massachusetts and New Hampshire (where they hold their judgeships until age seventy), and Rhode Island (where they are elected by the legislature for life terms; Rottman et al., 2000, pp. 26–29).

## Methods for Selecting State Trial Court Judges

Trial court judges at the court of general jurisdiction level are much more likely than appellate judges to be selected through elections (see Box 7.4 for a breakdown of the methods used to select trial court judges). In twelve states, they are selected using the merit system or modified form of the merit system in which judges are selected using input from a judicial nominating commission but are not required to stand for popular retention elections (Rottman et al., 2000, pp. 34–49). In addition, judges in the District of Columbia are selected using the modified form of the merit system. It is not always clear what methods of selection are used for trial court judges, as some states employ multiple methods as noted in the table in Box 7.4. What is clear, however, is the merit selection is used far less often than it is with appellate court judges.

Elections seem to be the norm for trial court judges. In the majority of states (a total of thirty-one of fifty), judges are chosen through popular elections, on either partisan (eleven of fifty) or nonpartisan (twenty of fifty) tickets. In these states, potential judges campaign for their positions, much like candidates for other elected positions (although they are expected to refrain from the "mudslinging" associated with other campaigns). In one state (South Carolina), judges are elected by the legislature, bringing the total number of states that rely on elections to thirty-two.

In four states, trial court judges at the general court level are appointed by the governor, sometimes with input from the legislature (Rottman et al., 2000, pp. 34–49). These appointments are politically oriented in some states, while some states attempt to eliminate favoritism from their selection processes by utilizing nonbinding recommendations made by their state bar or other associations. In the remaining two states, the general court level judges are appointed by the legislature.

The path to a lower court judgeship is much more complicated because many states have multiple methods of selection for lower court judges, depending on district or court type. Elections seem to be the most common form of selection; eleven states rely on partisan elections, twelve on nonpartisan elections, and two on both partisan and nonpartisan elections (Rottman et al., 2000, pp. 34–49). In addition, another four states have elections for at least some of their lower court judges, while the other lower court judges in the state are selected through other means. The judges in the courts of limited jurisdiction are appointed by the governor in eight states, the local governing body (e.g., mayor) in three states, higher court justices in three states, the legislature in one state, and a special magistrate commission in one state. Two states' rules for judicial selection are locally determined, and two states (Illinois and Minnesota) have no courts of limited jurisdiction (while South Dakota has no courts of limited jurisdiction, it does have judges who hear traffic and other "limited jurisdiction" type cases).

Trial court judges sit for terms varying from two to fifteen years, depending on state and level of court, except in Massachusetts and New Hampshire (where they are appointed until age seventy) and Rhode Island (where they are appointed for life; Rottman et al., 2000, pp. 34–49).

## Comparison of the Four Methods of Judicial Selection

The manner in which judges are selected has elicited some interest from citizens and scholars alike. The four selection styles have different advantages and disadvantages. The benefits of appointing judges are that the individuals making the appointments will try to avoid selecting inadequate candidates due to fear of embarrassing themselves or their political party. Only a foolish political leader would appoint a personal friend whose qualifications were weak and whose decisions would attract a lot of unwanted attention from citizens' groups and the media. A drawback of the appointment system is that it is typically very partisan (i.e., Democrats tend to appoint Democrats whereas Republicans favor Republicans), and that many good candidates are never even considered because they do not have connections to the individual making the appointments. If a political leader is unaware of a particular individual, for example, that person certainly cannot be appointed no matter how good a judge he or she would make. Finally, the public may feel that a judge has been imposed on them by a political leader for the duration of the appointment.

Elections, on the other hand, give the judges legitimacy through being chosen by the public. Citizens may be more likely to accept decisions made by a judge whom they elected (versus one who was appointed for them). Partisan elections, due to their political nature, often mean that local party leaders play a strong role in who gets elected. This means that although the judges are technically "appointed" by the local leadership through their selecting which judges are able to run in an election, those leaders have a much lower level of accountability than those who appoint judges directly. Of course, political party leaders are unlikely to support those who might cause their party great embarrassment, but this level of accountability is greatly reduced. Nonpartisan elections remove the party politics, but provide no accountability by an outside individual (i.e., there is no individual who screens the judges prior to election). In addition, the candidates in a nonpartisan election are on their own when it comes to financing and running their campaigns, thus eliminating some candidates from the contest who do not have those resources.

In addition, elections are not always as democratic as they appear. A quick case study will help illustrate the dynamics of partisan elections. Philadelphia lawyers who wanted to become judges in the early 1980s had to "suck up" to Democratic leaders who were in charge by doing pro bono work for them and by paying $20,000 directly to the Democratic City Committee (Ferrick, 1999). Once they got noticed, they could be included on the ballot, and because most people vote by party, the candidate was a shoe-in. Now, the process is more complex because not all districts use the same ballot. This means that judicial hopefuls must pay the general endorsement fee ($30,000 in 1997) and win over enough of the sixty-nine ward leaders, each of whom requires endorsement fees of $500 to $3000, to guarantee their election (Ferrick, 1999). In 1967, Blumberg (p. 120) noted that the "going rate" for judgeships in New York City was two years' salary "contributed" to one's political party and that "buying" judicial positions was a common practice; even those jurisdictions that did not require outright "buying" involved huge amounts of time and money being donated to party activities in order to build the political base required to win an election. Some people might liken this to buying a judgeship, which may erode their faith in the judges who serve them. Regardless of your opinions about the process, however, this illustration shows how the citizens of Philadelphia do not *really* select their judges, despite their participating in what appears to be a clean election.

The fourth selection type, the merit system, was designed to combine the best of appointments and elections, while eliminating the disadvantages associated with both methods. The merit system is not without its drawbacks, however. The judges selected through the merit system tend to represent the values and interests of the judicial nominating commission or bar association leadership. And, all traces of politics are not removed as some judicial nomination commissioners are appointed by the governor, and the governor is presented with a list of candidates from which he or she is free to choose. In the end, the role of politics is merely transformed rather than truly eradicated.

## Does Method of Judicial Selection Affect Justice?

One scholar's research on judges in two cities illustrates how justice may be based, at least in part, on the characteristics of judges and judicial selection methods. Levin (1977, p. 48) noted that judges in Minneapolis, Minnesota, were essentially selected by the local bar association, a method that largely precluded influences based upon political affiliation. Due to the bar's involvement in approving candidates, the Minneapolis judges were usually from private legal practice, many from large law firms. The Minneapolis Bar Association had even sponsored a law in the 1950s that forced new candidates for judgeships to name which incumbent he or she sought to replace in upcoming elections; this law prevented judicial candidates from running against "the entire field of incumbents up for re-election in the hope of at least receiving more votes than the lowest incumbent" (Levin, 1977, p. 53). In general, the Minneapolis judges tended to be legalistic and society-oriented; that is, they emphasized protecting society rather than protecting defendants' rights (Levin, 1977, p. 101).

In Pittsburgh, Pennsylvania, however, Levin found a very different situation. The Pittsburgh judges were elected on a partisan basis for ten-year terms. Local politics dominated the selection of judges and restricted the role played by the local bar association. In fact, the local county bar association often "considered the party committee's candidate unacceptable," but it never "even attempted to support an opposing candidate" (Levin, 1977, p. 55). Judicial selections were heavily party-oriented, meaning that governors generally appointed judges from their own political parties (Levin, 1977, p. 55). The Pittsburgh judges tended to be defendant-oriented; that is, they emphasized protecting defendants' rights and "giving defendants a break" when they deserved leniency (Levin, 1977, p. 117).

As might be expected given the differences discussed above, the punishment philosophies of the judges in the two cities also varied immensely. The more defendant-oriented Pittsburgh judges felt that prison was not an effective punishment because it did not address the true causes of crime (Levin, 1977, p. 124). The more society-oriented Minneapolis judges, on the other hand, readily used incarceration because they felt it was a useful penalty due to its deterrence and incapacitative value (1977, p. 109). By these two examples, we can see that the process for judicial selection may play an important role in how judges dispense justice in their courtrooms.

In general, judges who are elected may be more likely to represent local sentiment, as they must gather the local population's support to win enough votes to secure their judgeships. Appointed judges, on the other hand, may vary in their levels of agreement with the attitudes of those in the communities they serve, as they may be chosen by agents who do not live in those same communities (e.g., governors). Of course, judges who are appointed to temporarily fill slots (vacated by elected judges who retired or resigned) must some day be subject to some form of election themselves, but research has shown that judicial incumbents have a strong upper hand in elections and that fewer than 10 percent are voted out of office (e.g., Vines, 1962, pp. 114–15).[4] In addition to affecting sentences, selection method may be fundamental when determining the type of person who chooses to become and is chosen to become a judge. As previously mentioned, for example, minority and women judges may stand a better chance of obtaining a judicial position under schemes that rely on appointment rather than election.

## JUDICIAL TRAINING

Our country's justice system seems to place a high value on the input of amateurs. In addition to utilizing jurors, who rarely have any training at all in law, our judicial selection methods sometimes seem to be designed to ensure that the least experienced individuals are selected to be judges. While the candidates are typically well-trained in the law itself, they usually have little experience in the courtroom, and law school provides minimal or no training on how to be a judge.

Until about forty years ago, there was very little training offered to those who wished to become judges. Due in part to complaints voiced by legal scholars and research teams about the quality and training of judges, judicial education programs were introduced and are still offered today. These programs, however, tend to be short in duration. The National Judicial College (NJC), established in Reno during the early 1960s, for example, offers a number of judicial training and sentencing seminars to those judges whose jurisdictions can afford to send them. The NJC courses are typically three to five days long and cover a wide variety of topics. Some judges attend NJC on a regular basis as part of their ongoing education. Three states (Nevada, New Hampshire, and Wyoming) require their general jurisdiction judges to attend NJC before beginning their judgeships (Rottman, Flango, and Lockley, 1995, pp. 86–89). Another popular training source is the Administrative Office of the Courts (AOC); thirteen states require AOC training programs for their general jurisdiction court judges. Federal judges attend orientation sessions offered by the Federal Judicial Center.

Individual states also sponsor training programs, but these courses last only a few days and tend to focus on issues specific to the jurisdiction the judges will be serving, such as how to complete paperwork needed in that jurisdiction. Some jurisdictions now assign judges to observe other judges for a period of time, similar to an apprenticeship. Despite the trend toward judicial education, twenty states still require no specialized judicial education for those who will preside over their courts (Delaware, however, is currently developing a program, and all Arkansas judges attend training though it is not required; Rottman et al., 2000, pp. 60–63). When our nation's methods of training judges are compared to countries that offer special judicial tracks in law school or other forms of specific and sustained training for potential judges, one can readily see that our system has some room for improvement in this area.

Some judges have never even been in a courtroom before they are chosen to preside over one. The merit system, discussed earlier in this chapter, ranks judges based on their bar association qualification ratings. Those chosen through this method, though excellent attorneys, are often employed in business law or other noncriminal fields and may have no experience with the types of cases over which they will preside, including criminal cases. Of course, gubernatorial appointments and popular elections also result in judges who have little or no courtroom experience because the selection criteria seldom include whether the candidate is a seasoned courtroom participant (Vines, 1962, p. 116). See Box 7.5 for an anecdote about the problems caused by one attorney's inexperience in the criminal courts. Judges who preside over civil cases do not appear to be any more likely to have prior courtroom experience, meaning that the day-to-day concerns of their new career may be as foreign to them as they are to their brethren in the criminal courts.

---

## BOX 7.5
## One Attorney's Courtroom Nightmare

A probate attorney in rural New Jersey had registered under the state's mandatory pro bono law. Originally written in the wake of *Gideon v. Wainwright,* 1963 (which guarantees the right to free counsel), this law is still used to provide lawyers to criminal defendants in rural areas that cannot afford to fund a public defenders' office. The attorney was dismayed one day when he found in his mail an order to serve; in fact, he had been assigned to represent a drug offender. Rather timidly, he went to the local jail to meet his new client. He informed the client that he had never represented an accused in a criminal trial, knew very little about criminal law, and had never even been in a criminal courtroom. He then told the client he had one choice and one choice alone: plea-bargain. The attorney met with the prosecutor on the case and worked out a plea agreement, though he still admits he is not even sure if the bargain was a good one. In addition to influencing the justice outcome for his client, the attorney's inexperience in the criminal courts illustrates that attorneys who work in fields other than criminal law may have little criminal courtroom experience.

Ironically, it is often these very attorneys (those with little experience in the courtroom, that is) who receive high bar association ratings for judgeships due to a variety of factors, including the weight assigned to the schools from which candidates graduate. But graduates from the better law schools rarely go into criminal law due to perceiving that field of law as less desirable and less lucrative than other types of practice. Instead, they prefer to go into civil or other branches of law that guarantee them more prestige and upward mobility. In the end, attorneys in the criminal law arena may have more courtroom experience but significantly lower bar association ratings.

Even those who have previously held other courtroom roles as prosecutors or defense attorneys quickly find that their experience was in a vastly different capacity. Attorneys are expected to be zealous advocates, but judges are supposed to be neutral arbitrators. "Unlearning" that role may be difficult; one new judge reported that early in his judicial career, he kept jumping from his seat, prepared to object to a variety of legal issues (Wice, 1985, p. 120). It took this judge a while to overcome the ingrained desire to raise objections during the trials he was hearing. It is not hard to imagine that he faced other difficulties adapting to his new, more neutral, role.

## JUDICIAL DISCRETION AND RELATIONSHIPS WITH OTHERS

Judges have an incredible amount of discretion in their work. Unless their decisions are bizarre enough to warrant removal from office, most judges do not suffer ramifications from making the occasional bad choice. Despite the presence of mandatory sentencing schemes (e.g., "three-strikes" laws) and sentencing guidelines, the vast majority of their decisions are relatively unfettered by rules and regulations. Instead, judges are expected to apply the law in a fair manner. And, remarkably, judges seem capable of fulfilling that role. While some people may be unhappy with individual decisions made by judges, wholly corrupt or mean-spirited judges appear to be quite rare.

The public does become outraged at judges for their handling of specific cases or types of cases. One need only remember the ire incurred by Judge Lance Ito for his handling of the O.J. Simpson case. Then, when another judge granted O.J. Simpson custody of his children, enraged citizens mounted an unsuccessful campaign to have her removed from office (e.g., Attorney defends O.J., 1997). Like the two justices in the Simpson cases, other judges have attracted and survived their share of negative attention from the public when they made unpopular rulings. See Box 7.6 for the story of a justice whose unpopular written dissent nearly cost him his appellate judgeship.

Sometimes judges are attacked for decisions they make that go awry. One New York city judge, for example, attracted condemnation from the public and his governor when a domestic abuser he released on bail murdered his victim, who had implored the court to protect her. The judge had released the abuser because he was underwhelmed by the victim's injuries, saying "There is no actual physical injury, is there, other than some bruising? . . . I am not suggesting that bruising is nice, but there is no disfigurement" (Two ex-judges, 1996). And, another New York judge was removed from office after telling his clerk, "Every woman needs a good pounding every now and then," when a domestic violence victim asked for a protection order against her husband (Judge removed, 1997). Because her protection order was denied, her husband could not be removed from her home during a future violent episode, and the woman was forced to flee with her children.

---

### BOX 7.6
### A Judge Whose Unpopular Dissent Almost Cost Him His Job

While seated on the California Appellate Court, Justice J. Anthony Kline issued a dissenting opinion in a case in which he said he "cannot as a matter of conscience" support a state supreme court precedent regarding a controversial legal issue.[5] Within a few months, Justice Kline had formal charges filed against him by his state's judicial fitness commission, accusing him of "willful misconduct" for writing the dissent. It is important to point out two significant facts. First, Justice Kline's was merely one of several votes and the appellate court ruled as a whole to support the precedent. Second, his dissent was based soundly in legal reasoning. The only offensive action he engaged in was his asking the court to revisit and reconsider the controversial precedent. For this questioning of a prior decision by his state's supreme court, he faced termination by the judicial fitness commission. More than a year later, the commission formally dismissed the charges, possibly due to the immense support of the legal community given to Kline. The commission's final report mentioned the importance of judicial independence: "It is fundamental to our system of jurisprudence that they feel free to break new ground, challenge existing assumptions, present novel legal reasoning, and experiment with different approaches. In most instances they must be able to do so free from fear of discipline for the free expression of their ideas" (adapted from: Lubet, 1998; Ofgang, 1999).

(For the story of a Supreme Court justice whose unpopular rulings cost her her judicial position, see Box 15.5 in Step 15.)

---

Despite their extraordinary discretion, judges rely on others in the courtroom drama to help them make decisions. In many jurisdictions, judges count on probation officers to help them with sentencing concerns, but others also play a role in judicial decisions. In many cases, from mundane day-to-day concerns to serious rulings, judges rely heavily on their fellow judges, using informal and formal meetings to gather and share information (Meyer and Jesilow, 1997, p. 67). In addition, prosecutors and defense attorneys help shape every stage of each case, from whether or not bail should be allowed to what sentence is appropriate in a given case.

In addition to counting on them for assistance, most judges "play along" with the courtroom work group. Decisions that are out of line with how the other members of the courtroom work group choose to act can attract condemnation from them. Judges who gain reputations for being difficult to work with may find themselves the subject of courtroom gossip or suffer other sanctions. Some judges, on the other hand, have gone a bit too far in their congeniality toward the courtroom work group. A Washington judge resigned after an investigation showed that he drank beer with the prosecutor and defense attorney while a jury deliberated on a drunk-driving case, in violation of laws regarding the consumption of alcohol in the courthouse (Brandt, 1998).

# THE DILEMMAS OF BEING A JUDGE

## "Good" Versus "Bad" Judges

Bad judges are fairly easy to recognize. They are prejudiced or oppressive, hateful or corrupt. Some of them appear unable or unwilling to perform the duties of their office. They may sleep during trials (e.g., Reeves, 1997) or act bizarrely, such as the judge who signed court papers "Adolf Hitler" and threw firecrackers into his colleagues' offices (Bedlan, 1998). They may use their offices to line their pocketbooks with bribes (e.g., Two ex-judges, 1996), or they may wage private wars against individuals they dislike (e.g., McQuiston, 1996). Some of them use the sentence of jail illegally, such as the judge who repeatedly jailed poor workers until they made payments on their debts, although this use of incarceration is illegal in the United States (Dillon, 2000). Other bad judges put their needs before the needs of society or the defendants appearing before them. They are a generally despicable class of individuals whose decisions appear to be rooted in some anti-societal, self-serving sentiment. Well, not always, but truly bad judges are still fairly easy to spot.

Good judges, on the other hand, are much harder to identify. Try to design a way to recognize a good judge—it is hard to do. Those who do not to act in inappropriate ways are not necessarily *good* judges, further clouding our task. Are good judges those who vote their conscience? What if their consciences are not in line with the rest of society? Are good judges those who react to public wants and desires? What about those who do whatever the public wants to keep their constituents happy, even if what the public wants is unconstitutional or unfair (e.g., impose long prison terms on panhandlers because the public is tired of feeling harassed by them)? Are good judges those who are compassionate toward defendants? What about those whose compassion leads them to sentence to probation those convicted of serious offenses? As you can see, it is fairly hard to recognize a good judge.

## Judicial Ethics

One characteristic of good judges is that they behave in an ethical manner. There are canons of judicial conduct established by the American Bar Association and the Judicial Council, which regulate how judges must act.

First, judges are expected to remain dispassionate in the matters before them; that is, they must be neutral about their cases and apply the law in an impartial manner. It should not appear that judges are favoring their own beliefs or trying to make a name for themselves, like the judge who ordered $1 million bail for a ship captain who was charged with misdemeanor charges stemming from a serious oil spill off the Alaskan coast although the prosecutor had requested only $25,000 bail (King, 1989).

The second canon says that judges must be uninvolved in the actions they handle; that is, they must be impartial. If they cannot be impartial, they are expected to recuse themselves, as one judge did when the defendant's lawyer accused him of having Alzheimer's disease (Fried, 1997). He said he was afraid he could not be fair toward the defense given the comment, so he stepped down from the case as he should have. Another judge was asked to recuse himself from a number of breast implant cases he was hearing because his wife could benefit from class-action suits due to her own breast implants (Corneliussen, 1997). While he said his wife was healthy and that her implants would have no effect over his courtroom decisions, the case highlights the importance that judges maintain the *appearance* of impartiality. A third judge came under fire when he presided over a tobacco regulation case even though he had been a former lobbyist for the tobacco industry; to the relief of many, however, his decision to allow regulation of tobacco as a drug was based on what he felt the law required rather than on his own leanings toward the tobacco industry (Thompson, 1997).[6] Judges may be challenged if either the defense or prosecution questions their impartiality and can demonstrate that the judge might be too connected to the case to act in a fair manner. Judges who appear to be biased, regardless of whether they actually *are* biased, can find their decisions questioned by appellate courts. This is what happened to federal District Court Judge Thomas Penfield Jackson when his ruling to break up Microsoft was overturned and the case was remanded to another judge; he had appeared biased during and following the trial, going so far as to comment on the case to the press and discuss it in speeches, referring to Microsoft CEO Bill Gates and the corporation in rather unflattering terms.

It is not an admission of wrongdoing or favoritism when a judge recuses himself or herself from a case; it is the proper thing to do when questions exist about a judge's possible impartiality. If you were a criminal court judge, would you be able to ignore the fact that your best friend was appearing before you for sentencing? Surely not. Having friends is not the problem; trying to act as though friendships would not matter, on the other hand, is a serious issue. Recusal would be your best choice; no matter what sentence you imposed, people would assume your friendship played a role, and such perceptions erode the public's confidence in the judiciary.

A controversial example is the recent U.S. Supreme Court case in which presidential hopefuls Al Gore and George W. Bush challenged one another in a rapid whirlwind of legal challenges. *Bush v. Gore* (2000) may earn the distinction of moving from state court of general jurisdiction to U.S. Supreme Court in the shortest time interval, one month total. After issuing a ruling that the vote recounts then underway in Florida were not to be resumed, thus making George W. Bush president of the United States, the public maelstrom began. Accusations had already begun to fly that one of the justices (Antonin Scalia) should have recused himself because his son worked for the firm representing Bush. After the ruling was found to have been perfectly divided down political lines, with all five Republican appointees voting in favor of Bush and all four Democratic appointees voting in favor of Gore, the public was furious and the media complained about the role the U.S. Supreme Court played in the "stolen election."

This case demonstrates two important factors when dealing with the courts. First, no outcome in this case could have satisfied everyone—it was politically charged and on the forefront of every news channel in America as well as many of those in other countries. Regardless of our beliefs, we must recognize that the U.S. Supreme Court does not exist solely to make people happy; it exists to apply our legal principles to problems and to find legally responsible solutions to those problems. The second factor illustrated by this case is the important role of impartiality in justice. Regardless of whether politics played a role in this case, many members of the public felt it did. These individuals felt that the justices had not been impartial, and that they let their personal beliefs interfere with justice. Had all nine justices recused themselves based on personal connections or beliefs, as some individuals called for, however, no one would have been left to hear the case.

The third canon says that judges must avoid doing things that could bias them or create an appearance of bias. For this reason, they tend to avoid joining citizens groups, such as the NRA (National Rifle Association). They also avoid rallies, even for issues they support. Can you imagine having a drunk-driving case heard by a judge who is a vocal leader in MADD (Mothers Against Drunk Driving)? Unfortunately, avoiding potentially biasing actions also isolates judges from their friends and communities. Those who had prior legal careers find that they must discontinue close friendships with former colleagues lest they appear to be inappropriate (Morgenstern, 1994, p. 60). Sometimes, maintaining friendships with lawyers can get judges into hot water. Every year, several California judges are formally disciplined with advisory letters when it becomes known that they had social relationships with attorneys in their courts (e.g., Panel tells of judges', 1998). Judges who were former prosecutors, which is a popular path to take toward judgeships, must sever ties with law enforcement officials with whom they may have become friends. See Box 7.7 for one judge's view of the isolation being a new judge caused her; she had to break ties with former work associates and experienced problems with other acquaintances who were not certain how to treat her once she became a judge.

Once elected or appointed, judges often feel obligated to resign from board positions with such agencies as the YMCA and March of Dimes (Morgenstern, 1994, p. 61). When judges do not discontinue these activities, they may be accused of being biased on the bench. A recent appointment to Massachusetts' Supreme Court is illustrative; some citizen's groups had opposed one candidate's elevation to the court because she had once served on the board of trustees for an abortion clinic, and they felt she could not be impartial if she were asked to rule on an abortion case (McMillan, 1999). Judges also risk formal sanctions from ethics commissions if membership in a group "would cast doubt on their impartiality" (e.g., Egelko, 1995). In the end, the canon that judges have to avoid activities that could bias them often contributes to isolation that is overwhelming and contributes to judicial burnout.

## BOX 7.7

## One View of the Isolation
## Caused by Becoming a New Judge

The following interview excerpts with a judge who was recently appointed to a judgeship shows a few of the differences she saw between her career as a prosecutor and her new career as a judge. The greatest differences were that she could no longer socialize with other members of the criminal justice system and had to cope with the public's newfound view of her as a dignitary who inspired awe, rather than as the everyday person she strove to be.

JUDGE: It is funny because being a judge is so isolated.

*Is it more isolated than being a prosecutor?*

JUDGE: Oh, prosecutor or any of that. I had a gay old time; I would have police officers come in and we'd eat stuff from Taco Bell, or if we were doing a search warrant, we would order out for a pizza; we would sit there with everybody involved and we would talk about what we were going to do, how we were going to do it. I had defense counsel coming in saying "Oh, hey, someone bought some pie." We'd sit down and have some pie and discuss a case. I had victims come in even though their cases were closed. They'd come in and just to talk to me, just to have someone listen to them. I had a lot of kids that I took through court that would come in and tell me that they were doing okay, that they were doing fine. Oh gosh, just—I had all kinds of people. . . . I never told anyone, "I'm too busy, I'm sorry I can't talk to you." When people would come [and ask if I was busy, I would invite them into my office].

*How has that changed now?*

JUDGE: I don't have anybody [coming] back here [to her judicial chambers], it's really lonely. I compare myself to the Maytag repair man. I don't know the way people perceive you as a judge. People say, "So, what do we call you?" I say "I have never had my name changed or anything. The title that I have is just a new job that's from 8 to 5, that is just my job." But it carries beyond that, it's like, "Oh my gosh, you are a judge!" I went to a wedding recently, and they needed some people to help finish cooking and things like that. I am not one to stand there and watch people have a hard time, so I washed my hands, started cooking, started helping here and there, wherever I was needed. I did it because that is how I was taught. Someone looked at me and said, "Oh my gosh, that's a judge!" They were saying "Judge, that's all right." I said, "No, 'Judge' isn't my name, my name is [———]." I said, "Judge—I do that 8 to 5 Monday through Friday. I am on emergencies if someone needs something done right away, but if I'm not working, if it is after hours, and I am not doing an emergency case, this is what I do, this is how I handle things."

*Source:* Personal interview conducted by author, 1999.

Fourth, judges must not make comments on litigation before them. Even if they have strong opinions about a case, they are not allowed to grant interviews. They are also expected to keep details of cases confidential from their families and friends. Not making comments prevents the media and others from characterizing judges as biased. Consider the case of a New Jersey judge who was banned by his state's supreme court from serving as an unpaid commentator for *Court TV* and *Rivera Live;* the court reasoned that his appearances violated a state rule that bars judges from commenting on any case, even those in other jurisdictions: "By prohibiting judges from commenting on pending cases in any court, we avoid the possibility of undue influence on the judicial process and the threat to public confidence posed by a judge from one jurisdiction criticizing the rulings or technique of a judge from a different jurisdiction" (Curran, 1997).

Finally, judges must not allow themselves to be influenced by ex parte communications (i.e., communications from noncourt personnel). Generally, judges refuse to discuss their cases and try to avoid contact with those who might try to sway their opinions. The extent to which the courts may strive to protect judges from ex parte communications may sometimes appear excessive. When the Navajo Nation Supreme Court (many Native American tribes, including the Navajo Nation, have their own independent court systems) was invited to argue a case in 1999 at Harvard University, for example, a Harvard staffer stood outside the door when the chief justice used the restroom to prevent anyone from approaching him during that private moment. This was not only to provide him with additional privacy; the staffer was also to prevent potentially biasing contact from taking place.

## DEALING WITH CORRUPT OR INCOMPETENT JUDGES

As mentioned earlier, judicial corruption is infrequently reported. Despite its rarity, judges do commit crimes or become incompetent while in office. The question then becomes how to deal with those individuals.

Federal judges who are found to be corrupt can be removed by the Senate following impeachment by the House of Representatives. The process is similar to that experienced by President Bill Clinton following the Monica Lewinsky scandal. As detailed in the U.S. Constitution, a two-thirds vote by the Senate removes the judge from office. As we learned in the Clinton-Lewinsky scandal, impeachment is not an actual conviction. Instead, it is more like a grand jury indictment. Therefore, impeached judges must be tried for their crimes if they are to be punished beyond losing their judicial positions.

State judges can also be removed from office by impeachment, but that is not the only method of removal available. The most common method of removal is failure to re-elect the judge. Judges who invoke enough public condemnation can also be subject to a recall election, such as what some citizens tried to do to the judge who granted to O.J. Simpson custody of his children. To hold a recall election, enough signatures must be obtained on petitions asking for the procedure. The investigations branch of any state's judiciary can also suspend or remove judges for violating certain rules and laws. State legislatures, relying on processes outlined in their respective state constitutions, can remove judges from office, but this is rarely used; the Washington State legislature, for example, has attempted to remove only two judges since Washington became the forty-second state in 1889 (Stone, 1999). Finally, the court where the judge served can be eliminated, but this is extremely rare.

Incompetent judges are sometimes removed by their respective judicial branches, usually on the suggestion of a judicial council or fitness commission (discussed below) or some other decision-making committee. Judges who are incapacitated by illness or other means, for example, cannot serve as judges and may be asked to take a leave (e.g., disability leave) or retire early. Judges can be denied new cases if they refuse to obey orders to step down.

## Judicial Fitness Commissions and Their Role in Policing Judges

One important force in the supervision of judges was the creation of judicial fitness commission, known by various names (e.g., Commissions on Judicial Conduct, Commission on Judicial Performance, and other names). These commissions are legislatively created panels of lawyers, judges, and citizens who hear cases of suspected judicial misconduct and decide how to deal with the cases. The commission in New York, for example, was created through an amendment to the state constitution.

The first permanent judicial fitness commission was established in California in 1960, and by 1981, all fifty states and the District of Columbia had commissions (Lubet, 1998, p. 60). Although commissions differ in their "structure, composition, and procedure," their general purpose and processes are similar (Lubet, 1998, p. 60).

A judicial fitness commission is able to consider a range of reactions to complaints after conducting an investigation. It may privately reprimand a judge, by sending him or her a letter, sometimes ordering the judge to change his or her conduct. It may also publicly reprimand or censure an offending judge. In serious cases, a commission could suspend or dismiss a judge. Judges who are under investigation by a fitness commission are entitled to counsel, and some attorneys specialize in the field of judicial and lawyer misconduct proceedings.

Federal judges are supervised by Circuit Judicial Councils, but the councils are not as powerful as state fitness commissions due to the guarantee of lifetime positions for federal judges during good behavior. Circuit Judicial Councils may dismiss complaints, privately reprimand a judge, publicly censure a judge, order that no new cases be assigned to the judge for a specified period of time, or ask the offending judge to retire. In the case of suspected disabilities that would impair one's ability to serve as judge, the council may certify that a disability exists so the judge will be forced to retire.

Misconduct includes such things as accepting bribes, using one's judicial office to benefit friends or family, violating judicial canons of ethics, and other abuses of power. In those states that have adopted the Model Code of Judicial Conduct (which nearly every state has done), judges may be investigated for engaging in any action that "demeans" the judicial office (Canon 4A); writing or speaking publicly (Canon 4B); engaging in "government, civic, or charitable activities" that do not directly concern the law (Canon 4C); becoming involved in business or other financial ventures with attorneys or others who might come before the court on which the judge serves (Canon 4D); and many other actions that are obviously grey areas that might be difficult to police.

Misconduct does not, or at least should not, include making unpopular or incorrect rulings (unless the ruling resulted from bribery or other abuse of the office). Simply making bad decisions should not be enough to get a judge sanctioned. One of the hallmarks of American justice is the value we place on judicial independence; this is why federal judges are appointed for life. Some scholars argue that fitness commissions may overstep their bounds and try to intimidate judges whose views or rulings are unpopular (e.g., Lubet, 1998). When this happens, judicial independence is negatively affected.

## SOME EVERYDAY WORRIES OF TRIAL COURT JUDGES

Like other members of the courtroom work group, judges worry about legal and nonlegal issues in their lives. Much of their concerns deal with the day-to-day running of their courtroom. Judges are expected to clear their calendars of cases, and sometimes crushing caseloads interfere with their ability to easily accomplish that task. Lower court judges may have caseloads of several hundred cases per day, and they feel this affects their ability to effectively deal with defendants in a just manner. One judge complained: "I've got 3.8 seconds per personal encounter" (personal interview). Another judge said that his "personal record" was 400 cases in one day, which made him question his ability to do his job: "The nature of the judiciary has changed where we're less judges and more case processors" (personal interview). The caseload pressures are not limited to lower courts nor are they new; one felony court judge wondered in the 1960s: "Did John Marshall or Oliver Wendell Holmes ever have to clear a calendar like mine?" (Blumberg, 1967, p. 123).

Other judges worry about pressures put on them by their local and state legislatures. Mandatory sentences, for example, have attracted a lot of condemnation from judges who feel that discretion is important in their ability to dispense justice in their courtrooms: "Once you start doing mandatory minimum sentences, politics gets involved in it too much rather than justice and fairness, in my opinion. If you want to have mandatory sentences in everything, why need a judge? Just have a computer up there and when the guy is charged guilty, just punch the computer and it will pop up the sentence for it" (personal interview). Other judges worry about the pressures to extract money to support state projects from defendants who are otherwise "good" people: "I don't personally feel that I am under any obligation whatsoever to balance the budget on the backs of people like that coming into court. And I won't do it" (personal interview). As demonstrated by these quotes and research by others, judges often resent infringement on their discretion and particularly dislike mandatory minimums that they feel are unjust (e.g., Forer, 1994; Peyser and Foote, 1994; Mandatory minimums, 2000).

Like other individuals, judges have their pet peeves. Some dislike certain types of cases. One judge detested drunk-driving (DUI) cases, so she used the courtroom network to her advantage by starting a rumor that her daughter had been killed by a drunk driver; whenever she was assigned a drunk-driving case, the defense attorneys would do everything in their power to get the case switched to another judge (personal interview).[7] Other judges worry about cases that are emotionally difficult to deal with. A number of the judges interviewed by one of the authors mentioned their dislike for child abuse cases: "I'll tell you which ones I like the least—child abuse and child molestation cases. Those really hit close to home and emotionally because I have . . . kids of my own. . . . I'm too emotionally involved in those cases and I try to avoid those if I can" (personal interview). Real or imagined, these dislikes and others like them may have important effects on the justice doled out in courtrooms across the country. Some judges work around mandatory sentences through creative means, but this does not always work or sometimes attracts the attention of the legislature, which promptly closes the utilized loopholes (e.g., Meyer and Jesilow, 1997).

Some judges worry about defendants lying in court, which will be discussed further in Step 14, as it is a factor that may be used to enhance sentences. As was discussed earlier in this chapter, some judges worry about maintaining friendships and appearing impartial. Other judges worry about being reversed on appeal. A few worry whether they are doing what is right in their courtrooms. These are real concerns for judges and their presence can contribute to judicial burnout.

# CONCLUSION

In this chapter, we learned about judicial responsibilities and the many roles judges play in the justice drama from arrest to appeal by signing warrants, assigning bail, presiding over preliminary and pre-trial hearings, accepting plea bargains, overseeing jury selection, presiding over trials and ruling on objections, imposing sentences, and hearing appeals. We also examined briefly the demographic characteristics shared by judges and how they might affect justice. We looked at the increasing role played by women and minority judges and the pre-judicial education received by those who hear our disputes and settle our differences. Then, we turned our attention to the methods of selecting judges and the pros and cons of those methods. Finally, we explored judicial discretion and how it is shaped by the canons of judicial conduct. See Box 7.8 for some concluding observations on judges, written by students.

The next chapter will describe the roles played by other key players in the courtroom drama, such as defendants, victims, witnesses, bailiffs, clerks, jurors, bail bondsagents, translators, victim-witness assistants, spectators, and court-watchers. You will learn how these individuals are viewed by the criminal justice system and how they are important in shaping the face of justice.

---

### BOX 7.8
### Some Student Observations Regarding Judges

Anne S. (1997) noted that one judge, in addition to explaining the adversarial system to defendants, also seemed to encourage defendants to plead guilty:

> When the judge entered the courtroom, the first thing he did was set down his "ground rules." He stated that everyone was presumed innocent and that it was the job of the state to prove beyond a reasonable doubt that the defendant was guilty. He said that plea bargaining was permitted and also if anyone was not satisfied with the decision of the court that that person had twenty days to appeal the decision. The judge believed that "silence is golden" and anyone who thought that this rule did not apply to them would be "dealt with in the proper manner." Finally, he said that those who plan to plead guilty would be given preference and those cases would be handled first because those who plead guilty are people who "acknowledge their responsibility."

Herbert Nix III (1997) was surprised that a judge admitted in open court that jail overcrowding affected the sentences he imposed:

> XX is the next defendant to come forward. In this case, the defendant, who is in his mid-forties, has pled guilty to [threatening to hurt another person]. XX has no prior convictions. The judge sentenced the defendant to four years' probation. The judge said that threats should not be taken lightly, but unfortunately because of the over-crowdedness in the criminal justice system, his hands are tied and he was unable to impose the preferred sentence.

Stacy Walter (1999) noted that judges can get angry with defendants who act out of line or have bad days, both of which can spell trouble for defendants appearing before them:

> In comes the judge. All rise! Judge T takes his position overlooking the crowd from the bench. He looks to be in a good mood tonight. I have witnessed Judge T before

*(continued)*

and if he has had a bad day, I guarantee you will have a throat clenching evening. Opening [announcements] were made. No cell phones, beepers, stereo/radio equipment, and most importantly, no whiny children. It is a courtroom not a nursery. . . . The second case was another DUI charge. . . . [the defendant] talks back to the judge. How stupid can this guy be? Judge T threatens to send him to jail if he does not shut up. . . . After these two cases Judge T is perturbed, because he lashes out at the people coming in and out of the courtroom doors. Silence fell over the courtroom. . . . [Another defendant] leaves the courtroom and slams the door. Judge T sends an officer to go get her and bring her back into the courtroom. She comes back into the courtroom and the judge asks her why she slammed the door and she replies, "I didn't know the door was that light." Judge T tells her to respect others, and she is dismissed from the courtroom.

N.P. Rainey (1997) observed a judge socializing defendants to let their attorneys speak for them rather than bogging down proceedings by trying to speak themselves:

The judge recommends that if the defendant has an attorney that they let the attorney speak for them.

# DISCUSSION QUESTIONS

1. What do you feel is the most important of the roles fulfilled by judges? Could others in the justice system fulfill any of the other roles? Why are these roles assigned to judges?

2. Scan your local newspaper for stories that discuss decisions or actions by judges. Classify the actions based on the decision points at which judges are involved.

3. Do you feel that drug courts and community programs are a good investment? Do you feel that the roles filled by judges for these two programs could be fulfilled by others in the justice system? How does the "air of the judicial office" help these programs function?

4. Contact your local courts or find their Web page. How do the judges in your community "look" demographically? Are they similar to the demographic picture presented in this chapter? If they differ, why do you think that is true?

5. Why might female and minority judges be more "gender- and colorblind" than their male and white counterparts? Consider the research discussed that suggested that female judges and male judges might approach cases differently. Why might this be?

6. Why is judicial diversity important? How might it influence public perceptions of courts, judges, and the legal process?

7. It is clear from the table in Box 7.4 that merit selection is used far less often to choose trial court judges than it is with appellate court judges. Why do you think this is true?

8. Why is judicial independence important? How might each of the methods by which judges are selected help preserve or compromise judicial independence?

9. Consider the situation in those states where judicial hopefuls must come up with significant sums of money in order to qualify for selection as a judge. How might these financial requirements screen out good potential judges? How might such requirements threaten judicial independence?

10. How much does the public really know about the selection and training of judges? Were you surprised to learn that some judges may never have been in a courtroom prior to taking the bench? What kinds of training do you believe that judges should have before taking the bench?

11. How could judicial fitness commissions play a more active role in policing judges? Is this a good idea? What are the pros and cons of a process that more closely monitors judges?

## NOTES

1. Of the 11 percent of felons who were convicted in 1994 after a trial (the remaining 89 percent plead guilty), the proportion of jury (52 percent) and bench (48 percent) were roughly equal (*adapted from* Langan and Brown, 1997:8, Table 9). Many of those jury trials were for violent offenses; 83 percent of the trials resulting in convictions for violent offenses were heard by juries. For all other categories of offenses (i.e., property, drug, weapons, and other), bench trials were more common.

2. The seven states that do not specifically require that judges be admitted to their state bars before assuming their judgeships are: Illinois, Indiana, Iowa, Massachusetts, Nevada, Oklahoma, and Wyoming. We counted as requiring admission to the state bar eight states that require prior legal practice in the state, but do not specify if that is as a member of the state bar: Alabama, Alaska, Arizona, Arkansas, Mississippi, Nebraska, Ohio, and Texas. In addition, the state of Tennessee requires only that judges in that state be "qualified to practice law."

3. Whereas most states do not require a law degree for all judges in their courts of limited jurisdiction, only six states do not have this requirement for their general jurisdiction court judges: Kansas (about one-third of state's District Court judges are "District Court Magistrates" and the Kansas Supreme Court may approve those who do not have law degrees for this position), Maine, Massachusetts, North Carolina (which does not mandate law degrees for "special judges" or those who were elected prior to 1981), Oklahoma (about one-third of the state's district court judges are "special judges" who need not have a legal education), South Dakota (about three-fourths of the full-time judges are lay magistrates or clerk/magistrates and do not necessarily possess a law degree; Rottman et al., 2000, pp. 50–56). In addition, the state of New Hampshire does not specify whether judges must possess a law degree for general jurisdiction judges, but requires them for lower court judges, leading one to believe law degrees are required for general jurisdiction judges in practice even if not by law.

4. When judicial positions are vacated before the expiration of the judges' terms, the governor (or other legislatively selected individual or group) temporarily appoints a judge to fill in until the next election. This process may impact the justice system as it allows some individuals to bypass the formal structure of judicial elections; even temporary appointees actually run as incumbents during the next election (which means they are more likely to win the election). In some jurisdictions, a special election can be called to fill judicial vacancies.

5. The controversial practice was the use of "stipulated reversals," in which parties, as part of a settlement, ask an appellate court to reverse a trial court decision rather than dismiss an appeal, thus allowing the original defendant to better defend himself or herself in expected future claims. If an appeal is dismissed, the original decision stands, which means the original defendant cannot relitigate the issues brought up in the case. If the decision is reversed, on the other hand, the legal reasoning that attributed blame for the tortious behavior in question is eliminated.

6. Some could argue that his ruling was intended to show that he was not "biased" toward tobacco. To avoid any accusations of impropriety, the judge could have recused himself from the case altogether.

7. Although one could argue that the judge's integrity should be questioned for attempting to manipulate her caseload through false rumors, she may actually have done the defendants a service by
helping them get their cases heard before judges who did not share her dislike for DUI cases.

# REFERENCES

*Argersinger v. Hamlin,* 407 U.S. 25 (1972).

Ashman, A. (1975). *Courts of Limited Jurisdiction: A National Survey.* Chicago: American Judicature Society.

Attorney defends O.J.'s custody. (1997, February 17). *Associated Press Wire.*

Bedlan, B. (1998, March 24). Board: Fire suspended Omaha judge. *Associated Press Wire.*

Berkson, L. (1982). Women on the bench: A brief history. *Judicature,* 65: 286–293.

Boland, B., and Sones, R. (1986). *The Prosecution of Felony Arrests, 1981.* Washington, DC:
National Institute of Justice.

Blumberg, A.S. (1967). *Criminal Justice.* Chicago: Quadrangle Books.

*Bradwell v. Illinois,* 83 U.S. 130 (1872).

Brandt, A.L. (1998, April 7). Judge resigns after drinking flap. *Associated Press Wire.*

*Bush v. Gore,* 531 U.S. 98 (2000).

California Constitution, art VI, sec. 15.

Cappell, C.L. (1990). The status of black lawyers. *Work and Occupations,* 17: 100–121.

Carbon, S. (1982). Women in the judiciary: An introduction. *Judicature,* 65: 285.

Carbon, S., Houlden, P., and Berkson, L. (1982). Women on the state bench: Their characteristics and
attitudes about judicial selection. *Judicature,* 65: 295–305.

Corneliussen, A. (1997, January 17). Implant judge may step down. *Associated Press Wire.*

Curran, J. (1997, January 25). New Jersey judge fights TV ban. *Associated Press Wire.*

Davis, S., Haire, S., and Songer, D.R. (1993). Voting behavior and gender on the U.S. courts of
appeals. *Judicature,* 77: 129–133.

Dillon, S. (2000, January 30). Small-town Arizona judge amasses fortune, and indictment. *New York
Times Wire.*

Egelko, B. (1995, October 19). New ethics code for judges is shaping up: But panel drafting rules is
accused of secrecy. *San Diego Union Tribune,* p. A3.

Emmert, C., and Glick, H. (1987). Selection systems and judicial characteristics: The recruitment of
state supreme court judges. *Judicature,* 70: 228–235.

*Escobedo v. Illinois* 378 U.S. 478 (1964).

Feeley, M.M. (1979). *The Process Is the Punishment: Handling Cases in a Lower Criminal Court.*
New York: Russell Sage Foundation.

Feinblatt, J., and Berman, G. (2001). *Responding to the Community: Principles for Planning and
Creating a Community Court.* Washington, DC: Bureau of Justice Statistics.

Ferrick, T. (1999, January 31). The high cost of judgeships. *Philadelphia Inquirer.*

Flango, V.E., and Ducat, C. (1979). What differences does method of judicial selection make? Selection procedures in state courts of last resort. *Justice System Journal,* 5: 25–44.

Forer, L.G. (1994). *A Rage to Punish: The Unintended Consequences of Mandatory Sentencing.* New
York: Norton.

Fried, J.P. (1997, May 15). Judge recuses himself from Gigante mob case. *New York Times*.

Gebelein, R.S. (2000). *The Rebirth of Rehabilitation: Promise and Perils of Drug Courts*. Washington, DC: National Institute of Justice.

*Gideon v. Wainwright*, 372 U.S. 335 (1963).

Gilligan, C. (1982). *In a Different Voice: Psychological Theory and Women's Development*. Cambridge: Harvard University Press.

Glick, H., and Emmert, C. (1986). Stability and change: Characteristics of state supreme court judges. *Judicature*, 70: 107–112.

Graham, B.L. (1990). Judicial recruitment and racial diversity on state courts: An overview. *Judicature*, 74(1): 28–34.

Gruhl, J., Spohn, C., and Welch, S. (1981). Women as policymakers: The case of trial judges. *American Journal of Political Science*, 25: 308–322.

Holmes, M.D., Hosch, H.M., Daudistel, H.C., Perez, D.A., and Graves, J.B. (1993). Judges' ethnicity and minority sentencing: Evidence concerning Hispanics. *Social Science Quarterly*, 74: 496–506.

Judge removed for anti-woman remark. (1997, June 10). *Associated Press Wire*.

King, J. (1989, April 5). Spill tanker captain held on one million dollars bail. *Reuters Wire*.

Langan, P.A., and Brown, J.M. (1997). *Felony Sentences in State Courts, 1994*. Washington, DC: National Institute of Justice.

Levin, M.A. (1977). *Urban Politics and Criminal Courts*. Chicago: University of Chicago Press.

Lubet, S. (1998). Judicial discipline and judicial independence. *Law and Contemporary Problems*, 61: 59–74.

Mandatory minimums in drug sentencing: A valuable weapon in the war on drugs or a handcuff on judicial discretion? (2000). *American Criminal Law Review*, 36: 1279–1300.

Martin, E. (1982). Women on the federal bench: a comparative profile. *Judicature*, 65: 306–313.

Martin, E. (1990). Men and women on the bench: Vive la difference? *Judicature*, 77: 204–208.

Martin, E. (1993). The representative role of women judges. *Judicature*, 77: 166–73.

McMillan, J. (1999, October 13). Woman named Mass. chief justice. *Associated Press Wire*.

McQuiston, J.T. (1996, October 16). N.Y. court upholds judge's dismissal. *New York Times Wire*.

Meyer, J.F., and Jesilow, P. (1997). *'Doing Justice' in the People's Court: Sentencing by Municipal Court Judges*. New York: State University of New York Press.

*Miranda v. Arizona* 384 U.S. 436 (1966).

Morgenstern, B.L. (1994, July). An uncomfortable distance. *ABA Journal*: 60–61.

Myers, M.A., and Talarico, S.M. (1988). *The Social Contexts of Criminal Sentencing*. New York: Springer/Verlag.

New York criminal court judge faces removal. (1996, February 16). *Washington Times Wire*.

Ofgang, K. (1999, August 20). CJP formally dismisses misconduct charges against Court of Appeal Presiding Justice J. Anthony Kline. *Metropolitan News-Enterprise*, p. 1.

Panel tells of judges' misdoings: 58 in California disciplined last year. (1998, April 14). *San Diego Union Tribune*, p. A3.

Peyser, M., and Foote, D. (1994, August 29). Strike three, you're not out. *Newsweek*, p. 53.

Reeves, J. (1997, September 17). Alabama suspends blind judge. *Associated Press Wire*.

Rottman, D.B., Flango, C.R., and Lockley, R.S. (1995). *State Court Organization 1993*. Washington, DC: National Institute of Justice.

Rottman, D.B., Flango, C.R., Cantrell, M.T., Hansen, R., and LaFountain, N. (2000). *State Court Organization, 1998.* Washington, DC: U.S. Department of Justice.

Smith, V. (1998, May 7). Ex-judge acquitted in civil case. *Associated Press Wire.*

Spohn, C. (1990). The sentencing decisions of black and white judges: Expected and unexpected similarities. *Law and Society Review,* 24: 1197–1216.

*State of Florida ex rel. Argersinger v. Hamlin,* 236 So. 2d 442 (1970).

Stone, G. (1999, November). External trends affecting the practice of law in Washington State: State legislative impacts. *Washington State Bar News,* pp. 37–40.

Thompson, E. (1997, April 26). FDA-Case judge had tobacco ties. *Associated Press Wire.*

Two ex-judges and lawyer guilty of tainting California court. (1996, October 20). *New York Times.*

U.S. Bureau of the Census, Census of the Population 1970. (1973). *Subject Reports: Occupational Characteristics.* Washington, DC: Government Printing Office.

U.S. Bureau of the Census, Census of the Population 1990. (1992). *Supplementary Reports: Detailed Occupation and Other Characteristics from the EEO File for the United States.* Washington, DC: Government Printing Office.

Vines, K. (1962). The selection of judges in Louisiana. *Tulane Studies in Political Science,* 8: 99–119.

Warrick, L. (1993). *Judicial Selection in the United States: A Compendium of Provisions* (2nd ed.). Chicago: The American Judicature Society.

Welch, S., Coombs, M., and Gruhl, J. (1988). Do black judges make a difference? *American Journal of Political Science,* 32: 126–136.

Wheaton, E. (1997). *Myra Bradwell: First Woman Lawyer.* Greensboro, NC: Morgan Reynolds.

Wice, P.B. (1985). *Chaos in the Courthouse: The Inner Workings of the Urban Criminal Courts.* New York: Praeger.

# Step 8

# Jurors and Other Key Participants in the Courtroom Play Their Roles

Imagine a job description that looks something like this:

**Wanted:** People needed to play a crucial role in the legal system. You will be responsible for jointly deciding issues of critical importance, perhaps even life or death significance. No prior knowledge of the legal system or how to make important decisions is required; in fact, the less knowledge of the legal system you have, the better. Depending upon the assignment you receive, the position may require you to sit through weeks, months, or (in rare instances) even years of testimony, and to remember what you hear and see without taking any notes. You must also be able to follow legal instructions to the letter, even when you are not sure what they mean.

*Potential job benefits:* An inside look at the workings of your legal system, and a feeling of pride and satisfaction in your work; the opportunity to participate meaningfully in the business of government.

*Potential job side effects:* You might be left wondering whether you made the correct decision; you may experience physical and emotional symptoms of stress; and your decisions may be strongly criticized by a number of people who are highly interested in the work that you perform.

*Eligibility criteria:* U.S. citizen at least eighteen years of age who can speak and understand English, who has never been convicted of a felony. You must be able to make decisions in a fair and impartial way. You must be available for the position during weekday business hours for an indefinite period of time (the average time for each assignment is three days; but occasionally assignments of several months or even years occur).

*Pay:* Depending on your state, you will be paid from $5.00 to $40.00 per day. You will not be paid for your first day of service, and you will not be reimbursed for any expenses you incur in connection with this work. However, in some instances, free bus passes may be available.

*Job Title:* Juror.

Now imagine that instead of applying for this job, you receive a notice in the mail that your local court is summoning you for jury duty. The notice gives none of the information that the "job description" above provided; but this is indeed a job and it is not optional—it's mandatory. In fact, if you toss that jury summons, you are committing a misdemeanor. Depending upon the policies and resources in your county, you could find yourself in jail for not showing up for jury duty.

If you are like many people, your reaction to receiving a jury summons in the mail may be "I don't have time for this!" (see Box 8.1 for one juror's lament about jury duty). Yet while the job of a juror is often quite demanding and underappreciated, it is critically important. Jurors play a central role in our legal system, and as such they are key participants in the courtroom process. This chapter will describe the role of jurors and briefly discuss the roles of other participants in the courtroom process.

---

## BOX 8.1

## A Bird's-Eye View from the Jury Impaneling Room

The following timeline, kept by a woman who was asked to show up for jury duty, illustrates why citizens are sometimes disappointed when notices for jury duty appear in their mailboxes. As you read her account, think about ways the courts could make her "duty" less onerous.

Monday, January, 24, 2000

| | |
|---|---|
| 8:30 A.M.: | Sit down in jury impaneling room. |
| 8:45 A.M.: | Judge M starts talking to us, telling us what to expect of our day, and telling us how happy he is that we "chose" to be there. |
| 9:00 A.M.: | District Clerk Billy X starts talking to us, telling us what to expect of our day and how happy he is that we "chose" to be there, tells jokes, some that he's obviously gotten off the Internet. Note to self: Send Billy some new jokes. |
| 9:40 A.M.: | Note to self: Don't drink that second cup of coffee tomorrow morning. |
| 10:00 A.M.: | District Clerk assigns us to courtrooms. I don't have to be in the courtroom until 1:30 P.M. |
| 10:25 A.M.: | Leave courthouse and drive across town to get home. Have lunch while I'm home, pick up the house, clean up the kitchen. |
| 1:30 P.M.: | Arrive back in courtroom, find assigned (by juror number) seat. Pass juror information card to my right, placing my juror information card on top of stack as per bailiff's instructions. |
| 1:33 P.M.: | Go stand outside in the hall and wait as per bailiff's instructions. |
| 2:05 P.M.: | Note to self: Bring a better book to read tomorrow. |
| 2:13 P.M.: | Forty minutes after sending us to wait in the hall, bailiff comes out and asks us to please wait ten more minutes. |
| 2:24 P.M.: | Fifty four minutes after arriving back at courthouse at 1:30 P.M., called back into courtroom, seated in assigned seats. Handed juror information card and told that in the previous fifty minutes all ten cases on the Judge docket were cleared (they either plea-bargained or pled guilty) and we can go home for the day. But we have to be back at 8:30 A.M. tomorrow morning to do this all over again. |

Total intake for the day: $6.00 and a headache. Don't get me wrong, I'm not so much complaining about the jury system, but they just don't seem to understand why no one looks forward to jury duty.

Approximately 1,800 jurors were called today; approximately 1,100 showed up, however many of them were late because they could not find parking places because there are only about 850 parking spaces in the county courthouse parking lot. The courthouse is in the middle of downtown and with all the other people going downtown to work, it created a minor traffic jam at the corner of the courthouse with nowhere for these people to go. Then, when they did get inside the courthouse (an hour and half late) into the jury impaneling room, there was nowhere for them to sit; it was standing room only because the room only holds 1,000 people. I'm still wondering what would have come of it if the Fire Marshall had been there. Would he have ticketed the county for exceeding the occupancy limit in the jury impaneling room?

And no one understands why people don't want to go to jury duty. Summon me to a building under the penalty of a $100 fine (or in some cases jail time) if I don't show up, don't give me any place to park and nowhere to sit for the day, and I'll "volunteer" for it every time (Ener, 2000).

## JURORS: KEY PLAYERS IN THE COURTROOM

Jurors are key participants in the criminal justice system even though most cases are plea-bargained before trial because most cases are plea-bargained "in the shadow of the jury," with great concern for what a jury might think if the case did come to trial. Prosecutors' decisions about whether or not to pursue a case are often based on assessments of how jurors would respond. For this reason, the influence of the jury system extends far beyond the actual verdicts rendered in courtrooms.

As we'll see in the chapter on trials, jury selection and the jury's decision-making processes are major phases in the trial process. But before discussing those, this chapter takes a look at the role that jurors are expected to play in court.

## JUROR: A MULTIPURPOSE ROLE

The opportunity for ordinary folks to participate in the legal process as jurors is one of the key aspects of a democratic government in its most basic form. But why should we have juries composed of ordinary citizens, especially when so many people do not want to take the time to serve as jurors? The answers lie in looking at the role that jurors play in our legal system.

Juries in colonial America were intended to be a bulwark against government oppression of citizens, especially citizens whose political activities displeased the government. This central role for juries continues today.

American jurors have always been the **"triers of fact"** at trial. Historically, jurors in America were empowered to decide both the law and the facts in a given case. In contrast, modern-day jurors are restricted to deciding only the facts in a case, while judges determine the law. Was the defendant near the area at the time of the crime? Does the evidence put the defendant at the scene? Did the accused have a motive for the offense? An opportunity to commit the crime? How does the defense's portrayal of events compare to the prosecution's?

But jurors are not simply fact finders. If this were the only function of juries, why not use professional fact finders with expertise in investigation, or professionals known for logical thinking or specialized knowledge (for example, blue ribbon juries in complex technical cases)? The use of laypeople instead of fact-finding professionals illustrates the highly political and symbolic aspects of the role that jurors play.

Indeed, the framers of the Constitution considered **trial by a jury of peers** (members of the defendant's community) to be an important constitutional right because of the unique status of jurors as legal amateurs rather than hired officials. A critical facet of the role that jurors play in the court system is serving as "the conscience of the community," bringing community values and beliefs to bear on the process of justice. This provides yet another protection against government oppression insofar as citizens serving as jurors can send a message about the law and the way it is applied. Thus, for example, jurors in Michigan acquitted Dr. Jack Kevorkian on charges of assisted suicide in four separate trials, although he was later convicted of murder after he videotaped an assisted suicide and his own participation in the event (Silverglate, 1999).

## COURTROOM PARTICIPANTS: OTHER KEY ROLES IN THE COURTROOM

### The Defendant

Consider the possibility that you might become a defendant in a criminal or civil case. "No way," you say, "I have done nothing wrong!" Yes, quite true. But that does not mean that you cannot be suspected, charged, and tried for a crime, or sued civilly. The key legal concept that a suspect must be considered "innocent until proven guilty" is actually an explicit reminder that innocent people can and do become defendants—and that erroneous convictions of innocent people can occur (Radelet, Bedau, and Putnam, 1992; Connors et al., 1996). Circumstances or prejudices can create the appearance of guilt, and due process protections may be insufficient to protect someone accused of a crime. In some circumstances, simply having been accused can lead some people to assume that "where there's smoke, there's fire" (Willis, 1992). This is the major challenge that people accused of a crime must battle.

What are the typical characteristics of defendants? That depends upon what type of offense one considers. For "white-collar crimes," depending upon what types of offenses are included in this definition, the typical individual defendant is usually a white, middle-aged, middle-class male (Daly, 1989). But corporations can be defendants in white-collar crime cases as well (see Box 8.2), so describing the "typical" white-collar crime defendant must take this into account. For "street crimes," defendants are typically young, male, and disproportionately likely to be ethnic minorities.

Let's break down this profile by its components. Statistically, defendants are more likely to be from the fifteen to twenty-five age group than any other age group (Uniform Crime Reports, 1994, p. 227). Research shows that offenses drop significantly after age thirty (Steffensmeier and Harer, 1991); many possible reasons have been put forth as potential explanations for this, including the possibility that offenders may simply "mature out of crime," or may find better access to legitimate income-generating activities, or may feel more risk-averse as they grow older, start families, and form stronger ties to the community.

The vast majority of street crime defendants are male, especially in the cases of violent crime (Bureau of Justice Statistics, 2001). While the percentage of females who are charged with a crime has increased relative to both their numbers in the past and to the number of males charged with crimes, increasing gender equality has not brought a large overall increase in female criminality, contrary to

---

## BOX 8.2

## Corporate Defendants

Can a corporation be found culpable for a criminal or civil offense? Not the people who created the corporation, or the people who are employed by it, but the corporation itself, as a legal entity? Yes, indeed. While you are an example of a "natural person" in the eyes of the law, a corporation can be considered a "legal person," and as such it can be charged with violating the law and held responsible. Of course, it's a bit difficult to sentence a corporation; imagine trying to send one to prison. But this legal concept of the corporation as defendant recognizes that in many instances, corporate crimes cannot be tied to any one particular person or group of people; perhaps the original people who set the crime in motion have long since left the company, or the organization's size and complexity masks the human agents behind the crimes. Corporate crimes often unfold over long periods of time and may reflect the actions of many people, making it very difficult to determine the degree to which individual offenders within the corporation may be culpable.

How does one sentence a corporation found guilty of a criminal offense when there are no "natural persons" charged with the crime? The most common sanction is to fine the corporation. The idea is to make the people responsible for conducting corporate business accountable for preventing future crimes. Furthermore, since a corporation is first and foremost a business, a large fine can directly affect a company's profitability and public image. However, the effectiveness of fines as a corporate sanction is a subject of continuing debate.

the expectations of some theorists (Donziger, 1996, p. 148). Why are defendants so much more likely to be male than female? This question raises a host of other questions and controversial issues, from the nature of gender and the relative influence of social and biological influences on behavior (the "nature versus nurture" question) to the question of whether females and males are equally likely to be defined and sanctioned as criminals.

Although the gender question is far from being conclusively answered, three things seem clear from research on crime, gender, and legal system responses: first, females can and do commit serious crimes, including violent crimes; second, notwithstanding this, males commit the vast majority of violent and nonviolent crimes; third, females are sometimes treated more leniently and sometimes treated more severely than males for their crimes, depending upon the nature of the crime, the historical era, and other factors. The "war on drugs" has resulted in disproportionate increases in the number of women incarcerated for relatively minor drug crimes in recent years (U.S. Department of Justice, 1994; Bloom, Chesney-Lind, and Owen, 1994). However, recent research shows that overall, women tend to be treated more leniently than men for their crimes (Bureau of Justice Statistics, 1994).

The fact that people from ethnic minorities are disproportionately likely to be represented among street crime defendants raises some very important questions. Does this reflect a difference in actual rates of offending; a difference in rates of arrest, prosecution, and conviction; or a combination of both? If so, what are the possible reasons for such disparities? The evidence suggests that the answer varies with the type of offense. Young minority males are disproportionately likely, compared to their numbers in the general population, to be both perpetrators *and* victims of homicide (Pallone and Hennessy, 1999; Snyder and Sickmund, 1999, p. 54). For other crimes, much evidence suggests that differences in the commission of crime between ethnic groups do not explain the disproportionate representation of people of color as defendants. America's "war on drugs" has disproportionately affected minority people and minority communities, especially African Americans and Hispanics (Tonry, 1995). For example, African Americans represented 35 percent of defendants arrested for drugs, 55 percent of those convicted, and 74 percent of those sentenced to prison, despite the fact that they represented only 15 percent of illegal drug users (Mauer, 1992). In California, research shows that African Americans and Hispanics are significantly more likely to be subjected to arrests that are later "unfounded" due to lack of evidence than whites (Schmitt, 1991; Miller, 1996). Government research on drug interdiction efforts by the U.S. Customs Service reveals that use of racial profiling in searches of airline passengers was not only invasive of passengers' privacy, it was also ineffective (Watson, 2000). The following excerpt from the United States General Accounting Office report, which examined over 100,000 incidents of passenger searches at major U.S. airports, illustrates this:

Generally, searched passengers of particular races and gender were more likely than other passengers to be subjected to more intrusive types of personal searches (being strip-searched or x-rayed) after being subjected to frisks or patdowns. However, in some cases those types of passengers who were more likely to be subjected to more intrusive personal searches were not as likely to be found carrying contraband. Specifically, White men and women and Black women were more likely than Black men and Hispanic men and women to be strip-searched rather than patted down or frisked, but they were less likely to be found carrying contraband. The most pronounced difference occurred with Black women who were U.S. citizens. They were 9 times more likely than White women who were U.S. citizens to be x-rayed after being frisked or patted down in fiscal year 1998. But on the basis of x-ray results, Black women who were U.S. citizens were less than half as likely to be found carrying contraband as White women who were U.S. citizens (General Accounting Office, 2000, p. 2) Hispanic women . . . were 4 times as likely to be x-rayed as White women were, but they were about two thirds as likely to have contraband found during an x-ray. (GAO, 2000, p. 15).

Such findings suggest that the disproportionate representation of African Americans among drug defendants is a complex phenomenon requiring examination of factors that result in disparate treatment of African Americans (Harvard Law Review, 1988). What kinds of things could result in disparate treatment? Such factors could include individual discrimination by criminal justice system actors such as police, as well as "legitimate contextual factors" (Walker, Spohn, and DeLone, 2000), such as bail policies and visibility factors. For example, bail decisions favor middle-class rather than poor defendants. A greater percentage of African Americans and Hispanics (compared to other ethnic groups) are poor, so these groups are disproportionately affected by bail guidelines. Another example of this is provided by sentencing policies for crack versus powder cocaine use. Sentencing policy for crack versus powder cocaine has a disparate impact on African American dealers; despite research showing that roughly the same percentage of people from both ethnic groups use cocaine. Why the disparity? Research also shows that whites deal and use powder cocaine, while blacks deal and use crack cocaine. Therefore, federal sentencing guidelines that are much harsher on crimes involving crack cocaine (a mandatory five-year prison sentence for five grams of crack versus five hundred grams of powder) have disproportionately affected African Americans (Reiman, 2001, p. 130).

Box 8.3 provides more detail on the concepts of discrimination and disparity. The key point to keep in mind is that differences in treatment may or may not reflect individual bias, depending on the context. As one scholar notes, ". . . a racial disparity is not necessarily indicative of a racial discrimination. A disparity is often evidence of discrimination. But one must keep in mind that a racial disparity may stem from causes other than disparate treatment" (Kennedy, 1997, p. 9).

## White-Collar Defendants

The disproportionate impact of the "war on drugs" on poor and minority communities illustrates the fact that inequities in the criminal justice process reflect differences

## BOX 8.3

## Discrimination and Disparities in Treatment of Defendants

When considering reasons for disparities (that is, differences) in treatment of defendants by demographic characteristics, such as social class, ethnicity, and gender, it is important to be aware of the distinction between *individual* discrimination and *institutional* discrimination. Individual discrimination is what most people typically think of when they hear the word "discrimination." If a police officer, a prosecutor, a judge, or a juror treats someone differently (more harshly or more leniently) because of the person's ethnicity, gender, social class, sexual orientation, or other demographic characteristics, then this is an example of bias on the part of the individual. This bias may be consciously prejudiced; or it may be the result of unconscious stereotyping on the part of the individual: In other words, an individual may or may not realize they are acting in a biased manner.

For example, the phenomenon of the "self-fulfilling prophecy" can come into play. This is the idea that your observations reflect your expectations, and that this selective observation then serves to support your expectations. For example, if you are a shopkeeper who believes that teenagers are more likely to shoplift than people of other ages, then you are probably going to watch teens much more closely than other people when they enter your store. Of course, because you are closely monitoring teenagers, you are more likely to detect incidents of shoplifting by people in that age group, and correspondingly less likely to detect shoplifting by people in other age groups. Thus, your selective focus on teens means you catch them shoplifting more frequently than you catch senior citizens or middle-aged people who are shoplifting. Given this, your experiences will thus confirm your personal theory that when it comes to theft from your store, "teens are the problem." Thus even if most of the shoplifters in your store are *actually* people in their thirties, you won't discover that unless you change your observation strategies.

Similarly, some police officers' expectations that certain types of people (young men dressed in a certain way, for example) are more likely than others to be troublemakers may mean that police selectively focus more attention on them rather than others. Naturally, this means that police are more likely to spot illegal behavior by those "under the microscope," so to speak, than by others less closely watched. An illustration of this idea is provided by the words of the National Criminal Justice Commission, commenting on the war on drugs: "Police found more drugs in minority communities because that is where they looked for them. Had they pointed the drug war at college campuses, it is likely that our jails would now be filled overwhelmingly with university students" (Donziger, 1996, p. 115).

Institutional discrimination refers to the idea that the policies, practices, and customs of social institutions can be discriminatory in either intent or impact. For example, laws or policies prohibiting women from working as lawyers or correctional officers, or from serving as jurors, are an example of institutional discrimination that reflect discriminatory intent. That is, such laws or policies on their face reflect the intention to discriminate. On the other hand, some institutional policies or practices may have a discriminatory impact even when they are facially neutral. For example, recruitment policies specifying a height requirement for becoming a police officer have a disproportionate impact on women who would like to become officers. Although the policy is neutral with respect to gender, so that it screens out all applicants, whether male or female, who do not meet height requirements, given the fact that women on average are shorter than men, many more women will be screened out by such a policy in comparison to male applicants (this is the reason police departments have by and large lowered or eliminated height requirements).

So, do disparities in treatment reflect discrimination? The concept of contextual discrimination refers to the idea that discrimination in the criminal justice system is not systematic; rather, its occurrence, nature, and frequency depends upon the context. For example, some police departments are more likely to engage in racial profiling than others; some judges are more likely than others to be biased in sentencing. Thus, disparities might reflect individual or institutional discrimination, or some combination of both. Institutional policies, such as bail policy, discussed above, can have a disparate impact, which does not reflect discriminatory intent on the part of individual policymakers. In this case, contextual factors, such as whether a bail candidate has steady employment and ties to the community, may account for differences in treatment of defendants by social class and ethnicity. Therefore, the answer to the question of whether disparities reflect discrimination is "it depends"—on contextual factors.

in treatment by both ethnicity and social class. For example, much research has documented the fact that the criminal justice system focuses on "crime in the streets" rather than "crime in the suites"—that is, white-collar crime. The question of how to define white-collar crime is a lively controversy in the academic community, and different definitions of white-collar crime exist. However, the classic definition remains that of Edwin Sutherland, whose landmark work focused attention on the crimes committed by elite businesspeople. Sutherland defined white-collar crime as "crime committed by a person of respectability and high social status in the course of his occupation" (Sutherland, 1949, p. 9).

The legal system usually categorizes white-collar offenses as violations of civil rather than criminal law, and thus white-collar offenders are far less likely to face the possibility of incarceration than "street" criminals. In those cases where a white-collar offense is treated as a crime (instead of or in addition to being classified as a violation of civil law), the penalties prescribed for white-collar crime are far less severe than those for street crimes (Johnson, 1986; Hagan and Palloni, 1986). This disparity in treatment of white-collar and street crimes does *not* accurately reflect the toll exacted by white-collar crimes on society and individual victims. Far from being "just paper crimes," white-collar crimes are estimated to cost society significantly more than street crimes in economic costs alone (Conklin, 1977; Cullen, Maakestad, and Cavender, 1987; Levi, 1987). A recent government report estimated the costs of fraud and other economic crimes (which constitute only one category of a wide range of white-collar crimes) to be in the range of $40 *billion* annually (U.S. Department of Justice, 2000, p. 1).

White-collar crime also has equally significant (some would say more significant) actual or potential "secondary costs," such as the corrosion of public trust in government, business, and economic institutions (Moore and Mills, 1990) and higher costs of insurance, goods, and services (Shenk and Klaus, 1984). Contrary to common misconceptions, white-collar crime can and does involve physical harm, injury, and death; it is a myth that white-collar crime is nonviolent. For example, crimes involving unsafe workplaces, faulty consumer products, medical malpractice, and environmental crimes produce injuries, disease, and deaths on a broader scale than street crimes (Reiman, 2001, pp. 78–98).

## The Victim

The victim's participation in the legal process reflects the fact that they were thrust into a role they would never have chosen. It may seem odd to refer to the "role" of victims, as if victims somehow simply play an assigned part in the courtroom drama. Undoubtedly, the experience of being victimized can be a life-altering experience. In that sense, victimhood doesn't feel like a "role" in the conventional sense of the word. Indeed, the victim has no formal legal role in the criminal justice system (Walker, 2001).

Yet in another important way, the role of victim is a central one in the legal system. Victims must report crimes in order for the legal process to function. Whereas prosecutors represent society as a whole in their condemnation of the crime and the defendant, the harms suffered by individual victims (and those who care for them) are potent reminders of the gravity of the proceedings taking place in court. The victim's role helps turn abstract notions of "justice" and "harm" into concrete realities. A recent study by the Department of Justice estimated the cost of victimization at $450 billion (yes, billion) per year, and further calculated that 75 percent of this cost reflected harm to "quality of life" (Miller, Cohen, and Wiersma, 1996). Although this study was based on data from the National Crime Victimization Survey, this figure probably underestimates the costs of victimization for a variety of reasons. For one thing, it is difficult to accurately measure the length and scope of consequences, including physical and psychological harm, financial losses, and life changes such as the effect on the victim's relationships with other people. But statistics such as the one above become "humanized" when victims enter the courtroom. The victim's role is to personalize the otherwise bureaucratized, formal nature of the legal proceedings, serving as a reminder to all participants of the reasons why they are gathered in court.

In recent years, public attention to the experiences and opinions of crime victims has resulted in a vocal victims' rights movement. In response, the federal government and many state governments have passed legislation intended to give crime victims a greater voice in the criminal justice process (see Boxes 8.4 and 8.5 for more information). In 2000, the Violence Against Women Act (VAWA) was signed into law, providing $185 million each year from 2001 through 2005 for programs and services to prevent victimization and assist victims (National Center for Victims of Crime, 2001). This major piece of victims' rights legislation builds on provisions outlined in its predecessor, the 1994 VAWA. The new legislation is groundbreaking in the scope of violence that it addresses through providing authorization for the creation and funding of a wide array of programs designed to prevent victimization and provide services to victims, including (National Center for Victims of Crime, 2001):

- Programs to provide training for judges and other court personnel on domestic violence, stalking, sexual assault, and child abuse
- Programs to provide training for police, prosecutors, and judges on violence against people with disabilities
- Programs designed to address the problem of dating violence
- A directive to the U.S. Attorney General to help develop standardized guidelines for forensic exams in sexual assault cases
- Funding and assistance for the maintenance and development of shelters for battered women and their children
- Programs to assist law enforcement and victims deal with the crime of stalking
- Provision of funds to develop services to provide victims with assistance on related civil legal matters

People who are victimized may discover that others are unsure of how to act around them. Victims, particularly those whose experiences have left physical or emotional scars too visible to be ignored, may find other people responding to them primarily in terms of their status or role as a victim. They may find that they share the experience

---

## BOX 8.4
## Recent Victims' Rights Developments

States vary in the rights that people have as crime victims, but there are many specific examples of legislation aimed at acknowledging the victim's rights and role in the legal process. Some examples include:

- Legislation providing victim assistance funds to help victims deal with the aftermath of crime (e.g., funds for counseling or medical assistance or to replace damaged property).
- Victim notification provisions, whereby crime victims can receive notification when the person convicted of harming them is released from incarceration. With this information, victims can lobby parole boards to attempt to keep convicted criminals incarcerated.
- Legal rulings allowing victims and their advocates to make victim impact statements at sentencing hearings (and parole board hearings).
- Court-ordered restitution by offenders to victims.
- The opportunity to participate voluntarily in victim–offender mediation programs.

---

## BOX 8.5

## Resources for Victims

The National Center for Victims of Crime (NCVC) maintains a Web site with information, publications, and links for people interested in victims, victims' rights, and related issues. The toll-free number is 1-800-FYI-CALL. The NCVC Web site is www.ncvc.org.

At the state level, the attorney general's office for your state is usually a good source of information on legislation, policies, resources, and information related to victimization and victims' rights.

At the county and city level, police and prosecutors can provide information on services available to victims and legal policies relevant to victims in that particular jurisdiction.

Colleges and universities have a variety of campus resources, depending upon the institution's size and resources. Sources of information, help, and referrals on victimization issues include the campus police department; the campus health center/counseling center; the campus women's center (not all campuses, however, have such a center); and student organizations (on campuses where these exist) dedicated to raising awareness and providing information about violence and safety-related issues, such as sexual assault, drunk driving, and drug use.

---

of being defined in terms of "victimhood" with people who are victims of illness or accident; in both instances, the individual's misfortune may become a defining characteristic. If this occurs, people who have been victimized may find that this new "role" robs them of their individual identity to some degree.

People who have been victimized may respond to being labeled in a variety of ways. Sadly, some respond by avoiding contact with others in order to avoid the pain, discomfort, or embarrassment of others' reactions to their victim status. This may be especially likely if victims are blamed by others for their misfortunes to some degree (see Box 8.6). Unfortunately, societal reactions to victims are often colored by the nature of the relationship between the victim and attacker; for instance, were they

---

## BOX 8.6

## You Don't Always Get What You Deserve—or Deserve What You Get

Have you ever left something of value unattended in a public place? Perhaps you left your backpack on a table in the library for a few minutes while you made copies on the machine at the other end of the shelves. Perhaps you left your bicycle parked in front of the student union for just a minute while you ran in to buy a bottle of juice from the café. You may have forgotten your $90.00 biology textbook in your classroom after a particularly interesting discussion of photosynthesis; or perhaps you were reading outside at a table and accidentally left your book on the bench when you decided to leave. There was that camera you left on your beach towel when you and a group of friends decided to play volleyball a few yards away.

Hopefully, you've never had something stolen from you as a result of circumstances such as these. But if you have, then you know the feelings of regret and anger that being a victim of theft can create. You have been victimized by a crime. Someone, a thief, stole your property. Yes, your actions may have provided the opportunity for the thief to commit the crime, but the thief is the one who decided to commit the crime. Therefore, it doesn't matter if you left your backpack, forgot your book, or even left your living room window open on a sunny afternoon—and a thief spotted your new laptop computer sitting on the coffee table, came in, and stole it while you were out of the room. The point is, you are not to blame: The fact that your actions may have helped provide the thief with the opportunity to commit the crime does not mitigate the fact that the thief is the one who is responsible for the crime.

Unfortunately, however, victims sometimes find themselves blamed to some degree for their misfortunes by other people. Why? Surely people can recognize that poor judgment (such as leaving your belongings unattended or leaving the window wide open) is something that most of us have exhibited at some time or another—but that this doesn't mean we should be blamed when we are victimized. However, the pervasive practice of victim-blaming suggests people often add insult to injury by holding victims at least partially responsible for what happened to them. This may be the case even when it is clear that the victim's actions in no way provided an opportunity for the crime to occur; such as when women and girls assaulted by soldiers during war are shunned afterwards by some members of their communities. We are back to the question of "why?" Why blame the victims?

Part of the answer may lie in our need to try and make sense of the world, our need to believe that the world is a just, fair place where people get what they deserve—and where they deserve what happens to them (Lerner, 1980). In such a world, "good people" have good things happen; and "bad people" presumably reap the consequences of their behavior. In a fair and just world, then, being victimized by crime would only happen to people who somehow deserved such misfortune: that is, people "get what they deserve."

Whether such a world exists is a philosophical question, but whether people believe in such a world is a question social psychologists have examined. Their research shows that individuals vary in the degree of their need to believe in a just world (Lerner, 1980). For some people who have a high need to believe that the world is a just and fair place, it may be psychologically comforting to believe that crime victims "must have" done something to bring misfortune upon themselves. To think otherwise would suggest that the world is unfair and unjust, that bad things can happen to good people . . . in fact, it would suggest that bad things can happen to anyone, which is a scary thought. Thus, people with a high need to believe in a just world may search for explanations for crime in the behavior of victims in an attempt to make sense of the event in a way that is psychologically reassuring (Foley and Pigott, 2000; Hafer, 2000; Kleinke and Meyer, 1990). Nonetheless, whatever the reasons, too often victims are forced to cope with victim-blaming in the aftermath of a crime.

strangers, acquaintances, or intimates? Most violent crimes, however, are perpetrated by someone known to the victim, such as a family member, friend, neighbor, coworker, or acquaintance. More murder victims in the United States, for example, are killed by someone they know than by a stranger, although the number of homicides committed by intimates is decreasing (Fox and Zawitz, 2000, p. 2).

Victims may respond to their experiences in a variety of ways that are beyond the scope of this discussion to describe. For example, people who have suffered a crime may experience cognitive, emotional, and physical effects that last for years. However, one method of coping that appears to have become more frequent as society moves toward more open discussion of the experiences and needs of victims is to emphasize the victim's status as a survivor. In choosing to emphasize their strengths in the face of their ordeals, people who have been victimized can redefine their victimhood in the eyes of others. Emphasizing survivorship rather than victimization may potentially provide survivors with an improved sense of control over their lives, which is particularly critical for people who have experienced traumatic events.

## VICTIMS, DEFENDANTS, AND RIGHTS: A CONFLICT?

Although there have been major advances in societal and legal recognition of victims, their rights, and their needs, these changes have not been without controversy. Some have raised concerns that the enhancement of victims' rights may come at the expense of due process protections for people accused of a crime. For example, in the last decade victims have gained the right to participate in the sentencing phase of death penalty cases and describe the impact the crime has made on their lives (*Payne v. Tennessee*, 1991). But critics have raised questions about how such "victim impact statements" may influence legal proceedings. Should the testimony of an emotionally distraught victim be taken into account in determining a defendant's plea bargain, parole chances, or sentence? To what degree should the impact on the victim be considered legally relevant to such determinations?

Another example of a controversial change in the law designed to assist victims occurred in California. Until 1994, the **statute of limitations** allowed prosecutors to file charges against an individual suspected of child molestation up to six years after the crime allegedly occurred. In 1994, the California legislature passed a law changing the statute such that prosecutors could file charges against a molestation suspect up to one year after the victim *reported* the crime, regardless of when it had occurred (Dolan, 1999). This effectively extended the statute of limitations, because the new provisions allowed prosecutors to file charges based on victim allegations that they had been molested decades earlier (see Step 1 for a discussion of related statutes in Michigan and Washington). The statute was changed in recognition of the fact that molestation victims often do not report their victimization at the time that it is occurring. Under the new law, which is targeted toward crimes involving "substantial sexual contact," the victim's allegations must be corroborated by independent evidence, and the testimony of a mental health expert is not considered such evidence.

After 1994, prosecutors filed charges in several cases for which the old statute of limitations had previously run out. Defendants challenged this practice as an unconstitutional application of a law *ex post facto* (after the fact), but lost on appeal in *People v. Frazer* (Dolan, 1999). Critics have raised questions about whether the prosecution of cases that may be decades old presents due process issues.

## OTHER COURTROOM PLAYERS

### Court Administrator and Staff

The court administrator and other staff are key players, yet primarily unseen. Court administrators perform a variety of important tasks. With their staff, they create statistical reports issued from the court, such as those documenting the courts' various dockets (e.g., number of protection orders sought and awarded). They also provide administrative support for the judges, and interact with the public. One court administrator, for example, was asked by the judges in his courthouse to project what their caseload would be in ten years. Court administrators sometimes schedule training for courtroom staff, including judges.

### Bailiffs

Bailiffs assist the judge or magistrate in the courtroom, performing a variety of functions. Depending upon the jurisdiction, bailiffs may be staff members of the court, or they may be sheriff's deputies or police officers who are periodically assigned to perform the duties of the bailiff. The bailiff's duties include providing security and helping maintain order in the courtroom. Bailiffs are occasionally required to physically restrain people who become disruptive, aggressive, or threatening to others during court proceedings. For example, defendants may try to escape, or victims of crimes may try to exact revenge in the courtroom, as Ellie Nesler did when she shot and killed her son's alleged molester during court proceedings (Arax and Dolan, 1997).

During a trial, the bailiff escorts the defendant to and from the courtroom, and in many courtrooms, bailiffs swear in witnesses before they testify from the witness box. The bailiff also watches over jurors by escorting them to and from the courtroom, and sometimes to the parking lot after the day's proceedings. This helps ensure that jury tampering is prevented by discouraging people from contacting jurors while they are on break. If jurors have questions about courtroom proceedings or the judge's instructions to the jury, they are instructed to contact the bailiff, who will then bring their questions to the judge. And when jurors have finished deliberating, it is the bailiff who takes charge of the official verdict form that the jurors have filled out. As one student who learned about bailiffs from her criminal justice course project put it:

> The bailiffs that I interviewed did not feel that their job was underappreciated, but they did suggest that the public may not realize all of their duties. The bailiff's main responsibility is

to maintain peace and protect the safety of people in the courtroom, but this explanation does not provide due credit to the bailiff's vital role. Bailiffs help fill out the large amount of administrative paperwork for each case, and make sure people are in the correct court and are on the calendar for that day. In general, bailiffs help make the court run smoothly. . . . Once a bailiff becomes familiar with a particular judge, he often becomes an irreplaceable asset to the court. Judges and bailiffs who work closely with one another can eventually communicate with a series of verbal and nonverbal cues. (Huntington, 1993)

## Court Clerks

Court clerks assist judges with issues such as scheduling the court calendar, entering evidence into the trial record, and communicating with other members of the courthouse. For example, court clerks communicate with jury managers to determine how many prospective jurors are needed in that particular courtroom, and when. Court clerks maintain the paperwork that is necessary to keep the courtroom functioning, such as the case materials. When forms are necessary, the court clerk is usually the one who ensures that they are in the case file, available to the judge or others who need them. Without the court clerk, the voluminous paperwork that keeps the justice system moving smoothly would have to be filed and preserved by judges or others in the courtroom drama.

## Court Reporters

Court reporters are probably best known from their regular appearance in courtroom docudramas. Court reporters are the individuals who make a record of what is said during the trial. Because appeals will be based on the record made by the court reporter, precision and accuracy are absolutely necessary; the transcript must include every word that is spoken. When attorneys or judges say, "let the record reflect that. . . ," they are ensuring that certain items, especially nonaudible items, are included in the transcription. If a witness, for example, moves his head in response to a question, one of the attorneys will typically say something like "let the record reflect that the witness nodded his head 'yes'" so that readers of the transcript will know what the witness was doing.

As seen in docudramas, many court reporters use a stenotype, a typewriter with only twenty-two keys, to type in shorthand. If a transcript of the hearing or trial must be made, the shorthand notes can be transcribed into standard English. Some stenotype machines are computerized, so the machine will automatically "translate" the shorthand information into standard English. In fact, some computerized stenotypes can display the information keyed in by the court reporter moments after it is said; in addition to serving the court's needs, these machines allow for "close captioning" whenever deaf individuals appear in court as defendants, victims, witnesses, or in other capacities. Some new methods of making a record of hearings or trials include audiotaping or videotaping the proceedings.

Using audiotapes or videotapes makes the recording less expensive, but then someone must ultimately transcribe all the tapes if a printed record is needed for any reason (e.g., an appeal). Some people feel that voice dictation software may someday be a feasible way to create transcripts without hiring court reporters. At the present, however, that software is not accurate enough to replace court reporters.

## Jury Commissioners and Their Staff

These are the folks who help translate the ideal of "trial by jury" into a daily reality in courthouses across the nation. They handle the practical aspects of summoning citizens to the courthouse for jury duty and ensure that the steps of jury selection are carried out in accordance with the law's requirements for representativeness. Defense attorneys can and do challenge the representativeness of the jury selection process, and when this occurs the jury management personnel must provide evidence rebutting such allegations.

Jury managers also face public relations challenges, for they must deal skillfully with citizens who can be irate at the prospect of spending hours or days in the jury assembly room, waiting to be called to a courtroom and then possibly chosen

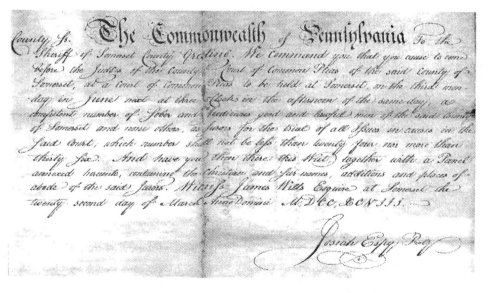

This 1798 handwritten document commands the Sheriff of Somerset County, Pennsylvania, to "cause to come before the Judges of the county Court of Common Pleas" no fewer than twenty-four nor more than thirty-six "Sober and Judicious good and lawful men . . . and none others, as Jurors for the trial of all Issues in causes in the Said court." Jury service is an important way that common citizens can participate in the justice system, and this document shows this process in action. The actual jurors supplied to the court consisted of twenty-nine farmers, a watchsmith, a tanner, and a carpenter. There were, of course, no women on the list.   SOURCE: Courtesy of documents collection of Jon'a Meyer.

for jury questioning—only to find they are not needed. Jury management person-nel are faced with the task of soothing irritated citizens for, as some see it, frivo-lously wasting people's valuable time for no reason. Rarely does anyone realize that one of the main reasons this occurs is that cases scheduled to go to trial are often plea-bargained at the last minute, sometimes even well after the trial has begun. Because of the unpredictability associated with whether cases will be tried versus plea-bargained, and the fact that it is uncertain how many people will need to be questioned during jury selection in order to obtain a jury for any particular case, jury managers must summon a greater number of prospective jurors than may actually be needed.

## Witnesses

In general terms, witnesses are people who provide evidence that helps establish what the facts are in a particular case. There are several different types of witnesses, distinguished by the specific nature of the testimony they present from the witness box. Some witnesses testify voluntarily; some are legally compelled by a **subpoena** (a legal document that commands a witness to appear in court under penalty for fail-ure to do so). The origin of the subpoena process is the Sixth Amendment's provi-sion that a defendant has the right to "have compulsory process for obtaining witnesses in his favor." Regardless of the type of witness or the circumstances that bring them to the witness box, the purpose of having witnesses testify is to provide the court with evidence that is legally relevant. Witnesses swear under oath that their testimony will be truthful. Let us look at specific types of witnesses and some of the issues associated with witness testimony more closely.

### Eyewitnesses

Eyewitnesses are often thought to be the most persuasive source of evidence in the courtroom because of the powerful impact from hearing someone say "I saw what happened." Research shows that jurors weigh the testimony of eyewitnesses quite heavily in reaching a verdict, and in fact often give *too much* weight to eyewitness testimony (Cutler, Penrod, and Dexter, 1990; Loftus, 1979; Loftus and Schneider, 1987; Wells and Seelau, 1995).

"Too much weight?" you might ask. "What does *that* mean?" What it means is that a large and solid body of research on eyewitness accuracy has demonstrated that eyewitnesses are far less accurate than most people assume (Cutler and Penrod, 1995). In addition, the more confident an eyewitness appears to be while testifying, the more credible observers such as jurors find the witness (Cutler, Penrod, and Dex-ter, 1990). Research has shown, however, that greater confidence is not necessarily indicative of greater accuracy as an eyewitness (Smith, Ellsworth, and Kassin, 1989).

This does not mean that an eyewitness who swears without hesitation that he or she is "absolutely, positively 110 percent sure" that the defendant is the person they saw committing the crime is necessarily wrong. Rather, eyewitnesses are simply far less accurate and reliable than the legal system assumes, and this has critical implications for the process of justice. For example, research looking at why mistaken convictions of innocent defendants occur has found that erroneous eyewitness testimony was the primary factor in a large percentage of these cases (Wells and Seelau, 1995).

Can eyewitnesses really be so fallible? Research has consistently demonstrated that the answer is "yes," and that the fault lies in the difference between how people expect human memory to work and how it actually functions. One of the premier researchers in the area of eyewitness accuracy describes the issue this way:

> Eyewitness testimony, which relies on the accuracy of human memory, has an enormous impact on the outcome of a trial. Aside from a smoking pistol, nothing carries as much weight with a jury as the testimony of an actual witness. The memory of witnesses is crucial not only in criminal cases but in civil cases as well—in automobile accident cases, for example, eyewitness testimony carries great weight in determining who is at fault. Implicit in the acceptance of this testimony as solid evidence is the assumption that the human mind is a precise recorder and storer of events. . . .
>
> Truth and reality, when seen through the filter of our memories, are not objective facts but subjective, interpretive realities. We interpret the past, correcting ourselves, adding bits and pieces, deleting uncomplimentary or disturbing recollections, sweeping, dusting, tidying things up. Thus our representation of the past takes on a living, shifting reality; it is not fixed and immutable, not a place way back there that is preserved in stone, but a living thing that changes shape, expands, shrinks, and expands again, an amoebalike creature with powers to make us laugh, and cry, and clench our fists. Enormous powers—powers even to make us believe in something that never happened.
>
> Are we aware of our mind's distortions of our past experiences? In most cases, the answer is no. As time goes by and the memories gradually change, we become convinced that we saw or said or did what we remember. We perceive the blending of fact and fiction that constitutes a memory as completely and utterly truthful. We are innocent victims of our mind's manipulations. (Loftus and Ketcham, 1991. Reprinted by permission)

### Expert Witnesses

An expert witness is a person with "special knowledge of the subject" (Gifis, 1984, p. 171). The court determines whether a person qualifies as an expert witness based on the person's education and/or experience with the subject matter. The court must also decide whether the issue in question is one that requires the testimony of an expert witness in order to help jurors better understand the issues in the case.

In essence, expert witnesses help provide context, whether by educating jurors about the general issues in an area (e.g., how victims of domestic violence may react to abuse, or discussing research on eyewitness accuracy and fallibility) or providing specific information on a key issue in the case (e.g., whether the defendant was insane at the time of the crime).

Expert witnesses often provide critical information to the jurors, but the use of expert witnesses is not without its problems. Questions raised by their use include:

---

## BOX 8.7

## Eyewitness Accuracy In and Out of the Lab

In one study (Loftus, 1979), research participants were shown a film showing two cars that collided, resulting in some damage to the cars. Participants were then asked to recall the scene they "witnessed," and to estimate how fast one of the cars had been traveling when it passed the barn along the country road. A week later, the participants were asked whether they remembered the barn, and 17 percent said they did.

There was no barn in the film. However, the suggestion that there was a barn had been sufficient to alter the recollections of some of these "eyewitnesses," and many other studies have consistently found the same results.

Unfortunately, real cases of mistaken identity are too easily found as well. In these cases, the honest belief of a sincere eyewitness or eyewitnesses has resulted in a miscarriage of justice. In Lenell Geter's case, several eyewitnesses conclusively identified him from photographs as the person who was present at the robbery of a chicken takeout restaurant. Despite having a solid alibi provided by nine coworkers who verified that the young engineer had been with them at work during the time of the crime, and despite the fact that Geter's workplace was forty miles away from the crime scene, he was convicted and given a life sentence. Geter served almost two years in state prison before the real robber was identified and apprehended (Clarke, 1994).

---

- How will jurors respond if each side's respective experts present contradictory testimony, leading to a "battle of the experts"?
- What if one side has the resources to hire an expert witness, but the other side cannot? Does this raise issues of fairness and due process?
- What if the testimony of the expert witness is so technical that jurors have trouble understanding it?
- Can expert witnesses sometimes simply be "hired guns" available for a fee, whose testimony may appear to reflect the interests of the side that retained them, regardless of relevant scientific evidence and the facts of the particular case?

### Character Witnesses

Character witnesses can offer evidence about a trial participant's character in one of two ways: by giving an opinion of the person's character, or by describing the person's reputation in the community with respect to relevant character traits (e.g., honesty or peaceableness).

Character evidence is typically offered to help prove a person's *good* character and is usually considered inadmissible to prove "evil" character. There are numerous exceptions to this general legal rule, however; also, well-meaning character witnesses can unintentionally present damaging evidence, as the following example illustrates (*People v. Hurd,* 1970):

In this case, the defendant Mr. Hurd was brought to trial on charges of sexually abusing his daughter, including committing sodomy and oral copulation. He offered his priest as a good character witness; the priest stated that he had known Hurd for approximately four years and stated, "In my opinion, Mr. Hurd has good moral character. He is honest, fair, upright, and has never done anything to indicate otherwise." However, during cross-examination, the prosecutor posed the following questions to the priest in order to test the depth of his knowledge of Mr. Hurd:

> Do you know that twenty years ago Mr. Hurd was arrested for transporting a stolen car across state lines?
>
> Are you aware that ten years ago Mr. Hurd was arrested for armed robbery?
>
> Are you aware that five years ago Mr. Hurd was arrested for forcible rape?
>
> Do you know that two years ago Mr. Hurd was arrested for child beating, in which the victim was the daughter involved in the present case?[1]

Needless to say, Mr. Hurd was convicted. On appeal, the California appellate court held that such inquiries were proper, given the witness' broad assertion that Mr. Hurd possessed good character.

## THE DEFENDANT AS WITNESS

Should the defendant testify at trial on his or her own behalf? That depends on the circumstances of the case and the defendant's history. If the defendant testifies, he or she can be impeached by character evidence just like any other witness, with the consequent dangers of creating negative perceptions among jurors (Wissler and Saks, 1985; Willis, 1992; Grant, 1996). But if the defendant elects not to testify, jurors may feel that silence is indicative of guilt, despite the fact that the prosecutor is legally prohibited from encouraging the jury to make such an inference (*Griffin v. California,* 1965). Therefore, with regard to the decision to take the stand, the defendant may be between a rock and a hard place.

### Court Interpreters

Court interpreters also play an often overlooked but integral role in the courtroom. In some cases, interpreters using American Sign Language serve as translators on behalf of deaf participants in legal proceedings. In an increasing number of cases, interpreters are needed in order to communicate with defendants, witnesses, and

---

## BOX 8.8
### Children As Witnesses

When children serve as witnesses in court, it raises a host of troubling questions. How reliable are child witnesses, especially very young children (Bruck, Ceci, and Hembrooke, 1998; Ceci and de Bruyn, 1993; Meyer, 1997)? Can young children remember significant details associated with stressful and traumatic events (Peterson, 1996)? Can adults confuse or mislead children by the use of suggestive questioning (Bruck, Ceci, and Hembrooke, 1998)? Can the questioning style used to elicit testimony and accounts from children lead them to tailor their stories to what they believe the questioner wants to hear (Meyer, 1997)? How will testifying in court affect the child, especially if the child is describing details about his or her own victimization at the hands of a molester? What if a child must testify as a witness against an adult member of his or her own family who is accused of a horrendous crime?

---

victims. In order to be a court interpreter, people must not only be fluent in both English and a second language, but they must also be able to translate legal terms and concepts accurately and swiftly.

In many jurisdictions, there is a serious shortage of qualified court interpreters. When a qualified court interpreter is not available, court proceedings may stop in their tracks. Worse, due process may be compromised: In some cases, faulty or incomplete translations by people who were pressed into service as interpreters due to a lack of qualified, certified translators have resulted in courtroom errors (Yesko, 2000). See Box 8.9 for more information on the role of interpreters.

## Victim-Witness Assistants

Victim-witness assistants include people who act officially in that capacity, such as staff members of a victim assistance office who help people seeking restraining orders. However, assistants are also often volunteers who have been trained through a community organization (e.g., a battered woman's shelter) to provide support to victims.

One of the best-known examples of volunteer victim assistants is the national Court-Appointed Special Advocates (CASA) program, which trains community volunteers. CASA volunteers serve as advocates for abused and neglected children by serving in the legal capacity of *guardian ad litem*. In this role, the volunteer seeks to represent the best interests of the child by investigating the child's circumstances and using the information to help advise the judge on what course of action would best serve the child's interests.

## BOX 8.9

## One Student's Views Based on Observations and Interviews with Two Interpreters (Devin Howell, 1993)

Some foreigners do not understand why their actions are a matter for the law, because it is not considered that way where they come from. . . . Interpreters play the key role in dealing with foreign defendants. The interpreter is sometimes the defendant's only source of information about our legal system and its many terms. Defendants can use an interpreter for plain translation verbatim, or for moral support and a source of legal knowledge to help in their case. The interpreter is often used as a "buffer" between the judge and defendant. The interpreter controls the communication between the defendant and the judge by his or her style of translation.

When translating, the interpreter should know the cultural background of the defendant. This allows for more understanding by the defendant as opposed to just a verbatim translation. A "plain style" interpretation does not give the defendant an equal understanding of the proceedings or the law in many cases. . . . Both [of the interpreters I interviewed] informed me that many subjects have little understanding of our legal system. They also have trouble interpreting "legal terms." This comes from never having to face a legal system of our magnitude. Many times, a subject has come from a third-world country and the court process is very simplistic in that country. . . . The interpreters told me that often these people will fall back onto their knowledge of the justice system where they come from. When defendants take this action, it changes the process of justice for them, and in some instances, the outcome. Foreigners acting on legal knowledge learned from foreign courts, or no knowledge, lose advantages given to them by [our] system (e.g., right to free defense, trial by jury, innocent until proven guilty). The interpreters revealed that in many instances the defendant believes he or she cannot afford an attorney, even after being told he or she will be granted one. I observed this in a number of cases, and only after thorough explanation did the subject understand it is his or her right.

*Source:* Devin Howell (1993); used with permission.

## Courtroom Spectators

By their very presence in the courtroom, spectators illustrate the public accountability of the courts to the community. Whether courtroom observers are merely casual watchers, members of the media, or people with a strong personal stake in the outcome of the proceedings, their perceptions of courtroom proceedings represent one of the major links between a court and members of that community. Sometimes, interest groups such as MADD (Mothers Against Drunk Driving) will send courtwatchers to observe and make note of hearings and sentences handed down to defendants. Another common source of courtroom spectators is classes on courts and law, as many professors send their students to observe some "real justice" in action to complement their viewing of primetime docudramas.

## CONCLUSION

We've examined some of the key roles played by various participants in courtroom legal proceedings. The roles vary in their depth and demands on the participants who fulfill them. Some of the roles represent professional choices and responsibilities, such as the roles played by court officials. In contrast, some of the roles are thrust upon people—certainly the "role" of victim is chosen by no one. In addition, defendants, jurors, and some witnesses may be surprised to find themselves playing their parts in the courtroom drama; and the degree to which these participants choose (or are forced to) assume these roles varies widely.

Now that we have been introduced to the key and supporting participants in the courtroom process, let us go to the next chapter to take a close look at the next question: Which cases make it to court, which cases do not, and why?

## DISCUSSION QUESTIONS

1. Given that most criminal cases never go to trial, why are jurors and jury trials an important part of the criminal courts?

2. What is a "jury of your peers"?

3. Considering the role of the defendant, in what ways is gender linked to offending?

4. What are some potential explanations for the disproportionate number of minorities represented among street crime defendants?

5. When someone says "white-collar crime," what kinds of offenses do you think of? Why would you consider these white-collar rather than "street" crimes? Who is victimized by these crimes, and in what ways?

6. What are some examples of "legitimate contextual factors" that may explain disparities (differences) in treatment of defendants from different ethnic groups?

7. Why is it important to consider race (ethnicity) and social class together when looking at disparities in the treatment of minority and nonminority defendants?

8. Although victims have no formal role in the legal process, they play a critical part in the legal system nonetheless. Can you think of some examples of this?

9. The victims' rights movement has grown enormously in the last two decades. What are some examples of ways that society and the legal system pays attention to the plight of victims, their needs, and their rights?

10. Consider the examples you read that discussed possible legal conflict between the rights of victims and the rights of defendants. Are there other examples of this tension between victims' rights and due process that you can think of?

11. Courtrooms function only with the cooperative effort of several key players, including staff members such as clerks, bailiffs, administrators, jury management staff, and interpreters. In what ways do the people in these positions provide crucial support to the courtroom work group?

12. What role do witnesses play in the courtroom? What are the different types of witnesses?

13. Considering what you learned about issues surrounding eyewitness identifications, do you believe that defendants should be convicted solely on the basis of such evidence (i.e., when there is no other evidence linking the accused to the crime)? Why or why not?

14. In this chapter we examined the way that the varied "players" on the courtroom "stage" have parts in the courtroom drama. One role you can try out for yourself is that of courtroom spectator. Courtrooms are public arenas (with few exceptions, such as juvenile court hearings), and you should consider visiting a few courtrooms to observe the proceedings and compare your observations to what you learn in this book.

## NOTE

1. Questions cited in Wydick, p. 148.

## REFERENCES

Abramson, J. (1994). *We, the Jury: The Jury System and the Ideal of Democracy.* New York: Basic Books.

Arax, M., and Dolan, M. (1997, October 2). Ellie Nesler apologizes as she is released. *Los Angeles Times,* p. A1.

Bloom, B., Chesney-Lind, M., and Owen, B. (1994, May). *Women in California Prisons: Hidden Victims of the War on Drugs.* San Francisco: Center on Juvenile and Criminal Justice.

Bruck, M., Ceci, S.J., and Hembrooke, H. (1998, February). Reliability and credibility of young children's reports: from research to policy and practice. *The American Psychologist,* 53(2): 136 (Special Issue: Applications of Developmental Science).

Bureau of Justice Statistics. (1994). *Violence Between Intimates.* Washington, DC: U.S. Department of Justice.

Bureau of Justice Statistics. (2001). *Criminal Offenders Statistics.* Washington, DC: U.S. Department of Justice.

Ceci, S.J., and de Bruyn, E. (1993, January/February). Child witnesses in court: A growing dilemma. *Children Today,* 22(1): 5.

Clarke, J. (1994, March 27). Lenell Geter's false conviction leaves him "between love, hate." *Houston Chronicle,* p. 12.

Conklin, J.E. (1977). *"Illegal but not Criminal": Business Crime in America.* Englewood Cliffs, NJ: Prentice Hall.

Connors, E., Lundregan, T., Miller, N., and McEwan, T. (1996). *Convicted by Juries, Exonerated by Science: Case Studies in the Use of DNA Evidence to Establish Innocence after Trial.* Alexandria, VA: U.S. Department of Justice, National Institute of Justice.

Cullen, F.T., Maakestad, W., and Cavender, G. (1987). *Corporate Crime Under Attack: The Ford Pinto Case and Beyond.* Cincinnati, OH: Anderson.

Cutler, B.L., and Penrod, S.D. (1995). *Mistaken Identification: The Eyewitness, Psychology, and Law.* New York: Cambridge University Press.

Cutler, B.R., Penrod, S., and Dexter, H.R. (1990). Juror sensitivity to eyewitness identification evidence. *Law and Human Behavior,* 14: 185–191.

Daly, K. (1989). Gender and varieties of white-collar crime. *Criminology,* 27(4): 769–93.

Developments in the law—race and the criminal process. (1988, May). *Harvard Law Review,* 101(7): 1473–1641.

Dolan, M. (1999, August 31). Rescinding of molestation case deadline upheld. *Los Angeles Times,* p. A1.

Donziger, S. (ed.). (1996). *The Real War on Crime: The Report of the National Criminal Justice Commission.* New York: HarperCollins.

Ener, M.L. (2000). Personal communication with author.

Foley, L., and Pigott, M. (2000, May). Belief in a just world and jury decisions in a civil rape trial. *Journal of Applied Social Psychology,* 30(5): 935.

Fox, J.A., and Zawitz, M.W. (2000, March). *Homicide Trends in the United States: 1998 Update.* Washington, DC: Bureau of Justice Statistics Crime Data Brief (NCJ 179767).

General Accounting Office. (2000, March). United States General Accounting Office Report to the Honorable Richard J. Durbin, United States Senate. *U.S. Customs Service: Better Targeting of Airline Passengers for Personal Searches Could Produce Better Results.* GAO/GGD-00-38.

Gifis, S.H. (1984). *Barron's Law Dictionary.* Woodbury, New York: Barron's Educational Series.

Grant, D.R. (1996). *From Prior Record to Current Verdict: How Character Evidence Affects Jurors' Decisions.* Dissertation.

Grant, D.R. (2000, March). The phenomenology of jury service: Jurors' experiences, questions, and suggestions. Presentation made at the American Psychology-Law Conference, New Orleans.

*Griffin v. California,* 380 US 609 (1965).

Hafer, C.L. (2000, August). Do innocent victims threaten the belief in a just world? Evidence from a modified Stroop task. *Journal of Personality and Social Psychology,* 79(2): 165.

Hagan, J., and Palloni, A. (1986). "Club Fed" and the sentencing of white-collar offenders before and after Watergate. *Criminology,* 24(4): 603–621.

Hans, V., and Vidmar, N. (1987). *Judging the Jury.* New York: Plenum.

Howell, D. (1993). Personal communication from author.

Huntington, C. (1993). Functions of the Courtroom Bailiff. Personal communication from author.

Johnson, K. (1986). Federal court processing of corporate, white collar, and common crime economic offenders over the past three decades. *Mid-American Review of Sociology,* 11(1): 25–44.

Kennedy, R. (1997). *Race, Crime, and the Law.* New York: Vintage Books (Random House).

Kleinke, C.L., and Meyer, C. (1990, September). Evaluation of rape victim by men and women with high and low belief in a just world. *Psychology of Women Quarterly,* 14(3): 343(11).

Lerner, M.J. (1980). *The Belief in a Just World: A Fundamental Delusion.* New York: Plenum Press.

Levi, M. (1987). *Regulating Fraud—White Collar Crime and the Criminal Process.* London: Tavistock.

Levine, J. (1992). *Juries and Politics.* Pacific Grove: Brooks/Cole.

Loftus, E. (1979). *Eyewitness Testimony.* Cambridge, MA: Harvard University Press.

Loftus, E., and Ketcham, K. (1991). *Witness for the Defense: The Accused, the Eyewitness, and the Expert Who Puts Memory on Trial.* New York: St. Martin's Press.

Loftus, E., and Schneider, N.G. (1987, June). Challenging eyewitness testimony; jurors believe confident witnesses even when they are wrong. *Trial,* 23(6): 40.

Mauer, M. (1992). *Americans Behind Bars: One Year Later.* Washington, DC: The Sentencing Project.

Meyer, J. (1997). *Inaccuracies in Children's Testimony: Memory, Suggestibility or Obedience to Authority?* New York: Haworth Press.

Miller, J. (1996). *Search and Destroy: African American Males in the Criminal Justice System.* New York: Cambridge University Press.

Miller, T., Cohen, M.A., and Wiersma, B. (1996). *Victim Costs and Consequences: A New Look.* Washington, DC: Government Printing Office.

Moore, E., and Mills, M. (1990, July). The neglected victims and unexamined costs of white collar crime. *Crime & Delinquency,* 36(3): 408–418.

National Center for Victims of Crime. (2001). Public Policy Issues. Available at www.ncvc.org/law/issues/VAWA_main.htm.

Pallone, N., and Hennessy, J. (1999). Blacks and whites as victims and offenders in aggressive crime in the U.S.: Myths and realities. *Journal of Offender Rehabilitation,* 30(1–2): 1–33.

*Payne v. Tennessee,* 501 U.S. 808 (1991).

*People v. Frazer,* 21 Cal. 4th 737 (1999).

Peterson, C. (1996). The preschool child witness: Errors in accounts of traumatic injury. *The Canadian Journal of Behavioral Science,* 28(1):36–42.

*People v. Hurd,* 5 Cal. App. 3d 865, 85 Cal Rptr. 718 (1970).

Personal communication between Diana Grant and Don Vera, Deputy Jury Commissioner, Stanislaus County, California (1999).

Radelet, M., Bedau, H., and Putnam, C. (1992). *In Spite Of Innocence: Erroneous Convictions in Capital Cases.* Boston: Northeastern University Press.

Reiman, J. (2001). *The Rich Get Richer and the Poor Get Prison: Ideology, Class, and Criminal Justice* (6th ed.). Boston: Allyn and Bacon.

Schmitt, C. (1991, December 9). Ethnic disparities start with arrests. *San Jose Mercury News,* p. 8A.

Shenk, J.F., and Klaus, P.A. (1984). *The Economic Cost of Crime to Victims.* Special Report, U.S. Department of Justice: Bureau of Justice Statistics.

Silverglate, H. (1999, April). Tipping evidence scales. *The National Law Journal,* p. A30.

Smith, V.L., Ellsworth, P.C., and Kassin, S.M. (1989, April). Eyewitness accuracy and confidence: Within versus between-subjects correlations. *Journal of Applied Psychology,* 74(2): 356.

Snyder, H., and Sickmund, M. (1999). *Juvenile Offenders and Victims: 1999 National Report.* Washington, DC: U.S. Department of Justice, Office of Justice Programs, Office of Juvenile Justice and Delinquency Programs.

Steffensmeier, D., and Harer, M.D. (1991, August). Did crime rise or fall during the Reagan presidency? The effects of an "aging" U.S. population on the nation's crime rate. *Journal of Research in Crime and Delinquency,* 28(3): 330–359.

Sutherland, E. (1949). Is "white collar crime" crime? *American Sociological Review,* 10: 132–139.

Tonry, M. (1995). *Malign Neglect: Race, Crime, and Punishment in America.* New York: Oxford University Press.

Uniform Crime Reports. (1994). Washington, DC: Federal Bureau of Investigation.

U.S. Department of Justice, Bureau of Justice Statistics. (1994). *Women in Prison.* Bulletin. Washington, DC: U.S. Government Printing Office.

U.S. Department of Justice, Office of Justice Policy, Office for Victims of Crime Bulletin. (2000, May). *Victims of Fraud and Economic Crime.* Washington, DC: U.S. Department of Justice.

Walker, S., Spohn, C., and DeLone, M. (2000). *The Color of Justice* (2nd ed.). Belmont, CA: Wadsworth/Thomson Learning.

Walker, S. (2001). *Sense and Nonsense About Crime and Drugs: A Policy Guide* (5th ed.). Belmont, CA: Wadsworth/Thomson Learning.

Watson, R. (2000, April 13). Report on racial profiling reveals it just doesn't work. *The Buffalo News,* p. 2B.

Wells, G.L., and Seelau, E.P. (1995). Eyewitness identification: Psychological research and legal policy on lineups. *Psychology, Public Policy, and Law,* 1: 765.

Willis, C.E. (1992). The biasing of culpability judgments with evidence of prior bad acts. Paper presented at the 1992 meeting of the American Psychology-Law Society, San Diego, CA.

Wissler, R.L., and Saks, M.J. (1985). On the inefficacy of limiting instructions. *Law and Human Behavior,* 9(1): 37–47.

Wydick, R. (1987). Character evidence: A guided tour of the grotesque structure. *U.C. Davis Law Review,* 21: 123–195.

Yesko, J. (2000, March 1). Broken English: MD court translators criticized. Allegro Web Communications. Available at www.charm.net/~marc/chronicle/translators_mar00.html.

# PART III

# Courtroom Processes

# Step 9

## Some Cases Don't Make It to Court

---

❖

---

We've just seen how some of the participants in the criminal justice drama play key roles in the court system. But as this chapter will demonstrate, some of the participants may not get the opportunity to play their roles, as some cases never make it to the courtroom. As one team of researchers studying the **attrition** of felony cases noted, "half or more of all arrests for serious crimes end without convictions" (Feeney, Dill, and Weir, 1983). In addition, a certain percentage of felony charges are reduced to misdemeanors, depending on the nature of the case and local prosecutorial policies.

Why does attrition occur? In this chapter we will look at what activities do—or do not—become grist for the criminal justice process. Some actions, for example, are not legally defined as crimes, and therefore they cannot result in arrest until and unless the legislature acts to change this. After reading this chapter, you should have a good understanding of some of the reasons why some cases never enter the criminal justice process, or are weeded out of the process before reaching the courtroom. In particular, we will take a close look at the key role that the police play in determining which cases and suspects make it to court.

## MODELS OF THE CRIMINAL JUSTICE PROCESS: FUNNELS, CAKES, AND NETS

What do you think of when you think of the criminal justice process? In order to help you visualize it, there are a variety of analogies available. One common model of the criminal justice process likens it to a funnel: wide at the top, tapering down to a narrow end. The funnel model illustrates the fact that the number of crimes that are processed through the system decreases at each step due to case attrition (see Figure 9.1). For example, the criminal process begins with a crime being committed. But as we learned earlier, *many* crimes are not reported by victims for a variety of reasons. Of those reported, some are processed further through the legal system,

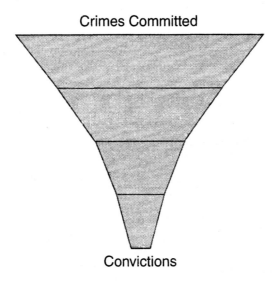

Crimes Committed

Convictions

FIGURE 9.1    The funnel model of the criminal justice process.

but at each stage of the process fewer and fewer cases are handled by the system because cases are shunted out of the system at a variety of points along the way.

Another model for conceptualizing how cases are processed in the criminal justice system uses the "wedding cake" analogy (see Figure 9.2) (Friedman and Percival, 1981; Gottfredson and Gottfredson, 1988). The wedding cake model illustrates how cases are sorted into layers depending upon their seriousness, with less serious cases forming the bottom layer of the cake and more serious cases forming the smaller layers on top. At the very top of the cake, the smallest layer represents famous (or rather, infamous) cases that attract a lot of publicity and, unfortunately, often contribute to public misinformation about the criminal justice process. Such notorious cases are not representative of the vast majority of cases in the criminal justice system.

The layers of the "criminal justice wedding cake" illustrate two important points about case processing: First, cases at different layers are accorded quite different treatment, in keeping with the differences in case seriousness. Thus, misdemeanors at the bottom layer of the cake are handled quite differently than serious felonies in the third layer. Second, within each layer, cases are similar and therefore should be handled consistently (Walker, 2001). Under the wedding cake model we expect minor cases to receive less attention, and thus there is greater attrition at this level, represented by the bottom layer of the cake. More serious offenses, however, are more likely to be pursued through all stages of the criminal justice process.

Another model of the criminal justice process that can help us understand why some cases don't get to court requires us to think of the criminal justice system as a

**FIGURE 9.2**  The wedding cake model of the criminal justice process.  SOURCE: Adapted from Walker, 2001.

net. The net has characteristics that allow some offenders to exit the net at certain points, while others struggle fruitlessly to get free but merely further entangle themselves. For example, police may decide to let an individual who has committed an offense remain in circulation so that the person can serve as an informant and provide information on the "bigger fish" of primary interest to the police. Or, as we will see when we look at plea bargaining in Step 11, defendants with little information to trade with the prosecutor may get less attractive plea deals than their accomplices in crime who have more knowledge with which to bargain. In these situations, the medium-sized "fish" may swim out of the net faster than the littlest fish, who get stuck with longer sentences. Some of the exit points from the net are built in so that some cases are routed out of the net. Other exits represent rips and tears in the net, places where it has frayed and has yet to be repaired adequately (see Figure 9.3).

## THE WINNOWING PROCESS

The common theme illustrated by the funnel, cake, and net models of the criminal justice process is that at each stage in the process cases are winnowed out (i.e., sifted out). These models illustrate case attrition graphically, which raises two important questions: (1) *How* does this happen at each stage or point in the process? (2) *Why* does this happen?

These questions require us to step back and take a look at the key decision points in the criminal justice process, and to examine the critical role that decision-making **discretion** plays in the criminal justice system. Discretion is the power to

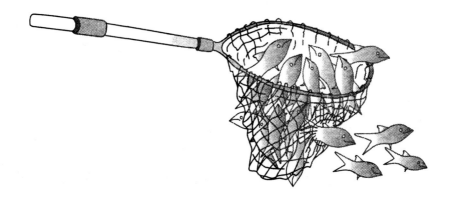

**Figure 9.3**  The net model of the criminal justice process.

make choices: to exercise one's decision-making abilities to choose between alternatives. The decision points in the criminal justice process are places where decisions are made that determine whether and how an individual's actions are defined as a crime and whether a criminal case is pursued. We must therefore look at the decisions made even before the "gatekeepers" of the criminal justice system—the police—are involved. At each of these decision-making stages, the choices of the actors in the legal system determine which cases make it to court and which cases do not. At each of these stages, criminal justice actors must exercise their discretion in order to reach a decision.

What are these "decision points," and what are the issues they raise for legal decision-makers? Let's take a look (see Figure 9.4).

## CASE ATTRITION AND KEY POINTS IN THE CRIMINAL JUSTICE PROCESS

The criminal justice process has key stages, points in the process of funneling cases through the system where case attrition can occur. Let's take a look at this process and how case attrition occurs at each point.

**1. What determines whether an action is defined as a crime or not?** Legislators, voters, and courts all serve as sources of decisions that determine whether or not it is a crime for a husband to beat his wife, for someone to steal another person's identity, or to surreptitiously take intimate photos of people's bodies in public, or to fail to provide safety training for workers in hazardous industrial positions, for example.[1] As our discussion in Step 8 concerning differential treatment of white-collar and street crimes demonstrated, white-collar offenses are usually treated as violations of civil law rather than criminal law. In addition, prosecutorial policies

**Legislators**
Congress and state legislatures are responsible for enacting statutes defining crimes and their potential penalties. The substance and format of federal and state public policies on crime and criminal justice reflect key decisions made at different points in the legislative process.

**Police**
Police departments create department policies on police actions. Individual officers make many decisions, such as whether, and whom, to stop, search, arrest, or warn; whether to initiate pursuit of a suspect, charges pursuant to an arrest, and other decisions.

**Victims**
Decide whether to report the crime, and whether to participate in the criminal justice process to the extent there are opportunities for participation.

**Prosecutors**
Responsible for critical decisions about cases, such as the sufficiency of the evidence, the type of charges to be filed, winnability, considerations of resources, the interests of justice, and other important decisions.

**Defense Counsel**
Responsible for critical decisions such as what to advise the client, how best to handle the case, and how to locate potentially exculpatory evidence through the legal process of discovery, among other key decisions.

**Prosecution and Defense Counsel**
Both make key decisions about possible plea bargains, jury selection in the event of a trial, and how best to assemble the evidence and the witnesses in a case and challenge the opposition's account of events.

**Judges**
Responsible for many critical decisions, such as those associated with the preliminary hearing, the question of bail, the admissibility of evidence, the conduct of the trial (for example, ruling on objections presented by counsel), and the sentencing process.

**Juries**
As the triers of fact, juries are responsible for assessing whether the prosecution has proved the government's case beyond a reasonable doubt. In most death-penalty cases, the jurors determine whether a defendant found guilty of a capital crime should receive a life sentence or the death penalty.

FIGURE 9.4    Decision-making in the criminal justice process

may not emphasize aggressive pursuit of white-collar offenses, whether from lack of resources, perceived public apathy, or other reasons.

Of course, if a particular action is not defined as a violation of criminal law, then that action, no matter how ethically objectionable it might be, will not become part of a criminal court's caseload (recall David Cash, who failed to intervene on behalf of Sherrice Iverson, the little girl killed in a casino restroom by Cash's friend, Jeremy Strohmeyer?). Thus, you can see how decisions about how crimes are defined directly contribute to the "case winnowing" process.

**2. When a crime is committed, is it detected?** As we saw earlier in this book, there is a large "dark figure" of unreported crime, and many reasons for the lack of reporting. Victims may be reluctant to report crimes due to fear, shame, a desire for privacy, or other reasons. In some instances, victims of crime may be unaware of their victimization and therefore unable to report it, as for example with people who have been subjected to illegal environmental pollution from companies in their neighborhood, or people whose identities are stolen without their knowledge, or people who do not realize that violence perpetrated against them by their intimates constitutes a crime (e.g., marital rape).

In other cases, victims are well aware of their aggressor's crimes, but are fearful of the consequences of reporting them (e.g., victims of gang violence fearing retaliation; victims of domestic violence fearing retaliation or fearing loss of family income if the abuser is incarcerated). The use of "date-rape drugs," such as Rohypnol, to render sexual assault victims helpless can sometimes cause amnesia effects that interfere with the victim's ability to determine exactly what happened, thus making reporting less likely in some cases (Fitzgerald and Riley, 2000). Some victims are less able than others to report crimes committed against them, such as children, the mentally impaired, or people who are institutionalized (e.g., residents of nursing homes, inmates in correctional facilities). Depending on the context, the impediments to reporting will vary. Hence, the inability to report victimization, or the decision not to report, is a significant reason why some crimes do not become part of the criminal justice system caseload.

**3. When a crime is discovered, will it become a criminal case?** The vast majority of crimes known to police are reported by citizens rather than initially discovered by police. Police must then determine whether or not a crime has actually been committed, and if so, who the culprit is (although this chapter assumes that the police complete criminal investigations, in some jurisdictions investigators with the prosecutor's office may complete most of an investigation). The discovery of an apparent crime does not necessarily mean that a criminal case will result, or that a criminal case will make it all the way through the courts to conviction or acquittal. There are many reasons for this. Some crimes, such as child abuse, may be reported to child welfare agencies rather than the police. Police records therefore do not accurately depict the extent and nature of child abuse, although the

Many individuals other than those directly involved with the courts may screen cases before they reach the courts. Victims may not detect or report offenses. Police officers may exercise discretion in selecting which cases result in arrest. Many of the cases law enforcement officers screen out of the courts' docket involve minor offenses that are not supported by evidence, or offenses that an officer feels do not warrant further involvement in the justice system (for example, issuing warnings to disorderly teenagers). Situations like the one shown in this photograph, where an officer obtains information from a victim of a crime, can result in many outcomes.   SOURCE: Courtesy of Jon'a Meyer.

implementation of new reporting methods will help improve the reporting situation in future (Finkelhor and Ormrod, 2001).

Perhaps the action that was discovered and reported as a crime is not actually a violation of criminal law after all. Or, there may be insufficient evidence that a crime has actually occurred. For example, worried relatives may contact police to report that a family member is missing and urge police to investigate. However, if the person reported missing is a competent adult, and there is no indication of foul play, the police must wait a certain period of time after the disappearance occurred before investigating. The reason is that it is not crime for an adult to voluntarily decide to "disappear," unless he or she is legally obligated to stay put (e.g., probationers), and every year many families discover that this is just what their loved ones did. Of course, if a juvenile decides to "run away," this is a **status offense** (i.e., an action that is an offense when committed by a minor). The police call reports of crimes that cannot be sufficiently substantiated "unfounded" reports. There are also many instances where behavior that is technically a crime is diverted from the criminal justice system by police decisions not to pursue the matter. There are a variety of reasons for this, which we will discuss in detail shortly.

**4. When a crime is substantiated by police investigation and reported to the prosecutor, will it become a criminal case?** Here is where the quantity and quality of the evidence and the prosecutor's discretion are critically important. As you'll recall from Step 5, prosecutors must use their discretion to decide which cases to pursue. In some cases, a crime has clearly been committed but the evidence is insufficient to permit identification of the culprit, so the case remains in the filing cabinet, awaiting further developments. In other cases, the victim may be unwilling to press charges; this has been a very common reason for prosecutorial failure to pursue charges in domestic violence cases. In recent years, however, many prosecutors' offices have instituted "**no drop**" policies in domestic violence cases. In jurisdictions with such policies, prosecutors will pursue charges based on other evidence even where the victim refuses to press charges (or agrees to cooperate by signing a complaint, but later asks that charges be dropped).

A certain percentage of cases reflect arrests of the wrong person, where despite police investigation, the person apprehended is not the actual culprit. As you'll recall from Step 5, in some instances prosecutors decide that the case is not "winnable," or that in the interests of justice, the case should not be pursued. At the federal level, for example, U.S. attorneys may decline to prosecute cases not only for insufficient evidence, but for reasons such as lack of resources, lack of criminal intent, alternative resolution of the matter, or the fact that the nature of the case makes it of "minimal federal interest" (U.S. Department of Justice, 2000, p. 24). Thus, for a variety of reasons, reflecting both case factors and organizational factors (e.g., resource limitations), prosecutors decline to file charges in a certain percentage of cases, or request dismissal of cases that haven't "panned out" after further investigation.

Prosecutorial policies on case screening, case filing, and case priorities are therefore a central source of case attrition. However, it is important to keep in mind that case attrition *in and of itself* is not necessarily a problem; whether it is problematic depends upon what kinds of cases fail to make it through the criminal process, and the reasons why they are weeded out. Cases where there is insufficient evidence that a crime has occurred, or insufficient evidence that the suspect arrested is the actual culprit, are appropriately screened out by prosecutors. In contrast, prosecutorial resources may be focused on identifying and pursuing repeat violent offenders. However, these are often difficult goals to achieve, for example, because it is often hard to accurately pinpoint the most serious repeat offenders due to lack of information and resources (Chaiken and Chaiken, 2000). The words of Feeney, Dill, and Weir, (1983) discussing attrition, illustrate this concept well:

> A high prosecutorial conviction rate may be a sign of excellent prosecutorial performance or of overly conservative charging policies; the best test is not the rate itself but the kind of charges not filed. A high attrition rate may be a sign of lax performance by either the police or the prosecutor, illegal or highly aggressive police work, or a very careful police command and control system that keeps unusually detailed records of police arrest activity.

**5. Suppose the prosecutor pursues a case.** As we saw in Step 3, at the preliminary hearing the prosecutor must present sufficient evidence that there is probable cause to believe that the accused committed the alleged crimes in order for a judge to order the case bound over for trial. If the prosecutor does not meet this burden of proof, the judge will dismiss the case. In instances where the matter has gone to a grand jury, the prosecutor will present evidence to grand jury members and ask them to return an indictment. As you'll recall from Step 5, grand juries are frequently criticized as being "rubber stamps" for prosecutors, but in some cases grand juries have refused to return an indictment. This is another avenue, then, through which cases may not make it to court.

---

## BOX 9.1

## Resurrected Cases: Cases That (Almost) Didn't Make It to Court

In 1981, Sylvia Edgren, a mother of two, was kidnapped, sexually assaulted, and murdered in Monterey, California. Police collected physical evidence and stored it, but at the time there were few leads in the case. DNA analysis, the scientific technology that would help pinpoint the identity of criminal perpetrators, was in its infancy, so the case remained open in police files. In the two decades since Ms. Edgren's murder, developments in DNA testing have begun to revolutionize the criminal justice process. The newspapers report stories almost daily of DNA analysis being used to identify criminal suspects, and to exonerate those mistakenly convicted of a crime. In the Edgren case, Monterey police took advantage of a new Justice Department DNA databank of known felons to see if the evidence in the case matched the samples from the individuals in the databank. In January 2001, police arrested suspect Michael Adams after the database reported a match between the Edgren case evidence and Adams' DNA profile, which had been filed in the databank after a 1987 conviction (Goodyear and Hallissy, 2001).

The Justice Department databank has produced several other "cold hits" that reveal a possible match between DNA from case evidence and DNA profiles in the databank. One such case is that of David McIntosh, who was about to be released from state prison after serving his sentence in one case when the databank identified him as the suspect of interest in the 1984 murder of thirteen-year-old Heidi Marie Fredette. McIntosh has been charged with capital murder in her death, and the case is proceeding at this writing (Goodyear and Hallissy, 2001).

In the midst of this technological revolution, however, it is important to remember that DNA evidence is not infallible; if not collected and preserved properly, it may become degraded or contaminated. And DNA evidence, like fingerprint evidence, is not proof per se that a suspect committed a crime: it is relevant to the question of whether or not the suspect was present at the crime scene, but it does not reveal when or why the suspect was there (National Institute of Justice, 1999).

*Source:* Copyright © The San Francisco Chronicle. Reprinted with permission.

# POLICE: THE "GATEKEEPERS" OF THE CRIMINAL JUSTICE SYSTEM

The most publicly visible representatives of our legal system, and arguably of our government as a whole, are the police. Police officers are front and center in the frequency and range of their contacts with members of the public; in 1999, for example, about 21 percent of U.S. residents had at least one contact with the police. About half of these contacts were traffic stops, and another 19 percent of police-public contacts were for the purpose of reporting a crime (Bureau of Justice Statistics, 2001, p. 1). Police play a critical role in the legal process because their actions influence those of all other legal actors in the court system. Police are the "gatekeepers" of the criminal justice system in the sense that their decisions determine who "gets in" to the system and who does not, and police evidence-gathering activities form the basic foundation for a criminal case. Thus, the decisions that police officers make determine which cases go into the "funnel" or the layers of the "cake" (or are caught in the criminal justice "net") and shape the "raw material" that the prosecutor has to work with. Unlike many bureaucracies, in the criminal justice system some of the most critical discretionary decisions are made by line-level officers in the bureaucracy rather than higher-level officials (Tonry, 1993, p. xiv). Given their importance, let's look at the role police play in more detail.

There are social, legal, and ethical dimensions to police conduct that are unique to the occupation of law enforcement, although the ethical dilemmas inherent in police work share similarities with other occupations (e.g., medicine and law). Police work is unique in that it is characterized by the twin themes of *authority* and *danger* (Skolnick, 1966). Police are the only members of society who are legitimately authorized to use force, including deadly force, to respond to conflicts in both the public and private realms. Therefore, police have unparalleled authority, which carries with it commensurate responsibilities to exercise such life-or-death power in a lawful manner. The concept of danger is also central to policing, because although most police work does not involve actively chasing dangerous criminals (contrary to popular depictions on television cop dramas), the potential for an officer to encounter a dangerous situation characterizes much police work.

Police spend most of their time maintaining order and providing service to community members, and the least amount of time performing law enforcement activities (Richardson, 1974). However, these three categories of police activity are highly interrelated, and effective police work depends upon all three types of activities. This also highlights the very broad variety of tasks that police in our society are asked to perform; in essence, police wear many and varied "hats." When something appears to be amiss, police are usually the first people called, and as such they respond to an infinite variety of problems requiring them to do something in response. The complex nature of police work is captured in one researcher's conceptualization of police as a "regulatory agency": "They regulate relationships between citizens and between citizens and institutions" (Klockars, 1985, p. 105). Yet, police must often act with little information and little time to gather, evaluate, and consider information; police must often "run roughshod over ambiguity" (Herbert, 1996). As one researcher summarizing the results of extensive field studies of police work notes: ". . . field observations document . . . the realization that the police had to improvise their way through many situations" (Goldstein, 1993, p. 33).

There are contradictions inherent in the role of the police in our society. As a democratic society, we place a high emphasis on individual freedom and liberty. Yet totally unconstrained liberty would result in civil disorder, with people constantly infringing on the rights of their neighbors; thus your right to enjoy peace and quiet at midnight on a Sunday so that you can do well on your Monday morning exam requires that I refrain from playing music too loudly at that hour. Should I fail to recognize this, you may decide to call your local police to help impress this fact upon me. Police therefore must help maintain the *balance* of order and liberty, of restraints on individuals' activities in the interests of the greater good, and of respect for individual freedom and civil liberties that are the essence of a democratic society. While maintaining order in our diverse, pluralistic society, with its consequently localized and sometimes conflicting norms about what constitutes "order," police must wield their authority and their power to exercise discretion (i.e., to make choices) in determining how to perform their work very carefully. For if police do not observe constraints on their behavior, we risk having infringement on our liberties by police themselves.

It is clear that police work involves many dimensions, and police activities directly influence the work of other actors in the criminal justice process, most notably the prosecutor and defense attorneys. The quality of the evidence gathered by police in their investigation of a potential crime determines whether the prosecutor will be able to file charges in a particular case. Yet, one study found that most case attrition occurs between the time of arrest and the filing of charges (Petersilia, Abrahamse, and Wilson, 1987). It is important, then, that police and prosecutors have a good working relationship and communicate clearly about how to achieve mutually desired goals. For example, research on the effectiveness of police procedures has noted that whereas police only need probable cause to arrest, prosecutors may be reluctant to pursue a case if the evidence won't meet the reasonable doubt standard. This suggests that successful prosecution efforts require better communication between police and the district attorney's office; for example, the development of guidelines that clearly indicate to police officers what types of evidence and information are needed by the prosecution in order to successfully pursue a case (Petersilia et al., 1987). This would help avoid breakdowns in communication, which is another reason why some potential cases don't make it to the courtroom.

The multifaceted nature of police work means that police are frequently called upon to exercise their decision-making abilities. For example, perhaps you have been pulled over for speeding. If so, the officer may have given you a speeding ticket. However, the officer may have let you go with only a warning. This is one of the most common examples of police discretion in action, and it illustrates how discretion is a key feature of police work (Goldstein, 1960; Davis, 1975; Bordner, 1983). Discretion is inherent in police work both at the level of police department policies and priorities, and in the daily decision-making of individual officers. For example, police departments must decide how to allocate their personnel and other resources, which means deciding what kinds of crimes should receive high-priority attention by police and which ones can be de-emphasized. In setting such priorities, police departments must consider the priorities of other agencies that they work with and the needs of the communities in their jurisdiction.

At another level, individual officers must decide whether or not to initiate a vehicle pursuit of a suspect, and if the pursuit becomes a high-speed chase that poses a danger to the public, whether and when to discontinue the pursuit. Officers also make daily decisions about whether to stop and question people, whether to offer assistance to stranded motorists, and whether to ask loitering teenagers or homeless people camped out on public property to "move along." A useful definition of police discretion is the following (Davis, 1969):

> A police officer or police agency may be said to exercise discretion whenever effective limits on his, her, or its power leave the officer or agency free to make choices among possible courses of action or inaction.

Far from being an aberration representing a departure from the "ideals" of law enforcement, then, the exercise of discretion is part and parcel of policing and is thus a fundamental feature of police work. An officer who decides to take action where she or he has the choice of whether to do so, such as deciding to stop or arrest someone, rather than simply letting the matter rest, is exercising discretion. But the officer who decides to avoid action, by choosing not to pursue a case, or not to enforce the law to the limit in a particular situation, is also exercising discretion; in such situations, the decision not to pursue the matter means that some incidents (and therefore some suspects) will never make it to court. However, police failure to take action can sometimes result in civil liability lawsuits against police departments. Police departments have been sued for failure to arrest in cases of domestic violence, for failure to stop and offer aid to motorists, and for failure to arrest suspected drunk drivers who were stopped but merely warned by police (Kappeler, 1997). The success of such lawsuits varies depending upon the circumstances of the case, the legal theory underlying the lawsuits, and the nature of the applicable precedents.

The central role that discretionary decision-making plays in policing is due to the nature of the institution of policing and the nature of police work. Due to lack of resources, police cannot practice full enforcement of the law: it is not possible to investigate all crimes and pursue all lawbreakers. It is also arguably not desirable from a societal perspective for police to take a "total enforcement" approach, as this would ignore public sentiments that support more vigorous enforcement of some laws than others. For example, if the police were to suddenly begin earnestly attempting to enforce all violations of the speeding laws, public outcry would almost certainly result. Many people in society would not appreciate full enforcement of the gambling laws, either, if it meant that the charity bingo event held in the local church had to be canceled, or that people gathered in a private home with friends to wager modest sums on a hot poker game would be arrested and hauled off to court.

Even if police possessed the resources to enforce most laws "to the letter," scholars of policing and sometimes police themselves can point to circumstances where police probably should not practice full enforcement. For example, both the actual security of the public, and residents' *feelings* of safety and security, may be better served when police choose not to enforce the law at a particular time and place (Cohen and Feldberg, 1991). For example, Cohen and Feldberg discuss the dilemma faced by police providing security at a large rock concert. The concert is well under way, with thousands of fans jammed into the area in front of the stage. Some of the concert-goers are drunk or drugged, and there are cash drug transactions openly occurring in this area during the concert. Police can see this, and some fans may wonder why the police do not immediately move in and grab the suspects. However, this situation poses a dilemma for police, because they must consider the possible risks to public safety if they should attempt to nab the dealers right then and there. Police action under the circumstances might spark hostility and result in drunk, drugged fans becoming enraged and battling police and each other, with innocent people harmed in the process; this is the exact opposite of the police goal of maintaining public safety and security at this concert. Thus police should consider whether a better alternative from a public safety perspective might be to wait until the concert is over and try to catch the suspects as they leave (Cohen and Feldberg, 1991, pp. 70–88). In the words of one researcher, "police discretion often means choosing between enforcing the law or maintaining public order" (Vick, 1985).

The increasing emphasis on police-community relations fostered by a shift toward "community policing" also raises the question of the degree to which officers should take local norms and customs into account in exercising their discretion. For example, if city regulations prohibit alcohol consumption in public, should police enforce this law to the same extent in all neighborhoods in that city? What if it is a common, generally accepted custom in some neighborhoods for residents to sit out on their front porches on a hot summer evening while drinking beer? In this context, police enforcement of the law may elicit a different reaction from residents of this community than in another community with different local customs. It could thus be argued that policing that is responsive to the community should take community norms into account, and that this is preferable to "across the board" enforcement of the law without the reasoned exercise of discretion

(Kelling, 1999). However, this argument makes the questionable assumption that there are shared community norms, despite the fact that there may actually be little community consensus on which behaviors are acceptable or not. Such situations raise important challenges for police departments and individual officers, challenges that once again illustrate the central role that police discretion plays.

Police departments and individual officers alike must consider how best to use their limited resources to focus on the most pressing needs of their jurisdiction. Which problems pose the greatest threat to the community? Which problems are of greatest concern to the community? Sometimes, problems of concern to many in the community may not be actual crimes, but rather issues of maintaining order, such as residents' perceptions that loitering teenagers pose a threat. In Berkeley, California, a city famous for its history of political activism, merchants reported concern to police about the growing number of "day laborers" seeking work on the streets. The merchants complained about the presence and activities of the day laborers, many of them illegal immigrants whose sole means of support consists of participating in the daily scramble when a driver pulls up to offer a job (usually involving unskilled or semi-skilled labor for very modest compensation). Is this a matter for the police to address, or should the Berkeley City Council instead (or in addition) try to come up with a solution that addresses the needs of the merchants, their customers, and the laborers themselves?

The nature and extent of crime and public order problems facing police vary from area to area, and police priorities reflect this fact. Police officers must frequently exercise their discretion during the course of the situations they encounter daily, and the local context provides different challenges. In large urban areas, for example, police are far less likely to be concerned by the discovery of a window box sporting cannabis plants among the marigolds than they might in a small town. Similarly, police in rural areas must deal with crimes that urban police officers probably rarely encounter, such as crop and livestock thefts. A farmer whose valuable avocado crop has been harvested and trucked away by midnight thieves faces a significant loss of livelihood, and a rash of such crop thefts is likely to be a high priority for the police or sheriff in agricultural areas.

Because police are the "gatekeepers" of the criminal justice system, their decisions affect the criminal justice system and society as a whole. Police officers' decisions about how to respond to domestic violence calls, for example, determine whether and how public policies designed to deter domestic violence (e.g., mandatory arrest) are actually implemented. This example illustrates why the role of the police, and police discretion, is so central in the criminal justice process: Police are the ones who translate "law on the books" into "law in action" through the decisions they make in the course of their work. The most carefully thought out crime policy will have little meaning if it is not put into practice by criminal justice actors, such as the police (and members of the courtroom work group).

Police discretion, and community perceptions of how police exercise their powers of choice, have important implications for police-community relations. For example, police policies and practices regarding traffic stops may be a key influence on community perceptions of police and the criminal justice system, as controversies over the issue of racial profiling illustrate.

Due to the individualized nature of the situations police encounter in their work, they must make decisions about how to respond in each case; although the actions of police are in theory guided by the law and by police department policies and guidelines, in practice police officers must determine which rules are relevant and how to apply them to the particular situation at hand. Discretion, therefore, is an inherent and necessary characteristic of police work. It allows police to tailor their responses to individual situations and to prioritize which tasks they should focus on. For instance, going back to our traffic violation example, an officer who stops you for speeding may decide not to ticket you because you have no prior moving violations, you were only going a few miles over the speed limit, and you promise not to speed again. If any of these factors were different, however, the officer might decide instead to issue a ticket. Therefore, you can see how discretion opens up the potential for selective enforcement of the law, for favoritism and bias.

## THE PROS AND CONS OF DISCRETION

Herein lies a recurring societal dilemma: we want personalized justice rather than mechanized, across-the-board rote application of the law by our police, but we also want equal treatment of similar cases and offenders. This is the dilemma of "equality versus discretion" (Wrightsman, Nietzel, and Fortune, 1994). Sometimes, we appear to want police officers to use their discretion to fail to enforce the letter of the law when we believe that this is appropriate. If you have received a warning about speeding instead of a ticket, you probably feel the officer acted appropriately in exercising discretion in your case; and many people would approve such discretion by an officer who stops a speeding car only to discover that the anxiety-racked driver is a husband trying to make it to the hospital before his wife gives birth in the back seat. Yet discretion by police often brings cries of "foul!" as well, as when police appear to be favoring certain individuals or groups. The way we perceive police discretion (or discretion by other criminal justice system actors, for that matter) may depend upon how we conceptualize justice. Cohen describes two different views: the idea that justice represents treatment particularized to an individual; and the idea of justice as equal treatment (Cohen, 1985). However, think about the concept of "equal treatment" for a moment. Does equal treatment necessarily mean identical treatment of all similar cases? Alternatively, if we conceptualize "equal" treatment as meaning "fair" treatment, this might suggest that we could—and perhaps should—treat everyone fairly *not* by handling all cases in an identical manner, but by customizing justice to take into account the particular circumstances of the case. Thus, for example, under this definition of "equal" treatment, we might want a police officer to respond differently to a driver who was weaving slightly because he or she was distracted by the earsplitting caterwauls of an unhappy cat in its backseat carrier, versus a driver who was weaving due to imbibing during lunch. On the other hand, differential treatment raises the specter of bias (whether negative or positive, in the sense of favoritism), and therefore police discretion is a source of continuing controversy.

## What Influences Police Exercise of Discretion?

Now that we've seen how important police discretion is in determining which cases make it to court and which do not, let's look at some of the evidence on *how* police exercise their discretion. How often, and in what types of situations, do officers actually choose to exercise discretion? What factors influence the way that police use their discretion?

Research has shown that the nature and extent of the exercise of discretion by police varies according to the characteristics of the officer, the police department, the nature of the offense, the relationship between the victim and offender, and possible penalties for the offense.

## Officer/Department Characteristics Influencing Discretion

Studies of police discretion have found that organizational characteristics of the police department and the characteristics of officers themselves can influence how officers exercise discretion. For example, the likelihood of officers arresting a suspect rather than choosing not to arrest may vary by the organizational structure and size of the police department (Smith and Klein, 1984; Mastrofski, Rilti, and Hoffmaster) 1987). A study of Maine police officers' use of discretion in handling driving offenses found that officers who felt that penalties for such offenses were too harsh were less likely to cite or arrest offenders, and that officers with fewer years in service were also more likely to exercise discretion (Meyers, Heeren, and Hingson, 1989).

## The Nature of the Offense/Offender

Police perceptions of the members of the public they encounter can influence their exercise of discretion as well. Research examining police discretionary decisions in nonfelony cases in three selected Southern cities and towns in the United States found that African American suspects were treated less favorably than white suspects by police (Powell, 1990). However, other research did not find this effect for race (Klinger, 1996). Another study found that Danish police were more lenient with citizens they perceived as respectable and law-abiding, in contrast to those for whom they made less favorable attributions (Holmberg, 1998). An experiment examining influence on discretion with Australian police found that officers' perceptions of the credibility of victims alleging that they had been raped varied with the victim's level of inebriation (Schuller and Stewart, 2000). While the results of such studies may not be applicable in other locations, they are instructive in illustrating the vast range of potential influences on police discretion. As Brooks (2001, p. 25) discusses, there are conflicting interpretations of research examining the relationship between citizen demeanor and the responses of police officers.

Not surprisingly, officers' perceptions of the nature and seriousness of the activities they encounter in their work affects their reactions. For example, police encounters with juvenile offenders reveals that juveniles suspected of a felony are usually arrested, but those suspected of less serious crimes are usually not arrested, but are handled through "informal" means (Berger, 1996). In another study, approximately half of police officers who witnessed elder mistreatment reported the problem, and an even smaller percentage reported exploitation of elders (Daniels et al., 1999). Another study illustrated the complexity of police decisions about how to handle people who appeared to be mentally ill and in need of assistance (Green, 1997). Police decisions about whether to arrest people who appeared to be mentally ill, versus other options, such as transporting them to a hospital or simply trying to talk to the person and calm him or her down, depend upon a variety of factors. For example, the officer's estimate of the probability that the person presents a danger, and the officer's perception that the person's behavior might escalate into a situation requiring further police intervention, influenced officers' responses in such situations (Teplin, 2000).

As has been mentioned earlier in this book, the nature of the relationship between a victim and an offender has historically been an important determinant of police response to certain kinds of crimes (Black, 1980). Police have traditionally been less likely to arrest the suspect the closer the suspect's relationship to the victim, especially in cases of domestic violence or rape. In recent years, public attention and activism has illuminated this situation, and thus the disparity in police response to these kinds of cases (versus other kinds of cases) is less than it used to be. Nonetheless, as is discussed in the following section, police discretion ultimately determines how and when the law is applied by officers working the streets. For example, Buzawa and Buzawa (2001) discuss research showing significant variation in the degree to which police officers have actually implemented mandatory arrest policies in domestic violence cases.

## Police Discretion and Offense Penalties

Crime policies that mandate that certain actions be taken in response to a potential or actual offense provide an illuminating example of the importance of discretion in criminal justice decision-making. For example, research has shown that "mandatory arrest" policies requiring police to arrest suspected abusers in cases of domestic violence are not necessarily enforced 100 percent by the police; that is, in some cases, despite such policies, arrests may not be made (Lerman, 1992). Similarly, statutes mandating police arrest of suspected drunken drivers may not be fully implemented by some police departments and officers (Meyers et al., 1987). In one state, when a new law was passed mandating that anyone caught carrying a handgun under certain circumstances faced a mandatory jail term of no less than one year, observers questioned how this influenced the likelihood of arrest. Some critics of the law suggested that some officers may have altered their behavior in order to avoid subjecting citizens unfairly to the perceived harsh penalties of the new law. Research does suggest that police enforcement of the law varies according to community norms and values (Goldstein, 1960).

## THE ARGUMENT OVER POLICE DISCRETION

Some argue that police have too much discretion, and this results in bias, discrimination, and favoritism in the types of cases and offenders who make it to court. A related criticism is that when police exercise discretion in deciding how to enforce or not enforce the law, they are taking the law into their own hands and in effect usurping the power of the legislature to determine what the law is (Klockars, 1985). For example, critics cite evidence from law enforcement files, which shows the practice of racial profiling by police in some jurisdictions (American Civil Liberties Union, 1999; Zamora, 2001) (see Box 9.2). Others point to the reluctance of some police departments to pursue certain kinds of cases, such as rape cases.

The coercive authority of police to place an individual under arrest raises many questions about the nature and impact of police discretionary decisions associated with this power. Police sometimes choose not to make an arrest even when there is sufficient evidence that a crime has been committed and the suspect is known (Goldstein, 1993, p. 34). For example, we saw that police are less likely to make an arrest in assault cases when the victim and the suspected offender have a close relationship (Black, 1980). At the other end of the spectrum, when police officers arrest someone without intending to prosecute the person (for example, in order to compel a witness to reveal what they know to the police, or to intimidate suspected gang members), this raises ethical and legal questions about the appropriate purposes of the power to arrest (Goldstein, 1993, p. 35).

In contrast to those concerned that the police possess too much discretion to interpret and apply the law, some people argue that police have too little discretion, and that this lets some offenders slip through the cracks because police cannot use certain tactics. For example, adherents of this position argue that the Fourth Amendment prohibition on unreasonable searches and seizures, and the concomitant exclusion of evidence that is illegally obtained under the Exclusionary Rule, serve as undesirable constraints on police. However, the evidence does not support this assertion (Fyfe, 1983; Nardulli, 1983). Similarly, it has been argued that police

---

## BOX 9.2

## The California Highway Patrol and Racial Profiling

"You kiss a lot of frogs before you find a prince." Although this statement might remind you of a child's fairy tale, it actually represents the words of a California Highway Patrol (CHP) Supervisor testifying under oath at a legal deposition (Zamora, 2001, p. A1). The supervisor was discussing the CHP practice of stopping motorists in the search for drugs, and asserting that many stops must be made in order for officers to successfully locate a driver transporting illegal drugs. The supervisor was testifying in response to a 1999 lawsuit against the California Highway Patrol by the American Civil Liberties Union (ACLU), alleging that the CHP selectively targeted minority drivers for traffic stops. In response to the allegation of racial profiling, in 2001 many internal CHP documents were turned over to the ACLU as part of the process of discovery. According to the CHP's own statistics, in some parts of California, Latino and black drivers were two to three times more likely than white drivers to be stopped, and more likely once stopped to be asked by CHP officers if their cars could be searched. This was particularly notable because of the fact that the California Highway Patrol had released a public report the previous year (2000) that concluded that there was little evidence to support concerns about racial profiling by the CHP (California Highway Patrol, 2000). However, in response to the CHP supervisor's "frog" reference, one ACLU official noted: "The obvious problem is that most 'frogs' the CHP is stopping are Latino and African American . . . who are forced to endure the loss of personal liberties because of their skin color . . ." (Zamora, 2001, p. A1).

*Source:* Copyright © The San Francisco Chronicle. Reprinted with permission.

---

should have greater leeway in the interrogation techniques that they may legally use to obtain a confession from a suspect. Others argue, however, that police are already allowed too much leeway in this regard.

A realistic perspective on police discretion recognizes that it is an inherent and inevitable aspect of police work that can be used to achieve both desirable and undesirable legal and social ends. For example, in addition to allowing police to "tailor justice" to accommodate mitigating circumstances, police discretion may help blunt the impact of "bad laws"; that is, statutes which may be ill-considered in design or application, perhaps because the law is outdated or reflects hasty policy-making by lawmakers (Klockars, 1985). However, police discretion also allows police misconduct and abuse of power to occur. For example, decisions to selectively enforce or not enforce the law with respect to certain categories of people (certain ethnic groups, students versus seniors, poor compared to affluent people) can not only have life-changing consequences for the individuals involved, but can harm public perceptions of the legitimacy and fairness of the criminal justice system as well.

One thing is clear concerning police discretion: The manner in which police discretion is exercised is critically important, for a number of reasons. Police decision-making about which goals to pursue and what means can or should be used to achieve these goals influence a number of stakeholders, including individuals who come in contact with the police, the general public, agencies and individuals that comprise the legal system, and the police themselves. However police determine which tasks take priority, and which crimes and suspects merit more or less attention, the consequences will be felt in a number of ways. Thus, for example, police decisions about which kinds of crimes are top priority determine what cases prosecutors and other members of the courtroom work group eventually see; police discretion determines the degree to which public policies on crime are implemented (e.g., mandatory arrest policies); and police discretion has an enormous impact on police community relations, and the perceived legitimacy of the criminal justice system. Police discretion can result in decisions that raise legal as well as social issues for police departments (e.g., "hot pursuits" of vehicles by police can expose police departments to civil liability lawsuits by third parties who are injured in such chases).

Given this, it is not surprising that an enduring topic of both theoretical and applied research on police and policing is the question of how police discretion can be regulated. How much discretion should police officers have? How can officers be

---

## BOX 9.3
## Free Coffee and Pie?

You are an officer who occasionally stops by a café for a coffee on your break. After several visits during which you and the café owner, "Ted," make pleasant small talk, the friendly owner begins to insist you take free coffee and pie whenever you stop by. "I just want to show my appreciation for the hard job you folks in blue are doing for our community," says Ted.

Should you accept? Why or why not?

Now suppose one night you pull over a driver who just ambled slowly through a bright red light. No other cars were around, so no one was hurt. You recognize that the driver is Ted, the café owner. He apologizes repeatedly for running the light, explaining that he was tired from having slept poorly the previous night. After explaining, Ted says "Hey, you aren't going to give your old pal here a ticket for a little mistake like that, are you?" What are your options as an officer responding to this incident?

1. How are you going to handle the ticketing decision?
2. Should you keep going to the café and accepting free food after this?

Remember that *perceptions* are critical: your perception, as an officer, of the café owner's intent; the owner's perception of you in your role as a representative of the government; and other onlookers' perceptions of your actions. Given this, what do you think are the possible consequences of your decisions about the issues in (1) and (2) above?

trained to develop their abilities to exercise good judgment during crucial decision-making tasks? Even the most seemingly trivial decisions facing a police officer can have significant repercussions for police–community relations, as the example of the "free coffee" dilemma in Box 9.3. How can discretion that is abused be sanctioned? What methods are available for regulating, reducing, monitoring, or otherwise influencing the amount of discretion officers have and the opportunities they have to use discretion? Attempts to regulate police discretion have formed the substance of many of our landmark criminal justice decisions (such as the Miranda doctrine). The existence of police misconduct illustrates all too well the power of discretion and the potentially deadly consequences of its abuse. However, there is also cause for optimism to be found in that efforts to regulate police discretion and prevent its abuse have shown some success (Walker, 1993).

## CONCLUSION

Clearly, many, if not most, potential criminal cases never actually make it to court, for a variety of reasons. Regardless of which model of the criminal justice process one uses, the evidence shows that only a fraction of possible cases remains after the "winnowing process." Some actions are not defined as crimes at all; other crimes are not reported to police for some reason. Police discretion to make decisions about what incidents and individuals to focus on, and how to respond to potential crimes, has a huge impact on which cases make it into the criminal justice process. Prosecutorial discretion, as we saw earlier in Step 5, is the key to determining which cases brought by the police ultimately make it to court, and which cases do not. The cases that do appear in court, therefore, are only a sample, and not a representative sample at that, of the crimes that occur in our society.

### DISCUSSION QUESTIONS

1. Consider the discussion at the beginning of the chapter on how some actions are not defined as crimes under the law. Can you find examples in your newspaper of current controversies that illustrate this? For example, should human cloning be against the law? How might political and societal pressures influence whether or not a particular activity is defined as a crime?

2. What are some of the reasons that crimes fail to come to the attention of police? What steps could be taken to address this situation (e.g., what might encourage victims to report)?

3. Why is it important that the police and prosecutors have a good working relationship in order for the criminal justice process to function effectively? What kinds of problems can result from a lack of communication between police and prosecutors?

4. Consider some of the difficulties of measuring case attrition. How should we count "lost" cases? For example, how would you account for prosecutorial overcharging when trying to determine an attrition rate? How would you figure out how many cases that "fell out of" the criminal justice system were cases that should have resulted in a conviction, and how many cases were those that were appropriately dropped (e.g., evidence exonerated an innocent suspect)?

5. What are the advantages and disadvantages of police discretion? How (and why) is discretion integral to the practice of policing? Why is police discretion difficult to regulate?

6. How is police discretion is linked to issues such as police misconduct, including the problem of racial profiling.

7. Why is the exercise of police discretion a critical influence on police–community relations and public perceptions of the legitimacy of the criminal justice system?

# NOTE

1. For example, historically the "rule of thumb" in English law has been said to condone domestic violence by allowing a man to beat his wife for the purpose of "disciplining her" as long as the man chastised her with a stick no bigger in diameter than his thumb. Another example is this: Identity theft was not a crime in some jurisdictions until recently, when legislators quickly passed laws to address this gap in the statutes so that prosecutors could pursue cases of identity theft. Similarly, the practice of photographing people's bodies without their knowledge, for example, by positioning tiny microcameras so as to shoot footage of women's bodies underneath their skirts, then posting the result on the Internet, is relatively recent and poses an interesting example of the crime definition issue. Finally, the lack of adequate safety training for workers facing occupational hazards is often considered an offense, but is rarely denoted as a crime under current laws. Instead, it is usually defined as a violation of civil law (administrative regulations).

# REFERENCES

Berger, R. (1996). Legal and extralegal factors in police and court processing of juveniles. In Ronald J. Berger (ed.), *Sociology of Juvenile Delinquency,* 2nd ed., pp. 403–416. Chicago: Nelson-Hall Publishers.

Black, D. (1980). *The Manners and Customs of the Police.* New York: Academic Press.

Bordner, D.C. (1983). Routine policing, discretion, and the definition of law, order, and justice in society. *Criminology,* 21(2): 294–304.

Brooks, L. (2001). Police discretionary behavior: A study of style. In R. Dunham and G. Alpert (Eds.), *Critical Issues in Policing: Contemporary Readings,* pp. 117–131. Prospect Heights, IL: Waveland Press.

Bureau of Justice Statistics. (2001, February). *Contacts between police and the public: findings from the 1999 national survey.* U.S. Department of Justice. NCJ 184957.

Buzawa, E., and Buzawa, C. (2001). Traditional and innovative police responses to domestic violence. In R. Dunham and G. Alpert (Eds.), *Critical Issues in Policing: Contemporary Readings,* pp. 216–237. Prospect Heights, IL: Waveland Press.

California Highway Patrol. (2000). *Public contact demographic data summary.* California Highway Patrol report to Governor Gray Davis. Sacramento: California Highway Patrol.

Chaiken, M., and Chaiken, J. (2000). Priority prosecution of high-rate dangerous offenders. Chapter 14 in Barry Hancock and Paul Sharp (Eds.), *Public Policy, Crime, and Criminal Justice,* 2nd ed., pp. 227–239. Upper Saddle River, NJ: Prentice-Hall.

Cohen, H. (1985). A dilemma for discretion. In William Heffernan and Timothy Stroup (Eds.), *Police Ethics: Hard Choices in Law Enforcement,* pp. 69–80. New York: John Jay Press.

Cohen, H. and Feldberg, M. (1991). *Power and Restraint: The Moral Dimension of Police Work.* New York: Praeger.

Daniels, S., Baumhover, L., Formby, W., and Clark-Daniels, C. (1999). Police discretion and elder mistreatment: A nested model of observation, reporting, and satisfaction. *Journal of Criminal Justice,* 27(3): 209–25.

Davis, K. (1969). *Discretionary Justice.* Baton Rouge, LA: Louisiana State University Press.

Davis, K. (1975). *Police Discretion.* St. Paul, MN: West Publishing.

Feeney, F., Dill, F., and Weir, A. (1983). *Arrests Without Conviction: How Often They Occur and Why.* Washington, DC: U.S. Department of Justice.

Finkelhor, D. and Ormrod, R. (2001, May). *Child Abuse Reported to the Police.* Office of Juvenile Justice and Delinquency Prevention. NCJ 187238.

Fitzgerald, N. and Riley, K.J. (2000, April). Drug-facilitated rape: Looking for the missing pieces. *National Institute of Justice Journal.* NCJ 181731.

Friedman, L.M. and Percival, R.V. (1981). *The Roots of Justice: Crime and Punishment in Alameda County, California, 1870–1910.* Chapel Hill: University of North Carolina Press.

Fyfe, J.J. (1983). The NIJ study of the Exclusionary Rule. *Criminal Law Bulletin,* 19: 253–60.

Gottfredson, M.R. and Gottfredson, D.M. (1988). *Decision Making in Criminal Justice: Toward the Rational Exercise of Discretion,* 2nd ed. New York: Plenum.

Goldstein, H. (1993). Confronting the complexity of the policing function. In Lloyd Ohlin and Frank Remington (Eds.), *Discretion in Criminal Justice: The Tension Between Individualization and Uniformity.* Albany, NY: State University of New York Press.

Goldstein, J. (1960). Police discretion not to invoke the criminal process: Low visibility decisions in the administration of justice. *Yale Law Review,* 69: 543–594.

Goodyear, C. and Hallissy, E. (2001, June 25). State boosts felon's DNA database: Crime-fighting cache becomes largest in U.S. *San Francisco Chronicle,* p. A1.

Green, T.M. (1997). Police as frontline mental health workers: The decision to arrest or refer to mental health agencies. *International Journal of Law and Psychiatry,* 20(4): 469–86.

Harris, D. (1999, June). Driving while black: Racial profiling on our nation's highways. An American Civil Liberties Special Report. Available at www.aclu.org/profiling/report/index.html.

Herbert, S. (1996). Morality in law enforcement: Chasing "bad guys" with the Los Angeles Police Department. *Law and Society Review,* 30(4): 799–818.

Holmberg, L. (1998). Policing the customers: How Danish community policy officers label the people they work among. *Criminal Justice Policy Review,* 9(2): 169–84.

Kappeler, V. (1997). *Critical Issues in Police Civil Liability.* Prospect Heights, IL: Waveland Press.

Kelling, G.L. (1999). *Broken Windows and Police Discretion.* Washington, DC: U.S. Department of Justice, Office of Justice Programs, National Institute of Justice.

Klinger, D. (1996). More on demeanor and arrest in Dade County. *Criminology,* 34: 61–82.

Klockars, C. (1985). *The Idea of Police.* Beverly Hills, CA: Sage.

Lerman, L.G. (1992). The decontextualization of domestic violence. *The Journal of Criminal Law and Criminology,* 83: 217–40.

Mastrofski, S.D., Rilti, R., and Hoffmaster, D. (1987). Organizational determinants of police discretion: The case of drinking-driving. *Journal of Criminal Justice,* 15: 387–402.

Meyers, A., Heeren, T., Hingson, R., and Kovenock, D. (1987). Cops and drivers: Police discretion and the enforcement of Maine's 1981 OUI law. *Journal of Criminal Justice,* 15(5): 361–68.

Meyers, A.R., Heeren, T., and Hingson, R. (1989). Discretionary leniency in police enforcement of laws against drinking and driving: Two examples from the State of Maine, U.S.A. *Journal of Criminal Justice,* 17(3): 179–86.

Nardulli, P. (1983, Summer). The societal costs of the Exclusionary Rule: An empirical assessment. American Bar Foundation Research Journal, pp. 585–690.

National Institue of Justice. (1999). Commission on the future of DNA evidence. Department of Justice, BC 000614.

Petersilia, J., Abrahamse, A., and Wilson, J.Q. (1987). *Police Performance and Case Attrition.* Santa Monica, CA: RAND Corporation.

Powell, D. (1990). A study of police discretion in six southern cities. *Journal of Police Science and Administration,* 17(1): 1–7.

Richardson, J.F. (1974). *Urban Police in the United States.* Port Washington, NY: Kennikut Press.

Schuller, R. and Stewart, A. (2000, October). Police responses to sexual assault complaints: The role of perpetrator/complainant intoxication. *Law and Human Behavior,* 24(5): 535–51.

Skolnick, J. (1966). *Justice without Trial: Law Enforcement in Democratic Society.* New York: Macmillan.

Smith, D., and Klein, J. (1984). Police agency characteristics and arrest decisions. In G. Whitaker and C. Phillips (Eds.), *Evaluating Performance of Criminal Justice Agencies.* Beverly Hills: Sage.

Teplin, L. (2000, July). Keeping the peace: Police discretion and mentally ill persons. *National Institute of Justice Journal;* pp. 8–15.

Tonry, M. (1993). Foreword in Lloyd Ohlin and Frank Remington (Eds.), *Discretion in Criminal Justice: The Tension between Individualization and Uniformity.* New York: State University of New York Press.

U.S. Department of Justice, Office of Justice Programs, Bureau of Justice Statistics. *Compendium of Federal Justice Statistics, 1998.* (2000). NCJ 180258.

Vick, C. (1985). An introduction to aspects of public order and the police. In J.R. Thackrah (Ed.), *Contemporary Policing: An Examination of Society in the 1980s.* London: Sphere, pp. 161–72.

Walker, S. (1993). Taming the system: The control of discretion in criminal justice, 1950–1990. New York: Oxford University Press.

Walker, S. (2001). *Sense and Nonsense about Crime and Drugs,* 5th ed. Belmont, CA: Wadsworth.

Wrightsman, L.S., Nietzel, M., and Fortune, W. (1994). *Psychology and the Legal System,* 3rd ed. Pacific Grove, CA: Brooks/Cole Publishing Company.

Zamora, J. (2001, April 20). CHP stops more minorities: Agency admits law-abiding blacks, Latinos run greater risk of being pulled over. *San Francisco Chronicle,* p. A1.

# Step 10

# "You Ring, We Spring": The Role of Bail in the Court System

❖

In the last chapter, we examined the screening process through which cases must go and learned that all cases must make it through several levels of scrutiny before going to trial. Because these procedures (and pre-trial motions and preliminary hearings) may take a great deal of time, the vast majority of defendants seek pre-trial release. The means by which defendants can be released before trial usually involves posting bail.

By the end of this chapter, you will be able to explain how the bail process works and present a short history of bail. You will be able to recognize the different types of bail systems in use in the United States, and discuss the influences of others in the justice drama concerning this issue. You will be able to list several problems associated with the bail system and will be able to relate what influences pre-trial detention can have on defendants.

## THE BAIL SYSTEM

Bail is a unique guarantee system by which the courts try to ensure that defendants will show up for their trials by forcing them to deposit money or other collateral with the courts in exchange for release before trial. If defendants do not return for their trials, the money or collateral is forfeited. If they do return, defendants are entitled to a return of their collateral regardless of the trial outcome. That means that even persons who are found guilty after trial, or who plead guilty, must still get whatever bail they posted returned to them.

Judges or magistrates usually set bail, but the police or the district attorney can set bail in some jurisdictions. Even in jurisdictions where judges set bail, others in the justice drama (e.g., police, prosecutor, or victim) may have influence on whether bail is granted and the amount required for bail (Feeley, 1979, pp. 209–210; Wice, 1985, p. 55). In most jurisdictions, law enforcement agencies follow bail guidelines established by the court so that accused individuals can post bond and be released from custody. If these guidelines were not used, every arrested person would have to wait for a judge to set bail, which would be an unnecessary delay and would needlessly crowd the jails and courtrooms. These guidelines, for example, are how most drunk drivers get out of jail before trial. The police consult the guidelines and allow accused persons to post bail and leave. Those who wish to see a judge, perhaps to get their bail amount reduced, must wait until their initial hearing.

Interestingly, the U.S. Constitution does not guarantee any person bail, only that it not be excessive if it is granted.[1] Although no person is automatically entitled to bail, most defendants are granted bail in some form. Proponents of the bail system argue that bail amounts are often "excessive," but the Supreme Court has not defined an exact amount that is fair. For this reason, we sometimes see defendants whose bail is a million dollars or more, especially if their alleged crimes are serious.

Although bail was initially designed to release defendants from incarceration so that criminal justice system personnel were no longer obligated to house, feed, or clothe them, high bail amounts have been used throughout American history as a way to keep defendants in jail prior to their trials. Lester (1965), for example, details how civil rights activists in the 1960s were detained in lieu of $4,500 bonds for disturbing the peace. Now, bail is strongly tied to the seriousness of the offense, the accused's prior record, or other legal factors. See Box 10.1 for criteria commonly used in deciding whether or not to grant bail.

Even now, however, extra-legal factors affect bail. Those who have few ties to the community (e.g., work, family, or home ownership) sometimes have to post higher bail amounts because of the court's perception that, when substituting financial ties to the court in place of formal ties to the community, the financial incentives to remain in the jurisdiction need to be higher than usual. Ironically, those who are unemployed or who do not own their homes may be less likely to be released without having to post bond or may be asked to post a higher bond than a similarly situated defendant who has a job or home in the community. At first glance, these disparities appear to be based on the reality that bail is often set higher for individuals who are considered by the court to be a high flight risk. The reasoning here is that would-be absconders will think twice before risking the loss of a significant amount of money or collateral. Some people feel this is unfair because there is no flight risk predictor that is 100 percent accurate. In some respects, however, setting higher bail for those who appear to pose a high flight risk is similar to automobile insurance companies that charge (and keep) higher premiums regardless of whether "high-risk" drivers are ever involved in an accident.[2] Belonging to groups that have higher rates of absconding (e.g., those without community ties, the unemployed, and those with prior records) may mean that an individual who would never consider fleeing the jurisdiction must post higher bail or remain jailed until he or she can obtain the funds or a **surety** (i.e., a person who will guarantee, often through posting of funds or collateral, that the defendant will show up for trial). An interesting twist to this rule is that bail is sometimes set

# BOX 10.1
## Common Bail Guidelines

The 1966 Bail Reform Act established specific criteria to be used in federal pre-trial release decisions. Because many states adopted these same criteria, they are important. One criticism of these guidelines is that they do not provide weighting factors, meaning that one judge could base 90 percent of his or her decision on just one of the factors, while another may assign significant values to each criterion (Harmsworth, 1996). As you read these criteria, think about which you would "score" highly on and which you might not do so well on. Would you qualify for bail? Although you may not have a record of convictions or previous flights to avoid prosecution, how long have you lived in your community (especially salient for students who relocate for college)? Do you have a stable work record? What changes would you recommend to a commission that is studying fairness in bail decisions? What are the differences between the 1966 and 1994 guidelines? Why do you think the guidelines changed? What criteria do you feel should be included that are not on either of the two lists?

1966 guidelines: 18 U.S.C. section 3146(b):
1. the nature of the offense charged
2. the weight of the evidence against the accused
3. the accused's family ties
4. employment
5. financial resources
6. character
7. mental health
8. the length of residence in the community
9. a record of convictions; and
10. a record of failure to appear at court appearances or of flight to avoid prosecution

The current (1994) federal guidelines: 18 U.S.C. section 3142(g):
1. the nature and circumstances of the offense charged, including whether the offense is a crime of violence or involves a narcotic drug;
2. the weight of the evidence against the person;
3. the history and characteristics of the person, including—
   (A) the person's character, physical and mental condition, family ties, employment, financial resources, length of residence in the community, community ties, past conduct, history relating to drug or alcohol abuse, criminal history, and record concerning appearance at court proceedings; and
   (B) whether, at the time of the current offense or arrest, the person was on probation, on parole, or on other release pending trial, sentencing, appeal, or completion of sentence for an offense under Federal, State, or local law; and
4. the nature and seriousness of the danger to any person or the community that would be posed by the person's release (taken from Harmsworth, 1996).

higher for wealthy individuals because the court may feel they are willing to forfeit traditional bail amounts.

Most bail amounts are relatively reasonable, with half of felony defendants receiving bail that is $10,000 or less (Hart and Reaves, 1999). Due in part to their increased likelihood of jail time, those charged with violent offenses tend to get higher bail amounts; 40 percent of such defendants receive bonds that are $25,000 or higher (Hart and Reaves, 1999). Murder cases, of course, usually involve the highest bail amounts. When it is required at all, bail for misdemeanor cases tends to be even lower.

Sometimes, bail can be very high, even for cases that do not involve homicide. When heavy metal singer Tommy Lee was arrested for domestic violence against his wife, his bond was set at a whopping $1 million because he was already on probation for attacking a photographer and guidelines called for $500,000 initial bail (Rocker Tommy Lee jailed for abuse, 1998). In addition to the probability that his probation might be revoked, Lee's disregard for the conditions of his bail may have been interpreted by the judge as a general nonchalance toward court orders. Another recipient of a $1-million bond was a Nebraska man who was believed to have raped women at several college campuses. When setting the high bond, the judge acknowledged that the defendant posed a flight risk, in part because he had no ties to the area (i.e., family or job; [Bond set for campus rape suspect, 1997]). One of the highest bail amounts in a relatively petty case, however, was $3 million for Sterling Crumblin of New Jersey (McHugh, 2000). Why was his bail so high? It was not because the judge who imposed bail was a "hanging judge," as the same judge set bail at $750,000 for an accused murderer. It was not to protect the community since his charges were relatively minor, some drug charges and theft. From the court's point of view, Crumblin had committed an egregious error by skipping bail several times before, making him a severe flight risk. All three cases illustrate how high bond amounts may be used selectively to raise the costs for those defendants felt by the court to represent a risk of becoming absconders. This use of high bail bonds is not without its drawbacks. As discussed later in this chapter, bail is sometimes used in a biased manner to punish people rather than ensure that they return for trial.

Although no defendant has the right to bail, those accused of capital offenses are less likely to be granted bail because of their increased flight risk. Indeed, it would be difficult to place any price on a defendant's life (or his freedom in the event of a life sentence). We saw this in the O. J. Simpson, Unabomber, and Timothy McVeigh cases; no amount of money or collateral could have purchased their freedom. This does not mean that accused murderers cannot be granted bail. It simply means that they need not be granted bail. In one rare case, a California woman who had already been convicted of second-degree murder was allowed to stay out on bail pending her sentencing hearing, despite complaints from the prosecutor that witnesses in the case feared retaliation (Convicted killer released pending sentence, 1995).[3] In another case, involving a juvenile, a young man was allowed to remain out on bail pending his sentencing hearing for two murders that occurred during a robbery. After sentencing him, however, the judge revoked his bail and ordered him incarcerated even though he was appealing the decision (Davis, 1998). In both cases, the judges felt that the low flight risk posed by the individuals justified allowing them to remain free on bail. However, when the circumstances changed, both judges revoked the bail and returned the defendants to custody. That either individual received bail in the first place was rather unusual, as those accused of murder generally have high bail amounts and may also have to submit to other conditions, such as being required to wear an electronic anklet to monitor his or her whereabouts (e.g., to enforce conditions such as curfew or house arrest). The general thought is that those who have been convicted of murder have little to lose by fleeing because the sentences they face are so harsh.

Defendants who are believed by the court to represent a danger to the community or to the safety of any other person (e.g., a victim or witness) may be subjected to **preventative detention**. This alternative to release means that the accused will be held until trial or until the court feels the person is no longer a threat to others. In other words, a person can be denied bail when there is little evidence that he or she will flee the jurisdiction but there are indicators that he or she poses a threat to others. Preventative detention was ruled constitutional by the U.S. Supreme Court in the 1987 case, *United States v. Salerno*. In that case, Salerno and a co-defendant had been held without bail before trial because it was felt that they posed a danger to the community on the basis of their leadership positions in an organized crime "family" as well as allegations that they had used violent means to cover up their past criminal activities. Many states now include provisions for denying bail to those who pose a significant risk to the public or to specific individuals (e.g., victims or witnesses). This does not mean that bail has been transformed from a method to ensure a defendant's appearance at trial into a mechanism to protect the community; instead, protection of the public is one factor that can be used to increase bail amounts or deny it altogether.

Preventative detention can be utilized with nonviolent as well as violent offenses. In one North Carolina case, a woman who was accused of harboring a fugitive (she helped hide a suspect in a botched robbery-murder) was ordered to be held without bail (Cops Say Woman Hid Standoff Suspect, 1998); the fact that the fugitive was still at large probably played a significant role in the court's decision to deny her bail. Most preventative detention cases involve serious crimes, in particular those with significant harm to another person. In general, only about 6 percent of defendants are denied bail, but the majority (61 percent) of murder defendants are denied bail (Hart and Reaves, 1999).

## HISTORY OF BAIL

Bail has been around for quite a while and has its roots in the common law system in England. It began as a way to release defendants before their trials, in part because sheriffs hoped to avoid the responsibility associated with detaining prisoners. Maintaining prisoners was more than simply a costly annoyance; it was also a potentially fatal obligation. Sheriffs were hanged if their charges were able to escape from the often poorly constructed jail facilities (Holmes, 1881, pp. 249–50). This and other unfortunate realities formed the impetus for sheriffs to push for the release of defendants.

In addition to problems facing sheriffs, the court system itself needed a mechanism to free defendants who awaited trial. Up until the early 1900s, trials were conducted by justices who traveled from jurisdiction to jurisdiction to con-

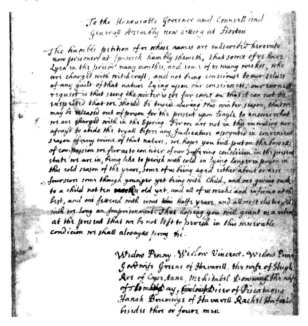

This 1692 handwritten request for bail was drafted by several accused witches, both male and female, who had already been incarcerated "many months" at the Ipswich jail. At the beginning of the petition, the accused witches state their innocence, then ask to "be released out of prison for the present upon Bayle to answer what we are charged with in the Spring. For we are not in this unwilling nor afrayd to abide the tryall before any Judicature." Obtaining "bayle" was important to the defendants because they were all "weake and infirme at the best" and felt they would "perish with cold" in the freezing Massachusetts winter while awaiting trial, which would not take place until the following spring. One can see the importance of bail, especially in circumstances where semi-annual court days meant waiting long periods in unheated prisons with inadequate food, water, and supplies. In fact, these defendants wrote that they were "all most distroyed with soe long an imprisonment," indicating that the conditions of their confinement left something to be desired.    Source: Library of Congress, Manuscript Division, LC-MSS-12021-1, John Davis Batchelder Autograph Collection.

duct trials. Accused persons, then, could expect unusually long waits between arrest and trial. Something had to be done to allow defendants to secure their own releases during these lengthy interims. Because the conditions of confinement were often quite harsh (e.g., lack of sanitation and heat), it was all the more important for the accused to secure release. Some individuals accused of witchcraft during the Salem witch trials, for example, hoped to use bail as a way to escape the terrible conditions of their confinement.

The original bail system consisted of the accused's friends or family coming forward to assure that the accused would appear for trial: "Indeed, in its strict sense, the word 'bail' is used to describe the person who agrees to act as surety for the accused . . . and becomes responsible for his later appearance in court" (Williams, n.d., p. 1). This was no light duty; if the accused was not present for trial, the accused's sureties could be punished in the same manner as were sheriffs of the day or at least fined substantially (Holmes, 1881, pp. 249–250). Oliver Wendell Holmes (1881, p. 248) noted that the common law bail system was linked to an ancient practice in which accused individuals submitted actual hostages to be held until their return. The hostages were killed if the orders to appear for trial were disobeyed.

Not all defendants were eligible for bail under common law, including those accused of crimes such as treason, murder, and arson (Blackstone, 1962, p. 353). Sometimes, the strength of the evidence played a role in whether defendants could receive bail. In manslaughter cases, for example, the accused was not eligible for bail if he was "clearly the slayer," but could receive bail if he was only "barely suspected" of the crime (Blackstone, 1962, pp. 353–354).

Over time, the bail system evolved from one in which advocates agreed to assume the burdensome duty of ensuring the accused's return for trial into a system in which the accused's sureties deposited a specified sum of money or property with the court. It was felt that the **bailee**'s connections to his sureties would prevent him from absconding and that the sureties' risk of losing their property would motivate them to adequately supervise the accused while he or she was out on bail (Williams, n.d., p. 3). No longer were the sureties bound "body for body" to the accused bailee (i.e., they might lose their property, but could no longer lose their lives). This cleared the path for professional bondsagents, who have only financial interests in the accused, to enter the bail process. The development of professional bondsagents has been traced to colonial America, because defendants there were unable to rely on family and friends to bail them out (Chamberlin, 1998), possibly because friends and family may have remained in England, leaving accused individuals to find other ways of securing their release before trial. The bail system, then, has undergone a great deal of change from its early roots to its current form.

The courts have not, however, substantially altered their interpretation of the sureties' obligations to the court, or of the sureties' powers over their bailees. If a bailee does not show up for trial, the surety is liable for the total amount of the bond because he or she voluntarily assumed that obligation. When the bond is forfeited, the surety has the right to track down the bailee and forcefully return him or her to court. The basis for this right rests in the view that the bailee was transferred into the custody of the surety when he or she was released from jail. The surety, therefore, is a sort of metaphysical or abstract jailer, who can recommit the accused whenever it becomes necessary to do so. This view was explained in further detail by the U.S. Supreme Court in *Taylor v. Taintor* (1872):

> When bail is given, the principal is regarded as delivered to the custody of his sureties. Their dominion is a continuance of the original imprisonment. Whenever they choose to do so, they may seize him and deliver him up in their discharge, and if that cannot be done at once, they may imprison him until it can be done. They may exercise their rights in person or by agent. They may pursue him into another state; may arrest him on the Sabbath; and if necessary, may break and enter his house for that purpose. The seizure is not made by virtue of new process. None is needed. It is likened to the rearrest, by the sheriff, of an escaping prisoner. (p. 371)

In some respects, a bail surety's powers exceed those granted to law enforcement personnel. Whereas jurisdictional boundaries represent difficult barriers to law enforcement, who must rely on good public relations and extradition orders to capture absconding suspects, a surety (or his or her agent) can easily cross even state lines in pursuit of a bailee. Similarly, sureties may break into homes in most jurisdictions to secure their bailees, whereas law enforcement personnel must carefully follow meticulously designed policies governing their uninvited entry into homes (e.g., knock notices). Sureties are also able to circumvent search warrant requirements if the search is part of their attempt to locate someone who failed to honor his or her promise to return for trial.

Bail sureties' common law "right to arrest" has been preserved by state and federal statutes (William, n.d., p. 9). The federal Bail Reform Act of 1984, for example, specifically empowers sureties to "arrest" their bailees and deliver them to federal marshals who must bring them before the appropriate court (18 U.S.C., sec. 3149). There is no requirement that the bailee break any laws before their sureties can "revoke" their bail and recommit them to detention, either. Remember that in case your parents or friends ever post bail for you: They can recommit you to jail for no reason other than the fact that they no longer wish to be responsible for your return to court. To further assist sureties, some jurisdictions have created bail jumping statutes as an added disincentive to those considering absconding while out on bail. These statutes provide for the incarceration and/or fining of defendants for the offense of jumping bail as well as their punishment for their original crime.

Like others in the justice drama, however, bail sureties and their agents must be careful not to overstep their bounds. Although they are granted additional powers to assist them in recovering bail skippers, they are liable if they make a mistake or go too far in their attempts to return someone to custody. Most bail sureties leave the task of physically tracking down and returning bail skippers to **bounty hunters** or skip tracers, who perform this service for a fee, usually 10 percent of the bond

ABC Bail Bonds, in Camden, New Jersey, is directly across the street from the county detention center. The agency is open twenty-four hours a day and, for a price, will post bonds for those who meet their screening criteria. Bail bond agencies fulfill a valuable role in criminal justice, allowing those accused of crimes to secure their freedom before trial. Research has shown that those who are detained before their trials are less able to assist with their own defenses. Despite this reality, about half of inmates held in jails are unconvicted and awaiting trial.   SOURCE: Courtesy of Jon'a Meyer.

amount. A sometimes gruff group of individuals, bounty hunters are basically an unregulated bunch. All skip tracers can track bail jumpers, but only two states, Indiana and Nevada, license bounty hunters (Kelley, 1997).

This lack of regulation sometimes lands skip tracers themselves in court—the result of their efforts to track and return bail absconders. After being mistaken for a bail absconder, one New York woman was abducted by bounty hunters and transported against her will to Alabama; although they released her and bought her a bus ticket for the 900-mile journey back to her home as soon as they realized their mistake, she sued in federal court[4] and received a $1-million settlement (Panel considers bounty hunters law, 1998). In another case, a California bounty hunter was arrested for assault with force likely to produce great bodily injury after he broke a bail skipper's neck, nose, and collarbone (Thornton, 1993). Yet another skip tracer was arrested for assault with a deadly weapon after he shot an absconder (Pierce, 1996). It is cases such as these that have led to calls for additional oversight of bounty hunters.

## TYPES OF BAIL

There are many bail systems in use across the United States. The form that is most like the roots of our current system is **fully secured bail**. Under this system, the accused person deposits with the court either the full bail amount or property (e.g., real estate deeds) worth the full bond amount. Once this is done, the accused is freed pending appearance at trial. If the accused does not show up for trial, he or she forfeits the entire amount and will still have to stand trial if found. Of course, many defendants do not have access to large sums of money, so several alternative approaches have been developed over time.

Currently, the most common type of bail is **privately secured bail** or **surety bail**. More than one fourth (28 percent) of defendants who are released before trial use this mechanism (Hart and Reaves, 1999). Defendants wishing to utilize this system of bail must contact a bail bondsagent, who, for a nonrefundable fee, posts a bond for the full bail amount with the court. Generally, this fee is 10 percent of the total bail amount. Most bail bondsagents also require some form of collateral before bailing out a client. The bondsagent then takes a portion of the defendant's fee and purchases a bond from an insurance company who agrees to pay the full amount if the defendant does not show up for trial. The remaining funds become the bail bondsagent's payment for service as an insurance broker. A few bondsagents do not rely on insurance companies, but they become personally responsible for the full amount if any of their clients fails to show up for trial. Box 10.2 contains a brief synopsis of a typical day in one California bondsagent's life. The bondsagent explains how the bail process works and mentions some of the problems he typically faces in his field.

A third type of bail is **percentage bail** or **deposit bail**. Under percentage bail, defendants deposit with the court a percentage, generally 10 percent, of the total bail amount. Percentage bail is the third most common form of pre-trial release, used by 11 percent of defendants who are released (Hart and Reaves, 1999). Defendants who show up at their hearings get their deposits back. Those who fail to return to court lose the 10 percent deposit and are billed for the remaining 90 percent. If the absconder leaves any money or property behind, the court can file liens and seize the forfeited amount. Defendants' initial financial outlay for this type of bail is similar to privately secured bail, except that the deposit is returned to the defendant rather than going to a bondsagent as payment for his or her services.

The final form of bail is **unsecured bail**. This type of bail does not require defendants to deposit any money or collateral with the courts. If the defendant does not return to court, however, the full bail amount is forfeited and payable upon demand. Unsecured bail is similar to a judge suspending the bond amount; the judge first sets the bail amount and then allows the defendant to leave without paying, but liable for the full amount in the event he or she does not appear at trial. Unlike the other three bail systems, which are implemented jurisdiction-wide, unsecured bail may be used on a case-by-case basis within a jurisdiction. For those defendants about whom a judge is uncertain about their likelihood of returning to court, a bail amount can be required.

Most nonserious defendants are not required to post bail or to put up a bond. Instead, they are **released on their own recognizance** (ROR), which means they

---

## BOX 10.2

## A Day in the Life of a Bondsagent

"King" Stahlman Bail Bonds never closes; the office is open twenty-four hours a day, 365 days a year, even on holidays and when business is slow. To secure Stahlman's services, the defendant or his or her family and friends "front" ten percent of the total bail amount to Stahlman. In exchange for this fee, Stahlman agrees to pay the court the full bail amount if the bailee fails to appear for trial, then the bailee is released. If the bailee flees, Stahlman gets six months to "produce the fugitive" before he is held responsible for the bail. Sometimes, Stahlman sues bail skippers to get his money back, but this is not always effective.

Most of Stahlman's clients show up for trial after securing his services and getting out of jail, but some do not. Regardless of whether they show up for trial, some cause Stahlman and his staff some worry. Says Stahlman of some of his clients: "It's amazing how you can bail somebody out of jail and three weeks later the phone is disconnected and the co-signer is gone."

Stahlman does not play soft with his clients. Before posting the bond, he informs all clients that excuses for missing trial are not tolerated: "There's only three reasons you miss a court appearance . . . You're in jail, you're in the hospital—or you're dead." He also takes pictures of them in case they skip and he has to hire a bounty hunter to track them down. He also requires some clients to check in from time to time to keep him informed about their cases and whereabouts.

Despite his warnings and efforts to screen clients before posting bonds for them, a few bailees do skip town. Like many other bondsagents, Stahlman employs the services of bounty hunters to track down and return bail jumpers. Bounty hunters ultimately end up satisfying two agencies, because their services return the defendant to trial (satisfying the court) and free the bondsagent from paying the full bond (satisfying Stahlman). Stahlman says that bounty hunters prefer to "call themselves skip tracers . . . [to give themselves] a little class."

Most of the bonds Stahlman provides are moderate amounts ($5,000 to $10,000), for those accused of assault, domestic violence, drug dealing, and residential burglaries. On occasion, he provides larger bonds. In one case, he provided a bond for half a million dollars for a man accused of attempted murder for shooting his nephew. Stahlman acknowledges that there is risk that someone will flee: "I had a bookmaker tell me the risk is so bad he wouldn't be in this business."

Sometimes, attorneys come by Stahlman's office to request his services for their clients. Status in the community might help, but does not guarantee that Stahlman will post bond for wealthy individuals. He once turned down a doctor's son because the son's attorney could not guarantee that the son would show up for trial. Those who have no resources at all, however, should not expect charity from bondsagents, including Stahlman.

After a full, eleven-hour day, Stahlman goes home to relax and catch the evening news.

*Source:* Story adapted from Steinberg, 1997.

---

simply promise to return to court for their hearing. According to recent government statistics, the highest number of all pre-trial releases, 38 percent, are ROR releases (Hart and Reaves, 1999). There is no money or collateral forfeited if the defendant does not appear, but a warrant can be issued for his or her arrest if he or she fails to appear. This form of release is usually used for individuals who have ties to their

## BOX 10.3

## New Mexico Court Order Setting Conditions of Release

The order depicted here allows courtroom personnel to quickly check off applicable conditions for bail. This form is from New Mexico, but its format is not uncommon and resembles the layout used in other jurisdictions. It includes three important components: (1) the type of and amount of the bond; (2) the defendant's promise to appear; and (3) any conditions of release. As you read over the conditions, try to think of cases for which they would be appropriate. Would any case merit *all* of the conditions?

*STATE OF NEW MEXICO*          *(COUNTY OF ...........................)*
                                        *(CITY OF ...............................)*

                *IN THE ......... COURT*

*(STATE OF NEW MEXICO)*
*(CITY OF ......................)*
         *v.*                            *No. ..............*
    John Doe

### ORDER SETTING CONDITIONS OF RELEASE
### BAIL BOND

*(This form is to be used if the defendant is to be released on a secured appearance bond or bail bond. If a surety provides bond for the defendant, Form 9-304 must also be completed. If the defendant personally deposits cash as required, no other form is required.)*

*It is ordered that the defendant be released on bail in the amount of ....................*
*dollars ($ .........) provided that the defendant executes this order and agreement and:*

**(check and complete applicable alternatives)**

[ ] *deposits with the court the sum of .................... dollars ($ .........) in cash being .........% of the required bond to secure its performance. (A paid surety may post cash with the court provided the paid surety executes an agreement that upon forfeiture the paid surety will pay the balance of the full amount of the bail set forth above.)*

[ ] *executes a bail bond on a form approved by the supreme court in the sum of .................... dollars ($ .........) or deposits with the clerk of the court, in cash, one-hundred percent (100%) of the amount of the bail set. (If a surety posts bond for the defendant the defendant and the surety must also execute Form 9-304.)*

[ ] *it is ordered that the defendant report to (name) .................... (set forth designated entity or pretrial services agency agreeing to supervise the defendant) ......... (set forth telephone number of entity).*

### DEFENDANT'S BOND

*I .............., defendant in the above-entitled matter, do hereby bind myself to the following conditions of release:*

**(court or designee must complete before
the defendant reads and signs this bond)**

    *I agree to appear before the above court on .............., at ..... (a.m.) (p.m.) in courtroom .............. and at such other places as I may be required to appear, in accordance with any and all orders and directions relating to my appearance in the above-entitled matter as may be given or issued by the above court or any magistrate, district or appellate court to which the above entitled case may be removed or the cause transferred.*
    *I further agree to pay the (State of New Mexico) (City of ..............) the full amount of the bail set forth above in the event that I fail to appear as required or comply with the additional conditions checked below.*

*Agreement to Comply with All*
*Additional Conditions of Release*

I further agree that:

*(court or designee must complete*
*applicable conditions prior*
*to signature by the defendant)*

[ ] I will remain in the custody of the above named third-party custodian who has agreed to report any violation of a release condition to the court;

[ ] I understand that my release is subject to my maintaining my employment. If my employment is terminated I agree to immediately report such termination to the court;

[ ] I will actively seek employment;

[ ] I will attend classes at .............;

[ ] I will not associate with the following persons .............;

[ ] I will not leave the (city of .............) (this county) (the county of .............) (this state) (the state of .............) without further permission of the court;

[ ] I will reside at ............. unless otherwise agreed to by the court;

[ ] I will avoid all contact with ............. and ............. (set forth the names of the alleged crime victim or any potential witness to the crime);

[ ] I will not leave my residence between the hours of ..... (p.m.) and ..... (a.m.) without prior permission of the court;

[ ] I will not possess a firearm, destructive device or other dangerous weapon without prior permission of the court;

[ ] I will:

    [ ] refrain from excessive consumption of beer, wine and other alcoholic beverages;

    [ ] not drink any alcoholic beverages;

[ ] I will not take or use any narcotic drugs without a prescription by a licensed medical practitioner;

[ ] I will submit to any urine analysis or alcohol test upon the request of .............;

[ ] I agree to the following (medical) (psychological or psychiatric) treatment for ............. (set forth treatment such as treatment for drug or alcohol dependency);

[ ] I will remain at (set forth institution) ............. for the following treatment ............. for a period of .............;

[ ] I agree that if I am released for the purpose of (employment) (schooling), I will return to ............. (set forth place of detention) each day immediately after (work) (school) (classes).

I understand the above conditions of release and agree to them.

I understand that the court may have me arrested at any time, without notice, to review and reconsider these conditions.

I understand, that if I fail to appear as required, I may be prosecuted and sent to (jail) (the penitentiary) for the separate offense of failure to appear. I agree to comply fully with each of the conditions imposed on my release and to notify the court promptly in the event I change the address indicated below.

I understand that my conditions of release may be revoked and I may be charged with a separate criminal offense if I intimidate or threaten a witness, the victim or an informant or if I otherwise obstruct justice.

I further understand that my conditions of release will be revoked if I violate a federal, state or local criminal law.

.........................................................
*Defendant*

.........................................................
*Address*

.........................................................
*City and State*

.........................................................
*Telephone Number*

*(Continued)*

## BOX 10.3 *(continued)*

*The above conditions of release are hereby approved. The defendant shall be released from custody upon the execution of this agreement and the posting of the required bail bond.*

.................................................................
*(Judge)  (Designee)*
.................................................................
*Date*

**FIGURE 10.3**   *Source:* New Mexico Supreme Court Rules 1986, Criminal Forms, Judicial Pamphlet 9, 1990 Replacement, pp. 38–40.

communities (e.g., those who own their homes or whose family is local) that would presumably keep them from fleeing the jurisdiction. Those with good reputations in their communities (e.g., city councilpersons, church officials, and teachers) may also be released on their own recognizance. No matter how much standing one has in his or her community, however, this form of release is seldom used for serious offenses like drug trafficking or murder (e.g., 18 U.S.C., sec. 3142).

In addition to posting bail, defendants may be classified as **conditional release**, which means they are required to comply with certain conditions prior to being released. See Box 10.3 (pages 278–280) for a court order form that lists some conditions of bail release. Nearly one tenth (9 percent) of releasees are released on conditional release (Hart and Reaves, 1999). These conditions often involve staying away from one's victim (e.g., in domestic violence or stalking cases) or to seek care in a substance abuse or other treatment program. A variety of conditions may be required, as long as they are reasonably tied to protecting the community or ensuring that the accused shows up for trial. Sometimes, defendants are ordered to comply with electronic monitoring so that their whereabouts can be tracked. Even though their families posted bonds of $300,000, for example, Amy Grossberg and Brian Peterson, accused of killing their newborn, were required to wear electronic monitoring devices and observe a strict curfew (Hoffman, 1997).

In fact, the Grossberg-Peterson case illustrates several important issues with respect to bail. Despite the fact that they had been charged with capital murder and faced the death penalty if convicted, the prosecutor dropped his opposition to bail because he felt that neither was a danger to the community. The judge allowed bail on the basis of their character references, ties to the community, and lack of criminal records. In response to fears that they might abscond, however, the judge ordered them to submit to the conditions mentioned above and to surrender their passports. The case is also interesting in that they were allowed to return to their families' homes in New Jersey despite facing trial in Delaware.

Another form of release is **third-party custody**. This form of release is most similar to the common law system in which bail sureties assumed the responsibility for ensuring the accused's presence at trial (except that the sureties no longer risk death if the bailee absconds). This form of release is generally used with juveniles or defendants who the court fears may not return to court due to mental illness or other issues. Under this system, a third party (e.g., a parent, family member, or friend), promises to assure that the defendant will return for his or her hearing. This form of release is relatively uncommon.

## INFLUENCES ON BAIL BY THE COURTROOM WORK GROUP AND OTHERS IN THE JUSTICE DRAMA

Although judges are usually responsible for actually granting bail and determining the amount, this decision is by no means made in a vacuum. Other members of the courtroom work group strive to affect the final decision. The prosecutor may argue that the defendant represents a danger to the community or victim if released, or may argue that the alleged crimes warrant a high bail amount because of the increased flight risk associated with more severe penalties. The defense attorney, on the other hand, will attempt to present his or her client in a favorable light, arguing instead that bail should be granted and that the defendant deserves a minimal bond, due either to indigence, lack of prior record, or mitigating personal conditions (e.g., the defendant is ailing or is the main source of support for his or her family). Research shows that judges are more likely to "side with" prosecutor's recommendations rather than those made by defense attorneys (Feeley, 1979, p. 67; Wice, 1985, p. 58).

The police also have an effect on bail. In some jurisdictions, they alone set bail in misdemeanor cases and in some felony cases. In others, they establish, through the charges they list on arrest reports, an initial bail amount that may be paid by defendants who wish to secure their release immediately. Those who do not pay the initial bail or who are not granted bail at the police level are entitled to a bail hearing before a magistrate within a specified amount of time, usually forty-eight hours. In any case, the charges that are filed against defendants are at least initially selected by the police and these charges are closely related to the final bail amounts.

Bondsagents deserve special mention for their influences on the bail process. They depend on the courts for their business, and at the same time assist the courts by allowing defendants who would ordinarily be forced to remain in jail. This is no unimportant function, considering that more than half of all jail inmates in the United States are awaiting trial (Perkins, Stephan, and Beck, 1995). In a very real sense, then, the courts and bondsagents need each other. It is quite possible that the bail system would have undergone many more court-mandated changes had it not been for the development of the private bond business. Instead of suing for their release under habeas corpus actions, defendants pay a bondsagent's fee and are released.

As discussed earlier, situational justice may play an important part in bail decisions. Bail may be denied to particularly loathsome defendants who are charged with only moderately severe offenses, or bail amounts may be set far above individual defendants' means simply to prevent them from achieving release prior to their trials (Davis, 1969, p. 10; Feeley, 1979, p. 210). This practice was common in the southern states as a way to "penalize" blacks who challenged the dominant white power structure (e.g., Lester, 1965). Unfortunately, the use of high bail to achieve situational justice did not vanish with the abuses during the Civil Rights movement.

In 1989, a judge set bond at $1 million for the captain of the Exxon Valdez (which was involved in an 11-million gallon oil spill in Prince William Sound, just off the Alaskan coast), although the prosecutor requested only $25,000 bond and the captain faced only misdemeanor charges of being drunk and below deck when the accident occurred (King, 1989). The bond was reduced to $25,000 the next day, and it has since been argued that the presence of the media on the day of the initial hearing led the judge to set the unusually high bail, passionately comparing the captain's actions to the bombing of Hiroshima: "It is a misdemeanor of such a magnitude that has probably never been equalled anywhere in this country. We have a destruction, a man-made destruction that has not been equalled since Hiroshima" (King, 1989). Even more recently, a judge set bail at $5 million for former savings and loan chief Charles Keating despite the prosecutor agreeing that he could be released on his own recognizance (Granelli, 1990). In both of these cases, and others like them, it appears that the judges simply wanted to ensure that the defendants were unable to make bail, forcing them to get a "taste" of jail before the bail amounts were reduced on appeal (Chambers, 1990).

Bail policies and the factors taken into consideration in setting bail have a disproportionately heavy impact on not only poor defendants, but also defendants of ethnic minority groups. In one study of 150,000 criminal cases in Connecticut, researchers found that African American and Hispanic defendants had their bail set at double the amount for white defendants. In some drug cases, minority defendants had bail set at four times the amount of that as white defendants in comparable cases (Ewing and Houston, 1991).

## THE MANHATTAN BAIL PROJECT

No discussion of bail would be complete without mentioning the Manhattan Bail Project, administered by the Vera Institute of Justice. The project's goals were to determine if those who could not meet the financial requirements for bail (i.e., they were granted bail but were too poor to post bond) could be depended upon to return without putting up bail (Ares, Rankin, and Sturz, 1963, p. 71). To achieve this goal, the program staff designed a classification scheme to help them rate the likelihood of defendants absconding. The approach contained many of the same criteria used by the courts in determining bail (e.g., ties to the community, presence of family nearby, employment history, and prior record; Rubin, 1976, p. 56). To evaluate the potential of the program, indigent defendants who met the program's criteria were randomly assigned to one of two groups: an experimental group (which was sponsored by the Vera Institute for pre-trial release) or a control group (which was not sponsored and remained in jail between arrest and trial).

The results of the evaluation were enlightening. As expected, the project found that, with proper screening, almost all defendants showed up for trial. This finding was instrumental in initiating the Bail Reform Act of 1966, which declared that defendants in federal cases should be entitled to bail whenever possible. Although the Bail Reform Act of 1966 applies only to federal courts, state courts tend to agree that defendants should be offered bail when it is feasible to do so without risking the community's safety or a failure to appear on behalf of the accused.[5] Box 10.4 demonstrates this idea by presenting the guidelines followed by Virginia magistrates with respect to bail decisions (Virginia magistrates perform many of the functions once completed by justices of the peace). The guidelines also emphasize the value assigned by judges to characteristics of the offense and the accused's community ties as indicators of his or her likelihood of absconding.

Equally important to demonstrating the efficiency of the Vera Institute's screening strategy, the evaluation showed that although the defendants had been

---

## BOX 10.4
## Bail Guidelines Followed by Virginia Magistrates

Bail procedures exist to enable an accused to stay out of jail and to insure that the accused will appear for trial. Magistrates decide the terms of bail by examining certain facts about the accused, such as the nature and circumstances of the offense charged, whether a firearm is alleged to have been used in the offense, weight of the evidence, character of the accused, the accused's family ties, employment, financial resources, length of residence in the community, involvement in education, and past record. If possible, the magistrate will release the accused on a written promise to appear in court with or without an unsecured bail bond. If, after examination of these facts, magistrates are not reasonably sure that the accused will appear for trial, the magistrates, in their discretion, will require the execution of a bail bond with surety in a reasonable amount and may impose such other conditions deemed reasonably necessary to insure appearance at trial. The monetary sum of the bail bond can be forfeited as a penalty if the accused fails to appear in court or violates any condition of bail (Supreme Court of Virginia, n.d.).

randomly assigned to the pre-trial release group (i.e., there was no bias in who was assigned to the two groups), those who were released were substantially less likely to be convicted (59 percent of the experimental group was acquitted versus 23 percent of the control group) and if they were convicted, they were considerably less likely to be incarcerated (21 percent of the convicted experimental group was jailed versus 96 percent of the control group [Ares, Rankin, and Sturz, 1963, pp. 86–87]). The evaluators concluded that being detained before trial affected future decisions in the criminal justice system. The evaluation certainly lent some support to the assertion that incarcerated defendants are less able to assist with their own defenses. This reality will be covered in greater detail later in the next section of this chapter.

## "DON'T PAY MEANS YOU STAY": PROBLEMS WITH BAIL

The bail process is not without its critics. In fact, there are a number of problems noted with the current system, most of which are noted by commentators who feel the bail system is an important institution. Despite their support of the process, they still recognize that the system needs reform.

One of the most persistent criticisms of the bail process is that it discriminates against the poor (e.g., Ares, Rankin, and Sturz, 1963; Burns, 1973; Lizotte, 1978). Due to their access to funds and greater likelihood of owning property that can be used for collateral, the rich are better able to deposit the full amount of their bail with the court. The poor, on the other hand, are often unable to gather the funds to post and instead must rely on private bondsagents who charge a fee for their service. See Box 10.5 for statistics regarding whether defendants were able to secure pre-trial release by type of attorney (publicly funded or privately secured); these statistics tend to show that those who qualify for publicly funded attorneys are less able to make bail when it is allowed. In cases where bail amounts are high, the fees paid to bondsagents can be quite costly: For example, in securing his release, Charles Keating's family paid $30,000 cash to a bondsagent after his bail was reduced to $300,000 (Granelli, 1990). The important distinction is that those who post the full amount of their bail have it returned in its entirety when they appear for trial, whereas those who rely on bondsagents are not entitled to any refund. Keating's family, then, stood to lose the entire $30,000 they posted. There are countless examples of indigent defendants who cannot post even moderate bonds, much less very high bail amounts.

It is also important to realize that bondsagents do not accept as clients everyone who solicits their services (e.g., Professional Bondsmen of New Mexico, n.d.). Like any other individual in the criminal justice system, bondsagents have discretion regarding for whom they choose to issue bonds. They are unlikely, for example, to accept defendants who have no property whatsoever, defendants who they feel might

# BOX 10.5
# Release Prior to Trial by Type of Counsel

The following table presents statistics regarding whether defendants were able to secure pre-trial release by type of attorney (publicly funded or privately secured). Taken together, these statistics show that those who qualify for publicly funded attorneys are less able to make bail when it is allowed because approximately the same percentage of defendants in each category are denied bail (meaning that the others were unable or unwilling to post bail). The table also presents statistics on the case outcomes broken out by attorney. The numbers should not surprise you, given the findings discussed in Step 6.

### Release Before Trial and Disposition of Case with a Felony Charge, by Type of Counsel, for Convicted Jail Inmates, 1996

|  | Type of counsel | |
|---|---|---|
|  | Public | Private |
| **Release before trial*** |  |  |
| Released | 22.5% | 54.5% |
|    Without bail or bond | 3.8 | 4.1 |
|    With bail or bond | 18.7 | 50.4 |
| No release | 77.5 | 45.5 |
|    Bail or bond set | 57.0 | 26.0 |
|    Bail or bond not set | 20.5 | 19.5 |
| **Disposition of case** |  |  |
| Not guilty | 14.0% | 20.7% |
|    Bench trial | 7.6 | 8.7 |
|    Jury trial | 5.0 | 10.7 |
|    Unknown type of trial | 1.4 | 1.3 |
| Guilty/no contest plea | 85.9 | 79.3 |
|    With plea bargain | 53.5 | 48.7 |
|    Without plea bargain | 32.4 | 30.6 |

*Counsel may have been appointed or hired after bail hearing.

*Source:* C.W. Harlow, 2000. *Defense Counsel in Criminal Cases.* Washington, DC: Bureau of Justice Statistics, p. 7.

abscond, or those whom they dislike in any way. One bondsagent (Vigil, 1994) explained that she usually avoids first-time felony offenders because they might get "skittish" and leave town due to fear about the trial outcome, cases where bail is very high because there is more money to lose if the client skips, and those charged with violent offenses because they represent possible harm to the bondsagent or her staff. Unlike the rich, who simply post their bonds and leave, the poor must subject themselves to a separate and distinct process to gain liberty before their trials.

Further, some people have decried the remarkable powers that bondsagents have over their clients, as previously discussed. These powers stem from the fact that the process is essentially a civil rather than criminal one. Remember, if the defendant fails to appear at trial, the bondsagent forfeits the 90 percent he or she posted or the insurance bond that he or she purchased. To prepare for that possibility, they have clients sign a release form authorizing the bondsagent to send skip tracers after them to locate and bring them back before the court. Skip tracers, given their unique status in the criminal justice system (i.e. that they are not government agents, but they have significant arrest powers), are not bound by the same due process concerns as law enforcement officers.

A few critics point to the corruption that the bail process seems to engender. Judges have been known to set very high bail in exchange for kickbacks from bondsagents. This can happen because bondsagents get a percentage of the bail as commission, so higher bonds mean higher fees. Another form of corruption happens when bondsagents bribe officials in order to be able to solicit clients inside the jails. Although it is not necessarily corruption, bail bondsagent companies and representatives sometimes lobby against the use of ROR (release on own recognizance) because they make no money off defendants who are released on ROR.

Some scholars argue that allowing bondsagents to get involved in the bail system taints its true purpose. As originally conceived, bail was to ensure the defendant's appearance at trial. When bondsagents bail their clients out of jail, however, the risk is transferred from the defendant to the bondsagent. The accused does not stand to lose much if he or she fails to appear, and under current law, bondsagents are no longer punished (except for forfeiture of the bond) if the bailee fails to appear. And, some critics argue that, because of reliance on insurance companies, even the bondsagents do not stand to lose much. The only thing most bondsagents risk is the cancellation of their insurance policies. This, too, runs counter to the purpose of bail (which is to ensure the defendant appears at trial) because neither the accused nor the bondsagent incurs much risk.

Some commentators have noted that forfeited bonds are not always collected when defendants fail to appear. Sometimes the courts do not wish to irritate the bondsagents on whom they depend to ease jail overcrowding. These critics ask why such a perverted system is maintained, which allow bonds agents to retain their fee and the bond, even when their clients do not show up.

A final critique of the bail system is that some defendants commit crimes due to bail; that is, they commit crimes to obtain the funds to pay off their bail or bondsagent fees. This is not to be confused with new crimes committed while out on bail, which is an argument against allowing bail at all. Instead, this critique centers on the supposition that forcing defendants to buy their way out of jail leads them to commit crimes in order to secure the funds needed to do so. This is similar to the Florida case in which a probationer was robbing banks in order to pay his monthly probation fees (Man robs bank to pay probation, 1997). Although these incidents seem to attract media attention, this type of case is rare.

# WHEN BAIL IS NOT MET: THE INFLUENCE OF PRE-TRIAL DETENTION

When defendants cannot meet the bail assigned to their cases, they must remain in detention until they obtain the necessary funds or until trial, whichever comes first. Those for whom bail is denied, of course, must wait out their trials behind bars. Pre-trial detention has been shown to have many negative effects on defendants, as illustrated by the Manhattan Bail Project and other research.

First, although pre-trial detainees are presumed innocent in theory, they are mixed in with offenders sentenced to jail for their crimes. Pre-trial detainees are subjected to the same conditions of incarceration as other inmates, including the sometimes awesome loss of privacy and dignity, and isolation from family and loved ones. The psychological effects of incarceration cannot be overestimated. Prisoners have been shown to experience increased levels of stress due to the uncertainty added into their lives and the inability to establish adequate sleep patterns. Apprehension, tension, frustration, feelings of isolation, and fear are likely to befall the inmate (e.g., Boudouris and Brady, 1980; New York State Defenders Association, 1985; Wojda, 1991). Worry about physical predation may also affect inmates of both genders. Although these fears are probably exaggerated by the media, men are still more likely to be raped in jail than in the free world (Cotton and Groth, 1982).

Further, pre-trial detainees can suffer the stigmas of incarceration that are normally reserved for convicted offenders. They may lose their jobs because they miss days at work, especially when one considers that pre-trial detainees are likely to be employed in secondary sector jobs that depend on the defendant's presence at work, such as waiters and waitresses, hair stylists, and other service-oriented jobs. A number of these employers rely on a "three strikes and you're out" approach; those who miss three days of work are terminated. Those employed in secondary sector jobs are also unlikely to have vacation time they can use while in jail.

Pre-trial detainees can also lose their families and friends because of their incarceration. Spouses may need to move in with other family members or friends for financial and other support, children sometimes must be transferred to the temporary custody of others, and friendships are difficult to attend to while defendants are in jail awaiting trial. Some family and friends may not recognize that an accused defendant is not necessarily guilty, and so may shun even those who have not yet been tried. In reality, the mere bringing of charges against an individual is enough to raise the suspicions of many family members and friends.

Financial debts, including housing rentals, utility bills, and credit card payments, continue to accrue while defendants await their trials (Knowles and Prewitt, 1969, p. 72). Sometimes, defendants are released only to find that they have lost their housing due to nonpayment of rent, their utilities have been turned off, their credit cards canceled, or their credit history ruined by only a short pre-trial detention.

Finally, and possibly most important, research shows that defendants who are held before their trials are less able to assist in their own defense. They cannot seek out witnesses or meet freely with their attorneys (Knowles and Prewitt, 1969, p. 72). Because they are held in jail, they are unable to meet with prosecutors to negotiate plea bargains or other reductions in the charges they face.

Persons detained before trial are also more likely to be further processed and convicted, even when other factors are controlled (Albonetti, 1986, 1991; Ares, Rankin, and Sturz, 1963; Ebbesen and Konečni, 1981; Holmes and Daudistel, 1984; Lizotte, 1978; Uhlman, 1979, pp. 90–92; Wheeler and Hissong, 1988). They are also more likely to waive their right to trial and enter a guilty plea, especially if the crimes with which they are charged will result in probation or a short jail sentence (Feeley, 1979, p. 134; Knowles and Prewitt, 1969, p. 72). The same research shows that sentences imposed on pre-trial detainees are harsher than those imposed on defendants who were released (e.g., Ares, Rankin, and Sturz, 1963). Because we also know that the bail amount is tied to likelihood of release before trial (i.e., that bailees' bonds are three times lower than those for pre-trial detainees; Hart and Reaves, 1999), this points to an area where significant reform is necessary.

To compound matters, pre-trial detainees often appear at their trials in detention center issued jumpsuits, and shackled to other prisoners. Men may be unshaven, and defendants of both genders may not be able to create a favorable impression due to exhaustion from lack of sleep or anxiety. Defendants' appearances have been linked to negative impacts on judges, and especially on juries (Knowles and Prewitt, 1969; Rubin, 1976; Uhlman, 1979, p. 92).

## CONCLUSION

From its roots as a system in which bail sureties agreed to take the accused's place if the bailee absconded, our current bail system has evolved into a popular form of release for those accused of committing crimes. Those who cannot meet bail themselves can call on others, including professional bondsagents (for a fee), to help them do so. Many of the problems noted about the bail system are tied to its potentially discriminatory structure, but reforms have been implemented in some jurisdictions to assuage those difficulties. Due in part to the symbiotic (i.e., mutually beneficial) relationship between bondsagents and the courts, one can safely conclude that the bail system can withstand even zealous attempts to eradicate it.

The next chapter will explain the history and types of modern plea bargains. We will learn about how plea bargains are initiated and processed, and how they affect justice, the actors in the justice drama, and the public.

## DISCUSSION QUESTIONS

1. Look at the two sets of guidelines in Sidebar Box 10.1. What are the differences between the 1966 and 1994 guidelines? Why do you think the guidelines changed? What criteria do you feel should be included that are not on either of the two lists?

2. Imagine that you are a defendant in colonial America. In addition to the possible absence of loved ones and family who could post bonds with the court, what other hardships would exist for you if you wanted to be released before trial?

3. Should all accused persons be allowed to post bail? Why or why not?

4. Consider the plight of people awaiting trial who are not granted or cannot make bail. Jails often house a volatile mix of pre-trial detainees: people convicted of crimes and sentenced to a year or less of incarceration; and people convicted of serious, violent crimes and sentenced to state prison who are held in jail pending transfer to state prisons. Often these groups of inmates are mixed together, rather than separated. Is this fair to people who have not yet been tried? What would be some problems that could arise if you were arrested for nonpayment of parking tickets and put in jail along with hardened criminals?

5. Make a list of all the ways that pre-trial detention negatively affects a defendant's legal prognosis (i.e., the final outcome in the defendant's case)? Why does pre-trial detention have this effect?

6. How might pre-trial detention help explain the disproportionate conviction and incarceration of poor and minority defendants?

7. Think about what you learned about bounty hunters and skip tracers. Why do they have fewer Fourth Amendment constraints on their power than police officers? What problems does this present? What reforms would you suggest to eliminate these problems?

## NOTES

1. The Eighth Amendment to the U.S. Constitution reads: "Excessive bail shall not be required, nor excessive fines imposed, nor cruel and unusual punishments inflicted."

2. Thanks to an anonymous reviewer who suggested this analogy.

3. After the prosecutor filed a motion asking the judge to reconsider the release, the judge ordered her into jail until the sentencing hearing. The judge said he had not yet seen the police report in her case or her arrest record, which detailed a prior offense for assault with a deadly weapon (Murderer free on bail but not for long, 1995).

4. She sued the skip tracers, the bondsman that hired them, several officers in New York and New Jersey who failed to order her release, and the city of New York.

5. Not showing up for trial can also net you a charge of a separate crime, Failure to Appear (FTA).

## REFERENCES

Albonetti, C.A. (1986). Criminality, prosecutorial screening, and uncertainty: Toward a theory of discretionary decision making in felony case processings. *Criminology,* 24: 623–644.

Albonetti, C.A. (1991). An integration of theories to explain judicial discretion. *Social Problems,* 38: 247–66.

Ares, C., Rankin, A., and Sturz, H. (1963). The Manhattan bail project: An interim report on the use of pretrial parole. *New York University Law Review,* 39: 67–92.

Blackstone, W. (1962). *Commentaries on the Laws of England: Of Public Wrongs.* Adapted by R.M. Kerr. Boston: Beacon Press.

Bond set for campus rape suspect. (1997, May 19). *Associated Press Wire.*

Boudouris, J., and Brady, H.J. (1980). Attitudes of prison inmates. *Journal of Offender Counseling Services and Rehabilitation,* 5: 67–77.

Burns, H. (1973). Black people and the tyranny of American law. *Annals of the American Academy of Political and Social Science,* 407: 156–166.

Chamberlin, J.A. (1998). Bounty hunters: Can the criminal justice system live without them? *University of Illinois Law Review, 1998:* 1175–1205.

Chambers, M. (1990, November 12). When judges set high bail indignantly. *National Law Journal,* p. 13.

Convicted killer released pending sentencing. (1995, December 10). *San Diego Union-Tribune Wire.*

Cops say woman hid standoff suspect. (1998, May 1). *Associated Press Wire.*

Cotton, D.J., and Groth, A.N. (1982). Inmate rape: Prevention and intervention. *Journal of Prison and Jail Health,* 2: 47–57.

Davis, G.W. (1998, March 31). No bail for teen in cab killings: Risk of flight still great during appeal, judge says. *Beacon Journal Wire.*

Davis, K.C. (1969). *Discretionary Justice: A Preliminary Inquiry.* Baton Rouge: Louisiana State University Press.

Ebbesen, E.B., and Konečni, V.J. (1981). The process of sentencing adult felons: A causal analysis of judicial decisions. In B. Sales (Ed.), *The Trial Process.* New York: Plenum.

Ewing, J., and Houston, B. (1991, June 17). Some judges punish people without benefit of trial. *Hartford Courant,* p. A1.

Feeley, M.M. (1979). *The Process Is the Punishment: Handling Cases in a Lower Criminal Court.* New York: Russell Sage Foundation.

Granelli, J.S. (1990, October 19). Keating freed after U.S. judge slashes bail. *Los Angeles Times Wire.*

Harlow, C.W. (2000). *Defense Counsel in Criminal Cases.* Washington, DC: Bureau of Justice Statistics.

Harmsworth, E. (1996). Bail and detention: An assessment and critique of the federal and Massachusetts systems. *New England Journal on Criminal and Civil Confinement,* 22: 213–290.

Hart, B.A., and Reaves, T.C. (1999). *Felony Defendants in Large Urban Counties, 1996.* Washington, DC: Bureau of Justice Statistics.

Hoffman, J. (1997, January 22). Bail granted to teen-agers in baby death. *New York Times Wire.*

Holmes, O.W. (1881). *The Common Law.* Boston: Little, Brown.

Holmes, M.D., and Daudistel, H.C. (1984). Ethnicity and justice in the Southwest: The sentencing of Anglo, Black, and Mexican origin defendants. *Social Science Quarterly,* 65: 265–277.

Kelley, M. (1997, September 3). Killings by bounty hunters stir an outcry: Calls for regulation rise after 2 die in tragic error. *San Diego Union Tribune Wire.*

King, J. (1989, April 5). Spill tanker captain held on one million dollars bail. *Reuters Wire.*

Knowles, L.L., and Prewitt, K. (1969). *Institutional Racism in America.* Englewood Cliffs, NJ: Prentice Hall.

Lester, A. (1965). *Justice in the American South.* London: Amnesty International.

Lizotte, A.J. (1978). Extra-legal factors in Chicago's criminal courts: Testing the conflict model of criminal justice. *Social Problems,* 25: 564–80.

Man robs banks to pay probation. (1997, June 14). *Associated Press Wire.*

McHugh, M. (2000, November 14). Judge sets $3 million bail for drug suspect. *Newark Star-Ledger,* p. 47.

Murderer free on bail but not for long. (1995, December 12). *San Diego Union-Tribune Wire.*

New York State Defenders Association. (1985). *What Prisons Do to People.* Albany, NY: New York State Defenders Association.

Panel considers bounty hunters law. (1998, March 12). *Associated Press Wire.*

Perkins, C.A., Stephan, J.J., and Beck, A.J. (1995). *Jails and Jail Inmates 1993–94: Census of Jails and Annual Survey of Jails.* Washington, DC: Bureau of Justice Statistics.

Pierce, E. (1996, June 9). Shooting leads to jail for one bounty hunter. *San Diego Union-Tribune Wire.*

Professional Bondsmen of New Mexico (n.d.) *Bail Agent Code of Ethics.* Albuquerque: Professional Bondsmen of New Mexico.

Rocker Tommy Lee jailed for abuse. (1998, February 25). *Associated Press Wire.*

Rubin, T.H. (1976). *The Courts: Fulcrum of the Justice System.* Pacific Palisades, CA: Goodyear.

Steinberg, J. (1997, February 28). Longtime "king" of bail bonds keeps busy courting the public. *San Diego Union-Tribune Wire.*

Supreme Court of Virginia. (n.d.). *The Office of the Magistrate: Virginia Information Pamphlet.* Richmond, VA: Supreme Court of Virginia.

*Taylor v. Taintor,* 83 U.S. 366 (1872).

Thornton, K. (1993, June 27). Bounty hunter is charged with beating fugitive. *San Diego Union-Tribune Wire.*

Uhlman, T.M. (1979). *Racial Justice: Black Judges and Defendants in an Urban Trial Court.* Lexington, MA: Lexington Books.

*United States v. Salerno,* 481 U.S. 739 (1987).

Vigil, S. (1994). Personal Interview with author.

Wheeler, G.A., and Hissong, R.V. (1988). A survival time analysis of criminal sanctions for misdemeanor offenders: A case for alternatives to incarceration. *Evaluation Review,* 12: 510–527.

Wice, P.B. (1985). *Chaos in the Courthouse: The Inner Workings of the Urban Criminal Courts.* New York: Praeger.

Williams, G. (n.d.) *The Bondsman's Right to Arrest.* Davenport, IA: Crown.

Wojda, G.L. (1991). *Behind Bars.* Laurel, MD: American Correctional Association.

# Step 11

# Plea Bargaining

---

❖

---

In the last chapter, we examined bail and its use to release defendants before trial. We also examined how bail (or the inability to make bail) can affect individual defendants' access to justice. In this chapter, we move to the next step, plea bargaining. Technically, plea-bargain negotiations may occur at any stage in the trial process, and they often follow pre-trial motions aimed at discovery (e.g., requests for statements made by the defendant to police), dismissal of charges, or exclusion of evidence. Once the rulings have been issued on pre-trial motions, the attorneys for the two sides are better able to assess their cases and their possible need to engage in plea bargaining.

Plea bargains are estimated to occur in some 90 percent of criminal cases in the United States (e.g., Miller, McDonald and Cramer, 1978, p. 17). In 1996, 91 percent of all felony convictions in the state courts were disposed of through guilty pleas (Brown, Langan, and Levin, 1999, p. 7; Maguire and Pastore, 1999, p. 432, Table 5.42). Although not all guilty pleas are the result of formal bargains, many are, and those that do not follow negotiations often involve some sort of leniency expected by the defense.

Despite their frequent use, plea bargains are one of the most controversial issues in the justice system. The public abhors them, but the justice system appears to embrace them. Editorial after editorial condemns their very existence, but plea bargains are still firmly ensconced in American justice. Plea bargains are defined by the public as a "soft on crime" policy or proof of laziness by prosecutors, by members of the justice system as a way to deal with crushing workloads and vague concepts of justice and fairness, and by defendants as a way to fashion more palatable sanctions for their actions. As defined by *Black's Law Dictionary*, the leading law dictionary, **plea bargaining** is:

> The process whereby the accused and the prosecutor in a criminal case work out a mutually satisfactory disposition of the case subject to court approval. It usually involves the defendant's pleading guilty to a lesser offense or to only one or some of the counts of a multi-count indictment in return for a lighter sentence than that possible for the graver charge (Black, 1991, p. 798).

A group of federal attorneys discuss their cases. It is in informal sessions such as these that plea bargains are wrought. Sometimes the product of hallway encounters, plea bargains are typically initiated by defense attorneys and involve some sort of concession by the prosecutor in exchange for a guilty plea. Though plea bargains are subject to judicial review, they are seldom rejected, meaning that American justice depends heavily on negotiation between attorneys.   SOURCE: Library of Congress, Prints & Photographs Division, FSA-OWI Collection, LC-USW3-030791-D DLC, Marjory Collins, photographer.

This definition illustrates the process in formal plea bargaining, which may involve detailed negotiations in which both sides in a case haggle back and forth, or the bargains may involve offers that are simply accepted or rejected by the other side. Formal bargains, called **explicit plea bargains**, are those in which some concession has been granted to the defendant in exchange for his or her agreement to plead guilty (Weninger, 1987, p. 280). This type of bargain will be discussed at length in this chapter. The second category of negotiations, **implicit plea bargains**, involve no direct promises of leniency. Although there is no "explicit" agreement entered into by the prosecution, there is still pressure on the defendant to plead guilty in exchange for ambiguous hopes of leniency (Guidorizzi, 1998, p. 756).

The United States is not alone in its use of plea bargaining. Many countries have some form of "abbreviated" approach for routine cases, including Scandinavia, West Germany, and several other European countries (Felstiner, 1978, p. 309). Similar to the United States, some 85 percent of British defendants plead guilty, and "informal plea negotiation" is common in England (Baldwin and McConville, 1978, pp. 287, 292).

## TYPES OF PLEA BARGAINS

There are three main categories of plea bargains. Each type involves sentence reductions, but those reductions are achieved in very different ways. One common type is **charge bargaining**, in which a defendant pleads guilty in exchange for a reduction in the severity of charges he or she faces. In a fairly typical scheme, for example, a Rhode Island defendant faced with felony charges of receiving stolen goods was allowed to avoid a felony proceeding by pleading guilty to misdemeanor charges (Reputed mobster gets probation, 1999). Similarly, cases in which defendants are allowed to plead guilty to necessarily included offenses (e.g., aggravated assault) rather than attempted murder charges are examples of charge bargains—the actual charges are decreased, thereby reducing the maximum sentence that may be imposed in the case.

Another common type of plea negotiation is **sentence bargaining**. Those who engage in this type of plea negotiations are promised lighter or alternative sanctions in exchange for pleading guilty (e.g., Guidorizzi, 1998, p. 756; Weninger, 1987, p. 280). Sentence bargains are relatively common in homicide cases where defendants will plead guilty to avoid the death penalty or life without parole sentences.[1] One defendant who was on trial for murder and other serious charges avoided the death penalty when he pleaded guilty in exchange for receiving six consecutive life terms (Ziegler, 1996). A New Mexico woman did the same when she pleaded guilty in exchange for two life terms instead of the death penalty (Herrera, 1997). Sentence bargains are also employed in cases less serious than homicide. When a 1997 California defendant pleaded guilty to a felony drug charge in exchange for a promise that he would serve no more than three years in prison (Drug rap dropped, 1997), he was engaging in sentence bargaining. Even the lower courts have their share of sentence bargains, where defendants agree to plead guilty in exchange for having a few months shaved off of their jail terms, a lower fine, or fewer points added to their driving records (Meyer and Jesilow, 1997, p. 111). Sometimes, prosecutors agree not to make a sentence recommendation, thus leaving the sentence up to the judge (e.g., *Santobello v. New York*, 1971); the assumption is that the sentencing judge will sentence more leniently than he or she would have in the absence of a guilty plea. However, with sentence recommendation bargains, the defendant has no guarantee that the judge will accept the prosecutor's recommendation for a reduced sentence. Therefore, this type of plea bargain is less attractive to defendants. Defendants are also not guaranteed legal relief if their expectations of leniency in exchange for a plea are not met (e.g., Komitee, 1995). In sentence bargaining, it is the sentence itself that is transformed, resulting in a reduced penalty.

The final type of plea negotiation is **count bargaining**, in which the number of charges is reduced. Instead of being charged with three separate counts of drunk driving in one night, for example, one California defendant was allowed to plead guilty to just one (Meyer, 1993). Similarly, some defendants will have one or more charges dropped in exchange for pleading guilty to the remaining offenses. Count bargaining is less common than the other two forms (Weninger, 1987, p. 280), in part because it is limited to those offenders who amass multiple charges. Although it simplifies matters, a defendant's charges need not be identical for count bargaining to occur. Any charge(s) may be dropped by the prosecutor in exchange for a guilty plea on the remaining charge(s). In count bargaining, the actual number of charges is decreased, thereby reducing the maximum sentence that may be imposed in the case.

The defense, of course, hopes that the end result of any plea bargain is a reduced penalty. In general, scholars have noted that those who plead guilty receive more lenient sentences than their counterparts who go to trial (Acevedo, 1995, p. 997; Guidorizzi, 1998, p. 775; Heumann, 1978; Weninger, 1987, p. 295). According to government statistics, the average sentence following a felony conviction by jury trial was 150 months in 1996, compared to only 54 months for defendants who pled guilty (Levin, Langan, and Brown, 2000, p. 39, see Box 11.1 for the sentences broken down by offense). Sometimes, lenient penalties are reserved for those who plead guilty; informal courthouse norms in one jurisdiction stated that only defendants who had pled guilty could be eligible for probation, meaning that those who insisted on their day in court often served their day in jail, too (Neubauer, 1974, p. 240).

Because of the greater interest accorded to them by the public, murderers deserve special mention. Murderers convicted by juries are more likely than those who plead guilty to receive death sentences or life sentences compared to more lenient sentences. In 1996, 5 percent of jury trials for murder ended with death sentences and an additional 43 percent ended with life sentences, whereas only 3 percent of those who pled guilty received death sentences and only 14 percent got life terms; the remaining 86 percent of defendants who pled guilty received less serious penalties (Brown, Langan, and Levin, 1999, p. 8).

Ironically, the sentences imposed in individual plea bargains sometimes differ little from what defendants would receive after trial, especially when one considers that the statistical differences mentioned above may be attributable to defendants refusing bargains that call for harsh penalties but receiving those severe sentences after conviction (this would inflate the severity of sentences imposed after trial when compared with those willingly accepted by defendants who plea bargained). In count bargains, the dropping of charges may not reduce the sentence at all; the prosecution gives up "very little" since most sentences are served concurrently (Neubauer, 1974, p. 203). Receiving **concurrent** terms means that multiple sentences are served at the same time, so the offender spends only the longest term in detention; **consecutive** terms, on the other hand, means that the offender must serve the terms one after the other so that when one term is completed the next begins. Receiving a jail term of six months, then, requires the same amount of time behind bars as three concurrent six-month terms. The reality of concurrent sentences led one prosecutor to comment, after agreeing to dismiss several misdemeanor counts against an accused sex offender, "If we had gone to trial and he had been convicted of all the charges he would have faced 64 years in prison. He still faces 64 years in prison" (Callahan, 1996, p. B1).

# BOX 11.1

## Average Felony Sentence Lengths

As you look over the following table, compare the sentences imposed for guilty pleas to other types of "convictions." Generally, which type of conviction yields the highest average sentence? For which offense(s) is the difference between guilty pleas and bench or jury trials the greatest? For which offenses is the difference the least? Are there any offenses for which pleading guilty yields a *higher* average sentence than either bench or jury trial? What factors do you feel could account for the differences shown in this table?

### Average Felony Sentence Length in State Courts, by the Type of Conviction, Type of Sentence Imposed, and Offense, 1996

| Most serious conviction offense | Maximum sentence length (in months) for convictions by — | | | | | | | | | |
|---|---|---|---|---|---|---|---|---|---|---|
| | Total | | Trial | | | | | | Guilty plea | |
| | | | Total Trial | | Jury | | Bench | | | |
| | Mean | Median | Mean | Median | Mean | Median | Mean | Median | Mean | Median |
| **SENTENCES TO PRISON** | | | | | | | | | | |
| **All offenses** | 61 mo | 36 mo | 107 mo | 60 mo | 150 mo | 120 mo | 70 mo | 48 mo | 54 mo | 36 mo |
| **Violent offenses** | 104 mo | 68 mo | 170 mo | 139 mo | 205 mo | 180 mo | 116 mo | 84 mo | 86 mo | 60 mo |
| Murder[a] | 237 | 300 | 314 | 720 | 332 | ** | 258 | 240 | 191 | 182 |
| Sexual assault[b] | 117 | 72 | 170 | 120 | 215 | 180 | 83 | 60 | 100 | 70 |
| Robbery | 102 | 72 | 158 | 120 | 180 | 144 | 128 | 120 | 90 | 70 |
| Aggravated assault | 70 | 48 | 118 | 72 | 144 | 96 | 89 | 60 | 59 | 37 |
| Other violent[c] | 57 | 36 | 92 | 60 | 124 | 72 | 51 | 36 | 48 | 36 |
| **Property offenses** | 48 mo | 36 mo | 69 mo | 48 mo | 93 mo | 66 mo | 58 mo | 48 mo | 46 mo | 36 mo |
| Burglary | 61 | 48 | 92 | 60 | 112 | 84 | 74 | 60 | 57 | 46 |
| Larceny[d] | 39 | 29 | 50 | 36 | 65 | 48 | 47 | 36 | 38 | 25 |
| Fraud[e] | 39 | 29 | 46 | 32 | 65 | 60 | 46 | 33 | 39 | 28 |
| **Drug offenses** | 50 mo | 36 mo | 78 mo | 48 mo | 100 mo | 70 mo | 61 mo | 43 mo | 46 mo | 36 mo |
| Possession | 36 | 24 | 49 | 36 | 79 | 48 | 35 | 24 | 35 | 24 |
| Trafficking | 55 | 36 | 87 | 60 | 106 | 72 | 72 | 60 | 50 | 36 |
| **Weapons offenses** | 40 mo | 24 mo | 66 mo | 40 mo | 91 mo | 60 mo | 46 mo | 36 mo | 36 mo | 24 mo |
| **Other offenses[f]** | 41 mo | 36 mo | 51 mo | 36 mo | 83 mo | 48 mo | 34 mo | 24 mo | 40 mo | 36 mo |
| **SENTENCES TO JAIL** | | | | | | | | | | |
| **All offenses** | 6 mo | 6 mo | 8 mo | 6 mo | 7 mo | 6 mo | 8 mo | 6 mo | 6 mo | 6 mo |
| **Violent offenses** | 7 mo | 6 mo | 9 mo | 6 mo | 9 mo | 6 mo | 10 mo | 9 mo | 7 mo | 6 mo |
| Murder[a] | 9 | 12 | 9 | 6 | 9 | 6 | 8 | 9 | 9 | 12 |
| Sexual assault[b] | 8 | 6 | 11 | 12 | 12 | 12 | 10 | 12 | 7 | 6 |
| Robbery | 10 | 9 | 14 | 12 | 10 | 12 | 17 | 12 | 10 | 9 |

| Most serious conviction offense | Maximum sentence length (in months) for convictions by — | | | | | | | | | |
|---|---|---|---|---|---|---|---|---|---|---|
| | Total | | Trial | | | | | | Guilty plea | |
| | | | Total Trial | | Jury | | Bench | | | |
| | Mean | Median | Mean | Median | Mean | Median | Mean | Median | Mean | Median |
| Aggravated assault | 7 | 6 | 8 | 6 | 8 | 6 | 9 | 6 | 7 | 6 |
| Other violent[c] | 6 | 6 | 6 | 6 | 5 | 4 | 8 | 6 | 6 | 6 |
| **Property offenses** | 6 mo | 6 mo | 8 mo | 6 mo | 6 mo | 6 mo | 9 mo | 6 mo | 6 mo | 6 mo |
| Burglary | 7 | 6 | 8 | 6 | 5 | 2 | 10 | 11 | 7 | 6 |
| Larceny[d] | 6 | 5 | 8 | 6 | 6 | 6 | 8 | 6 | 6 | 5 |
| Fraud[e] | 5 | 5 | 9 | 6 | 6 | 6 | 10 | 12 | 5 | 5 |
| **Drug offenses** | 6 mo | 6 mo | 8 mo | 6 mo | 7 mo | 8 mo | 8 mo | 6 mo | 6 mo | 6 mo |
| Possession | 6 | 6 | 7 | 6 | 6 | 6 | 7 | 6 | 6 | 6 |
| Trafficking | 6 | 6 | 9 | 8 | 8 | 8 | 9 | 6 | 6 | 6 |
| **Weapons offenses** | 6 mo | 6 mo | 7 mo | 6 mo | 7 mo | 6 mo | 6 mo | 4 mo | 6 mo | 5 mo |
| **Other offenses[f]** | 6 mo | 6 mo | 7 mo | 6 mo | 7 mo | 6 mo | 7 mo | 3 mo | 6 mo | 6 mo |
| **SENTENCES TO PROBATION** | | | | | | | | | | |
| **All offenses** | 41 mo | 36 mo | 48 mo | 60 mo | 50 mo | 54 mo | 48 mo | 60 mo | 41 mo | 36 mo |
| **Violent offenses** | 48 mo | 36 mo | 50 mo | 60 mo | 58 mo | 60 mo | 46 mo | 60 mo | 48 mo | 36 mo |
| Murder[a] | 71 | 60 | 243 | 360 | 281 | 360 | 60 | 60 | 68 | 60 |
| Sexual assault[b] | 66 | 60 | 52 | 60 | 61 | 60 | 50 | 60 | 67 | 60 |
| Robbery | 52 | 60 | 58 | 60 | 74 | 60 | 55 | 60 | 52 | 60 |
| Aggravated assault | 41 | 36 | 45 | 48 | 49 | 54 | 38 | 36 | 41 | 36 |
| Other violent[c] | 43 | 36 | 50 | 60 | 36 | 36 | 51 | 60 | 42 | 36 |
| **Property offenses** | 40 mo | 36 mo | 46 mo | 60 mo | 44 mo | 48 mo | 47 mo | 60 mo | 40 mo | 36 mo |
| Burglary | 45 | 36 | 45 | 48 | 43 | 60 | 50 | 60 | 45 | 36 |
| Larceny[d] | 39 | 36 | 48 | 60 | 40 | 36 | 48 | 60 | 38 | 36 |
| Fraud[e] | 39 | 36 | 45 | 60 | 52 | 60 | 45 | 60 | 39 | 36 |
| **Drug offenses** | 42 mo | 36 mo | 49 mo | 60 mo | 56 mo | 60 mo | 49 mo | 60 mo | 41 mo | 36 mo |
| Possession | 36 | 36 | 44 | 60 | 50 | 60 | 43 | 48 | 36 | 24 |
| Trafficking | 45 | 36 | 54 | 60 | 57 | 60 | 56 | 60 | 45 | 36 |
| **Weapons offenses** | 34 mo | 25 mo | 36 mo | 36 mo | 41 mo | 36 mo | 34 mo | 24 mo | 34 mo | 24 mo |
| **Other offenses[f]** | 40 mo | 36 mo | 49 mo | 60 mo | 41 mo | 36 mo | 51 mo | 60 mo | 40 mo | 36 mo |

See note on tables 1.1, 1.2, and 1.3. Some estimates in this table are based on as few as 1 case and are therefore unreliable.

**Because the median includes felons sentenced to life in prison, the median sentence to prison is greater than 50 years.

[a]Includes nonnegligent manslaughter.

[b]Includes rape.

[c]Includes offenses such as negligent manslaughter and kidnaping.

[d]Includes motor vehicle theft.

[e]Includes forgery and embezzlement.

[f]Composed of nonviolent offenses such as receiving stolen property and vandalism.

*Source:* Levin, Langan, and Brown, 2000, pp. 39–40.

In addition, some research suggests that sentences are based on the severity of offenders' actions rather than the specific charges for which they are convicted. Thomas Uhlman (1977, p. 36; 1979, p. 91), for example, found that defendants who were sentenced following charge reductions were more likely to receive sentences at the high end of the range for those charges, whereas defendants who had been convicted on the original (and more serious) charges received sentences that were lower in the range. In the end, the terms ended up being fairly close, leading him to conclude that "plea 'bargains'. . . may be more apparent than real" (Uhlman, 1977, p. 36). Other researchers have noted similar phenomena, with sentences being raised so that they reflect the gravity of the actual offenses rather than simply the label placed upon them by bargaining prosecutors (Ferdinand, 1992, p. 110; Matheny, 1980). See Box 11.2 for an example illustrating how this may occur.

In some cases, bargains reflect the legal reality or worth of a case. One scholar noted that grand juries in New York during the early 1900s issued indictments for murder "in almost every" homicide case in the event that evidence showed up at trial that justified the more serious charges (Train, 1922, p. 224). If prosecutors did not reduce the charges where appropriate, serious injustices would undoubtedly result. Even today, some prosecutors overcharge and reduce the charges after reviewing the case and meeting with defense attorneys to bargain (Holten and Lamar, 1991, p. 208; Lindquist, 1988, p. 171).

## HISTORY OF PLEA BARGAINING

The history of plea bargaining is one of the least documented elements in the criminal justice system. One reason for plea bargaining's obscure past may be that bargaining was considered inappropriate by the judiciary until the late 1960s.

One of the earliest documented plea bargains may have taken place in 1431, when Joan of Arc was offered the opportunity to save herself from being burned at the stake as a heretic by recanting her statements that she had heard the voices of three saints sent by God and was acting on holy directions to help free France from the English (Sackville-West, 1936, p. 330). In this case, admitting the crime of heresy temporarily spared her from the death penalty.[2]

Another early form of plea bargaining took place during the 1692 witch trials in Salem, Massachusetts. In those cases, accused witches were told if they confessed they would live, but if they failed to do so, they would be hung; the judges did this both to encourage confessions and because they wanted the "admitted" witches to testify against others in an attempt to uncover more witches (Hill, 1995, p. 137). Conceding that they had practiced witchcraft spared many accused witches from execution; in fact, no accused witch who confessed was put to death.[3] Those who refused to plead guilty met with less savory fates; nineteen individuals were hung and one was pressed to death (Giles Corey, who was mentioned in Step 4).

## BOX 11.2

## How Reduced Charges May Not
## Necessarily Mean Reduced Sentences

To some, it is difficult to understand how lowering charges does not always mean more lenient sentence outcomes. To illustrate this concept, let us consider a hypothetical burglar's sentence in New Jersey. If a weapon is used in the offense or an injury occurs, burglary is a second-degree felony in New Jersey (which carries a term of five to ten years under New Jersey guidelines), otherwise burglary is a third-degree felony (which carries a term of three to five years). Assume Joe Burglar successfully bargains to have his burglary bumped down a notch (i.e., the prosecutor agrees to "ignore" the presence of a weapon or injury and charges Joe with a run-of-the-mill burglary).

If Joe is sentenced on the reduced charges, the sentencing judge, after reviewing the case, may give him a sentence near the maximum for the charge, in this case, five years in prison. The judge may do this because Joe's actions are serious for a third-degree crime.

If Joe is sentenced on the more serious charges, however, the sentencing judge may review the case and give him a sentence toward the lower end of the sentencing range for the charge, in this case, five years in prison. The judge may do this because, when compared to other second-degree offenders, Joe's actions are less serious.

Either way, Joe ends up spending five years in prison. His record, however, shows a conviction on the reduced charge and there is a chance that the outcome will be more lenient than the maximum term. Most important, from Joe's point of view, is that he has reduced the maximum sentence he can receive from the judge. And, we do know that certainty is a value held in great regard by defendants facing sentences.

In retrospect, the Salem witch trials illustrate one of the harshest criticisms of plea bargains—that they sometimes induce the innocent to plead guilty.

A third example of an early plea bargain appears to have occurred in England in the 1704 case of Daniel Defoe. Defoe pled guilty "on the promise of pardon secretly given to him" to the charge of writing a "scandalous and seditious pamphlet" (Andrews, 1890/1991, p. 99). It is important to remember that such a charge was considered quite serious at the time. Defoe was fined, ordered to make three appearances in the pillory, and incarcerated "during the Queen's pleasure"; after a year in prison, the Queen sent Defoe's wife the money to pay the fine (Andrews, 1890/1991: pp. 100–101). It is unlikely that any formal written agreement was drawn up, but this case appears to illustrate an early plea bargain. At the very least, the defendant pled guilty because he expected leniency in exchange for his plea, as per the secret promise.

Although these three examples seem to illustrate plea bargains, they are very different from the plea bargains that take place today. One similarity that ties these three examples together is that, in each case, the courts valued a confession above punishment. In fact, the courts seemed to value a confession more than a conviction.

In the first two cases, which were heard in **ecclesiastical courts** (i.e., church courts) rather than criminal courts, confessions legitimized the trials by showing the public that the accuseds' crimes were real rather than fiction. In the third case, Defoe admitted that his pamphlets were scandalous and seditious rather than having any scholarly value. In all three cases, the confessions legitimized the accusations and the courts' role in prosecuting them. Today's plea bargains, on the other hand, appear to have developed out of a desire for convictions (due to a systemic pressure to efficiently dispose of cases).

This is not to say that there were no instances of jurisdictions or time periods in which plea bargaining was the norm. One researcher uncovered a curious 1485 English hunting law that stated that defendants who confessed to violating the statute would be fined as misdemeanants, while those who failed to confess would be tried as felons (Langbein, 1974, p. 70); other researchers have found "specific indications" of true plea bargaining in early times (Alschuler, 1978, pp. 221–222), but these examples do not suggest a regular pattern of plea negotiation. It is examples such as these, however, that have led some scholars (e.g., Dash, 1951, p. 396) to assert that plea bargaining was a method used by prosecutors in the seventeenth and eighteenth centuries to reduce the severity of sentences from death to other options, such as transportation to a penal colony.

If they existed at all, plea bargains were rare in early America. In 1804, in response to a young man's guilty plea to murder and rape, the trial judge was so surprised that he informed the defendant that he "was under no legal or moral obligation to plead guilty" and that he had the right to deny the charges and force the government to prove them, but the defendant insisted on pleading guilty (*Commonwealth v. Battis*, 1804, pp. 95–96). This led the judge to inform the defendant that he would be given some time to think about his actions and to direct the court clerk not to record the guilty pleas. Later that afternoon, the defendant again pled guilty when he was brought into court, leading the judge to question those who had contact with the defendant:

> Upon which the Court examined, under oath, the sheriff, the jailer, and the justice, (before whom the examination of the prisoner was had previous to his commitment) as to the sanity of the prisoner; and whether there had not been tampering with him, either by promises, persuasions, or hopes of pardon, if he would plead guilty. On a very full inquiry, nothing of that kind appearing, the prisoner was again remanded, and the clerk directed to record the plea on both indictments. (*Commonwealth v. Battis*, 1804, p. 96)[4]

By the 1830s, however, plea bargains had become routine in Boston, Massachusetts. As early as 1832, public ordinance violators could expect more lenient sentences in the city's police court (i.e., a misdemeanor level court) if they pled guilty (Ferdinand, 1992, p. 89). After the defendants entered "not guilty" pleas, whoever prosecuted the cases could begin negotiations, offering to drop some of the charges and impose minor fines for the remainder of the charges in exchange for guilty pleas (Ferdinand, 1992, p. 94). The rate of police court guilty pleas more than quadrupled between 1834 and 1844, increasing from 8.1 percent of the cases to 35.1 percent (Ferdinand, 1992, p. 89).

From public ordinances, the practice spread to higher courts, including those that handled misdemeanors and felonies (Ferdinand, 1992, p. 95). Part of the popularity of plea bargaining in the general jurisdiction courts may have been the rapid increases in caseload, from some 300 cases a year to 1,500 cases a year by 1850 (Ferdinand, 1992, pp. 99, 101). It became normal for defendants to plead not guilty, then to switch their plea to guilty in exchange for the dismissal of charges or other "suitable agreement[s]" arranged with the prosecutor (Ferdinand, 1992, p. 101).

It is important to note that the first negotiated pleas in Boston were for offenses that did not have a clear victim (Ferdinand, 1992, p. 93). In victimless cases, such as gambling, the prosecutor does not have to factor in victim concerns, including the victim's safety or sentence preferences. Instead, criminal justice officials are the complainants, and their interests are more easily accommodated by plea bargaining. Haller (1978, p. 274) noted that the development of professional police and prosecutors' offices in the mid-1800s meant that responsibilities such as issuing arrest warrants and charging defendants were taken away from the courts, which further facilitated the growth of plea bargaining as individuals who were not trained in the law began to look for ways to handle their caseloads. From its humble beginnings as a way to dispose of *mala prohibita* crimes that were illegal only because they were legally prohibited (e.g., prostitution or public drunkenness), plea bargaining expanded to encompass *mala in se* crimes in which the harm and victim are more clear (e.g., battery or theft).

Even if they were routine before the Civil War, it was only after that war that cases in which plea bargains had been negotiated began to appear in the appellate court docket (Alschuler, 1978, pp. 223–224). No longer confined to the trial courts, plea bargains needed to be considered at this higher level of review. The appellate courts reacted with shock and began to decry the practice whenever given the opportunity.

By 1878, plea bargaining had become such an issue that one state's supreme court reversed a conviction because the trial court had not made an independent examination of the case facts before accepting a defendant's guilty plea (*Edwards v. People,* 1878). Apparently, the state legislature had enacted a statute specifically directing judges to vacate guilty pleas they felt were erroneous (i.e., that the defendant was factually innocent of the crime) or the product of "undue influence" (*Edwards v. People,* 1878, p. 761). Because the text of the Michigan Supreme Court decision illustrates so well the fears held by some that plea bargains were perverting the criminal justice system, a few excerpts are presented in Box 11.3. From those excerpts, one can easily see that the legislature sought to address two primary criticisms of plea bargaining: (1) that innocent defendants will be induced to plead guilty and (2) that sentences will not adequately reflect the crimes committed by offenders.

---

## BOX 11.3

### A Few Excerpts from *Edwards v. People* (1878)

The Legislature of 1875, having in some way had their attention called to serious abuses caused by procuring prisoners to plead guilty when a fair trial might show they were not guilty, or might show other facts important to be known, passed a very plain and significant statute designed for the protection of prisoners and of the public. It was thereby enacted as follows:

> That whenever any person shall plead guilty to an information filed against him in any circuit court, it shall be the duty of the judge of such court, before pronouncing judgment or sentence upon such plea, to become satisfied, after such investigation as he may deem necessary for that purpose, respecting the nature of the case, and the circumstances of such plea, that said plea was made freely, with full knowledge of the nature of the accusation, and without undue influence. And whenever said judge shall have reason to doubt the truth of such plea of guilty, it shall be his duty to vacate the same, direct a plea of not guilty to be entered, and order a trial of the issue thus formed. (pp. 761–762)

It is contrary to public policy to have any one imprisoned who is not clearly guilty of the precise crime charged against him, and it is equally contrary to policy and justice to punish any one without some regard to the circumstances of the case. By confining this statute to informations and not extending it to indictments,[5] it is easy to see that the Legislature thought there was danger that prosecuting attorneys, either to save themselves trouble, to save money to the county, or to serve some other improper purpose, would procure prisoners to plead guilty by assurances they have no power to make of influence in lowering the sentence, or by bringing some other unjust influence to bear on them. It is to be presumed they had evidence before them of serious abuses under the information system which in their judgment required checking by stringent measures.

Every one familiar with the course of criminal justice knows that those officers exercise very extensive and dangerous powers, that in the hands of an arbitrary or corrupt man are capable of great abuse. And unless the general impression is wrong, great abuses have been practiced by this very device of inveigling prisoners into confessions of guilt which could not be lawfully made out against them, and deceiving them concerning the precise character of the charges which they are led to confess. And it has also happened, as is generally believed, that by receiving a plea of guilty from a person whose offense is not aggravated, worse criminals who have used him for their purposes remain unpunished, because the facts which would convict them have not been brought out. (pp. 762–763)

---

One legal historian notes that plea bargains in the nineteenth century differed from their current counterparts in that the majority of historic bargains involved reducing charges, whereas current bargains are more likely to consist of dropping one or more of the defendant's charges (Friedman, 1978, p. 251). He cites the example of an Alameda County, California, man who was charged in 1880 with embezzling $52.50. At first, he pled "not guilty," but he changed his plea to "guilty" after the prosecutor reduced the charge to theft of less than $50.00. Another defendant pled "not guilty" to charges of grand larceny, but also changed his plea when the charges were reduced to petty larceny. It appears that plea bargains were possible for serious property crimes in Alameda County, even in the nineteenth century.

By 1900, the majority of cases in New York County, New York, were disposed of by guilty pleas. One scholar tracked guilty pleas for the county and found that between 77 percent and 83 percent of defendants pled guilty between the years of 1900 and 1907 (Train, 1922, p. 226). And, the pleas were not always due to defendants' spontaneous decisions to plead guilty. Train (1922) noted that some court officials negotiated with defendants for pleas and built reputations based on their ability to do so:

> Court officers often win fame in accordance with the ability as 'plea getters.'. . . Accordingly each morning some of them visit the pens on the floor below the court-room and negotiate with the prisoners for pleas. The writer suspects that the assistant in charge of the Part is usually depicted as a fierce and relentless prosecutor and the jury as a hardened, heartless crew who would convict their own mothers on the slightest pretext. (p. 223)

By the 1920s, plea bargains had become standard practice in other jurisdictions, but they still were not fully endorsed by appellate courts. Two scholars in that decade, Justin Miller and Raymond Moley, each published articles decrying the practice. According to statistics uncovered by the two, plea bargains were everyday routine nearly everywhere. In Cook County, Illinois, for example, 96 percent of felony prosecutions in 1926 resulted in guilty pleas (Moley, 1928, p. 97). In fact, of twenty-four jurisdictions for which Moley was able to obtain data, five (St. Paul, Syracuse, Omaha, Yonkers, and Minneapolis) had guilty plea rates of 90 percent or higher, six had rates between 80 percent and 89 percent, ten had rates between 70 percent and 79 percent, and only three had rates below 69 percent (Moley, 1928, p. 105). Although Moley was unable to ascertain exactly how many of the guilty pleas resulted from plea bargaining, he concluded that giving prosecutors discretion "has made it possible for the practice of 'bargaining for pleas' to assume very large proportions in the administration of criminal justice, particularly in the large cities" (Moley, 1928, p. 109).

Moley (1928, p. 103) referred to the process as "compromising" of cases or "bargaining for pleas" and likened the practice to baseball players' batting averages. Possibly because of his effective analogy, modern court scholars talk about prosecutors' "batting averages" as a driving force behind the prevalence of plea bargaining. See Box 11.4 for some other insights provided by Moley.

In his article, Miller (1927) spent less time documenting the existence of plea bargaining, instead focusing on the process itself and the motivations behind it. He noticed that judges varied in their amenability to bargains; some refused to allow them in their courts, others suggested bargaining to the attorneys, and a few

## BOX 11.4

## Moley's Wisdom and Insight Regarding Plea Bargains

As a quick perusal of the following quotes readily shows, Moley's insight regarding plea bargaining demonstrates the nature of the practice, even as it is practiced today.

Lists gains to the prosecutor and uses the phrase "batting average":

> [There is no] onerous and protracted [trial, no risk of loss at trial, no risk of having to oppose an appeal, bargains count as convictions] and when he goes before the voters for re-election he can talk in large terms about securing convictions when, in reality, these "convictions" include all sorts of compromises. The district attorney's "record," as he usually interprets it to the public, rests upon the ratio of convictions to acquittals and means as much to him as a batting average means to a baseball player. (p. 103)

Even mandatory sentencing laws can be circumvented:

> Here, then is exactly what the operation of the Baumes Law [a mandatory sentencing scheme] in the largest city of the United States finally came down to. It indicates that in cases where the evidence was fairly conclusive and the accused persons were willing to plead guilty, the discretion of the district attorney, with the consent of the court, permitted half of the cases in which guilt was established to escape the legislators' well made plans. (p. 113)

Bargains represent perverse logic:

> Either a person is guilty of the crime charged, or he is not. It does not satisfy the requirements of justice to punish him for one crime because it is impossible to punish him for the correct one. (p. 124)

The importance placed on prosecutors' records facilitates bargaining:

> With present methods of establishing his "efficiency" before the public, he is able through compromising large numbers of cases to appear to be getting large numbers of convictions when, in fact, his convictions are to a large extent merely theoretical. Moreover, it is easy for the prosecutor to avoid labor in the way merely for the purpose of expending his best energies upon sensational and politically advantageous exploits in court. (p. 125)

Plea bargaining is not rational and its goals are not justice:

> It is in its methods and its implications a process of driving a bargain—a game of wits. It is psychologically more akin to a game of poker than to a process of justice. . . . It is not a search for truth; it is an attempt to get as much from an unwilling giver as is possible. (p. 125)

*Source:* R. Moley, 1928, "The Vanishing Jury," *Southern California Law Review,* 2: 98–127.

"bargain[ed] openly, in court, with the accused person" (Miller, 1927, p. 10). He felt some of the blame for the practice lay with increases in caseload because of the "prolific creation of new crimes" (i.e., the outlawing of more and more behaviors by the legislature). More recently, Mather (1978, p. 283) noted that the creation of new laws during Miller's day affected caseloads in two ways; increases in caseloads were obvious, but the creation of new laws also transformed caseloads because the new cases were of a "distinctly different type." The new laws (e.g., Prohibition laws) did not enjoy total support by the public, so juries sometimes refused to convict those accused of breaking them. This reality made prosecutors even more inclined to bargain (Haller, 1978, p. 273; Mather, 1978, p. 283).

Other legal historians have attempted to explain the evolution of plea bargaining in terms of caseload differences. Langbein (1978, p. 263) noted that Old Bailey (a famous court in England) heard a dozen cases a day in the 1730s compared to current estimates of several days per case. Why the huge increase in processing time? Langbein argues that the shift lies in the transformation of legal procedures. In the 1700s, the rules of evidence were far less formal than current ones, and there were no attorneys, which meant there were no motions or extended cross-examination sessions (Langbein, 1978, p. 263). In other words, the number of trials is not as important as the time consumed by each one. It isn't just that there are more trials now than in the past; indeed, the trials of yesterday were very different from today's notion of trials and due process.

It is also important to acknowledge the differences between methods used to determine guilt in earlier times and those used today. Looking back to the early history of courts (see Step 4), trial by ordeal and battle now seem like little more than legally sanctioned guessing games but were once considered to be effective methods to determine the guilt of accused lawbreakers. There were no video surveillance cameras to capture incriminating footage of robberies, no DNA tests, no hair analysis, and no expert scientists whose abilities to unravel complex mysteries dazzle even prime-time television audiences. Instead, early courts relied on divine intervention, and later courts relied on jury trials in which both sides presented evidence to support their claims about what happened on some night in question. The rationale behind the adversarial process was that the truth would emerge through careful analysis of the evidence presented by the defense and prosecution. Current scientific analysis, on the other hand, reduces at least some of the doubt regarding the guilt of the accused. This realization led one distinguished legal historian (Friedman, 1978, p. 257) to comment: "In a system run by amateurs . . . without technology or police science—no fingerprints, blood tests, ballistics reports—the classical trial might be as good a way as any to filter out the innocent from the guilty."

Regardless of how plea bargaining got its foot in the door, it is clear that it has been a regular part of American criminal justice since the nineteenth century, despite not being recognized as "legal" by the appellate courts. Even until the 1960s, plea bargains were still treated as the justice system's "dirty little secret."

Defendants who had bargained were not allowed to acknowledge this in court; instead, they were expected to be "thespians who would affirm in court, before attorneys and judges who knew better, that guilty pleas were wholly voluntary, the consequences of contrition, and not induced by assurances of leniency" (Cohen and Tonry, 1983, p. 308). In 1967, an important report, *The Challenge of Crime in a Free Society* documented the presence of plea bargaining and recommended bringing it out of the shadows and into open court (President's Commission on Law Enforcement and Administration of Justice, 1967/1968, pp. 333–338). Partly as a result of this report, plea bargaining is now officially recognized and defendants no longer have to put on fraudulent performances in court. In fact, plea bargaining has its own case law, as we will see later in this chapter.

## EFFECTS OF PLEA BARGAINING ON COURTROOM WORK GROUPS

There is no doubt that plea bargaining plays a central role in the American justice system. That some 90 percent of defendants plead guilty means that even a reduction of 10 percent in that number could double the number of trials and significantly overtax the court system. For this reason, and others, the courtroom work group views plea negotiation as attractive, and as a team fashions the sentences imposed on the majority of defendants. One courts scholar summed up the importance of bargains, calling them "the most critical stage in the criminal justice system. [They are] the most important determinant of who gets what from the criminal justice process" (Neubauer, 1974, p. 195).

Plea bargaining is the principal mechanism that allows judges, prosecutors, and defense attorneys to cooperate and work together toward their individual and collective goals (Blumberg, 1967; Eisenstein and Jacob, 1977; Nardulli, 1978; Weninger 1987, p. 266). Courts observer and scholar Maureen Mileski (1971) explained the importance of cooperation for the smooth functioning of the courtroom work group:

> The prosecutor balances his need to prosecute cases against his need to maintain good relations with the judge, public defender, and many other attorneys who frequently take cases to court; all are members of the "team" that maintains orderly operations of the court. They share a worksite. Together they can make their worksite a fractious, turbulent one or an orderly and predictable one. Though the interest of some of the parties are formally at odds, in operation they share common interests. A certain level of cooperation between them [develops]. (p. 488)

To understand why courtroom work groups rely so heavily on plea bargaining, it is important to understand how each member of the courtroom work group benefits from them. The primary motivation is that bargains represent a "done deal"; there is no risk of loss at trial for either prosecution or defense. In cases in which there is no "smoking gun" evidence, bargains may be a way for both sides to minimize their losses through negotiations. All members of the courtroom work group benefit in some way from plea bargains. See Box 11.5 for a writeup about a courtroom work group that emphasized cooperation and excluded those who failed to participate with the other members of the courtroom work group.

Plea bargains are a major boon to prosecutors because they allow them to improve their "batting averages" (Blumberg, 1967, p. 179). In a system that places more value on convictions than actual sentences, prosecutors can easily view plea bargaining as a way to increase their conviction rates (Moley, 1928, p. 103; Kunkle, 1989). Through plea bargaining prosecutors can avoid trials that, in addition to consuming great amounts of time and requiring much work, can result in acquittals (Blumberg, 1967, p. 179). Of course, even the most politically insulated

---

## BOX 11.5
## The Value of Cooperation to the Courtroom Work Group

One of our students, Constance O'Connor, was invited by the judge she was observing to attend normally private in-chambers sessions during which she observed and interviewed members of the courtroom work group. Her findings are below. As you read them, consider how this courtroom work group would treat newcomers, especially those who failed to cooperate with the others:

All of the subjects [I] interviewed stressed that with group cooperation, the system works efficiently and smoothly. There is a continuing need to work together with required reasonableness that helps maintain the group's cohesion. Mutual understanding, trust, and a reciprocal give and take are the necessary components of the work group if it is to operate at full efficiency. Cooperation is the cornerstone of the system functioning at its maximum capabilities.

According to those involved in this work group, without cooperation the system bogs down to the detriment of all. To quote the words of a probation officer that I interviewed, "If someone's not cooperating with the others, it throws a monkey wrench into the whole thing." Interestingly, all of the subjects personally felt that a certain type of personality was the biggest obstacle to group cooperation. This personality was variously described as one who is a "stickler for details," intent upon career advancement often at the expense of others, or just a "plain jerk." This type of personality does not share the common goals and values of the work group and is predominantly concerned with his individual successes, not the success of the group as a whole. Group cooperation and cohesiveness are not a priority to this type of individual. It was noted by several subjects that this type of individual "doesn't last long around here." In fact, it was specifically mentioned that the judge in this work group was especially intolerant of this type of personality and had "gotten rid of anyone who wouldn't work within her system."

prosecutor cannot bargain all cases away, lest he or she incur the wrath of an angry public.

Mileski (1971) noted that both public and private defense attorneys pushed plea bargains as a way to protect the court from defendants' requests for trials. Since public defenders are part of the criminal justice system, they may decide it is expedient or wise to serve the system's interests rather than those of their clients. Even private attorneys may be swayed to work for the court through preferential scheduling of their cases or harsh punishment of their clients who refuse to bargain. Scheduling preferences allow attorneys to maximize the use of their time, whereas harsh punishment of their clients affects their reputations. Cooperative defense attorneys are able to achieve other rewards, including the granting of continuances to allow for fee collection or the scheduling of cases before a "favorable" judge (Blumberg, 1967, pp. 105, 144). These controlling actions serve to coax defense attorneys to "play the [plea bargain] game in order to get along" (Blumberg, 1967, p. 106).

Defense attorneys can maximize their efficiency and profit through careful use of plea bargaining. Through cooperating with the court, defense attorneys can dispose of cases quickly, an important consideration in that public defenders are part of the bureaucracy and private attorneys are usually paid on a case-by-case basis. Many private attorneys find that plea bargaining is cost-effective because it requires less time and effort than going to trial (Knowles and Prewitt, 1969; Moran and Cooper, 1983, p. 75). In fact, when plea bargaining was banned in Alaska, defense attorneys reported that they had to increase their fees to make up for the additional work they had to do (Rubinstein and White, 1978, p. 371). Sometimes, attorneys discuss the possibility of plea bargaining with a client and "if the defendant is amenable to a deal, [they are] hired (in fact) for this purpose rather than as an actual courtroom defense" (Moran and Cooper, 1983, p. 75).

Plea bargaining becomes all the more attractive to defense attorneys when one considers that the majority of defendants are presumed by the courtroom work group to be guilty. Through plea bargaining, defense attorneys are able to counteract overcharging by prosecutors and get charges reduced to reflect the legal worth of a case (Holten and Lamar, 1991, p. 208; Lindquist, 1988, p. 171). The ability to obtain lenient sentences, or apparently lenient, in the face of overwhelming evidence of guilt is another way attorneys can boost their reputations.

Even judges benefit from the process. Plea bargaining allows judges to "avoid the time-consuming, expensive, unpredictable snares and pitfalls of an adversary trial" (Blumberg, 1967, p. 65). The benefit of saved time is obvious, but what "unpredictable snares and pitfalls" could await a judge? Remember that one role of judges is to issue rulings on pre-trial motions and objections during the trial itself. Every ruling is subject to review by a higher court, and judges' decisions are sometimes overturned on appeal, which they dislike (Heumann, 1978, p. 66). Plea bargaining avoids this embarrassing possibility. On a similar note, judges also avoid having to make difficult rulings on vague issues that come up during the trial.

Plea bargains also allow judges to "engage in a social-psychological fantasy" in which the defendant has already admitted his guilt and stands "repentant" before the judge (Blumberg, 1967, p. 65). Some judges place a high value on admissions of culpability, so defendants who plead guilty may receive more lenient sentences. One judge told a defendant who had pled guilty that he was giving him a lenient sentence because he did not get on the witness stand and tell "some perjured tale"; the same judge gave one felon probation after he pled guilty, but imposed a five-year prison term on his co-defendant who refused to admit his guilt and insisted on going to trial (Friedman, 1978, pp. 253–254). Admitting one's culpability could make a huge difference in the sentence outcome when appearing before that judge, and it sometimes affects the sentences in other judges' courtrooms, too.

Finally, plea bargaining allows judges to avoid shouldering the burden of sentencing alone. As we read in Step 7, judges often feel underprepared to sentence the offenders who appear before them. Plea bargains eliminate this responsibility because they typically involve ratifying a sentence deal that has already been worked out in advance. In addition, judges need not worry that the sentences they impose during plea bargains will be held against them. When Alaska banned plea bargains, for example, sentences became more severe, but not because bargains had been used to gut sanctions; instead, judges could no longer blame unpopular sentences on prosecutors, so they increased the overall severity of sentences in order to appease the public (Rubinstein and White, 1978, p. 378). Transferring the blame for sentences to plea bargaining may be even more appealing to judges who wish to keep their positions during upcoming elections.

Although they are not members of the courtroom work group, defendants also benefit from plea bargains. They are able both to limit the severity of the sanctions they face and to add a level of certainty to the criminal justice process. For guilty individuals, the threat of going to trial is sometimes used to coax prosecutors into making "sweetheart deals" (Weninger, 1987, p. 270), but even innocent defendants sometimes plead guilty because they are overwhelmed by the evidence against them (or what the police and prosecution say is evidence against them) or by the justice system itself. Sometimes, plea bargains are too good for even innocent defendants to pass up, especially if they have been held in jail before trial. After spending ten months in custody awaiting trial, for example, one defendant insisted he was innocent but agreed to a bargain that offered a sentence of one year, which meant he would be immediately released, saying "You mean if I'm guilty I get out today? . . . But if I'm innocent I got to stay in?" (Mills, 1971, p. 62). If deals aren't sweet enough, on the other hand, the defendants may decide to take their chances at trial.

Sometimes, defendants plead guilty because they wish to avoid further stigma or inconvenience. One defendant, for example, pled guilty because he knew a trial would be reported in the newspaper and he worried about the effects on his family (Baldwin and McConville, 1978, p. 294). The above-mentioned defendant who insisted he was innocent pled guilty because fighting the charges would involve waiting in jail until trial, whereas a guilty plea ensured his immediate release (Mills, 1971, p. 62). When we consider that the average case takes about seven months from the time of arrest to sentencing, and jury trial cases average a year from arrest to sentencing (Brown, Langan, and Levin, 1999, p. 8), we can understand the motivation to just plead guilty and go home, despite the effect on one's record.

## THE HOW AND WHY OF PLEA BARGAINING

Now that we know a little about the types, history, and motivations behind plea bargaining, we need to look at how they take place. Before any communication takes place between the defense attorney and prosecutor, the two adversaries go through the case files to determine what the case is "worth." Items that increase worth include solid evidence, serious harm, vulnerable victim, extreme culpability, and other factors that strengthen the case against the defendant. The presence of weak evidence, uncooperative witnesses, reluctant victims (e.g., in some domestic violence cases), dubious harm, or reduced culpability (e.g., due to youth or mental impairment) decreases the legal worth of the case. Fairness also fits into the picture, as the goal of both sides is supposed to be justice.

In some respects, the prosecutor begins the plea bargaining process since he or she makes the first statement regarding what the case is worth through the charges he or she files. If the defense attorney disagrees with the charges, he or she may decide to bargain with the prosecutor.

Although either side may broach the possibility of plea bargains, they are typically initiated by defense attorneys, who approach prosecutors with offers to negotiate cases. In a system that depends heavily on guilty pleas, the initiation and continuation of plea bargaining sessions is one of the defense attorney's primary roles. If the defense attorney's offer is consistent with a prosecutor's perception of the "worth of the case" it will usually be accepted; the prosecutor is usually more concerned about convictions than sentences (McCall, 1978, p. 99). If the offer does not seem appropriate, the prosecutor may negotiate further (McCall, 1978, p. 99). If the prosecutor won't agree, the defense attorney may threaten to "work [the prosecutor] to death" through filing motions (Heumann, 1978, p. 39) or otherwise putting on a zealous defense that, through exercising as many of the defendant's rights as possible, will make the prosecutor work hard to obtain any conviction.

The bargain may involve dropping charges, reducing the severity of individual charges (e.g., from grand larceny to larceny), or making specific sentence recommendations. Even where the negotiation does not include the recommendation of a specific sentence, bargains allow the defense to limit the discretion of "hanging" judges (who are known to be tough on offenders) by lowering the maximum sentence that may be imposed.

Once the attorneys are in agreement, it is the defense attorney's job to "sell the offer to the accused" (Moran and Cooper, 1983, p. 75). It is this role in plea bargaining that has attracted much criticism. Blumberg (1967) likened the defense attorney's role in persuading the defendant to accept negotiated justice to the work of a "double agent" or someone participating in a "confidence game":

> Criminal law is a unique form of private practice. It simply appears to be private practice. Actually, it is bureaucratic practice, because of the lawyer's role in the authority, discipline, and perspective of the court organization. . . . [T]he lawyer in the criminal court is a double agent, serving higher organizational rather than professional ends. The lawyer-client "confidence game," in addition to its other functions, helps to conceal this fact. (pp. 114–115)

In the end, the bargains must meet with judicial approval, but the recommendations of the prosecutor and defense attorney are rarely rejected (Cramer, 1981, p. 185; Feeley, 1979; Neubauer, 1974, p. 93; Ryan and Alfini, 1978, p. 486). Typically, judges confine themselves to determining whether the defendant appears to be guilty of the offense and whether the plea was entered into voluntarily (Ryan and Alfini, 1978, p. 486). This tendency to endorse the attorneys' work reflects the fact that judges typically know far less about the case than either attorney, which leads them to honor the attorneys' assessment regarding the "worth" of a case (Meyer and Jesilow, 1997, p. 65).

When the recommended sentences appear too harsh or too lenient, some judges will refuse the bargain and send the attorneys back to the drawing room to design a more appropriate sanction (Meyer and Jesilow, 1997, p. 55). Some judges get more involved in plea bargains than simply reviewing the finalized bargain. About one third of judges attend plea bargaining sessions and some even "participate in the substance of plea negotiations with counsel, and in doing so influence, sometimes even dominate, the sentencing decision" (Ryan and Alfini, 1978, pp. 501–502). See Box 11.6 for one judge's assessment of his role in plea bargaining.

In cases where defense attorneys or prosecutors are absent, which is common in misdemeanor level courts, judges sometimes play an important role in plea bargaining. In courts where there is no prosecutor, judges may "take on the trappings of the prosecutorial role, including negotiation" (Ryan and Alfini, 1978, p. 495). In one jurisdiction characterized by lack of defense counsel at misdemeanor-court sessions, plea bargains were "routinely manufactured by prosecutors and judges" during the defendants' arraignments (Meyer and Jesilow, 1997, p. 11). One lower court judge made his intentions clear when addressing a man accused of presenting false information to a police officer and violating probation: "If you plead guilty, I'll give you credit for time served. That's what you want to do, right?" (Meyer, 1992b). The hearing lasted one minute from start to finish, and the defendant was sentenced to the two days he had already served in jail.

If the attorneys are unable to work out a deal that satisfies both of them (and the defendant), or the judge rejects the bargain, the case must go to trial. Offense

---

## BOX 11.6

## One Judge's Assessment of His Role in Plea Bargaining

The following interview segment with a judge tells a little about how judges can get involved in the plea bargaining process in the lower courts as well as the supervisory function judges must fulfill:

> They [the attorneys] make offers and counter-offers and often the judge in that court will sort of get into it. We'll have a conference in chambers and will talk about the case.... The judge's duty there is similar to the arraignment court—make sure there's justice.... The judge says, "Given the facts that you've given me, this is what I would probably sentence." The defense attorney comes back and says, "That's what he [the defendant] wants.".... The judge's role at that point is to be careful and not give some low-vault [i.e., unnecessarily lenient] indicated sentence. You've got to watch that. Give the same sense of fairness. (Meyer, 1992a)

---

seriousness is only one factor considered by the parties when negotiating plea bargains, but it should come as no surprise that those accused of violent offenses are less likely than other defendants to give up their right to trial by pleading guilty (Brown, Langan, and Levin, 1999, p. 7). Certainly, any offers acceptable to prosecutors in violent offenses are less attractive to the defense, who may decide to try for an acquittal at trial. See Box 11.7 for the breakdown of conviction type (i.e., plea bargain versus following a trial) by offense type.

Typically, the prosecutor is less likely to budge on cases with strong evidence, and is more likely to bargain when the chances of conviction are low. If there is clear evidence of guilt, such as a videotape of the offense or strong scientific evidence, the prosecutor will be unwilling to concede much unless there are other problems with the case (e.g., the victim is afraid or does not wish to testify at the trial). Bargains are also unlikely in cases where there is significant public ire, even if the offense is minor.

Defense attorneys are less likely to give up much in terms of a plea bargain if there is a decent chance of acquittal (e.g., because of public sentiment for a crime victim accused of killing a burglar) or if the culpability for the offense may be blamed on another person (e.g., a killing that may have been in self-defense). If the bargain involves little gain (e.g., a reduction of only a few years off a lengthy prison sentence), many defense attorneys would rather take their chances at trial.

---

## BOX 11.7

### Percent of Felons Convicted in State Courts, by Offense and Type of Conviction, 1996

| Most serious conviction offense | Total | Percentage of felons convicted by— | | | Guilty plea |
|---|---|---|---|---|---|
| | | Trial | | | |
| | | Total Trial | Jury | Bench | |
| **All offenses** | 100% | 9% | 4% | 5% | 91% |
| **Violent offenses** | 100% | 17% | 11% | 7% | 83% |
| Murder[a] | 100 | 46 | 40 | 7 | 54 |
| Sexual assault[b] | 100 | 19 | 11 | 7 | 81 |
| Robbery | 100 | 16 | 10 | 7 | 84 |
| Aggravated assault | 100 | 14 | 7 | 7 | 86 |
| Other violent[c] | 100 | 15 | 7 | 8 | 85 |
| **Property offenses** | 100% | 6% | 2% | 5% | 94% |
| Burglary | 100 | 8 | 3 | 5 | 92 |
| Larceny[d] | 100 | 6 | 2 | 4 | 94 |
| Fraud[e] | 100 | 6 | 1 | 5 | 94 |
| **Drug offenses** | 100% | 8% | 3% | 5% | 92% |
| Possession | 100 | 9 | 2 | 7 | 91 |
| Trafficking | 100 | 8 | 3 | 4 | 92 |
| **Weapons offenses** | 100% | 9% | 4% | 5% | 91% |
| **Other offenses[f]** | 100% | 8% | 2% | 6% | 92% |

Note: Detail may not add to the total because of rounding.
Data on type of conviction were available for 629,593 cases.
Table includes estimates for cases missing a designation of type of conviction.
[a]Includes nonnegligent manslaughter.
[b]Includes rape.
[c]Includes offenses such as negligent manslaughter and kidnaping.
[d]Includes motor vehicle theft.
[e]Includes forgery and embezzlement.
[f]Composed of nonviolent offenses such as receiving stolen property and vandalism.

*Source:* Brown, Langan, and Levin, 1999, Table 10.

# THE U.S. SUPREME COURT'S VIEW OF PLEA BARGAINING

By now, it is relatively easy to see that plea bargains save money and time and that they help the two sides avoid the risks of losing at trial, but these considerations should not be the only ones that determine whether the practice should be continued. Saving time and money is a good thing, but appellate courts will not tolerate fiscally sound features that result in injustice; for example, eliminating the right to counsel would certainly save a lot of time and money, but would also result in unconstitutional unfairness. Likewise, plea bargaining would have to be discontinued if it were to be used in a patently arbitrary or discriminatory fashion without regard for the seriousness of the crimes alleged to have been committed by the defendants. The following cases illustrate the Supreme Court's views regarding the propriety of plea bargaining.

First, the U.S. Supreme Court had to determine whether there must be evidence of defendants' voluntary entrance into plea bargains. In the 1969 case of *Boykin v. Alabama,* the court reversed the conviction of a man who had received five death sentences after pleading guilty to five counts of robbery, not because death was an unfair penalty for robbery,[6] but because the trial judge had not ensured that Boykin's guilty pleas were voluntary. As a result of this case, judges are now expected to make sure guilty pleas are voluntary; of course this does not always happen. See Box 11.8 for an example of Amy Grossberg's post-bargain hearing in which the judge *did* try to ensure that she willingly agreed to plead guilty.

---

## BOX 11.8

### A Judge Ensures That Amy Grossberg's Plea Bargain Is Acceptable

The following is a transcript of the hearing following Amy Grossberg's acceptance of a plea bargain that would reduce the charges she faced in connection with the death of her newborn from capital murder to manslaughter. She and her boyfriend were catapulted into infamy after their newborn son was found dead in a Delaware trash dumpster in 1996. Because Ms. Grossberg provided the same answer to every question (i.e., "Yes, your honor"), only her first answer is included to minimize space.

As you read the transcript, look for how the judge ensures that the bargain is acceptable (e.g., that it was knowingly and voluntarily entered into by the defendant).

*Superior Court Judge Henry duPont Ridgely:* Miss Grossberg, you've heard the statements to the court by your counsel, Mr. Malik, regarding the guilty plea which is tendered today. Was everything he said correct?

*Grossberg:* Yes, your honor.

Do you understand that you have the right to a speedy trial with the assistance of a lawyer, and that you will give up that right by pleading guilty?

Do you understand you will have the assistance of a lawyer at sentencing if your guilty plea is accepted?

You are charged by an amended indictment to include a lesser-included offense, manslaughter . . . It reads: Amy S. Grossberg, on or about the 12th day of November, 1996, in the County of New Castle, State of Delaware, did recklessly cause the death of the newborn baby of Amy S. Grossberg and Brian C. Peterson Jr. Do you understand the nature of this charge?

Are you, in fact, guilty of this charge?

Do you understand that the statutory penalty is up to ten years in jail and such fine or other conditions as the court may order?

Has anyone threatened you or forced you to plead guilty?

I show you a guilty plea form. Did you go over this form carefully with your attorneys?

And did you give true answers to each of the questions on this form?

Do you understand each of the constitutional rights that are listed on this form?

Do you understand that you will give up all of these rights by pleading guilty?

I show you now a two-page plea agreement. Did you go over this document carefully with your attorneys?

And did you read and sign it?

Is this the entire agreement between you and the prosecution?

Do you seek to voluntarily enter this plea of your own free will because you are guilty of this charge?

Have you discussed this matter fully with your attorneys?

And have you discussed it fully with any other family member that you care to discuss it with?

Do you seek to voluntarily enter a plea of your own free will, of your own free accord?

Are you satisfied that your attorneys have done all that they can reasonably do for you?

Do you understand that the next proceeding before this court will be your sentencing?

*Source:* Courtesy of The News Journal, Delaware, April 23, 1998.

Then, the high court addressed the question of whether it is constitutionally permissible to reward defendants who plead guilty by offering them reduced penalties, ruling that this was acceptable in *Brady v. United States* (1970, pp. 752–753). During the same year, the high court agreed to review a case involving another important issue in plea bargaining, protestations of innocence by defendants who accept plea bargains. In *Carolina v. Alford* (1970), Alford was charged with first-degree murder, but was given the option of pleading guilty to second-degree murder. Despite the strong evidence against him, Alford insisted he was innocent, but pled guilty to the reduced charge because he feared being executed:

> I pleaded guilty on second-degree murder because they said there is too much evidence, but I ain't shot no man, but I take the fault . . . and I just pleaded guilty because they said if I didn't they would gas me for it, and that is all. (p. 29)

In upholding the validity of Alford's plea and sentence of thirty years in prison, the Supreme Court held that defendants may plead guilty without admitting culpability.[7]

Of course, as mentioned earlier in this chapter, some judges may refuse to accept this type of plea bargain if they feel the defendant is not guilty of the offense (e.g., Ryan and Alfini, 1978, p. 486).

The next year brought *Santobello v. New York* (1971), which held that defendants are entitled to a legal remedy if prosecutors break conditions specified in plea bargains. In that case, Santobello pled guilty after the prosecutor promised not to recommend a specific sentence. As a result of time delays, a new prosecutor was assigned to the case who hadn't realized that his predecessor had made the promise, so he recommended the maximum sentence. Even though the sentencing judge said he would have imposed the maximum in the absence of the prosecutor's recommendation, the Supreme Court sent the case back with instructions for the trial court to send the case to another judge or to offer Santobello the option of withdrawing his guilty plea.

Another landmark plea bargaining case, *Bordenkircher v. Hayes* (1978) held that prosecutors can threaten to bring additional charges against defendants who refuse plea bargains. A prosecutor had threatened to re-indict Hayes under Kentucky's habitual offender law (which had a mandatory sentence of life in prison) if he did not accept a plea bargain for five years in prison for writing a forged check for $88.30. Hayes refused, the prosecutor kept his word, and Hayes received the mandatory life term. In 1982, the Supreme Court added to *Bordenkircher* in *United States v. Goodwin,* when it ruled that prosecutors may file additional charges against defendants if they back out of plea bargains that call for fewer charges.[8]

Taken together, these cases illustrate the Supreme Court's view that plea bargaining is a valid form of justice, and that the agreements are valid like other contracts (i.e., they cannot be broken without consequences). The cases also demonstrate that the negotiation process does not prohibit efforts by prosecutors to seek enhanced charges against defendants who are unwilling to admit their guilt in plea bargains. Finally, they show the value the criminal justice system assigns to plea bargaining; even the U.S. Supreme Court said the practice is desirable given the resource savings it can generate (*Santobello v. New York,* 1971, p. 260). In the end, it is clear that plea bargaining progressed from America's dirty little secret to an accepted and desirable routine in just a few decades.

See Box 11.9 for an example of the form that must be signed by defendants who wish to plead guilty. Even a quick perusal clearly shows the influence of the U.S. Supreme Court decisions regarding plea bargains (see Box 11.10).

## ARGUMENTS FOR AND AGAINST PLEA BARGAINING

The Supreme Court has approved of plea bargaining, going so far as to call it "an essential component of the administration of justice" and stating that "properly administered, it is to be encouraged" (*Santobello v. New York,* 1971, p. 260), but this is only one argument in favor of bargaining. Another argument for the practice

# BOX 11.9

# A Sample Guilty Plea Proceeding Form

To ensure that guilty pleas are voluntarily entered, the following form (or one similar to it) may be used. In some jurisdictions, defendants read and initial the forms themselves. In New Mexico, however, the judge presiding over the guilty plea is required to complete the form, initialing that each condition was met before allowing the plea. As you read over the facts that must be ascertained, consider the U.S. Supreme Court decisions that may have inspired each of them.

9-406                          CRIMINAL FORMS                          9-406

*9-406. (Effective September 1, 1990.)*

[5-303, 6-502, 7-502, 8-502]

STATE OF NEW MEXICO                          COUNTY OF ..................

IN THE ............ COURT

STATE OF NEW MEXICO
      *v.*                          No. .............
John Doe

### GUILTY PLEA PROCEEDING

*The defendant personally appearing before me, I have ascertained the following facts, noting each by initialing it.*

*Judge's*
*Initial*

........ 1. *That the defendant understands the charges set forth in the (complaint) (information) (indictment).*

........ 2. *That the defendant understands the range of possible sentence for the offenses charged, from a suspended sentence to a maximum of ................................*

........ 3. *That the defendant understands the following constitutional rights which the defendant gives up by pleading (guilty) (guilty but mentally ill):*

........ (a) *the right to trial by jury, if any;*

........ (b) *the right to the assistance of an attorney at all stages of the proceeding, and to an appointed attorney, to be furnished free of charge, if the defendant cannot afford one;*

........ (c) *the right to confront the witnesses against him and to cross-examine them as to the truthfulness of their testimony;*

........ (d) *the right to present evidence on his own behalf, and to have the state compel witnesses of his choosing to appear and testify;*

........ (e) *the right to remain silent and to be presumed innocent until proven guilty beyond a reasonable doubt.*

........ 4. *That the defendant wishes to give up the constitutional rights of which the defendant has been advised.*

........ 5. *That there exists a basis in fact for believing the defendant is (guilty) (guilty but mentally ill) of the offenses charged and that an independent record for such factual basis has been made.*

........ 6. *That the defendant and the prosecutor have entered into a plea agreement and that the defendant understands and consents to its terms. (Indicate "NONE" if a plea agreement has not been signed.)*

........ 7. *That the plea is voluntary and not the result of force, threats or promises other than a plea agreement.*

........ 8. *That under the circumstances, it is reasonable that the defendant plead (guilty) (guilty but mentally ill).*

........ 9. *That the defendant understands that a conviction may have an effect upon the defendant's immigration or naturalization status.*

*On the basis of these findings, I conclude that the defendant knowingly, voluntarily and intelligently pleads (guilty) (guilty but mentally ill) to the above charges and accept such plea. A copy of this affidavit shall be made a part of the record in the above-styled case.*

........................................          ........................................
    *District Judge*                          *Date*

---

### CERTIFICATE BY DEFENDANT

*I certify that the judge personally advised me of the matters noted above, that I understand the constitutional rights that I am giving up by pleading (guilty) (guilty but mentally ill) and that I desire to plead (guilty) (guilty but mentally ill) to the charges stated.*

...............................................
*Defendant*

*Subscribed and sworn to*
*before me this ........*
*day of ....., 19....*
...............................................................................................
Clerk, Notary or Other Officer Authorized to Administer Oaths

*The undersigned attorney hereby certifies that he has conferred with his client with reference to the execution of this affidavit and that he has explained in detail its contents.*

...............................................
*Defense Counsel*

[As amended. effective September 1, 1990.]

*Source:* New Mexico Supreme Court Rules 1986, Criminal Forms, Judicial Pamphlet 9, 1990 Replacement, pp. 63–64

---

is that it allows courts to devote scarce resources to the cases that require them, by processing routine cases through bargains. When cases are relatively ordinary, the members of the courtroom work group may feel their time is better spent on the more uncommon cases, making plea bargains all the more attractive to them. See Box 11.11 for one student's observations of a court of limited jurisdiction. The student notes several issues that play important roles in plea bargains.

Defenders of plea bargains also point out that they are used only in cases where conviction at trial is less likely, so the agreements ensure some form of penalty for defendants who might be acquitted on technicalities. This is the "half a loaf is better" argument (Moley, 1928, p. 123). Cutting deals with defendants enables the prosecutor to better do the job because he or she can use the time saved to pursue other criminals (Easterbrook, 1992, p. 1975). Sometimes, plea bargains are offered to those who testify against others, enabling prosecutors to successfully go after "bigger fish" who mastermind crimes.

One scholar[9] argues that plea bargains are "superior" to trials for "separating the guilty from the innocent" (Easterbrook, 1992, p. 1972). He defends the practice, in part on grounds that prosecutors are better able than jurors to ascertain guilt, and plea bargains can consider evidence that might be excluded from trials (p. 1971).

Victims, too, sometimes prefer plea bargains. By avoiding trial, they need not testify in court, which may be a frightening experience for victims of violent crimes. Victims also avoid the emotions associated with the possible acquittal of

## BOX 11.10

## Some Important Passages from U.S. Supreme Court Cases on Plea Bargaining

Judges must ensure that guilty pleas are entered voluntarily:

> It was error, plain on the face of the record, for the trial judge to accept petitioner's guilty plea without an affirmative showing that it was intelligent and voluntary (*Boykin v. Alabama*, 1969, p. 242).

Guilt need not be admitted for a plea to be valid:

> Thus, while most pleas of guilty consist of both a waiver of trial and an express admission of guilt, the latter element is not a constitutional requisite to the imposition of criminal penalty. An individual accused of crime may voluntarily, knowingly, and understandingly consent to the imposition of a prison sentence even if he is unwilling or unable to admit his participation in the acts constituting the crime. Nor can we perceive any material difference between a plea that refuses to admit commission of the criminal act and a plea containing a protestation of innocence when, as in the instant case, a defendant intelligently concludes that his interests require entry of a guilty plea and the record before the judge contains strong evidence of actual guilt. Here the State had a strong case of first-degree murder against Alford. Whether he realized or disbelieved his guilt, he insisted on his plea because in his view he had absolutely nothing to gain by a trial and much to gain by pleading (*Carolina v. Alford*, 1970, p. 37).

Bargaining is "an essential component" of the justice system:

> The disposition of criminal charges by agreement between the prosecutor and the accused, sometimes loosely called "plea bargaining," is an essential component of the administration of justice. Properly administered, it is to be encouraged. If every criminal charge were subjected to a full-scale trial, the States and the Federal Government would need to multiply by many times the number of judges and court facilities (*Santobello v. New York*, 1971, p. 260).

Plea bargains are "highly desirable":

> Disposition of charges after plea discussions is not only an essential part of the process but a highly desirable part for many reasons. It leads to prompt and largely final disposition of most criminal cases; it avoids much of the corrosive impact of enforced idleness during pretrial confinement for those who are denied release pending trial; it protects the public from those accused persons who are prone to continue criminal conduct even while on pretrial release; and, by shortening the time between charge and disposition, it enhances whatever may be the rehabilitative prospects of the guilty when they are ultimately imprisoned (*Santobello v. New York*, 1971, p. 261)

Prosecutors must honor conditions of bargains:

> On this record, petitioner "bargained" and negotiated for a particular plea in order to secure dismissal of more serious charges, but also on condition that no sentence recommendation would be made by the prosecutor. It is now conceded that the promise to abstain from a recommendation was made, and at this stage the prosecution is not in a good position to argue that its inadvertent breach of agreement is immaterial. The staff lawyers in a prosecutor's office have the burden of "letting the left hand know what the right hand is doing" or has done. That the breach of agreement was inadvertent does not lessen its impact (*Santobello v. New York*, 1971, pp. 261–263).[10]

Threats to seek enhanced charges are valid in plea bargain negotiations:

> After arraignment, Hayes, his retained counsel, and the Commonwealth's Attorney met in the presence of the Clerk of the Court to discuss a possible plea agreement. During these conferences the prosecutor offered to recommend a sentence of five years in prison if Hayes would plead guilty to the indictment. He also said that if Hayes did not plead guilty and "saved the court the inconvenience and necessity of a trial," he would return to the grand jury to seek an indictment under the Kentucky Habitual Criminal Act, . . . which would subject Hayes to a mandatory sentence of life imprisonment by reason of his two prior felony convictions. . . . It may be helpful to clarify at the outset the nature of the issue in this case. While the prosecutor did not actually obtain the recidivist indictment until after the plea conferences had ended, his intention to do so was clearly expressed at the outset of the plea negotiations. Hayes was thus fully informed of the true terms of the offer when he made his decision to plead not guilty. This is not a situation, therefore, where the prosecutor without notice brought an additional and more serious charge after plea negotiations relating only to the original indictment had ended with the defendant's insistence on pleading not guilty. As a practical matter, in short, this case would be no different if the grand jury had indicted Hayes as a recidivist from the outset, and the prosecutor had offered to drop that charge as part of the plea bargain (*Bordenkircher v. Hayes*, 1978, pp. 358–361).

the defendant, especially in crimes where the defendant claims the victim is at fault or shares the blame for the offense (e.g., some sex crimes).

Of course, there are also arguments against the practice. One common argument is that plea bargaining allows offenders to escape the punishment that is legislated for their crimes: "Men charged with crimes carrying heavy penalties are treated as if they have committed only minor offenses carrying light penalties. . . . Justice seems to be bought on the cheap" (Rosett and Cressey, 1976, p. 3). The widespread use of plea bargaining to reduce penalties may lead "seasoned criminal" to "conclude that it is worth his while" to break the law and pay the reduced price for his actions (Dash, 1951, p. 395). However, other commentators assert that

---

## BOX 11.1

## "A Front Row Seat into the Legal System": A Student's Observations Regarding Plea Bargaining

Stacy Walter, one of the author's students, was a regular observer at her local court. The following excerpts from her observations show several factors that are important in plea bargaining. First, the cases are run-of-the-mill routine cases, which increase the likelihood that plea bargains will be viewed favorably by key justice decision-makers:

> The night's docket list read like a never-ending saga of operating an unsafe vehicle in the borough of XX, disregarding a police signal and siren, and failure to appear. The first case called was a failure to appear. This was not the first time this offender had skipped court. Judge T issued a warrant $500.00 and no 10% [bail]. Next up, operating a motor vehicle without insurance. The defendant pled "it was a friend's car, your honor." Guilty, $31.00 fine $30.00 court costs. . . .

The defendants also valued plea bargains. Stacy Walter noted that a fourth member of the courtroom drama in this jurisdiction was the court liaison, who actually worked out the deals:

> On a side note, as these proceedings were going on, people were constantly wandering in and out of the courtroom doors. They had formed a line to speak to the court liaison, who was plea bargaining their charges.

The members of the courtroom work group got along well. Even the private attorneys were friendly with the other members of the courtroom work group. Because they got along, the judge and attorneys (and the courtroom liaison) were able to work as a team to efficiently dispose of cases:

> Judge T and prosecutor K seemed like a tag team, with their secret teammate, the court liaison, out in the hallway cutting deals. . . . Many of the private attorneys hired by the defendants seemed to know Judge T. Judge T wished one attorney good luck as his wife was expecting a baby any day. Overall, I would say the environment was well-connected.

The courtroom regulars justified bargaining, saying it kept the courtroom operating smoothly:

> Then we began to talk business. They [the court liaison and two police officers she was interviewing] told me . . . why there are so many plea bargains. They said there are so many because they want to keep the court running smooth.

Stacy Walter noted the links between assembly-line justice and plea bargaining:

> A great deal of what I observed in court was similar to that which I had read in the textbook. The interaction of the courtroom work group could not have been better explained or demonstrated. The "assembly line of justice" was up and running in full speed. Shortcuts were taken in order to keep the docket list running smoothly. Plea bargains were cut left and right.

The prosecutor benefitted from the regular use of bargains, making him likely to continue the practice:

> The prosecutor racked up a batting average like no other. . . . I have always wanted to be an attorney. . . . Watching prosecutor K rack up a batting average made me envious. I want a batting average, too.

"plea bargaining has proven to be a phantom loophole" because the evidence shows that plea bargaining does not let serious criminals escape with light sentences (Walker, 2001, p. 159).

Even in 1927, Miller worried that plea bargains meant that defendants' rights were trampled because prosecutors, mindful of their records, would "overlook" the rights of the poor and uneducated by persuading them to give up their right to trial by pleading guilty. It is important to recognize that most defendants in Miller's day were not represented by counsel, as that right was not guaranteed to defendants until *Gideon v. Wainwright* in 1963. Miller theorized that defendants without resources would be targeted for abuse by prosecutors who felt they needed to improve their conviction rates. Another important distinction between then and now is that many jurisdictions did not then allow bench trials, so any trials in the 1920s had to be conducted in front of juries (Moley, 1928, p. 102).

In modern times, the practice of plea bargaining has been attacked not for its use per se, but on grounds that defendants of color often receive less desirable plea deals than white defendants (Donziger, 1996, p. 112). In California, for example, two defendants with similar nonviolent criminal histories, accused of burglary and receiving stolen property in separate incidents, received very different plea deals: The white defendant was convicted of one count of burglary after the DA dismissed the other three charges, and was sentenced to sixteen months in state prison; the African American defendant was convicted on all four charges and was sentenced to eight years in state prison (Donziger, 1996, p. 112). A recently released comparison of plea bargains for white and African American defendants in 146 capital cases found that 60 percent of white defendants charged with capital crimes avoided the death penalty through plea bargains in comparison to 41 percent of black defendants (Dorning, 2000). The Justice Department noted that this disparity alone does not necessarily indicate discrimination, but leading death penalty researcher David Baldus believes that the results ". . . raise a red flag. . . . the magnitude of the disparity is very strong" (Dorning, 2000, p. 1).

Another criticism of plea bargaining is related to its use by prosecutors to pursue "bigger fish," as mentioned above. This has led to cases in which offenders who had more information to offer a prosecutor received significantly lighter sentences than their less culpable co-defendants who had little knowledge with which to bargain. For example, in a number of drug cases, women who were peripherally involved in drug distribution networks received sentences that were years longer than their heavily involved boyfriends, who used their knowledge to plea bargain their sentences down (e.g., Johnson, 1995).

Modern critics of plea bargains are more likely to complain that the practice encourages overcharging by prosecutors (so they can reduce the charges without hesitation) and that it penalizes those who seek trial (e.g., Felstiner, 1978, p. 309). These are serious criticisms that may soon be the substance of a petition to the Supreme Court to review a case dealing with these issues. It is criticisms such as these that have led to bans on plea bargaining in some jurisdictions. Through the implementation of strict sentencing guidelines, for example, the federal system has attempted to do away with plea bargains, but it has been shown that the process continues (Wray, 1993, pp. 7–8). One way federal prosecutors circumvent mandatory sanctions and thus engage in quasi-bargains is to charge drug couriers under statutes that do not involve mandatory sentences. Federal prosecutors in eastern New York say they must do this because most couriers have "limited culpability," most judges dislike harsh mandatory sentences for "low-level offenders," and charging offenders with crimes that involve mandatory penalties increases the likelihood of trials that would "overwhelm" the courts (Wray, 1993, p. 7).

Individual jurisdictions have also banned plea bargaining. The best known are Alaska and El Paso, Texas. Alaska's attorney general banned plea bargaining in 1975 (Rubinstein and White, 1978, p. 367). Within a few years, the policy increased the number of trials but did not affect the rate of guilty pleas or the time from arrest to the end of trial. Sentences became more severe, but only for those accused of minor offenses or who had no prior convictions; these "clean kids" received longer prison terms after the ban (Rubinstein and White, 1978, p. 376). Sentences for violent offenders, on the other hand, remained the same because they had been receiving harsh sentences before the ban. The lack of change in the rate of guilty pleas leads some scholars to surmise that implicit bargaining was still taking place (Guidorizzi, 1998, p. 775), and some researchers found evidence of explicit bargains despite the ban (Rubinstein and White, 1978, pp. 370–371). Alaska removed the ban in 1993, but plea bargaining had been fairly rampant since a 1980 change in charging policy that allowed prosecutors to reduce charges to reflect "the essence of the conduct engaged in" rather than what the prosecutor "could prove" (Guidorizzi, 1998, p. 775).

The ban on plea bargaining in El Paso, Texas, lasted only six years (Acevedo, 1995, p. 988). Within three years, the trial rate had doubled and backlog had increased by 250 percent (Weninger, 1987, p. 277). Some judges complained bitterly that they wanted bargaining to return so they could reduce their dockets and the backlog (p. 306). The backlog was so great that the jurisdiction had to reorganize its courts to enable the civil court judges to assist with the increases in criminal trials. Despite the intention to bring about sentencing uniformity, the ban did not appear to have any effect on judges' sentence severity (p. 303). The ban did, however, increase the length of pre-trial detention (p. 309).

There have been other temporary bans, including Bronx County (New York), Detroit (Michigan), and the state of California's ban on bargaining for defendants charged with "serious" offenses (Acevedo, 1995, p. 988). Undoubtedly, there will be many bans on the practice in the future; whenever plea bargaining is viewed as allowing the premature release of offenders, there will be attempts to eradicate its existence. Any ban will be ineffective, however, unless those who set it in motion fully understand the effects it will have on the justice system and commit the resources necessary to deal with those changes.

# CONCLUSION

Although not formally recognized until relatively recently, plea bargains have existed for at least two hundred years and their popularity does not appear to be waning. If anything, the courtroom work group has come to depend on them as a way to efficiently dispose of the majority of cases that form their workload. But plea bargaining is more than a way to speed up the assembly line of justice; in many ways, it has become a way to do justice by mitigating the punishment imposed on many offenders in exchange for admissions of culpability and testimony against others.

In the next chapter, we finally move to the trial itself. It has been a long process with many steps, but the trial is finally ready to begin. After the jury has been selected, the two attorneys will present their cases and the judge or jury will decide the outcome. You will see how all the preceding steps come together for this—the finale.

## DISCUSSION QUESTIONS

1. Some people have said that American justice is no longer adversarial because 90 percent or more of cases involve guilty pleas. What are some ways that justice can remain adversarial even in cases where defendants plead guilty?

2. In a class taken by one of the authors of this book, the professor offered a "B" on the final paper to anyone who did not submit a paper.[11] This scenario is somewhat similar to plea bargaining by prosecutors because the professor would save the time necessary to grade the papers, while the students would save the time and effort necessary to write the papers. Assuming that offer were made in this class, would you accept your instructor's offer? Why or why not? What factors would influence a student's choice to take the "B" versus writing the paper? Which students would be more likely to accept such an offer? Which ones would turn down the offer? How does this example relate to plea bargaining in the criminal justice system by defense attorneys and prosecutors?

3. Scan your local newspaper for stories involving plea bargains. What reasons were offered by the prosecution for engaging in plea bargains? What reasons did defense attorneys offer for the defendant's accepting a bargain?

4. Classify the plea bargains you found for question 3 into the three categories: charge, count, and sentence bargaining. Do you notice any patterns in the types of bargains offered?

5. Scan your local newspaper for stories involving rejected plea bargains. What were the reasons behind the rejections, and which party was unsatisfied with the bargains?

6. Search your local newspaper for ten stories on recent crimes, trying to find those that present enough detail so you understand what happened. Assuming you are the local prosecutor, and you are able to try only eight cases, which two cases would you bargain away? What factors influenced your decisions? For those that lacked enough details for you to be comfortable with a bargain, what factors did you want to know (e.g., level of planning in the offense, personal background of the offender, etc.)?

7. What effects do modern technology and developments in investigations (e.g., DNA tests) have on a defendant's likelihood of accepting a plea bargain versus taking one's chances at trial? What do you think will happen as more and more new technologies become available to the American justice system?

8. How could a prosecutor design a bargain that satisfies his or her needs, the defense's needs, and the public?

9. Oh, lucky you! You have just been appointed to the plea-bargaining reform commission for your state. What guidelines would you suggest to remedy the ills of plea bargaining (you might want to first think about the problems your state faces with respect to plea bargaining)?

10. Consider what you've learned regarding the process of plea-bargaining. Recall that the Supreme Court held that it was constitutionally acceptable for prosecutors to threaten to add charges against defendants who refused plea bargains (*Bordenkircher v. Hayes,* 1978). In this same case, the Court stated that plea bargaining is a "give-and-take negotiation . . . between the prosecution and defense, which arguably possess relatively equal bargaining power" (p. 362). Do you think that the two sides do in fact possess relatively equal leverage during plea negotiations? What are some of the reasons for your answer? Even if this were true in general across cases, could there be cases where the government has significantly more power? In such circumstances, how would this affect plea bargaining?

## NOTES

1. Of course, some defendants who plead guilty still receive the death penalty because plea bargains often don't guarantee a particular sentence. The sentencing agent, typically a judge, does not always follow suggestions made by the prosecution.

2. Though she initially agreed and signed a confession which saved her life, she later recanted, saying she had confessed only because of "fear of the fire" and that she had heard again from the voices that she was damning herself by recanting (Sackville-West, 1936, p. 336). She was burned at the stake as a heretic on May 30, 1431, but was canonized as a saint in 1920.

3. This was probably due to officials' ultimate recognition that the witch scare was in error, rather than any intended long-term lenience.

4. The defendant was sentenced to death for his crimes, showing that pleading guilty does not ensure lenient treatment from the court.

5. Author's Note: Remember that indictments are handed down by grand juries, so that any presumed abuses by prosecutors should be less likely.

6. Remember, it was once legal to impose death sentences for crimes other than murder or offenses with serious harm. It was only in 1977, in the case of *Coker v. Georgia,* that the death penalty was ruled

unconstitutional for the rape of an adult woman and in 1982, in *Enmund v. Florida* (1982, p. 797), the death penalty was held to be an "excessive penalty" for robbers who do not kill their victims.

7. It is important to point out that the evidence in the Alford case was overwhelmingly against him. One witness testified that Alford had left his house with his gun, saying he was going to kill the victim, then returned home and stated that he had "carried out the killing" (*Carolina v. Alford,* 1970, p. 28).

8. Of course, some may argue, based on the Santobello and Goodwin cases, that defendants are not as "free" to reject bargains as initially assumed, meaning that the practice is not always completely voluntary.

9. The scholar Frank H. Easterbrook is also a judge, as he is both senior lecturer at Yale law school and a judge on the United States Court of Appeals.

10. Subsequent cases have shown that depending upon constitutional issues, such as whether a defendant's plea was made "in reliance on" a prosecutor's offer of leniency, prosecutors sometimes are not held to the terms of their deals (e.g., Ejzak, 1991, p. 107). In one case, for example, the prosecutor offered a reduced penalty in exchange for the defendant acting as an informant against others; the defendant cooperated, but the prosecutor withdrew the offer (*People v. Navarroli,* 1988). In another case, a defendant was promised reduced charges if he cooperated in the prosecution of another individual; his cooperation resulted in the arrest of the sought-after killer, but the prosecutor never called him to testify and failed to honor the agreement (*People v. Marquez,* 1981). In both cases, the courts upheld the prosecutions' actions as acceptable. What distinguished these two cases from plea bargains was that neither involved the actual pleading guilty in exchange for a reduced penalty (Ejzak, 1991). Since no constitutional rights were involved in the deals, the prosecutors were not legally obligated to honor their deals.

11. We will never know whether the professor was serious when he made the offer because none of the students in the class accepted the deal. They all chose to write a paper.

# REFERENCES

Acevedo, R. (1995). Is a ban on plea bargaining an ethical abuse of discretion? A Bronx County, New York case study. *Fordham Law Review, 64*: 987–1013.

Alschuler, A. (1978). Plea bargaining and its history. *Law and Society Review, 13*: 211–245.

Andrews, W. (1991). *Old Time Punishments.* New York: Dorset Press. (Originally published in 1890, London: Simpkin, Marshall, Hamilton and Kent).

Baldwin, J., and McConville, M. (1978). Plea bargaining and plea negotiation in England. *Law and Society Review, 13*: 287–307.

Black, H.C. and publisher's editorial staff. (1991). *Black's Law Dictionary* (abridged 6th ed.). St. Paul, MN: West.

Blumberg, A.S. (1967). *Criminal Justice.* Chicago: Quadrangle Books.

*Bordenkircher v. Hayes,* 434 U.S. 357 (1978).

*Boykin v. Alabama,* 395 U.S. 238 (1969).

*Brady v. United States,* 397 U.S. 742 (1970).

Brown, J.M., Langan, P.A., and Levin, D.J. (1999). *Felony Sentences in State Courts 1996.* Washington, DC: Bureau of Justice Statistics.

Callahan, B. (1996, June 11). Ex-teacher angrily tries to withdraw guilty plea. *San Diego Union Tribune,* p. B1.

*Carolina v. Alford,* 400 U.S. 25 (1970).

Cohen, J., and Tonry, M.H. (1983). Sentencing reforms and their impacts. In A. Blumstein et al. (Eds.), *Research on Sentencing: The Search for Reform,* vol. II. Washington, DC: National Academy Press.

*Coker v. Georgia,* 433 U.S. 584 (1977).

*Commonwealth v. Battis,* 1 Mass. 95 (1804).

Cramer, J.A. (1981). Judicial supervision of the guilty plea hearing. In J.A. Cramer (Ed.), *Courts and Judges.* Beverly Hills, CA: Sage.

Dash, S. (1951). Cracks in the foundation of criminal justice. *Illinois Law Review,* 46: 385–406.

Donziger, S. (Ed). (1996). *The Real War on Crime: The Report of the National Criminal Justice Commission.* New York: HarperPerennial.

Dorning, M. (2000, July 24). Federal death sentences show race gap more plea deals for white suspects. *Chicago Tribune Wire.*

Drug rap dropped against ex-deputy. (1997, May 22). *Associated Press Wire.*

Easterbrook, F.H. (1992). Plea bargaining as compromise. *Yale Law Journal,* 101: 1969–1978.

*Edwards v. People,* 39 Mich. 760 (1878).

Eisenstein, J., and Jacob, H. (1977). *Felony Justice: An Organizational Analysis of Criminal Courts.* Boston: Little, Brown.

Ejzak, W.M. (1991). Plea bargains and nonprosecution agreements: What interests should be protected when prosecutors renege? *University of Illinois Law Review, 1991:* 107–136.

*Enmund v. Florida,* 458 U.S. 782 (1982).

Feeley, M.M. (1979). *The Process Is the Punishment: Handling Cases in a Lower Criminal Court.* New York: Russell Sage Foundation.

Felstiner, W.L.F. (1978). Plea contracts in West Germany. *Law and Society Review,* 13: 309–325.

Ferdinand, T. (1992). *Boston's Lower Criminal Courts, 1814–1850.* Newark: University of Delaware Press.

Friedman, L.M. (1978). Plea bargaining in historical perspective. *Law and Society Review,* 13: 247–259.

*Gideon v. Wainwright,* 372 U.S. 335 (1963).

Guidorizzi, D.D. (1998). Should we really "ban" plea bargaining?: The core concerns of plea bargaining critics. *Emory Law Journal,* 47: 753–783.

Haller, M. (1978). Plea bargaining: The nineteenth century context. *Law and Society Review,* 13: 273–279.

Herrera, P. (1997, April 28). Killer apologizes at sentencing. *Associated Press Wire.*

Heumann, M. (1978). *Plea Bargaining: The Experiences of Prosecutors, Judges, and Defense Attorneys.* Chicago: University of Chicago Press.

Hill, F. (1995). *A Delusion of Satan: The Full Story of the Salem Witch Trials.* New York: Doubleday.

Holten, N.G., and Lamar, L.L. (1991). *The Criminal Courts: Structures, Personnel, and Processes.* New York: McGraw-Hill.

Johnson, P.C. (1995). At the intersection of injustice: Experiences of African American women in crime and sentencing. *The American University Journal of Gender and the Law,* 4: 1–76.

Knowles, L.L., and Prewitt, K. (1969). *Institutional Racism in America.* Englewood Cliffs, NJ: Prentice Hall.

Komitee, E.R. (1995). Bargains without benefits: Do the sentencing guidelines permit upward departures to redress the dismissal of charges pursuant to plea bargains?" *New York University Law Review*, 70: 166–195.

Kunkle, W.J. (1989). Punishment and the criminal justice system: A prosecutor's viewpoint. In F.E. Baumann and K.M. Jensen (Eds.), *Crime and Punishment: Issues in Criminal Justice*. Charlottesville: University Press of Virginia.

Langbein, J.H. (1974). *Prosecuting Crime in the Renaissance: England, Germany, France*. Cambridge, MA: Harvard University Press.

Langbein, J. (1978). Understanding the short history of plea bargaining. *Law and Society Review*, 13: 261–272.

Levin, D.J., Langan, P.A., and Brown, J.M. (2000). *State Court Sentencing of Convicted Felons, 1996*. Washington, DC: Bureau of Justice Statistics.

Lindquist, J.H. (1988). *Misdemeanor Crime: Criminal Trivial Pursuit*. Newbury Park, CA: Sage.

Maguire, K., and Pastore, A.L. (Eds.). (1999). *Sourcebook of Criminal Justice Statistics, 1998*. Washington, DC: Bureau of Justice Statistics.

Matheny, A.R. (1980). Negotiations and plea bargaining models: An organizational perspective. *Law & Policy Quarterly*, 2: 267–284.

Mather, L.M. (1978). Comments on the history of plea bargaining. *Law and Society Review*, 13: 281–285.

McCall, G.J. (1978). *Observing the Law: Field Methods in the Study of Crime and the Criminal Justice System*. New York: Free Press.

Meyer, J.F. (1992a). Personal interview with a lower court judge in California.

Meyer, J.F. (1992b). Personal observation during a lower court hearing in California.

Meyer, J.F. (1993). Personal interview with a lower court judge in California.

Meyer, J., and Jesilow, P. (1997). *'Doing Justice' in the People's Court: Sentencing by Municipal Court Judges*. New York: State University of New York Press.

Mileski, M. (1971). Courtroom encounters: An observation study of a lower criminal court. *Law and Society Review*, 5: 473–538.

Miller, H.S., McDonald, W.F., and Cramer, J.A. (1978). *Plea Bargaining in the United States (Phase I report)*. Washington, DC: Government Printing Office.

Miller, J. (1927). The compromise of criminal cases. *Southern California Law Review*, 1: 1–31.

Mills, J. (1971, March 12). I Have Nothing to Do with Justice, *Life*, 70(9): 56–68.

Moley, R. (1928). The vanishing jury. *Southern California Law Review*, 2: 98–127.

Moran, T.K., and Cooper, J.L. (1983). *Discretion and the Criminal Justice Process*. Port Washington, NY: Associated Faculty Press.

Nardulli, P.F. (1978). *The Courtroom Elite: An Organizational Perspective on Criminal Justice*. Cambridge, MA: Ballinger.

Neubauer, D.W. (1974). *Criminal Justice in Middle America*. Morristown, NJ: General Learning Press.

*People v. Marquez*, 644 P.2d 59 (Colo. Ct. App. 1981).

*People v. Navarroli*, 121 Ill. 2d 516 (1988).

President's Commission on Law Enforcement and Administration of Justice. (1968). *Challenge of Crime in a Free Society*. New York: Avon Books. (Reprinted from *Challenge of Crime in a Free Society*, Washington, DC: Government Printing Office, 1967).

Reputed mobster gets probation. (1999, April 14). *Associated Press Wire.*

Rights explained to the defendant. (1998, April 23). [Delaware] *News Journal.*

Rosett, A., and Cressey, D.R. (1976). *Justice by Consent: Plea Bargains in the American Courthouse.* Philadelphia: J.B. Lippincott.

Rubinstein, M.L., and White, T.J. (1978). Alaska's ban on plea bargaining. *Law and Society Review,* 13: 367–383.

Ryan, J.P., and Alfini, J.J. (1978). Trial judges' participation in plea bargaining: An empirical perspective. *Law and Society Review,* 13: 479–507.

Sackville-West, V.M. (1936). *Saint Joan of Arc.* New York: The Literary Guild.

*Santobello v. New York,* 404 U.S. 257 (1971).

Train, A.C. (1922). *The Prisoner at the Bar: Sidelights on the Administration of Criminal Justice.* New York: Charles Scribner's Sons.

Uhlman, T.M. (1977). The impact of defendant race in trial-court sanctioning decisions. In J.A. Gardiner (Ed.), *Public Law and Public Policy.* New York: Praeger.

Uhlman, T.M. (1979). *Racial Justice: Black Judges and Defendants in an Urban Trial Court.* Lexington, MA: Lexington Books.

*United States v. Goodwin,* 457 U.S. 368 (1982).

Walker, S. (2001). *Sense and Nonsense about Crime* (5th ed.). Belmont, CA: Wadsworth.

Weninger, R.A. (1987). The abolition of plea bargaining: A case study of El Paso County, Texas. *UCLA Law Review,* 35: 265–313.

Wray, H.R. (1993). *Mandatory Minimum Sentences: Are They Being Imposed and Who Is Receiving Them?* Washington, DC: Government Accounting Office.

Ziegler, N. (1996, December 14). Life terms for fatal car heist. *Associated Press Wire.*

# Step 12

## Your Day in Court: The Trial Begins

If you are the defendant in a trial, you are probably not in the state of mind to appreciate the fact that you are about to participate in a rather remarkable courtroom proceeding that represents both the ideals and the (sometimes quite different) realities of our legal system. Although you have the choice of being tried by a judge without jurors in a **bench trial**, if you are like most defendants who go to trial, you have probably opted for trial by a jury of your peers. As you may recall from Step 7, only 3 percent of trials are bench trials (adapted from Boland and Sones, 1986, pp. 6, 26). As you face the prospect of trial by jury, however, you may well appreciate the differences between the modern trial you are about to experience and the trials of olden days, including trial by ordeal and trial by battle (see Step 4).

In this chapter, we will briefly continue tracing the development of modern American jury trials from pre-Revolutionary times, and then focus on the modern trial process from the perspective of the jury. Since what matters most in a jury trial is how jurors perceive the unfolding criminal justice drama and its key actors, a jury-focused perspective will help illuminate the realities of the trial process. As we go through the steps of the modern trial process (see Figure 12.1), it will help to keep in mind what we already know about the duties and dilemmas of key players, such as the judge, the prosecutor, and the defense attorney.

As we watch the process of trial unfold, it may become clearer why trials can sometimes be quite lengthy. The length of the average criminal trial varies by jurisdiction, but commonly ranges between three days and one week. Occasionally, a trial might last much longer, depending upon the number of witnesses called to testify and the amount of physical evidence presented. The longest and costliest trial in America was the McMartin preschool case, which lasted thirty months, and was then followed by two additional trials because of hung juries on some of the charges, making the total length of the case seven years.

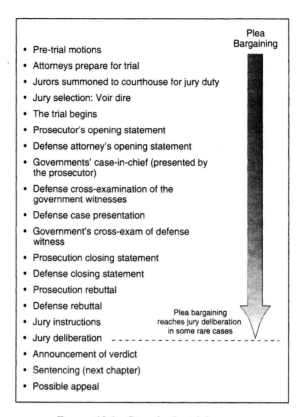

- Pre-trial motions
- Attorneys prepare for trial
- Jurors summoned to courthouse for jury duty
- Jury selection: Voir dire
- The trial begins
- Prosecutor's opening statement
- Defense attorney's opening statement
- Governments' case-in-chief (presented by the prosecutor)
- Defense cross-examination of the government witnesses
- Defense case presentation
- Government's cross-exam of defense witness
- Prosecution closing statement
- Defense closing statement
- Prosecution rebuttal
- Defense rebuttal
- Jury instructions
- Jury deliberation
- Announcement of verdict
- Sentencing (next chapter)
- Possible appeal

Plea Bargaining

Plea bargaining reaches jury deliberation in some rare cases

**FIGURE 12.1   Steps in the trial process**

## TRIAL BY JURY IN PRE-REVOLUTIONARY AMERICA

When the colonists came to America, they imported the concept of trial by jury as part of the package of English legal concepts and procedures. Since America was still a colony of the British Crown, the colonists' early experiences with trial by jury were often filled with difficulty. When a colonist was accused and tried, jurors were generally chosen by the King's officials, not from the accused's neighbors (or peers). These officials usually chose jurors partial to the Crown's interests, so getting justice was nearly impossible in the eyes of independence-minded colonists. Yet the colonists could see the potential for the jury trial, if the jurors were impartial or consisted of even numbers of those partial to the prosecution and those partial to the defense (Abramson, 1994).

## TRIAL BY JURY AFTER INDEPENDENCE

After the American Revolution, the framers of the Constitution considered trial by a jury of peers so important that the Constitution provides the right to trial by jury for all crimes except impeachment; the Sixth Amendment (1791) provides the right to be tried by an **impartial** jury, meaning a fair and unbiased one; the Seventh Amendment (1791) grants this right in civil cases involving twenty dollars or more.

The Supreme Court originally interpreted these constitutional provisions as applicable only in federal trials, reasoning that trial by jury was not a "fundamental" right, and thus was not applicable to the states through the Fourteenth Amendment's due process clause (*Palko v. Connecticut,* 1937). This meant that states were not required to provide jury trials, but could choose to do so. In *Duncan v. Louisiana* (1968), the Court reversed its position, ruling that trial by jury in criminal cases is a fundamental right applicable to the states. The justices' reasoning in the *Duncan* case emphasized the importance of jury trials as part of due process and as a significant aspect of a participatory democracy.

In subsequent cases, the Supreme Court clarified the scope of the right to trial by jury, finding it applicable in any case involving a minimum possible sentence of six months' incarceration, and even in some cases with a shorter penalty. In *Lewis v. United States* (1996), however, the Supreme Court ruled that defendants who are convicted of multiple petty offenses for which the combined total length of incarceration would be greater than six months are *not* entitled to a jury trial. For civil matters, however, the Court has not extended the Seventh Amendment requirement of trial by jury to the states, instead leaving state governments to decide whether they wish to require juries in civil trials.

## MODERN-DAY TRIALS

We've seen the reasons why the right to trial by jury is a fundamental part of due process in our court system. Now let's take a closer look at the trial itself, beginning with a fundamental question: What is the purpose of a jury trial? Many people might answer "To find the truth, of course." That is indeed the purpose, yet this presumes that there is a single true version of events, and that the adversarial format of a criminal trial is the best way to discover the truth.

However, a trial can also be conceptualized as a forum where differing interpretations of events are offered by each side, and jurors sift and sort and select the version of events that seems most plausible. The jurors then begin the complicated process of reconciling the facts of the case as they perceive them with the provisions of the law, the dictates of their consciences, and the compromises hammered out during jury deliberations. The resulting verdict, therefore, reflects a particular subjective construction of "the truth" as much as—perhaps more than—it represents a discovery of an "objective" truth. In this sense, the purpose of a jury trial may be to provide a forum for presenting competing versions of the truth, and provide a means both practical and symbolic of pronouncing that justice has been served. This illustrates the role that trials play as social dramas where larger societal issues can be examined and addressed in the context of specific cases.

# THE TRIAL PROCESS: PRE-TRIAL ACTIVITIES

## Discovery

This is the process whereby the prosecution and the defense exchange information in order to prepare for trial. As part of discovery, each side may interview and take **depositions** from witnesses. A deposition is an "out-of-court statement given under oath by any person involved in the case" (American Bar Association, 2001). Although the goal of discovery is to enable each side to anticipate the evidence the other side will present, in order to avoid unpleasant surprises (American Bar Association, 2001), sometimes surprises occur nonetheless. For example, it may be revealed later that information that should have been disclosed to the defense was not, either inadvertently or deliberately. Sometimes, a subpoena requesting all relevant papers is answered with a slew of unsorted papers crammed into cardboard boxes. This tactic may cut into the opposition's preparation time, by requiring them to spend time wading through a paper flood to identify relevant documents.

## Ongoing Negotiations Between Defense and Prosecution

As we saw in the last chapter, most criminal charges are settled through plea bargaining. When the defense opts to go to trial, however, that does not necessarily mean the end of negotiations. Even as the defense and prosecution prepare to go to trial, ongoing attempts to reach a settlement occur, and negotiations can continue even as the trial begins and after it is well underway. In one case, for example, a man pleaded guilty to stealing Malcolm X's diary three days into his trial for the theft (Finkelstein, 2000). In some rare cases, plea bargains are finalized while the jury is out deliberating.

## Pre-Trial Motions

Before the trial actually begins, the defense and prosecution will submit relevant pre-trial **motions** to the court for the judge to decide upon. Motions are requests to the court for a ruling on a legal matter. For example, the defense may file a motion asking the judge to dismiss the case on the basis of insufficient evidence. The prosecution will then file a rebuttal requesting the court not grant the motion, and explaining why the case should proceed. Attorneys for either side may file a motion requesting that the trial date be postponed in order to give them more time to study the issues in a case or locate a key witness. Another common petition is a motion to discover, which is used to seek information held by opposing counsel. See Box 12.1 for an example of a pre-trial motion that is relatively uncommon, except in cases attracting intense publicity.

## BOX 12.1

## Pre-Trial Motions for Change of Venue in the Oklahoma City Bombing Trial

The bombing of the federal building in Oklahoma City, in which 168 people died, received extensive and in-depth media coverage before and after the trial of suspects Timothy McVeigh and Terry Nichols. News media around the world described the wreckage of the building, possible motives for the bombing, the search for survivors, and the horror and grief of victims and their families. The horrific and unique nature of the crime made the smallest details of the event the subject of widespread coverage, which was often emotionally laden and intensely detailed. Not surprisingly, local media in Oklahoma, especially in Oklahoma City itself, provided saturation coverage of the bombing and its aftermath, including the capture and identification of Timothy McVeigh.

As McVeigh's defense team prepared for trial, people around the world saw images of the death and destruction caused by the bombing. Given such intense and emotionally evocative coverage, the defense team questioned whether defendants McVeigh and Nichols could receive a fair trial in the Oklahoma City venue. Could a truly impartial jury be drawn from citizens of the local community, given the widespread impact of the bombing and the extensive media coverage?

The defense attorneys hired social scientists to investigate this question through empirical research on the newspaper coverage in four potential trial venues: Oklahoma City, Tulsa, and Lawton (all in Oklahoma), and Denver, Colorado. Researchers at the University of Nebraska, Lincoln, conducted a content analysis of newspaper media coverage of the bombing. They assessed the nature and emotional content of the coverage, as well as the sheer volume of coverage in each locale, by reading a random sampling of 939 articles about the bombing published in the newspapers of each city between April 20, 1995, and January 8, 1996. Each newspaper article was systematically coded along a number of dimensions, including whether McVeigh and Nichols were portrayed as the embodiment of evil or in other demonic imagery, clearly negative characterizations of the defendants.

The results of the study showed that the nature of the media coverage in the Oklahoma cities was substantially more emotionally laden and prejudiced than that which appeared in the Denver paper. The scientists concluded that the nature and extent of the pre-trial publicity in the venue where the trial was to be held was such that it would be substantially impossible to seat an impartial jury.

The defense attorneys decided to file a motion for change of venue—that is, a request to change the location of the trial. For both legal and practical reasons, a request for change of venue often requires the defense to provide solid evidence supporting the argument that the trial should be conducted at another location. The research demonstrated that there was more intense media coverage of the issues in Oklahoma, and that not surprisingly Oklahomans were more familiar with and had stronger attitudes about the bombing, the guilt of the suspects, the nature of the evidence that had been amassed, and other associated issues. The defense motion for change of venue, using this evidence in support of the motion, was granted. Thus, the trial was ultimately held in Denver, and both defendants were found guilty (Studebaker, Robbennolt, Pathak-Sharma, & Penrod, 2000).

## Jury Selection: The Legal Foundations

The right to trial by an "impartial" jury raises many questions concerning jury selection and composition. A common method of jury selection before 1968 was the "key man" system, relying on prominent citizens in the community to serve. This meant many citizens were excluded from jury duty, despite being legally eligible. Most notably, in *Strauder v. West Virginia* (1880), the Supreme Court struck a state law excluding African American men from jury duty as a violation of equal protection. Thus, by law, the importance of fair jury selection was explicitly established. However, in fact, the practice of excluding minorities from jury service continued unacknowledged by the Court, as illustrated by its decision in *Swain v. Alabama* (1965) allowing exclusion of potential jurors on the basis of race.

Similarly, although women became jury eligible between 1870 and 1940 (depending on locale), most states continued to exclude women from **jury pools** (from which jurors are drawn) (Abramson, 1994). The Supreme Court addressed this in *Taylor v. Louisiana* (1975), striking the practice of including women in jury pools only if they had contacted the court and asked to have their names included on jury lists.

One of the first Vermont juries to include women as well as men was convened in Barre Municipal Court. Women were not allowed to serve as jurors in Vermont until 1943. The issue of whether women could or should serve as jurors was debated until well into the twentieth century. Some people argued that women should be protected from the unpleasantness of courtroom trials, while others argued that women were intellectually or morally unfit to serve as jurors. The debate over women's jury service clearly illustrates the central role that gender stereotyping has played in shaping women's participation in the criminal justice system, whether as jurors, judges, attorneys, or police and correctional officers.   SOURCE: Courtesy of the Aldrich Public Library, Barre, Vermont.

In 1968, Congress enacted the Jury Selection and Service Act, requiring that federal jury pools be comprised of citizens drawn at random "from a representative cross section of the community." In *Taylor v. Louisiana* (1975), the Supreme Court extended this requirement to states. The random selection requirement substantially changed the methods used to create jury pools, but did not address how individual jurors are selected during **voir dire** (jury questioning).

In *Holland v. Illinois* (1990), the Supreme Court clarified that it is the *process* of selecting the jury pool that must be representative, rather than juries themselves. This is a crucial distinction to keep in mind. Many people mistakenly think that a "jury of one's peers" refers to a jury made up of people who share the defendant's ethnic and gender background. This is *not* the case! If the definition of "peers" referred to similarities between defendant and jurors, then a defendant with a prior criminal conviction could surely make the case to have some ex-felons on his or her jury. Instead, a **jury of one's peers** refers to the idea that defendants should be tried by fellow citizens from the same community. Therefore, if the process of jury selection has been carried out in accordance with legal requirements, the resulting jury is considered a jury of one's peers, even if the defendant is an Asian American woman in her twenties and the jury consists of mostly white middle-aged men.

## THE GOAL OF REPRESENTATIVENESS

Why do we care about the representativeness of the jury selection process? What are the legal assumptions underlying the requirement of a representative jury selection process?

One of the major assumptions is that the selection process, if drawing from a representative cross section of the community, will lead to a more diverse jury (though the jury itself will not be representative). Another assumption is that jurors from different demographic groups may have significantly different perspectives on the case: Women may see the issues differently than men, for example, and people from different ethnic groups sometimes bring differing perspectives.

Yet research shows that jurors' demographic characteristics, although significant influences on the verdict in some cases, are less important than the evidence in many cases. The key question is *how* (to what degree) such characteristics are important in any particular case. The assumption that jurors' verdicts can almost always be accurately predicted based on demographic characteristics is *not* supported by research: Not only do jurors not necessarily vote according to their demographic characteristics, but demographic groups are themselves not uniform in their beliefs. In addition, every juror simultaneously represents a variety of different demographic groups defined by age, ethnic background, gender, education level, sexual orientation, political and religious attitudes, social class, and others.

However, the assumption that demographics have nothing to do with verdict choices is inaccurate as well; since we are a product of our experiences, diversity

Who will fill these seats? The process of jury selection illustrates the complexities involved in drawing jurors from a "representative cross-section of the community," as required by law. Consider the importance of the jury in both criminal and civil cases. Who would you want to fill these seats in your trial? SOURCE: Courtesy of Jon'a Meyer.

matters. For example, if a juror shares the same ethnicity as the defendant, it may increase the likelihood that the juror will acquit or, on the other hand, convict. Although often assumed, "group loyalties" may not exist in reality. For example, women jurors are not necessarily the "ideal juror choice" for the prosecution in a rape case. While some women may indeed be more likely to sympathize with a female victim, under some circumstances women may actually be less sympathetic toward the victim. For example, some women may imagine themselves in the situation and feel that they would have acted differently, thus increasing the likelihood that they may blame the victim.

The fact that juror demographics are not necessarily tightly linked to their verdict choices is in fact quite appropriate, given that verdicts are not supposed to reflect the influence of extra-legal factors. We can recognize that personal experiences influence jurors' perspectives but do not necessarily determine jurors' behavior. Whether experiences are such a powerful influence that they essentially determine a juror's verdict choice depends upon a complex constellation of factors, including the political and social atmosphere at that time and place, and the issues in the case. Certainly, all-white juries in the American South during the first half of the twentieth century illustrated all too well how racism in the jury box—which was a reflection of the racism in the larger community—sometimes left little chance for African American defendants to receive a fair trial.

However, it is also critically important to avoid assuming that all members of a given demographic group share the same perspective, attitudes, or experiences. Certainly, they may share some common experiences, but individual differences also exist. Just as all teenagers and young people do not think alike, all women or all men or all members of a given ethnic group do not have the same attitudes or identical experiences.

Public controversy surrounding high-profile criminal cases, in particular cases raising questions about the relationship between race, ethnicity, and the fairness of the legal process, suggests another reason for caring about representativeness. While verdicts from relatively homogenous juries may be greeted with skepticism by significant segments of the public, verdicts from more diverse juries could potentially—although not necessarily—be perceived as having more legitimacy.

## Steps in the Process of Jury Selection

So, just how is a jury selected? To begin with, using lists from voter registration and the Department of Motor Vehicles, each county's jury management personnel create a master list of county residents. From this list, the names of people who will receive a summons for jury service are randomly drawn. Folks whose names are not on these lists have no chance of being called for jury duty, so people who are homeless or who move frequently, such as students or seasonal employees, are often underrepresented on the lists. In an attempt to capture a larger cross-section of residents, some jurisdictions use additional sources, such as lists of people receiving social security, general assistance (welfare), or unemployment benefits.

After the jury summonses are sent out, more prospective jurors are in effect "weeded out" of the jury selection process in the following ways:

- The person does not respond to a summons for jury service.
- The person is not eligible for jury duty (e.g., he or she moved to another county).
- The person is exempt (e.g., a peace officer, in some jurisdictions).
- The person is excused (e.g., for medical reasons).

The folks who remain after this stage comprise the **venire** (the jury panel). This is where the process of **voir dire** begins—where the judge and/or the attorneys question prospective jurors to determine whether they should be seated on the jury. "Voir dire" means "to speak the truth" in French, and therefore implies the process of identifying any biases or prejudices on the part of the jury panel.

## "Traditional" Jury Selection

How are jurors typically selected? "Traditional" jury selection is based on lawyers' experiences, intuitions, hunches, and implicit personality theories—that is, their

BOX 12.2

Excuses, Excuses . . .

Some people will say almost anything to avoid their civic duty, and jury managers and their staffs have heard just about every excuse in the book. One jury manager recalls that late one morning, a group of people summoned to the courthouse for jury duty was still sitting around the jury assembly room, waiting to see if they would be called to a courtroom. As the morning wore on, a young couple from the group came up to the counter to ask the jury manager whether the woman could be excused. Time was of the essence, the young woman explained, because she and her boyfriend were trying to become parents. That meant, she said, that they were timing their attempts to coincide with particular times of day when the woman's fertility was likely to be greatest—and here the young couple hugged and kissed to demonstrate the sincerity of their intentions. So, said the young woman, the morning was wearing on, and the best timing for potential parenthood was going to be sometime soon—in the next few hours, in fact. So, could she please be excused so that she and her boyfriend could go and proceed with parenthood plans?

"You'll have to tell it to the judge," said the jury manager, explaining that the law requires that citizens who wish to be excused on the scheduled day of their jury duty must make this request to a judge. (Personal communication with author.)

beliefs that juror characteristics, such as ethnicity, gender, age, certain experiences, and even nonverbal demeanor indicate potential attitudes and behavior that may or may not favor their side. Box 12.3 shows how Clarence Darrow, the famous defense lawyer, chose jurors in his cases.

## Scientific Jury Selection

This refers to the use of social science techniques to assist attorneys in selecting jurors and/or developing persuasive trial strategies to present the case. The goal is to systematize jury selection, in order to help maximize the chances of avoiding jurors unfavorable to one's side while identifying jurors who are favorable.

Common techniques of scientific jury selection (SJS) include surveying community members and holding focus groups (discussion groups) to gauge their attitudes and reactions on issues crucial to the trial. For example, both sides in the criminal trial of O.J. Simpson were interested in potential jurors' attitudes and experiences with domestic violence, their beliefs about scientific evidence (such as DNA samples), their perceptions of police officers and police credibility, their feelings about celebrities, and their potential race or gender sympathies. Research with residents of the community in which the trial will be held should help identify the types of citizens who would make the most favorable jurors. The research is conducted with residents in the community from which the actual jurors will later be drawn; research is not done with actual jurors themselves, for legal and ethical reasons. However, the use of scientific jury selection techniques with potential jurors

# BOX 12.3

# Traditional Jury Selection

*Clarence Darrow was a famous defense attorney who represented controversial defendants such as Socialist presidential candidate Eugene Debs, Tennessee school teacher John Scopes, and teenaged murderers Leopold and Loeb. Darrow, an ardent opponent of capital punishment, was known for his fiery oratory in the courtroom and his skill as a litigator. As you read this excerpt from Darrow's writings, think about what kinds of stereotypes appear to be illustrated by his assertions.*

Choosing jurors is always a delicate task. The more a lawyer knows of life, human nature, psychology, and the reactions of the human emotions, the better he is equipped for the subtle selection of his so-called "twelve men, good and true." In this undertaking, everything pertaining to the prospective juror needs to be questioned and weighed: his nationality, his business, religion, politics, social standing, family ties, friends, habits of life and thought; the books and newspapers he likes and reads, and many more matters that combine to make a man; all of these qualities and experiences have left their effect on ideas, beliefs and fancies that inhabit his mind. . . . Involved in it all is the juror's method of speech, the kind of clothes he wears, the style of haircut, and, above all, his business associates, residence and origin. If a criminal case, it is practically always the poor who are on trial. The most important point to learn is whether the prospective juror is humane. This must be discovered in more or less devious ways. As soon as "the court" sees what you want, he almost always blocks the game.

Let us assume that we represent one of "the underdogs" because of injuries received, or because of an indictment brought by what the prosecutors name themselves, "the state." Then what sort of men will we seek? An Irishman is called into the box for examination. There is no reason for asking about his religion; he is Irish; that is enough. We may not agree with his religion, but it matters not, his feelings go deeper than any religion. You should be aware that he is emotional, kindly and sympathetic. If he is chosen as a juror, his imagination will place him in the dock; really, he is trying himself. You would be guilty of malpractice if you got rid of him, except for the strongest reasons.

If a Presbyterian enters the jury box and carefully rolls up his umbrella, and calmly and critically sits down, let him go. He is cold as the grave; he knows right from wrong, although he seldom finds anything right. He believes in John Calvin and eternal punishment. Get rid of him with the fewest possible words before he contaminates the others; unless you and your clients are Presbyterians you probably are a bad lot, and even though you may be a Presbyterian, your client most likely is guilty.

If possible, the Baptists are more hopeless than the Presbyterians . . . you do not want them on the jury, and the sooner they leave the better. The Methodists are worth considering; they are nearer the soil. Their religious emotions can be transmuted into love and charity. They are not half bad; even though they will not take a drink, they really do not need it so much as some of their competitors for the seat next to the throne. If chance sets you down between a Methodist and a Baptist, you will move toward the Methodist to keep warm.

Beware of the Lutherans, especially the Scandinavians; they are almost always sure to convict. Either a Lutheran or Scandinavian is unsafe, but if both in one, plead your client guilty and go down the docket. He learns about sinning and punishing from the preacher, and dares not doubt. A person who disobeys must be sent to hell; he has God's word for that.

As to Unitarians, Universalists, Congregationalists, Jews and other agnostics, don't ask them too many questions; keep them anyhow, especially Jews and agnostics. . . .

*Source:* From *How to Pick a Jury* by Clarence Darrow, quoted in *Esquire,* May 1936.

during voir dire is illustrated by the use of detailed jury questionnaires and probing questions from attorneys. Such detailed information gathering has led to charges that such practices may intrude on the privacy of potential jurors.[1]

Scientific jury selection rests upon several critical assumptions, including the following:

- Jurors' behavior reflects or is at least consistent with their attitudes.
- Links between individual characteristics and attitudes on case issues in community members will be similar for actual jurors.
- Use of questionnaires, surveys, and questioning during *voir dire* can accurately measure attitudes and uncover biases.
- Juror attitudes significantly influence the verdict.

In most of the criminal cases where SJS techniques have been used by the defense, defendants have been acquitted, convicted on lesser charges, or the jury deadlocked. For example, in the McMartin preschool case, the defense used scientific jury selection techniques to help identify the most promising types of jurors in an attempt to combat the potentially prejudicial effects of extensive pre-trial publicity. Based on this research, the defense attempted to get jurors from certain ethnic groups (African American, white, or Asian) rather than others (Hispanic, Native American). The defense also focused on male jurors, and jurors with a relatively high education level. The McMartin defense also attempted to choose jurors with particular attitudes on issues relevant to the case; for example, jurors who believed that it was possible for children to be taught to testify about things that never happened (Fukurai, Butler, and Krooth, 1993). In the end, the McMartin defendants were acquitted on most charges. The jury deadlocked on fourteen other charges against one of the defendants.

Scientific jury selection is a controversial practice for several reasons, and it is employed relatively rarely in criminal trials compared to its use in civil trials. Some proponents of SJS believe it is very effective, but the results of the limited amount of research experimentally comparing traditional and scientific selection strategies suggests it's a toss-up (Horowitz, 1980; Nietzel and Dillehay, 1986). However, in some circumstances, SJS might be significantly more effective than traditional jury selection techniques: in cases where the evidence is equivocal; for certain types of civil litigation or political cases; where community sentiment

---

**BOX 12.4**

**SJS and the O.J. Simpson Criminal Trial**

During jury selection for the criminal trial of O.J. Simpson, prosecutor Marcia Clark selected juror Jeannette Harris. Clark thought that the domestic violence issues the prosecution would raise in the case would resonate with Harris, because of Harris's identity as an African American woman. Clark's decision went against the recommendation of the prosecution's jury consultant, who argued that this was a questionable assumption (Davis and Davis, 1995).

---

about the case has been shaped by extensive media coverage. The use of SJS techniques together with traditional methods, so that jurors selected only if both methods indicate they would be acceptable, can boost chances of making good juror selection. Perhaps the most effective role for SJS is in helping attorneys develop the best case presentation. For example, SJS can provide invaluable data to help attorneys decide the best, clearest, and most accessible way to present complex or technical legal and scientific information, or the most understandable way to arrange the sequence of arguments and evidence presentation.

The debate over the effectiveness of SJS raises complex ethical questions that are not resolvable through empirical research. To the extent that scientific jury selection is an effective tool in some circumstances, does this provide some defendants with an unfair advantage over those without the resources to employ "scientific" techniques? The response most often heard is that defendants already vary in the resources available to them to marshal tools for their defense, such as the most competent counsel, the services of defense investigators, and the services of expert witnesses. To the extent that defendants with greater resources enjoy an advantage over other defendants, the issue of inequality is an old and persistent one, and access to SJS research is merely another example of an already entrenched problem.

## Voir Dire: "To Speak the Truth"

The purpose of **voir dire** is to question prospective jurors in order to weed out people who would not be impartial. In reality, voir dire also provides the attorneys the opportunity to try to identify jurors who will be sympathetic to their side, and those who may favor the opposition. The process of questioning prospective jurors can also provide each side with a better idea of the "game plan" the opposition will use at trial. For example, during jury selection in a case where a woman stands accused of killing her husband, the prosecution team may learn that the defense is planning to present information that the accused was a victim of domestic violence as part of its trial strategy.

Depending upon the jurisdiction, the judge may do most of the juror questioning, or the attorneys may be the primary questioners (see Box 12.6). In some

---

## BOX 12.5

## The Unwanted Juror

Some years ago in a Massachusetts prosecution for assault with intent to murder, one seat remained to be filled on the jury after the defense had expended its final challenge. The man called to occupy it was, as his informational questionnaire disclosed, a police lieutenant. In the "Remarks" section he had written: "I once investigated and prosecuted a case of assault with intent to murder."

Before the lieutenant could enter the jury box, defense counsel was, understandably, asking the judge to excuse the juror "for cause." However, because the juror had sworn to his impartiality during the usual pre-empanelment routine the judge denied the request.

As the trial went on, the evidence seemed to the judge to be exceptionally strong, and he silently anticipated a conviction. At the end he did not pick the foreperson for the jury (as many judges do) but instead left that choice to the jurors. They selected the lieutenant and returned after only an hour's deliberation.

"What say you, Mr. Foreman?" the clerk intoned in language unchanged since John Adams's day. "Is the defendant guilty or not guilty?"

Promptly and loudly the lieutenant replied, "Not guilty." After the defendant's discharge several jurors, including the lieutenant, asked to speak to the judge. "We were wondering," said a woman, "why the government brought this case; it seemed pretty weak to us." "I'll second that," said the lieutenant. "It's the worst, sloppiest investigation I've seen in seventeen years as a police officer. They should be ashamed at having wasted everyone's time."

"Well," said the judge, "cases aren't always predictable." And, he might have added, neither are juries—or jurors. (Zobel, 1995)

*Source:* Reprinted by permission of American Heritage, Inc., 1995.

---

cases, prospective jurors are asked to fill out questionnaires indicating their attitudes and experiences with issues in the case. Jury questionnaires can run from a few pages to dozens of pages, depending upon the complexity of issues in the case. For example, in the trial of John DeLorean, the forty-two-page jury questionnaire contained ninety-nine questions (Brill, 1989, p. 232)

The voir dire phase of jury selection provides an interesting contrast to earlier steps in the process of jury selection, where the focus on the representativeness of the selection process requires *random* selection of prospective jurors. In contrast, jury selection during voir dire is anything *but* random, as attorneys for each side attempt to choose jurors they favor and exclude those they believe could be biased against their case. So how does the juror selection process become so selective?

Attorneys have two ways they can "strike" a prospective juror off the panel. First, an attorney can "challenge" a juror "for cause." Attorneys have an unlimited number of challenges for cause. This means that the attorney asks the court to excuse the juror from service because the attorney believes that the juror would be biased for a particular reason. For example, voir dire may reveal that a potential

## BOX 12.6

## A Personal View of Voir Dire

The courtroom was full, with about sixty people sitting on the plain wooden benches. Some were looking around with interest, obviously curious about the jury selection process that was about to begin. Others had already opened their paperbacks and resumed the reading they had begun that morning in the jury assembly room. As prospective jurors, we knew only that we had been assigned to go to a courtroom where a criminal case was to be tried; we knew no other details. After the bailiff led us to the courtroom and we were seated, the judge introduced himself and explained that some of us would be randomly selected to come up and be seated in the jury box, so that the attorneys in the case could begin the process of questioning the jury. The jury selection process would continue until there were twelve jurors and two alternates selected for the case.

I was one of the people called during the first round of jury questioning, and I could feel my fellow citizens' eyes on me and the other prospective jurors as we took our seats in the jury box. The palpable but unspoken question was "will I be next?"

The prosecutor and defense attorneys introduced themselves, and we got our first look at the defendant. The judge explained a little bit about the process, and asked if there was any reason that we could not serve, if selected. One man quickly raised his hand and asked to be excused, stating that he had a lower back condition that prevented him from sitting in the same position for long periods of time. The judge asked him a few questions about this but quickly granted his request to be excused. A few other people wanted to be excused, and the judge granted most of these requests.

The judge and attorneys then began systematically questioning each person in the jury box, one individual at a time. During questioning, all eyes in the courtroom—the attorneys, the judge, the defendant, the other potential jurors in the courtroom—were focused on the individual responding from the jury box. "What's your name? What is your occupation?" the judge would ask, and then the attorneys would take turns asking questions that could give them a sense of who we were, what our attitudes toward the key issues in the case would be. "Do you have children?" asked the defense. Both sides asked questions about gun ownership and attitudes. As the questioning continued, the questions provided an interesting glimpse of the case. It appeared the defendant was an ex-felon who was being charged with possession of a firearm, which had been left unattended and could have endangered a child who came upon it. However, no one had actually been injured.

At some point in the questioning, an attorney for one side or the other might stop and confer with someone else, and after that the attorney might ask the judge to excuse the potential juror who had just been questioned; alternatively, the attorneys for both sides would state that "This juror is acceptable to us," and the questioning would begin with a new prospect. Now it was my turn, and I was surprised at the hint of nervousness I felt. I had long been accustomed to public speaking, usually in front of far larger groups than this; yet the solemnity of the circumstances felt quite different than anything I'd experienced before.

"What is your occupation?" "Criminal justice professor? How interesting . . ." "What kind of courses do you teach?" "Oh, you say you teach a course on jury selection and decision-making?" "And your dissertation topic was jury decision making in criminal cases?" (Audible titters from members of the courtroom audience).

To my surprise, I was not challenged for cause, and I happily settled in to watch as my fellow prospective jurors were questioned. However, as the nature of the case became clearer, I started to have misgivings. The case appeared to present issues that were startlingly similar to the issues I had researched for my dissertation.

At this point, the judge ended the questioning of this batch of potential jurors by asking all of us if we knew anyone else in the courtroom. A young man seated two rows in front of me in the jury box raised his hand. "I know Dr. Grant. She was one of my instructors . . ."

I peered from the back row of the jury box. I had thought the fellow looked vaguely familiar, but only vaguely. One of the attorneys apparently found this connection interesting. "So tell us," he asked the young man "what course did you take with Dr. Grant?" "When was that—a couple of years back?"

I still had little memory of this particular former student, but I felt for him as his academic life was being probed in front of a whole bunch of interested and evidently amused strangers. I was not prepared for the next question the attorney asked of my former student: "What grade did you get in Dr. Grant's class?" "You got a 'C,' you say?" At this, I could hear suppressed giggles from some members of the audience. Oh dear, I thought. And anyway, how was *that* relevant to the person's potential to be a good juror?

After that, it appeared that both the student and I were going to be on the same jury, because neither attorney objected to our university connection. But I knew what I had to say when the judge asked a final question of all of us. "Is there any reason you feel you could not serve on this jury? If so, please speak up."

I raised my hand. I briefly explained my increasing misgivings about serving as a juror in this particular case, because while I believed that I could be a fair and impartial juror, I knew that my fascination with the particular issues presented in this case from a research perspective could distract me if I were to serve. Not only would I be thinking about the issues of the case from the perspective of a citizen serving as a juror, I would also be examining the issues from the perspective of a jury researcher who had spent much time studying cases that presented very similar issues to this one: "Looking in from the outside," as it were. Regretfully, I asked to be excused, and I was. As I left the jury box, I wondered how the case would turn out and what the experience of serving in the case would be like for the other people selected as jurors. I silently wished them good luck as I walked out of the courtroom, feeling rather wistful.

juror had been a crime victim, or knows one of the participants in the case. During voir dire in a civil case observed by one of the authors, one man was dismissed after he told the judge that he himself had a lawsuit pending against the defendant, and a woman was excused when she announced that she knew the plaintiff's attorney from church. It is easy to see how these individuals may be less than fully impartial because of such connections.

Much more controversial is the use of **peremptory challenges** to "strike" prospective jurors. Attorneys for each side have a limited number of "peremptories" that they can exercise, depending on the jurisdiction and the complexity of the case. Peremptory challenges are "ace in the hole cards" because they allow attorneys to exclude a prospective juror who could not be removed from the panel using a challenge for cause. Traditionally, attorneys can exercise peremptory challenges without giving any reason for wanting to remove a particular person. Historically, the attorney's reasoning was legally irrelevant; perhaps the attorney had a "gut hunch" that the person would favor the opposing side, or the attorney wished to select jurors in keeping with his or her personal stereotypes of the "ideal" juror.

However, in recent years the issue of the purposes for which peremptory challenges are employed, especially by the prosecution, has become very controversial. Research suggested that prosecutors used peremptory challenges to systematically strike prospective jurors who were African American, especially in death penalty cases where the accused was African American. In Philadelphia, a prosecutor conducting a videotaped training session urged new district attorneys to use peremptory challenges to strike poor African Americans as jurors (Johnson, 1998).

Questions about the role of peremptory challenges in jury selection have come into sharp focus recently, given the new emphasis on inclusiveness in jury selection that took hold after *Duncan v. Louisiana.* Controversy focused on the "race-based" use of peremptories, because such challenges directly conflict with the goal of representativeness in jury selection.

A major change in the Supreme Court's perspective on the use of peremptory challenges became evident in 1986. In *Batson v. Kentucky* (1986), the Court reversed its earlier position in *Swain v. Alabama* (1965), holding that using race to strike a prospective juror violated the defendant's equal protection rights. Thus, peremptory challenges cannot be used to exclude potential jurors *solely* on the basis of race. In the Court's written opinion, the justices discussed the potential harm to the ideal of representativeness posed by the use of peremptories to strike people of a **cognizable group** (a group of people recognizable as having a high likelihood of sharing common experiences and attitudes). In *Batson,* the Court decreed that when it appears that the prosecution may be engaging in a "race-based" use of peremptory challenges, the court can require the prosecutor to provide a "nondiscriminatory" explanation for the pattern. Critics charge, however, that this has not ended the race-based use of peremptory challenges (Morehead, 1994; Swift, 1993). Following *Batson,* the Supreme Court decided a series of cases representing a consistent perspective on the purposes for which peremptory challenges can be used. The Court forbade the use of race-based peremptories in civil cases in 1991 *(Edmonson v. Leesville Concrete Company)* and ruled that the use of race-based peremptories by *defense* counsel in criminal cases is unconstitutional in 1992 *(Georgia v. McCollum).* In 1994, the Court extended its reasoning on peremptory challenges in a case arising out of a child custody dispute *(J.E.B. v. Alabama ex rel. T.B.),* forbidding the use of peremptories to strike prospective jurors *solely* on the basis of gender.

Although the U.S. Supreme Court has thus far not extended its ban on the use of peremptory challenges solely on the basis of race or gender to other potential "cognizable groups," it may be only a matter of time. In 2000, the California Supreme Court ruled that sexual orientation is another indicator of a cognizable group, and thus peremptory challenges cannot be used to remove prospective jurors solely on the basis of their sexual orientation (Chiang, 2000). This ruling applies only in California, of course.[2]

What is the future of peremptory challenges? This jury selection technique may have a limited lifespan, because of the increasing realization that there is an inherent conflict between the ideal of representation and the use of peremptory challenges. Another factor in the potential future demise of peremptory challenges is that it seems quite likely the U.S. Supreme Court may recognize additional cognizable groups in the future. For example, religious beliefs or occupational status could arguably represent group distinctions meriting designation as a cognizable group. It might even be argued that students could be considered a cognizable group. Would you agree?

## We Have a Jury!

During the voir dire phase of jury selection, prospective jurors have been "weeded out" for a variety of reasons. The attorneys for both sides have challenged some for cause, and have used peremptory challenges to unseat others. A notable number of citizens may have asked the judge to be excused from serving in this case, citing a variety of reasons: health problems or a change of circumstance that the requester was not aware of when summoned. Depending on the judge's discretion, hopeful citizens may or may not have their request granted. At the conclusion of this process, the folks who survived this long winnowing process comprise the jury, along with a couple of alternate jurors who can step in if a juror has to leave (commonly for health reasons, or possibly due to actual or alleged juror misconduct).

So is the jury drawn from a "representative" cross-section of the community? Consider all of the mechanisms by which folks are "weeded out" of the jury selection process (see Figure 12.2). These are all threats to the representativeness of the selection process, leading some jury scholars to decry the process as the "myth of representativeness" (Abramson, 1994).

## THE TRIAL BEGINS

"All rise!" the bailiff commands, and everyone in the courtroom stands. As the defendant, the attorneys, the court staff, the jurors, and the courtroom spectators watch, the judge enters the courtroom and sits, and thus the trial begins. "Court is in session!" says the bailiff. Thus begins the next phase of the trial after jury selection.

The judge has lists of the items that each side wishes to have admitted as **evidence** in the case. Evidence includes "any type of proof that is legally presented at

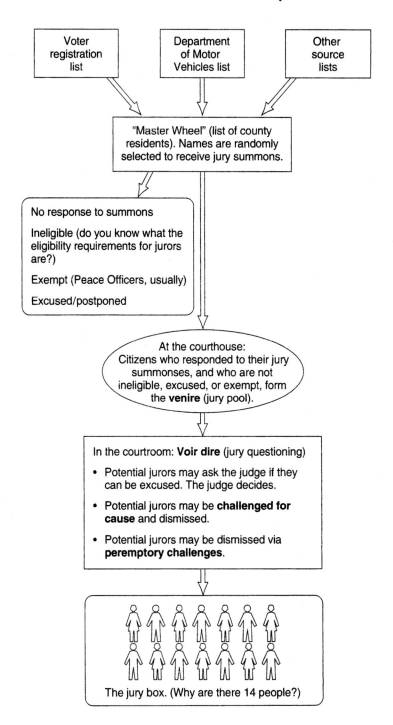

FIGURE 12.2 The jury selection process in criminal trials

trial through witnesses, records, and/or exhibits" (Courtinfo, online). Some of these items will meet the legal requirements for admissibility as evidence without much difficulty. Other items may be far more problematic. Is the evidence relevant and **probative**, that is, tending to prove or disprove the legal issues at hand?

Some of the material offered as evidence may be inadmissible because of questions about the legality of methods used to obtain it. For example, should the confession of a defendant who was interrogated by police without an attorney present be admitted? The defense wants the confession thrown out on grounds that it was not given voluntarily; the prosecution argues that the confession was given freely by the defendant. The judge considers legal precedent on the admissibility of confessions and information on the circumstances under which this confession was obtained in deciding whether it is admissible or not.

What about information that is so relative that it could prejudice the jurors against the defense? Assume, for example, that a judge must decide whether to allow the prosecution to introduce evidence of the defendant's prior arrest for a crime similar to the one in the current trial. The prosecution cannot present this information as proof that the defendant is a "bad person," and therefore likely guilty of the current charge. This is prohibited by the rules of evidence (Federal Rule of Evidence 407). But the prosecutor states that he is asking that evidence of the defendant's prior arrest or conviction be admitted to help jurors assess the credibility of the defendant's testimony (if he or she takes the witness stand) because he wants the jurors to consider whether someone with an arrest or conviction is a believable witness.

The defense has filed a motion opposing the introduction of evidence of the prior arrest or conviction, arguing that it will unnecessarily prejudice the defendant's case. The defense attorney currently plans to call the defendant to the stand to testify on his or her own behalf, but may change that plan depending upon how the trial proceeds. The defense faces a dilemma: If the defendant testifies and the prosecutor is allowed to tell the jury about his or her prior arrest, jurors may perceive the defendant as having little credibility, or worse, as having a propensity for criminal behavior (Grant, 1996). Yet, (if the defendant does not take the stand) and testify about events during the night in question, the jurors may wonder about this and might interpret the defendant's silence as an indication of guilt, despite the judge's admonition to jurors not to make such an inference.

The judge scans the courtroom, looking at the faces of the participants and spectators. After opening remarks to the audience, the judge turns to look at the expectant faces in the jury box. From this point on, almost everything that is said and done in the courtroom by the participants in the case is done with an eye to how it will influence the jurors. How will the jurors perceive the evidence that is presented? How will they be influenced by the witnesses whose testimony they hear? Will the defendant's demeanor and facial expression have a favorable or unfavorable impact? Will the jurors' impressions of the attorneys and the judge color their attitudes about the facts in the case? What impression will the victim—or the family and friends of the victim—make on jurors as they sit in the spectator section of the courtroom or testify on the witness stand?

## OPENING STATEMENTS

The purpose of opening arguments is to provide a framework for jurors to consider the evidence to come. The opening arguments are not part of the evidence, yet they are considered critical factors (along with closing arguments) in the jury's decision. The prosecution begins the presentation of the evidence at trial by outlining the government's **"case in chief"** (the government's theory and evidence in the case) for the court. The prosecution bears the burden of proving its case beyond a reasonable doubt. The defense then presents its opening arguments; it may be more difficult for the defense to construct a persuasive opening argument because much of the defense case will consist of attacking the credibility of the prosecution's version of events rather than providing a distinct alternative explanation for events (Faculty, 2000).

As the excerpt from the prosecution's opening statements in the *McVeigh* case illustrates, opening statements can be emotionally compelling presentations, consistent with the dramatic nature of a criminal trial (see Box 12.7). As the famous

---

### BOX 12.7

### Excerpts from the Prosecution's Opening Statements in the Oklahoma City Bombing Trial

Ladies and gentlemen of the jury, April 19th, 1995, was a beautiful day in Oklahoma City—at least it started out as a beautiful day. The sun was shining. Flowers were blooming. It was springtime in Oklahoma City. Sometime after 6 o'clock that morning, Tevin Garrett's mother woke him up to get him ready for the day. He was only 16 months old . . . and as some of you know that have experience with toddlers, he had a keen eye for mischief. . . .

That morning, Mrs. Garrett got Tevin and her daughter ready for school and they left the house at about 7:15 to go downtown to Oklahoma City. She had to be at work at 8 o'clock. Tevin's sister went to kindergarten, and they dropped the little girl off at kindergarten first; and Helena Garrett and Tevin proceeded to downtown Oklahoma City. . . . Tevin attended the day-care center on the second floor of the federal building.

When she went in, she saw that Chase and Colton Smith were already there, two years old and three years old. Dominique London was there already. He was just shy of his third birthday. So was Zack Chavez. He had already turned three. When she turned to leave to go to her work,

Tevin, as so often, often happens with small children, cried and clung to her; and then, as you see with children so frequently, they try to help each other . . . one of the little Coverdale boys— there were two of them, Elijah and Aaron. The youngest one was two and a half. Elijah came up to Tevin and patted him on the back and comforted him as his mother left.

As Helena Garrett left the Murrah Federal Building to go to work across the street, she could look back up at the building; and there was a wall of plate glass windows on the second floor. You can look through those windows and see into the day-care center; and the children would run up to those windows and press their hands and faces to those windows to say good-bye to their parents. And standing on the sidewalk, it was almost as though you can reach up and touch the children there on the second floor. But none of the parents of any of the children that I just mentioned ever touched those children again while they were still alive.

At nine o'clock that morning, two things happened almost simultaneously. In the Water Resources Building—that's another building to the west of the Murrah Building—an ordinary legal proceeding began in one of the hearing rooms; and at the same time, in front of the Murrah Building, a large Ryder truck pulled up into a vacant parking space in front of the building and parked right beneath those plate glass windows from the day-care center.

What these two separate but almost simultaneous events have in common is that they both involved grievances of some sort. The legal proceeding had to do with water rights. . . . It was a tape-recorded proceeding, and you will hear the tape recording of that proceeding. It was an ordinary, everyday-across-America, typical legal proceeding in which one party has a grievance and brings it into court or into a hearing to resolve it, to resolve it not by violence and terror, but to resolve it in the same way we are resolving matters here, by constitutional due process.

And across the street, the Ryder truck was there also to resolve a grievance; but the truck wasn't there to resolve the grievance by means of due process or by any other democratic means. The truck was there to impose the will of Timothy McVeigh on the rest of America and to do so by premeditated violence and terror, by murdering innocent men, women and children, in hopes of seeing blood flow in the streets of America.

At 9:02 that morning . . . a catastrophic explosion ripped the air in downtown Oklahoma City. It instantaneously demolished the entire front of the Murrah Building, brought down tons and tons of concrete and metal, dismembered people inside, and it destroyed, forever, scores and scores and scores of lives—lives of innocent Americans: clerks, secretaries, law enforcement officers, credit union employees, citizens applying for Social Security, and little kids.

All the children I mentioned earlier, all of them died, and more; dozens and dozens of other men, women, children, cousins, loved ones, grandparents, grandchildren, ordinary Americans going about their business. And the only reason they died, the only reason that they are no longer with us, no longer with their loved ones, is that they were in a building owned by a government that Timothy McVeigh so hated that with premeditated intent and a well-designed plan that he had developed over months and months before the bombing, he chose to take their innocent lives to serve his twisted purpose.

In plain, simple language, it was an act of terror, violence, intended to serve selfish political purpose.

The man who committed this act is sitting in this courtroom behind me, and he's the one that committed those murders.

*Source:* Associated Press, 1997. Reprinted with permission.

jurist Judge Learned Hand once wrote: "It is impossible to expect that a criminal trial shall be conducted without some show of feeling; the stakes are high, and the participants are inevitably charged with emotion. Courts make no such demand; they recognize that a jury inevitably catches this mood . . ." (*United States v. Wexler,* 1935). For this and other reasons, opening arguments can have a powerful influence on jurors, and in some cases jurors may decide their opinion of the case simply on the basis of hearing the "opener," before the evidence is presented (Perrin, 1999). For both sides, the opening statements provide the opportunity to develop the framework of the case, focus on relevant themes, and present a theory of what occurred. These three elements—frame, themes, and theory—define the contours of the case (see Box 12.8 for an example of this). As one article on trial advocacy advises:

> Opening statement is especially demanding because it requires counsel to present facts in a compelling manner. Counsel must emphasize from the beginning that they are "telling a story" to the panel. "Telling a story" is the best way to structure an opening statement, that is, to present the opening statement with a compelling recitation of the facts, using inflection and language to highlight some facts and minimize others, and to create empathy with the panel for counsel's theory of the case. Counsel can also use devices to add emphasis and to suggest disbelief. Such devices include repetition, vivid imagery, and oratorical techniques such as dramatic pauses and pacing. (Faculty, 2000, p. 35)

---

## BOX 12.8
## Key Elements of the Case

*Steven Lubet describes why it is critically important to set up the framework of a case in order to set the context within which the triers of fact will evaluate all subsequent pieces of evidence:*

That act of imagination or vision constitutes a story frame, the context in which the factfinder determines what must have happened in the incident described by the evidence. To use a contemporary example, recall that the prosecution in the O.J. Simpson case labored long and hard to create what might be called a "domestic violence" frame. At the very outset of the trial, prosecutors introduced evidence of Mr. Simpson's ill treatment of his wife, his past threats, and her fear of him. The purpose of this evidence was to support the conclusion that, given his jealousy, anger, and violent nature, he must have been the murderer. In contrast, the defense developed a counter-story, the "police prejudice" frame, intended to advance the theory that the officers must have contrived or mishandled the DNA and other evidence against Mr. Simpson.

Neither side had the benefit of direct evidence, which increased the importance of the competing frames. . . . Instead, the jurors were asked to reach a conclusion based upon an accumulation of circumstances, in light of their own judgment and past experiences. (Lubet, 2001)

*Source:* Reprinted with permission of the University of Colorado Law Review.

There are limits to what attorneys can say as part of opening (and closing) statements, however. According to the rules of trial procedure and professional ethical guidelines, for example, attorneys should not make factual claims that will not be supported by the evidence, make prejudicial remarks about any of the parties in the case, attack opposition witnesses or counsel, or refer to jurors by their names (Sinclair, 1990). While examples of violations of such rules by both defense counsel and prosecutors are obviously troubling, instances of inappropriate claims by prosecutors during opening statements raise special concerns because of the fact that prosecutors may have greater credibility in the eyes of jurors.

## THE EVIDENCE IS PRESENTED

After opening statements by the prosecution and defense, the trial then proceeds with the prosecution's presentation of evidence. There are two types of evidence:

1. **Direct evidence** usually is that which speaks for itself: eyewitness accounts, a confession, or a weapon.

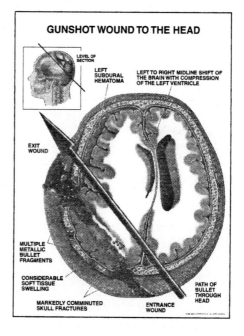

Many prosecutors and defense attorneys present evidence to a jury or judge through the use of courtroom exhibits. This exhibit illustrates the injuries received by a shooting victim in a comprehensive and informative graphic, to help a juror or judge see the negative effects of the crime. By looking at this graphic, created by Medical Legal Art, one can easily imagine the harm to the victim. Technology has greatly changed the nature of courtroom exhibits by providing graphics such as computer-generated animations to demonstrate shootings, car accidents, and other incidents.   SOURCE: Courtesy of Medical Legal Art, Atlanta, Georgia.

2. **Circumstantial evidence** usually is that which suggests a fact by implication or inference: the appearance of the scene of a crime, testimony that suggests a connection or link with a crime, physical evidence that suggests criminal activity. (American Bar Association, 2001)

After the prosecution has presented the government's case, the defense then presents its case, and the prosecution has a brief opportunity for rebuttal. As you will recall from Step 8, there are a variety of key players at trial, and this is the

---

## BOX 12.9

## The Confrontation Clause: Confronting Controversies

The Sixth Amendment provides a person accused of a crime many key due process rights, some of which we discussed in Step 4. A key provision of the Sixth Amendment is the **confrontation clause**, which specifies a defendant's right "to be confronted with the witnesses against him." This provision was intended to ensure that the trial process was conducted in an open and fair manner so that the accused would be able to respond to the charges alleged. For this reason, the defendant has the right to be present at his or her trial during all phases of the proceeding, and to confront the witnesses against him or her. In most trials, no special issues relating to the confrontation clause arise, but in some trials very difficult legal and ethical issues do occur in connection with these rights.

Suppose, for example, that a defendant is repeatedly disruptive at trial. Perhaps the defendant tries to attack others, or constantly interrupts the judge or other parties in the case. Perhaps the court's admonitions to the defendant and defense counsel are insufficient to stop the disruptions, which are so problematic that the trial cannot proceed unless the defendant behaves. Yet, the defendant continually defies the judge. The constitutional question is whether or not the trial can continue if the defendant has been removed from the courtroom in order to prevent disruption of the legitimate legal proceeding taking place. Can you think of some of the arguments for and against allowing the trial to proceed in the absence of a disruptive defendant?

Cases involving child witnesses have also posed constitutional challenges to the confrontation clause. In cases involving child witnesses who testify in court about their experiences as victims of sexual abuse, courts have grappled with the question of whether it is constitutionally permissible for child witnesses to avoid direct visual contact with the defendant through testifying from behind a screen or via closed-circuit television. This difficult issue implicates the rights of the defendant, concerns for victims, and the interests of the government in ensuring that key prosecution witnesses are able to testify. Are such "screening" mechanisms acceptable? If so, why? If not, why not? What are the implications of allowing such screening mechanisms? What might the jury miss if such mechanisms are allowed?

Should witnesses who fear retribution be allowed to testify anonymously? Prosecutors argued (in *California v. Alvarado,* 2001) that the witnesses would face danger from violent gang members if they testified in a murder trial while using their real names. Prosecutors argued that the witnesses should be allowed to testify anonymously despite the fact that the weight of precedent on the issue did not favor their position.

point at which many take the stage, so to speak. All the major parties to the case should be present, although in a small percentage of trials the defendant may not be present (see Box 12.9 on the confrontation clause). During the course of the trial, a wide variety of witnesses may be called to testify, including the victim, the defendant, police officers, government investigators (such as Drug Enforcement Administration agents), expert witnesses, character witnesses, and other witnesses attesting to key facts in the case (for example, that the defendant was at work with them at the time of the crime). A **witness** is a person who can give a firsthand account of something they saw, heard, or experienced. Each time a person takes the witness stand to testify, the bailiff swears the person in by administering the oath to be truthful. The witness then testifies on **direct examination**; that is, in response to questions from the attorney representing the party that called the witness. A pattern quickly becomes apparent: After each side presents a witness, opposing counsel then steps in and questions the witness, asking probing questions designed to challenge the witness' testimony. This is the process of **cross-examination**, a basic and powerful tool in the adversarial process because it can help reveal inconsistencies, contradictions, and gaps in testimony. During cross-examination, attorneys may ask leading questions, but the scope of their questioning should be restricted to the matters the witness testified to on direct examination. Sometimes a witness' testimony appears to surprise the attorney who called the witness, and the value of the old legal saying that one should "never ask a question unless you know the answer" becomes evident (see Box 12.10 for a humorous example).

Cross-examination has been called "the heart and soul of a criminal trial" (Swerling, 1999, p. 753). The power of cross-examination lies in its use as a tool

---

## BOX 12.10

## Never Ask a Question Unless You Know the Answer

An attorney questioning a doctor on the witness stand asked the following questions (Sevilla and Lorenz, 1993, online):

*Question:* Doctor, before you performed the autopsy, did you check for a pulse?

*Answer:* No.

*Q:* Did you check for blood pressure?

*A:* No.

*Q:* Did you check for breathing?

*A:* No.

*Q:* So, then it is possible that the patient was alive when you began the autopsy?

*A:* No.

*Q:* How can you be so sure, Doctor?

*A:* Because his brain was sitting on my desk in a jar.

*Q:* But could the patient have still been alive nevertheless?

*A:* Yes, it is possible that he could have been alive and practicing law somewhere.

for developing evidence that supports the cross-examining attorney's case and illuminates contradictions in the opposition's case:

> The possible purposes of cross-examination include discrediting the witness, impeaching the witness, undermining the damaging testimony of a witness or another adverse witness by cross-reference, eliciting favorable testimony to your position, drawing or creating favorable inferences with other testimony, corroborating favorable testimony for your position, damaging your adversary's case, advancing your case, injecting or enhancing your theme, and tying down an important issue or unanswered question (Swerling, 1999, p. 764).

For example, cross-examination allows the jury to assess the credibility of a witness when it is used to impeach the witness. As one court Web site states in its information for prospective jurors:

> As you listen to the testimony, there are a few questions you might keep in mind: Does this witness have an interest in how the case comes out? Does he or she "forget" when its convenient to do so, and only remember what is favorable? Are the statements of the witness reasonable—or improbable? Could the witness simply be mistaken about what he or she saw, heard, smelled, or felt?
>
> Remember that witnesses often remember different details, especially when an event happened quickly, and involved emotions. Cross-examination of witnesses will also help you in considering evidence. Cross-examination often points up weaknesses, uncertainties, and improbabilities in testimony that might have sounded convincing at first. You should keep an open mind to the end of the trial, when you have heard all the evidence (Santa Clara County, 2001).

Cross-examination is sometimes referred to as a "double-edged sword." On one hand, an effective cross-examination can be the key to winning a case, whereas a less skillful cross-exam carries the potential to weaken a case if it reveals information that wasn't anticipated by the cross-examining attorney. On the other hand, cross-examination is not without potential costs of several types. For example, although the legal rationale for cross-examination of a defense character witness is to help the jury assess the credibility of the character witness' testimony, it can weaken the defendant's case by painting an unflattering portrait of the defendant's criminal history. "So what?" you may well ask. The problem is that it is legally impermissible for jurors to draw an inference that the defendant has a propensity for criminal behavior on the basis of information about prior criminal history of the defendant. Yet research suggests that jurors are quite likely to make such an inference, and that it may significantly influence their verdicts (Grant, 1996). Thus, cross-examination in such instances may carry an unintended "legal cost" to the defendant.

Cross-examination of victims in sex crimes cases provides a different example of the potential costs of the "double-edged sword." Research and observation of cross-examination of victims in rape cases illustrates that searching questions posed by defense counsel can contribute to rape victims' feelings that they have been "revictimized" by their courtroom experiences.

When counsel for one side believes that the other side is making statements that are irrelevant, prejudicial, or misleading, the attorney will interject with an **objection**. If the judge sustains the objection, the offending attorney will be instructed in accordance with the judge's ruling, such as requiring the attorney to rephrase a question or discontinue an offensive behavior, such as harassing a witness. If the judge decides the objection lacks merit, the objection will be overruled, sometimes after the action in question has been explained by the errant attorney. At various times, the attorneys and the judge will call a **sidebar** if there is a legal question that needs to be briefly discussed at the judge's bench, out of earshot of the jury. If the issue requires more extensive discussion, the judge may call a recess and hear from both attorneys in chambers.

During the presentation of evidence, counsel for both sides must focus on how the proceedings appear to jurors (see Box 12.11). An interesting example of jurors' perspectives on the legal process illustrates this point: Louisiana Judge W. Ross Foote interviewed more than 400 jurors to ask them their opinions on the judicial process. Following are the jurors' "top ten pieces of advice" to lawyers (Foote, 1995, quoted in Anderson, 1999, p. 621):

---

## BOX 12.11
## Some Tips, Tricks, and Techniques of Trial Presentation

During a trial, attorneys must consider the most persuasive way to present the evidence, the witnesses, and the arguments they present. The literature on trial tactics is replete with examples of appeals to jurors' emotions. The attorney might appeal to jurors' sense of right and wrong, or ask them to think about how their verdict will affect their community. Prosecutors and defense attorneys alike may remind jurors of the victim's character; how the death of such a person of sterling qualities represents a loss to society; or how the victim's abusive, violent characteristics contributed to his or her own demise. Attorneys may ask jurors to put themselves in the shoes of the victim or the defendant, and to imagine how they would respond in similar circumstances.

If the families and friends of the victim and the defendant can appear in court to show support, so much the better. The silent message that this is a person whom others judge worth supporting, or a person who is much loved and much missed, is worth more than a thousand words.

During cross-examination, one of the attorneys may "accidentally" mention information that is not admissible, such as the fact that the defendant or the witness has a prior criminal record. Despite the objection from opposing counsel and an admonition from the judge to jurors to ignore the forbidden fact, the cat is already out of the bag.

Another technique used to reduce the impact of damaging information about the credibility of your witness is to beat the opposition to the scoop by acknowledging the issue at the outset of the witness' testimony. This tactic of "stealing thunder" deprives opposing counsel of the opportunity to claim that your side tried to conceal the witness' credibility flaws from the jury.

1. Be brief, succinct and accurate. Get to the point.
2. Don't repeat evidence, questions and other points so often.
3. Don't confuse the jury. Establish as many facts as possible, leaving no questions or doubts. Give more background on some points. Cover all bases of a case sufficiently.
4. Be more organized and prepared and familiar with the information required. Make sure your client also is prepared with factual information at hand.
5. Keep in mind a lay person's lack of knowledge of legal and . . . medical terminology. Speak in simple terms and have witnesses do so, also.
6. Do not underestimate the intelligence and ability of the jury.
7. Be factual, fair and courteous. Don't make the other attorney's questions look stupid and ridiculous. Don't show hostile attitudes, at least not to the jury.
8. Don't object so often.
9. Try to settle out of court.
10. Use fewer theatrics. Don't be a big fake. Be nice but don't take it to extremes. (Louisiana Bar Association; reprinted with permission)

## CLOSING STATEMENTS

After the presentation of evidence by both sides is finished, including direct examination, cross-examination (and, sometimes, more questions during redirect and re-cross-examination), the trial concludes with the prosecution and defense closing statements. These carefully crafted presentations to the jury are designed to persuade the triers of fact to draw particular inferences from the facts that support a specific conclusion favoring the speaker's side. As with presentation of the evidence, the prosecution usually presents its closing argument first, followed by the defense. After the defense's closing argument, the prosecution is allowed a brief period of rebuttal and the defense can make a surrebuttal.

There is much debate and some study on the question of the relative advantage to the government of being allowed the first chance to frame the issues during closing arguments, in contrast to the defense's position of following the prosecution and yet being subject to the prosecution's opportunity for rebuttal (Mitchell, 2000). During the closing, counsel will summarize the case, in the process reminding the jury of the strength of their arguments and the weaknesses in the opponent's case. Closing arguments cannot be used to present new evidence, but they provide an opportunity for counsel to present the jury with a new "twist" on the conclusions they are asked to draw from the evidence presented. In this context, the effective trial counsel, whether defense or prosecution, may want to consider the Story Model's paradigm (Pennington and Hastie, 1993) of juror decision-making while constructing a persuasive narrative during closing statements (Meyer, 1999). The effectiveness of closing arguments thus depends upon the rhetorical skills of the attorneys in presenting their arguments persuasively. Therefore, closing arguments are an opportunity for counsel to demonstrate their efforts at zealous advocacy in the adversarial arena. Yet for this very reason, critics charge that closing arguments often illustrate "adversarial excesses" when attorneys overstep the boundaries of appropriate advocacy (Nidiry, 1996). For just as we saw in the section on opening statements, attorneys are prohibited from doing certain things—such as referring to facts not admitted as evidence, introducing new evidence, or invoking racial, ethnic, or gender stereotypes about the defendant, the victim, or witnesses during "closers"—but in practice, attorneys may flout such rules with relative impunity (Nidiry, 1996). For example, defense attorneys in most jurisdictions are not permitted to ask jurors to nullify the law, but in other jurisdictions this is permissible, and in practice this may occur in any jurisdiction.

Given the prosecutor's role as a "minister of justice" and the possibility that prosecutors' assertions may have greater credibility than the claims of defense counsel in the eyes of some jurors, the problem of prosecutorial misconduct during closing statements raises special concern. Prosecutors who use inflammatory language—for example, calling defense witnesses "liars," making prejudicial references to the defendant's ethnic background or sexual orientation, or arguing that the jury must help the government "win the war on drugs" by convicting the defendant—may be shifting the emphasis of the argument from evidence to emotion. Such a shift would signal a potential "legal impropriety" on the part of counsel (Nidiry, 1996). The issue of what kinds of statements may be allowed as part of closing arguments has been particularly controversial in death penalty cases in which prosecutors have made religious arguments in favor of the death penalty. For example, one prosecutor's closing arguments to the jury during the penalty phase of a capital trial included the following statements:

> You are not playing God. You are doing what God says. This might be the only opportunity to wake [the defendant] up. God will destroy the body to save the soul. Make him get himself right. . . . Let him have the opportunity to get his soul right. (*People v. Sandoval*, 1992, p. 193)

Although courts have consistently held that such arguments are improper for a variety of reasons, the courts have rarely offered any remedy to defendants (Duffy, 1997). Actual and proposed remedies for attorney misconduct during closing have proven insufficient to address the problem, and in some cases appear merely to perpetuate the problem. For example, in some cases the improper assertions of defense counsel during closing arguments have been "remedied" by the court allowing the prosecution to make similar arguments in rebuttal (Nidiry, 1996).

However, while defense counsel misconduct during closing is much less often subject to appellate review (given that the government cannot appeal acquittals),[3] prosecutorial misconduct during closing argument can be the basis for an appellate court overturning a conviction. For example, in *People v. Hill* (1998), the defendant's convictions for murder and attempted murder in a death penalty case were overturned after prosecutorial misconduct was held by the appellate court to represent a denial of the defendant's right to a fair trial. In this unusual case, the prosecutor had previously been rebuked (although not formally disciplined) by the same appellate court for using a variety of inappropriate tactics during closing arguments in other cases, including one in which the defendant's conviction for child molestation was overturned as a result of an appellate finding that the prosecutor's misconduct included misstating the law and making "unjustified inferences" (Spiegelman, 1999). In the *Hill* case, the court found that the prosecutor had misstated the evidence, referred to inadmissible evidence during closing, mischaracterized the testimony of an eyewitness, misstated the law, intimidated defense witnesses, and displayed contempt for opposing counsel both verbally and nonverbally (Spiegelman, 1999) (see Box 12.12).

---

## BOX 12.12

## Prosecutorial Misconduct in *People v. Hill*

The Hill prosecutor's misconduct is illustrated by a couple of examples discussed in Spiegelman (1999). In one instance, the prosecutor misstated the evidence when she directed the victim of attempted murder to show the jury a ten-inch scar on his chest, which the prosecutor later referred to in her closing argument to the court:

> You saw the scar. Take a look at it, and you will remember how far across the chest it went. If you stick it in him two times and rip his chest open, you are planning to kill him. (*People v. Hill*, 1998, p. 686)

The defense counsel objected, providing hospital records showing that the scar that the jury had seen was not the result of the attack, but instead was a scar resulting from surgery the defendant had undergone earlier. Nonetheless, the prosecutor refused to acknowledge this (Spiegelman, 1999).

The prosecutor also smeared the defendant's character by claiming that:

> Everything [the defendant] ever did one way or another, he got away with. He has killed. He has stabbed. He has robbed. He has gone to prison for it. He has not been rehabilitated under any guise or thought. (*People v. Hill*, 1998, p. 693).

However, this was not in fact the case, because the defendant did not have any prior convictions for homicide, attacks involving stabbing, or robbery. The prosecutor was reported to the state Bar Association for disciplinary proceedings. (Spiegelman, 1999, reprinted with permission)

## JURY INSTRUCTIONS

"Ladies and Gentlemen of the jury. . . ." It's time for the judge to issue instructions to jurors about their duties before the jury retires to the deliberation room. The nature and length of jury instructions varies with the type of case; in some cases, they may take several hours (or even longer). The judge's **charge** to the jury in a criminal case will outline the elements of the crime that must be proven, and remind jurors that the prosecution carries the burden of proving the defendant's guilt beyond a reasonable doubt. The judge will tell the jurors what their verdict choices are: For example, in a particular case, jurors may have a choice between verdicts of first-degree murder, second-degree murder, manslaughter, or acquittal. The instructions will remind jurors that they must base their verdict on evidence presented in court, and apply the law as instructed by the judge. In addition to the standard jury instructions given, jurors may also be given additional instructions on specific issues that the defense or the prosecution has requested. For example, jurors may be reminded that information they learned about the defendant's prior convictions should only be used to assess his or her credibility, not to infer a general propensity for criminal behavior.

It seems obvious that it is important for jurors to be able to understand the instructions the judge reads to them concerning the case. After all, how can the jurors apply the law to the facts of the case if they don't understand what they are supposed to be doing? Yet, research demonstrates that jurors may not comprehend jury instructions accurately, and often fail to follow them (Severence and Loftus, 1982; Tanford, 1990; Diamond, 1994). Some jurors may believe that the defendant must prove innocence, despite direct instructions to the contrary. In addition, jurors sometimes have trouble with instructions about the burden of proof. The fact that jurors are instructed on the law only after hearing the case, rather than being given such instructions at the outset, may lessen the impact of the instructions. Some jury researchers have suggested that instructions should be given at both the beginning and end of a case in order to maximize their usefulness to jurors.

The consequences of a failure of understanding are not trivial matters. Researchers interviewing jurors who had served in death penalty cases discovered that some of the former jurors were confused about the difference between "aggravating" and "mitigating" factors (Eisenberg and Wells, 1993; Garvey, 1998). Other researchers have found similar results (Luginbuhl, 1992; Blankenship et al., 1997). The distinction is a critical one, for jurors are instructed in capital cases to decide whether the defendant receives life or death on the basis of such factors. **Aggravators** include factors that weigh in favor of a death sentence, such as whether the victim was tortured before death or the victim was a child. **Mitigators** include factors that weigh in favor of giving a life sentence, such as the defendant's past history of abuse or mental incapacity.

Despite the significance of jurors' lack of comprehension, appellate courts have not been receptive to appeals based on this argument. Although an appeal based on the fact that the jury was not given the appropriate legal instructions may well result in a conviction being overturned and a new trial ordered, it is a different matter if the jury simply did not understand an instruction that was properly given. In one case, the appellate court noted that: "It has never been held error in California to instruct in terms of [a jury instruction] due to lack of intelligibility" (*John B. Gunn Law Corp. v. Maynard*, 1987). See what you think of the jury instructions in Box 12.13. How understandable are they? Do you think these instructions would raise any questions in the minds of jurors?

---

## BOX 12.13

## Deciphering Jury Instructions: Would It Help to Be Psychic?

*In the state of New York, if you are a juror in the trial of a defendant accused of misdemeanor fortune-telling, these are some of the instructions the judge will read to you:*

The count is Fortune Telling.

Under our law, a person is guilty of Fortune Telling when, for a fee or compensation which he or she directly or indirectly solicits or receives, that person claims or pretends to tell fortunes [or holds himself or herself out as being able, by claimed or pretended use of occult powers, to answer questions (or give advice on personal matters) (or exorcise, influence or affect evil spirits or curses)].

[This charge does not apply to a person who engages in such conduct as part of a show or exhibition solely for the purpose of entertainment or amusement.] In order for you to find the defendant guilty of this crime, the People are required to prove, from all the evidence in the case, beyond a reasonable doubt, both [each] of the following two [three] elements:

1. That on or about (date), in the county of (county), the defendant, (defendant's name), claimed or pretended to tell fortunes [or held himself/herself out as being able, by claimed or pretended use of occult powers, to answer questions (or give advice on personal matters) (or exorcise, influence or affect evil spirits or curses)]; and
2. That the defendant directly or indirectly solicited or received a fee or compensation for such conduct; and
3. [That the defendant did not engage in such conduct as part of a show or exhibition solely for the purpose of entertainment or amusement].

Therefore, if you find that the People have proven beyond a reasonable doubt both [each] of those elements, you must find the defendant guilty of Fortune Telling as charged in the count.

On the other hand, if you find that the People have not proven beyond a reasonable doubt either one or both [any one or more] of those elements, you must find the defendant not guilty of Fortune Telling as charged in the count.

# JURY DECISION-MAKING: LEGAL AND EXTRA-LEGAL INFLUENCES

How do jurors decide on a verdict? Although the verdict should reflect only the evidence in the case, research has revealed that many factors other than the evidence can significantly influence jurors' thoughts and emotions, and thus potentially their verdicts. Jurors' attitudes and beliefs about human nature, the law, and legal processes are potentially significant (but not necessarily inevitable) influences on their verdicts (Levine, 1992). Jurors' perceptions of the character, motives, and behavior of key players in the legal drama—the defendant, the victim, the judge, the attorneys—represent one category of extra-legal factors that can significantly influence the verdict. Jurors' beliefs about the defendant's future dangerousness, the proportionality of the defendant's potential sentence to the crime, and other legally irrelevant factors can also influence the verdict (Levine, 1992). In one survey of potential jurors, "A significant minority of respondents said that they could not be impartial if a party were gay or lesbian (31 percent); Hispanic (25 percent); black (24 percent); Asian (24 percent); or Caucasian (23 percent)" (Van Voris, 2000, p. 1). Although this finding does not guarantee that such biases would significantly influence such jurors' verdicts, it seems quite plausible that it would. A recent examination of white jurors' bias against black defendants, for example, found evidence of racial bias, and the authors conclude that the evidence suggested that racial bias was particularly apparent in cases where race was *not* an explicit issue in the trial (Sommers and Ellsworth, 2001).

At a broader level, the political climate and the tide of public opinion on crime are also significant influences in some cases (Levine, 1992). Because of the fact that by law, jury verdicts should reflect only the evidence in the case, factors such as these are referred to as "extra-legal" or sometimes "extra-evidential" influences on the jury in order to emphasize that they are legally irrelevant. Let's look more closely at an example of this.

What if public opinion about a particular case is so volatile that it threatens the defendant's right to a fair trial? Can justice truly be served when courtroom proceedings occur in an atmosphere of palpable tension? Can jurors freely deliberate without consideration of how their decision will be received? If jurors are to serve as "the conscience of the community," what happens when the community wants blood, not justice?

In 1913, during the trial of Leo Frank, a northerner of Jewish heritage accused of murdering a young girl, newspaper accounts described the uproar that existed in the southern community of Atlanta, Georgia, over the case. At the conclusion of Frank's trial in an emotionally charged courtroom, the jurors found Frank guilty and sentenced him to death. The defense appealed the sentence, but it was affirmed by a majority of judges of the Georgia Supreme Court. However, two judges dissented: Judge Oliver Wendell Holmes (who later became a member of the U.S. Supreme Court) and judge Charles Evans Hughes. Judge Holmes' description of Leo Frank's trial make the reasons for the dissent clear:

> The trial began on July 28, 1913, at Atlanta, and was carried on in a court packed with spectators and surrounded by a crowd outside, all strongly hostile to [Frank]. On Saturday, August 23, this hostility was sufficient to lead the judge to confer in the presence of the jury with the Chief of Police in Atlanta and the Colonel of the Fifth Georgia Regiment stationed in that city, both of whom were known to the jury. . . . The judge before beginning his charge had a private conversation with [Frank's] counsel in which he expressed the opinion that there would be 'probable danger of violence' if there should be an acquittal or disagreement [i.e., a hung jury], and that it would be safer for not only [Frank] but his counsel to be absent from Court when the verdict was brought in.
>
> At the judge's request they agreed that [Frank] and they should be absent, and they kept their word. When the verdict was rendered, and before more than one of the jurymen had been polled there was such a roar of applause that the polling could not go on till order was restored. The noise outside was such that it was difficult for the judge to hear the answers of the jurors although he was only ten feet from them. . . .
>
> Mob law does not become due process of law by securing the assent of a terrorized jury. We are not speaking of mere disorder, or mere irregularities in procedure, but of a case where the processes of justice are actually subverted. . . . Any judge who has sat with juries knows that . . . they are extremely likely to be impregnated by the environing atmosphere. (Zobel, 1995. Reprinted with permission of American Heritage, Inc.)

Despite the Georgia appellate court's affirmation of Leo Frank's death sentence, the governor exercised his legal option to commute the sentence to life imprisonment. But a few weeks later, an angry mob stormed the local jail where Leo Frank was being held, kidnapping and then lynching him (Zobel, 1995).

---

## BOX 12.14
## Legal Assumptions about Jury Decision-Making

What are the law's assumptions about jury decision-making, and are these assumptions realistic in light of research on how jurors and juries actually function? Imagine that you are a juror in a felony trial involving a defendant charged with a serious crime. In the courtroom, you watch and listen as lawyers present the opening arguments, refer to pieces of important evidence, and cross-examine witnesses. You may listen to testimony from the victim, expert witnesses for one or both sides, and possibly the defendant as well. Throughout all this, you are forbidden to take any notes. Fortunately, the court reporter records the proceedings while making a transcript of the trial. While the trial is proceeding, you are not allowed to talk to anyone—including your fellow jurors—about any aspect of the case. You are not supposed to come to a conclusion about the defendant's guilt or innocence until you gather with the other jurors to deliberate, yet your mind keeps coming back to the guilt question every night as you go to sleep. You know that you should not let sympathy or prejudice influence your assessment of the evidence; but you sometimes find it hard to ignore your feelings as you think about the case.

What do you think is the purpose of these restrictions on your behavior as a juror? Wrightsman, Nietzel, and Fortune (1994) assert that the law expects jurors to act in a certain way, and that these expectations are embodied in such regulations and restrictions on juror conduct. Wrightsman and his colleagues identify five assumptions and assess their viability in light of research on human behavior. They discuss how such research casts serious doubt on the accuracy of these assumptions.

1. *Jurors are accurate and complete information processors.* This assumption is reflected in the fact that typically jurors are not allowed to take any notes on the trial. Instead, they are expected to rely on their collective memories. Imagine if you were required to remember all the things you've learned in your courses without the benefit of taking any notes or audiotapes. The judge has discretion to allow jurors to take notes, and an increasing number of courts are allowing this.

    Research on human cognitive biases, memory, and decision-making processes suggests this assumption is questionable at best. Research on judgmental heuristics (decision-making) demonstrates that human decision-making is typically distorted by cognitive biases (Nisbett and Ross, 1980). Jurors' accuracy as information processors is subject to question according to research showing that jurors give too much weight to certain types of evidence (such as eyewitnesses) but give too little weight to statistical and probabilistic evidence. In addition, jurors often have difficulty understanding and/or adhering to jury instructions.

2. *Jurors can suspend judgment until they hear all the evidence.* This assumption is clearly reflected in the court's charge to jurors to avoid coming to a conclusion on the defendant's culpability until jury deliberations.

    However, research on human decision-making suggests that people typically evaluate information as it is received, and that it may be difficult for people to separate the acquisition and evaluation of information because the two processes are so intertwined. Recall that jurors sometimes make initial judgments simply based on the opening statements, despite the fact that "openers" are not part of the evidence.

3. *Jurors are "blank slates" with no or few preconceptions.* The law's emphasis on impartial, unbiased jurors appears to reflect the assumption that it is possible, given appropriate jury selection procedures, to impanel a jury whose members have few preconceptions about the participants and events in the trial.

    Yet this assumption is belied by the very techniques used during voir dire to select jurors, where attorneys actively seek jurors whose biases will favor their side. An attorney might also try to use voir dire to try to begin to sway members of the panel toward his or her side, by asking questions in such a way that prospective jurors get a slanted portrayal of the case.

    The assumption that jurors bring few preconceptions with them to the jury box is further eroded if you consider that the process of voir dire may not identify and weed out biased jurors for a number of reasons. Jury questioning does not always uncover the biases of jurors who should have been challenged for cause, whether this is due to the fact that the questioning simply did not uncover the issue or the juror actively concealed—or was even unaware of—his or her biased preconceptions or attitudes.

---

## BOX 12.14 *(continued)*

4. *Jurors base their verdict only on the evidence.* The legal system's admonition to jurors to avoid discussing the evidence with anyone during the trial, including other jurors, and the concern with the possible biasing effects of jurors' exposure to media sources of information on the trial are two indicators of this assumption about jurors.

   However, research on jury decision-making provides much evidence to the contrary; in fact, it appears that jury verdicts can and do reflect the influences of many things other than simply the evidence presented in the case. Such influences can come from an almost limitless array of sources, including jurors' attitudes and experiences, the characteristics and behavior of the participants in the case, the political climate surrounding the trial, and media coverage of case-related issues.

5. *Jurors are unaffected by group pressures.* Ideally, jury deliberations involve jurors discussing the evidence and sharing their views as they attempt to reach consensus. But where should we distinguish between attempts to persuade that are not coercive and attempts that are perceived by the target, and perhaps others, as coercive or even intimidating? The law's assumption that jurors will engage in a cooperative process as they deliberate seems to reflect the implicit assumption that this process will not reflect pressures toward conformity. Yet, group dynamics are such that the minority faction on a jury, especially if this consists of a sole juror, may be subject to intense pressures to conform to the majority faction's view of the case. (Adapted from Wrightsman, Nietzel, and Fortune, 1994, with the permission of Brooks/Cole)

---

# HOW DO JURORS DECIDE?

The "Story Model" of jury decision-making (Pennington and Hastie, 1993) presents a detailed theory of how juror decision-making occurs. In this model, jurors are portrayed as active manipulators of evidence and information who construct an account of events related to the crime, not merely passive recipients of information presented at trial. According to the story model, each juror constructs a story or stories in three steps, and this ultimately determines which verdict is chosen.

First, jurors use trial evidence and real-world knowledge to construct one or more stories that link the events described during the trial in some causal way. Jurors actively imagine themselves in the position of participants in the crime ("How would I have behaved in this situation?") as they seek to understand what happened. While constructing a story (or possibly more than one story) that links events in some causal way, the jurors rely on their own experiences to make inferences, such as the inference that the sight of a knife would cause fear (Pennington and Hastie, 1993). For example, mock jurors in the case of a defendant accused of a stabbing constructed different types of stories to account for the fact that a defendant was in possession of a knife at the time of the crime. The jurors' inferences varied depending upon their class backgrounds. Middle-class jurors were more likely to feel that the defendant's possession of a knife at the time of the crime indicated that he planned the attack, whereas working-class jurors were more likely to infer that the defendant had probably simply been carrying a knife routinely for purposes of self-defense. In the second step of the story model, the juror learns a set of "verdict representations," such as the legal distinction between first- and second-degree murder. In the final step, the juror compares the narrative story or stories he or she has constructed with the verdict choices to check for a match. The verdict that best matches the story is chosen, and if no good match is found, the juror should return a "not guilty" verdict. What determines which story is finally chosen? Pennington and Hastie's model describes four "certainty principles" governing the choice:

1. Coverage (How well does the story explain the evidence?)
2. Coherence (Are the parts of the story internally consistent? Is the story plausible; does it fit with the juror's knowledge of what happens in the real world? Is the story complete; does it cover all the main issues, without leaving too many gaps or requiring too many inferences?)
3. Uniqueness (Is this story the best explanation of events? Or are there other accounts that explain the evidence just as well?)
4. Goodness of fit (how well do the elements of the story match elements of the verdict choices? For example, if one of the verdict choices is self-defense, do the elements of the story fit with this?)

The Story Model suggests some implications for attorneys' trial strategies. Presenting evidence in the form most amenable to story construction appears more likely to lead to a verdict consistent with the potential story, compared to other methods of presentation, such as presenting evidence out of temporal sequence, organized around the order in which witnesses appear, or thematically organized around legal issues. Jurors have more confidence in a given story when they have heard both defense and prosecution evidence presented in story order versus hearing only one side, or neither side, present in story order. One attorney put it thus:

> The best trial lawyers are storytellers. They take the raw and disjointed observations of witnesses and transform them into coherent and persuasive narratives. They develop compelling theories and artful themes, all the better to advance a client's cause. . . . But trial lawyers are not only storytellers. In addition, they are legal technicians, taking the raw observations of witnesses and organizing them into coherent, legally meaningful narratives. You can tell a terrific story and nonetheless lose your case—especially if you have failed to shape it in a way that will be convincing to the trier of fact. (Lubet, 2001, p. 2)

## JURY DELIBERATIONS

In California, the Judicial Council Web site has this advice for potential jurors:

> Quite often in the jury room the jurors may argue and have a difference of opinion. When this occurs, each juror should try to express his or her opinion and the reasoning supporting it. It would be wrong for a juror to refuse to listen to the arguments and opinions of the others or to deny another juror the right to express an opinion. Remember that jurors are not advocates, but impartial judges of the facts. By carefully considering each juror's opinion and the reasons behind it, it is usually possible for the jurors to reach a verdict. A juror should not hesitate to change his or her mind when there is a good reason. But each juror should maintain his or her position unless conscientiously persuaded to change that opinion by the other jurors. Following a full and free discussion with fellow jurors, each juror should vote only according to his or her own honest convictions. (Judicial Council of California, 2000)

When jurors begin the process of deliberation, their first task is to choose a foreperson, unless the judge has already done so. The jurors can make this choice however they wish: They can take a vote, ask for a volunteer, or draw lots. The foreperson's task is to help organize the deliberation process, to ensure that the group considers all the issues, and that the opinions of all are heard. Research finds that men are more likely than women to become jury forepersons, but it is not clear whether this is because they are chosen or volunteer more often.

The next task jurors have is deciding how to begin deliberating. In some cases, jurors will take an initial ballot at the beginning or early on in deliberations, revealing where the group stands. Research on both jury simulations and the results of actual trials finds that the verdict typically, but not always, reflects the initial ballot results (Kalven and Zeisel, 1966).

As the jurors consider the evidence, they may go back and re-enact details of the crime that were presented in trial or reread important items of written evidence. Through the bailiff, the jurors may ask the judge for clarification on some of the evidence, testimony, or jury instructions. The judge's response may be limited to simply restating the confusing testimony or instructions again, without adding further clarification. By adhering strictly to procedure, the judge may avoid providing information that could serve as possible grounds for appeal.

Jurors may also attempt to get information that they believe is relevant to their decision, but which is not a legally permitted factor for consideration. A classic example of this is the length of the sentence. Jurors are not supposed to consider the potential sentence the defendant may face if convicted, yet many jurors are very interested in this. This is perhaps not surprising, reflecting a natural concern with the proportionality of the punishment in relation to the offense.

Their desire to know may be particularly acute in capital cases, where many jurors faced with the task of choosing life or death for a convicted defendant want to know "Is life *really* life, or is there the possibility the defendant could get out on parole?" In some cases, jurors in capital cases would have preferred to give a life sentence, but chose the death sentence because they could not be sure that a life sentence would keep the defendant off the streets for good (Bowers and Steiner, 1998). Requests to the judge for this information were answered with the instruction that they could not be told and should not consider the issue of how long a life sentence in their particular jurisdiction would actually be.

## GROUP DYNAMICS

Juries provide good examples of group dynamics in action. Juries are an example of groups that are convened for a specific purpose rather than formed naturally. Thus, juries illustrate groups of people who are brought together for a common purpose—the task of "doing justice." Jurors know little about each other before they begin deliberating, except for whatever information they gleaned about their fellow panelists during voir dire and perhaps from idle small talk during breaks in the trial. They cannot be entirely certain how long they will have to spend working together on their common task, but they know that once their task is done, they may never see each other again. Therefore, the jurors may not behave in the same way that they would if they anticipated future interactions with each other.

As the jurors begin deliberating, they may learn that some of them are first-time jurors, while others may have served before. Regardless, most group members will be acutely aware of the stakes involved for the parties in the case, especially in a felony case.

So how do these factors influence the group dynamics of jury decision-making during deliberations? Recall that according to Wrightsman and colleagues (1994), the law assumes that jury decisions will be "unaffected by group pressures or personal wishes." However, much research on jury decision-making demonstrates that too often this is not so; in fact, juries provide classic illustrations of the power of group pressures toward conformity.

Idealized portrayals of jurors, such as the classic Henry Fonda movie *Twelve Angry Men,* show jurors arguing passionately to persuade each other on their views on the basis of the evidence. The arguments use appeals to logic and reason, with the goal of genuinely convincing the audience of the inherent superiority of the speaker's view of the case.

In reality, research shows that the line between *persuasion* and *coercive pressure* can be very thin. Jurors in the minority faction face intense pressures to conform, varying with the individual makeup of the people on that jury. Jurors do not want to deadlock because they cannot reach consensus; they want to finish the task. A lone juror faces especially strong pressures, but having even one other ally is quite effective in helping a nonconformist resist pressures from jurors in the majority faction. Research cannot tell us how often undue pressure to conform is placed on jurors in actual cases. But anecdotal information from interviews with actual jurors demonstrates that not infrequently, jurors may be subjected to expressions of disgust, angry comments, taunts, and pleas to change their verdict decision. In one case, several women jurors reported that the jury foreman and other male jurors called them "stupid females" and told them that because they were women, they "didn't have minds" (Duffy, 1996). In the most extreme examples, a few jurors have reported that they voted to convict a criminal defendant when they really wished to acquit (*State v. Kaiser* [1996]; *M.S. v. Stansfield* [1996]).

While majority jurors are prevailing upon those in the minority to join them, they may provide psychological rationales to holdouts that help them to retain dignity while joining the majority. Levine (1992) describes this phenomenon occurring among the jurors in the trial of serial murderer Juan Corona:

> Respect is sometimes a two-way street, with the dominant group helping the holdout to relent by acknowledging the right to dissent and the legitimacy of alternative viewpoints. This "stroking" process can ease the way to capitulation by enabling the dissenter to maintain self-esteem at the same time he or she is crumbling. This was the tactic of what had become an 11-person majority for conviction in the Juan Corona mass murder case. Rather than steamroll the remaining resister into compliance with them, the jury took a day off from voting after six full days of deliberation and told her to go with her convictions. On the 8th day she switched, remarking: "I think I've changed my mind. Yesterday you gave me a day's rest and I relaxed and I saw things differently . . . basically, I now think you people are right and I do think Corona guilty." (Levine, 1992, p. 155. Reprinted by permission of James Levine)

However, Wrightsman, Nietzel, and Fortune (1994) question the true rationale for this juror's change of heart, noting that earlier during the Corona jury's deliberations, this same juror had exclaimed "Please, I'll change my vote. Just don't hate me. I'll change my vote so you can go home to your wife" (Wrightsman, Nietzel, & Fortune, 1994, p. 334). Regardless of the reasons for this juror's decision to join her fellow jurors in convicting Corona, the phenomenon of holdout jurors illustrates classic conformity pressures. As with any divided group, once someone from the minority makes the decision to join the majority viewpoint, this "legitimates the idea of capitulation so that others with similar views almost always follow suit" (Levine, 1992, p. 154). Despite the deliberative ideal embodied in the law, such conformity pressures do not necessarily invalidate the jury's verdict under the rules of evidence. In one case where a juror who voted to convict reported that she did so after being pressured during deliberations, the defendant's conviction was upheld by an appellate court, which noted that such pressure ". . . is an inherent and intrinsic part of the deliberative process" (Nadvorney and Cantu, 1987, p. 32).

## BARGAINING BETWEEN JURY FACTIONS

Because juries often have several verdict choices, there is often room for compromise between different factions on the jury. For example, jurors may have to choose between convicting the defendant of second-degree murder, manslaughter, or acquitting. Given such verdict choices, there is room for negotiation. Similar opportunities for negotiation and compromise exist in cases involving multiple counts of the same crime, or multiple charges varying in seriousness. The group dynamics of jury-room bargaining play an important role in preventing hung juries, as the case of Joel Steinberg illustrates (see Box 12.15).

"Logrolling" is a particular form of jury group compromise: when there are multiple defendants accused in the same incident, juries may convict one defendant but not the others, even though the evidence is the same in the joint trial of all defendants. For example, in one case several police officers were tried on charges of brutality stemming from an interrogation of a suspected killer of a fellow officer.

---

## BOX 12.15
## Bargaining in the Jury Room

*James Levine describes the negotiations that occurred during the infamous trial of a lawyer on charges of killing his daughter.*

Steinberg, a disbarred lawyer and routine cocaine user, was accused not only of striking a severe blow to the back of the girl's head but of failing to get help for 12 hours while she was still alive. Complicating the trial was the situation of Hedda Nussbaum, Steinberg's live-in lover, who allegedly had been viciously brutalized by Steinberg for years. She, too, waited to call medical authorities until it was too late. At first Nussbaum was also charged with murder, but later the charges were dropped and she became a witness against Steinberg.

From the beginning of deliberations, the jury was deeply divided . . . the allocation of moral responsibility between the two principals was a source of dispute. The jury initially split evenly into 3 factions: those who thought Steinberg guilty of murder (the "hard liners"), those who favored first-degree manslaughter (the "middle of the roaders"), and those who opted for second-degree manslaughter because they thought Nussbaum had struck the fatal blow (the "softies") . . . in the foreman's words, 'we were almost hopelessly divided.' After eight days . . . the jury arrived at a verdict. They opted for first degree manslaughter, the in-between outcome.

Although at one point the pro-murder contingent reached ten . . . the hardliners eventually realized that they would never get all 12 jurors to agree on a murder conviction. They then willfully deviated from the judge's instructions that they first dispense with the murder charge before going to the lesser ones, and they concentrated on getting the "softies" to accept the first-degree manslaughter charge—no mean feat considering that some continued to feel that Hedda Nussbaum might have been the more culpable. Having accomplished that, the hardliners themselves relented on the murder charge, even though in their hearts they believed it was warranted. The alternative was a hung jury, and it was thought preferable to establish some culpability and assure punishment rather than give Steinberg another opportunity to get exonerated. (Levine, 1992, p. 158)

*Postscript: One of the "hardliner" jurors in the case would later say that she regretted not being able to bring in a murder conviction.*

*Source:* Reprinted by permission of James Levine.

The jury acquitted four of the officers, but returned verdicts of guilty against three other officers, although all the officers were tried together, and the evidence was the same for each defendant (Levine, 1992). How can this seemingly inconsistent result have occurred? "The verdict seems baffling unless we bring in a plausible political explanation: defendants were traded off so that neither the pro-police nor the pro–civil rights forces would come away empty-handed. Defendants are treated differently to secure a resolution that gives something to both sides in a split jury" (Levine, 1992, p. 160).

The group dynamics of jury deliberations reflect the influence of psychological and political pressures, strategies, and solutions. Jurors bring their own experiences, attitudes, and beliefs with them to the deliberations, and work together as a group to fashion a verdict that reflects the facts as they perceive them. This means that even when jurors agree on a verdict, they may vary in their reasons for agreement. For example, interviews with jurors in one case revealed that some jurors voted to acquit the defendant because they believed he was not guilty of any crime; others felt he may have been guilty but felt that the government had not met its burden of proving guilt beyond a reasonable doubt (Brill, 1989).

When the jurors are ready to announce their decision, it's time to call the bailiff and prepare to re-enter the courtroom, all eyes upon them as they take their seats in the jury box one last time.

---

## BOX 12.16

### How Do Jurors Perceive Each Other?

In one study, jurors in felony cases generally reported being favorably impressed with the seriousness and sense of purpose shown by their fellow jurors. Many were quite pleased and even proud of how their jury had come together as a group to tackle the task at hand. However, some jurors were distressed at what they knew or suspected was misconduct on the part of a member of the panel, such as when a juror attempted to discuss the case during trial breaks. In another case, a juror announced upon entering the deliberation room for the first time that he had made up his mind about the verdict. One juror described how another juror on the panel had refused to participate in deliberations and instead spent three days reading her book while the others deliberated. (Grant, 2000)

---

## THE JURY DECIDES: THE VERDICT

Historically, jury service could sometimes be hazardous to the health, as we saw in Step 4's discussion of the treatment of jurors who refused to find William Penn and William Mead guilty. As we saw, the Penn and Mead trial was a turning point in the history of juror independence, and today, jurors are free to return the verdict as they see fit. They do not need to discuss their reasons for their verdict with anyone. However, in cases where the jury returns a guilty verdict, the defense may request that individual jurors be "polled" (questioned) as they sit in the jury box, in order to affirm that the decision was indeed unanimous. If the jury returns an acquittal, the decision is final. If the jury convicts, a judge has the power to overturn the verdict if it appears the evidence would not support a conviction. In practice, however, judges rarely exercise this power.

In approximately five percent of cases, the jury is unable to agree on a verdict. If the jury informs the bailiff that they are "hung," the judge may order the jurors to deliberate further and try their best to reach an agreement. If they are still unable to reach a verdict, the judge declares a **mistrial**. Mistrials can occur for other reasons as well, such as the death of a key party (e.g., an attorney), juror misconduct, or a fatal procedural error that would prejudice the outcome. For example, in one case a mistrial was declared after it was disclosed that jurors examining some documents during deliberations had learned about the defendant's prior convictions, which was information that they were not supposed to have. This happened because jurors had noticed that certain sections of testimony in the document had been covered with correction fluid, and they held the papers up to the light to decipher what had been concealed (Gotthelf, 1994).

What does this mean for the defendant? Because the defendant's trial was not completed, the prosecutor has the right to decide whether to retry the case, which

---

### BOX 12.17
### The Impact of Jury Service on Jurors

Interviews with a small group of jurors who served in felony cases provide a glimpse into the jurors' experiences (Grant, 2000). The jurors in this study almost uniformly reported a sense of pride and satisfaction in performing their civic duty, often describing the experience as a "fascinating" opportunity to get an inside look at the workings of the legal system.

In contrast, the jurors' perceptions of negative aspects of jury service varied greatly. Pragmatic aspects of jury service, such as lack of parking and poor juror pay, were mentioned often. Major substantive concerns reported by these jurors included experiencing doubts about the jury's decision. For example, some former jurors reported that over a year after their service, they remained "haunted" by doubts and questions. One former juror reported thinking about the trial every day and wondering whether he had made the right decision in a complex murder trial. Another person said it took weeks to "readjust" after serving as a juror in a murder case, and another described worrying about whether she was being followed by gang associates of the defendant. One man described how he and his fellow jurors had convicted a teenaged defendant of attempted murder. Later, said this former juror, he discovered that the young defendant had received a very long sentence. Upon learning this, said the juror, "I felt like I had killed a child," because he believed strongly that such a long sentence was not merited. (Grant, 2000)

would not violate double jeopardy. The prosecutor's decision will depend upon a number of things, including the seriousness of the crime, the resources that would be required for a retrial, and the prosecutor's assessment of why the current jury could not reach agreement. For example, in an unusual case in California, defendant Taufui Piutau was tried on misdemeanor charges of driving under the influence of kava (a type of tea with relaxing properties, typically sold in health food stores). The jury could not reach agreement, and a mistrial was declared when jurors reported they were hung ten to two in favor of acquittal. The district attorney, asked whether he would retry the case, commented that "with a split like that in a misdemeanor case, I can't remember the last time a case was retried" (Stannard, 2000, p. A17).

## JURY NULLIFICATION

In the 1735 trial of John Peter Zenger, a publisher who was accused of printing seditious material, jurors refused to convict even though it was clear that Zenger had violated the law. This is often cited as a classic example of **jury nullification**. Jury nullification, broadly defined, refers to juries returning a verdict that is inconsistent with the evidence; in essence nullifying the law by taking it into their own hands. For example, a jury that acquits a defendant accused of sexual assault not because of lack of evidence, but due to juror perceptions of the victim, is practicing jury nullification.

A narrower conception of jury nullification would refer only to jurors' ability to decide not to apply the law in certain cases, thus acquitting the defendant or returning a verdict of guilty on a lesser charge than the facts of the case would support (Abramson, 1994). One possible example here might be the failure of four different Michigan juries to convict Dr. Jack Kevorkian of assisting suicide on four separate occasions. He was later convicted of murder by a jury after he videotaped his role in a patient's death and gave the tape to the *60 Minutes* newsmagazine for broadcast (Silverglate, 1999).

As we saw earlier, juries historically held the power to decide both the law and the facts in a case. In *Sparf and Hansen v. United States* (1896), the Supreme Court confined the power of the jury to deciding the facts in the case, leaving the judge to decide the law. This meant that juries no longer possessed the legal *right* to nullify the law; however, to this day juries retain the *power* of nullification.

Controversy exists over the question of whether juries should be informed of their power to nullify. Proponents argue that jury instructions should explicitly inform jurors that they have the right to nullify, but there is disagreement over how nullification should be defined. If nullification were narrowly defined, jurors could be informed that they possess the power to refuse to apply the law. In essence, juries would have the power to bestow leniency on a defendant, but not to convict a defendant where the evidence does not support a conviction. Proponents of informing juries of their nullification powers argue that juries should be able to decide the law for themselves, because the laws might be unjust, out of date, or not applicable in certain cases. Another argument favoring nullification is the idea that because laws are made to express general principles, the task of jurors is to apply the law to the specific circumstances of the case. In turn, this requires that they sometimes interpret the law anew, or ignore it.

Opponents, however, argue that informing juries about nullification defeats the very purpose of having a system of laws. Allowing juries to practice nullification would amount to condoning injustice, as juries might be more likely to return verdicts based on personal or political biases rather than the evidence. This perspective is evident in a California appellate decision upholding a defendant's conviction for statutory rape. At trial, the judge had replaced a juror who didn't believe in the law with an alternate. The defendant appealed, but the appellate court's decision illustrated judicial concerns about jury nullification: "A nullifying jury is essentially a lawless jury, . . . Jury nullification is contrary to our ideal of equal justice for all and permits both the prosecution's case and the defendant's case to depend upon the whims of a particular jury" (Chiang, 2001, p. A3).

However, research on the potential consequences of giving jurors instructions that inform them of their power of nullification suggests juries do not appear to take law into their own hands very frequently, or for no reason. Informing jurors of their power to nullify does not appear to result in the "jury anarchy" which concerns many critics of nullification (Jacobsohn, 1976; Horowitz, 1985; Niedermeier, Horowitz, and Kerr, 1999).

Ironically, the practice of jury nullification may be enhanced by the trend toward mandatory sentences. For example, reports have surfaced of cases where jurors learned that the defendant, on trial for a relatively minor, nonviolent crime, was actually facing a third-strike sentence of twenty-five years to life if convicted. In response, the jurors apparently decided to acquit instead (Chiang, 1996). This has raised the prospect of a scenario where the defense attorney whose client is being tried for a crime such as check kiting, may seek ways to subtly "cue" the jury, hoping they will realize that this is a "three-strikes" case and that they will choose to acquit the defendant despite having sufficient evidence to convict.

There are indications that jury nullification may be growing, with some cases suggesting individual jurors and sometimes juries use their decision-making power to send messages about their perceptions of the criminal justice system in general or specific laws (Biskupic, 1999). This raises a very interesting question: When a jury refuses to apply the law, is this a worrisome deviation from the ideals underlying trial by jury—or is it the very embodiment of the jury's role as the conscience of the community?

## CONCLUSION

The announcement of the verdict in a criminal trial is frequently simply a culmination of one phase of the criminal courts process. If the defendant is found "not guilty," then the prosecution cannot appeal the verdict.[3] In the aftermath of an acquittal, the former defendant returns to society, the defense attorney may contemplate the lessons learned from a successful defense, and the prosecutor may try to ask the jurors why they voted for acquittal. Victims, or their families, will undoubtedly replay the trial in their minds as they contemplate the verdict. The jurors must now return to their everyday lives, where they can reflect on their experiences and the impact that serving as a juror has made on them.

However, most felony criminal trials result in a verdict of "guilty" (Hart and Reaves, 1999). In these cases, the verdict is actually a signal for the next critical steps in the process to begin: the task of determining the appropriate sentence, and for the defense, the question of whether there are grounds for an appeal. Let us turn our attention now to the next phase: the question of sentencing.

## DISCUSSION QUESTIONS

1. What did you think of Clarence Darrow's jury selection strategies (presented in Box 12.3)? Do you think that group members generally share the same attitudes, or not? What does the research on the relationship between juror characteristics, attitudes, and behavior suggest? Given the research on the relationship between juror characteristics, attitudes, and behaviors, why do you think Darrow believed his strategies for juror selection were successful? Is it possible that Darrow's skill as an advocate for his client, rather than his jury-picking techniques, accounted for his success as a defender?

2. What do you think of the use of peremptory challenges? Take a position:
   a. Do you think the use of peremptory challenges *increases* the likelihood of an impartial jury?
   b. Do you think the use of peremptory challenges *decreases* the likelihood of the impartial jury?

3. Should peremptory challenges be abolished? Why or why not? Give specific reasons.

4. Should students be considered a "cognizable group"? Why or why not?

5. Is the jury's power, if not their right, to nullify a necessary part of flexibility in the jury system, an illustration of jury discretion that gives the system its value in tailoring justice? Or is it an opportunity for citizens to do an "end run" around the law by disregarding the law and the facts?

6. Amar, discussing jury decision rules, comments: "Preserving unanimity might also be undemocratic, for it would create an extreme minority veto unknown to the Founders" (1995, p. 1190). What do you think he means? Do you think this statement has merit? Why or why not?

7. Consider the issue of religious appeals by prosecutors during closing arguments. Why might such arguments be considered improper by courts? Think about how such arguments could influence the jury and then discuss reasons. Would religious appeals to mercy on the part of defense counsel pose similar problems? Why or why not?

## NOTES

1. Note that the use of jury questionnaires does not in and of itself mean that scientific jury selection strategies are being used. Depending upon how such questionnaires are constructed and interpreted, they may simply represent attempts to gather information about prospective jurors, rather than being part of a concerted strategy based on social science techniques. The use of jury

questionnaires illustrates the fact that there is no hard and fast distinction between "scientific" and "nonscientific" jury selection techniques; rather, the distinction is a matter of degree reflecting not only how information is gathered but how it is analyzed and applied.

2. The reason that gender orientation can be considered a cognizable group in California, when it has not been designated as such by a U.S. Supreme Court decision, is straightforward: While states may not provide fewer constitutional protections than those provided by the U.S. Constitution, U.S. Supreme Court decisions, or federal statutes that are nationally applicable, states can choose to provide *greater* constitutional protections.

3. There are a few very narrow exceptions where the government may be able to appeal an acquittal, such as when the acquittal was obtained through judicial corruption.

## REFERENCES

Abramson, J. (1994). *We, the Jury: The Jury System and the Ideal of Democracy.* New York: Basic Books.

Amar, A. (1995). Edward L. Barrett, Jr., Lecture on Constitutional Law: Reinventing juries: Ten suggested reforms. *U.C. Davis Law Review,* 28: 1169–1194.

American Bar Association. (2001). *How Courts Work: Steps in a Trial.* Available online: www.abanet.org/publiced-dd/courts/trials/eps.html.

Anderson, J.F., Jr. (1999). Trial advocacy: Setting yourself apart from the herd: A judge's thoughts on successful courtroom advocacy. *South Carolina Law Review,* 50: 617–38.

Associated Press (1997). Transcripts of Thursday's court session in the trial of Timothy McVeigh as prepared by the official court reporter and distributed by PubNETics Inc. of Denver.

*Batson v. Kentucky,* 106 S. Ct. 1712 (1986).

Biskupic, J. (1999, February 8). In jury rooms, a form of civil protest grows. *Washington Post,* p. A1.

Blankenship, M., Luginbuhl, J., Cullen, F., and Rexlick, W. (1997). Juror comprehension of sentencing instructions: A test of Tennessee's death penalty process. *Justice Quarterly,* 14: 325–51.

Boland, B. and Sones, R. (1986). *The Prosecution of Felony Arrests, 1981.* Washington, DC: National Institute of Justice.

Bowers, W.J. and Steiner, B.D. (1998). Death by default: An empirical demonstration of false and forced choices in capital sentencing. *Texas Law Review,* 77: 605–717.

Brill, S. (1989). *U.S. v. John DeLorean:* Entrapped? In Brill, S. (Ed.), *Trial by Jury.* New York: American Lawyer Books/Touchstone, pp. 201–29.

*California v. Alvarado,* 121 S. Ct. 1644 (2001).

Chiang, H. (2001, May 8). Top state court says jurors must honor law: They'll be removed from case if they put conscience first. *San Francisco Chronicle,* p. A3.

Chiang, H. (2000, February 3). Ruling protects gay juror rights: Dismissals can't be based on sexual orientation, state court says. *San Francisco Chronicle,* p. A1.

Chiang, H. (1996, September 24). Some jurors revolt over 3 strikes: Penalty prospects sway their verdicts. *San Francisco Chronicle,* p. A1.

Courtinfo. Available online at www.courtinfo.ca.gov.

Darrow, C. (1936, May). "How to Pick a Jury." *Esquire,* p. 36.

Davis, M., and Davis, K. (1995, December). Star rising for Simpson jury consultant. *American Bar Association Journal,* 81: 14.

Diamond, S.S. (1994, June 6). Instructions frequently baffle jurors. *The National Law Journal*, p. C1.

Duffy, B.C. (1997). Note: Barring foul blows: An argument for a per se reversible-error rule for prosecutors' use of religious arguments in the sentencing phase of capital cases. *Vanderbilt Law Review*, 50: 1335–74.

Duffy, S. (1996, December 3). Despite sexist remarks, pressure, female jurors' guilty votes stand. *The Legal Intelligencer*, p. 1.

*Duncan v. Louisiana*, 391 US 145 (1968).

*Edmonson v. Leesville Concrete Company*, 500 US 614 (1991).

Eisenberg, T., and Wells, M. (1993, November). Deadly confusion: Juror instructions in capital cases. *Cornell Law Review*, 79: 1–17.

Faculty, the Judge Advocate General's School, U.S. Army. (2000, June). The art of trial advocacy: "It's like déjà vu all over again!" Yet another look at the opening statement. *Army Lawyer*, 34: 39.

Finkel, N.J. (1995). *Commonsense Justice: Jurors' Notions of the Law*. Cambridge, MA: Harvard University Press.

Finkelstein, K.E. (2000, July 18). Ex-court clerk admits stealing Malcolm X diary. *New York Times*, p. B4.

Foote, W.R. (1995). $6,000,000 deposition . . . and other jury observations: Things that bug juries. *Louisiana Bar Journal*, 42: 526.

Fukurai, H., Butler, E., and Krooth, R. (1993). *Race and the Jury*. New York: Plenum Publishing.

Garvey, S. (1998). Essay: Aggravation and mitigation in capital cases: What do jurors think? *Columbia Law Review*, 98: 1538–1539.

*Georgia v. McCollum*, 505 US 42 (1992).

Gibson, D. (2000). Jury instructions. Available at www.stu.edu/lawlib/Reference/Research/Jury%20 Instructions.htm.

Gotthelf, B. (1994, September 5). Jury sees right through the evidence. *New Jersey Law Journal*, p. 14.

Grant, D.R. (1996). From prior record to current verdict: How character evidence affects jurors' decisions. Unpublished dissertation. University of California, Irvine. Irvine, CA.

Grant, D.R. (2000). The phenomenology of jury service: Jurors' experiences, questions, and suggestions. Presentation made at the American Psychology-Law Conference, New Orleans, March 2000.

Hart, T., and Reaves, B. (1999, October). Felony defendants in large urban counties, 1996. U.S. Department of Justice, Office of Justice Progams, Bureau of Justice Statistics, p. 26.

*Holland v. Illinois*, 110 S. Ct. 803 (1990).

Horowitz, I. (1980). Juror selection: A comparison of two methods in several criminal cases. *Journal of Applied Social Psychology*, 10: 86–99.

Horowitz, I. (1985). The effect of jury nullification instruction on verdicts and jury functioning in criminal trials. *Law and Human Behavior*, 9: 25–36.

Jacobsohn, G. (1976). The right to disagree: Judges, jurors, and the administration of justice in Maryland. *Washington University Law Quarterly*, 1: 571–607.

*J.E.B. v. Alabama*, ex rel. T.B. 511 U.S. 127 (1994).

*John B. Gunn Law Corp. v. Maynard*, 189 Cal. App. 3d 1565 (1987).

Johnson, S.L. (1998). Symposium on race and criminal law: Batson ethics for prosecutors and trial court judges. *Chicago-Kent Law Review*, 73: 475–507.

Judicial Council of California. (2000). Available at www.courtinfo.ca.gov/jury/step4.htm.

Kalven H., Jr., and Zeisel, H. (1966). *The American Jury.* Chicago: University of Chicago Press.

Kassin, S.M. and Wrightsman, L.S. (1981). The construction and validation of a juror bias scale. *Journal of Research in Personality,* 17: 423–41.

Levine, J. (1992). *Juries and Politics.* Belmont, CA: Brooks/Cole Publishing.

*Lewis v. United States,* 518 U.S. 322, 325-26 (1996).

Litan, R.E. (Ed.). (1993). *Verdict: Assessing the Civil Jury System.* Washington, DC: The Brookings Institute.

Lubet, S. (2001, Winter). The Forgotten Trial of Wyatt Earp. *University of Colorado Law Review,* 72: 1–51.

Luginbuhl, J. (1992). Comprehension of judges' instructions in the penalty phase of a capital trial. *Law and Human Behavior,* 16: 203–18.

Meyer, P. (1999, Spring). Trial Advocacy: "Desperate for Love III": Rethinking Closing Arguments as Stories. *South Carolina Law Review,* 50: 715–50.

Mitchell, J.B. (2000, Spring). Why should the prosecutor get the last word? *American Journal of Criminal Law,* 27: 139–215.

Morehead, J. (1994, Spring). When a peremptory challenge is no longer peremptory: Batson's unfortunate failure to eradicate invidious discrimination from jury selection. *DePaul Law Review,* 43: 625–43.

*M.S. v. Stansfield,* 101 F.3d 909 (3rd Circuit, 1996)

Nadvorney, D. and Cantu, M. (1987, September 28). Alleged pressure by members does not overturn conviction. *The National Law Journal,* p. 32.

Nidiry, R. (1996, June). Note: Restraining adversarial excess in closing argument. *Columbia Law Review,* 96: 1299–1334.

Niedermeier, K., Horowitz, I., and Kerr, N. (1999). Informing jurors of their nullification power: A route to a just verdict or judicial chaos? *Law and Human Behavior,* 23(3): 331–51.

Nietzel, M. and Dillehay, R.C. (1986). *Psychological Consultation in the Courtrooms.* New York: Pergamon Press.

Nisbett, R., and Ross, L. (1980). *Strategies and Shortcomings of Social Judgment.* Englewood Cliffs, NJ: Prentice Hall.

*Palko v. Connecticut,* 302 U.S. 319 (1937).

Pennington, N. and Hastie, R. (1991). A cognitive theory of juror decision making: The story model. *Cardozo Law Review,* 13: 519–21.

Pennington, N., and Hastie, R. (1993). The story model for juror decision making. In Reid Hastie (Ed.), *Inside the Juror.* New York: Cambridge University Press.

*People v. Hill,* 952 P.2d 673, 685 (Cal. 1998).

*People v. Hurd,* 5 Cal. App. 3d 865, 85 Cal Rptr. 718 (1970).

*People v. Sandoval,* 4 Cal. 4th 155, 841 P.2d 862, 883 (1992).

Perrin, T. (1999). From O.J. to McVeigh: The use of argument in the opening statement. *Emory Law Journal,* 38: 107–15.

Personal communication in 1999 with Mr. Don Vera, Deputy Jury Commissioner, Stanislaus County, California.

Santa Clara County Superior Court Jury Service Information, available online. Accessed 2001: www.claraweb.co.santa-clara.ca.us/sct/jury/index.html.

Severence, L.J. and Loftus, E.F. (1982). Improving the ability of jurors to comprehend and apply criminal jury instructions. *Law and Society Review,* 17: 153–97.

Sevilla, C., and Lorenz, L. (Illustrator). (1993). *Disorder in the Court: Great Fractured Moments in Courtroom History.* New York: W.W. Norton. Excerpt was found online at: http://www.national-center.org/LB14.html.

Silverglate, H. (1999, April). Tipping evidence scales. *The National Law Journal,* p. A30.

Sinclair, D.K. (1990). *Trial Handbook* (2nd ed). New York: Practising Law Institute.

Sommers, S., and Ellsworth, P. (2001, March). White juror bias: An investigation of prejudice against Black defendants in the American courtroom. *Psychology, Public Policy, and Law,* 7(1): 201–29.

*Sparf and Hansen v. United States,* 156 U.S. 151 (1896).

Spiegelman, P.J. (1999, Winter). Prosecutorial misconduct in closing argument: The role of intent in appellate review. *The Journal of Appellate Practice and Process,* 1: 115–84.

Stannard, M. (2000, October 28). Criminal case involving kava drinker ends in mistrial. *San Francisco Chronicle,* p. A17.

*State v. Kaiser,* 260 Kan. 235, 918 p. 2d 629 (1996).

*Strauder v. West Virginia,* 100 US 303 (1880).

Studebaker, C., Robbennolt, C., Pathak-Sharma, M., and Penrod, S. (2000). Assessing pretrial publicity effects: Integrating content analytic results. *Law and Human Behavior,* 24(3): 317–336.

*Swain v. Alabama,* 380 US 202 (1965).

Swerling, J.B. (1999, Spring). Trial advocacy: "I can't believe I asked that question": A look at cross-examination techniques. *South Carolina Law Review,* 50: 753–97.

Swift, J. (1993, January). Note: Batson's invidious legacy: Discriminatory juror exclusion and the "intuitive" peremptory challenge. *Cornell Law Review,* 78: 336–69.

Tanford, J.A. 1990. The law and psychology of jury instructions. *Nebraska Law Review* 69: 71–111.

*Taylor v. Louisiana,* 419 US 522 (1975).

*United States v. Wexler,* 79 F.2d 526, 52930 (2d Cir. 1935).

*United States v. Stansfield,* 101 F.3d 909 (3rd Cir. 1996)

Van Voris, B. (2000, October 23). Jurors to lawyers: Dare to be dull. *National Law Journal,* 23(9): p. A1.

Wrightsman, L., Nietzel, M., and Fortune, W. (1994). *Psychology and the Legal System* (3rd ed.). Pacific Grove, CA: Brooks/Cole Publishing.

Zobel, H. (1995, July–August) The jury on trial. *American Heritage,* 46(4): 42 (10).

# PART IV

# Post-Conviction Processes

# Step 13

# The Punishment Dilemma

In the previous chapter, we learned about the important events in a criminal trial. Once an individual has been convicted or has pled guilty, the focus of the court changes from determination of guilt to the determination of an appropriate penalty. This role is generally believed to be a sentencing agent's (i.e., a judge's or jury's) most difficult task. The violation of all laws carries some potential penalty, even if the sentence is ultimately suspended. Before we can discuss the imposition of penalties, however, we must first examine where sentencing agents derive their power, what philosophies guide sentencing, and what options are available at sentencing. This chapter focuses on these three areas.

## DISCRETION

Determining penalties is yet another stage in the court system that allows for and requires **discretion** (i.e., the power or ability to act according to one's judgment or beliefs). Just as prosecutors need to make choices about what charges to file, sentencing agents need to be able to make reasoned choices about which sentences fit the crime. Of course, they cannot make choices that are ludicrous or unconstitutional. The choices they make must fit within the limits of their discretion (that is, how they can legally exercise their discretion) or they run the risk of being overturned or changed at the appellate level.

The first factor that limits judges and juries in the sentencing process is the U.S. Constitution. According to the Eighth Amendment, sentences must not be "cruel and unusual." Generally, this means that sentences cannot involve torture or other brutal practices. An early U.S. Supreme Court case that involved this issue was *Weems v. United States* (1910). Among other things, Weems had been sentenced to fifteen years of "hard and painful labor" in chains for making false entries into official records while working for the U.S. government in the Philippine Islands. The Supreme Court ruled that the sentence was not proportionate to

Weems' offense and thus invalidated it. Sentencing agents, then, have to ensure that the sentences they impose are not too disproportionate to offenders' crimes. Beyond *Weems*, however, the Court has not offered much of a definition of what constitutes cruel and unusual punishment.

A more recent usage of the Eighth Amendment includes cases in which overcrowding at prisons is an issue. In essence, some appellate and supreme courts have ruled that double- and triple-celling of inmates is a cruel punishment. Judges know they cannot sentence offenders to prisons that are under a decree to reduce their populations unless other offenders are released to make room for the new arrivals (e.g., Meyer and Jesilow, 1993). This may mean that offenders who judges feel deserve jail are sentenced with other options.

A second factor that limits sentencing agents is criminal statutes. All criminal statutes list the potential penalties for engaging in the proscribed activity. Those who burglarize homes in California, for example, face a sentence of two to six years in prison. New Jersey burglars can expect a sentence of three to five years in prison. Burglars in other states face penalties set by their state's legislature. Judges cannot sentence burglars to the death penalty because penal codes do not allow this sentence for burglars.

The third factor is related to the second, and is the role played by compulsory sentencing laws. Although they will be discussed more in the next chapter, it is important to mention that sentencing agents must, in theory, heed whatever compulsory sentencing laws have been put in place by their legislative bodies. The most common compulsory sentencing schemes are mandatory sentencing laws, which require judges to impose mandatory minimum sentences. Compulsory schemes also include sentencing guidelines designed to narrow judges' discretion and sentence enhancements, which mandate additional penalties for certain offenders (e.g., the use of a gun or specific type of weapon while committing another crime may result in the imposition of additional time in prison).

The fourth factor in discretion is society's role. Before imposing sentences, judges need to consider what the public wants for particular offenders or types of offenders. Elected judges need to remain responsive to their constituents' needs in order to get re-elected. Even if they are appointed, judges must consider the political ramifications of imposing sentences that are not consistent with the public's wishes. Some scholars argue that judges in small communities are most affected by these constraints because each judge "knows the content of his sentencing remarks will be on page one of the local paper" (Kunkle, 1989, p. 75).

The final factor limiting discretion is the sentencing philosophy to which the court or state legislature ascribes. Sentencing philosophies embody the purposes we have for punishing criminals and are very important, as they sometimes dictate which punishments are appropriate.

# PUNISHMENT PHILOSOPHIES

There are four generally recognized punishment philosophies: deterrence, incapacitation, rehabilitation, and retribution. Some scholars argue that there is a fifth punishment philosophy, restoration (e.g., Branham and Krantz, 1994, p. 6). Although the goal of each philosophy: is to prevent crime, they differ dramatically in their approaches. We will discuss each of the five in turn. Boxes 13.1 through 13.5 will present a number of interview segments with judges to illustrate the sentencing philosophies.

## Deterrence

According to the principle of deterrence, the purpose of punishment is to prevent crime by convincing or scaring individuals not to commit crimes because they or others have been punished for violating a law. When people decide not to park in a handicapped space because they have been fined or do not want to be fined, they have been deterred from the illegal activity.

One early scholar who wrote about deterrence was Cesare Bonesana, Marchese de Beccaria (1738–1794). Beccaria was a classical theorist who argued that criminals are rational human beings who make choices based on free will. He said criminals choose to commit crimes because the benefits outweigh the costs. The way to prevent crime, then, is to raise the "costs" of crime. Among other things, he recommended that certainty, celerity (speed), and severity be considered when designing an effective system of punishment (Beccaria, 1775/1983).

Certainty means the assurance with which one can expect to be punished following a crime. Beccaria argued that criminals could not be deterred from crimes unless they felt certain they would be punished. If only a small percentage of criminals are punished for violating a particular law, others may be likely to break the same law with the assumption that they will not be caught. This is one reason why motorists are more likely to speed when they do not see police officers. Similarly, I have had students tell me they are less likely to cheat when their professor brings in extra proctors to help keep an eye on things; they feel the chances of getting caught and punished are higher when the proctors are present. In a nutshell, these students are talking about certainty.

But, many factors contribute to the fact that the certainty of punishment for any given crime is not at optimally high levels. First, fewer than half of crimes are reported by victims (Harlow, 1985; Bureau of Justice Statistics, 2000, p. 94), so the perpetrators of the unreported crimes never face the specter of arrest or punishment. Certain crimes, especially white-collar offenses, might go undetected by the victims so they are not even reported, much less prosecuted. Cases are eliminated at various stages in the justice system by officials exercising their discretion (e.g., police officers may sometimes issue warnings rather than taking more formal

Cesare Beccaria (1738–1794) is considered the father of classical theory. Beccaria and his followers argued that criminals are rational human beings who make choices based on free will. To prevent crime, Beccaria felt punishments must be swift and certain, and sufficiently severe to deter would-be offenders.    SOURCE: Illustration courtesy of the Granger Collection.

actions, or prosecutors may decline to prosecute in some cases because of evidentiary or other concerns). Given these realities, certainty of punishment does not exist for all crimes.

Celerity is the swiftness with which criminals are punished. Beccaria argued that people are less able to attach meaning to punishments that are long overdue. For example, children who are told to "Wait till your father gets home" may forget why they are being punished once daddy finally gets home. Further, some criminals may break laws because they know they will not be punished for months, sometimes years, after their crimes.

Severity refers to the harshness of the penalties imposed on offenders. Beccaria felt that penalties should be severe enough to deter people from crimes, but reasonable enough that all guilty parties will be reported and punished; that is, sentences must not be too lenient nor too strict. To illustrate, consider the penalty for cheating on papers. If the penalty was to rewrite the paper, some people would be willing to turn in their classmates, and professors would agree to penalize the cheaters. On the other hand, if the penalty was expulsion from the school, even on a first offense, very few students would be turned in and punished because many people would consider that penalty to be unreasonable. Only cheaters who were already outcasts would be subjected to such a system of justice, leading to disparities in sentences. Another example of this is the reluctance of some juries to convict defendants accused of nonviolent crimes if the jurors suspect the case is a "three strikes" case that will result in a very long sentence for the defendant. Beccaria argued that certainty and celerity were far more important than severity. Even if the penalties were mild, knowing that all offenders would be detected and punished would still deter people from crime.

There are two types of deterrence: general and specific. **Specific deterrence** (also known as individual deterrence) occurs when criminals are deterred from future crimes because they themselves have been punished. My friend Elena does not jaywalk because she once received a ticket for doing so. Whenever she starts to jaywalk, she hears money trickling from her bank account to pay the fine. Another of my students told me he will never park in a handicapped space because he was given 100 hours of community service for a past infraction. Both of these individuals had been affected by specific deterrence. Whenever convicted criminals say they wish to avoid going back to jail, specific deterrence is operating.

**General deterrence**, on the other hand, takes place when others (the community in general) are deterred because they know criminals are punished. Although I have never been ticketed, I do not jaywalk because my friend Elena received an expensive ticket for jaywalking. In fact, none of her friends jaywalk because we do not want to get tickets. Whenever would-be offenders decide they do not want to be punished because they have seen others receive distasteful penalties, general deterrence is at work. Sometimes, judges will acknowledge the value of general deterrence during sentencing. For example, one low-level money launderer was told by a federal judge that she was sentenced to two weeks incarceration, even though the prosecutor had not called for any incarceration, because he wanted to "send a message that if you commit a crime of this sort, you will go to jail" (Neumeister, 2000). The judge felt she did not deserve a longer sentence because the role she played was minimal, but wanted to emphasize deterrence in the minds of other would-be criminals.

In summary, under deterrence, criminals are hypothesized to be rational individuals who weigh the costs and benefits of illegal acts and decide that the benefits of crime outweigh the costs (Blumstein, Cohen, and Nagin, 1978, p. 19). Offenders are punished, then, to maintain the perception that crime has high costs, thus thwarting the commission of illegal acts.

Critics of deterrence point to its seeming inconsistencies with popular thought and the findings from research on the psychology of decision-making. Because the philosophy is rooted in the concept of the greatest good for the greatest number, certain offenders should go unpunished, according to deterrence theorists. Jeremy Bentham (1823, 1948, p. 177), for example, argued that crimes committed by offenders whose skills were needed by the rest of society (e.g., a community's only doctor) should go unpunished. We see hints of this phenomenon today when doctors who work in low-income areas are not prosecuted or are not punished for medical fraud because the system is not able to readily replace them (e.g., Jesilow, Pontell, and Geis, 1993). Bentham also held that punishments—executions

A tangible example of deterrence in Dorset, England. This sign from the early 1700s illustrates two important concepts in punishment. First, the sign represents a clear attempt to deter would-be offenders from damaging the bridge through the threat of severe punishment. Second, the sign mentions the penalty of transportation for life for those who damage the bridge. Between 1718 and 1776, some thirty to forty thousand offenders were sentenced to transportation from England to America. Between 1787 and 1869, approximately 162,000 criminals were transported from England to Australia (Newbold, 1999).  SOURCE: Courtesy of Jon'a Meyer.

or other penalties—that would anger the populace or other governments should not be carried out (e.g., the uproar by the United States to reduce Michael Faye's punishment after he was sentenced to be caned in Singapore). These ideas are repugnant to those who argue that criminals should not escape punishment solely because of their status in society.

Other critics argue that it is impossible to know whether the impact of punishment (the costs of crime) deters potential offenders because we cannot accurately determine how much benefit a certain crime represents to an offender or how much cost a given punishment delivers. This is due to the fact that according to deterrence theory, each offender theoretically weighs the costs and benefits of committing a crime according to his or her own subjective perception. Thus, there will be individual differences between potential offenders in how they perceive the risks and rewards of crime. For example, which is considered worse by offenders, a year of intensive supervision probation or a year in prison? Several research teams have found that offenders (especially recidivists and single men) report that they would prefer prison due to their belief that probation is stricter or more difficult to complete (Crouch, 1993; McClelland and Alpert, 1985; Petersilia and Piper Deschenes, 1994). Their preference for jail cannot be blamed merely on difficulties in making such decisions without facing them; Petersilia and Turner (1990) found that nearly one fourth of a sample of offenders who were offered the opportunity to participate in an intensive probation program preferred instead to go to prison!

Another difficulty in assessing deterrent value of punishments is that punishments affect different people in dissimilar ways. A fine, for example, may be of little consequence to a wealthy business owner but may be overwhelming to an unemployed person. Other penalties also affect people differently. Some individuals are traumatized by even short jail terms, whereas others seem able to tolerate prison terms of several years. To some, community service is a way to serve their communities; others view it as a shameful, stigmatizing punishment. Some scholars believe that although deterrence (especially general deterrence) has not worked well for reducing street crimes, it may be more effective when applied to white-collar criminals, who are arguably more likely to consciously contemplate the consequences of their crimes (e.g., Braithwaite and Geis, 1982). The list of comparisons could go on if we had unlimited space to consider them here.

Others argue that not all people act of their own free will. The mentally ill, for example, may commit crimes due to reasons other than their exercise of clear thought; that is, they may commit crimes that reflect the influence of their illness on their thinking processes. It may also be difficult to deter crimes of passion, in which offenders are so incensed that they are temporarily unable to act in a rational manner. Individuals who catch their spouses in bed with other lovers, for example, are unlikely to weigh the costs and benefits of a criminal act before taking sometimes lethal actions. Consider the last time you wanted to punch someone. Chances are you were furious and were not in the mood to consider the pros and cons of crime. Modern laws take this lack of free will into account by allowing complete or partial defenses for the mentally ill and for crimes committed in the heat of passion. If a reasonable person would be incensed by the situation faced by the defendant, then the defendant might qualify for a lesser charge or lower degree of the crime (e.g., second-degree rather than first-degree assault).

Other critics argue that this utilitarian philosophy allows for the sanctioning of innocent people (e.g., Rawls, 1955). Because deterrence relies on making examples of others, it would not be evil to punish an occasional innocent to deter others if the sanctioning meant the greatest good for the greatest number. Bentham (1823/ 1948, p. 183), for example, advocated punishing offenders for crimes that had not yet been detected because it was often difficult to uncover all crimes committed by offenders. This criterion is less likely to be cited as good policy today, but there are some offenders who were "made an example of," even if their actions were not necessarily the most egregious, in order to keep the perceived costs of punishment high. For example, after a man who falsely claimed he had provided Columbine shooters Eric Harris and Dylan Klebold with bomb-making materials was arrested and booked into jail for making a false report, the local sheriff commented, "Maybe this will slow down some of these crackpot calls that we're getting" (Vogt, 1999). The sheriff's comments show that the man was essentially being made an example of to prevent others from making such calls, especially as he was the only one (of presumably many offenders, given the sheriff's comments) charged with such an offense. In fact, he could have received a harsher sentence than others who played a role in facilitating the offense. See Box 13.1 for three interview segments that illustrate deterrence as a sentencing philosophy.

---

# BOX 13.1

## Judges' Comments on Deterrence

*This and the following four boxes presents extracts from interviews with eleven judges to illustrate each of the five sentencing philosophies. As you read the following interview segments, think about how they demonstrate deterrence.*

*General deterrence:*

[Regarding driving-under-the-influence (DUI) cases]: You hear cases on both sides, does incarceration really help? Should we put these people in home confinement because the jails are so crowded? I feel really strongly that punishment is a deterrent on DUI cases. I think that this is demonstrating that people are drinking less at noon, people are very aware of designated drivers. I think a lot of this has to do with fear of going to jail.

*Specific deterrence:*

[Regarding littering offenses]: A $271.00 fine and picking up trash for eight hours is heavy enough, don't you think? The point of the law is deterrence, so a person will never, ever do it again. And I don't think you have to fine somebody $500.00 to accomplish that purpose. If a $271.00 fine and picking up trash for eight hours doesn't do it that guy or gal is crazy. I have not had a repeat littering offender; maybe if I did I would jack it up a little.

*Both specific and general deterrence:*

With respect to deterrence, I think we have to look at a couple of aspects of it. One, is this particular defendant going to be deterred from committing future similar crimes, or from committing future crimes at all? Is the punishment here strong enough to make the guy understand? . . . The next aspect of deterrence is whether or not other people in similar circumstances might be deterred from this type of crime because of the type of sentence this kind of defendant gets in this situation. So, deterrence is something that has to be considered when you're indicating somebody's punishment. The thing of sending a message out of this room is not just between me and the defendant. Society is all involved in this, so I have to justify society's sense of fairness and I have to think of the deterrent value of the sentence.

## Rehabilitation

**Rehabilitation** is an effort to end criminal behavior by "curing" offenders of their criminality. According to this philosophy, punishment is a form of treatment administered to criminals (MacNamara, 1977).

Advocates of rehabilitation agree with Beccaria that humans act of their own free will, at least most of the time (Menninger, 1959). However, rehabilitation efforts often reflect a positivist approach to crime and punishment, that is, an approach that asserts that human behavior is at least partially determined or influenced by a variety of factors. Thus, crime cannot be deterred by the mere threat of punishment. Consider drug abuse and sales. Would any rational person use and sell drugs when the penalties are so harsh? What about murder? Only a "crazy" person would commit murder. This gets to the core of the rehabilitation model.

Crime occurs when "sick" people do illegal things. They may be suffering from physical illnesses (e.g., chemical imbalances), psychological disorders (e.g., compulsive obsessions), addictions (e.g., drugs or alcohol), or social disorders (e.g., inability to control their anger). Consider, for example, kleptomaniacs, whose shoplifting results from a psychological illness. Whatever the cause, rehabilitation advocates argue that society owes it to itself and individual offenders to try to cure them before releasing them back into society. The treatment sometimes consists of administration of drugs, psychotherapy, or retraining and education programs.

Of course, rehabilitation does not mean that we should try a few cures and then give up and release the offender. The model assumes that if we cannot cure a given offender, we need to "provide for his indefinitely continued confinement" to protect society (Menninger, 1959, p. 62). It is this belief that leads advocates of the rehabilitation model to support indeterminate sentences where offenders are **paroled** (i.e., released into the community under supervision after being incarcerated) after they can demonstrate that they have been cured. Karl Menninger (1959), an eloquent supporter of rehabilitation, once said:

> With more use of the indeterminate sentence and the establishment of scientific diagnostic centers, we shall be in a position to make progress in the science of *treating* antisocial trends. Furthermore, we shall get away from the present legal smog that hangs over the prisons, which lets us detain with heartbreaking futility some prisoners fully rehabilitated while others, whom the prison officials know full well to be dangerous and unemployable, must be released, *against our wishes,* because a judge far away . . . said that five years was enough. (pp. 63–64)

This is where many criticisms of rehabilitation arise. First, how do we know when an offender has been cured? Many offenders who are paroled commit new crimes. At best, this shows how difficult it is to predict with any accuracy whether individuals will recidivate. Further, the rehabilitation model is based on the premise that we *can* cure offenders, and some doubt whether this assumption is accurate because of the difficulty in reliably predicting human behavior. Research evaluating a variety of programs intended to rehabilitate has not given cause for optimism; however, the evidence does show that some rehabilitative efforts are quite effective for particular types of offenders (e.g., Walker, 2001).

Second, how is the nature of the treatments utilized? Some inmate writers, like Jack Abbott (1981), have written of the terrors of the medical model. Some offenders have been forced into painful medical procedures (e.g., lobotomies or drug treatments) that may not be successful or whose side effects are worse than the disease, all in the name of finding a cure for crime.

Third, some employees of the criminal justice system doubt that rehabilitation can be effective in reducing crime if participation in programs is voluntary (MacNamara, 1977), and argue that therapies undertaken involuntarily are less likely to be effective. Still others contend that we cannot force criminals to undergo therapies that might not work. This is complicated by the fact that a number of criminals do not want to be cured of what the rest of society determines to be criminal. To illustrate, consider my friend Sylvia, who showed me some blurry pictures she had taken. When I told her to stand farther from her subject when using her instamatic camera, she told me that she liked the pictures somewhat blurry because they looked more surreal. She considered the photos to be artistic and did not want the problem to be ended! Like Sylvia and her preference for out-of-focus photographs, alcoholics and drug addicts often do not feel that their preference for substance use needs to be cured. Some criminals, such as prostitutes and gamblers, may not even view their activities as criminal and resent efforts by those appointed by the justice system to prescribe suitable remedies.

Other people have taken issue with the idea of judges surrendering their sentencing power to psychologists and social workers. They feel that judges have been given the power to sentence and should fulfill that obligation. Criminals should not be given the opportunity to avoid culpability by turning to social workers who can absolve them of their responsibility by arguing that crime results from the actions of "sick" people who need to be healed, so criminals cannot be blamed for their actions (if criminals cannot be held responsible, then they certainly should not be penalized for their crimes).[1] Some scholars argue that this medicalized view is untrue; not all criminals commit crimes attributable to one or more assorted maladies, and those who do break laws deserve to be punished for their transgressions (Dalrymple, 1992; Wasserstrom, 1980). See Box 13.2 for two interview segments that illustrate rehabilitation as a sentencing philosophy.

## Incapacitation

**Incapacitation** involves attempts to physically restrain offenders from victimizing others. For the most part, incapacitation is the belief that we can prevent crimes by

---

## BOX 13.2

### Judges' Comments on Rehabilitation

*This is the second in a series of five boxes that present extracts from interviews with eleven judges to illustrate each of the five sentencing philosophies. As you read the following interview segments, think about how they demonstrate rehabilitation.*

People to me that are into substance abuse are really abusing themselves. . . . When they have been arrested three or four times, it is a despairing thing because it's hard to find help for them. If you can get those people in a day-to-day facility, you can change their outlook toward using these substances. I am concerned if we are really doing any good with putting people in jail for Health and Safety Code violations. Some of these sentences are a mandatory ninety days. These people go right out and do crimes again and if they are not getting some kind of help, I don't know what good jail sentences do. I also realize that people who are abusing drugs are also stealing, etc. It is all compounded.

In the misdemeanor range, you're concerned that "Hey, this person isn't a bad person; they can be salvaged.". . . You take a look at the individual defendant, whether he has a drug problem, an alcohol problem, or he has an unemployment problem or whatever's causing him to do this. We have some programs, such as Domestic Violence Diversion Program, which I believe is the most successful rehabilitation type program. Everyone that goes to this program comes back reporting how fantastic it is. . . . It feels good to see a husband and wife smiling again with their children, coming back with a progress report—they have it working again. Whatever the factors were that were causing the problems, this program appears to help people face those factors and get rid of them and get on with their lives.

---

isolating offenders from the rest of society, thus preventing them from committing further crimes against the populace (Blumstein, Cohen, and Nagin, 1978, p. 64). When offenders are behind bars, they cannot victimize the rest of society. Prosecutors have long understood the importance of incarceration in their efforts to protect the public from offenders (Kunkle, 1989).

Adherents of incapacitation argue that the benefits of incarceration need not include deterrence or rehabilitation (Blumstein, Cohen, and Nagin, 1978, p. 64). The value of prison, in and of itself, is protection of the public. Under this philosophy, it is irrelevant whether prison-based treatment programs work or potential offenders are deterred by the prospects of going to prison. The value of incapacitation lies in its ability to restrain offenders who would otherwise victimize society.

In theory, incapacitation is not limited to prison or jail. House arrest and commitment to in-patient drug treatment programs, for example, keep offenders off the streets for the duration of their sentence. Nonincarcerative approaches may also serve the ideals of incapacitation. Newly developed Intensive Supervision Programs (ISPs) may so closely monitor offenders that it is difficult for them to continue committing crimes. Innovative devices like breath-testers, which require convicted drunk drivers to "blow clean" before starting their cars, are based on incapacitation. Prescription drugs such as antabuse serve to prevent alcoholics from drinking because they are made ill if they do. Regardless of its effectiveness, castration is an incapacitation-based attempt to prevent sexual deviants from recidivating.[2]

Some followers of incapacitation believe that a majority of crimes are committed by relatively few individuals, and argue that crime rates will go down if these few offenders are selectively incarcerated (e.g., Wilson, 1985). There is some truth to this argument. Wolfgang, Figlio, and Sellin (1972, p. 88) found that "chronic recidivists" (juveniles who had committed at least five earlier offenses) accounted for more than half of all new offenses in their Philadelphia sample. Similarly, Blumstein and Cohen (1987) found that one tenth of a sample of imprisoned robbers admitted to committing seventy or more robberies a year before being incarcerated. It appears, then, that some offenders commit crimes at a higher rate than others. It is this rationale that underlies many "three strikes and you're out" policies; unfortunately, current prediction techniques are inadequate for the task of identifying these "career criminals."

Critics of incapacitation argue that incarceration does not prevent crime; it merely relocates it to the inside of prisons. Many violent offenders continue to victimize others while in prison. And, once they are released, nothing stops them from resuming their criminal behavior. Further, inmates are introduced to new crimes, such as gang membership and smuggling ventures, that they may not have committed while in the free world.

Other critics note offenders' amazing abilities to circumvent incapacitative measures. Some offenders on house arrest find ways to leave their homes undetected. Forced prescriptions cannot work when offenders do not take them. Breath-testers installed in drunk drivers' cars cannot determine who is "blowing clean" (the offender or a friend or family member recruited to blow into the device) before igniting the ignition. Even castration does not always work; Robert Martinson (1974, p. 36) once remarked, "Where there's a will, apparently there's a way" when discussing rapes committed by castrated men. In short, incapacitation cannot work if offenders bypass their sentences. Of course, as offenders find ways to outwit their sentences, the criminal justice system is quick to refine the conditions or devices that were designed to incapacitate.

Another criticism of incapacitation is that policies such as preventive detention, which were designed to incapacitate, raise grave due process questions. Critics argue that because even the most sophisticated techniques currently available are not very accurate at predicting behavior, incapacitation policies result in the unnecessary confinement of many people who would not actually have committed a future crime. See Box 13.3 for two interview segments that illustrate incapacitation as a sentencing philosophy.

---

## BOX 13.3
### Judges' Comments on Incapacitation

*This is part of a series of five boxes that present extracts from interviews with eleven judges to illustrate each of the five sentencing philosophies. As you read the following interview segments, think about how they demonstrate incapacitation.*

Especially on . . . DUI cases, we are looking at protecting the public by suspending licenses. . . . If we have a very dangerous person, it is important that he is put somewhere so the public will be safe.

In terms of sentences, violent crimes . . . generally warrant incarceration for protection of the victims, and not only [the] victim of that crime, [but] potential victims who may testify.

---

## Retribution

**Retribution** is one of the most misunderstood punishment theories. Some people mistakenly believe that retribution, also referred to as **just deserts**, justifies *any* penalty, no matter how harsh.

Retribution is based on the concept of *lex talionis* ("an eye for an eye"). During the very earliest eras of justice, what we now call crimes were treated as private wrongs; victims or their families were allowed and expected to exact vengeance against the individuals who caused them harm (e.g., Schafer, 1977). This resulted in blood feuds, which impeded civilization's progress, so the existing system of justice was transformed into one in which offenders were tried and punished by their communities, rather than relying on informal norms of justice that had resulted in blood feuds. In many respects, punishment of offenders by the government is society's replacement of the right of the victim or the victims' family to seek vengeance (except through civil suits).

Ancient law and justice codes reflect the initial stages of this transformation and clearly illustrate the idea of "an eye for an eye." In ancient times, one who wronged someone else met with the same fate he had bestowed on his victim (e.g., knocking out the tooth of an equal meant that one's own tooth would be knocked out). Other penalties were tied to the crime itself, such as barbers who had their hands amputated for destroying a slave's markings. *Lex talionis* is best seen in the following excerpt from the Code of Hammurabi (circa 1700 B.C.):

- If a son strike his father, his hands shall be hewn off.
- If a man put out the eye of another man, his eye shall be put out.
- If he break another man's bone, his bone shall be broken.

According to retributive theory, we punish offenders to take away any advantages they might have gained from their illegal acts. Under this way of thinking, criminals deserve to be punished for the wrongs they have committed (Hawkins, 1944; Kant, 1797/1995). In fact, this is the only acceptable justification for punishment, according to retribution theory. Offenders must be guilty of the crime for which they are to be punished and may only be given the amount of punishment that they deserve (Hawkins, 1944; von Hirsch, Wasik, and Greene, 1989). It would be unacceptable, for example, to harshly penalize parking violators simply because society wants to rid itself of this problem.

Supporters of retribution argue that it is morally wrong to allow a guilty party to escape punishment (Hawkins, 1944). Plato (circa 380 B.C./1953), in his dialogue, *Gorgias,* argued that because punishment cleared the conscience that a criminal should "run to the judge, as he would to the physician, in order that the disease of injustice may not be rendered chronic" (p. 573). Punishment, then, is something to which mankind is *entitled.* To allow the guilty to avoid punishment is to deny them the dignity of choosing their actions, a dignity expressly reserved for man (Hawkins, 1944; Morris, 1968).

Retribution does not allow for the punishment of innocent parties or for the discipline of those who for some reason cannot be held responsible for their actions (Morris, 1968). The insane, for example, should not be punished for actions tied to their mental illness. Further, the crimes must result from voluntary actions (Berns, 1989). Even the ancient Code of Hammurabi recognized that some people would commit crimes for which they should not be punished (e.g., unintentional injuries caused during a quarrel were not punished if the offender paid the victim's physician's fees).

By punishing offenders, we restore the balance society seeks and satisfy society's desire for revenge (Berns, 1989; Hawkins, 1944). Criminals have misappropriated society's benefits for themselves and have thus gained an "unfair advantage" over law-abiding citizens (Morris, 1968). Punishment based on retribution removes that advantage and attempts to restore balance to society, while establishing proper parameters of behavior (Grupp, 1971, pp. 5–6). Adherents of retribution theory assert that, in some respects, offenders punished under retribution undergo a limited form of rehabilitation. Punishing "bad" people for misconduct places their activities outside the boundaries of what "good" people do. When offenders realize that they have done wrong and deserve their punishment, they "ought to amend [themselves] accordingly" (Hawkins, 1944, p. 206).

Critics of retribution argue that "just deserts" is outdated, that as a civilized society, we have moved beyond the need for simple vengeance. And, punishing some people simply because they have done wrong does not address the underlying problem. These critics argue that withholding necessary treatment from offenders is not the solution to crime.

Other critics argue that it is impossible to set up a satisfactory punishment scale. While it is easy to say that offenders should receive no more punishment than they deserve, how much do they deserve? Such scales, once created, cannot

---

**BOX 13.4**

**Judges' Comments on Retribution**

*This is part of a series of five boxes that present extracts from interviews with eleven judges to illustrate each of the five sentencing philosophies. As you read the following interview segments, think about how they demonstrate retribution.*

[Regarding factors used in sentencing]: Way down the line, but it's there and hopefully it doesn't happen very often, is just vengeance. This asshole has beaten up on fifteen different girlfriends and you don't want him to do it again, but you want to hurt him, too, because he's an asshole. I'd say that's true only where someone has inflicted physical pain on someone else. Then, you want that victim to know you couldn't horsewhip the son-of-a-bitch, but you gave him a horsewhip sentence. . . . I don't like people who hurt people who are physically less strong than they are. And hammering someone in that situation may be a deterrent, but probably not, but it feels good. You have to admit it; it just does. If you read about some outrageous behavior in some news article and something bad happens to the actor, it kind of makes you feel warm inside. Vengeance isn't just the Lord's. We all have it. Not a need for it necessarily, but we all like to feel that the rascal got what was coming to him. And, we all hope the price is painful enough that it might deter him, but whether it does or not, he got what was coming to him.

[Regarding sentencing philosophy]: Since it's a misdemeanor, it's not going to be in the paper, [so] no one is going to read about it and it's not going to deter other people except [those] in the courtroom. . . . My primary concern is the person before me, that this person get punished appropriately for what they did, and their background and the whole picture of this person.

---

take into account offenders' differing roles and motivations in offenses. In short, retribution-based policies do not recognize as different the actions of thieves who steal bread to feed their families and thieves who steal to feed their illicit drug habits. At the heart of retribution is a sense of deservedness that requires individualized sentencing that recognizes offenders' differing culpabilities. See Box 13.4 for two interview segments that illustrate retribution as a sentencing philosophy.

## Restoration

**Restorative justice** is by no means a new philosophy. In fact, it is "as old or older" than retribution. In ancient times, crimes were considered violations of other people. It was not until the twelfth century that offenses took on a new meaning, that of crimes against the king or government (Umbreit, 1994, p. 1). Before this time, punishment served retributive and restorative functions.

It was around 1116 that King Henry I redefined offenses as crimes against the king or government by declaring in his *Leges Henrici* that the crown should be compensated for crimes because offenders had breached "the king's peace" (Stubbs, 1900, 1906). This important distinction meant that the king was entitled to the compensation that was once given to victims. To that existing system of restitution, King Henry I appended the notion of fines payable to the king as head of government; this supplementary sanction made offenders responsible for both restitution and fines. As time progressed, however, fines began to replace restitution in toto. Victims of crime were still entitled to sue for damages, but otherwise lost out on automatic restitution that was once standard. With King Henry I's interventions (he also established a system of sheriffs and justices of the peace whose duties were to oversee the crown's interest in criminal sanctions), the government began to have a vested interest in justice outcomes. As those interests became normal, restoration began to fade as the dominant justice policy.

Returning to the Code of Hammurabi (circa 1700 B.C.), we can see how some penalties were designed to try to make victims whole again through payments. If a building collapsed due to poor workmanship, the architect was expected to replace any slaves who were killed or any goods that were destroyed. Many harms were translated into specific monetary payments to be made to the victims, as in the payment of ten shekels if a "freed man strike the body of another freed man." Careless crop watering usually meant paying for any damages, as in the following passages:

- If any one open his ditches to water his crop, but is careless, and the water flood the field of his neighbor, then he shall pay his neighbor corn for his loss.
- If a man let in the water, and the water overflow the plantation of his neighbor, he shall pay ten gur of corn for every ten gan of land.

Under restorative justice, we return to the concept of crime as a violation of another person. The victim, then, becomes central to the sentencing process. Instead of punishing criminals, the intent of restorative justice is to "restore" victims through restitution in the form of money or service. Sometimes, offenders are asked to "undo" their crimes, as in the case of juveniles ordered to remove graffiti. Other offenders are ordered to make symbolic restitution through community service.

Restoration also seeks to restore offenders. Through restoration of the victim, the offender "makes good" on his crime and restores himself to his pre-crime status. Sometimes, the two parties are brought together in victim–offender mediation sessions where together they design a restitution plan (Umbreit, 1994). It is during these sessions that victims can be returned to a sense of safety as the offender describes why a particular victim was targeted; generally, the selection of a victim involves a pragmatic choice by the offender (e.g., burglarizing the first house without cars in the driveway) versus a clear case of stalking or following as many victims believe to be the case.

Perhaps an example will clarify how restoration occurs when offenders undo the specific harm they caused. Some years ago, a retired police officer caught a group of teens spray-painting one of the buildings on his property. He was more frustrated than furious when he caught them, because of the expense and time he would have to take to fix the damage, which was visible from the street. But instead of attacking the youths, he asked if they would be willing to paint over their graffiti with a mural of his choosing. Possibly skeptical at first, the kids still agreed to do so, and the mural was enjoyed by the retired officer and all who drove past until the paint was faded by the sun and elements. The victim in this case was happy with the outcome and his new mural, and the kids gained the satisfaction of knowing that they had "done good" for a local community member and learned that their artwork would be appreciated if it was limited to appropriate situations. Most importantly, however, under restorative justice, the victim was made whole again and the youths were able to undo their criminal acts and regain their status in the community as nondelinquents. In this case, of course, the harm was easily repaired, and some critics of restoration argue that "undoing" other offenses, especially crimes of violence, is much harder to accomplish. To those critics, some restorative justice policymakers counter that the principles they advocate have been successfully implemented even in homicides.

Other critics of restoration complain that ordering offenders to pay their victims does not make them whole. Instead, it teaches us that every crime has a dollar value, and that mere financial payments can restore victims. Victims of violent crimes often complain that restitution payments, usually paid at a rate of a few dollars a week, do not make up for their losses in dignity or feelings of safety. Sometimes, victims protest that such schemas can readily return offenders to their pre-crime status, but cannot really make bona fide breakthroughs in restoring victims to that same plateau.

Others complain that the program only works for a few offenders. That is, that some criminals will continue to victimize others unless there are penalties in addition to returning what they have taken or reimbursing individuals for their out-of-pocket expenses. These critics complain that restitution alone lets criminals off lightly, and may teach offenders that crime has little cost. See Box 13.5 for two interview segments that illustrate restoration as a sentencing philosophy.

## AVAILABLE SANCTIONS

No matter what the sentencing agent's preference or what the stated punishment philosophy is, the endorsed sanction must be available before it can be imposed on any offender. A judge, for example, may feel a certain offender requires intensive

---

## BOX 13.5
## Judges' Comments on Restoration

*This is the last of five boxes that present extracts from interviews with eleven judges to illustrate each of the five sentencing philosophies. As you read the following interview segments, think about how they demonstrate restoration.*

I don't think we do rehabilitation on a local level. . . . In the cases where I put them [offenders] on probation, then the purpose that I do have in mind is either to provide restitution for a victim who has been damaged or to force the defendant to be subject to some stricter rules.

[The concept of] nalyeeh[3] is not necessarily property or money; it's what you can do to redeem yourself. [*(Interviewer questions are in italics) So, "that which is necessary"?*] If you say, "Okay, I will go to counseling and at the next squaw dance [i.e., traditional ceremonial gathering], I will make a public apology to you," you know that is my way of redeeming myself. [*Therefore, an agreement to go into counseling and the speech at the squaw dance could be nalyeeh?*] Yes; then I say, "Okay, now I feel better now. You understand what you did and now I know what you are going to go for. We won't expect this problem any more." [*What if I volunteered to cut wood for an elder? Would that be nalyeeh, too?*] Yes, it would be something you do for somebody to make them feel right or what they say [to] set things right. [*So, if I hurt you, I could cut someone's wood near (here)?*] Yeah, or I might have you cut wood for all the squaw dances for the summer. [*That's a lot of woodcutting*] . . . To a big degree, the size of the nalyeeh would be set to where a [victim] feels comfortable that it [i.e., the offending behavior] is not going to happen again and they are [at] ease. I know that a lot of times, judges will say nalyeeh means money and I will say, "No, not from where I was raised. It was different things.". . . The main idea was harmony, . . . to restore that feeling and also to restore the harmony of the family and of the community.

*The first ten interviews (including all of those from the previous four boxes) were with municipal court judges in California. The final extract is from an interview with a criminal court judge of the Navajo Nation. A number of Native American tribes have returned to their restorative justice roots. The Navajo Nation operates a Peacemaking Court that relies on the use of traditional justice methods to restore harmony to individuals, families, and communities. In peacemaking, victims and offenders meet with a mutually chosen peacemaker to discuss how to "undo" the harms suffered by victims and how to prevent future harms from occurring. The program is successful and enjoys a low recidivism rate. (Yazzie and Zion, 1996, pp. 170–172)*

---

therapeutic intervention, but if there are no programs available or no funds to pay for such programs, the judge will have to choose another sentence.

Before the twentieth century, punishments were quite harsh, even for minor offenses. Penalties tended to be **corporal** (i.e., physical and applied to the body, such as whippings), and were sometimes gruesome by today's standards of decency. Prehistoric sanctions tended to rely on banishment or ritualistic executions to placate any gods who would be angry about the broken norm. These penalties were designed to remove the offender from society so that the gods would not bring unfavorable conditions to the rest of the society due to harboring the norm-breaker.

Early European sanctions typically fell into one of four general classifications: humiliatory, corporal, death, or exile. Humiliatory penalties were used for minor offenses and included the cucking stool (i.e., offenders were seated at their own front doors to expose them to ridicule); branks (which were odd contraptions that fit over one's head, usually used for women who scolded their husbands or who spread rumors); stocks and pillories; the jougs (which were iron collars fastened around offenders' necks to hold them on a platform); drunkards' cloaks (barrels worn by habitual drunks); scarlet letters (e.g., those worn by adulterers such as Hester Prynne in Hawthorne's *The Scarlet Letter*); riding the stang (a curious penalty often reserved for domestic abusers in which the offender was paraded through town seated on a donkey or other beast of burden while townspeople followed beating pots and pans and blowing horns and singing poems about the abuses the offender heaped on the victim); and other penalties designed to shame offenders into conforming with societal norms (Andrews, 1890/1991).

More serious crimes demanded harsher sentences. Corporal penalties were also common and included whipping, branding, boring of the offender's tongue, cutting off an offender's ears, and other bodily penalties. Legal decision-makers in early Europe were also quite fond of slow, painful executions of a variety of styles, sometimes preceded by torture. One reason penalties were so harsh was the belief that crime and disorder stemmed from the devil's influence, and must be punished harshly (see Box 13.6 for an illustration from 1616 that shows the presumed influence of the devil on a woman who killed her two children, aged two and five). And, for those who were adjudged incorrigible, what better penalty than to exile them to the New World or other colonies that needed citizens?

Fortunately far from our historical roots, today's judges tend to impose financial and supervision-oriented sanctions. Discussed below are several sanctions, including noncustodial, custodial, and other punishments.

## Financial Penalties: Fines and Restitution

**Fines** involve paying a sum of money to the government after breaking a law. Fines have been used for a long time and were originally a way to raise money for the British Crown. Now, a certain portion of fines is sometimes earmarked for special accounts, such as victims' compensation funds, in addition to supplementing road construction accounts, general welfare monies, and similar government resources. Most individuals have paid fines for parking tickets and other minor offenses. In the lower courts, fines are the most frequently applied sanction (Lindquist, 1988, p. 26; Mileski, 1971, p. 501, President's Commission Task Force Report on the Courts,

BOX 13.6

## The Devil and Margret Vincent

This 1616 illustration, taken from the cover of a leaflet that discussed the infanticides committed by Margret Vincent, demonstrates clearly the belief held by individuals of that time that Satan influenced those who were not strong in their Christian faith to commit crimes. The publication mentions that she was "assisted by the Devill" and that she was "more cruell than the Viper, the invenomd Serpent, the Snake, or any Beast whatsoever" (Anonymous, 1616, p. 4).

Transport yourself back in time to the early 1600s. How should we sentence someone who acts at the behest of the devil and does his "evil" bidding by strangling her own children with cordage provided by Satan himself? Only the harshest sentences were considered acceptable in order to deal with this omnipresent and diabolic force.

FIGURE 13.3  *Source:* Anonymous, 1616 (cover).

1967, p. 18). Felony courts also impose fines, although far less often (Eisenstein and Jacob, 1977, p. 274). Federal courts nearly always impose some form of fine.

Borrowing an idea from Europe, a few American jurisdictions have begun to experiment with **day fines**. This special type of fine is adjusted to the offender's ability to pay (Winterfield and Hillsman, 1993). The way they work is simple in theory, but hard to put into practice. Each criminal violation is assigned a value in day-fine units. Let us assume for the purposes of illustration that shoplifting is assigned a day-fine unit value of three days, and that Joe and Joanne each shoplift a CD from a music store and are fined three day-fine units. Joe makes $30 a day at his job, so his fine would be $90. Joanne makes $50 a day at her job, so her fine would be $150.[4] The reasoning behind fining the different offenders different amounts is that Joe and Joanne should feel the same effects on their pocketbooks. Just because Joanne has a higher paying job should not mean that she has to work fewer days to make the money to pay her fine.

Of course, this can mean extremely high fines for minor offenses when laws are violated by very wealthy individuals. When Nokia executive vice president Anssa Vanjoki was caught going 15 miles above the speed limit in Helsinki, Finland, he was assessed a $103,000 fine, and Internet entrepreneur Jaakko Rytsola was ordered to pay a $74,600 traffic fine (Turula, 2002). The reason the fines were so high is that the jurisdiction relies on day fines and the two mens' incomes topped several million dollars a year.[5]

Sometimes confused with fines is **restitution,** because both result in offenders paying money out of their pockets. Restitution differs from fines, however, in that it is paid to the victim, typically as part of an attempt to achieve restorative justice. Because the payments are often made through the court or probation office, offenders may feel they are simply paying a higher fine. Restitution is supposed to reimburse victims for damages or for medical and counseling expenses they incur due to the offenses, or for other costs associated with being victimized. Some victims are reimbursed for the time they had to take off work and for daycare costs for their children while they attended hearings. Some offenders, especially juveniles, are assigned to work for the person or business they victimized. One young man, for example, found himself cleaning a bookstore's bathrooms every weekend for a year when he was caught shoplifting valuable comic books.

## Community Service

Prior to 1971, indigent offenders who had been ordered to pay fines were jailed, hence the old adage "thirty dollars or thirty days." The U.S. Supreme Court ruling *Tate v. Short* (1971), however, outlawed that practice so that only offenders who could afford fines but refused to pay them could be sent to jail for nonpayment. *Tate v. Short* meant that an alternative sanction had to be utilized for indigent offenders and community service filled that need. Those sentenced to **community service** are assigned to work without compensation for various nonprofit or governmental agencies. Typical community service placement sites include charities, schools, parks, and programs that service youths or elders (Meeker, Jesilow, and Aranda, 1992, p. 200). Through the work they provide, offenders make symbolic restitution to the community they harmed by their criminal actions. Community service had been used on a fairly consistent basis since the 1960s but increased in popularity after *Tate v. Short.* This type of sentence has been called a panacea by some because there are many benefits associated with community service: jail overcrowding is minimized, the offender may learn basic work skills or discipline, and the community benefits from the labor of the offender (Klein, 1988, pp. 173–78). The work completed by these offenders is useful to the placement agencies; for example, estimates of the value of the work provided by community service workers assigned to work for the California Transit Authority in just two counties in California (Los Angeles and Ventura) indicate that they provide free labor worth more than $30 million a year (Webber and Nikos, 1992).

## Probation

**Probation** is another common sanction used for both misdemeanors and felonies. Probation owes its development to retired Boston shoemaker John Augustus, who in 1841 asked a local judge to assign a drunk to him for supervision and education in the trade of making shoes. Instead of jailing the drunk, the judge agreed to let Augustus try his hand at reformation. Augustus' intervention was successful so the court assigned him to work with more drunks. Those humble beginnings set the stage for the popularity of probation—a sanction that now applies to more than three million offenders (Bonczar and Glaze, 1999).

Unlike other sanctions, probation is "not designed to provide punishment" (McDonald, 1992, p. 189). Instead, its goal is rehabilitation of offenders through a combination of supervision and assistance through social programs. As evidence of the push for programming, 41 percent of all probationers in 1996 were ordered into drug or alcohol treatment as a condition of their receiving probation (Bonczar, 1997). Offenders of all types receive probation terms, even violent offenders. In fact, more than half (57 percent) of those who are put on probation were convicted of a felony (Bonczar and Glaze, 1999), and one in 100 homicide offenders receives probation (Bonczar, 1997). The major dilemma faced by probation departments across the nation is staff shortages, which affect their ability to supervise and rehabilitate offenders (Wice, 1985, p. 22). See Figure 13.1 for a graph showing trends in the use of probation, parole, and incarceration.

There are several forms of probation. The first, **informal probation**, can be just that—very informal. Sometimes, offenders are only told to avoid future involvement in crime and are required to mail in monthly postcards so their probation officers can keep track of them. Individuals on informal probation may only encounter problems if they end up back in court, at which time they may face additional penalties. The second form, **regular probation**, involves more supervision, usually regular in-person visits and telephone contacts in addition to periodic unannounced visits to the offender's home or workplace. Regular probation often involves mandated programming that is tailored to the offender's specific needs (e.g., completion of substance abuse programs or personal counseling). As caseloads have increased, however, probation officers have found themselves with less

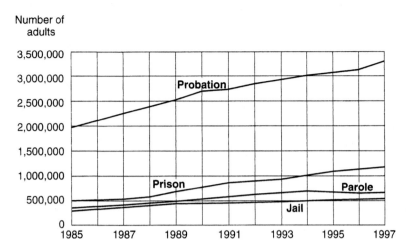

**FIGURE 13.1 Trends in the use of probation, parole, jail, and prison**   *Source:* Bureau of Justice Statistics, 1997, p. iii.

and less time to devote to supervision, meaning that many probationers get little individualized attention.

In response to the criticisms that probation is a "slap on the wrist" that does not work because large caseloads prevent probation officers from supervising their clients, a number of jurisdictions have developed **intensive supervision programs** (**ISPs**). In addition to increased contact with probation officers, these programs typically include rigorous conditions (e.g., routine and/or random drug testing). Sometimes, ISP is combined with day reporting services to ensure that high-risk offenders receive programming they need coupled with the supervision the community deserves. True to its being designed primarily as a rehabilitation program, stakeholders in one survey reported that the most important purpose of day reporting services was to provide offenders with access to the treatment services they need to prevent their return to crime (Latessa et al., 1998, pp. 12–13).[6] Evaluations of the effectiveness of ISPs are inconclusive, however; when compared to traditional probation, some ISP programs appear to reduce recidivism while others may actually increase it (Gowdy, 1993, p. 5). The increased recidivism for ISP participants, however, may be strongly related to the increased attention and supervision such offenders are given; the more regular contact and more consistent drug tests certainly net some crimes that could easily escape detection in an informal or regular probation setting. ISP is often augmented with electronic monitoring, as discussed below.

## Custodial Sentences (Incarceration and Home Confinement)

There are also custodial sentences, including prison and jail. **Prisons** are state operated (or federally operated for federal offenses) and only those convicted of felonies may be sent to prison. The history of prison is interesting. In early Rome (A.D. 533), it was illegal to imprison offenders after conviction—only those awaiting trial could be held in detention facilities. England's use of prisons was mainly limited to debtor's prisons where those who owed debts were held until the arrears were satisfied (a strong incentive for one's family to meet the financial obligation!). Prison as a sentence for crimes (rather than a holding place for those awaiting trial or execution) was strongly advocated by the famous Quaker reformer, William Penn, in 1682. It is important to recognize that until the seventeenth century, penalties were very harsh and many offenses resulted in execution. Penn felt that imprisoning offenders was more humane than executing them; he argued instead that they could be housed in facilities where they could read the Bible and reform themselves. After Penn died in 1718, there was regression back to corporal sanctions and executions, but the Quakers lobbied the legislature and a law was passed in 1776 allowing imprisonment for all crimes except murder, rape, treason, and arson.

The first prison in America, the Walnut Street Jail, was established in 1790 in Philadelphia and emphasized penitence and solitary confinement. This approach (i.e., stimulus deprivation, or the privations of solitary confinement twenty-four hours a day) drove several inmates insane, so the practices were abandoned in favor of those that allowed silent interaction with other inmates in common work areas. Now, there more than two million prisoners in the United States alone, leading some to comment on the "prisonization of America." Overcrowding is a major factor that limits use of prison as a sanction. See Figure 13.1 for a graph showing trends in the use of probation, parole, and incarceration.

Instead of prison, those who are convicted of misdemeanors may be sent to **jail**. Jails are locally operated by counties, and are usually for sentences of less than one year.[7] Because they operate within the counties they serve, jails are more flexible than prisons so that offenders may receive **weekend sentences** (i.e., where offenders serve their time on the weekends but are released during the week), or **work release** or **study release** sentences (i.e., where offenders are incarcerated at night but may work or go to school during the day). Jails are also overcrowded, limiting their use as a sentence. See Figure 13.2 in Box 13.7 for a graph showing a ten-year breakdown of jail and prison sentences.

A special form of custodial sentence is **home detention**, a sanction that, as of the mid-1980s, is increasingly coupled with **electronic monitoring** (Renzema and Skelton, 1990). In fact, Gowdy (1993, p. 5) argues that home confinement may be enjoying a new popularity because the availability of electronic monitoring is believed to make the sanction "practical and affordable." Electronic monitoring, rumored to have been invented by Stan Lee for use in a Spiderman comic,[8] involves offenders wearing electronic anklets or wristlets that alert supervisory authorities if they leave their homes. Although not everyone feels electronic monitoring is a panacea, they still see it as appropriate for certain offenders, such as

# BOX 13.7

## Graph Showing a Ten-Year Breakdown of Jail and Prison Sentences

From year-end 1990 to midyear 2000, the nation's prisons and jails grew by 783,157 inmates, an annual increase of 5.6 percent.

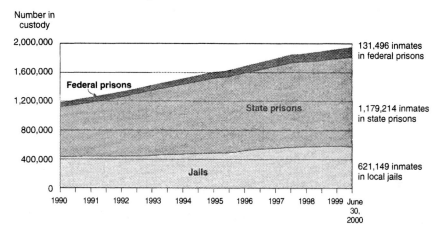

FIGURE 13.2

### From year-end 1990 to midyear 2000:

- The rate of incarceration in prison and jail increased from 1 in every 218 U.S. residents to 1 in every 142.

- State, federal, and local governments had to accommodate an additional 82,438 inmates per year (or the equivalent of 1,585 new inmates per week).

### In the year ending June 30, 2000:

- The number of inmates held in jail rose by 15,206, in state prison by 27,953, and in federal prison by 13,501. In the three largest state prison systems, the number dropped in California (down 33 inmates) and New York (down 2,269 inmates), while it rose in Texas (up 890 inmates).

### On June 30, 2000:

- Privately operated prison facilities held 76,010 inmates (up 9.1 percent since year-end 1999).

- Local jails were operating 8 percent below their rated capacity. In contrast, at year-end 1999 state prisons were between 1 percent and 17 percent above capacity, and federal prisons were 32 percent above their rated capacity.

- An estimated 12 percent of black males, 4 percent of Hispanic males, and 1.7 percent of white males in their twenties and early thirties were in prison or jail.

- There were 110 female inmates per 100,000 women in the United States, compared to 1,297 male inmates per 100,000 men.

*Source:* Beck and Karberg, 2001, p. 1.

those who are severely ill, disabled, or whose presence in their home is essential to others. Said one lower court judge about the sanction:

> You gonna ask me about my favorite topic, which is electronic confinement? . . . You know what I call it? Commit-a-crime-go-to-your-room. No, I don't like it. No, I don't do it. I have used it quite frequently with people who are extremely ill; I've used it with a lot of AIDS patients.

## Creative Sanctions

In addition to the customary penalties, there are a number of creative sanctions employed by judges who are frustrated with the inability to fashion appropriate responses from available sentencing options. Creative sentences involve such sanctions as ordering doctors to perform medical services at a free clinic, having business owners give lectures or mentor minority businesses to help their companies survive, directing offenders to establish organizations or funds, ordering drunk drivers to install breathalyzers in their cars to prevent them from driving drunk, and requiring offenders to write letters of apology or essays. There was even a judge who sentenced a man who starved his dog to death to live on bread and water alone for a weekend.

A number of innovative penalties focus on embarrassment or shame, such as requiring drunk drivers to display bumper stickers on their cars identifying them as such, or ordering people to make public apologies for the harm they have caused. Some judges now hope to "remind" offenders of the harm they have perpetrated by ordering them to carry pictures of those they have killed in drunk-driving accidents or to pay $1.00 a month to the victim.

Creative penalties tend to be imposed either in special cases or by judges who make a hobby of innovative sanctioning. One famous judge who designs and imposes creative sanctions is Judge Ted Poe, who has served as a criminal court judge in Houston, Texas, since 1981. His sentences have included public apologies delivered from the city hall steps, offenders carrying signs to apologize to businesses they have victimized, mandated signs posted on child molesters' lawns explaining that no children are allowed on their property, and a hairdresser who was ordered to give free haircuts at centers that serve the disabled (Connelly, 1999). See Box 13.8 for some other creative sanctions.

## The Death Penalty

The most severe penalty that can be applied by any court is the **death penalty**. Although it is allowed in thirty-eight states, it is relatively uncommon. Despite this rarity, however, the death penalty has strong symbolic value and affects plea bargains and defendants' decisions to seek trial by jury.

---

## BOX 13.8
## A Few Creative Sanctions Imposed During February, 1998

*As you read about these three sentences, all imposed during February of 1998, think of the sentencing philosophies each could address. Some of the sentences illustrate more than one sentencing philosophy.*

*Man must carry photo of victim* (2/11/98, Associated Press)
A twenty-one-year-old Oklahoma man who killed a young woman when his vehicle crashed into another automobile was sentenced to carry the victim's photo with him for a year in addition to serving 20 days in jail. He was not under the influence of drugs or alcohol at the time of the accident, but had run a stop sign, so he pled guilty to negligent homicide. The victim's mother had requested that he be ordered to carry her photograph.

*Man ordered to post DUI sticker* (2/21/98, Associated Press)
After serving a five day jail sentence and losing his driver's license for drunk driving, a 36-year-old Kansas man with multiple priors for drunk driving requested that a judge reinstate his license. The judge agreed and told him he could get his driver's license back in a few months if he complied with an interesting condition: he had to put a "bright" red-and-orange sticker on the rear window of his car that said "Convicted DUI." The judge told him that he faced a year in jail if he removed the sticker.

*Thief ordered to send birthday card* (2/22/98, Associated Press)
When a twenty-year-old Pennsylvania man stole a stereo system out of a car he had broken into, he was arrested for that crime and several others. After he had pled guilty to theft, receiving stolen property, and conspiracy to commit theft, the judge noticed that the automobile break-in occurred on her birthday. So he would not quickly forget the crime, she ordered him to send her a birthday card for two years in addition to paying restitution to his victims and completing twenty-three months of probation.

---

At present, there are five methods of executing those convicted of capital offenses. The most common method, by far, is lethal injection. The remaining methods are electrocution, lethal gas, hanging, and firing squad. See Table 13.1 for a breakdown of execution methods. In the vast majority of states, defendants must be charged with murder to even face the death penalty, but a few states allow capital punishment for other offenses. See Table 13.2 for a list of offenses that qualify for the death penalty.

**TABLE 13.1    Method of Execution, by State, 1999**

| Lethal injection | | Electrocution | Lethal gas | Hanging | Firing squad |
|---|---|---|---|---|---|
| Arizona[a,b] | New Hampshire[a] | Alabama | Arizona[a,b] | Delaware[a,c] | Idaho[a] |
| Arkansas[a,d] | New Jersey | Arkansas[a,d] | California[a] | New Hampshire[a,e] | Oklahoma[f] |
| California[a] | New Mexico | Florida | Missouri[a] | Washington[a] | Utah[a] |
| Colorado | New York | Georgia | Wyoming[a,g] | | |
| Connecticut | North Carolina | Kentucky[a,h] | | | |
| Delaware[a,c] | Ohio[a] | Nebraska | | | |
| Idaho[a] | Oklahoma[a] | Ohio[a] | | | |
| Illinois | Oregon | Oklahoma[f] | | | |
| Indiana | Pennsylvania | South Carolina[a] | | | |
| Kansas | South Carolina[a] | Tennessee[a,i] | | | |
| Kentucky[a,g] | South Dakota | Virginia[a] | | | |
| Louisiana | Tennessee[a,i] | | | | |
| Maryland | Texas | | | | |
| Mississippi | Utah[a] | | | | |
| Missouri[a] | Virginia[a] | | | | |
| Montana | Washington[a] | | | | |
| Nevada | Wyoming[a] | | | | |

Note: The method of execution of Federal prisoners is lethal injection, pursuant to 28 CFR, Part 26. For offenses under the Violent Crime Control and Law Enforcement Act of 1994, the method is that of the state in which the conviction took place, pursuant to 18 U.S.C. 3596.

[a] Authorizes 2 methods of execution.

[b] Arizona authorizes lethal injection for persons whose capital sentence was received after 11/15/92; for those sentences before that date, the condemned may select lethal injection or lethal gas.

[c] Delaware authorizes lethal injection for those whose capital offense occurred after 6/13/86; for those whose offense occurred before that date, the condemned may select lethal injection or hanging.

[d] Arkansas authorizes lethal injection for those whose capital offense occurred on or after 7/4/83; for those whose offense occurred before that date, the condemned may select lethal injection or electrocution.

[e] New Hampshire authorizes hanging only if lethal injection cannot be given.

[f] Oklahoma authorizes electrocution if lethal injection is ever held to be unconstitutional, and firing squad if both lethal injection and electrocution are held unconstitutional.

[g] Wyoming authorizes lethal gas if lethal injection is ever held to be unconstitutional.

[h] Kentucky authorizes lethal injection for persons whose capital sentence was received on or after 3/31/98; for those sentenced before that date, the condemned may select lethal injection or electrocution.

[i] Tennessee authorizes lethal injection for those whose capital offense occurred after 12/31/98; those whose offense occurred before that date may select lethal injection or electrocution.

*Source:* Snell, 2000, p. 5.

## TABLE 13.2 Capital Offenses, by State, 1999

**Alabama.** Capital murder with a finding of at least 1 of 10 aggravating circumstances (Ala. Code § 13A-5-40 and § 13A-5-49).

**Arizona.** First-degree murder accompanied by at least 1 of 10 aggravating factors.

**Arkansas.** Capital murder (Ark. Code Ann. 5-10-101) with a finding of at least 1 of 10 aggravating circumstances; treason.

**California.** First-degree murder with special circumstances; train wrecking; treason; perjury causing execution.

**Colorado.** First-degree murder with at least 1 of 14 aggravating factors; treason. Capital sentencing excludes persons determined to be mentally retarded.

**Connecticut.** Capital felony with 9 categories of aggravated homicide (C.G.S. 53a-54b).

**Delaware.** First-degree murder with aggravating circumstances.

**Florida.** First-degree murder; felony murder; capital drug trafficking.

**Georgia.** Murder; kidnaping with bodily injury or ransom where the victim dies; aircraft hijacking; treason.

**Idaho.** First-degree murder; aggravated kidnaping.

**Illinois.** First-degree murder with 1 of 15 aggravating circumstances.

**Indiana.** Murder with 16 aggravating circumstances (IC 35-50-2-9). Capital sentencing excludes persons determined to be mentally retarded.

**Kansas.** Capital murder with 7 aggravating circumstances (KSA 21-3439). Capital sentencing excludes persons determined to be mentally retarded.

**Kentucky.** Murder with aggravating factors; kidnaping with aggravating factors.

**Louisiana.** First-degree murder; aggravated rape of victim under age 12; treason (La. R.S. 14:30, 14:42, and 14:113).

**Maryland.** First-degree murder, either premeditated or during the commission of a felony, provided that certain death eligibility requirements are satisfied.

**Mississippi.** Capital murder (97-3-19(2) MCA); aircraft piracy (97-25-55(1) MCA).

**Missouri.** First-degree murder (565.020 RSMO).

**Montana.** Capital murder with 1 of 9 aggravating circumstances (46-18-303 MCA); capital sexual assault (45-5-503 MCA).

**Nebraska.** First-degree murder with a finding of at least 1 statutorily-defined aggravating circumstance.

**Nevada.** First-degree murder with 14 aggravating circumstances.

**New Hampshire.** Six categories of capital murder (RSA 630:1 and RSA 630:5).

**New Jersey.** Purposeful or knowing murder by one's own conduct; contract murder; solicitation by command or threat in furtherance of a narcotics conspiracy (NJSA 2C:11-3C).

**New Mexico.** First-degree murder in conjunction with a finding of at least 1 of 7 aggravating circumstances (Section 30-2-1 A, NMSA).

**New York.** First-degree murder with 1 of 12 aggravating factors. Capital sentencing excludes persons determined to be mentally retarded.

**North Carolina.** First-degree murder (N.C.G.S. 14-17).

**Ohio.** Aggravated murder with at least 1 of 8 aggravating circumstances. (O.R.C. secs. 2903.01, 2929.01, and 2929.04).

**Oklahoma.** First-degree murder in conjunction with a finding of at least 1 of 8 statutorily defined aggravating circumstances.

**Oregon.** Aggravated murder (ORS 163.095).

**Pennsylvania.** First-degree murder with 18 aggravating circumstances.

**South Carolina.** Murder with 1 of 10 aggravating circumstances (§ 16-3-20(C)(a)). Mental retardation is a mitigating factor.

---

**TABLE 13.2    Capital Offenses, by State, 1999 *(continued)***

---

**South Dakota.** First-degree murder with 1 of 10 aggravating circumstances; aggravated kidnaping.

**Tennessee.** First-degree murder.

**Texas.** Criminal homicide with 1 of 8 aggravating circumstances (TX Penal Code 19.03).

**Utah.** Aggravated murder (76-5-202, Utah Code annotated).

**Virginia.** First-degree murder with 1 of 12 aggravating circumstances (VA Code § 18.2-31).

**Washington.** Aggravated first-degree murder.

**Wyoming.** First-degree murder.

---

*Source:* Snell, 2000, p. 3.

The death penalty is by far the most controversial sanction available on the sentencing palette. Those who support it argue that it has a strong deterrent value, and often cite research by Isaac Ehrlich (1975) whose research found that every execution in the United States resulted in "7 or 8 fewer murders" (p. 414). However his study has been criticized by many scholars (e.g., for incorrectly using statistics) and other research has found no reductions in homicide associated with use of the death penalty (e.g., Lempert, 1983; Sellin, 1959). Other death penalty supporters focus on the cost savings over imprisoning offenders for life in prison, but those individuals do not take into consideration the significant cost of appeals. Yet a third group of supporters argues that murderers deserve to die; this retribution-based argument is supported by surveys of the general population.

On the other side of the coin are those who oppose the death penalty, who cite the irreversibility of the penalty—the execution of an innocent person cannot be "undone." One research team (Bedau and Radelet, 1987) examined capital cases between 1900 and 1985 and found that an innocent person had been convicted in 350 cases and that 139 of those parties were given the death sentence; of those 139 innocent individuals, twenty-three were executed. Of course, it is expected that some errors will creep into the justice system, but even one wrongfully executed person a year is considered to be too many by death penalty opponents. The now famous Innocence Project started by Barry Scheck and Peter Neufeld in 1992 at the Cardozo Law School (at Yeshiva University in New York) has responded to requests from thousands of inmates who seek their assistance in proving their innocence; the Project has successfully demonstrated the innocence of a number of convicts by relying on testing of DNA evidence found at crime scenes. The work by the Innocence Project and its fellow projects have clearly demonstrated that at least some convictions were wrongful, casting doubt on many others.

A second camp of death penalty opponents argues that the death penalty itself is cruel and unusual punishment, and that modern standards of decency prove the death penalty to be archaic, but polls of the public show that many citizens continue to support the death penalty despite any evolving standards. A third camp of opponents notes that the penalty is discriminatory because blacks are more likely than whites to receive death and those who kill whites (versus blacks) are more likely to get the death penalty, as is discussed below. Supporters of the death penalty counter this argument by pointing out that those whose crimes are more heinous deserve the death penalty, and blacks may commit more violent crimes (e.g., Green, 1964).

The death penalty has undergone quite a legal battle, and several cases from the past few decades have nearly eradicated it. The first of those legal challenges was the 1968 decision rendered in *Witherspoon v. Illinois.* The defense in the *Witherspoon* case argued that the defendant's death penalty jury was biased because people who had indicated that they had any objection to the death penalty were excluded from the jury under an Illinois law that allowed challenges for cause "of any juror who shall, on being examined, state that he has conscientious scruples

A belief in divine intervention may have encouraged some early jurists to impose harsh sentences, because the innocent were expected to be rescued by divine intervention. Truly innocent people could even be saved from execution. When Anne Greene was "miraculously" revived in 1650 after being taken down from the scaffold from which she was hung for killing her newborn, a contemporary scholar argued that she must certainly have been innocent because she had been prevented from dying; that she truly had not known she was pregnant and had delivered a stillborn child, as she had claimed at trial (Watkins, 1651). Similarly, this early 1500s English wall painting in Winchester Cathedral shows the Virgin Mary supporting Ebbo on the scaffold. Sentenced to die for a crime he did not commit, Ebbo's death was prevented by the divine Virgin who held him up for three days to demonstrate his innocence. The Virgin and other divine beings are also credited with restoring unjustly amputated hands and intercepting in a multitude of wrongfully imposed death sentences. SOURCE: Courtesy of Jon'a Meyer.

against capital punishment, or that he is opposed to the same." Using that law, the prosecution had eliminated "nearly half" of the potential jurors (1968, p. 512). The defense felt this was unfair because those who support the death penalty were both more likely to vote "guilty" and were more likely to impose the death penalty.

The Supreme Court agreed with Witherspoon that it was unfair to have a **penalty phase jury** (the jury that decides between imposing the death penalty or other sentences, such as life in prison) that favored capital punishment, but held that states could exclude those who could *never* consider giving the death penalty (e.g., because of their strong moral beliefs against capital punishment). This case was very important because it meant that potential jurors could no longer be excluded "simply because they voiced general objections to the death penalty." Those who were unable to ever consider capital punishment could still be excluded because they would be unable to consider all the options available to them (i.e., they would automatically exclude death without regard for the crime). If you have ever seen the political buttons that say "Witherspoon excludable" on them, they show that the wearer would never impose the death penalty on anyone, no matter what the facts in a case were, meaning that they could legally be excluded from a punishment phase jury in a capital case.

The Supreme Court did not, however, agree with Witherspoon's argument that those who support the death penalty are more likely to convict, and would therefore be unfit to judge guilt. Witherspoon had based that claim on three research studies showing those who favored capital punishment were also more likely to believe the prosecution and vote "guilty." The court was not swayed by those particular studies, however, possibly because none of the three had yet been published and two involved college student samples. In the end, the court held that the "presently available information" was "too tentative and fragmentary to establish that jurors not opposed to the death penalty tend to favor the prosecution in the determination of guilt" (*Witherspoon v. Illinois,* 1968, p. 517).

Later that same year, the Eighth Circuit Court of Appeals (which hears appeals from Arkansas) heard the *Maxwell v. Bishop* case in which a black man who had been sentenced to death for rape[9] demonstrated through historical evidence that capital punishment had been used in rape cases almost exclusively against blacks who had raped whites (89 percent of executed rapists were black). The appeals court held that historical evidence is not enough, that a defendant must show that discrimination existed in his or her particular case. Of interest, the U.S. Supreme Court vacated the judgment and sent the case back to the federal district court two years later for that court's decision on whether Maxwell should get a new sentencing hearing, but the rationale had nothing to do with racial bias. Instead, the high court was dismayed to learn that at least seven jurors had been excluded from Maxwell's penalty phase jury on the basis of "grounds held impermissible in the Witherspoon case" (1970, p. 264). See Box 13.9 for the answers that resulted in the exclusion of three of the potential jurors.

The third major attack on the death penalty came three years later in *McGautha v. California* (1971). The defense in *McGautha* focused on the guidelines given to death penalty jurors, or rather the lack of them. This issue had been raised in *Maxwell v. Bishop* (1970), but was essentially ignored by the U.S. Supreme Court because its focus was on whether jurors had been improperly excluded from his trial, but McGautha raised them again. The lack of guidelines, McGautha argued, made it impossible to determine why a particular person received the death penalty. Many offenders on death row had committed crimes that were less severe than those who were sent to prison. In some cases, co-defendants received different sentences for the same crime. In other words, McGautha argued, the death penalty is arbitrary and unfair because there is little ability to predict what penalty a given murderer will receive. The Supreme Court, however, said that the argument did not present sufficient legal grounds for overturning the death penalty.

---

## BOX 13.9

### *Witherspoon* Excludables?

Although the issue was not raised by Maxwell, at least seven jurors had been excluded from his jury based only upon the following answers they provided to questions. As you read their answers, consider why the U.S. Supreme Court did not approve of the challenges for cause. Could one or more of these jurors actually have been a *Witherspoon* excludable? How could the trial judge have determined whether they were excludable under the *Witherspoon v. Illinois* (1968) case?

*Potential juror #1:*
QUESTION:   If you were convinced beyond a reasonable doubt at the end of this trial that the defendant was guilty and that his actions had been so shocking that they would merit the death penalty do you have any conscientious scruples about capital punishment that might prevent you from returning such a verdict?
ANSWER:   I think I do.

Potential juror #2:
QUESTION:   Do you entertain any conscientious scruples about imposing the death penalty?
ANSWER:   Yes, I am afraid I do.

Potential juror #3:
QUESTION:   Mr. Adams, do you have any feeling concerning capital punishment that would prevent you or make you have any feelings about returning a death sentence if you felt beyond a reasonable doubt that the defendant was guilty and that his crime was so bad as to merit the death sentence?
ANSWER:   No, I don't believe in capital punishment.

*Source:* Quotes taken from *Maxwell v. Bishop*, 1970, pp. 264–265).

Then came *Furman v. Georgia* (1972), the landmark decision that shook up the country's use of the death penalty. The defense in this case argued that the death penalty was given in an arbitrary and capricious manner and was a violation of the Eighth Amendment (which bans cruel and unusual punishments). Furman claimed that juries imposed the death penalty without any real guidance, and that made the decisions unpredictable and unfair. The Supreme Court agreed with Furman and declared the death penalty unconstitutional as it was being administered at that time. All death sentences in the country were immediately overturned and changed to life in prison. That is how Robert Lee Massie was released in 1978—his sentence was converted due to *Furman.* The Court in *Furman* did not say the death penalty itself was unconstitutional, but rather that it could not be imposed in such an arbitrary manner. A number of states, especially in the South, began rewriting their death penalty statutes to provide guidance to juries regarding who should get the death penalty. In general, they created a list of aggravating and mitigating factors that should be considered.

The test of the new guidelines came four years later in *Gregg v. Georgia* (1976). Here, Georgia argued its new jury guidelines removed the arbitrary and capricious element from the death penalty, so that Gregg's sentence of death was valid. The Supreme Court agreed that the new guidelines meant that the death penalty was not as arbitrary and capricious as those struck down in *Furman.* This allowed other states to rewrite their statutes to provide guidance to jurors. See Box 13.10 for a chart showing the number of executions from 1930 to 1999, which shows the effect of *Furman* and *Gregg* on capital punishment.

One of the most recent substantive attacks on the death penalty came in 1987. *McCleskey v. Kemp* resurrected the issue of discrimination by adding in a new factor, victim race. In this case, evidence from the famous Baldus study (named after the primary researcher) was presented. In this study, three social science researchers examined more than 2,000 murder cases in Georgia in the 1970s. They found that murderers who killed whites were 4.3 times more likely to get the death penalty than those who killed blacks, even when other factors, such as offense seriousness, were statistically controlled for using multivariate statistics. The researchers also found that prosecutors were more likely to seek the death penalty when the defendant was black and the victim white; prosecutors opted to seek the death penalty in 70 percent of cases involving this racial mix versus fewer than a third of other cases (1987, p. 287). The defense argued that the death penalty statistics, in and of themselves, demonstrated a bias in its usage. The U.S. Supreme Court took the position seen two decades earlier in *Maxwell v. Bishop* (1968): Statistical discrepancies do not indicate that the death penalty is unfairly imposed in any particular case. While it recognized the Baldus study as "sophisticated," the court noted that it did not point to discrimination against McCleskey himself:

> Thus, to prevail under the Equal Protection Clause, McCleskey must prove that the decisionmakers in his case acted with discriminatory purpose. He offers no evidence specific to

## BOX 13.10

### Persons Executed, 1930–1999

As you look over this graph, notice the nearly decade-long span that was nearly devoid of executions. It is clear that the *Furman* and *Gregg* cases had some impact on capital punishment, but a closer look reveals that the number of executions had declined rapidly *before* the 1972 *Furman* decision. What do you think could contribute to this drop?

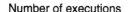

**Persons executed, 1930–1999**

Number of executions

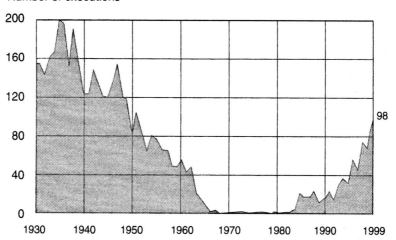

*Source:* Snell, 2000, p. 11.

his own case that would support an inference that racial considerations played a part in his sentence. Instead, he relies solely on the Baldus study. McCleskey argues that the Baldus study[10] compels an inference that his sentence rests on purposeful discrimination. McCleskey's claim that these statistics are sufficient proof of discrimination, without regard to the facts of a particular case, would extend to all capital cases in Georgia, at least where the victim was white and the defendant is black. (1987, pp. 292–293)

*McCleskey* was the last major general attack on the death penalty and is the most recent case that stood a chance of invalidating the death penalty across the nation. Capital appeals are constantly being raised, however, so the ultimate penalty may someday be a relic of the past. Recent public opinion polls suggest that Americans are increasingly questioning the death penalty, and its support may be decreasing (e.g., Entzeroth, 2001; Gallup, 2000).

## HOW DO THE OPTIONS "STACK UP" UNDER THE FIVE PUNISHMENT THEORIES?

Now that we have examined the philosophies of punishment and some available punishment options, it is important to see how sentencing options and philosophies are intertwined. Think about each of the sentencing options discussed in this chapter and which philosophy each best reflects. Fines, for example, have little incapacitative value but could be effective deterrents and could also fulfill retributive goals. Jail and prison can be excellent forms of incapacitation and also serve retributive and deterrent functions. Rehabilitation is probably best served by regular or intensive supervision probation, whereas restoration is best served by restorative justice initiatives such as restitution and community service.

Judges who adhere to a particular philosophy are logically more likely to pick penalties that suit that approach. Rehabilitation-oriented judges, for example, are more likely to rely on sentences they feel will help offenders get back on the right track, such as probation. Retribution-oriented judges may favor jail terms (Meyer and Jesilow, 1997, p. 108). This does not mean that judges are hemmed in by one philosophy. Instead, judges are likely to follow the philosophy they feel is appropriate for the individual offenders before them (Meyer and Jesilow, 1997, p. 61). One shoplifter, for example, may get probation coupled with a referral to social services agencies to help him or her get a job while another finds himself or herself in jail for the same offense. Even with these differences, however, sentencing philosophies still affect sentences. After you figure out which options are best suited for the five philosophies, take a look at Table 13.3 at the end of this chapter to see how your answers compare.

## CONCLUSION

In this chapter, we first looked at discretion and its role in sentencing, differentiated the five major theories of punishment, and looked at several options available to sentencing agents, including the controversial death penalty. Without discretion, judges cannot fashion penalties, but too much discretion may be abused. An individual judge's sentencing philosophy may have a lot to do with the penalties imposed in his or her courtroom, especially when discretion is sufficient to allow some leeway. A third factor that helps determine sentences are the specific options available to judges and the public's perception of those options. As more and more alternatives are developed, the sentences imposed in American courts may change dramatically.

In the next step, we will delve deeper into the art of sentencing, examining, for example, how judges set penalties and the factors that are associated with sentences.

**TABLE 13.3    How Well a Sample of Sentencing Options "Stacks Up" Under the Five Punishment Theories**

*(Note: Sentencing goals will [and should] vary with every crime,*
*so a particular punishment's failure to "stack up" under a particular*
*sentencing philosophy is not necessarily a problem)*

| Penalty | Deterrence | | Incapacitation | Rehabilitation | Retribution | Restoration |
|---|---|---|---|---|---|---|
| | General | Specific | | | | |
| Fines | Acceptable if the fine deters others from committing crimes (e.g., if drivers do not park in handicapped zones so as to avoid the fines). | Acceptable if the fine deters future crimes by the offender. | Unacceptable because fines do not protect society. In some respects, they endanger it by causing some offenders to commit additional crimes such as theft to pay their fines. | Unacceptable because it does not address offenders' underlying needs for interventions. In no way do fines seek to "cure" the criminal. | Acceptable for nonserious offenses where fines are appropriate. Often, fines are enough of a penalty to punish. | Because fines go to the state, restorative justice is not met. Restitution is a better choice because victims are restored to some degree and offenders play a role in the restorative process. |
| Community Service | Acceptable if the community service deters others from crime. | Acceptable if the community service deters the individual offender from future crime. | Barely acceptable. Offenders are incapacitated for only the hours they are actually completing the work. | Acceptable if offenders need to learn work skills or work habits. | Good for nonserious offenses because it is a tax on offenders' free time, which makes it a punishment. | Excellent, especially when offenders work directly for victims, as in removing their graffiti from walls. |
| Informal Probation | Not very good. Who is deterred by having friends and acquaintances told to stay out of trouble? | May work if offenders do not commit future crimes because they fear future involvement with the justice system. | Not acceptable. Informal probation does not protect the rest of society. | Not acceptable unless offenders' needs are met. A better choice is regular probation with mandated programs. | Not acceptable because it does not penalize the offender. Some say it is a slap on the wrist. | Not good. It does not address the needs of offenders or victims. |

| Penalty | Deterrence | | Incapacitation | Rehabilitation | Retribution | Restoration |
|---|---|---|---|---|---|---|
| | General | Specific | | | | |
| Regular Probation with Mandated Programs | Not very good, but better than informal probation. Some potential offenders may avoid crime so they will not be forced into programs they feel are a hassle or are not appropriate for them. | Not very good, but better than informal probation. Some offenders consider participation in the programs to be a hassle not worth repeating, so they avoid further offenses. Consider, for example, lengthy drunk driver education courses. | Not acceptable. Probation does not protect the rest of society, except during the actual time offenders spend participating in programs. | Appropriate, especially if programs to which offenders are sent are effective in reducing recidivism. Some programs also address family needs, such as parenting skills training, thus reducing the criminality of others, too. | Not acceptable because rehab programs are not supposed to be punishment, although some offenders may feel punished by having to participate in them. | Not acceptable because probation addresses offender's problems, but often ignores the victims. If conditions include restitution or other restorative justice initiatives, this option may be an excellent way to address restoration. |
| Intensive Supervision Probation (ISP) | Not very good, but better than other forms of probation. The conditions tend to be onerous (e.g., curfews and limits on associates) so some potential offenders will avoid crime to avoid them. | Not very good, but better than other forms of probation since some may avoid crime just to avoid the sometimes onerous conditions (e.g., curfews). In fact, when given the choice, some offenders choose prison over ISP, so it has some deterrent power. | Acceptable if the conditions limit offenders' abilities to engage in crime. Since it is often coupled with electronic monitoring and close supervision, ISP can protect the community. | Appropriate if the conditions include rehabilitation-oriented options such as substance abuse programs. In fact, knowing that one's relapses are more likely to be detected may motivate offenders to participate fully in rehab programs. | Appropriate if the conditions are onerous (e.g., limits on who offenders may associate with and random drug testing). When given the choice, some offenders choose prison over ISP, which shows that offenders view ISP as punishment. | Acceptable only if conditions involve participation in restorative justice initiatives. |

| Penalty | Deterrence | | Incapacitation | Rehabilitation | Retribution | Restoration |
|---|---|---|---|---|---|---|
| | General | Specific | | | | |
| Jail Term | Good if the term is sufficient to deter others from commiting crimes | Good if the term is sufficient to deter the individual offender from future crimes. | Good for the length of the term because the offender is kept off the streets during this time. Unfortunately, some offenders continue to commit crimes in jail, but their ability to do so is greatly curtailed. | Unacceptable because most jails do not have necessary programs available for offenders who need them and sentences are too short to bring about meaningful change. | Excellent. Even short jail terms are considered a strong punishment. | Not acceptable. Actually, jail is usually opposed by restoration advocates because there is no attempt to restore either party and two wrongs do not make a right. |
| Prison Sentence | Good if the term is sufficient to deter others from commiting crimes | Good if the term is sufficient to deter the individual offender from future crimes. | Excellent. Protects public from offenders' future crimes. Drawback is that other prisoners can still be victimized, and some offenders still engage in crimes against the public (e.g., scams). | Good prospect under indeterminate sentences because members of psychological and social work communities can determine when offenders are ready to re-enter society. Acceptable under determinate sentencing because programming can be implemented. | Excellent. Even short prison terms are considered a strong punishment. | Not acceptable. Actually, prison is usually opposed by restoration advocates because there is no attempt to restore either party and two wrongs do not make a right. If offenders work while in prison and send the money to their victims, some restoration is achieved, however. |

*(continued)*

TABLE 13.3   How Well a Sample of Sentencing Options "Stacks Up" Under the Five Punishment Theories *(continued)*

| Penalty | Deterrence | | Incapacitation | Rehabilitation | Retribution | Restoration |
|---|---|---|---|---|---|---|
| | General | Specific | | | | |
| Death Penalty | Acceptable because it deters at least some members of the public from committing capital offenses. | Some say it is the ultimate specific deterrent, although in truth it does not deter those who are put to death; it incapacitates them. | Definitely protects society from future crimes by the offender. Also protects other prisoners who would be incarcerated with them. | Totally unacceptable because it does not address the offender's illness. In fact, it is an admission that society is unable to treat offenders effectively. | Good, reflects the ideal of *lex talionis*, that those who kill deserve to be killed. | Unacceptable. Does not make victim or offender whole again. |

# DISCUSSION QUESTIONS

1. Think of the last time you were tempted to violate some norm (e.g., to speed, park illegally, or cheat in a class). Did your perception of certainty play a role in your decision to engage or not engage in the violation of that norm?

2. How could a sentence be a specific deterrent but not a general deterrent? Could a sentence be a general deterrent, but not a specific deterrent? Provide examples for your answers.

3. Look over the interview segments in Boxes 1–5. Each quote is from a different judge, but can you imagine some quotes being provided by the same judge? How could this be possible?

4. Chris Cross has stolen a CD from his local music store. Can you imagine some circumstances that would make you lean toward each of the five sentencing philosophies? For example, if you learned that Chris was eleven years old, which philosophy might you lean toward? If you learned that he was stealing CDs to sell so he could buy pornographic materials, which philosophy would seem most appropriate? Think of circumstances that would cause you to lean toward each of the sentencing philosophies.

5. Would you support bringing back any historic penalties? If so, which ones and why? If not, why? Which legal challenges would likely be raised against the penalty you reinstituted?

6. How could probation be reformed to make it more palatable to the public? Would the changes increase or decrease its effectiveness as a rehabilitation strategy?

7. Scan your local news or the major newswires (such as the Associated Press or Reuters) for creative sanctions. Why do you think the judges imposed those specific penalties? Could you think of instances where creative penalties were used inappropriately? Can you imagine some creative penalties that you think might work?

8. What current attacks on the death penalty are in the news? How much of a chance do you think those cases have to invalidate capital punishment? Assume your opinion is being solicited at a general forum on the death penalty. If you were allowed to state just one important rationale for *or* against capital punishment, what would you say?

9. Label each of the following five quotes from actual municipal court judges with the sentencing philosophy you feel it best illustrates. Each philosophy is used only once. Explain why you feel the interview segment illustrates the philosophy to which you matched it.
   A. [When talking about cases that are suitable for picking up trash along the highways]: A real jerk who's done something so bad, but it's not serious enough to get them a felony, or not serious enough to get them jail time. But it's such a bad thing he did, that you want to punish him, almost eye for an eye. So, you find something for that person to do.
   B. Hopefully [a sentence] keeps you from doing it again and possibly keeps somebody else from doing the same thing again. . . . If I just slap you on the hand right now and don't really hit you a little hard, you're going to do it again and your friends are going to do it again.
   C. I feel that [community service sentences are] a good alternative. Most of the people we see, I would rather have them working rather than sitting in their dayroom watching TV. They will feel better about themselves and we are getting something physically done—cleaning up graffiti, for example.
   D. I'd like to have some residential treatment programs for mentally ill people who come into the criminal justice system and can't find access to the mental health system because they're borderline, so that they drift between the systems and end up doing lots of jail time because they're marginally handicapped. And, I'd like to have some long-term residential protected placements for those people so that I can stabilize them and either reintegrate them or put them into low supervision mental health programs, otherwise they end up in the street, addicted to alcohol and any other street drug that they can get their hands on. I would like to have more of those kinds of alternatives.

E. The chief recipient of the harm of the DUIs would be the common ordinary citizen like you and me who is around the roadway. . . . I do have to keep in mind that there are a lot of children [and] citizens out there, and they need to be protected from this type of thing.

# NOTES

1. Remember that our system dictates that those who lack culpability should not be punished. See the discussion of *mens rea* and criminal defenses in Step 2 for more information on this important concept.

2. Unfortunately, castrated men are still able to commit sexual assaults that do not involve intercourse.

3. "Nalyeeh" is a Navajo word for that which undoes any harm done to a person; it includes monetary and other forms of compensation, apologies, promises to reform, acknowledgement of harm, and so forth.

4. Actually, day-fine units are a percentage of one's daily salary, so that fifteen or so units make up one day. This allows greater flexibility in fining options, especially for very minor offenses, such as letting one's parking meter run out. So, while our example is designed to be easy to understand, it is not entirely precise.

5. At the time of this writing, Vanjoki was appealing the fine amount because his income had dropped dramatically in the year prior to his receiving the ticket. Rytsola had already paid the $74,600 fine.

6. The other purposes of day reporting services were reducing overcrowding at detention facilities, building political support for the program itself, and providing supervision for safety of the public.

7. Some offenders may be sentenced to jail on multiple misdemeanors, resulting in sentences of more than one year. In addition, a few jurisdictions allow sentences in excess of one year for misdemeanors. Jails also house a number of individuals who are awaiting transfer to a state or federal prison to serve their sentences.

8. It has been reported that Albuquerque-based Judge Love read a Spiderman comic in which a device similar to the modern-day electronic monitoring anklets was used. The judge thought the idea might work for those on home detention and asked an engineer if he could manufacture such a device. The rest of the story is history.

9. One could be executed for rape of an adult woman until 1977, when the United States Supreme Court disallowed that practice in *Coker v. Georgia*. Louisiana still allows the death penalty for rape, but only if the victim is under the age of twelve.

10. The study was named after the authors, professors David Baldus, Charles Pulaski, and George Woodworth.

# REFERENCES

Abbott, J.H. (1981). *In the Belly of the Beast*. New York: Random House.

Andrews, W. (1991). *Old Time Punishments*. New York: Dorset Press. (Originally published in 1890, London: Simpkin, Marshall, Hamilton and Kent.)

Anonymous. (1616). *A pittilesse mother. That most vnnaturally at one time, murthered two of her owne children at Acton within six miles from London vppon holy thursday last 1616. The ninth of May. Being a gentlewoman named Margret Vincent, wife of Mr. Iaruis Vincent, of the same towne.*

*With her examination, confession and true discouery of all the proceedings in the said bloody accident. Whereunto is added Andersons repentance, who was executed at Tiburne the 18. of May being Whitson Eue 1[161] Written in the time of his prisonment in Newgate.* London: Printed by G. Eld for J. Trundle, and sold by J. Wright.

Beccaria, C. (1983). *An Essay on Crimes and Punishments.* Brookline Village, MA: Branden Press Inc. (Translated and reprinted from *Dei delitti e delle pene* [4th ed.], 1775, London: F. Newberry.)

Beck, A.J., and Karberg, J.C. (2001). *Prison and Jail Inmates at Midyear 2000.* Washington, DC: Bureau of Justice Statistics.

Bedau, H.A., and Radelet, M.L. (1987). Miscarriages of justice in potentially capital cases. *Stanford Law Review,* 40: 21–90.

Bentham, J. (1948). *The Principles of Morals and Legislation.* New York: Hafner Publishing (reprinted from the 1823 edition).

Berns, W. (1989). Retribution as the ground for punishment. In F.E. Baumann and K.M. Jensen (Eds.), *Crime and Punishment: Issues in Criminal Justice.* Charlottesville: University Press of Virginia.

Blumstein, A., and Cohen, J. (1987). Characterizing criminal careers. *Science,* 237: 985–91.

Blumstein, A., Cohen, J., and Nagin, D. (Eds.). (1978). *Deterrence and Incapacitation: Estimating the Effects of Criminal Sanctions on Crime Rates.* Washington, DC: National Academy of Sciences.

Bonczar, T.P. (1997). *Characteristics of Adults on Probation, 1995.* Washington, DC: National Institute of Justice.

Bonczar, T.P., and Glaze, L.E. (1999). *Probation and Parole in the United States, 1998.* Washington, DC: Bureau of Justice Statistics.

Braithwaite, J., and Geis, G. (1982). On theory and action for corporate crime control. *Crime & Delinquency,* 28: 292–314.

Branham, L.S., and Krantz, S. (1994). *Sentencing, Corrections, and Prisoners' Rights in a Nutshell* (4th ed.). St. Paul, MN: West.

Bureau of Justice Statistics. (1997). *Correctional Populations in the United States, 1997.* Washington, DC: U.S. Department of Justice.

Bureau of Justice Statistics. (2000). *Criminal Victimization in the United States, 1995.* Washington, DC: U.S. Department of Justice.

*Coker v. Georgia,* 433 U.S. 584 (1977).

Connelly, R. (1999, November 11). Shame, shame, shame. *Houston Press Wire.*

Crouch, B.M. (1993). Is incarceration really worse? Analysis of offenders' preferences for prison over probation. *Justice Quarterly* 10: 67–88.

Dalrymple, T. (1992, June 20). Beyond sympathy, beneath contempt. *The Spectator.*

Ehrlich, I. (1975). The deterrent effect of capital punishment: A question of life and death. *American Economic Review,* 65: 397–417.

Eisenstein, J., and Jacob, H. (1977). *Felony Justice: An Organizational Analysis of Criminal Courts.* Boston: Little, Brown.

Entzeroth, L. (2001). Putting the mentally retarded criminal defendant to death: Charting the development of a national consensus to exempt the mentally retarded from the death penalty. *Alabama Law Review,* 52: 911–941.

*Furman v. Georgia*, 408 U.S. 238 (1972).

Gallup Poll Surveys. (2000, August 29–September 25). Gallup social series: Crime. Available online at: www.gallup.com/poll/surveys/2000/topline000829/topline000829.asp (accessed 4/22/01).

Gowdy, V.B. (1993). *Intermediate Sanctions*. Washington DC: National Institute of Justice.

*Gregg v. Georgia*, 428 U.S. 153 (1976).

Green, E. (1964). Inter- and intra-racial crime relative to sentencing. *Journal of Criminal Law, Criminology and Police Science, 55*: 348–358.

Grupp, S.E. (1971). Introduction. In S.E. Grupp (Ed.), *Theories of Punishment*. Bloomington: Indiana University Press.

Hammurabi, King of Babylonia. (1958). The Code of Hammurabi. In J.B. Pritchard (Ed.), *The Ancient Near East: Volume 1, An Anthology of Texts and Pictures*. Princeton, NJ: Princeton University Press. (Translated by T.J. Meek, originally written circa 1700 B.C.E.)

Harlow, C.W. (1985). *Reporting Crimes to the Police*. Washington, DC: U.S. Department of Justice.

Hawkins, D.J.B. (1944). Punishment and moral responsibility. *The Modern Law Review, 7*: 205–208.

Jesilow, P.D., Pontell, H.N., and Geis, G. (1993). *Prescription for Profit: How Doctors Defraud Medicaid*. Berkeley: University of California Press.

Kant, I. (1995). On the right to punish and to grant clemency. In J.G. Murphy, *Punishment and Rehabilitation* (3rd ed.). Belmont, CA: Wadsworth. (Translated from *The Metaphysics of Morals*, 1797, reprinted by Cambridge: Cambridge University Press, 1991).

Klein, A.R. (1988). *Alternative Sentencing: A Practitioner's Guide*. Cincinnati: Anderson.

Kunkle, W.J. (1989). Punishment and the criminal justice system: A prosecutor's viewpoint. In F.E. Baumann and K.M. Jensen (Eds.), *Crime and Punishment: Issues in Criminal Justice*. Charlottesville: University Press of Virginia.

Latessa, E.J., Travis, L.F., Holsinger, A., and Hartman, J. (1998). *Evaluation of Ohio's Pilot Day Reporting Programs: Final Report*. University of Cincinnati. (Funded by a grant from the Bureau of Justice Assistance, Office of Justice Programs, U.S. Department of Justice, through the Ohio Office of Criminal Justice Services).

Lempert, R. (1983). The effect of executions on homicides: A new look in an old light. *Crime and Delinquency, 29*: 88–115.

Lindquist, J.H. (1988). *Misdemeanor Crime: Criminal Trivial Pursuit*. Newbury Park, CA: Sage.

MacNamara, D.E.J. (1977). The medical model in corrections: Requiescat in pace. *Criminology, 14*: 439–447.

Man must carry photo of victim. (1998, February 11). *Associated Press Wire*.

Man ordered to post DUI sticker. (1998, February 21). *Associated Press Wire*.

Martinson, R. (1974, Spring). What works: Questions and answers about prison reform. *Public Interest, 35*: 22–54.

*Maxwell v. Bishop*, 398 F.2d 138 (1968).

*Maxwell v. Bishop*, 398 U.S. 262 (1970).

McClelland, K.A., and Alpert, G.P. (1985). Factor analysis applied to magnitude estimates of punishment seriousness: Patterns of individual differences. *Journal of Quantitative Criminology 1*: 307–318.

*McCleskey v. Kemp*, 481 U.S. 279 (1987).

McDonald, D.C. (1992). Punishing labor: Unpaid community service as a criminal sentence. In J.M. Byrne, A.J. Luvigio, and J. Petersilia (Eds.), *Smart Sentencing: The Emergence of Intermediate Sanctions.* Newbury Park, CA: Sage.

*McGautha v. California,* 402 U.S. 183 (1971).

Meeker, J.W., Jesilow, P., and Aranda, J. (1992). Bias in sentencing: A preliminary analysis of community service sentences. *Behavioral Sciences and the Law,* 10: 197–206.

Menninger, K. (1959). Verdict guilty—Now what? *Harpers Magazine,* 219 (1311): 60–64.

Meyer, J., and Jesilow, P. (1993). "Doing justice": Judicial attitudes toward community service sentences. *The IARCA Journal on Community Corrections,* 5(5): 10–12.

Meyer, J., and Jesilow, P. (1997). *"Doing Justice" in the People's Court: Sentencing by Municipal Court Judges.* New York: State University of New York Press.

Mileski, M. (1971). Courtroom encounters: An observation study of a lower criminal court. *Law and Society Review,* 5: 473–538.

Morris, H. (1968). Persons and punishment. *Monist,* 52: 475–501.

Neumeister, L. (2000, July 11). Ex-bank worker gets 2-week sentence. *Associated Press Wire.*

Newbold, G. (1999). A chronology of correctional history. *Journal of Criminal Justice Education,* 10: 87–100.

Petersilia, J., and Piper Deschenes, E. (1994). What punishes? Inmates rank the severity of prison vs. intermediate sanctions. *Federal Probation* 58(1): 3–8.

Petersilia, J., and S. Turner. (1990). *Diverting Prisoners to Intensive Supervision: Results of an Experiment in Oregon.* Santa Monica, CA: Rand.

Plato. (1953). *The Dialogues of Plato.* Oxford: Clarendon Press. (Translated by B. Jowett from *Gorgias,* c. 380 B.C.).

President's Commission on Law Enforcement and Administration of Justice. (1967). *Task Force Report: The Courts.* Washington, DC: Government Printing Office.

Rawls, J. (1955). Two concepts of rules. *The Philosophical Review* 64: 3–32.

Renzema, M., and Skelton, D.T. (1990). *Use of Electronic Monitoring in the United States: 1989 Update.* Washington DC: National Institute of Justice.

Schafer, S. (1977). *Victimology: The Victim and His Criminal.* Reston, VA: Reston.

Sellin, T. (1959). *The Death Penalty: A Report for the Model Penal Code Project of the American Law Institute.* Philadelphia: Executive Office, American Law Institute.

Snell, T.L. (2000). *Capital Punishment, 1999.* Washington, DC: Bureau of Justice Statistics.

Stubbs, W. (Ed.). (1900). *Selected Charters and Other Illustrations of English Constitutional History: From the Earliest Times to the Reign of Edward the First* (8th ed.). Oxford: Clarendon.

Stubbs, W. (1906). *Lectures on Early English History* (edited by A. Hassall). New York: Longmans, Green.

*Tate v. Short,* 401 U.S. 395, 91 S.Ct. 668, L.Ed.2d 130 (1971).

Thief ordered to send birthday card. (1998, February 22). *Associated Press Wire.*

Turula, M. (2002, January 15). Nokia exec hit with six-figure fine. *Associated Press Wire.*

Umbreit, M.S. (1994). *Victim Meets Offender: The Impact of Restorative Justice and Mediation.* Monsey, NY: Criminal Justice Press.

Vogt, K. (1999, April 30). Deputy was watching gunman. *Associated Press Wire.*

von Hirsch, A., Wasik, M., and Green, J. (1989). Punishments in the community and the principles of desert. *Rutgers Law Journal* 20: 595–618.

Walker, S. (2001). *Sense and Nonsense about Crime* (5th ed.). Belmont, CA: Wadsworth.

Wasserstrom, R.A. (1980). *Philosophy and Social Issues.* Notre Dame, IN: University of Notre Dame Press.

Watkins, R. (1651). *Newes from the Dead.* Oxford: Printed by Leonard Litchfield [and H. Hall] for Tho. Robinson.

Webber, D., and Nikos, K. (1992, November 16). Dwindling service sentences to cost millions in free labor. *Daily News,* pp. 1, 6.

*Weems v. United States,* 217 U.S. 349; 54 L. Ed. 793; 30 S. Ct. 544 (1910).

Wice, P.B. (1985). *Chaos in the Courthouse: The Inner Workings of the Urban Criminal Courts.* New York: Praeger.

Wilson, J.Q. (1985). *Thinking about Crime* (Rev. ed.). New York: Vintage Books.

Winterfield, L.A., and Hillsman, S.T. (1993). *Staten Island Day-Fine Project.* Washington, DC: National Institute of Justice.

*Witherspoon v. Illinois,* 391 U.S. 510 (1968).

Wolfgang, M.E., Figlio, R.M., and Sellin, T. (1972). *Delinquency in a Birth Cohort.* Chicago: University of Chicago Press.

Yazzie, R., and Zion, J.W. (1996). Navajo restorative justice: The law of equality and justice. In B. Galaway and J. Hudson (Eds.), *Restorative Justice: International Perspectives.* Monsey, NY: Criminal Justice Press.

# Step 14

## $30 or 30 Days:
## Setting the Penalty

In the last chapter, we set the stage for sentencing by looking at judicial discretion and its limits, the different punishment philosophies held by individual judges, and the sanctioning options available to all judges. We now know that these factors play an important role in the eventual sentences imposed on offenders. This chapter takes up where we left off and discusses the art and process of sentencing itself.

By the end of this chapter, you will understand how judges fashion penalties for those who are convicted of crimes. You will know the role of the pre-sentence investigation report, and will recognize the influences of other factors on sentences. You will understand the mechanics of a sentencing hearing and how it resembles and differs from a trial. Finally, you will be able to discuss discrimination in sentencing and some reforms that have been suggested to eradicate it.

## SENTENCING IS A DIFFICULT TASK

Once a defendant has been convicted, the court must then turn its attention to establishing an appropriate penalty. This process, known as sentencing, is generally believed to be a judge's most difficult task (President's Commission on Law Enforcement and the Administration of Justice, 1967, p. 141; Wice, 1985, p. 145). Indeed, consider for a moment that you are a judge who has been assigned the task of determining what to do with a young man who has shoplifted a CD player from a department store. It is his first conviction. Your goal is to tailor a sentence to the specific offender before you, one that will show him that society disapproves of his actions and will deter both him and others from future crimes, but that considers any mitigating factors that may be present in his life. Will you send the thief to prison? Most state statutes say you can if the CD player is worth enough to be classified as a felony (e.g., whereas most state laws say that goods must be valued at $400 or more for grand theft, Virginia considers theft of property worth more than $200 to be a felony). Would you send him to jail for a shorter term of incarceration? Will you instead order him to work as a volunteer in a non-profit organization? What about probation? What are you going to do? These are the same questions that many judges ask themselves every day.

Despite the difficulty of sentencing, there is little preparation of judges for this task (Wice, 1985, p. 143), who must instead rely heavily on other judges to teach them the ropes of the robes or learn such items on their own (Alpert, 1981). Some judges depend on each case's attorneys to help them decide suitable sentences, but attorneys are seldom impartial and often have their own interests at stake. Those judges who do receive training often feel that the typical two-day program is not enough. In the end, judges are seldom taught how to sentence, what factors are important, and what to consider when imposing sentences. One federal judge, Marvin Frankel (1973), greatly criticized this system:

> They [judges] receive almost no instruction pertinent to sentencing. They may hear some fleeting references to the purposes of criminal penalties—some generalities about retribution, deterrence, etc. But so far as any intentional consequences of their legal education are concerned, they are taught by people and exposed to curricula barren of even food for thought about sentencing. (p. 13)

Despite the limitations on judges' training for sentencing, it is still a necessary part of the court process. Few other court activities are as important to offenders as the sentences they receive. Society, too, has a vested interest in whether penalties prevent crime. The remainder of this chapter will examine how penalties are determined, which factors are used in sentencing, whether discrimination exists in sentencing, and how sentencing laws have changed over recent years.

## PRE-SENTENCE REPORTS AND THE PROCESS OF SENTENCING

In theory, sentencing is a well-planned, time-consuming task. The court sets a sentencing date, typically a month or two after conviction. During this time, a probation officer spends as much time as necessary to prepare a thorough, useful pre-sentence report that incorporates the probation officer's professional assessment of the offender (Klein, 1988). This report is distributed to the judge, prosecutor, defense attorney, and defendant, who carefully read the report before the sentencing hearing. At least, that is how the process is supposed to move along. In practice it tends to be a great deal more harried, with individuals paying as much attention as their busy schedules will allow.

Because there is a high rate of agreement between judicially imposed sentences and the recommendations made by probation officers, it is important to take a few minutes to discuss the issues surrounding pre-sentence reports.

## Pre-Sentence Investigation Reports: What Are They?

The **Pre-Sentence Investigation** report (PSI) contains a variety of information about the offender and his or her offense and also presents a professional opinion concerning an appropriate penalty. PSIs are not requested in every case; this is especially true for cases adjudicated in the lower courts (Alfini, 1981, p. 8). Some judges request PSI reports when they feel they do not have enough information to determine a just sentence (Blumberg, 1967, p. 137). In cases where judges know little about offenders and their offenses, the PSI may be the primary source of information on which the ultimate sentence is based. For this reason, they are particularly useful in cases that are plea bargained.

Some probation departments have specialists who prepare PSIs, whereas others have a more vertical approach in which the probation officer who would actually be assigned to supervise the probationer completes the investigation and writes up the PSI (Henningsen, 1981). Some jurisdictions even allow privately prepared pre-sentence reports (Immarigeon, 1985), which routinely offer to the court creative sentencing options, such as one team did when it recommended that a rabbi convicted of fraud either establish a high school program focusing on Jewish education or "take charge of a Committee on Holocaust Studies" (*United States v. Bergman,* 1976, p. 500).[1] In addition to regular PSI reports, there is a shorter form called a selective PSI report that "contains only essential information" (Henningsen, 1981, p. 35). Regardless of the type of form implemented in a given case, the PSI should always be as honest, objective, and thorough as possible.[2]

## Pre-Sentence Reports: When Are They Completed?

Pre-sentence investigations are prepared after a defendant has been convicted or after she or he has agreed to plead guilty. This procedure is followed for four important reasons (Henningsen, 1981). First, the PSI report involves many sensitive questions of family, friends, and employers that may represent an unnecessary invasion of the defendant's privacy if he or she is acquitted at trial. Second, it is theoretically difficult for defendants to plead not guilty and then to cooperate and admit guilt to their probation officers. Third, a PSI report could not be admitted into court before sentencing anyway, because it could be prejudicial to the judge or jury. Finally, the report would be a needless use of scarce probation resources if the defendant is ultimately acquitted.

There are other times when it may be difficult to complete a thorough pre-sentence investigation. For example, even after conviction, some defendants will not admit their guilt to probation officers because they have appeals pending (Frankel, 1973, p. 27). It would not be in defendants' best interests to provide probation officers with detailed confessions while maintaining their innocence during their appeals. In order to demonstrate their appropriateness for lenient penalties, however, offenders must admit their culpability to their offenses and express feelings of remorse. This happened when a New York judge said he would consider a plea bargain for three months in jail and five years of probation only if the defendant in a vehicular manslaughter case had no serious prior convictions and "he demonstrates sufficient contrition and indicates remorse when the probation department conducts the pre-sentence investigation" (Breakey, 2000).

## Contents of the PSI

The PSI contains considerable information that judges may use when deciding sentences. First, a one-page summary of the offender's demographic characteristics is presented. This page, sometimes called the "face sheet," lists such information as the defendant's age, marital status, attorney's name, and sentencing date. The report then details the charges against the defendant and the penalties possible under statutory law. If probation is available, the report will note this.

The PSI also presents information regarding the defendant's past arrests and convictions. This section of the report may be a few lines or may extend several pages, and serves to show whether the offense was a rare occurrence or evidence of an individual's dedication to a life of crime.

A very important part of the PSI provides information on the instant offense (i.e., the offense for which the offender is currently being sentenced). First, the report presents the official version of the offense, generally gathered from police reports. This is followed by the defendant's version of the offense, which can serve to show any mitigating circumstances or the offender's acceptance of culpability. Statements from victims and/or police officers may be included in this part. Any mitigating or aggravating circumstances also will be detailed here.

The next major part of the report is a case history of the defendant. Generally, this information can help the judge view the defendant as an individual. Information about the defendant's family history, education, employment, religion, military service, financial information, interests and activities, and physical and mental health status (including any possible addictions) is included in this section.

At the conclusion of the report, the probation officer makes a sentencing recommendation on the basis of his or her professional assessment of the offender and the offense. Judges do not have to follow the recommendations, but the advice is generally weighted heavily (Ebbesen and Konečni, 1981; Henningsen, 1981). One reason that reliance on probation officers' recommendations may be discretionary is that the quality of the PSI reports would have to be policed much more closely if they were mandatory (Jones, 1981, p. 549). There is evidence that the courts have already considered this possibility. If a death sentence is based even in part on information contained in a PSI, for example, the U.S. Supreme Court has ruled that the information must be disclosed to the defense so the defendant can "deny or explain" the contents (*Gardner v. Florida,* 1977).

Box 14.1 presents a portion of Erik Menendez's PSI (Erik was the younger of two brothers who were convicted of murdering their parents in California). The

## BOX 14.1

## Portions of Erik Menendez's PSI report

Superior Court of California County of Los Angeles
Probation Officer's Report

Defendant's name(s): Erik Galen Menendez          Age: 25
Address (present): Los Angeles County Jail          Birthdate: 11/27/70
Sex: M                                             Race: W, White

[... *many other descriptors here, including custody status and sentencing judge*]

Charged with the crimes of (include priors, enhancements or special circumstances):
   I & II: 187 (a) PC (Murder)
Further alleged
   190.2 (A) (15) PC (Committed while lying in wait)
   190.2 (A) (3) PC (Committed multiple murders)
   III. 181 (1) PC (Conspiracy to commit murder)
Convicted of the crimes of (include priors, enhancements or special circumstances): Same

[... *other information here, including dates of conviction and arrest, etc.*]

**Elements and relevant circumstances of the offenses:**
The defendants conspired together and murdered Jose Enrique Menendez (age 45) and Mary
Louise "Kitty" (Andersen) Menendez (age 48), their parents at their Beverly Hills home. . . .
On the night of August 20, 1989, the defendants loaded their guns with rounds of 4 buck each.
At about 10:00 or 10:15 p.m., the defendants burst into the family den where the victims were
sitting on the couch. All ten rounds were fired at the victims and all but one found their
marks. . . . Because victim "Kitty" appeared to be still moving, the defendants then went to the
co-defendant's car where the defendant retrieved one or two shells of birdshot. He gave the
shell to the co-defendant who returned to the scene of the crime and shot victim "Kitty" in the
face at point blank range. After picking up the empty shells, they left to get rid of the guns and
bloody clothing and attempted to establish an alibi by meeting with a friend. When they were
unsuccessful in establishing contact with this person, they returned to the house and called the
Beverly Hills Police Department at 11:47 p.m. to report the murders. After being questioned by
the police, they returned to the house.

**Personal history:**
Substance abuse: No record, indication, or admission of alcohol or controlled substance abuse.
Type residence: Apartment          Length of occupancy: 4 months          Rent: $1,750
Residential stability last five years: Good
Formal education: He graduated from Beverly Hills High school in June, 1989.
Employment status: Unemployed
Employment stability last 5 years: N/A
Types of previous employment: None
Recommendation: It is recommended that probation be denied and that the defendant be
sentenced as prescribed by law.

*Source:* Adapted from Nidorf (1996).

PSI contains all of the parts discussed above, including the probation officer's recommendation at the end. When you read the excerpted report, think about each of the elements and the role that it plays in the sentencing process. In the end, both brothers were sentenced to two consecutive life terms without parole.

## THE SENTENCING HEARING

### Sentencing Hearings Compared to Trials

In some respects, the sentencing hearing may be compared to a fact-finding trial. Sentencing agents, whether judges or juries, may hear from character witnesses (e.g., the defendant's family and friends) or from victims (e.g., victim impact statements). These witnesses may testify at sentencing hearings; however, they do not testify about what they saw or heard. Instead, they tell the court about their feelings regarding the offender or his or her actions. In rare cases, defendants may call eyewitnesses whose testimony is "highly relevant" and who are likely to be truthful when they testify; for example, in one case the U.S. Supreme Court upheld the testimony of one eyewitness who testified that someone other than the convicted murderer had admitted to the killing (*Green v. Georgia,* 1979).

The defendant may also speak at the hearing, called exercising one's **right to allocution** (*Hill v. U.S.,* 1962), although judges nearly always impose whatever sentences they had tentatively assigned to the case before the sentencing hearing (Frankel, 1973, p. 36). Defendants can also try to demonstrate mitigating circumstances (e.g., that there was no intention to distribute the drugs found in the defendant's house at the time of his or her arrest), but the burden of proof at this stage is on the defendant (*Walton v. Arizona,* 1990). This is an importance difference: at trial, the burden of proof is on the prosecution. After conviction, the burden switches to the defense to prove any mitigating factors or to demonstrate that aggravating factors were incorrectly applied.

The defendant is not the only person the judge or jury may hear from during a sentencing hearing. In most states, the victim, or victim's family, may also speak at the sentencing hearing. Input from the victim or family members is typically included in the pre-sentence investigation, but most states also allow victims to make a victim impact statement (VIS) in court. Every state allows some form of VIS, ranging from written statements read in court to oral statements to more creative options, such as picture or video collages set to music. Ruled acceptable by the U.S. Supreme Court in *Payne v. Tennessee* (1991), VISs allow the justice system to pause and focus on the victim and to acknowledge the impact of the crime on his or her life. VISs are not without controversy, however, as some scholars question whether they will inappropriately introduce emotionalism into the sentencing process. VISs are discussed in greater detail in Step 8.

There are other important differences between trials and sentencing hearings. First, the purpose of the sentencing hearing is to establish the proper penalty rather than determine guilt, and its focus is to maximize the amount of information available to the sentencing agent. This means that information does not have to pass the strong criteria used for admission as evidence in a trial.

Unlike one's right to trial by jury, defendants have no right to be sentenced by juries; indeed, judges may overrule the sentences imposed by juries in states whose state legislatures have enacted laws permitting this (*McMillan v. Pennsylvania,* 1986) even in capital cases (*Spaziano v. Florida,* 1984). Such overrides are not common, but they do happen. In Joseph Spaziano's case (mentioned above), the jury voted for life imprisonment, but the judge overruled their recommendation and instead imposed the death penalty.[3] The Spaziano case, of course, involved a very rare sentence change. When judges overrule jury sentences, it is usually in the direction of leniency; for example, imposing a life sentence despite a jury's recommendation that a defendant receive the death penalty.

Likewise, in most states, defendants have no right to cross-examine witnesses who testify at their sentencing hearings because this may impede the testimony of intimidated witnesses (*Williams v. New York,* 1949). The convicted offender has the right to be present during their testimony, but cannot cross-examine the witnesses.

A fourth difference between trials and sentencing hearings is the level of proof required. Because guilt was established beyond a reasonable doubt for the defendant's conviction at trial, evidence presented at the sentencing hearing need only meet the civil standard of preponderance of evidence (*McMillan v. Pennsylvania,* 1986). It is also important to point out that the exclusionary rule does not apply to sentencing hearings. This means that evidence that was excluded at trial may be presented at the sentencing hearing. In other words, that 35 kilos of cocaine that was excluded from your trial after the judge ruled it was illegally seized because the police did not have probable cause to search your vehicle's trunk could very well end up on the evidence table at your sentencing hearing.

## Judicial Enhancement of Sentences

Judges may enhance sentences under many circumstances, according to the U.S. Supreme Court. First, judges who believe that defendants committed perjury, regardless of whether this is true, may enhance the sentences (*United States v. Grayson,* 1978). Defendants who refuse to cooperate with authorities (e.g., refusing to name one's drug suppliers) may find themselves facing more serious penalties than their counterparts who shared this information (*Roberts v. United States,* 1980). The reasoning behind these two enhancements is that telling the truth in court and cooperating with the authorities are ways to show that one has repented and has begun the journey toward rehabilitation. Lying and refusing to participate in the further detection or punishment of crime, on the other hand, are proof that one is not ready for lenience. How do judges know when they are being lied to? They often rely on their past experiences with other defendants and cases, but there is still an element of guesswork to it and that disturbs some judges. One judge, when asked what he would request if there were a Santa Claus of courts, told one of the authors he would ask for a truth dial because it would make his job much easier (see Box 14.2 for his quote and quotes from two other judges on the topic of lying).

It is not surprising that prior convictions can be used to enhance sentences, but most individuals do not know that prior crimes can be held against defendants even if they were never convicted (*Williams v. New York*, 1949). In the District of Columbia, defendants' sentences can be increased even if they were *acquitted* of prior charges (*United States v. Boney*, 1992)! These apparent contradictions are allowed because the level of proof used at sentencing hearings is lower than that required to establish criminal guilt at trial. One judge sentenced an Arizona man convicted of a nonfatal drive-by shooting to twelve years in prison in part because of his own belief that the young man's previous acquittal was an error on the part of the jury (see Box 14.3 for more details).

---

## BOX 14.2
## Three Lower Court Judges' Comments on Lying in Court

*As you read the following excerpts from interviews with lower court judges, think about how these judges view lying and the problems it poses for them. How is perceived perjury tied to satisfaction with career and how could it affect verdicts or sentences?*

*A criminal court judge:*
[If there were a Santa Claus of courts, I would ask for] a truth dial. I'd just like to have a little thing that, if you were talking, I could point it at you and if you're telling the truth it's blue and if you're not, it's red. And then I'd just know. That would make my job a lot easier. If you could sit here and know who's telling the truth and who isn't, your job would be a whole lot easier.

*Another criminal court judge:*
I tell people I am lied to every day of my life. One thing I have to do, when I leave, is to leave my job behind me.

*A judge who presides over civil court trials:*
There are some situations where judges lose their objectivity and I guess towing companies are one of my weak spots because I've seen so [much] crummy lying. And, you sit back and say, "Maybe this guy will be different." [But,] on the first three or four sentences out of his mouth, you know he's going to make up some wild scenario how that person's wheel fell off two miles down the road after he came out and changed the tire or how this car that had no dents in it, all of a sudden, down at the tow yard, its fender is bashed in or valuable property that was in the trunk somehow mysteriously disappeared.

# BOX 14.3

## Previous Acquittal Used to Enhance Sentence

To many observers, the defendant wore "a smirk and an attitude of bored indifference" during his many court hearings on assault and battery charges stemming from a drive-by shooting. Even if there was no smirk, there was no doubt that the judge was less than thrilled with the young man's attitude in court and toward life in general. The judge demonstrated his disapproval of Gonzales' crimes when he sentenced him to the maximum term possible under Arizona state law, twelve years in state prison without a chance of parole. Gonzales probably expected a more lenient sentence, since he had no criminal record—or did he?

Before the sentence was imposed, Gonzales' attorney informed the court that his pre-sentence investigation report, completed by the local probation office, said that he "has no record, a previous vehicle arson case having been dismissed by a hung jury."

The judge, on the other hand, was not so quick to dismiss culpability in the vehicle arson case. "I believe you burned that car. . . . The jury decided otherwise, that's their prerogative; but, I believe you burned it. . . . I suspect that you didn't learn a damned thing . . . I think you think you got away with something."

The judge then said, "I choose to aggravate the term," meaning finding reason to impose the maximum sentence allowed. Arizona law allows judges to consider prior cases when imposing sentences, even cases that do not result in convictions.

*Source:* Adapted from H. Kitching (1995), Bite the bullet, judge tells drive-by triggerman. *Nogales International.*

## FACTORS IN SENTENCING

In theory, sentences are based on a combination of legal factors, including the seriousness of offenses for which the defendant has been convicted. Long ago, Cesare Beccaria (1775/1983) noted that sentence severity was not always based solely on the legal merits of criminal cases. Instead, sentences appeared somewhat capricious; elites received leniency while commoners faced severe sanctions.

Interest in sentencing did not die with Beccaria. Current researchers are still trying to understand how sentencing takes place. Many have searched for bias in sentencing and a number have found evidence that it exists. Other researchers have joined in the fray and argue that sentences are based on the legal merits of the cases, rather than any supposed biases. In general, factors that influence sentencing can be divided into three categories: legal, extra-legal, and organizational. The next three sections examine these factors in greater detail.

## LEGAL FACTORS IN SENTENCING

Legal variables, such as prior record and offense severity, are "those which the system may legitimately use to fix sentences" (Lizotte, 1978, p. 567). As citizens, we expect these variables to affect sentences. Most individuals would agree that those convicted of rape or robbery *should* be punished more harshly than shoplifters because the crimes are more serious and cause more harm. Similarly, few people would argue if those being sentenced for their fifth burglary received harsher sentences than first-time burglars. Such **disparities** (i.e., differences in sentences) would not necessarily reflect **discrimination** (i.e., difference in sentences that are attributed to prejudice). Legal variables, then, are legitimate influences on sentence severity.

There has been a great deal of research on the effects of legal variables on sentences. Scholars have consistently found that those convicted of more serious charges tend to receive harsher sentences (e.g.; Chiricos and Bales, 1991; Lizotte, 1978; Myers, 1987; Myers and Talarico, 1988; Petersilia and Turner, 1985; Spohn, 1990; Uhlman, 1977, 1979). This makes intuitive sense. Those who cause more harm to their victims or to society in general should be penalized more than those who cause less harm. See Box 14.4 for a breakdown of sentences by offense, which shows the influence of this factor.

The presence of mitigating or aggravating circumstances in the offense has also been associated with sentence severity. For example, offenders who use guns while committing their crimes typically receive harsher sentences than other offenders (Feeley, 1979, p. 212; Spohn, 1990), sometimes because they face mandatory penalties or **enhancements** (i.e., laws that authorize harsher sentences when certain criteria are met, such as use of a firearm during a crime or victimizing a vulnerable victim). Criminals whose cases involve mitigating factors (e.g., reduced mental competence, minor role in the offense, youthful offender), on the other hand, often receive lesser penalties.

In some cases, the age of the offender is a legal variable in sentencing. Juveniles, for example, cannot receive the death penalty in most states. Unless they are tried as adults, juveniles cannot be incarcerated beyond expiration of juvenile jurisdiction. To illustrate, California cannot imprison even serious offenders tried in the juvenile court system (e.g., murderers) beyond the age of twenty-five; other juvenile offenders must be released by age twenty-one. Other states mandate release at earlier ages; regulations regarding housing juveniles with adults require that Arkansas juveniles must be released by age eighteen. Because youths convicted in the juvenile courts must be released when they become adults (or shortly thereafter), some juveniles charged with serious crimes are certified to the adult courts. Had Lionel Tate, a twelve-year-old boy who argued that he was imitating professional wrestlers when he beat a six-year-old girl to death in Florida, been tried in the state's juvenile courts, he could only be held until age twenty-one. By transferring him to adult court, he faced, and received, a mandatory sentence of life in

# BOX 14.4
# Felony Sentences Imposed by State Courts

As you look over the following table, it is clear that offense severity has at least some impact on sentences. Which offenses are least likely to receive probation? Most likely to receive probation? What can you say about the effect of offense severity on sentences, after studying this chart?

**Types of Felony Sentences Imposed by State Courts: by Offense, 1996**

| Most Serious Conviction Offense | Total | Percent of felons sentenced to— | | | Probation |
|---|---|---|---|---|---|
| | | Incarceration | | | |
| | | Total | Prison | Jail | |
| **All offenses** | 100% | 69% | 38% | 31% | 31% |
| **Violent offenses** | 100% | 79% | 57% | 22% | 21% |
| Murder[a] | 100 | 95 | 92 | 3 | 5 |
| Sexual assault[b] | 100 | 79 | 63 | 16 | 21 |
| Robbery | 100 | 87 | 73 | 14 | 13 |
| Aggravated assault | 100 | 72 | 42 | 30 | 28 |
| Other violent[c] | 100 | 73 | 38 | 34 | 27 |
| **Property offenses** | 100% | 62% | 34% | 28% | 38% |
| Burglary | 100 | 71 | 45 | 26 | 29 |
| Larceny[d] | 100 | 63 | 31 | 32 | 37 |
| Fraud[e] | 100 | 50 | 26 | 24 | 50 |
| **Drug offenses** | 100% | 72% | 35% | 37% | 28% |
| Possession | 100 | 70 | 29 | 41 | 30 |
| Trafficking | 100 | 73 | 39 | 33 | 27 |
| **Weapons offenses** | 100% | 67% | 40% | 27% | 33% |
| **Other offenses[f]** | 100% | 63% | 31% | 32% | 37% |

Note: For persons receiving a combination of sentences, the sentence designation came from the most severe penalty imposed—prison being the most severe, followed by jail, then probation. Prison includes death sentences. Data on sentence type were available for 997,906 cases.

[a] Includes nonnegligent manslaughter.

[b] Includes rape.

[c] Includes offenses such as negligent manslaughter and kidnaping.

[d] Includes motor vehicle theft.

[e] Includes forgery and embezzlement.

[f] Composed of nonviolent offenses such as receiving stolen property and vandalism.

*Source:* Brown, Langan, and Levin (1999), p. 2.

prison without parole (Canedy, 2001).[4] See Step 16 for more information on certification and the treatment of youths in the juvenile courts.

Prior records have also been linked with harsher sentences (e.g., Gordon and Glaser, 1991; Mileski, 1971; Spohn, 1990; Zatz, 1984). Those who have been convicted of prior criminal acts usually receive harsher sentences than first-time offenders. With respect to "three strikes and you're out" policies, the number and type of priors may be the most important factor in sentencing. When sentencing guidelines are followed, one's prior record also has a significant effect on one's final sentence.

Similarly, those facing more charges tend to receive harsher sentences (e.g., Klein et al., 1991). One scholar even found that the number of charges a defendant faced was a better predictor of sentence severity than prior record (Green, 1961). Again, this is rather intuitive. Logic dictates that a burglar who is sentenced for burglarizing two homes should receive a more severe sentence than a similar burglar who burglarized only one home.

Another legal factor in sentencing is the recommendation made by a probation officer in the pre-sentence investigation. The recommendation itself is a legal factor, but some research has shown that the advice given to judges by probation officers may be the result of bias. One research team (Reese, Curtis, and Whitworth, 1988), for example, found that probation officers' attitudes affected whether they recommended commitment for a juvenile offender. Other scholars (e.g., Hagan, 1975, p. 635; see also Ebbesen and Konečni, 1981) note that offender characteristics such as race and socioeconomic status may affect probation officers more than judges and hence "introduce a channel of extra-legal influence" (Hagan, 1975, p. 635) into sentencing. Other scholars note that probation officers' recommendations may be based in part on the desire to legitimize their own role in the criminal justice system; to illustrate, some probation officers recommend probation so that their offices' budgets can be increased (Moran and Cooper, 1983). These possible biases by probation officers become very important when one notes that the concordance rate between judges' sentences and probation officers' recommendations is very high, often exceeding 80 percent (e.g., Ebbesen and Konečni, 1981; Hagan, 1975).

The final legal factor we will consider is whether a plea bargain was reached in the case. As mentioned in Step 11, judges are not necessarily bound to the sentence agreed to in a plea bargain, but judges rarely deviate from the recommendations that arise out of bargaining sessions. Because of this, the terms of the plea bargain may be strongly associated with, and may be the only determining factor in, the final sentence. Of course, the terms of plea bargains are usually related to the nature of the charges and other legal factors, so the final sentence should not be that much of a surprise. Because plea bargains involve discretion, however, it is also possible that the extra-legal and organizational factors discussed below have some impact on the final recommendations. Later in this chapter, we will discuss plea bargaining as an organizational factor because the practice was designed to serve the courts' needs to dispose of cases. It is included as a legal factor because some bargains dictate sentences and the U.S. Supreme Court has recognized the value of bargaining in American justice. See Box 14.5 for some legal factors considered by lower court judges when deciding and imposing sentences.

---

## BOX 14.5

## Some Legal Factors Considered by Lower Court Judges When Sentencing

*When you read the following excerpts from interviews with lower court judges, think about what the judges value and how they view their role in the courts. Do you agree with their reasoning?*

*Prior record and harm:*

I have enough experience to know what cases are worth, and so, this is kind of like a marketplace, and cases have certain values of their own. And based on independent things within the case, the value goes up or down, based on prior records, or based on aggravating circumstances like use of weapons or causing great risks.

*Prior record:*

A first-timer, [you want to] sentence them appropriately. You don't sentence them with thirty days in jail and give the heavy-weight guy with the bad record five days in jail. What message does that send out? There's a mixed message; it's useless. You better reverse it. Five days for the first-timer, thirty days for the second-timer.

*Mitigating/aggravating circumstances:*

Now, there are things, when we sentence felonies, for example, there are low-term, mid-term, and high-term. I like to say we start at the mid-term. Say it's 2, 3 or 4 years. [I] start at 3 years, and if there are mitigating circumstances, I move down, and if there are worse circumstances, I might move up.

*Nature/seriousness of the crime:*

[The factors I consider] depend on the situation. If you have a first-time offender on a petty theft or some such thing like that you don't usually get too excited about it. [If] you start having people who are using guns and holding up people or something that is of a more violent nature, you are most concerned.

*Role of plea bargaining:*

Most of the sentencing that I do is worked out by way of plea bargains with DAs. So, all of the sentencing that you saw me do [when you observed me] was based on a contract basically with the DA. It's rare that I have a lot of discretion in sentencing.

---

## EXTRA-LEGAL VARIABLES IN SENTENCING

Extra-legal factors are those which have *legally impermissible* influences on legal decisions such as charging, verdicts, and sentencing. The influence of extra-legal variables on sentencing suggests discrimination. Influences that result from these factors undermine our general concept of fairness and justice. When race is felt to determine which defendants receive the death penalty, for example, the public may feel that our criminal justice system is unfair. This may reduce the likelihood that people will comply with the law (Tyler, 1990), or increase the likelihood that people will "martyrize" criminals (Kennedy, 1997, p. 27).

## Extra-Legal Defendant and Offense-Related Variables in Sentencing

Race/ethnicity is by far the most controversial extra-legal factor in sentencing. One of the first empirical studies in this area was conducted by Thorsten Sellin (1928) who compared conviction and sentencing rates for black and white defendants in Chicago during the 1920s. His finding that blacks received heavier penalties than whites has been replicated by many other researchers. Some researchers, however, have quickly denounced the idea that racism plays a role in sentencing and instead point out that the offenses committed by minorities are often more serious than those committed by whites (e.g., Green, 1964; Kleck, 1981, 1985). We now know that racial discrimination affects at least some judges under at least some circumstances, but findings of systemwide bias are far less common than the media would lead one to believe. In some respects, media focus is actually distorted in two opposite directions. Media accounts tend to overplay any potential suggestion of race having been a factor in a case, but underplay the real issues of discrimination against minorities, the poor, and other groups. Because of its profound impact on justice and perceptions of justice, we will examine discrimination in greater detail later in this chapter.

Generally, research shows that women are treated less harshly than men by the courts. Some scholars believe this results from paternalism or a desire to preserve maternal bonds. This phenomenon may be especially salient when defendants' children are in the courtroom at the time of sentencing. As women move into the crime areas previously dominated by men (e.g., violent crimes and fraud), these differences are beginning to disappear. For now, however, women still tend to get lighter penalties overall (Bureau of Justice Statistics, 1994; Daly, 1994; Meeker, Jesilow, & Aranda, et al., 1992). Some scholars argue that it is not women, per se, who are treated leniently, but caregivers in families, who just happen to be female more often than male. These researchers have found that male primary caregivers are also treated leniently, meaning that "familied" defendants of either gender are usually punished lighter than defendants without family responsibilities (e.g., Daly and Tonry, 1997; Simpson, 1989).

Almost ironically, socio-economic status is one of the major influences on sentences. Harsher sentences are often imposed on the poor, sometimes because society fears that such offenders are particularly despicable or dangerous (Chambliss and Seidman, 1971, p. 475; Lizotte, 1978). This seems offensive in a nation that claims fairness for all and once proclaimed, "Send us your poor, your huddled masses yearning to be free." Some scholars argue that "crime" in the United States is a label for deviant acts committed by the poor, while the harms perpetrated by elites (e.g., white-collar crimes) go relatively unnoticed (e.g., Reiman, 1995). Because they are so unlike the middle- and upper-class judges who sentence them, and hence less likely to be empathized with, the poor are likely to get harsh treatment in the courts when it comes to sentencing. This is particularly true when defendants are detained before trial because they could not make bail.

One of the most predictable, yet unfair effects on sentencing may be the dress and appearance of the accused. It is for this reason that many defendants, even in minor traffic cases, wear their Sunday best to court. Likewise, defendants who appear polite and remorseful in court sometimes meet with leniency in the courts. Researchers like Alan Lizotte (1978) recognize the importance of dress and demeanor and how these traits may be tied to socio-economic status:

> In the courtroom, poorer defendants might not present the image of respectability evidenced by dress, demeanor, and social standing which a wealthy person could. Judges might convict more often; assign higher bail amounts; refuse to grant bail; and assign tougher sentences to blacks or persons in lower occupations. (p. 565)

Ties to the community can help offenders in several ways. First, those who have social standing in the community can expect at least some favorable media coverage, even if the community is outraged.[5] Then, those with family ties are sometimes labeled as better risks for probation. Finally, they are more likely to be released before trial, and therefore are better able to assist in their own defenses.

Although possibly the most important factor in criminality, an offender's motivation for committing a crime is technically an extra-legal factor. The law considers **intent** (i.e., what one plans to do) rather than **motivation** (i.e., the goal behind one's planned actions). To illustrate this difference, consider the husband who euthanizes his invalid wife at her request after years of pain and suffering. Despite his motivation to end his wife's suffering, his intent was still to end her life. The husband could be convicted of murder for this act, regardless of whether it was motivated by compassion. When it comes time to impose sentence, however, motivation is elevated to a legal factor. In sentencing, we expect that the compassionate husband's act of murder be treated as less serious than a brutal murder of a healthy wife to collect on life insurance, not because the victims differ, but because the depravity involved in the crimes differs. Likewise, those who steal to feed their hungry children generally receive lighter penalties than drug addicts who steal to feed their drug habits.

Many offender-related, extra-legal influences are less consistent. Some judges, for example, prefer to "hammer" young offenders with harsh sentences to "set them straight" whereas others feel that young offenders deserve leniency. Some judges are more likely to release on probation certain types of offenders such as students and high-profile individuals, but others harshly sentence these offenders, who should "know better" (see Box 14.6 for some extra-legal factors considered by lower court judges when deciding and imposing sentences).

# BOX 14.6

## Some Extra-Legal Factors Considered by
## Lower Court Judges When Sentencing

*When you read the following excerpts from interviews with lower court judges, think about circumstances when their rationales could be viewed as discrimination, or the beginnings of discrimination. Can you imagine at least one set of circumstances under which you would agree with the judges' reasoning?*

*Race/ethnicity:*

I think the [domestic] abuse is maybe increasing a little bit. We have [a] tremendously high proportion of Hispanic residents in this jurisdiction, and I think a lot of the Hispanic legacy is to treat women less as humans and more as property.

*Race/ethnicity:*

I do see Hispanic names. I tell you, though, one thing that really upsets me are illegals. I don't mind illegals coming across the border. I don't mind people coming from other countries to work. My parents did it, yours did, and so on. But what really upsets me is when they come to this country to violate the law. Not in order to, necessarily, but they violate it. And I mean they are cutting and shooting and drunk driving and getting chased by the cops and crashing into people. So I had a meeting with the immigration people to say we have to do something about this. And the immigration people said just taking them back does not do anything. But if they are convicted of a felony and two serious misdemeanors . . . then if they come back, then they can go to the federal penitentiary and do 90 percent of their sentence in 8–10 years. So, what I am saying is that we do not want those criminals.

*Age:*

Is this the tenth time he's been caught breaking in and taking someone's stereo out of their car or is it his first? And if it's the tenth time for a thirty-year-old and it's the tenth time for an eighteen-year-old, you've got a real dilemma because that person's still young. I'm probably never going to reach the thirty-year-old, but if I really crucify the eighteen-year-old, maybe it will stop him. I can give the thirty-year-old a year in jail and he'll be out with his slim-jim and screwdriver the day he gets out. So I can slam him real hard and it probably won't do any good, whereas if I slam the eighteen-year-old, who really is probably less culpable because he hasn't had as much time to mature, I may get his attention and he may go straight.

*Attitude:*

But also it is [influenced by] attitude. Is the defendant's attitude more of being sorry or is it belligerent? A lot of body language that I see in the defendant [is important].

> *Dress:*
> Times are so hard and things are so expensive, that you get people coming in here on parking tickets dressed in tie and jacket, . . . you know, dressed very nicely to save five bucks on a parking ticket. . . . And you get a lot of people coming in here who aren't John Dillinger, coming in on a first-time moving violation, those people deserve to be treated like the good people that they are.

## Extra-Legal Community Variables in Sentencing

Extra-legal community factors may also play a role. Jail or prison overcrowding may lead some judges to consider alternative sentences (Meyer and Jesilow, 1993). The presence of the media or people in the audience may influence sentencing, especially in notorious cases. The general community attitudes toward crime and criminals affect sentencing, especially for elected judges in rural areas (Kunkle, 1989). Finally, the presence of racial unrest or economic inequality in a community may mean that sentences are harsher than in less diverse areas (Myers, 1987).

## Extra-Legal Judicial Variables in Sentencing

Some important, yet often overlooked, sources of extra-legal influence are the characteristics of the sentencing judges themselves.[6] Research has shown, for example, that female offenders receive harsher sentences from female judges than from male judges (Gruhl, Spohn, and Welch, 1981; Myers and Talarico, 1988). Minority judges seem to be more impartial with respect to offender race; that is, offender race is less important in sentences imposed by minority judges, whereas white judges seem to impose more lenient terms on white offenders (Holmes et al., 1993; Welch, Coombs, and Gruhl, 1988). Former prosecutors have been found to impose harsher sentences than other judges (Myers and Talarico, 1988) and retribution-oriented judges are often harsher than judges who follow other punishment philosophies (Hogarth, 1971). Some judges dislike and hand out harsh sentences to drunk drivers, child molesters, or other specific categories of offenders. Judicial age, religion, and form of selection (i.e., elected versus appointed) may also have significant effects on sentences. It is meaningful to realize that judicial characteristics may be as important, if not more important than characteristics of offenders.

## ORGANIZATIONAL FACTORS IN SENTENCING

A third category of sentencing factors are organizational; these are tied to the courtroom itself. In general, they revolve around the strength of the "courtroom work group," composed of the judge, prosecutor, and defense attorney (for more information on courtroom work groups, see Part II [Steps 5–8] of this textbook). The better connected these three courtroom players are, the more likely they are to work as one unit to dispose of cases in an efficient manner, sometimes at the expense of individual defendants (Eisenstein and Jacob, 1977; Nardulli, 1978).

One important organizational factor is the type of plea. It is well known that those who force the state to prove their guilt receive harsher penalties than those who plead guilty (e.g., Albonetti, 1991; Bullock, 1961; Nardulli, 1978). In keeping with the idea of trials as uncalled-for obstacles to justice, attorneys sometimes refer to the harsher sentences imposed on those who are convicted after trial as "rent charged for use of the courtroom." Hence, plea bargaining, whether explicit or implicit, can have a significant impact on final sentence.

Following Abraham Blumberg's (1967) discussion of defense attorneys as "double agents" whose primary duty is to appease the court by persuading their clients to plead guilty and save the state the cost of a trial, scholars began to focus their attention on how the members of the courtroom work group interact with different types of defense counsel. Most researchers agree that public defenders, due at least in part to their high caseloads, are less able than private attorneys to secure acquittals or lenient sentences (e.g., Lizotte, 1978). On the other hand, some research has found that public defenders are better able to secure favorable sentencing outcomes for offenders, presumably because they are able to develop close ties to other courtroom regulars (Pruitt and Wilson, 1984; Wice, 1985, p. 65).

Research has shown that another way to incur the wrath of the courtroom work group is to claim an "unfair" slice of their time in court. Basically, defendants who "take some of the court's time" have some of theirs taken in the form of longer sentences. This has been found true for both the felony (Eisenstein and Jacob, 1977; Nardulli, 1978) and lower courts (Meyer and Jesilow, 1997; Mileski, 1971). Peter Nardulli (1978, p. 216), for example, found that for each defense-initiated legal motion, robbers' sentences increased; those who made one motion were typically incarcerated for 25 months, whereas those who initiated more motions were sent to prison for at least 64 months. At the lower court level, one research team (Meyer and Jesilow, 1997) found that offenders whose misdemeanor arraignment hearings lasted just four or more minutes were significantly more likely than those with shorter hearings to be jailed! Of course, some argue that a possibility exists that sentence outcome "causes" trial length because longer trials are necessary for the complex cases that often involve long sentences; but it is also possible that defendants are not receiving their right to due process. See Box 14.7 for some discussions about organizational factors from judges and court administrators.

# DISCRIMINATION

As discussed above, discrimination reduces the public's trust and faith in the courts. The question is not whether discrimination exists, but the identity of its

---

## BOX 14.7

## Some Comments on Organizational Factors from Lower Court Judges and Court Administrators

*As you read the following quotes, consider the value placed by the courtroom work group on efficiency and saving time.*

*A judge talking about the lack of attorneys in lower courts and judges having to ensure that bargains are not used too often by prosecutors looking to get rid of cases quickly:*

I think our job is to make sure that . . . no one is taking advantage of anyone. The DA is in there talking with *pro pers* all the time, criminal defendants without lawyers, and if we fall asleep at the switch, some people may get some pleas that they shouldn't be pleading to. Punishment that's too high. The DAs are honorable, ethical people, so our job is simple. We check every claim, take every plea, so we're sort of a check-and-balancing system. So, if they're taking advantage of people, or it seems like that, we stop it. "Pardon me, why are you doing this on this person? Why is the fine twice what you normally offer?" And if they tell us why, and there's a good reason for it, fine. If not, I just tear it up. . . . If the offer is low, based on this person before me, then I'll tear it up and say, "No, start over. Either raise up your offer or we'll get them a lawyer and then go to trial, because this person needs more punishment than you're giving them."

*A judge discussing types of bargains in his court which might be attractive to defendants:*

Your first-time petty theft, for example, is usually in plea bargain situations reduced to a trespass . . . so the petty isn't on their record even though the police report indicates it's a clear petty theft. A driving on a suspended license, if the person gets a license, might be reduced to driving without a license . . . the first time or so, but . . . the second, third or fourth time isn't going to be treated like that, and that is just a matter of common sense.

*A court administrator discussing calendaring to improve court efficiency:*

Some courts segment their calendars by all public court cases, and private attorney cases are on different calendars so that it is more efficient. . . . Many calendars are designed for lawyer efficiency to try the cases out in the shortest period of time.

*A judge lamenting about individuals who "waste" the court's valuable time:*

I do not think that it does people any good to just keep going through the front door and not accept responsibility for what got them there. If they can do that by a trip to the front door and pleading guilty, paying the fine, and that modifies their behavior, I'm happier than anybody. But if they continue . . . the behavior that got them there in the first place, then I want to know how much time I'm supposed to . . . waste with them before we take what we're going to do here seriously? This thing costs a lot of money to [operate], courts and all of this stuff.

sources and the nature and extent of its impact. Early studies (pre-1970s) on discrimination showed that minorities, in particular blacks, received harsher penalties than whites. Among these studies were some that included control factors, such as offense severity and prior record (e.g., Bullock, 1961; Lemert and Rosberg, 1948), but without computers to calculate statistics, they relied on bivariate comparisons (meaning they could only control for one factor at a time).

More recent studies (i.e., those after 1970) used more sophisticated research methods, and also found evidence of racial bias in sentencing, but not to the degree reported in earlier studies. One of the most noteworthy studies of the 1970s was a study done by Alan Lizotte. Lizotte (1978) used complex statistical models to examine sentencing outcomes and found that race did not affect sentences directly, but instead operated through minorities' reduced ability to post bail. Another notable study during the 1970s (Uhlman, 1977, 1979) found that blacks received harsher sentences for three reasons: Their crimes were more serious (i.e., their criminality differed), they were poor (i.e., that class status mattered), and they were black (i.e., racism happened). In the 1980s, some researchers focused on the effects of sentencing guidelines that were implemented during the 1970s (e.g., Petersilia and Turner, 1984, found that even racially neutral criteria were "racially tainted," meaning that some of the criteria were associated with race), whether the biases found for blacks extended to other minority groups such as Mexican Americans (e.g., Zatz, 1984, found that Mexican Americans were treated differently from blacks and whites), and whether ecological variables were important in sentencing (e.g., Myers and Talarico, 1988, found that blacks received harsher sentences in communities in which there was a large gap between the lowest and highest incomes but that blacks were treated more fairly in communities with a larger black population).

Current research suggests that discrimination in the criminal justice system is contexual rather than systematic (Walker, Spohn, and DeLone, 2000). That is, evidence suggests that discrimination occurs in the justice system, but that its occurrence, nature, and frequency depends on the context. For example, some police departments are more likely to engage in racial profiling than others, some judges are more likely to be biased in sentencing than others, and so on. Because discrimination is contextual, it may be harder to detect using standard research methods. Sometimes the bias is against minorities, such as when blacks get longer prison terms. Some researchers have found that bias works in favor of white offenders, such as when the criminality of whites was "graded downward by probation officers and judges" in one study so that they received probation or short jail sentences while non-white offenders were sent to prison (Lemert and Rosberg, 1948). The end result of both forms of bias, of course, is the same: Minorities get harsher sentences than whites.

The research on discrimination has become somewhat of a methodological battleground (Meyer and Jesilow, 1997). Instead of discussing the significance of each other's findings, researchers seem to prefer arguing about each other's

This 1941 photograph of inmates from the Greene County prison camp in Georgia attending their warden's funeral illustrates the biases that African Americans of that time faced. Research has shown that African Americans are sometimes more likely than similarly situated whites to be convicted and to be sentenced to incarceration, which might explain the lack of white inmates in this picture. Outright discrimination in sentencing is far less common now because of social changes in how African Americans are viewed following the Civil Rights movement, as well as guarantees of counsel to indigent defendants and other forms of justice system oversight. Instead, discrimination, where it is found, is more contextual and subtle. SOURCE: Library of Congress, Prints and Photographs Division, FSA-OWI Collection, LC–USF33–020874–M1 DLC, Jack Delano, photographer.

"flawed" methods. Now, researchers use complex formulas that require substantial knowledge about statistics to understand. However, it is also important to be aware of methodological issues and the strengths and limitations of criminal justice system data. For example, data showing differences in offending by race/ethnicity may or may not reflect *actual* differences in offending. Why? Because the practices and policies of actors, such as police and prosecutors, can lead to differential arrest and charging policies based on race. Based on available research, we know that some judges are racist. These judges, while relatively rare, sentence minorities harshly simply because they are not white.

Sentencing discrimination may also be reflected in equally important but more subtle ways. For example, research on murder cases shows that the race of the victim is an even more significant influence than the race of the defendant on sentencing (as discussed in Step 13, this argument was raised by McCleskey in his 1987 appeal following his capital sentence for killing a white). Research from several studies of sentencing in capital cases found that when the victim is white, the defendant is more likely to be charged with and convicted of a capital crime, and to receive the death penalty (Baldus, Pulaski, and Woodworth, 1983; Radelet,

1989; Walker, Spone, and DeLone, 2000). This also illustrates contextual discrimination because it suggests that "... crimes involving African-American victims are not taken very seriously. ... [and] the lives of African-American victims are devalued relative to the lives of white victims. Thus, crimes against whites are punished more severely than crimes against African-Americans regardless of the offender's race" (Walker, Spone and DeLone, 2000, p. 245).

Bias is probably most likely in two types of situations. First are those circumstances that occur far from public scrutiny, such as plea bargaining sessions that usually take place in private. Second are those situations where sufficient discretion exists to permit discrimination to take place. Judges must have enough leeway to hand out discriminatory sentences. James Meeker and colleagues (Meeker, Jesilow, and Aranda, 1992), for example, argued that bias is most likely to occur in non-legal decisions. He and his research team found that Hispanics and males were more likely to be sent to less desirable sites to complete their community service sentences (e.g., picking up trash along roads versus working in libraries or other non-profit organizations), and suggested that the placement bias was due to the ability of the judges to exercise their discretion for that decision. In contrast, the defendants' sentence lengths (i.e., the number of hours of service ordered), which were established by law, were not handed out in a discriminatory fashion.

The role of race in justice has become a controversial issue for Americans, but seems to be one they do not really want to seriously tackle, preferring instead to rely on personal opinions and national rhetoric. As aptly summarized by one news columnist, "When a black person breaks the law, it's a comment on race. When a white person commits a crime, it's a comment on society" (Gonsalves, 1998, p. L5). It seems hard for most Americans to seriously question a justice system that repeatedly nets minorities because they are not faced with the continual specter of discrimination themselves. As discussed in Step 8, minorities tend to be arrested more often for street crimes and serious drug offenses. Because such offenses are punished harshly, minorities often find themselves facing strict sentences. Even when compared to whites accused of similar offenses, poor minorities may be less able to post bail to achieve pre-trial release or less able to hire competent counsel, thus increasing their chances of conviction. And, in some cases, outright discrimination is, unfortunately, a factor. As discussed earlier and in Step 8, discrimination can occur at one or more of many points. We still have far to go in our understanding of how race affects the entire process of justice, from law-writing to law-breaking and beyond.

## SENTENCING REFORMS TO DEAL WITH DISCRIMINATION

Discrimination is by no means new to criminal justice. As noted earlier, Cesare Beccaria noted with disdain in the eighteenth century that sentences were sometimes based more upon characteristics of offenders than upon their crimes. Unfortunately, Beccaria's laments described more than just his nation's justice system. American justice in earlier centuries often legislated harsher treatment for African Americans. Some early American laws were actually designed to treat black offenders harsher than their white counterparts. For example, rapists in Georgia during 1861 were sentenced differently according to their race and the race of their victims; state laws at that time dictated that blacks who raped "free white" females "shall be" sentenced to death, whereas non-blacks who raped free white females faced sentences of two to twenty years in prison and those who raped black women were to be punished "by fine and imprisonment, at the discretion of the court" (*McCleskey v. Kemp,* 1987, pp. 329–330). Similarly, an 1848 Virginia statute required the death penalty for any offense committed by a black that could result in three or more years in prison for a white (Jones, 1981, p. 543). These two examples show that our system of justice has not always protected all Americans equally. Even the U.S. Supreme Court acknowledged how tolerable social inferiority for blacks was to nineteenth century white Americans when it ruled in *Plessy v. Ferguson* (1896) that courts could not be expected to guarantee equality to blacks: "If one race be inferior to the other socially, the Constitution of the United States cannot put them upon the same plane."[7] Complaints about the existence of discrimination did not vanish with the eradication of such racist laws as those discussed above, but the situation has improved immensely in this country.

Until a few decades ago, there were relatively few limits on sentencing. Most offenders were sentenced under **indeterminate sentencing**. Under this arrangement, judges decide whether or not offenders will be sent to prison. Later, a parole board determines when each offender will be released. The parole board meets with offenders and determines which are rehabilitated, and therefore "ready" to be released. Rehabilitation, however, lost its political support and people began to notice that discrimination lurked under the euphemistic guise of reforming offenders. It was harder for minorities to convince all-white parole boards they were ready for release, meaning they were held for longer terms.

In response to the realization that sentence length often depended on an offender's skin color or socioeconomic status, legislators began designing a strategy to deal with the problem. Several legislative attempts to restrain discretion were developed. The first was the move from indeterminate sentencing to determinate sentencing. This system replaced vague, open sentences with terms set by statutes. Instead of meaningless sentences of "one year to life," offenders could expect to know the number of years they would serve for their crimes. It was also hoped that such policies would limit judicial discretion and drive judges to impose similar sentences on defendants convicted of similar offenses.

Some states, such as California, chose to rewrite their penal codes to say that retribution was the new state policy, and that sentences were intended to punish, rather than reform, offenders. Merely eliminating rehabilitation from state penological purposes, however, did not delete it from individual judges' priorities. Some judges continued to follow the old directive that viewed offenders as reformable. It did not take long for people to perceive that judges (and, to some extent, parole boards) were letting offenders off with "slaps on the wrist." Angry, the public demanded accountability from its judges and sought ways to limit their discretion. They demanded more restrictions on judges' sentencing options. Such a move, they reasoned, would prevent judges from coddling dangerous offenders.

## Sentencing Guidelines and Mandatory Sentences

One such restrictive sentencing reform is the implementation of sentencing guidelines. Sentencing in the federal and many state felony courts is directed by these rules that dictate sentences based on legal factors present in a case. The type of offense, harm to victim, amount of damage, and the offender's prior record, for example, contribute to a narrowly defined sentence. Using the federal guidelines, a robber who held up someone for less than $10,000 without (1) using a firearm, (2) any resulting injuries, or (3) any prior convictions could expect a sentence of thirty-three to forty-one months (United States Sentencing Commission, 1998, pp. 72–73). Theoretically, extra-legal factors such as race and gender are not allowed to influence sentences because they are excluded from the complex formulas that determine offenders' ultimate fates.[8] Most critically, the use of race and/or gender as factors raises equal protection and due process issues. See Box 14.8 for the 1998 Sentencing Guidelines sentencing table.

Under sentencing guidelines, judges may depart upward (i.e., impose a harsher sentence than that provided by the guidelines) or depart downward (i.e., impose a milder penalty than called for by the guidelines). Judges utilizing either option, however, must provide the court with their reasoning. For this reason, departures are seldom made. At the federal level, most departures are made for cooperating with authorities and providing information about criminal associates (Wray, 1993).

The most restrictive sentencing reform is the adoption of mandatory penalties. Mandatory sentences force judges to impose certain penalties, usually by dictating the minimum sentence a judge may consider. Most mandatory minimums apply to violent crimes (e.g., California's mandatory minimum of twenty-five years in prison for rapists who injure their victims), habitual offenders (e.g., "three strikes and you're out" laws), drug offenses (e.g., many states' mandatory prison terms for drug users and dealers), or firearm use (e.g., "use a gun, go to jail" laws). A new trend is the imposition of mandatory penalties on drunk drivers. All fifty states have some form of mandatory sentences in place and they are a regular feature in federal statutes (Parent et al., 1997). Although mandatory sentences have been around for many years (e.g., see Box 14.9 for a number of early "three strikes"–style American legal codes), the "get tough on crime" movement has boosted their popularity (e.g., Whitman, 1998, pp. 71, 72). In fact, "three strikes"–style sentencing schemes were approved by the U.S. Supreme Court in 1980 in *Rummel v. Estelle.* See Box 14.10 for a brief synopsis of this important case.

# BOX 14.8

## The 1998 Federal Sentencing Guidelines

This table shows sentences, in months, under federal guidelines. To determine an offender's sentence, one need only find the intersection of the Offense Level (i.e., offense severity) and Criminal History Category (i.e., prior record). Each offense has a base value to which points are added if other factors made the crime more serious, for example if the offender used a weapon or inflicted injuries on others (United States Sentencing Commission, 1998). These values are explained in explicit detail in the Guidelines manual, which is nearly 600 pages long.

### Criminal History Category (Criminal History Points)

| Offense Level | I (0 or 1) | II (2 or 3) | III (4, 5, 6) | IV (7, 8, 9) | V (10, 11, 12) | VI (13 or more) |
|---|---|---|---|---|---|---|
| 1 | 0–6 | 0–6 | 0–6 | 0–6 | 0–6 | 0–6 |
| 2 | 0–6 | 0–6 | 0–6 | 0–6 | 0–6 | 1–7 |
| 3 | 0–6 | 0–6 | 0–6 | 0–6 | 2–8 | 3–9 |
| 4 | 0–6 | 0–6 | 0–6 | 2–8 | 4–10 | 6–12 |
| 5 | 0–6 | 0–6 | 1–7 | 4–10 | 6–12 | 9–15 |
| 6 | 0–6 | 1–7 | 2–8 | 6–12 | 9–15 | 12–18 |
| 7 | 0–6 | 2–8 | 4–10 | 8–14 | 12–18 | 15–21 |
| 8 | 0–6 | 4–10 | 6–12 | 10–16 | 15–21 | 18–24 |
| 9 | 4–10 | 6–12 | 8–14 | 12–18 | 18–24 | 21–27 |
| 10 | 6–12 | 8–14 | 10–16 | 15–21 | 21–27 | 24–30 |
| 11 | 8–14 | 10–16 | 12–18 | 18–24 | 24–30 | 27–33 |
| 12 | 10–16 | 12–18 | 15–21 | 21–27 | 27–33 | 30–37 |
| 13 | 12–18 | 15–21 | 18–24 | 24–30 | 30–37 | 33–41 |
| 14 | 15–21 | 18–24 | 21–27 | 27–33 | 33–41 | 37–46 |
| 15 | 18–24 | 21–27 | 24–30 | 30–37 | 37–46 | 41–51 |
| 16 | 21–27 | 24–30 | 27–33 | 33–41 | 41–51 | 46–57 |
| 17 | 24–30 | 27–33 | 30–37 | 37–46 | 46–57 | 51–63 |
| 18 | 27–33 | 30–37 | 33–41 | 41–51 | 51–63 | 57–71 |
| 19 | 30–37 | 33–41 | 37–46 | 46–57 | 57–71 | 63–78 |
| 20 | 33–41 | 37–46 | 41–51 | 51–63 | 63–78 | 70–87 |
| 21 | 37–46 | 41–51 | 46–57 | 57–71 | 70–87 | 77–96 |
| 22 | 41–51 | 46–57 | 51–63 | 63–78 | 77–96 | 84–105 |
| 23 | 46–57 | 51–63 | 57–71 | 70–87 | 84–105 | 92–115 |
| 24 | 51–63 | 57–71 | 63–78 | 77–96 | 92–115 | 100–125 |
| 25 | 57–71 | 63–78 | 70–87 | 84–105 | 100–125 | 110–137 |
| 26 | 63–78 | 70–87 | 78–97 | 92–115 | 110–137 | 120–150 |
| 27 | 70–87 | 78–97 | 87–108 | 100–125 | 120–150 | 130–162 |
| 28 | 78–97 | 87–108 | 97–121 | 110–137 | 130–162 | 140–175 |
| 29 | 87–108 | 97–121 | 108–135 | 121–151 | 140–175 | 151–188 |
| 30 | 97–121 | 108–135 | 121–151 | 135–168 | 151–188 | 168–210 |

*(continued)*

## BOX 14.8 *(continued)*

**Criminal History Category (Criminal History Points)** *(continued)*

| Offense Level | I (0 or 1) | II (2 or 3) | III (4, 5, 6) | IV (7, 8, 9) | V (10, 11, 12) | VI (13 or more) |
|---|---|---|---|---|---|---|
| 31 | 108–135 | 121–151 | 135–168 | 151–188 | 168–210 | 188–235 |
| 32 | 121–151 | 135–168 | 151–188 | 168–210 | 188–235 | 210–262 |
| 33 | 135–168 | 151–188 | 168–210 | 188–235 | 210–262 | 235–293 |
| 34 | 151–188 | 168–210 | 188–235 | 210–262 | 235–293 | 262–327 |
| 35 | 168–210 | 188–235 | 210–262 | 235–293 | 262–327 | 292–365 |
| 36 | 188–235 | 210–262 | 235–293 | 262–327 | 292–365 | 324–405 |
| 37 | 210–262 | 235–293 | 262–327 | 292–365 | 324–405 | 360–life |
| 38 | 235–293 | 262–327 | 292–365 | 324–405 | 360–life | 360–life |
| 39 | 262–327 | 292–365 | 324–405 | 360–life | 360–life | 360–life |
| 40 | 292–365 | 324–405 | 360–life | 360–life | 360–life | 360–life |
| 41 | 324–405 | 360–life | 360–life | 360–life | 360–life | 360–life |
| 42 | 360–life | 360–life | 360–life | 360–life | 360–life | 360–life |
| 43 | life | life | life | life | life | life |

Of course, the legislature must not go too far in imposing mandatory penalties. The resulting sentences must bear some proportionality to the harm caused or appellate courts may strike them down as unfair on review. Consider the 1983 U.S. Supreme Court case, *Solem v. Helm.* Although the charges Helm faced resembled those three years earlier in *Rummel v. Estelle,* the High Court said a mandatory life sentence without parole was disproportionate to his crimes and voided the sentence (1983, pp. 303–302):

> The Constitution requires us to examine Helm's sentence to determine if it is proportionate to his crime. Applying objective criteria, we find that Helm has received the penultimate sentence for relatively minor criminal conduct. He has been treated more harshly than other criminals in the State who have committed more serious crimes. He has been treated more harshly than he would have been in any other jurisdiction, with the possible exception of a single State [Nevada, which also authorized life sentences without parole, but had not yet imposed that sentence]. We conclude that his sentence is significantly disproportionate to his crime, and is therefore prohibited by the Eighth Amendment.

In general, judges and courtroom work groups dislike mandatory sentences because they preclude individualization of sentences. They feel some defendants (e.g., elderly or borderline mentally ill defendants) should not be sent to prison. They also agree that the sentences mandated by the law are sometimes unfair.

# BOX 14.9

## A Sample of Early American "Three Strikes" Laws

As the following laws show, the magical number "three" was established long ago as the cutoff point for determining when an offender's life of crime could be terminated. After one's third offense, one was executed to protect the community. This does not mean that all repeat offender laws seized upon the number three; some repeat offender laws require only two prior offenses to trigger enhanced sanctions ("A thug in prison cannot shoot your sister," 1995, p. 257).

1611   Under a 1611 military law in Virginia, the failure to attend religious services was a crime. One's first offense meant losing a week's rations. The second offense netted a whipping in addition to the loss of a week's rations. Those who dared to commit a third offense were put to death (Johnson, 1988, p. 99).

1648   Massachusetts laws in 1648 established another early "three strikes" law for burglary and robbery. One's first conviction resulted in branding the letter "B" on the offender's forehead (remember, sophisticated tracking technology was not around in the 1600s, so the only way the justice system knew it was dealing with a recidivist was the presence of special maiming or brands on the forehead, hands, or other parts of the body; the presence of the letter "B" on an offender's forehead alerted the courts that the offender had been previously convicted of burglary). A second conviction netted a "severe" whipping in addition to the placement of a second brand on the forehead. The third offense was proof of one's being "incorrigible" and resulted in the offender being put to death. Committing these crimes on the Lord's day resulted in additional penalties, namely the cutting off of one ear on the first offense and the remaining ear on the second offense (Farrand, 1648/1929).

1748   A 1748 Virginia law for hog theft made it clear that swine were protected livestock. One's first offense netted a fine and twenty-five lashes. A second offense was punished by a fine and a two-hour stint in the pillory with one's ears nailed to the device (offenders, by the way, were freed from the pillory by slicing off their ears). The third offense, proof of incorrigibility, was punished with the death penalty (Friedman, 1993, p. 42).

Even some Native American tribes relied on the magic number "three." Traditional Mohawk law punished a third offense of lying with banishment, which was essentially a death sentence (Ross, 1996, p. 162). Early Cherokee law punished rapists with fifty lashes and the removal of the left ear. Repeat rapists received one hundred lashes and had their right ears cut off. Three-time losers were put to death (Young, 1969, p. 23).

Judges in one California county, for example, complained bitterly that they were forced to jail drug addicts for being under the influence of drugs, although this penalty did nothing to help offenders deal with their addictions (Meyer and Jesilow, 1997). Mandatory minimums also disrupt the courtroom work group's routine use

---

## BOX 14.10

### A Summary of *Rummel v. Estelle* (1980), an Important Case in Validating "Three Strikes" Laws

William Rummel had already pled guilty to credit-card fraud in the amount of $80 and passing a forged check for $28.36 when he was charged with theft of $120.75 (*Rummel v. Estelle*, 1980). For this third offense, the prosecutor charged him under Texas' habitual offender law which read: "[Whoever] shall have been three times convicted of a felony less than capital shall on such third conviction be imprisoned for life in the penitentiary" (*Rummel v. Estelle*, 1980). After his conviction and sentence to life in prison, Rummel filed a writ of habeas corpus in United States District Court claiming that his sentence was grossly disproportionate to his crimes. The District Court rejected his claim, but he then asked for reconsideration by a panel of judges which ultimately sided with him. A third hearing by the whole court *en banc* vacated that decision, once again rejecting his claim. The fourth step was a request for the U.S. Supreme Court to hear the case, and that court ruled the sentence was not cruel and unusual punishment or "grossly disproportionate" as noted below:

> The purpose of a recidivist statute such as that involved here is not to simplify the task of prosecutors, judges, or juries. Its primary goals are to deter repeat offenders and, at some point in the life of one who repeatedly commits criminal offenses serious enough to be punished as felonies, to segregate that person from the rest of society for an extended period of time. This segregation and its duration are based not merely on that person's most recent offense but also on the propensities he has demonstrated over a period of time during which he has been convicted of and sentenced for other crimes. Like the line dividing felony theft from petty larceny, the point at which a recidivist will be deemed to have demonstrated the necessary propensities and the amount of time that the recidivist will be isolated from society are matters largely within the discretion of the punishing jurisdiction.
>
> We therefore hold that the mandatory life sentence imposed upon this petitioner does not constitute cruel and unusual punishment under the Eighth and Fourteenth Amendments. The judgment of the Court of Appeals is Affirmed. (*Rummel v. Estelle*, 1980, p. 284–285)

*Postscript:* Three years later, the U.S. Supreme Court did side with another property offender who had received a life term for writing a bad check (*Solem v. Helm*, 1983). Their reasoning was that Rummel had been eligible for parole, while Helm was not. This fact made Helm's sentence disproportionate.

---

of plea bargaining and increase the number of trials demanded by defendants facing mandatory penalties.

Some courtroom work groups find ways to remove the shackles of mandatory and guideline-based sentencing. As shown in Box 14.11, state-level judges sometimes use creative interpretations or purposeful misreadings of sentencing statutes to avoid their intended effects, convert mandatory fines or jail terms into community service hours, or recommend that the probation department allow alternative placements such as residential treatment programs for jail terms (Meyer and Jesilow, 1993). At the federal level, prosecutors have been known to "divide the load" between codefendants in order to reduce possible sentences (e.g., nine ounces of cocaine in the possession of three codefendants would be equal to three ounces each), agree not to seek enhancements, or seek conviction on a less serious charge (Wray, 1993).

Some judges report that they appreciate mandatory and guideline-based sentences. These judges tend to feel that such sentences are acceptable when they are for important causes, such as reducing the incidence of drunk driving. Other judges appreciate that they do not have to determine appropriate penalties in potentially difficult cases. Others feel that the decreases in their discretion are worth the reduced discrimination that accompanies mandatory and guideline-based sentences.

Some states operate under **presumptive sentencing**. Under this scenario, an appointed sentencing commission made up of criminal justice personnel and private citizens sets up varying sentences for individual offenses, similar in some ways to the federal sentencing guidelines discussed earlier. The guidelines are mandatory, though judges may depart from them if they provide their reasons for doing so. If someone is injured in a robbery, for example, the judge may impose a harsher term than is normally imposed for robbery; if the offender played a minor role in the offense, on the other hand, the judge may consider a lesser term.

The intent of efforts to curb discretion are to reduce discrimination and to prevent soft-hearted judges from releasing hard-core offenders onto the streets. Whether or not mandatory penalties and other structured sentencing strategies achieve those goals in a fair manner is a matter of debate. Some legal scholars argue that the past two decades of "get tough" policies in America reflected the fact that although serious crimes were already punished severely, media and government distortions of the extent of the crime problem and the nature of sentencing practices led to public misperceptions that the criminal justice system was "soft on criminals." In response, legislatures passed mandatory sentencing statutes (Donziger, 1996; Walker, Spone, and DeLone, 2000).

---

## BOX 14.11

## A Lower Court Judge in California on the Creative Interpretation of Mandatory Statutes by Judges

There is an interplay between the legislature and the courts. If the statute is ambiguous at all, the judges will try to use that to avoid the mandatory language when they feel it's appropriate. When the legislature hears that they'll go back and revise the language to try to make it more mandatory. So it's an interplay between the two branches on that. (Meyer and Jesilow, 1993)

# BOX 14.12

## Some Student Observations on Sentencing

*The following observations, made by two of the author's students, illustrate some important issues in sentencing. As you read them, think about how the observations illustrate the art of sentencing.*

*Input from the prosecutor is important when determining sentence (Stacy Walter, 1999):*
> Throughout the cases heard this evening I watched how everyone interacted. I noticed that Judge T relied on the prosecutor K for several of the sentencing options. Judge T took into great consideration prosecutor K's opinion.

*Sentences may depend on the courtroom work group (Constance O'Connor, 1993):*
> I was often invited to sit in the judge's chambers and allowed to observe the "behind the scenes" negotiations. Without this direct observation, I would not have been fully aware of the role good-natured cooperation plays in the dispensation of justice. At one point, when the judge decided to give a young defendant a break and sentence him to a rehabilitation center instead of the county jail, the public defender remarked "You must be getting soft, judge." The judge laughingly replied, "No, I just like you today and want you to be happy." The friendly banter between members of this particular courtroom work group seemed to be the rule rather than the exception.

*Efficiency is highly valued and may affect sentences (Constance O'Connor, 1993):*
> In the judge's chambers, one public defender remarked, "Let's get them out of here today. I've got things to do." This type of flippant attitude towards his clients may suggest that this particular public defender is not truly interested in "doing justice" (to borrow a term from Eisenstein and Jacob, 1977), but rather in getting the cases in and out as quickly as possible. This study may also suggest that the public defenders cooperate with the district attorneys to the detriment of the defendants in order to "speed things up."

*The courtroom work group cannot "do justice" without cooperation from all members (Constance O'Connor, 1993):*
> One work group member shared a story with me about a young, highly ambitious district attorney who only lasted a short time at this courtroom. This district attorney insisted on "playing strictly by the book" and refused to participate in the cooperation and negotiation that had become the hallmark of this work group. After several weeks, the courtroom was hopelessly bogged down and the number of cases moving through the system had slowed to a trickle. The judge went to the uncooperative district attorney's boss and had him transferred out and replaced by a more compliant DA. Life returned to normal in the courtroom. Clearly, this demonstrates that in this particular courtroom, cooperation is not only desirable but is required if one wishes to maintain a position within the work group.

## SUMMARY

In this chapter, we examined how sentencing happens, that is, which factors affect sentences and how the hearings progress. We learned that most judges find sentencing to be a difficult task, and that is no surprise given the multiplicity of items that play a role in sentencing outcomes. We also discovered that most judges are unable to keep extra-legal and organizational factors out of their sentences, no matter how well-intentioned they are. Finally, we explored discrimination in sentencing, its causes, and some reforms that have been developed to reduce its incidence. In the end, even after a number of reforms, sentencing is still a difficult task. See Box 14.12 for some student observations regarding sentencing.

"We're appealing!" How many times have you heard that yelled from the top of the courthouse stairs? The next chapter will present information on what appeals are and when they are allowed. It will also clarify the types of rulings available following an appeal. For many defendants, the process ends with this chapter, but for those defendants who are successful in getting their appeals heard, we have one more step. . . .

## DISCUSSION QUESTIONS

1. How could the contents of a PSI be biased or incorrect? Could such biases/inaccuracies be attributed to individuals other than the probation officer who made the report? Provide some examples to explain your answer.

2. What, in your opinion, is the best time to complete the PSI? Why do you feel that way?

3. What are some key ways sentencing hearings are similar to trials? Key ways in which the two processes differ?

4. Do you feel it is fair for judges to be able to increase sentences based on prior cases that did not result in convictions?

5. Read the interview excerpts in Box 14.2, considering how these judges view lying and the problems it poses for them. How is perceived perjury tied to satisfaction with career and how could it affect verdicts or sentences?

6. Read the interview excerpts in Box 14.5, considering what the judges value and how they view their role in the courts. Do you agree with their reasoning?

7. Read the interview excerpts in Box 14.6, considering circumstances when their rationales could be viewed as discrimination, or the beginnings of discrimination. Can you imagine at least one set of circumstances under which you would agree with the judges' reasoning?

8. Read the quotes in Box 14.7. How could efficiency and saving time affect justice?

9. Read your local newspaper to get a small sample of criminal sentences. What are some examples of disparities you noted that probably do not indicate discrimination? Do you see any disparities that might be rooted in discrimination? What criteria did you use to classify the sentences into the two categories?

10. Look over the factors that the judge, either attorney, or other individuals (e.g., commentators or family and friends of the defendant or victim) said were important in the sentences. Classify them into the three categories of factors: legal, extra-legal, organizational. Do you notice any

patterns between the factors that judges and prosecutors claim are used versus those mentioned by other individuals?

11. What are some ways that perceptions of discrimination affects faith in the justice system? How could a lack of faith among the public cause problems for the courts?

12. Why haven't the many sentencing reforms eliminated perceptions of discrimination in sentencing? Have the reforms been beneficial in any ways?

13. List five reasons that you support "three strikes" laws and five reasons you think they should be changed. Overall, what is your opinion about "three strikes" laws?

# NOTES

1. The recommended sentence was not imposed, as the sentencing judge (Judge Marvin Frankel, who was cited in the previous section) wanted to order something more punitive.

2. Some probation officers use the acronym H.O.T. to help them remember that PSIs should be honest, objective, and thorough.

3. Ironically, twenty-one years after his conviction the lead witness recanted his testimony, earning Spaziano a new trial (Another delay in battery trial, 1997).

4. At the time of this writing, Tate's case was under appeal and the governor of Florida had been requested to grant clemency in the case by vacating the sentence or imposing a shorter term of three years in prison that was offered in a plea bargain.

5. Of course, those with high social standing can also expect negative press coverage if their behavior shocks their community. News of the downfall of politicians, clergy, youth group leaders, school teachers, principals, and other individuals who are "in the limelight" or whose positions involve public trust who have been accused of even minor crimes can sometimes set off a negative publicity frenzy. When Karen Howard, wife of the public relations director for the Philadelphia Eagles, killed a man in a 1998 hit-and-run accident, public outcry was unbelievably negative, with members of the public saying they were glad that her wealth was unable to buy her out of jail time, and with some going so far as to say they hoped she was sexually assaulted while incarcerated and were glad that she would be unable to see her young son for a year. In fact, it is possible that Howard was charged and received the relatively harsh sentence because of her prominence in the community and the outcry against her.

6. As mentioned earlier in this chapter, probation officers' personalities and characteristics may affect their recommendations, and therefore, sentencing itself.

7. This decision was a civil judgment concerning "separate, but equal" policies and did not specifically address sentencing differences. It does, however, illustrate the institutionalized inequity of the time.

8. Some scholars argue that some of the criteria that are utilized to establish sentences are associated with race (Petersilia and Turner, 1985). Blacks, for example, are more likely to injure their victims or use weapons during their crimes.

# REFERENCES

Albonetti, C.A. (1991). An integration of theories to explain judicial discretion. *Social Problems,* 38: 247–266.

Alfini, J.J. (1981). Introductory essay: The misdemeanor courts. *Justice System Journal,* 66: 5–12.

Alpert, L. (1981). Learning about trial judging: The socialization of state trial judges. In J.A. Cramer (Ed.), *Courts and Judges.* Beverly Hills, CA: Sage.

Another delay in battery trial. (1997, September 16). *The Miami Herald Wire.*

Baldus, D., Pulaski, C., and Woodworth, G. (1983). Comparative review of death sentences: An empirical study of the Georgia experience. *The Journal of Criminal Law & Criminology,* 74: 709–710.

Beccaria, C. (1983). *An Essay on Crimes and Punishments.* Brookline Village, MA: Branden (Translated and reprinted from *Dei delitti e delle pene* (4th ed.), 1775, London: F. Newberry).

Blumberg, A.S. (1967). *Criminal Justice.* Chicago: Quadrangle.

Breakey, P. (2000, August 29). Guilty plea entered in fatal car accident. *Oneonta Daily Star Wire.*

Brown, J.M., Langan, P.A., and Levin, D.J. (1999). *Felony Sentences in State Courts, 1996.* Washington, DC: Bureau of Justice Statistics.

Bullock, H. (1961). Significance of the race factor in the length of prison sentences. *Journal of Criminal Law, Criminology, and Police Science,* 52: 411–417.

Bureau of Justice Statistics. (1994). *Violence Between Intimates.* Washington, DC: U.S. Department of Justice.

Canedy, D. (2001, March 10). A sentence of life without parole for boy, 14, in murder of girl, 6. *Associated Press Wire.*

Chambliss, W.J., and Seidman, R.B. (1971). *Law, Order, and Power.* Reading, MA: Addison-Wesley.

Chiricos, T.G., and Bales, W.D. (1991). Unemployment and punishment: An empirical assessment. *Criminology,* 29: 701–724.

Daly, K. (1994). Gender and punishment disparity. In G.S. Bridges and M.A. Myers (Eds.), *Inequality, Crime, and Social Control.* Boulder, CO: Westview.

Daly, K., and Tonry, M. (1997). Gender, race, and sentencing. *Crime and Justice,* 22: 201–252.

Donziger, S. (Ed.). (1996). *The Real War on Crime: The Report of the National Criminal Justice Commission.* New York: HarperPerennial.

Ebbesen, E.B., and Konečni, V.J. (1981). The process of sentencing adult felons: A causal analysis of judicial decisions. In B. Sales (Ed.), *The Trial Process.* New York: Plenum.

Eisenstein, J., and Jacob, H. (1977). *Felony Justice: An Organizational Analysis of Criminal Courts.* Boston: Little, Brown.

Farrand, M. (1929). *The Book of the General Lawes and Libertyes Concerning the Inhabitants of the Massachusets* (facsimile ed.). Cambridge: Harvard University Press. (Originally published in 1648).

Feeley, M.M. (1979). *The Process Is the Punishment: Handling Cases in a Lower Criminal Court.* New York: Russell Sage Foundation.

Frankel, M. (1973). *Criminal Sentences: Law without Order.* New York: Hill and Wang.

Friedman, L.M. (1993). *Crime and Punishment in American History.* New York: Basic Books.

*Gardner v. Florida,* 430 U.S. 349 (1977).

Gonsalves, S. (1998, April 14). Not all racists are created equal. *Tri Valley Herald,* p. L5.

Gordon, M.A., and Glaser, D. (1991). The use and effects of financial penalties in municipal courts. *Criminology,* 29: 651–676.

Green, E. (1961). *Judicial Attitudes in Sentencing: A Study of the Factors Underlying the Sentencing Practice of the Criminal Court of Philadelphia.* New York: St. Martin's Press.

Green, E. (1964). Inter- and intra-racial crime relative to sentencing. *Journal of Criminal Law, Criminology and Police Science,* 55: 348–358.

*Green v. Georgia,* 442 U.S. 95 (1979).

Gruhl, J., Spohn, C., and Welch, S. (1981). Women as policymakers: The case of trial judges. *American Journal of Political Science,* 25: 308–322.

Hagan, J. (1975). The social and legal construction of criminal justice: A study of the pre-sentencing process. *Social Problems,* 22: 620–637.

Henningsen, R.J. (1981). *Probation and Parole.* New York: Harcourt, Brace Jovanovich.

*Hill v. U.S.,* 368 U.S. 424 (1962).

Hogarth, J. (1971). *Sentencing as a Human Process.* Toronto: University of Toronto Press.

Holmes, M.D., Hosch, H.M., Daudistel, H.C., Perez, D.A., and Graves, J.B. (1993). Judges' ethnicity and minority sentencing: Evidence concerning Hispanics. *Social Science Quarterly,* 74: 496–506.

Immarigeon, R. (1985). Private prisons, private programs, and their implications for reducing reliance on imprisonment in the United States. *The Prison Journal,* 65: 60–74.

Johnson, H.A. (1988). *History of Criminal Justice.* Cincinnati: Anderson.

Jones, D.A. (1981). *The Law of Criminal Procedure: An Analysis and Critique.* Boston: Little, Brown.

Kennedy, R. (1997). *Race, Crime, and the Law.* New York: Vintage.

Kitching, H. (1995, January 20). Bite the bullet, judge tells drive-by triggerman—12 years, no parole. *Nogales International.*

Kleck, G. (1981). Racial discrimination in criminal sentencing: A critical evaluation of the evidence with additional evidence on the death penalty. *American Sociological Review,* 46: 783–805.

Kleck, G. (1985). Life support for ailing hypotheses: Modes of summarizing the evidence for racial discrimination in sentencing. *Law and Human Behavior,* 9: 271–285.

Klein, A.R. (1988). *Alternative Sentencing: A Practitioner's Guide.* Cincinnati: Anderson.

Klein, S.P., Ebener, P., Abrahamse, A., and Fitzgerald, N. (1991). *Predicting Criminal Justice Outcomes: What Matters?* Santa Monica, CA: Rand Corporation.

Kunkle, W.J. (1989). Punishment and the criminal justice system: A prosecutor's viewpoint. In F.E. Baumann and K.M. Jensen (Eds.), *Crime and Punishment: Issues in Criminal Justice.* Charlottesville: University Press of Virginia.

Lemert, E.M., and Rosberg, J. (1948). The administration of justice to minority groups in Los Angeles County. *University of California Publications in Culture and Society,* 2: 1–28.

Lizotte, A.J. (1978). Extra-legal factors in Chicago's criminal courts: Testing the conflict model of criminal justice. *Social Problems,* 25: 564–80.

*McCleskey v. Kemp,* 481 U.S. 279 (1987).

*McMillan v. Pennsylvania,* 477 U.S. 79 (1986).

Meeker, J.W., Jesilow, P., and Aranda, J. (1992). Bias in sentencing: A preliminary analysis of community service sentences. *Behavioral Sciences and the Law,* 10: 197–206.

Meyer, J., and Jesilow, P. (1993). "Doing justice": Judicial attitudes toward community service sentences. *The IARCA Journal on Community Corrections,* 5(5): 10–12.

Meyer, J., and Jesilow, P. (1997). *"Doing Justice" in the People's Court: Sentencing by Municipal Court Judges.* New York: State University of New York Press.

Mileski, M. (1971). Courtroom encounters: An observation study of a lower criminal court. *Law and Society Review,* 5: 473–538.

Moran, T.K., and Cooper, J.L. (1983). *Discretion and the Criminal Justice Process*. Port Washington, NY: Associated Faculty Press.

Myers, M.A. (1987). Economic inequality and discrimination in sentencing. *Social Forces,* 65: 746–766.

Myers, M.A., and Talarico, S.M. (1988). *The Social Contexts of Criminal Sentencing*. New York: Springer/Verlag.

Nardulli, P.F. (1978). *The Courtroom Elite: An Organizational Perspective on Criminal Justice*. Cambridge, MA: Ballinger.

Nidorf, B.J. (1996). Probation officer's report for Joseph Lyle Menendez. Superior Court of California County of Los Angeles.

Parent, D., Dunworth, T., McDonald, D., and Rhodes, W. (1997). *Mandatory Sentencing*. Washington, DC: U.S. Department of Justice.

*Payne v. Tennessee,* 501 U.S. 808 (1991).

Petersilia, J., and Turner, S. (1985). *Guideline-based justice: The implications for racial minorities*. Santa Monica, CA: Rand Corporation.

*Plessy v. Ferguson,* 163 U.S. 537 (1896).

President's Commission on Law Enforcement and Administration of Justice. (1967). *Task Force Report: The Courts*. Washington, DC: Government Printing Office.

Pruitt, C.R., and Wilson, J.Q. (1984). A longitudinal study of the effect of race on sentencing. *Law and Society Review,* 17: 613–35.

Radelet, M.L. (1989). Executions of whites for crimes against blacks: Exceptions to the rule? *Sociological Quarterly,* 30: 529–544.

Reese, W.A., Curtis, R., and Whitworth, J. (1988). Dispositional discretion or disparity: The juvenile probation officer's role in delinquency processing. *The Journal of Applied Behavioral Science,* 24: 81–100.

Reiman, J. (1995). *The Rich Get Richer and the Poor Get Prison: Ideology, Crime, and Criminal Justice* (4th ed.). Boston, MA: Allyn and Bacon.

*Roberts v. United States,* 445 U.S. 550 (1980).

Ross, R. (1996). Leaving our White eyes behind: The sentencing of Native accused. In M.O. Nielsen and R.A. Silverman (Eds.), *Native Americans, Crime, and Justice*. Boulder, CO: Westview.

*Rummel v. Estelle,* 445 U.S. 263 (1980).

Sellin, T. (1928). The Negro criminal: A statistical note. *Annals of The American Academy of Political and Social Science,* 140: 52–64.

Simpson, S. (1989). Feminist theory, crime and justice. *Criminology,* 27, 605–631.

*Solem v. Helm,* 463 U.S. 277 (1983).

*Spaziano v. Florida,* 468 U.S. 447 (1984).

Spohn, C. (1990). The sentencing decisions of black and white judges: Expected and unexpected similarities. *Law and Society Review,* 24: 1197–1216.

"A thug in prison cannot shoot your sister": Ohio appears ready to resurrect the habitual criminal statute—will it withstand an Eighth Amendment challenge? (1995). *Akron Law Review,* 28, 253–289.

Tyler, T.R. (1990). *Why People Obey the Law*. New Haven: Yale University Press.

Uhlman, T.M. (1977). The impact of defendant race in trial-court sanctioning decisions. In J.A. Gardiner (Ed.), *Public Law and Public Policy.* New York: Praeger.

Uhlman, T.M. (1979). *Racial Justice: Black Judges and Defendants in an Urban Trial Court.* Lexington, MA: Lexington Books.

United States Sentencing Commission. (1998). *Guidelines Manual.* §3E.1.

*United States v. Bergman,* 416 F. Supp. 496 (1976).

*United States v. Boney,* 977 F.2d 624 (D.C. Cir. 1992).

*United States v. Grayson,* 438 U.S. 41 (1978).

Walker, S., Spohn, C., and DeLone, M. (2000). *The Color of Justice: Race, Ethnicity, and Crime in America* (2nd ed.). Belmont, CA: Wadsworth.

*Walton v. Arizona,* 497 U. S. 639 (1990).

Welch, S., Coombs, M., and Gruhl, J. (1988). Do black judges make a difference? *American Journal of Political Science,* 32: 126–136.

Wice, P.B. (1985). *Chaos in the Courthouse: The Inner Workings of the Urban Criminal Courts.* New York: Praeger.

Whitman, C.T. (1998). Bringing balance to the criminal justice system. *Crime and Delinquency,* 44: 70–74.

*Williams v. New York,* 337 U.S. 241 (1949).

Wray, H.R. (1993). *Mandatory minimum sentences: Are they being imposed and who is receiving them?* Washington, DC: Government Accounting Office.

Young, R.W. (1969). *Historical Backgrounds for Modern Indian Law and Order.* Washington, D.C.: Bureau of Indian Affairs, Division of Law Enforcement Services.

Zatz, M.S. (1984). Race, ethnicity, and determinate sentencing: A new dimension to an old controversy. *Criminology,* 22: 147–171.

# Step 15

# Appeals

We have seen the human drama that accompanies trials and sentencing hearings. The intense emotional atmosphere that can develop during pivotal moments of the trial demonstrates the seriousness of the proceedings in the eyes of many of the participants and observers. The highly formal, ritualized nature of court procedures is the "official framework" of trials, yet the actual proceedings are often quite personalized, idiosyncratic, and charged with emotion.

A defendant's conviction, however, is often only the end of one phase of the legal process, with the most critical stage yet to come. How can this be? The answer is that a finding of guilt in a trial court may raise legal issues that are reviewable by an appeals court.

Trial courts at both the state and federal level are charged with finding out the facts in a case and deciding how the law applies in particular cases. In contrast, the function of appellate courts is examining claims that the law was improperly applied or that legal procedures were not correctly followed. An **appeal** is "a proceeding in which a case is brought before a higher court for review of a lower court's judgment for the purpose of convincing the higher court that the lower court's judgment was incorrect" (Merriam-Webster, 1996).

## WHY ARE APPEALS IMPORTANT?

At first glance, it may seem obvious that appeals are important to the parties in a case, and indeed this is true. The appeals process is part of the system of "checks and balances" designed to ensure that defendants have received due process at earlier stages of the criminal justice process. Thus, appeals are a critical means for pursuing specific legal goals in individual cases.

However, appeals are also important because they are one of the principal avenues by which legal issues in a particular area of law are shaped. The principle of **stare decisis** means that precedent is highly respected in the law, but at the same

465

time legal, societal, and technological changes bring new issues before the courts. These new issues often raise legal questions that become the subject of appeals, and each appellate decision in turn contributes to legal precedent on the issue. An appellate court's **holding** in a case provides the court's decision, the case facts that were the basis for the decision, and the judicial reasoning underlying the decision. The holding serves as a precedent that is then applicable to all similar cases arising in future in the appellate court's jurisdiction.

In contrast to a trial court's decision, which is binding only on the parties to a particular case, an appellate court's decisions serve as precedent that is legally binding on all lower courts within its jurisdiction. This means that all lower courts must decide cases in a manner consistent with the applicable precedent in that jurisdiction.

Appellate court decisions in one jurisdiction also often serve as a source of guidance to courts in other jurisdictions that are seeking ideas on how to address a particular legal issue. Because appellate decisions constitute legal precedent that lower courts in the appellate jurisdiction must adhere to when deciding similar cases, appellate courts are thus major sources of public policy on criminal justice issues.

This creates continuing controversy between those who argue that courts are deliberative forums that are well positioned to perform policymaking, because appointed appellate judges are comparatively immune to the political pressures surrounding elected officials, and others who disagree. Legislators, as elected officials, are susceptible to influence by well-organized interest groups and lobbyists, and must depend on the favor of a certain proportion of the electorate if they wish to continue to hold office (see Box 15.1 on Rose Bird). In contrast, courts are better able to protect the rights of the minority, which otherwise might be suppressed by majority rule (Smith, 2000). For example, the right of individuals who wish to trample and burn the American flag has been protected by the U.S. Supreme Court as an expression of free speech under the First Amendment (*Texas v. Johnson,* 1989). Therefore, legal protection of the exercise of free speech is not contingent on the popularity of the speech or the speaker. Thus, the right of civil rights activists to demonstrate and lead protest marches is protected by the First Amendment; but so is the right of extremist white supremacist groups to march and protest as well.

Critics argue that policymaking by courts usurps the legislative function, and that, in addition, courts are not well suited to policymaking for a number of reasons (Smith, 2000):

- Judges do not have expertise in specific policy issues.
- Courts can consider policy issues only if and when they arise in cases before the court.
- Courts must rule narrowly on the legal issues in a particular case.
- Courts cannot rule broadly on matters of policy outside the scope of the specific issues in a case.

---

### BOX 15.1

### Judicial Independence, Accountability, and the Death Penalty

Rose Bird was the Chief Justice of the California Supreme Court from 1977 to 1986. During that time, sixty-one California death sentences were appealed to her court, and she voted to overturn the sentence in each case. Many California voters were outraged by this, and legal and political commentators accused Justice Bird of extreme judicial activism—of letting her opposition to capital punishment color her judicial decisions. Bird supporters argued in rebuttal that her decision was based on the specific legal issues particular to each case. In 1986, Justice Bird and two of her colleagues on the court were removed from office after failing a routine "confirmation vote" by voters. During the acrimonious public debate over Bird's handling of capital cases, some of Bird's opponents touted the slogan "Bye, Bye, Birdie" (Balzar, 1985). After being ousted from the court, Rose Bird lived a life of quiet seclusion until her death in 1999.

---

The significance of appellate courts becomes even clearer if you consider that our legal rights have an impact only insofar as legislatures and courts choose to interpret what these rights mean in practice. In particular, federal and state constitutional rights often raise legal issues that are addressed through the appellate process. For example, does the Sixth Amendment right to trial by jury apply to minors whose cases are adjudicated in juvenile court (*McKeiver v. Pennsylvania, 1971*)? Does the Fourth Amendment's prohibition against unreasonable search and seizure allow police officers to fire in order to prevent a suspect from fleeing (*Tennessee v. Garner, 1985*)? The provisions of federal and state legislation can raise similar questions for appellate courts (see Box 15.2 on HUD [Housing and Urban Development] policies).

Public policymaking on crime and criminal justice raises questions about policy applicability, scope, and exceptions. We've actually looked at some examples of this already on our journey through the courts. For example, "three strikes and you're out" sentencing statutes raise questions about what counts as a "strike": Do juvenile offenses count? Do nonviolent offenses count? Should offenses committed ten or twenty years before the current offense count? Each of these questions has been asked on appeal. See Box 15.3 for another example of how legislative provisions can provide plenty of questions for appellate courts to consider.

Appellate decisions therefore serve as a bridge between legal theory and practice, as a means of translating abstract concepts into concrete policies, procedures, and requirements. For example, what does "due process" mean in practice for a person accused of a crime? As we saw earlier in the book, it was only after a series of appellate court decisions from different cases spread over a span of more than 150 years that the concept of due process came to include the right to have an attorney provided if you cannot afford to hire one.

---

## BOX 15.2

### You May Be Your Brother's Keeper, After All

Herman Walker was seventy-seven years old, disabled, and living in public housing. When the woman he hired to assist him was found with a crack-cocaine pipe in her possession, Mr. Walker faced eviction. In another case, a woman living in public housing faced eviction after her adult granddaughter was arrested by police for drug possession five blocks away from her apartment; another grandmother faced eviction when her grandkids were found in the parking lot of her public housing building smoking marijuana (Finz, 2000). Another tenant, a pregnant woman with a toddler, was awakened by police when they arrested an individual who was in her living room and allegedly had heroin in his jacket pocket. The police had a search warrant to enter the apartment and look for two people alleged to be drug dealers. The tenant says the people did not have permission to be in her living room, and that her young child had accidentally let them in while her mother was asleep. The woman and her daughter face eviction (Egelko, 2001).

What's going on here? The common thread linking these cases is a federal anti-drug policy. In 1991, the federal Department of Housing and Urban Development, the agency that controls public housing, initiated a "one-strike" policy for public housing tenants. In an effort to control crime, the policy stated that public housing tenants would be evicted if any member of the household, including visitors, were involved in illegal drug activity either on or off the premises (Egelko, 2001). The policy, which could affect approximately three million tenants in public housing across the nation (Egelko, 2001), is set up to encourage tenants to monitor the behavior of people who live with, work for, or visit them, and to punish criminal activity by loss of a scarce resource—subsidized housing. But critics charge that this simply punishes tenants for the crimes of others when the tenants had no knowledge of such crimes, and that the policy illustrates how the war on drugs disproportionately affects the lives of people who are poor and people of color.

Tenants and their lawyers challenged this policy in federal court, and a judge issued an injunction stopping the evictions, "saying the law appeared 'irrational' because the tenants had no idea of the drug use" (Finz, 2000, p. A20). However, as the appeals process continued, the U.S. Court of Appeals for the Ninth Circuit reversed the injunction, allowing the evictions to go forward. However, evictions were halted once again when the appellate court decided to rehear the case **en banc** (that is, with the full panel of judges rather than the typical three judge panel). The court later ruled that evictions were permissible only when the tenant "knew or should have known" about the drug activity (Egelko, 2001) (Egelko, 2001; Finz, 2000).

Upon appeal by the tenants, on March 26, 2002, the U.S. Supreme Court upheld the constitutionality of Congress's "zero tolerance" eviction policy for public housing tenants, even if the tenants were unaware of the drug use of their family members, friends, caretakers, or visitors (*HUD v. Rucker et al.*, 2002) (Egelko, 2001; Finz, 2000). The policy rests on the assumption that the behavior of family, friends, and visitors of the lease-holding tenant is under the tenant's control, even if the drug-related activity took place blocks from the actual premises of the apartment or the building. Do you think this is a reasonable assumption?

*Source:* Excerpts from the *San Francisco Chronicle* reprinted with permission.

---

## BOX 15.3

## What's the Right Meaning of "Wrong"?

In California, criminal defendants who wish to present an insanity defense have the burden of proving that they were insane at the time of the crime, under the following definition of insanity:

> In any criminal proceeding. . . . in which a plea of not guilty by reason of insanity is entered, this defense shall be found by the trier of fact only when the accused person proves by a preponderance of the evidence that he or she was incapable of knowing or understanding the nature and quality of his or her act and of distinguishing right from wrong at the time of the commission of the offense. (California Penal Code § 25 (2001)(b)).

This definition was the subject of appeals related to various aspects of the wording. For example, this definition of insanity is a variation of the famous M'Naghten standard (see Step 2). However, whereas the original M'Naghten standard required a defendant to prove only that she or he was incapable of understanding the nature and quality of the act *or* incapable of knowing right from wrong, California's version appears to require defendants to prove *both* of these things in order to pass the standard. When a defendant appealed this apparently stricter requirement, the appellate court determined that the legislature had not intended to depart from the original M'Naghten standard. Therefore, despite the wording of Penal Code Section 25 2001(b), only one prong of the test must be met; in essence, the appellate court found that "and" really should be interpreted as "or," a critical difference for defendants presenting an insanity defense (*People v. Horn*, 1984; *People v. Skinner*, 1985).

What does it mean to speak of "knowing right from wrong"? In another case stemming from the wording of California's insanity definition, the appellate court clarified that "wrong" refers to society's generally accepted moral standards, not the defendant's subjective moral standard of right and wrong (*People v. Stress*, 1988).

---

## BOX 15.4

## The Great Writ

"You have the body." That is the literal translation of the Latin phrase "**habeas corpus**," which is the name of the appeal filed by thousands of people incarcerated in jails and prisons. habeas corpus appeals reflect a long legal tradition dating back to medieval times; the *Magna Charta* refers to this appeal as "the Great Writ" in recognition of its power as a legal mechanism for prisoners to question the legitimacy of their confinement by the government. The basis of a "habeas appeal," as it is commonly called, is an assertion that the appellant is being held illegally by the government. The appeal lays out the legal arguments to support this assertion and requests that the court free the person who is unjustly detained.

How did the Great Writ come to be? Recall the appeal the incarcerated jurors in the Penn and Mead trial (discussed in Steps 4 and 12) used to attain their freedom: that they were

## BOX 15.4*(continued)*

wrongfully imprisoned by the English government. This was the landmark case that ultimately resulted in the Habeas Corpus Act of 1679 becoming law in England (Rosenn, 1983). American colonists imported the Great Writ, and thus Congress provided for federal habeas corpus petitions in the Judiciary Act of 1789. The scope of habeas corpus was expanded to state courts in later years (Rosenn, 1983).

## THE POWER OF JUDICIAL REVIEW

The power of appellate courts to review the decisions of government officials in the legislature, the executive branch, and lower courts is the power of "**judicial review**." This power allows the U.S. Supreme Court and the supreme courts of each state to review legislation, court decisions, and executive acts that are challenged in court to determine their constitutionality. Note, however, that the power of judicial review does *not* mean that courts can independently decide to oversee the laws enacted by the legislature and the executive branch. Instead, appellate courts can only consider the issues arising from cases brought before them. Although judicial review empowers appellate courts to consider the legal issues raised on appeal from trial courts, the legal basis of the right to appeal is not found in the Constitution. Rather, statutory provisions at both the state and federal levels provide the legal basis for appeals of trial court decisions. The most famous articulation of the concept of judicial review was by Alexander Hamilton in *The Federalist* (No. 78), and by the U.S. Supreme Court in *Marbury v. Madison* (1803). The *Marbury* opinion illustrates the court's reasoning on the logic of judicial review:

> It is emphatically the province and duty of the judicial department to say what the law is. Those who apply the rule in particular cases, must of necessity expound and interpret that rule. If two laws conflict with each other, the courts must decide on the operation of each.
>
> So if a law be in opposition to the constitution; if both the law and the constitution apply to a particular case, so that the court must either decide that case conformably to the law, disregarding the constitution; or conformably to the constitution, disregarding the law; the court must determine which of these conflicting rules governs the case. This is of the very essence of judicial duty. (p. 177–178)

## COURT HIERARCHY

As we saw in Step 4, courts are organized in a hierarchy that defines each court's jurisdiction in relation to the other courts. At the state level, the decision of its supreme court is legally binding on the lower courts (both appellate and trial) in that state. However, the court decisions of one state are not legally binding on courts in a different state.

Though tribal court systems are independent, the courtroom of the Navajo nation Supreme Court is typical of many state and federal appellate courts. Three judges hear cases, and if one of the judges cannot sit on a particular case (e.g., due to illness), a replacement judge is temporarily appointed. The five flags in the background represent the jurisdictions governing the Navajo Nation: the federal government; the states of New Mexico, Utah, and Arizona; and their own tribal laws. The Navajo Nation does not have an intermediate court of appeals; appeals are heard by the Navajo Nation Supreme Court. SOURCE: Courtesy of Jon'a Meyer.

At the federal level, the decisions of higher federal courts are binding on lower federal courts. With respect to Constitutional issues, the decisions of federal courts are usually binding on state courts. On Constitutional matters, the ultimate appellate court is the U.S. Supreme Court.

The appellate process follows an established progression, with appeals ascending up the ladder of the court hierarchy in sequence. After the trial, an appeal must be submitted to the appropriate lower appellate court; appeals cannot be directly submitted to a higher appellate court. Criminal convictions in state trials can be appealed to federal courts only if there is a federally guaranteed right at issue (i.e., a right guaranteed by the U.S. Constitution or federal legislation). Why? Under the framework specified in the Constitution, the task of defining crimes and punishments is primarily a matter for state legislatures rather than the federal government. Thomas Jefferson said in 1798 that: "The power to create, define, and punish such other crimes is reserved, and of right appertains solely and exclusively to the respective States, each within its own territory" (Jefferson, 1798). This is why most criminal cases (and thus appeals) arise at the state level, although in recent years there has been an increasing trend toward national legislation giving rise to federal cases (for example, RICO, the Racketeer-Influenced Corrupt Organizations statute passed by Congress as a crime-fighting mechanism).

Because the federal and state court systems have a parallel structure to address issues of federal and state law, respectively, state criminal courts are generally autonomous with respect to matters of state law. If, for example, a criminal defendant wishes to appeal on the basis that her rights as provided in state legislation were violated, then the appeal is a matter for state appellate courts. However, the **Supremacy Clause** of the Constitution (U.S. Constitution Article VI, paragraph 2) provides that federal laws take precedence over state laws when there is a conflict between the two. Thus a state criminal defendant may claim that his federally guaranteed rights were violated, and file an appeal in the state appellate court. If the appeal is decided in favor of the defendant, the prosecution may appeal this finding in a higher level appellate court. However, if the defendant loses the appeal after having exhausted all state court avenues, then (and only then) may the defendant appeal to the appropriate federal appellate court.

## APPELLATE JUDGES

Federal judges at both the trial and appellate levels are appointed by the President of the United States, as provided for in the Constitution. Nominees must be

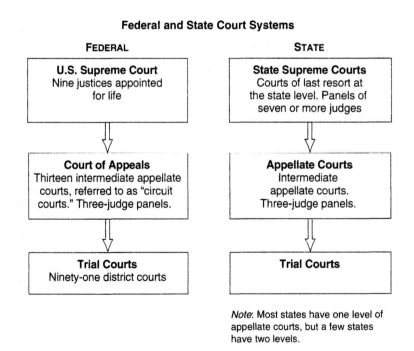

**FIGURE 15.1 Court hierarchy**

approved by the Senate. State appellate court judges are usually elected, but may be appointed in some jurisdictions (depending on the level of the appellate court).

## APPEALS OF LAW, NOT FACT

Appeals are made on the basis of matters of law, not fact. What this means is that the legal basis for an appeal must be a claim that the law was misapplied, either substantively or procedurally. An appeal cannot be made on the basis of disputes about the facts of the case, or dislike for the outcome of the case. For example, if you are convicted of a crime, you generally cannot appeal solely because you believe you are innocent. In rare cases, defendants have appealed their convictions using the argument that the evidence was not sufficient to support a conviction. However, such appeals are rarely successful. Rather, your appeal would have to be based on legal issues, such as whether your trial provided appropriate procedural safeguards.

Appellate courts thus usually *do not* relitigate factual issues that were brought up at trial. The facts as noted in the trial court's record of the proceedings are assumed to be correct (and this is why the court reporter's work is so important). This assumption reflects the belief that the judge (and jury, if there was one) would logically be in the best position to determine the facts of the case, compared to the judges of the appellate court. The issue for the appellate court is whether the law was properly applied to the facts in the case as they are described in the trial court records. Thus, appellate decisions are based on the facts and applicable law as described in the transcript of the trial proceedings, in the briefs and supporting documents filed by the parties to the appeal, and in oral arguments, which may be given in some appeals.

Under certain narrowly defined circumstances, an appellate court may hold an appeal **de novo** (anew). In this instance, "The appellate court uses the trial court's record but reviews the evidence and the law without deference to the trial court's rulings" (Black's Law Dictionary, 1999, p. 94).

## THE APPELLATE PROCESS: PROCEDURAL ISSUES

### Standing: Who Can Appeal?

In criminal cases, both prosecution and defense can appeal a court's decision on various motions (such as to exclude evidence). However, whereas defendants can always appeal a conviction if appropriate legal grounds exist, the government generally cannot appeal an acquittal (*State v. Jones,* 1809). Once a person is acquitted, they cannot be tried for the same crime. For example, recall the case of Mel Ignatow, the man who was acquitted of murdering his girlfriend, only to have photographs documenting his crime turn up later (see Step 5). In very limited circumstances, the government may be able to appeal an acquittal, such as when it was due to the defendant's bribery of the judge in a bench trial (*People v. Aleman,* 1994). In contrast, a number of other countries, such as Israel, Pakistan, Singapore, and Venezuela, allow the government to appeal acquittals (Office of Legal Policy, 1987).

However, note that the Fifth Amendment prohibition against double jeopardy does not mean that a person cannot be tried by two different types of courts on the same charges—for example, civil and criminal charges—or be prosecuted at both federal and state court levels.

In order for an appeal to proceed, the appellate court must determine that the **appellant** (i.e., the party bringing the appeal) has the legal right to bring the case; the opposing party, by the way, is called the **appellee**. This means that the court must determine whether the appellant has **standing**, meaning that the appellant has a legally recognizable interest in the case. Standing is defined as "the status of being qualified to assert or enforce legal rights or duties in a judicial forum because one has a sufficient and protectable interest in the outcome of a justiciable controversy and usually has suffered or is threatened with actual injury" (Merriam-Webster, 1996).

Here is an example of standing: In wrongful death lawsuits, people who are legally defined as family members of the deceased have standing to file the suit, whereas others generally do not. In San Francisco, the death of Diane Whipple, who was mauled to death by a neighbor's dog, raised the issue of standing. Whipple's long-term domestic partner, Sharon Smith, wanted to sue the owners of the dog for wrongful death but did not have legal standing to do so. Coincidentally, two months before Whipple was attacked, California legislator Carole Migden had introduced legislation to expand the California legal definition of family members to include domestic partners. If the legislation passes, domestic partners would have legal standing to sue for wrongful death in California (Hoppin, 2001). Box 15.5 describes a historic example of the controversy that the issue of standing can embody.

If a court determines that the appellant has standing, the case may proceed. If not, the court dismisses the case for lack of standing, which means only that this particular appellant cannot raise the issue. However, another appellant who has standing is free to raise the same issues as part of a new case.

## THE STEPS OF AN APPEAL

When a trial ends in conviction and the defense decides to appeal, there are certain steps which must be followed, as listed below. Depending on whether the appeal is filed in state or federal court, and the particular practices of the jurisdiction in which the appeal is filed, there will be variation in the amount of time allowed for each step, and the exact procedures the defense must take to complete each step:

---

## BOX 15.5

## Without a Leg to Stand On:
## The Issue of Standing in the Corn Tassels Case

The year was 1830, and the Cherokee Nation was in serious conflict with the state of Georgia (before the Trail of Tears, during which they were forcibly marched from their ancestral homeland to Oklahoma, the Cherokees lived in Georgia, where they were viewed as a nuisance by Georgians). Although the Cherokees, and other Native American nations, considered themselves to be sovereign, the state of Georgia had passed a law allowing them to assume jurisdiction when crimes occurred on Cherokee land.

Among those arrested by the state under its new law was Corn Tassels, a Cherokee Indian who was accused of killing another Cherokee. The Cherokee were understandably upset because they had intended to prosecute Corn Tassels themselves and viewed the state's actions as pure kidnapping. Imagine how upset Americans would be if a foreign nation came into this country and arrested and prosecuted an American citizen for a crime committed in the United States.

In September of 1830, the Georgia state court found Corn Tassels guilty and sentenced him to hang. An attorney working for the Cherokee Nation drafted an appeal, arguing that treaties signed with the Cherokees guaranteed them the right to self-government and that included control of their criminal justice system. The Cherokee fought, and predictably lost, appeals in the state of Georgia, and then sought a final appeal with the relatively new U.S. Supreme Court, filing a writ of error that argued that Georgia's actions were in error and violated the U.S. Constitution.

The U.S. Supreme Court granted the writ, and demanded that Georgia appear before their court to explain why the Corn Tassels situation "should not be corrected." But Georgia officials refused to submit themselves to any scrutiny, saying that "interference" by the U.S. Supreme Court "in the administration of the criminal laws of this state . . . is a flagrant violation of [Georgia's] rights." On December 24, 1830, ten days after the writ had been granted, Georgia officials executed Corn Tassels, rendering the appeal moot.

This case illustrates several concepts of courts. First is the idea of standing, which is possessed only by individuals who face actual injury or harm and who have a protectable interest in a case outcome. Even though the Cherokee Nation wanted the case to go forward, it could not because the individual with standing (i.e., Corn Tassels) could no longer press the case forward or benefit from the Court's intervention. It is irrelevant that his tribe and attorneys wanted to keep the case moving ahead in hopes that the U.S. Supreme Court would invalidate Georgia's law. It was also irrelevant that Georgia had directly interfered with the U.S. Supreme Court's review by prematurely executing the defendant. What was important was that Corn Tassels himself could no longer maintain the case and so the appeal was rendered moot.

The case also illustrates the relative powerlessness of the U.S. Supreme Court when faced with Georgia's extreme defiance. At that time, the High Court was fairly new and had not established its power or gained respect from the other branches of government or the American citizens. Instead, the High Court was somewhat afraid to anger the executive or legislative branches of a government that was rather hostile towards Native Americans. Today, this situation would not occur. If the U.S. Supreme Court ordered any state to appear and explain a situation, no state would feel that they could ignore such a request and act on their own (Norgren, 1996, pp. 60–62, 95–98).

- The appellant files a notice of appeal within the specified time after the conviction.
- The appellant files the trial court record (e.g., the transcripts) and supporting documents with the appellate court.
- The appellant and appellee each file **briefs**. A brief outlines the basic facts of the case, the argument being made by the party filing the brief, and lists cases serving as supporting precedents. Briefs are not so named because they are short memos; indeed they can be quite lengthy. Instead, the name reflects the fact that they "brief" the court on the case.
- In most courts, the judges will hear short oral arguments from the parties in the case. Typically, each side is given half an hour to present its case.
- When the court issues a decision, it is usually accompanied by a written opinion describing the court's reasoning for the decision.

## Timeliness of Appeal

Procrastination is not an option when seeking appellate review. Failure to file an appeal by the proper deadline will cause the appeal to fail regardless of its legal merits. The issue of timeliness is particularly important in capital cases, where clients can pay the ultimate price for their attorneys' failure to file the appropriate court

---

### BOX 15.6
### When Timing Is Everything

Russell Tucker was convicted of murder and sentenced to die. The defense attorneys handling his death penalty appeal failed to file some of the legal documents relating to his appeal by the deadline required in the state of North Carolina. When Tucker's execution date was set, attorney Steven Allen learned that he and the other attorney had missed the deadline by less than a week. Failure to meet the deadline meant their client faced certain execution. What Allen did not realize was that his co-counsel, David B. Smith, had sabotaged the client's appeal by deliberately missing the deadline and causing Allen to miss the deadline. Recall that earlier in Step 6 we read that David B. Smith had decided that their client "deserved to die" (Nowell, 2000, p. A14).

David B. Smith's misconduct came to light when he decided to reveal his role in the case, noting that he had "failed" and that he had to tell the truth. Smith reported that when he realized his fellow attorney Allen had misunderstood the filing deadline for the appeal, he avoided working on the case or correcting Allen's misperception about the deadline. After learning of Smith's admission, Allen appealed, arguing that Tucker should be allowed to have new attorneys appointed. The prosecution has opposed the appeal, and as of this writing the status of the appeal is not known (Nowell, 2000).

*Source:* Adapted from Nowell with permission of the Associated Press.

documents on time. Inexperienced and/or overworked attorneys have inadvertently missed such deadlines, but the case in Box 15.6 describes a very different story.

The issue of timeliness is particularly well-illustrated in death penalty cases where defendants sentenced to death later wish to appeal on grounds that new evidence will demonstrate "actual innocence." The incidence of such appeals has been increasing since the advent and improvement of technology such as DNA testing, which can be applied to evidence saved in cases prosecuted before DNA technology was available (or DNA analysis was sufficiently reliable) to be used to exculpate the defendant.

Whether through exoneration via DNA evidence or other types of evidence, a number of people have been freed after mistaken convictions: "Nationwide, eighty-five death-row inmates (or more than one percent of the approximately 6,000 men and women sentenced to death since the U.S. Supreme Court reinstated the death penalty in 1976) have been released from prison after their convictions were overturned by evidence of innocence" (Hart and Dudley, 2000, p. 2). As noted by one congressman, "innocent persons served an average of seven and one-half years on death row" (Leahy, 2000, S198). Nevertheless, such appeals are still relatively rare, and rarely successful. However, given increasing public concern with the possibility of mistaken convictions in death penalty cases, this situation could change in the future. The issue is also troubling to at least one Supreme Court jurist: Justice Sandra Day O'Connor commented at a speech to a lawyer's group that: "If statistics are any indication, the system may well be allowing some innocent defendants to be executed" (Whitworth, 2001, online). Justice O'Connor has supported the death penalty in most, although not all, cases involving capital punishment that have come before the court during her tenure.

An appeal based on the claim that evidence of "actual innocence" has been discovered post-trial must be filed within a specified time, which varies according to the nature of the appeal (e.g., an appeal for retrial, a writ of habeas corpus, or another type of appeal) and the jurisdiction. According to The Innocence Project, "thirty-three states require that claims of innocence based on new evidence be brought within six months of the final appeal" (Scheck, Newfield, and Dwyer, 2000). Of the remaining states, seven will permit such appeals at any time (Hart and Dudley, 2000).

So what happens if the evidence is not discovered until the deadline for appeal has passed? An inmate on death row cannot apply directly to a federal appellate court with a claim of new evidence of actual innocence. Instead, the inmate must first exhaust all state remedies, according to the U.S. Supreme Court (*Herrera v. Collins*, 1993). More critical from the defense perspective was the Supreme Court's ruling in *Herrera*, a capital case, which established that a mere claim of actual innocence is not sufficient in and of itself to trigger appellate review. Rather, the court held, there must be a violation of constitutional rights: "Few rulings would be more disruptive of our federal system than to provide for federal habeas review of free standing claims of actual innocence" (*Herrera v. Collins*, 1993, p. 401). The justices rejected appellant Herrera's claim that the constitutional issue at stake was the fact of his impending execution despite new evidence of his innocence. Herrera, who had been convicted of killing two peace officers on the basis of both physical evidence and his own confession, did not dispute the propriety of his conviction given the evidence presented at the time of trial. Rather, he contended that eight years after conviction, he now had exculpatory new information in the form of sworn affidavits attesting that his deceased brother was the actual killer of the officers: an affadavit from his nephew, who was nine at the time of the crime, swearing that he had seen his father killing the officers; and an affidavit from a family friend who stated that the dead brother had admitted the murders to him. Herrera argued that he was innocent and that therefore, his execution would constitute a violation of the Eighth and Fourteenth Amendments.

In the Court's opinion that affirmed Herrera's conviction and sentence, the justices noted that the original evidence presented at trial strongly indicated his guilt. They also questioned the fact that the affidavits consisted of hearsay and contained contradictory information, and that no explanation was offered for why the affidavits had not been produced years earlier at Herrera's trial. The Court, in denying his petition for examination of the claimed new evidence, stated that the proper avenue was to seek recourse in state courts, but that given that the timeline for filing such an appeal was long past, he should explore other options: "History shows that the traditional remedy for claims of innocence based on new evidence, discovered too late in the day to file a new trial motion, has been executive clemency" (*Herrera v. Collins*, 1993, p. 417).

## APPEAL OF ISSUES ALREADY ARGUED

The general legal principle underlying appeals of criminal law and procedure is that the issue being appealed must have been raised earlier at trial. For example, during the trial the defense may raise an objection to the prosecution's introduction of a particular witness. Another common basis for appeal is the assertion that the jury was not properly instructed. However, if there was no objection to the instructions given at the time of trial, there is generally no basis for raising the issue de novo. There are some exceptions, such as when the claimed error is so blatant that, if true, it would represent a fundamental deprivation of due process.

In general, only the final judgment of a trial court can be appealed. An exception to this is appeals that are made during the course of the trial, which are called **interlocutory appeals**. These address issues that require a decision by the trial judge before or during the course of trial, but which do not end the case (so-called interlocutory orders). In general, there is no right to interlocutory appeal except in certain specified circumstances. The procedural rules governing interlocutory appeals require that the trial court decision to be appealed must be final before it can be appealed, and the issue must be collateral to the merits of the case (which are appropriately the subject of trial). The issue must be so significant that waiting till the end of trial for review would significantly compromise an important right of the appellant; in other words, interlocutory appeals are used in situations where "immediate review is absolutely necessary to effectuate the purpose behind the claim" (Johns, 1982, p. 385).

For example, in cases where the defendant alleges that a retrial would violate the prohibition against double jeopardy, the defense will first file a motion in trial court seeking the case dismissal on those grounds. If the trial court denies, the defendant may then make an interlocutory appeal to the appropriate appellate court. If the procedural requirements are met, the appeal can be considered because the purpose of the prohibition against double jeopardy would be significantly undermined if the defendant had to await appeal until after trial (*Abney v. United States*, 1977).

## THE SOURCE OF THE ERROR

An appeal typically asserts that an error occurred in the trial judge's interpretation of the law, or in the conduct of trial proceedings. For example, the defense may argue on appeal that the judge improperly overruled a defense objection to the prosecutor's cross-examination. But what if the defense committed the error, by failing to present a crucial piece of exculpatory evidence, or failing to object to a prosecution tactic? As a general rule, the appellant cannot appeal on the basis of his or her own error.

So where does that leave defendants who wish to file an appeal on the basis of the claim that they were denied "effective assistance of counsel" during their trial? In this instance, the claim is generally filed by a new defense attorney handling the defendant's claim at the appeals stage. Of course, this raises the critical question of what constitutes "ineffective assistance of counsel." What if a defendant represents him or herself, and does a poor job of it? Can the defendant later claim that he or she was denied effective assistance of counsel?

### Harmless Error

The fact that an error occurred earlier in the criminal justice process does not in and of itself represent a denial of due process. If it is established that an error was made, the important question is whether it constitutes **harmless error**—that is, an error that the court determines did not significantly change the outcome of the case. In contrast, the court may determine that the problem constitutes **reversible error**—that is, a legal error that must be remedied by new legal proceedings.

In *Strickland v. Washington* (1984), a defendant convicted and sentenced to death for murder appealed on the basis that he had received ineffective assistance of counsel at trial, in violation of his Sixth Amendment right to counsel. The U.S. Supreme Court reviewed the case, and the Court's opinion discussed how this right should be evaluated. Does the right to counsel mean the right to a defense which is "effective"? What defines an effective defense strategy—one which is substantially free from error? Consider the *Strickland* court's perspective on effective assistance of counsel:

> A convicted defendant's claim that counsel's assistance was so defective as to require reversal of a conviction or death sentence has two components. First, the defendant must show that counsel's performance was deficient. This requires showing that counsel made errors so serious that counsel was not functioning as the "counsel" guaranteed the defendant by the Sixth Amendment. Second, the defendant must show that the deficient performance prejudiced the defense. This requires showing that counsel's errors were so serious as to deprive the defendant of a fair trial, a trial whose result is reliable . . . the defendant must show that there is a reasonable probability that, but for counsel's unprofessional errors, the result of the proceeding would have been different. A reasonable probability is a probability sufficient to undermine confidence in the outcome (*Strickland v. Washington*, 1984, HN10).

## You Be the (Appellate) Judges: Harmless Error?

In 1984, Calvin Burdine was tried for the murder of his former roommate. Because the killing occurred during the course of a robbery, the prosecutor filed capital murder charges, and Burdine faced the possibility of a death sentence if his jury convicted him. Burdine admitted participating in the robbery, but claimed that an accomplice committed the murder. Burdine's trial in a Texas state courtroom lasted a little over a week, at the end of which the jury swiftly convicted him, and shortly thereafter sentenced him to death. Throughout his trial and the initial unsuccessful appeal of his death sentence, Burdine was represented by an attorney named Joe Cannon.

More than a decade later, Burdine's new attorney, Robert McGlasson II, discovered that Burdine's trial attorney had napped at the defense table during the trial, sometimes for as long as ten minutes. Three jurors and the court stenographer attested to the fact that Cannon's eyes were closed and his head down, and the trial transcript documents long periods during the trial where Cannon made no objections or comments of any kind (Hoppin, 2000).

Does this constitute ineffective assistance of counsel? Yes, according to a Federal District Court judge, David Hittner, who overturned Burdine's conviction in 1999 after noting that "a sleeping counsel is equivalent to no counsel at all" (Robbins, 2000, online).

When the prosecution appealed this reversal, the matter went to the Court of Appeals for the Fifth Circuit. In a split decision, two of the three judges held that, despite the fact that Burdine's attorney had napped during "substantial portions" of his trial, this was not in and of itself proof that he was denied effective assistance of counsel. Rather, the court said, the question was whether his attorney's naps had in fact prejudiced his defense! Burdine had not proved that, the court ruled; therefore, the napping must be considered "harmless error."

McGlasson submitted a relatively rare type of appellate petition asking for further review of the case by the Fifth Circuit Court **en banc** (that is, a rehearing in front of the full panel of Fifth circuit judges). Burdine's appeal was supported, but Texas prosecutors appealed to the U.S. Supreme Court. In June, 2003, the Justices issued a ruling that allows Burdine to have a new trial (Egelko, 2002).

## The Burden of Proof

The appellant bears the burden of presenting and defending the legal worthiness of his or her appeal. After the appellant files the legal brief describing the facts of the case and the basis for the appeal, the appellee will file his or her own brief with the court in reply. The appellant will have the chance to file another document in response, and the court will decide the matter with or without hearing oral arguments from the parties, depending on how the court decides to handle the case. During oral arguments, appellate judges have the opportunity to question counsel for the government and the defense. Sometimes, the appellate justices on the panel begin firing questions at the attorneys well before they have completed their oral presentations. It is important therefore to present one's important points quickly, and to be able to think quickly on one's feet in order to answer questions that sometimes appear to be random and unrelated to the case at hand. Unlike the overt attempts to appeal to emotion that can characterize attorney presentations before a jury (or judge) at trial, appellate arguments have a distinctly different character, reflecting the difference in audiences.

Although appellate courts originally entertained oral arguments on appeals in virtually every case, the volume of appeals that are submitted to courts today precludes oral arguments in every case; in many cases the issues are sufficiently straightforward that oral arguments are not considered necessary. The trend toward

---

## BOX 15.7
## Why Spelling Matters

*American appellate courts in the nineteenth century could be sticklers for detail when they reviewed trial court records. Legal historian Lawrence M. Friedman provides an example of what he called "record worship" run amuck:*

Harwell, the defendant in a Texas case decided in 1886, had been arrested and convicted for receiving stolen cattle. The Texas court reversed, because, among other things, the jury found the defendant "guity" instead of "guilty." In 1877, the same court reversed a conviction because a jury carelessly wrote, "We, the jury, the defendant guilty," leaving out the word "find." This same court, however, magnanimously upheld a conviction of "guily" in 1879, proving that a "t" was less crucial than an "l" in the common law of Texas. (Friedman, 1985, p. 400)

"nonargument" appellate review has increased in recent years, and today most appeals are decided by the court without hearing arguments (Cecil and Stienstra, 1987).

## Standards of Appellate Review

How do appellate court judges evaluate the issues brought to them for review? It depends on the type of legal issue that is being appealed, and the nature of and context in which it is raised: An appellate court will use the appropriate standard of review, a legal standard of proof which is used to assess the arguments made in the appeal. It is important to understand the basis for appellate review: the assertion that a violation of a statute or constitutional provision has occurred. Depending on this, the legal issue is said to have arisen in a "statutory" or "constitutional" context. In turn, the context of the issue determines what standard of proof is applied during appellate review.

## THE OUTCOME OF THE APPELLATE PROCESS

The principle of *stare decisis* gears the appellate courts toward affirming lower court decisions, unless the appeal presents sound legal reasons for overturning the decision. Appellate courts appreciate the value of legal consistency and the importance of finality.

When an appellate court **affirms** (that is, confirms) a lower court's decision, the appellant has lost the case. When this happens, it may be possible to petition a higher-level appellate court to further review the matter. However, this is not an automatic process or a matter of right. The higher appellate court is free to deny the petition, and generally will grant the petition only if there are compelling legal issues at stake.

If the appeal is decided in favor of the appellant, a variety of possible outcomes may occur. The lower court's decision may be modified in part, rather than simply affirmed or reversed. The lower court's decision could be **reversed**, meaning that the appellate court has "set aside" the lower court's decision without requiring any further legal proceedings. In contrast, the case may be reversed and remanded (returned) to the trial court for further legal proceedings consistent with the opinion of the appellate court. This could mean that the defendant receives a new trial or sentencing hearing wherein the legal issues raised on appeal are relitigated consistent with the appellate court's decision. For example, if the defendant wins an appeal on the basis that testimony from an expert witness was improperly disallowed at the original trial, the new trial provides the opportunity for the expert witness to present the relevant testimony. Finally, an appellate court could simply **remand** the case back to the trial court without reversing the lower court's judgment. In this instance, the appellate court is essentially instructing the trial court to conduct further legal proceedings to address the issues raised on appeal. Figure 15.2 depicts the possible outcomes.

## THE "COURT OF LAST RESORT"

The United States Supreme Court was created pursuant to Article III of the Constitution, and serves as the ultimate interpreter of the U.S. Constitution. The Court also decides legal issues arising from federal statutes. The U.S. Supreme Court is the final appellate court, sometimes referred to as "**the court of last resort.**" The Supreme Court plays a unique role in the pantheon of American appellate courts because of its authority and influence on many of the most significant legal, political, and social

---

**BOX 15.8**

**Appellate Court Philosophy**

*According to one attorney, public expectations of the appellate process can be quite different from the reality of the process:*

Some clients, having been propagandized for years by movies and television programs showing people winning appeals on "technicalities," believe in the "magic wand" theory of the law. That is, a cunning lawyer will throw a mass of issues at an appellate court, wave a magic wand, and the judgment is reversed. Real life is different. Appellate courts try their hardest to uphold judgments, because there is a great social interest in the finality of judgments. Instead of looking for ways to reverse, appellate judges look for ways to affirm. The appeals that win are those which show the court that something fundamentally unfair or improper happened in the trial court, and the appellate court most likely will then reverse the judgment in order to preserve the integrity of our system of law. (Cox, 1997, online)

---

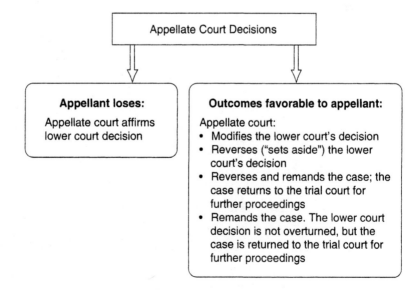

FIGURE 15.2 Appellate court decisions

issues in the nation. Although the Supreme Court usually operates in relative obscurity, the presidential election of 2000 focused worldwide attention on the court, raising public consciousness about the critical role of the court in the nation's legal and political affairs.

## U.S. Supreme Court Structure and Process

The U.S. Supreme Court includes nine justices, including a chief justice, who are appointed by the president of the United States for life. Unlike other appellate courts, which must review all cases submitted to them, each year the Supreme Court grants only a small proportion of the requests for **certiorari** (that is, requests for review) submitted for its consideration. For a case to be granted review by the Supreme Court, at least four of the nine justices must agree to accept the case. When the Court agrees to accept a case, the acceptance is referred to as "granting certiorari," commonly abbreviated as "cert."

The U.S. Supreme Court considers legal questions involving constitutional issues or matters involving federal laws; it does not review legal issues that concern only state constitutions or statutes. With hundreds of cases submitted to it each year, the Court must carefully select the cases that present legal issues of the greatest significance.

Cases that involve the application of constitutional rights in new contexts often merit the Court's attention. This is where the justices consider how to apply

This photograph shows the courtroom of the Supreme Court Building, where the U.S. Supreme Court has sat since 1935. In this country, there is no appeal available beyond the U.S. Supreme Court. Few cases make it this far—only about 100–200 a year—meaning that the majority of cases are governed by decisions rendered in lower federal courts or state supreme courts. SOURCE: Photograph by Franz Jantzen, collection of the Supreme Court of the United States.

constitutional principles, created more than two centuries ago, to modern-day issues. For example, how should the Second Amendment's right to bear arms, which was written in the era of muskets, be applied in a world with submachine guns (see Box 15.9)? How can the Fifth Amendment's privilege against self-incrimination be applied in cases where police request a DNA sample from an unwilling suspect? How can a defendant's Sixth Amendment right to a fair trial and impartial jury be protected in an age of widespread, detailed media reporting on criminal cases? How does the Fourth Amendment's prohibition against unreasonable search and seizure apply when law enforcement agents use new heat-sensing technology to track the movements of a suspect inside his or her home? These are just a few of the difficult questions that have been posed to the U.S. Supreme Court.

The U.S. Supreme Court also frequently reviews appeals that request the Court's assistance in resolving contradictory lower court precedents. For example, federal appellate courts in different circuits may have treated similar legal issues in very different ways, leading to inconsistent decisions between circuits. In some circumstances, the issue is of such significance that the Court will grant certiorari to a case that provides an opportunity to address jurisdictional inconsistencies (see Box 15.10 for insight into what the justices value when considering petitions submitted

---

## BOX 15.9
## The U.S. Supreme Court and the Second Amendment

Consider the following provision of the Second Amendment to the U.S. Constitution:
*The . . . right of the people to keep and bear arms shall not be infringed . . .*
These famous words are the source of the continuing and intense public controversy over gun crimes and gun control. What do these words mean? How should they be interpreted in the context of modern society? Questions such as these are at the heart of the debate over public policies on gun control. Many people argue that the intent of the framers of the Constitution is easily discernible in the language of the Second Amendment, and thus that the right to bear arms is absolute and cannot legally be subject to restraints in the form of gun control policies. Others argue that the framers never contemplated a world where sophisticated weapons that can kill scores of people exist—weapons which are relatively easy to obtain by members of the public.

Yet many people may be unaware of the fact that the U.S. Supreme Court has never interpreted the Second Amendment as providing an absolute right to bear arms, despite having considered the issue several times (Etzioni, 2001). Rather, the justices have determined that policies regulating various aspects of gun acquisition, ownership, and use are constitutionally acceptable. Thus, people can be subject to background checks before they purchase guns. Individuals can be required to apply for a permit before they are allowed to carry a concealed weapon. People can be restricted from carrying guns in particular places (for example, airports, public buildings, school); and restricted from owning certain types of guns or ammunition. State and local governments can ban certain types of firearms from being sold, transferred, or owned—as the District of Columbia did when it banned handguns in 1975 (Walker, 2001).

# BOX 15.10

## U.S. Supreme Court Rule 10: Considerations Governing Review on Writ of Certiorari

Review on a writ of certiorari is not a matter of right, but of judicial discretion. A petition for a writ of certiorari will be granted only for compelling reasons. The following, although neither controlling nor fully measuring the Court's discretion, indicate the character of the reasons the Court considers:

- (a) A United States court of appeals has entered a decision in conflict with the decision of another United States court of appeals on the same important matter; has decided an important federal question in a way that conflicts with a decision by a state court of last resort; or has so far departed from the accepted and usual course of judicial proceedings, or sanctioned such a departure by a lower court, as to call for an exercise of this Court's supervisory power;
- (b) A state court of last resort has decided an important federal question in a way that conflicts with the decision of another state court of last resort or of a United States court of appeals;
- (c) A state court or a United States court of appeals has decided an important question of federal law that has not been, but should be, settled by this Court, or has decided an important federal question in a way that conflicts with relevant decisions of this Court.

A petition for a writ of certiorari is rarely granted when the asserted error consists of erroneous factual findings or the misapplication of a properly stated rule of law.

*Source:* Supreme Court of the United States (online).

for possible review). For example, the Court has considered several cases involving conflicting federal circuit court definitions of various elements of federal crimes. The Court also granted certiorari to two cases to resolve a "circuit split" on the question of whether peace officers possess qualified immunity from civil lawsuits alleging federal civil rights violations. In one such case, police officers invited a *Washington Post* reporter to accompany them while they served a search warrant on a probationer at his home. Unfortunately, the home was actually the residence of the culprit's startled parents, who took exception to being awakened in the pre-dawn hours by several armed plainclothes officers, while the reporter snapped photographs. Although the photos were not published, the parents sued the police department, alleging that the media presence constituted a violation of their Fourth Amendment rights (see *Charles Wilson v. Harry Layne,* [1999] and *Hanlon v. Berger* [1998]).[1]

Another type of legal issue that may be appealed all the way to the Supreme Court is an instance where state or federal statutes clash with each other, or with the Constitution. One such example exists in California, where voters recently approved an initiative allowing marijuana use for medicinal purposes by patients whose health-care provider had authorized this. After passage of this measure, California police and prosecutors found themselves in an awkward position; if they continued "business as usual," pursuing possessors and purveyors of marijuana, they appeared to be violating the new state law; but if they failed to pursue such cases, they would not be complying with federal anti-drug laws. This has led to a variety of responses on the part of California police and sheriff's departments: In some locales, law enforcement proceeds against marijuana cases much as it did before the initiative passed; in other areas, police have issued "medical marijuana user" cards for patients to display to officers in the event they are stopped and marijuana is found in their possession (Hornblower, 1999).

In May 2001, the U.S. Supreme Court held unanimously that federal drug laws permit no exceptions for medical marijuana use. The justices rejected the argument that marijuana use for medicinal purposes should be permitted under a "medical benefits" exception to the Federal Controlled Substances Act, finding no conclusive evidence of such benefits. The Court did not directly address the legal viability of Proposition 215, but the Court's decision provides the legal go-ahead to California and federal authorities seeking to shut down marijuana clubs that provide marijuana for medical use by patients (Chiang, 2001). Despite this decision, related legal issues remain, such as whether patients can claim a "necessity" defense if facing prosecution for medicinal use of marijuana. Thus, it is likely that these issues will be part of the appellate docket, whether at the state or federal court level, in the future.

## CONCLUSION

The appellate process is a critical step in the journey of some criminal cases through the courts. Appellate review provides judicial oversight of trial proceed-

---

### BOX 15.11

### The "Volunteers"

Most death row inmates await the results of their appeals with baited breath, hoping for the opportunity for a new trial or at least a temporary stay of execution; others reject such appeals. Such "volunteers" for the death chamber insist that they want no appeals, that they want to get on with the business of death. Some say they crave some small element of control over their lives, or that they would prefer actual death to the living death of a "life" sentence. Some change their minds, or may never have been serious in the first place; others take matters into their own hands and commit suicide before they can be executed.

The truly dedicated "volunteers" are a breed apart. During the penalty phase of his trial, convicted killer Steven Judy had this to say to his jurors: "You better vote for the death penalty, because if you don't, I'll get out, and it may be one of you next, or your family." He was executed by the state of Indiana in 1981 (O'Neill, 1998).

Robert Massie was executed at San Quentin in California on March 27, 2001, after instructing his attorneys not to file appeals of his death penalty conviction. One newspaper account reported that Massie "was an eager participant in his execution this morning, helping medics find the veins needed to inject the lethal drugs that took his life." (Zamora et al., 2001, p. A1)

ings, precedent on new areas of law, and guidance to lower courts on the application of legal theory to new questions of fact. Although few criminal cases make it to trial and fewer still are reviewed by an appellate court, the impact of appellate rulings is felt throughout the criminal justice system as a whole. Appellate rulings shape both the substance and procedure of the criminal justice process, revealing as they do so the richness and complexity of the court system.

We have almost come to the end of our journey through the criminal court system, but we have one final, and very important, stop: the juvenile court system. Now that you are knowledgeable about the criminal courts and the steps of the criminal justice process for adult defendants (and juveniles who are prosecuted as adults), you are in a good position to learn about the juvenile courts. In the next chapter, you will learn how the juvenile justice system differs in significant ways from the adult criminal justice system, and the implications of this for both juvenile offenders and societal efforts to prevent juvenile crime.

## DISCUSSION QUESTIONS

1. How are appellate courts different from trial courts? How do the functions, roles, and outcomes of appellate courts set them apart from trial courts?

2. Given the starring role that stare decisis has in our legal system, how do appellate courts contribute to the dynamic, changing nature of the law?

3. Consider what you've learned about the controversy on appellate courts as policy-making forums. Do you think that courts have the ability to effectively shape policy, or not? Does judicial policymaking interfere with the legislative branch's function, or does it complement it?

4. In what ways are appellate courts dependent on other criminal justice actors, such as members of the courtroom work group, police, and corrections personnel, to implement the rulings that appellate courts produce? In what ways can the above-mentioned criminal justice players help translate "law on the books" into "law in action"?

5. In Box 15.1 you read about public-housing tenants who face possible eviction because of the drug crimes of people they knew. What are the constitutional issues raised by such a policy, and what is your opinion of the impact of this policy?

6. Why is the "Great Writ" a very powerful legal tool? What does "habeas corpus" mean (quick, think of the answer without peeking at the glossary)? When a petitioner makes a habeas appeal, what is he or she asking the government to do?

7. What is the basis for the power of judicial review, and what are the limitations of this power?

8. Imagine you are a defendant in a criminal case (again, just as you did before in Step 12). Unfortunately, your trial resulted in a conviction. You are convinced that if you can just tell a higher court about the strange circumstances that resulted in an innocent person such as yourself being charged with a felony, you'll win your freedom. But you know that you can't simply contest your conviction on the grounds that you're innocent, because you have no new evidence. Why not? What sorts of procedural issues are typically the basis for an appeal?

9. What does the concept of "standing" refer to, and why is it a key consideration in appellate litigation?

10. Consider what you've learned from earlier sections of the book about capital cases, the quality of defense representation in such cases, and the evidence that innocent people have been sentenced to death. Given this, what role do you believe the appeals process has in capital cases? Should

there be more avenues of appeal for defendants sentenced to death? Why or why not?

11. Consider the "sleeping lawyer" case. If you were an appellate judge, would you hold that a sleeping lawyer is by definition providing an inadequate defense, or would you require the defendant to prove that a napping counselor's actions—or rather, inaction—prejudiced the chance of a fair trial?

12. Why is the United States Supreme Court called the "court of last resort"? What is the role of the court in our legal system? In what ways do the Court's decisions influence everyone in America? Can you think of some examples?

## NOTE

1. On the issue of media presence, the Supreme Court held: "It is a violation of the Fourth Amendment for police to bring members of the media or other third parties into a home during the execution of a warrant when the presence of the third parties in the home was not in aid of the execution of the warrant" (*Wilson v. Layne,* 1999, p. 614).

## REFERENCES

Abadinsky, H. (1995). *Law and Justice: An Introduction to the American Legal System.* Chicago: Nelson-Hall.

*Abney v. United States,* 431 U.S. 651 (1977).

Balzar, J. (1985, April 7). Few rules to go by; Justice Bird's recall becoming epic battle. *Los Angeles Times,* p. 1.

*Black's Law Dictionary.* (1999). (7th ed.). St. Paul, MN: West Group.

California Penal Code § 25 (2001)(b).

Cecil, J. and Stiensra, D. (1987). *Deciding Cases Without Argument: An Examination of Four Courts of Appeals.* Federal Judicial Center, FJC–R–87–5.

*Charles Wilson v. Harry Layne,* 141 F.3d 111 (1999).

Chiang, H. (2001, May 15). Medicinal pot ruled illegal; Supreme Court says federal law allows no exception for prescription marijuana. *San Francisco Chronicle,* p. A1.

Cox, R.A. (1997, July). How appeals work: The basics for non-lawyers. Available online at www.appealslaw.com/haw.html.

Egelko, B. (2001, May 12). Hunters point case tests drug evictions. *San Francisco Chronicle,* p. A14.

Egelko, B. (2002, June 4). Man with sleepy lawyer can have a new trial. *San Francisco Chronicle,* p. A1.

Etzioni, A. (2001, April 6). Are liberal scholars acting irresponsibly on gun control? *The Chronicle of Higher Education (The Review),* pp. B14–B15.

Finz, S. (2000, September 20). Evictions of seniors assailed in court. *San Francisco Chronicle,* p. A20.

Friedman, L.M. (1985). *A History of American Law* (2nd ed.). New York: Simon & Schuster.

*Hanlon v. Berger,* 525 U.S. 981(1998).

Hart, J.L. and G.M. Dudley. (2000, Summer). Available post-trial relief after a state criminal conviction when newly discovered evidence establishes "actual innocence." *University of Arkansas Little Rock Law Review,* 22: 629–646.

*Herrera v. Collins,* 506 U.S. 390, 421 (1993).

Hoppin, J. (2000, November 3). Case of the sleeping lawyer splits two judges eyed for high court. *The Recorder,* available online at www.law.com.

Hoppin, J. (2001, March 16). Victim's partner files wrongful-death suit. *The Legal Intelligencer,* p. 4.

Hornblower, M. (1999, May 3). Here's my marijuana card, officer. *Time,* p. 7.

*HUD v. Rucker et al.,* No. 00-1770.

Jefferson, T. (1798). Draft Kentucky Resolutions, 1798. ME 17:380. Available online at etext.lib. virginia.edu/jefferson/quotations/jeff1275.htm.

Johns, P. (1982). Comment: Interlocutory appeals in criminal trials: Appellate review of vindictive prosecution claims. *University of Cincinnati Law Review,* 51: 373–385.

Leahy, Senator Patrick. (2000, February 1). Quoted in 146 Cong. Rec. S198 (daily ed.).

*McKeiver v. Pennsylvania,* 403 U.S. 528 (1971).

*Marbury v. Madison,* 5 U.S. (1 Cranch) 137 (1803).

*Merriam-Webster's Dictionary of Law.* (1996).

Norgren, J. (1996). *The Cherokee Cases: The Confrontation of Law and Politics.* New York: McGraw-Hill.

Nowell, P. (2000, November 3). Lawyer admits sabotaging appeal of death row client he didn't like. *San Francisco Chronicle,* p. A14.

Office of Legal Policy. (1987). Report to the Attorney General: Double jeopardy and government appeals of acquittals. pp. 49–50. Washington, DC: U.S. Department of Justice.

O'Neill, A.W. (1998, September 11). When prisoners have a death wish. *Los Angeles Times,* p. A1.

*People v. Aleman,* Nos. 93 CR 28786, 93 CR 28787, 1994 WL 684499 (Ill. Cir. Ct. Oct. 12, 1994).

*People v. Horn,* (1984, 3d Dist) 158 Cal App 3d 1014, 205 Cal Rptr 119.

*People v. Skinner* (1985) 39 Cal 3d 765, 217 Cal Rptr 685, 704 P2d 752.

*People v. Stress* (1988, 4th Dist) 205 Cal App 3d 1259, 252 Cal Rptr 913.

Robbins, M.A. (2000, November 3). Dozing lawyer case may go to U.S. Supreme Court. *Texas Lawyer.* Available online at www.law.com.

Rosenn, M. (1983, Spring). Symposium: State prisoner use of federal habeas corpus procedures: The Great Writ—a reflection of societal change. *Ohio State Law Journal,* 44: 337–XXX.

Scheck, B., Neufeld, P., and Dwyer, J. (2000). *Actual Innocence: Five Days to Execution and Other Dispatches from the Wrongly Convicted.* New York: Doubleday.

*Sawyer v. Whitley,* 112 S. Ct. 2514 (1992).

Smith, C. (2000). The capacity of courts as policy-making forums. In Hancock, B., and Sharp, B. (Eds.), *Public Policy, Crime, and Criminal Justice,* (pp. 240–256). Upper Saddle River, NJ: Prentice Hall.

*State v. Jones,* 5 N. Car 257 (1809).

*Strickland v. Washington,* 466 U.S. 668 (1984).

Supreme Court of the U.S.—Rules. Available online at www.supremecourtus.gov/ctrules/ctrules.html.

*Tennesse v. Garner,* 471 U.S. 1 (1985).

*Texas v. Johnson,* 109 S. Ct. 2533, 2536 (1989).

Vogel, K., and Stumpf, B. (2000). Preserving the record for appeal: Top ten mistakes. Available online at Findlaw.com.

Walker, S. (2001). *Sense and Nonsense about Crime and Drugs: A Policy Guide* (5th ed.). Belmont, CA: Wadsworth/Thomson Learning.

Whitworth, D. (2001, July 4). Reagan-appointed judge says innocent are being executed. *The Times.* Available online at www.thetimes.co.uk/.

*Wilson v. Layne,* No. 98-83, 526 U.S. 603 (1999).

Zamora, J., Podger, P., Chiang, H., and Squatriglia, C. (2001, March 27). Massie executed for 1979 S.F. murder. *San Francisco Chronicle,* p. A1.

# Step 16
## Juvenile Courts
### Phyllis B. Gerstenfeld

On June 8, 1964, Gerald Francis Gault and his friend, Ronald Lewis, spent the day making prank phone calls. When one recipient of their calls, Mrs. Cook, complained to the police, the county sheriff took Gault into custody. The next day he was questioned before a judge. On June 15, a second hearing was held. Mrs. Cook was not there, and no witnesses were sworn. No jury was seated; no lawyers were present. No Fifth Amendment warnings were given to Gault before he was questioned. At the end of the hearing, Gerry Gault was to be incarcerated for nearly six years. No appeal was permitted.

How could this be? The answer is that Gerry Gault was fifteen years old, and these hearings occurred in Juvenile Court. Had Gault been tried as an adult, he would have been entitled to many more procedural rights, and he would have faced a maximum sentence of $50 or two months in jail. But as we will see in this chapter, juvenile courts are quite different from ordinary courts.

## BEFORE JUVENILE COURTS

Until the industrial era, relatively few children were processed by the courts. Instead, fathers were given ultimate legal control and authority over their children. This worked well when most people earned their living from the land: A father could threaten to expel a disobedient child from the family farm, exposing the child to poverty and starvation. Moreover, even young children spent most of their waking hours working hard under their parents' watchful eyes, and so had little opportunity for mischief.

For those youths whom parents were unable to control, the rules were fairly clear. In both English and American common law systems, children under the age of seven could not be held criminally responsible for their acts because it was presumed

This chapter was written for this book by Phyllis B. Gerstenfeld, J.D., Ph.D.

that they were unable to form criminal intent. Children between the ages of seven and fourteen were also presumed to be unable to form intent, but this presumption could be overcome by evidence that the child knew what he or she was doing. If such evidence existed, or if the child was over age fourteen, he or she was treated like an adult. In the United States, some children as young as twelve have been subject to the ultimate adult penalty: death (Streib, 1987).

As more people moved to cities, the family became a less effective method of control. Furthermore, levels of urban poverty increased, leaving many children destitute. The first institution for wayward and destitute youths, the Bridewell, was established in London in 1555. The first youth correction institution in the United States was the **House of Refuge**, built in New York City in 1825. No court hearing was required to place a child in a House of Refuge, and children could remain there until their eighteenth or twenty-first birthday. A child could be committed by a parent or by a government agent, such as a constable. The idea behind these establishments was that adult prisons, rather than reforming delinquent youth, would merely make them worse.

In 1838, the mother of a minor named Mary Ann Crouse wished to commit her daughter to the Philadelphia House of Refuge. Mary Ann's father, who felt that she should remain at home, disagreed and argued that committing her amounted to punishing her without a trial. The Pennsylvania Supreme Court held in *ex parte Crouse* that Mary Ann's commitment was legal under the doctrine of **parens patriae** (the state as parent). The court stated that when a parent is unwilling or unable to control a child, the state has the power to step in and act in the child's and society's best interests. Houses of Refuge, the court wrote, are meant not for punishment but for reformation; therefore, the formal due process protections of criminal trials were unnecessary:

> The infant has been snatched from a course which must have ended in confirmed
> depravity . . . and not only is the restraint of her person lawful, but it would be an act of
> extreme cruelty to release her from it. (Roush, 1996)

The doctrine of *parens patriae* became the basis of the first juvenile court. In fact, although U.S. Supreme Court cases in the 1960s and 1970s made significant changes in how juvenile courts operate, *parens patriae* remains the courts' foundation.

## THE EARLY JUVENILE COURTS

As immigration, urbanization, poverty, and crime continued to increase, so did the pressure to do more to combat juvenile delinquency. Reformatories were overcrowded and their conditions were often deplorable, and many children were simply confined in adult institutions. Moreover, the emerging sciences of criminology and psychology argued that there were certain causes of crime; therefore, once the

A juvenile court in Denver, Colorado, in 1915 attended by the judge, court clerk, probation officer, and several boys. The charges faced by the boys might have ranged from incorrigibility to truancy to serious crimes, and they could expect sentences that reflected the rehabilitative ideals of the court, ranging from probation to detention in a reformatory. Now, young people must commit actual offenses (rather than so-called "status offenses") before they may be held in detention, and lawmakers are changing juvenile laws to allow certification of minors to adult courts in serious cases. SOURCE: Courtesy of the Library of Congress.

causes were discovered, offenders could be "cured" of their criminality. And so, at the urging of several prominent reformers, the juvenile courts were born. The first was the Cook County Juvenile Court, founded in Chicago in 1899. Within two decades, all but two states had followed Illinois's lead and established juvenile courts of their own (Ainsworth, 1991).

The early juvenile courts had several common features. The most important was that they operated under the *parens patriae* doctrine, and so were considered civil rather than criminal. The hearings were informal, with the stated goals being to discover the root of the child's problems and to solve those problems. Juvenile courts heard not only cases involving delinquency (in which the child was accused of violating a criminal law), but also status offenses (in which the child was generally wayward or a runaway), and cases where the child was neglected, abused, or destitute. No lawyers were involved and the hearings were nonadversarial. In fact, as late as 1965, more than one quarter of juvenile court judges had no formal legal training (Davis et al., 1997).

Because the purpose of juvenile courts (reformation) was different from criminal courts (punishment), the juvenile court proceedings did not include all of the due process trappings of criminal court. Not only were due process protections deemed unnecessary, it was argued, but they would interfere with the court's mission.

Therefore, there were no juries, and the child need not be found guilty beyond a reasonable doubt. As one of the creators of the juvenile court system wrote,

> The problem for determination by the [juvenile court] judge is not, Has this boy or girl committed a specific wrong, but What is he, how has he become what he is, and what can be done in his interest and the interest of the state to save him from a downward career. (Mack, 1909)

There were other differences as well. To protect children from the stigma that criminal convictions bring, juvenile court proceedings were closed to the public, records were kept confidential, and an entirely different terminology was constructed (see Box 16.1 for some important differences between the terminology used in adult and juvenile courts). Even the look of the courts was different: Rather than an imposing traditional courtroom, hearings were to take place in less formal settings with a table and chairs. Ideally, the judge, child, parents, and probation officer could sit informally around this table and determine what would be best for the child.

Juvenile court judges were also given a great deal of discretion in determining what was to happen to children who appeared before the court. Many more kinds of placements for minors were available than for adults. In addition, those

---

### BOX 16.1
### Adult versus Juvenile Court Terminology

| Adult Term | Juvenile Equivalent |
| --- | --- |
| Information, indictment | Petition |
| Trial | Adjudication hearing |
| Name of case: *State v. Doe* or *United States v. Doe* | Name of case: *In re Doe* |
| Defendant | Minor |
| Conviction | Delinquency adjudication |
| Guilty | Delinquent |
| Sentencing hearing | Disposition hearing |
| Sentence | Disposition |
| Jail | Juvenile Hall |
| Prison | Reformatory, reform school, youth authority, industrial school, and so on |

children who were confined to institutions such as reformatories were not given determinate sentences as are adults sent to prison. Instead, they were often ordered to remain incarcerated until they reached the age of majority (usually age eighteen or twenty-one), or until they were "cured." Thus did Gerry Gault face nearly six years (that is, until the age of twenty-one) in detention for a minor infraction.

# THE DUE PROCESS REVOLUTION

As originally conceived, the juvenile courts gave children a tradeoff: They were expected to give up their due process rights, and in return, their best interests were to be secured and they were to be given individualized treatment rather than punishment. The juvenile courts were to operate more like social service agencies than like places of justice.

Unfortunately, the promise of the juvenile courts was almost immediately broken. Understaffed courts were overburdened by heavy caseloads. Much of the staff was underpaid (or not paid at all—many were volunteers) and undertrained; many juvenile court judges were not formally trained in law at all. This ran contrary to the original intent of the system.

The courts were not the only problem. The hoped-for variety of dispositional alternatives did not materialize. In 1920, for example, only 55 percent of juvenile court systems provided any probation services (Ryerson, 1978). Conditions in many existing institutions remained appalling because of overcrowding and abuse. Again, this violated the original premise of the system. The continuing problems of the juvenile justice system, together with a Supreme Court inclined to promote constitutional rights, engendered a series of landmark cases, the most important of which was Gerry Gault's.

The first major U.S. Supreme Court case on juvenile justice was *Kent v. United States,* in 1966. Sixteen-year-old Morris Kent was transferred from juvenile to adult court to stand trial for rape. There was no transfer hearing, nor did the judge state the basis for his decision; he simply decided to transfer Kent on the basis (presumably) of the contents of Kent's probation files. The Supreme Court held that Kent's due process rights had been violated.

The direct impact of *Kent* was unclear. The case arose in Washington, DC, and the Supreme Court may have been acting in its role as overseer of the District of Columbia court system rather than as the nation's highest court. But *Kent* was significant in that it signaled the Court's dissatisfaction with the nation's juvenile justice system:

> There is much evidence that some juvenile courts . . . lack the personnel, facilities and techniques to perform adequately as representatives of the State in a *parens patriae* capacity, at least with respect to children charged with law violation. There is evidence, in fact, that there may be grounds for concern that the child receives the worst of both worlds: that he

gets neither the protections accorded to adults nor the solicitous care and regenerative treatment postulated for children.

Just a year later, the Court's skepticism reached a peak when it heard Gerry Gault's case (*In re Gault*, 1967). Although the Court questioned the concept of *parens patriae*, it did not discard it entirely. However, the Court held that whenever juveniles face the possibility of confinement, they are entitled to certain basic due process rights (see Box 16.2 for a list of rights accorded to juveniles, and a list of those that have not yet been extended to juveniles). "The condition of being a boy," Justice Fortas wrote for the majority, "does not justify a kangaroo court." Having been locked up for three years, Gerry Gault was finally free. He eventually became—what else!—a lawyer.

Some Justices expressed concern that affording juveniles due process rights would further hamper the success of the juvenile courts, and would effectively erase the distinction between the adult and juvenile systems (see Box 16.3 for some important excerpts from the *Gault* case). Nevertheless, in succeeding cases, the Supreme Court continued to grant additional rights. In *In re Winship* (1970), the Court held that the standard of proof beyond a reasonable doubt must be extended to juvenile as well as adult proceedings. In *Breed v. Jones* (1975), the Court held that the protection against double jeopardy applied in juvenile cases as well.

---

# BOX 16.2
## Due Process Rights and Juvenile Courts

*Juveniles **are** entitled to the following:*

| | |
|---|---|
| Transfer hearing before trial in adult court | *Kent v. United States,* 1966 |
| Notice of charges<br>Assistance of counsel<br>Confront witnesses and cross-examine them<br>Right against self-incrimination<br>Transcript of proceedings<br>Appellate review | *In re Gault,* 1967 |
| Proof beyond a reasonable doubt | *In re Winship,* 1970 |
| Double jeopardy protection | *Breed v. Jones,* 1975 |

*Juveniles are **not** entitled to the following:*

| | |
|---|---|
| Jury trial | *McKeiver v. Pennsylvania,* 1971 |
| Mandatory presence of parents during interrogation | *Fare v. Michael C.,* 1979 |
| Right against preventative detention | *Schall v. Martin,* 1984 |

---

# BOX 16.3
## Important Excerpts from *In re Gault* (1967)

*Justice Abe Fortas, writing for the majority:*
[Recent studies] suggest that the appearance as well as the actuality of fairness, impartiality and orderliness—in short, the essentials of due process, may be a more impressive and therapeutic attitude so long as the juvenile is concerned.

It is of no constitutional consequence—and limited practical meaning—that the institution to which he is committed is called an Industrial School. The fact of the matter is, that however euphemistic the title, a "receiving home" or an "industrial school" for juveniles is an institution of confinement in which the child is incarcerated for a greater or lesser time. . . . Instead of mother and father and sisters and brothers and friends and classmates, his world is peopled by guards, custodians, state employees, and "delinquents" confined with him for anything from waywardness to rape and homicide.

Under our Constitution, the condition of being a boy does not justify a kangaroo court.

*Justice Hugo Black, concurring:*
The juvenile court planners envisaged a system that would practically immunize juveniles from "punishment" for "crimes" in an effort to save them from youthful indiscretions and stigmas due to criminal charges or convictions. I agree with the Court, however, that this exalted ideal has failed of achievement since the beginning of the system.

*Justice Potter Stewart, dissenting:*
The inflexible restrictions that the Constitution so wisely made applicable to adversary criminal trials have no inevitable place in the proceedings of those social service agencies known as juvenile or family courts. And to impose the Court's long list of requirements upon juvenile proceedings in every area of the country is to invite a long step backwards into the nineteenth century.

---

But the Supreme Court would not grant juveniles *all* the rights that adults are afforded. In *McKeiver v. Pennsylvania* (1971), the Court declined to require jury trials in juvenile courts. This was not, as many lay people suppose, because requiring a jury of peers would mean that juveniles would have teenaged jurors; the "peers" language of the Sixth Amendment is not so strict. Instead, the Court expressed its fear that imposing a jury on the process would eliminate the last real boundary between the juvenile and adult courts. The Court was still extremely skeptical of the juvenile court system. Justice Blackmun wrote, "We must recognize . . . that the fond and idealistic hopes of the juvenile court proponents and early reformers of three generations ago have not been realized." *McKeiver v. Pennsylvania,* (1971; p. 543-4). However, even though the Court found the juvenile court system to be gravely ill, it was still unwilling to bury it. In the Court's eyes, juvenile courts still held promise. Jury trials, Justice Blackmun wrote, would not cure the system, but would only kill it. For this reason alone, the Court declined to require jury trials in juvenile courts.

In *McKeiver* the Court didn't require jury trials, but it didn't expressly prohibit them either. In fact, several states, such as Texas, have passed laws permitting or requiring jury trials in juvenile court cases. Furthermore, some areas have recently begun experimenting with "teen courts"; we'll look at those later in this step.

## JUVENILE COURT JURISDICTION

In many jurisdictions, the juvenile court is a subsidiary of the trial court of general jurisdiction (that is, the court in which adults are tried), or of other specialty courts such as probate courts (Rubin, 1985). In other places, the juvenile court is a separate entity altogether. Although they are most commonly called juvenile courts, they have other titles as well, such as family courts.

All juvenile courts have a judge of some kind. Today, most people presiding over juvenile court hearings have law degrees, but they may not technically be "judges." To accommodate spiraling caseloads, judges in many states are empowered to appoint referees or commissioners (the terms are virtually interchangeable). Referees have law degrees and act much like judges; however, most of their decisions are reviewable by their supervising judge. The office of referee brings less prestige than that of judge, and usually less pay.

Juvenile courts are courts of limited jurisdiction, in that they have the power to hear only certain types of cases. Usually, their jurisdiction is defined by the age and behavior of the offender. That is, they can hear cases involving people of certain ages who are suspected of performing certain (mostly criminal) acts. Depending on the location, they may hear cases involving abused and neglected children as well, and sometimes even divorce cases. The ages over which they have jurisdiction vary, but in most states the maximum age is seventeen; anyone who commits a crime after his or her eighteenth birthday becomes subject to the adult criminal courts. Some states also have minimum ages for juvenile court jurisdiction, and children below the minimum may not be prosecuted at all (although they may come under the auspices of Child Protective Services or similar agencies if the crime is serious or the child seems troubled).

In all states, youths may be tried in adult instead of juvenile courts under some circumstances: by statutory exclusion, judicial waiver, or concurrent jurisdiction.

**Statutory exclusion** means the legislature has passed laws that say certain juveniles who commit certain crimes will be tried as adults. These laws usually concern older offenders and serious or violent crimes. In recent years, states have been increasing the situations to which statutory exclusion applies by widening the number of crimes and lowering the minimum age. For example, California changed its laws in 1999 to require that children be tried as adults if they are four-teen or older and are accused of certain murders or sex offenses. Some states statu-torily exclude even more minors from juvenile status by setting the maximum age of juvenile court jurisdiction at age fifteen or sixteen instead of seventeen. In 1996, nearly a quarter million sixteen- and seventeen-year-olds were tried as adults in these states, and the number of juveniles who are tried as adults has been growing (Torbet and Szymanski, 1998).

**Judicial waiver** means that under certain circumstances, the juvenile court judge can choose to transfer the case to adult court. Usually, there are state statutes specifying which cases can be judicially waived and what factors the judge should consider. Because of the Supreme Court's ruling in *Kent v. United States* (1966), the judge must hold a waiver hearing in which certain due process protections are given to the minor. The Supreme Court has also held that due to double jeopardy protections, any waiver hearing must occur *before* a juvenile adjudication hearing. Once the adjudication hearing has been held, the minor can no longer be tried as an adult for that crime (*Breed v. Jones,* 1975). Today, all but four states allow judicial waiver (Torbet and Szymanski, 1998).

Finally, fifteen jurisdictions have **concurrent jurisdiction** (Torbet and Szy-manski, 1998). This means that both the juvenile and adult courts have jurisdiction over certain cases. The prosecutor can decide which court will hear the case. Unlike in cases of judicial waiver, no hearing is required, and the decision is within the prosecutor's discretion. Prosecutors are usually elected officials, and so their decisions in this regard may be swayed by public opinion. In Palm Beach County, Florida, for example, thirteen-year-old Nathaniel Brazill, an honor student with no delinquency record, was charged as an adult with first-degree murder for shooting his English teacher to death (Bragg, 2000).

In recent years, forty-four states have made it easier for children to be tried as adults by widening one or more of the transfer provisions. Most often, states did this by expanding the list of crimes eligible for statutory exclusion (Torbet and Szymanski, 1998). These changes were most likely a response to an increase in the juvenile crime rate in the 1980s and early 1990s, as well as several well-publicized cases of violent murders committed by teenagers. Ironically, however, by the time most of these laws were changed (1992 through 1997), the juvenile crime rate was decreasing steadily to historically low levels.

## THE OPERATION OF JUVENILE COURTS

Most of the American court system can trace its roots directly back to the English common law system, and, as a result, courts tend to be somewhat similar from state to state (see Step 4 for more information on the history and development of adult courts).

As we've seen, however, juvenile courts' roots instead lie more in social services. There is, therefore, much more variability in juvenile courts between jurisdictions.

How does a case proceed through the juvenile court system? Again, this varies from place to place, but Figure 16.1 illustrates a typical example. To begin with, a case has to be referred to the court. This referral can come from a number of different sources: schools, parents, social service agencies, victims, and so on. However, by far the most common referral source is law enforcement. In 1997, for example, 84 percent of delinquency cases came to the juvenile courts from law enforcement agencies (Puzzanchera et al., 2000).

Once a juvenile is placed under arrest, a law enforcement agency has several options. First, it can refer the child to juvenile court. In 1997, this happened in 67 percent of juvenile arrests, an increase in percentage of previous years (OJJDP, 2000). Second, it can send the case to social services or other agencies (26 percent of arrests in 1997). Finally, in some instances the case can be sent directly to adult court (7 percent of arrests in 1997).

When a case is sent to juvenile court, it usually goes to an intake officer, who often is a juvenile probation officer. In some states, it may go to a prosecutor instead. This person may decide to dismiss the case if it doesn't seem worth prosecuting. For example, in Blythe, California, prosecutors chose not to pursue a case against two girls, ages five and six, who suffocated a three-year-old (Gold, 2000). They declined to prosecute because they presumed that children so young were unable to truly understand what they had done. Or the intake officer may handle the case informally, such as through a referral to a social service agency or informal probation. Another option is diversion: Many jurisdictions have diversion programs for specific juveniles, such as first-time offenders or those with substance abuse problems. The idea behind diversion programs is to solve the child's prob-

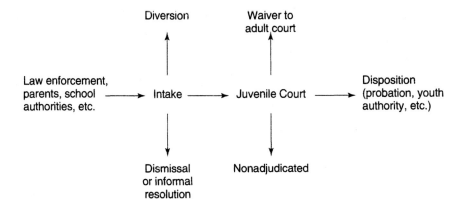

FIGURE 16.1 Typical juvenile justice process

lems without recourse to the more formal proceedings of juvenile court. If the offense and the age of the offender place the case under concurrent jurisdiction, a prosecutor may decide at this point to file the case in adult court. Finally, the intake officer may choose to refer the case to the juvenile court for formal processing, by filing a petition. The petition acts much like an indictment or information in an adult criminal case. At one time, more cases were handled informally than formally, but that changed in 1993. In 1997, 57 percent of intake cases were processed formally. Since then, the proportion of cases handled formally has been increasing steadily (Puzzanchera et al., 2000).

Once a petition is filed, the case is in the hands of the juvenile court judge (or referee). If judicial waiver is an option, a waiver hearing will be held. Relatively few cases at this point end up being transferred to adult court. In 1997, for example, there were 8,400 waivers from juvenile court, which was about 0.5 percent of the nearly 1.8 million cases nationwide (Puzzanchera et al., 2000).

If the case is not waived, an adjudication hearing will be held. As we've already learned, this is the juvenile equivalent of a trial. Today, this hearing includes many trappings of a criminal case, such as lawyers, transcripts, and sworn witnesses. Like adults, juveniles have the right a court-appointed attorney if they cannot afford one of their own, and the amount of assistance these lawyers provide can vary a great deal. In many jurisdictions, public defenders have enormous caseloads. Knowing that juvenile offenses often bring less harsh consequences than adult offenses, some public defenders may limit the time they spend with their youthful clients in order to have more time for the adults. In fact, especially for relatively minor crimes, the public defender may only meet his or her client for the first time a few minutes before the hearing begins. Furthermore, despite legal scholars' urging that children not be permitted to waive their right to counsel, children are allowed to do so, and often do (probably because it is more expedient and less expensive for the system).

Even when a juvenile is represented by counsel who has time to devote to the case, the attorney's role is unclear. Suppose a lawyer knows she can effectively defend her minor client in such a way that the minor will not be adjudicated delinquent. But also suppose that the lawyer believes that her client is troubled, and that it would be in his best interests to be adjudicated delinquent and receive treatment from the system. What is her legal and ethical duty? The answer is not entirely clear.

Depending on the jurisdiction, the case may be prosecuted by either a prosecutor or by a probation officer. In either case, a probation report on the child should be available to the judge. Thus, the decision in the case may depend not only on the evidence presented in the courtroom, but also on the child's history and present family circumstances. Since the 1970 *In re Winship* decision, juveniles have had the right to be found guilty beyond a reasonable doubt.

In actuality, especially in urban areas, juvenile court hearings may be extremely brief. Ayers (1997) reports that in Cook County Juvenile Court, the nation's original juvenile court, the average juvenile court hearing lasts twelve minutes. A typical judge there has 1,500 to 2,000 cases pending on his or her docket on any particular day. Clearly, the kind of careful, individualized treatment envisioned by the court's creators is impossible under these circumstances.

In 1997, juveniles were adjudicated delinquent in about 58 percent of cases (OJJDP, 2000). In the remainder of cases, the case was dismissed for lack of evidence, the juvenile was placed on probation pursuant to a plea bargain, other sanctions such as restitution or diversion were imposed, or the juvenile was placed in the care of a social service agency.

When a juvenile is adjudicated delinquent, the judge must choose a disposition, which is the equivalent of an adult's sentence. By far the most common disposition (54 percent in 1997) is probation (OJJDP, 2000). Juveniles may also be given other sanctions, such as restitution, or they may be placed in some confined setting.

As we learned, the architects of the juvenile court system imagined that there would be many different dispositional alternatives available, so that each child's individualized needs could be met. The degree to which this dream has been realized varies, but there are usually more options for children than for adults. Some alternatives include juvenile halls (which are essentially jails for youths), boot camps, wilderness programs, ranches, group homes, foster homes, residential treatment facilities, outpatient treatment programs, and youth correctional facilities. The availability of these resources varies by jurisdiction, with urban areas generally having more available alternatives.

Although a recommendation for placement is usually made by a probation officer, juvenile court judges have a great deal of discretion in these matters. Their decisions, as commentators have noted, may be affected by many factors:

> A judge's personal values and philosophy strongly affect his [sic] dispositions. Judges manipulate dispositions, and also are manipulated into particular dispositions by those who participate in hearings and by external community pressures. Judges are seen as independent decision makers, but their dispositions are made within the context of a system that may provide few options. (Rubin, 1985)

Therefore, which judge happens to hear a case may affect the case outcome (Podkopacz and Feld, 1996). Unfortunately, so may factors such as the offender's race (Bishop and Frazier, 1996).

The judge may have discretion not only over the kind of disposition, but also the length. As we've discussed already, juvenile dispositions were originally meant to be indeterminate. This made sense, if the purpose of the system was treatment rather than rehabilitation. After all, if you were seriously ill, your doctor would not admit you for a hospital stay of three days: He or she would keep you in the hospital until (and only until) you were cured! More recently, however, as the system has turned toward more punitive goals, many jurisdictions have required determinate sentences instead. Although juvenile courts' authority rarely extends past a person's eighteenth birthday, juveniles may be confined beyond that age. California is the most extreme example of this: People can remain subject to the California Youth Authority until their twenty-fifth birthday.

As you may recall, early reformers were appalled at the conditions within the Houses of Refuge. Unfortunately, problems persist in many juvenile facilities today. The most disturbing of these are overcrowding, violence, and lack of treatment programs. For an extensive discussion of these problems, see the Internet resources listed in Box 16.4 and on the text Web site under "juvenile courts."

---

## BOX 16.4

## Useful Internet Sites on Juvenile Courts

Below are a few Internet resources for juvenile courts. You may find others on the text Web site under "juvenile courts."

Office of Juvenile Justice and Delinquency Prevention
http://ojjdp.ncjrs.org/

Justice Information Center
http://www.ncjrs.org/

National Center for Juvenile Justice
http://www.ncjj.org/

Center on Juvenile and Community Justice
http://www.cjcj.org/

---

## THE CHALLENGES TODAY

In 1997, 2.8 million people under the age of 18 were arrested in the United States, and juvenile courts handled nearly 1.8 million cases. This was a 48 percent increase since 1988 and a 400 percent increase since 1960 (Stahl, 2000; Puzzanchera et al., 2000). As a result, juvenile cases are facing increasing delays in processing. The median time for case processing increased 26 percent between 1985 and 1994. Although professional standards recommend completing a juvenile case within 90 days, in the more populous jurisdictions, nearly half the cases in 1994 exceeded this limit (Butts, 1997).

If the juvenile court system was already overburdened in the early 1900s, what is the case today? Are juvenile courts giving youths either justice or help? Short of spending millions and millions more dollars, what is to be done?

One solution to juvenile court overcrowding is to transfer more youths to adult courts. Many states have done just that in recent years. As discussed above, in the last decade nearly every state has increased the circumstances under which juveniles can be transferred to criminal court, and the number of cases that have been transferred has increased as well (Snyder, Sickmund, and Poe-Yamagata, 2000). Of course, this doesn't really solve the overcrowding problem: It merely shifts the problem to the adult courts, which are already overcrowded themselves.

Furthermore, there are several fundamental arguments against treating juveniles as adults. First, many assert that it is inappropriate to treat children as adults when children are incapable of an adult's comprehension of the consequences of their acts and are unable to make adult-like decisions. This was the basis of the common law infancy defense (see Step 2 for more information on infancy and other defenses). Second, treating children as adults often means housing them with adult prisoners. This frequently leads to victimization of the children. Finally, it is argued, children are still malleable. Rather than lock them up in prisons, where they are only likely to become more criminal, why not try to reform them?

Besides overcrowding, juvenile courts are facing other significant challenges as well. One is the overrepresentation of minorities, and especially African Americans, in the juvenile justice system (Bishop and Frazier, 1996). At every stage, from arrest through disposition, black youths are overrepresented, and this cannot be entirely accounted for by differential offense rates. In 1999, the United States Office of Juvenile Justice and Delinquency Prevention concluded that, "There is substantial evidence of widespread disparity in juvenile case processing . . . [T]here is substantial evidence that minority youth are often treated differently from majority youth within the juvenile justice system" (Snyder and Sickmund, 1999, p. 193). Clearly, this is cause for great concern.

Another problem faced by the courts is how to deal with a wide variety of offenders. In 1997, 78 percent of juvenile arrests were for nonviolent offenses; 54 percent of males and 73 percent of females who enter the juvenile justice system never return a second time (Snyder and Sickmund, 1999). The most violent crimes—homicide, rape, robbery, and aggravated assault—comprised only 6 percent of arrests (Stahl, 2000). Can the same system effectively deal with this small minority while also dealing with the large majority of youths who are nonviolent and nonrepeat offenders?

Yet another issue confronting the juvenile courts today is a fundamental reassessment of their role. As we've discussed, the initial purpose of the courts was rehabilitative. In the 1990s, however, the focus became increasingly punitive, largely in response to inaccurate public perceptions that the juvenile crime rate was spiraling out of control (Feld, 1993; Lederman, 1999). But is this harsh approach appropriate, especially considering that most juveniles are nonviolent and will grow out of their criminal behavior (Klein, 1998)? And if the goal of the juvenile courts is to be punishment, why bother having them at all? They would be merely duplicating (poorly, some would argue) the purpose of the adult courts (Feld, 1993).

But if the punitive ideal is ultimately rejected and the courts return to the therapeutic ideal, substantial difficulties remain. Individualized treatment demands a great deal of discretion on the part of the courts; how can this be balanced with the due process protections required by *Gault*? Can justice and social work be dispensed by the same entity, especially if that entity is overloaded with cases? Some commentators have argued that this is simply impossible (see, e.g., Feld, 1993).

All of these challenges are so significant that it is unclear whether the juvenile courts will survive far into their second century. One commentator referred to it as a "bankrupt legal institution" (Melton, 1989). At the very least, it seems inevitable that they will be substantially reorganized, but the question remains of how to do this.

## ANSWERING THE CHALLENGE

One model that has been advocated is to simply abolish juvenile courts. As one criminologist (Feld, 1999) noted, "The fundamental shortcoming of the traditional juvenile court is not a failure of implementation but a failure of conception" (p. 358). Instead of a separate juvenile system, youths can be tried as adults and legislatures can create additional safeguards to protect them, such as providing for expungement of their records after they have served their sentences. "Full parity in criminal courts, coupled with alternative legislative safeguards for children, can provide the same or greater protections than does the current juvenile court" (Feld, 1999, p. 366).

A less drastic approach is to restructure the operation of juvenile courts. One recommendation is to extend juvenile court authority over a broad variety of youth and family concerns, including abuse and neglect (Lewis, 1999). The juvenile court was originally conceived to operate this way, as a large number of delinquent children are abuse or neglect victims. Increasing jurisdiction this way could improve prevention and increase treatment options.

A third recommendation is to increase the courts' use of early intervention programs (Lederman, 1999). Ideally, of course, intervention should occur before a child ever breaks the law. Improvement of services to at-risk youth could accomplish this. But once the law has been violated, the juvenile courts can still act to prevent future and more serious offenses.

One attempt at this has been the **drug court** movement. Most drug courts have been aimed at adults, but a significant minority have been created expressly for juvenile offenders. As with adults, many juvenile crimes can be traced to substance abuse. Drug courts employ intensive supervision, treatment programs, drug testing, and aftercare programs (Roberts, Brophy, and Cooper, 1997). Offenders who succeed at eliminating substance abuse and illegal behavior can avoid punitive sanctions. Although these programs can be expensive in the short run, the hope is that they will reduce recidivism in the long run. They also have the advantage of closely meeting the juvenile courts' rehabilitative ideals.

Another recent innovation is **teen courts** (sometimes called youth or peer courts). These are aimed at first-time offenders, and usually for relatively minor offenses. In a teen court, volunteer youths serve as attorneys (usually mentored by real lawyers), jurors, clerks, bailiffs, and sometimes judges. The offenders must admit their guilt, and the jury determines an appropriate sentence. Typical dispositions include community service, apology letters, teen court jury duty, substance abuse classes, and restitution (Butts, Hoffman, and Buck, 1999). Proponents of these courts believe that they will educate youths about the justice system and hold them accountable for their actions. It is also hoped that teens will be particularly responsive to the sanctions of their peers, as opposed to those of adults. As of 1999, there were more than 650 teen courts in the United States, with plans for many more in the works (OJJDP, 2000).

Because both drug courts and teen courts are new, it remains to be seen how effective they are in achieving their goals and also what other innovations for the juvenile courts are in store.

## THE FUTURE

What kind of courts will the Gerry Gaults and other youths of the future be facing? Will the juvenile justice system ever achieve what it promised to a century ago? If so, how? Or have the juvenile courts been merely a lengthy and unsuccessful experiment that should now be abandoned?

Nobody without a crystal ball can answer these questions today. One thing can be predicted with great certainty, however: Juvenile courts and the treatment of juvenile offenders will continue to be issues of great interest and importance to policymakers, researchers, and the public at large.

## DISCUSSION QUESTIONS

1. What is the relationship, historically and today, between the economy and delinquency?
2. The doctrine of *parens patriae* allows the government to step in and take over the parenting role, even against the wishes of a child's actual parent. When should the government be allowed to contravene parental power when it comes to raising a child?
3. What are the advantages and disadvantages of each of the distinctions between juvenile and adult courts?
4. What kind of educational and professional background should a juvenile court judge have?
5. Discuss the pros and cons of granting juvenile court judges broad discretion.
6. While the entire U.S. Supreme Court appeared highly skeptical of the juvenile justice system, the justices did not agree on how to "fix" it. Do you agree with the majority that the problems would be remedied through the imposition of due process protections?
7. Discuss whether juveniles should be granted the right to a jury trial. In some states, (e.g., California) juvenile court adjudications can count as the first two of a person's "three strikes." This

means the person need commit only one felony as an adult to receive life imprisonment. Should this affect juvenile's access to jury trials?

8. What factors should be considered in decided whether to try a juvenile as an adult? Who should make this decision: legislatures, prosecutors, or judges?

9. Should minors be permitted to waive their rights to counsel?

10. Given that severe budgetary restraints usually exist, how can we assure that juveniles receive effective assistance of counsel?

11. What can be done to address the overrepresentation of minority youths in the juvenile justice system?

12. What do you see as the role of juvenile courts today? How does that differ from the role of adult criminal courts?

13. Should juvenile courts be considered a failed experiment and abolished? If not, how should they be restructured?

14. How would you measure the effectiveness of a teen court program? Would you support such a program where you live?

15. What do you think the juvenile courts will be like 25 years from now? 100 years?

## REFERENCES

Ainsworth, J.E. (1991). Re-imagining childhood and reconstructing the legal order: The case for abolishing the juvenile court. *North Carolina Law Review,* 69: 1083–1100.

Ayers, W. (1997). *A Kind and Just Parent: The Children of Juvenile Court.* Boston: Beacon.

Bishop, D.M., and Frazier, C.E. (1996). Race effects in juvenile justice decision-making: Findings of a statewide analysis. *Journal of Criminal Law and Criminology,* 86: 392–413.

Bragg, R. (2000, June 22). When a child is accused of killing the law stays firm. *The New York Times,* p. A18.

*Breed v. Jones,* 421 U.S. 519 (1975).

Butts, J. (1997). *Delays in Juvenile Court Processing of Delinquency Cases.* Washington, DC: U.S. Department of Justice, Office of Justice Programs, Office of Juvenile Justice and Delinquency Prevention.

Butts, J., Hoffman, D., and Buck, J. (1999). *Teen courts in the United States: A profile of current programs.* Washington, DC: Department of Justice, Office of Justice Programs, Office of Juvenile Justice and Delinquency Prevention.

Davis, S., Scott, E.S., Wadlington, W., and Whitebread, C.H. (1997). *Children in the Legal System: Cases and Materials* (2nd ed.). Westbury, NY: Foundation Press.

*Ex Parte Crouse,* 4 Wharton Reports 9 (PA 1839).

*Fare v. Michael C.,* 442 U.S. 707 (1979).

Feld, B.C. (1993). Criminalizing the American juvenile court. *Crime and Justice: An Annual Review,* 17, 197–267.

Feld, B.C. (Ed.). (1999). *Readings in Juvenile Justice Administration.* New York: Oxford University Press.

Gold, S. (2000, August 24). Girls won't be charged in death of boy. *Los Angeles Times,* p. 3.

*In re Gault,* 387 U.S. 1 (1967).

*In re Winship,* 397 U.S. 358 (1970).

*Kent v. United States,* 383 U.S. 541 (1966).

Klein, E. (1998). Dennis the Menace or Billy the Kid: An analysis of the role of transfer to criminal court in juvenile justice. *American Criminal Law Review,* 35: 371–408.

Lederman, C.S. (1999). The juvenile court: Putting research to work for prevention. *Juvenile Justice,* 6(2): 22–31.

Lewis, J.D. (1999). An evolving juvenile court: On the front lines with Judge J. Dean Lewis. *Juvenile Justice,* 6(2): 3–12.

Mack, J. (1909). The juvenile court. *Harvard Law Review,* 23: 104–122.

*McKeiver v. Pennsylvania,* 403 U.S. 528 (1971).

Melton, G. (1989). Taking *Gault* seriously: Toward a new juvenile court. *Nebraska Law Review,* 68: 146–181.

Office of Juvenile Justice and Delinquency Prevention. (2000). *OJJDP Annual Report, 1999.* Washington, DC: U.S. Department of Justice, Office of Justice Programs, Office of Juvenile Justice and Delinquency Prevention.

Podkopacz, M.R., and Feld, B.C. (1996). The end of the line: An empirical study of judicial waiver. *Journal of Criminal Law and Criminology,* 86: 449–492.

Puzzanchera, C. Stahl, A., Finnegan, T., Snyder, H., Poole, R., and Tierney, N. (2000). *Juvenile Court Statistics 1997.* Washington, DC: U.S. Department of Justice, Office of Justice Programs, Office of Juvenile Justice and Delinquency Prevention.

Roberts, M., Brophy, J., and Cooper, C. (1997). *The Juvenile Court Movement.* Washington, DC: Department of Justice, Office of Justice Programs, Office of Juvenile Justice and Delinquency Prevention.

Roush, D.W. (1996) *Desktop Guide to Good Juvenile Detention Practice.* Washington, DC: U.S. Department of Justice, Office of Justice Programs, Office of Juvenile Justice and Delinquency Prevention.

Rubin, H.T. (1985). *Juvenile justice: Policy, practice, and law* (2nd ed.). New York: Random House.

Ryerson, E. (1978). *The Best-Laid Plans: America's Juvenile Court Experiment.* New York: Hill and Wang.

*Schall v. Martin,* 476 U.S. 253 (1984).

Snyder, H., and Sickmund, M. (1999). *Juvenile Offenders and Victims: 1999 National Report.* Washington, DC: Department of Justice, Office of Justice Programs, Office of Juvenile Justice and Delinquency Prevention.

Snyder, H., Sickmund, M., and Poe-Yamagata, E. (2000). *Juvenile Transfers to Criminal Court in the 1990s: Lessons Learned from Four Studies.* Washington, DC: U.S. Department of Justice, Office of Justice Programs, Office of Juvenile Justice and Delinquency Prevention.

Stahl, A.L. (2000). *Delinquency Cases in Juvenile Courts, 1997.* Washington, DC: Department of Justice, Office of Justice Programs, Office of Juvenile Justice and Delinquency Prevention.

Streib, V.L. (1987). *Death Penalty for Juveniles.* Bloomington: Indiana University Press.

Torbet, P., and Szymanski, L. (1998). *State Legislative Responses to Violent Juvenile Crime: 1996–1997 Update.* Washington, DC: U.S. Department of Justice, Office of Justice Programs, Office of Juvenile Justice and Delinquency Prevention.

# Glossary

❖

**acquittal** A defendant is acquitted if the prosecution fails to prove **beyond a reasonable doubt** that the accused is guilty. Acquittal is not the same as being found innocent; it merely implies that the prosecution was unable to prove legal guilt.

*actus reus*. An action (or omission of an obligatory action) that breaks the law. Compare to *mens rea,* which is a guilty state of mind. Both are required before an action can be considered a crime.

**administrative regulations** Rules enacted by regulatory agencies to govern certain activities, for example, FDA rules regulating food packaging or FAA rules regarding airline safety.

**adversarial system** A legal system in which opposing teams representing the prosecution and defense "battle" in court to try and determine the facts of a case. In an adversarial system, the judge's role is that of a neutral party who oversees the legal proceedings, and the accused is presumed innocent until proven guilty. Contrast with **inquisitorial system.**

**aggravators** Aggravating factors in a case are those that can serve as legal justifications for imposing a more serious sentence (e.g., serious harm to victim). Contrast with **mitigators.**

**allocution, right to** See **right to allocution.**

**appeal** A request to a higher court to review the decision of a lower court.

**appellant** The person or party an appealing a court's decision.

**appellee** The person or party named in appellate lawsuit. Sometimes called the "respondent."

**appellate court** A court that does not conduct trials; rather, appellate courts hear appeals arising from trials. Contrast with **trial courts,** which conduct trials to determine the facts of a case.

**arraignment** Hearing in court at which charges against the accused are formally read in court, and the accused has the opportunity to enter a plea.

**attrition** A decrease or lessening.

**bail bondsagent** Also known as a bail bonds person, bail bondsagents are professionals who, for a fee (typically, 10 percent of the total bond), will post bail on behalf of an accused person.

**bailee** A person who is released from jail on bail pending his or her next court hearing.

**bench trial** A trial where the accused waives the right to a jury trial and is tried by the judge instead.

**bounty hunter** Also known as skip tracers, bounty agents, and other terms. Refers to individuals who track down **bailees** who have skipped bail and fled.

**brief** A document that outlines the basic facts of the case, the argument being made by the party filing the brief, and lists cases serving as supporting precedents.

**burden of proof** The responsibility for meeting a legal standard of proof.

**case-in-chief** The main body of the case presented by the prosecution and the defense in court.

**cases of first impression** Cases raising new legal issues that have not previously appeared in court.

**celerity** Speed or swiftness of punishment.

**certification** Transfer of a juvenile from the jurisdiction of the juvenile court to an adult court. Typically, this is done only for certain serious crimes or for juveniles who have demonstrated that they are not amenable to the treatment that would be imposed in a juvenile court.

**certiorari** A request to the U.S. Supreme Court to review a case. If the Supreme Court decides to accept a case for review, it is commonly referred to as "granting cert."

**change of venue** A request to move a trial from the geographic jurisdiction where a crime occurred to one where there is a better chance of securing an impartial jury.

**charge bargain** A **plea bargain** in which a defendant pleads guilty in exchange for a reduction in the severity of charges she or he faces.

**charge to the jury** The judge's instructions to the jurors on their legal duties and responsibilities in the case.

**circuit court** One of the thirteen multi-state jurisdictions into which the federal courts have been divided.

**circumstantial evidence** Evidence from which an inference can be drawn that implies a fact. Compare with **direct evidence**.

**civil court** A court that has jurisdiction over civil matters and lawsuits resulting from **torts**, breaches of contracts, or other situations in which an individual seeks financial compensation from, or cease-and-desist orders against, another party following harm suffered at the other's hands.

**classicalism** Classical theorists believe that behavior is freely chosen and therefore reflects free will (and thus, may be deterred).

**codified law** Law based on written codes (statutes) that are maintained by the government. Modern codified laws are enacted by legislative bodies empowered to carry out that task. Compare with **common law**, which involves unwritten, but generally understood, law codes.

**cognizable group** A legal term referring to a group of people recognizable as having a high likelihood of sharing common experiences and/or attitudes.

**common law** Also called uncodified law. Law that is not written down in any one central place like a legal register. Common law is based on custom, tradition, and principles that govern behavior. Compare with **codified law**, which involves written law codes.

**community service** A penalty in which an offender is ordered to work without compensation for a charity or government agency.

**concurrent jurisdiction** When applied to the juvenile courts, this means that both the juvenile and adult courts have jurisdiction over certain cases.

**concurrent sentence** A type of sentence that allows offenders to serve multiple terms at the same time, so the offender spends only the longest term in detention. Compare with **consecutive sentences**.

**conditional release** Individuals who receive this form of release are expected to comply with the conditions set by the court (e.g., avoiding one's victim). Those who do not cooperate may be reincarcerated.

**confrontation clause** The Sixth Amendment's provision that the accused has the right to confront the witness(es) against him or her.

**consecutive sentence** A type of sentence in which offenders must serve multiple terms one after the other so that when one term is completed the next begins. Compare with **concurrent sentences**.

**conspiracy** The planning of or agreement to commit a crime by two or more people.

**corporal** Physical, applied to the body, as in physical punishment.

**count bargain** A **plea bargain** in which a defendant pleads guilty in exchange for a reduction in the number of counts she or he faces.

**courts of general jurisdiction** Trial courts that may hear all types of cases, including felonies and significant civil cases.

**courts of original jurisdiction** Trial courts.

**courts of limited jurisdiction** Trial courts that hear misdemeanors, small claims, and other less serious cases.

**courts of record** Courts in which official transcripts are made during the proceedings to serve as a record for potential future appeals.

**crime** An act of commission or omission that is legally prohibited. Requires presence of both *actus reus* and *mens rea*.

**Crime Control Model** A model, created by Herbert Packer, of the criminal justice process that emphasizes protecting society through reliance on an effective system that punishes crime. Contrast with the **Due Process Model**.

**cross-examination** When a witness testifying in court is questioned by the attorney opposing the party that called the witness to testify. In criminal trials, the prosecution is given the opportunity to cross-examine defense witnesses and the defense may cross-examine prosecution witnesses. Compare with **direct examination**.

**day fines** Financial penalties that are assigned based on day-units (i.e., a proportion of a person's daily income). Compare with **fines**.

**death penalty** Also referred to as capital punishment, the death penalty involves the taking of an offender's life by the state as a punishment for crime.

**defendant** The person accused of a crime or a civil offense.

**defense of others** A legal defense based on the principle that coming to the defense of others is permissible if the defendant believes that force is necessary to protect others or to prevent a violent felony.

**deposit bail** See **percentage bail**.

**deposition** A sworn statement given out of court by a person involved in the case.

**deterrence** See **general deterrence** and **specific deterrence**.

**direct evidence** Evidence that on its face directly indicates a fact. Compare with **circumstantial evidence**.

**direct examination** When a witness testifying in court is questioned by an attorney representing the party that called the witness to testify. In criminal trials, prosecution witnesses are directly examined by the prosecution, whereas direct examination of defense witnesses is completed by the defense. Compare with **cross-examination**.

**discovery** The process whereby prosecution and defense exchange information in order to prepare for trial.

**discretion** The power to choose among alternatives. In the legal system, it is the power or ability to act according to one's judgment or beliefs. Whenever legal system personnel have total discretion, they may do whatever they feel is appropriate. In contrast, those who lack discretion must act according to specific guidelines. Usually, when legal system personnel have discretion it is somehow circumscribed within at least some guidelines. No matter how vile a judge feels a burglar is, for example, she or he cannot sentence the burglar to death.

**discrimination** Differences in outcomes that may be attributed to prejudice or bias.

**disparities** Differences in outcomes, not necessarily due to **discrimination**.

**district courts** Federal courts of original jurisdiction.

**drug court team** Courtroom actors in specialized drug courts who work together as a team to ensure that drug addicts are provided with appropriate services and supervision to help them deal with their addictions. Drug court teams include judges, attorneys, probation officers, treatment center staff, and other personnel.

**Due Process Model** A model, created by Herbert Packer, of the criminal justice process that emphasizes protecting the due process rights of the accused. Contrast with **Crime Control Model**.

**duty to retreat** The legal requirement that an individual must attempt to retreat from the situation before acting in self-defense.

**ecclesiastical courts** Courts that hear cases arising in church settings, such as excommunication cases. Modern ecclesiastical courts are nonsecular and cannot impose criminal penalties.

**electronic monitoring** A technological advance that involves offenders wearing electronic anklets or wristlets that alert authorities if they leave their homes. Usually coupled with **home detention**.

**en banc.** Refers to the circumstance where an appeal is heard by all of the judges in the appellate court sitting together as a group rather than being heard by a smaller group, most often three judges per case. Typically, it is only particularly significant cases that are heard en banc.

**enhancements** Laws that authorize harsher sentences when certain criteria are met, such as the use of a firearm during the commission of a crime or evidence of a central role in the offense.

**evidence**  Material admitted to trial to support a fact introduced at trial.

**exclusionary rule**  A product of the 1914 U.S. Supreme Court decision in *Weeks v. United States*, this rule excludes illegally obtained evidence from being admitted at trial.

**explicit plea bargain**  A formal **plea bargain** in which a concession, typically for a reduced sentence, is offered to the defendant in exchange for his or her pleading guilty. Compare to **implicit plea bargain.**

*ex post facto*  Latin for "after the fact." *Ex post facto* laws are those that are retroactively applied to actions that took place before the law was enacted. Such laws are forbidden by the U.S. Constitution because defendants must have **fair notice** that their actions could result in punishment. Also refers to Constitutional prohibitions against retroactively applying a law.

**extra-legal factors**  Factors which legally should not influence legal decisions (such as the verdict or sentence) in a case. **Also called extra-evidential factors**.

**fair notice**  Refers to the legal requirement that individuals must be forewarned that actions they are planning will be treated as illegal, for example, through laws prohibiting and penalizing certain actions.

**felony murder rule**  Under this law, an offender can be prosecuted for a murder that occurred during the commission of certain serious felonies, such as rape or robbery, even if the offender did not intend the death.

**fines**  Financial penalties in which offenders are ordered to pay the state (or other level of government) a certain sum of money as punishment for breaking a law.

**foreseeability**  The idea that the offender knew or should have known that harm could occur from his or her behavior.

**fully secured bail**  A system whereby the accused deposits with the court either the full bail amount or property worth the full bond amount. If the individual absconds, the secured bail is forfeited.

**general deterrence**  General deterrence takes place when the community in general (as opposed to specific punished criminals) are deterred from criminal acts because they know criminals are punished and they do not wish to be punished. Compare to **specific deterrence**, which occurs when criminals themselves are prevented from committing future crimes because they have been punished and do not wish to be punished again. Deterrence is one of the five sentencing philosophies.

**general jurisdiction courts**  See **courts of general jurisdiction**.

**grand jury**  A panel of 12 to 23 citizens who are impaneled to serve a specified term of service, ranging from less than one month to two years, during which grand jury members may investigate a variety of different legal matters arising in their geographic jurisdiction.

*guardian ad litem* A person appointed by a court to safeguard the interests of a minor or incompetent individual in a lawsuit or other legal proceeding. Sometimes, a *guardian ad litem* is appointed in cases of suspected abuse or neglect, or in pending divorce cases.

**habeas corpus** Latin for "you have the body." A writ of *habeas corpus* is a legal document ordering the government to show that the incarceration of a certain person is legal.

**harmless error** A legal error that an appeals court determines did not change the outcome of the case.

**hierarchical jurisdiction** Refers to the hierarchical arrangement of the court system from lower courts to higher courts. Decisions rendered in higher courts are legally binding on the lower courts in the same geographic jurisdiction.

**holding** An appellate court's holding provides the court's decision, the case facts that were the basis for the decision, and the judicial reasoning underlying the decision. The holding in a case establishes a precedent for use in other cases.

**home detention** A sanction in which offenders are ordered to stay in their homes in place of incarceration in a facility.

**horizontal prosecution** Different prosecutors work on the case as it proceeds through each legal stage. In horizontal prosecution schemes, one prosecutor may handle the preliminary hearings while another handles the trial. Compare with **vertical prosecution.**

**hung jury** A jury that cannot reach agreement in a case requiring a **unanimous** verdict.

**impartial** Fair and unbiased.

**implicit plea bargain** An informal **plea bargain** in which a defendant expects, but has not been promised, some form of leniency in exchange for pleading guilty.

**incapacitation** Involves attempts to physically restrain offenders from victimizing others, e.g., through incarceration or other means designed to prevent the commission of crimes. Incapacitation is one of the five sentencing philosophies.

**indeterminate sentencing** Judges decide whether offenders will be sent to prison. A parole board later determines when each offender will be released, meaning that similar offenders may serve different sentences due to dissimilarity in their perceived suitability for release.

**indictment** A formal statement of charges issued when a grand jury determines there is sufficient evidence that the accused committed the crime to initiate a trial.

**informal probation** See **probation**.

**information** A document which formally lists the charges against the defendant.

**inquisitorial system** A system of justice in which an accused citizen is presumed guilty and may be required in court to prove his or her innocence. Contrast with **adversarial system** of justice.

**intensive supervision probation** See **probation**.

**intent** One's plans or purposes. May differ from one's **motivation** (i.e., the goal underlying one's purposeful actions). For example, one's motivation in some thefts could be to feed one's family, but the intent is still to steal.

**jail** County-operated facility for incarceration of those convicted of misde-meanors. Jails also hold offenders awaiting trial and those awaiting transfer to **prison**. Some variations of jail sentences include: **weekend sentences** (in which offenders serve time only on the weekends), **work release** (in which offenders are released to work, but return to the facility each evening), and **study release** (in which students are temporarily released to attend classes but return each evening). Sometimes, **home detention** is used in place of jail time.

**judicial review** This power allows the U.S. Supreme Court and the supreme courts of each state to review legislation, court desisions, and executive acts which are challenged in court in order to determine their constitutionality.

**judicial waiver** A waiver issued by a juvenile court judge under certain circum-stances, transferring a juvenile case to adult court.

**jury nullification** Refers to juries returning a verdict that is inconsistent with the evidence; in essence nullifying the law.

**jury of one's peers** A jury composed of members of the defendant's community (usually interpreted today to mean the county where the defendant resides).

**jury pool** The group of potential jurors from which actual jurors are drawn. Also called the **venire**.

**just deserts** See *lex talionis*.

**law in action** A term referring to how laws and legal procedures are actually implemented. Compare with **law on the books**.

**law on the books** A term referring to laws and legal procedures as they are writ-ten. Compare with **law in action**.

*lex talionis* Latin for "an eye for an eye." *Lex talionis* is sometimes described as "just deserts" and is based on the idea of retaliation, referring to whatever penalty a person deserves for the harm she or he caused another. The phrase comes from the ancient belief that anyone who put out the eye of a victim deserved to have his or her own eye put out. *Lex talionis* limited the retaliation to whatever harm was equal to that experienced by the victim. In other words, one could not expect to be put to death for damaging the eye of a victim.

**limited jurisdiction courts** See **courts of limited jurisdiction**.

**magistrate** Although "magistrate" is sometimes used interchangeably with the word "judge," magistrates are typically judicial officials who have limited powers (e.g., justices of the peace) or are authorized to conduct only certain functions (e.g., issue warrants, conduct preliminary or pretrial hearings).

*Magna Charta* Latin for "The Great Charter." A historic document providing certain due process rights to English subjects, signed by King John in 1215.

**mens rea** A (legally) guilty state of mind, sometimes referred to as having intent to do a certain act. Compare to *actus reus*, which is any action that breaks the law. Both are required before an action can be considered a crime.

**merit system** A method of selecting judges that relies, at least in part, on an assessment of their merits by a judicial nominating commission. Also called the **Missouri Plan**.

**Missouri Plan** See **merit system**.

**mistrial** A trial that is stopped by the judge because an unanticipated problem occurred that could prevent the accused from getting a fair trial. The defendant may be tried again in a new trial.

**mitigators** Mitigating factors in a case are those that can serve as legal justifications for imposing a more lenient sentence (e.g., playing a minor role in an offense). Contrast with **aggravators**.

**motion** A request to the court by an attorney asking for a ruling on a legal matter.

**motivation** The goals behind one's plans (e.g. one's motivation in stealing some items could be to prevent them from falling into the hands of minors or some other group, or one's motivation in vandalism could be to protest the fur trade). Motivation may differ from **intent**, or one's actual purpose in the behavior—to commit theft or to destroy property.

**negligent** Careless. There are different degrees of legal negligence in civil law, ranging from minor negligence to gross negligence.

**no drop policies** Refers to prosecutorial policies that specify charges will not be dropped even if the victim refuses to press charges.

**nolo contendere** A plea of "no contest" to a legal charge. Nolo contendere pleas are essentially guilty pleas.

**nonpartisan** Refers to elections in which the candidates are not identified by political party.

**objection** A legal tool used by an attorney to object to the content or format of an opposing attorney's statement in court.

**original jurisdiction, courts of** See **courts of original jurisdiction**.

*parens patriae* Refers to the state as parent.

**parole** When an offender is released from custody to be supervised in the community. Compare with **probation**, which is supervision in the community *instead of* (rather than *after*) incarceration.

**partisan** Refers to elections in which the candidates are identified by political party.

**penalty phase jury** A jury that decides between imposing the death penalty or other sentences, such as life in prison.

**percentage bail** Also known as **deposit bail**, this is a system in which the accused deposits a percentage (generally 10 percent) of the total bail amount with the court. If the individual absconds, the full amount is forfeited and payable on demand.

**peremptory challenge** A legal tool by which an attorney can ask that a potential juror be dismissed during **voir dire**, typically without giving any reason for the request.

**petit jury** Twelve (or sometimes fewer) people selected to hear the issues in a particular case. The formal term for "regular" juries; contrast with **grand jury**.

**plea bargaining** A negotiation process, typically between a prosecutor and defense attorney, in which the parties work together to obtain some concession (e.g., a reduced sentence) for the defendant in exchange for the defendant agreeing to plead guilty. The process avoids the need to go to trial, so it appeals to both attorneys, who typically seek to avoid the uncertainty represented by going to trial.

**positivism** The positivist perspective holds that behavior is influenced at least in part by a variety of factors (e.g., genetic makeup or environment), thus, behavior does not totally reflect free will.

**preliminary** (or **probable cause**) **hearing** A hearing at which the police must demonstrate that probable cause existed to arrest the suspect, and the prosecutor must demonstrate that there is sufficient evidence against the accused to proceed with the case. The judge may also set bail for the accused at the preliminary hearing.

**Pre-Sentence Investigation report** Also called a **PSI**, this report contains a variety of information about the offender and his or her offense for a judge to consider when imposing sentence. Written by a probation officer, the report also includes the author's professional opinion regarding an appropriate penalty.

**presumptive sentencing** Refers to a sentencing approach in which an appointed sentencing commission made up of criminal justice personnel and private citizens sets up varying sentencing for individual offenses. The guidelines are mandatory, although judges may depart from them if they provide their reasons for doing so.

**preventative detention** Refers to detaining a person suspected or convicted of a crime who is believed to pose a danger to another person or to the community in general. For pre-trial defendants, this may be achieved by refusing to grant bail to an individual accused of a crime. Legal mechanisms are sometimes employed to continue the incarceration of convicted felons who have finished serving their sentences, but who are still felt to pose a danger to others.

**prison** State-operated (or federally operated when discussing federal offenses) facility for incarcerating those convicted of felonies.

**privately secured bail** Also known as **surety bail**, this refers to a system in which the accused contacts a **bail bondsagent**, who, for a nonrefundable fee, posts a bond for the full bail amount with the court. Generally, this fee is 10 percent of the total bail amount; most bail bondsagents require some form of collateral before bailing out a client.

**pro bono** Refers to legal work done without a fee.

**probable cause** A reasonable belief, based on facts, that a particular person has committed a crime, that a particular crime has taken or will take place, or that a search will yield particular sought-after **evidence**. Probable cause is based on facts that can be written down and that would convince a reasonable person that the belief is logical and rational.

**probable cause hearing** See **preliminary hearing**.

**probation** The goal of probation is rehabilitation of offenders through a combination of supervision and programming. Probationers remain in the community, but are supervised by probation officers, and typically must complete programming and adhere to certain conditions (e.g., abstinence from drugs, avoiding one's victim, etc.). Those who do not obey the conditions of their probation or who commit other crimes may be re-sentenced. **Informal probation** typically involves very little supervision, whereas **regular probation** involves telephone or face-to-face meetings with probation staffers and more use of programming. **Intensive supervision probation** involves regular visits with probation staffers, routine drug and/or alcohol tests, and other sometimes rigorous conditions aimed at preventing **recidivism** among more serious offenders.

**probative** Tending to prove a fact in issue.

**proportionate force** Force that is proportionate to the perceived harm it is employed to prevent.

**PSI** See **Pre-Sentence Investigation report.**

**reasonable doubt, beyond a** The highest legal standard of proof. Prosecutors must prove the guilt of the accused beyond a reasonable doubt, which is defined in jury instructions.

**recidivism** A return or relapse to crime. Recidivists continue to break laws despite having been punished for previous offenses.

**regular probation** See **probation.**

**rehabilitation** An effort to end criminal behavior by "curing" offenders of their criminality. Under rehabilitative schemes, offenders are put through treatment programs of various types, depending on their individual need. Rehabilitation is one of the five sentencing philosophies.

**released on one's own recognizance (ROR)** A defendant who is released on his or her own recognizance promises to return to court for his or her hearing. There is no bail expected or forfeited if the individual absconds, but a **warrant** may be issued for the individual's arrest.

**remedial** An action intended to remedy a problem.

**restitution** Refers to compensation paid to the victim by an offender, typically as part of an attempt to achieve **restorative justice.**

**restorative justice** A philosophy of sentencing that emphasizes "restoring" victims through restitution in the form of money or service, rather than punishing offenders. True restorative schemes aim to restore all parties to a crime, that is, victims and offenders and their communities. Restorative justice is one of the five sentencing philosophies.

**retribution** A sentencing philosophy that relies on "just deserts," or what offenders deserve to receive as punishment. Based in *lex talionis*, retribution is one of the five sentencing philosophies.

**reverse and remand** Refers to an appellate court decision to send a case under review back to the trial court with directions for the trial court to follow in handling the case. The original outcome (e.g., verdict) will be replaced with the new outcome that is obtained following the directions provided by the appellate court (e.g., to allow a certain type of testimony or to prohibit certain evidence).

**reversible error** A legal error that must be remedied by new legal proceedings.

**right to allocution** The defendant's right to speak at his or her sentencing hearing.

**selective incorporation** Refers to the process by which the U.S. Supreme Court decided that most, but not all, of the guarantees provided by the Bill of Rights are incorporated within the meaning of due process, thus making them applicable to state as well as federal legal proceedings.

**sentence bargain** A **plea bargain** in which a defendant pleads guilty in exchange for a promise of lighter or alternative sanctions.

**self defense** A legal defense that force was necessary to protect the defendant from serious and imminent harm.

**sentence bargain** A **plea bargain** in which a defendant is promised a lighter or alternative sanction in exchange for pleading guilty.

**sidebar conference** A short meeting held at the judge's bench between the judge and the attorneys during a trial. During sidebars, the three parties discuss and resolve legal issues outside the hearing of the jurors.

**specific deterrence** Specific deterrence (also known as **individual deterrence**) occurs when criminals are prevented from committing future crimes because they have been punished and do not wish to be punished again. Compare to **general deterrence**, which occurs when the population as a whole is deterred due to the punishment imposed on criminals. Deterrence is one of the five sentencing philosophies.

**standing** Having "standing" means that an appellant has a legally recognizable interest in the case.

**stare decisis** From Latin, "let the decision stand." The legal principle of respecting legal precedent. *Stare decisis* involves deciding a case by applying the rules of law found in earlier cases, provided that the facts in the current case are similar. *Stare decisis* does not apply when compelling reasons exist to modify or overturn a prior decision.

**status offense** An action that is only an offense when committed by a person who is a minor (e.g., truancy or curfew violations).

**statute of limitations** The period of time defined by statute during which charges can be filed for a crime. The statute of limitations varies by jurisdiction and type of crime; there is no statute of limitations on murder.

**statutory exclusion** In juvenile justice, statutory exclusions occur when a legislature has passed laws dictating that certain juveniles who commit certain crimes will be tried as adults.

**strict liability** Refers to the idea that an individual can incur civil liability without *mens rea*. One can receive a speeding ticket, for example, even if one did not know she or he was exceeding the speed limit. Note: This is not the same concept as absolute liability.

**study release**  See **jail**.

**subpoena**  A legal document that commands a witness to appear in court under penalty for failure to do so. A subpeona *duces tecum* is an order to produce documents (e.g., receipts or accounting records) or other items for use in an investigation or at trial.

**surety**  Also known as **surety bail**. An individual or organization who guarantees that an accused will show up for trial. Typically, sureties deposit a specified sum of money or property with the court, which will be forfeited if the accused fails to show up for trial.

**third-party custody**  Under this system, a third party (e.g., a parent, family member, or friend), assures that the defendant will return for his or her hearing.

**tort**  An act or omission that results in harm or breaks a contract.

**trial by battle**  A historical form of justice in which the defendant in a civil or criminal case would literally do battle with his or her accuser (or hire someone to do battle for him or her). The outcome of the battle was thought to reflect divine influence, so that the honest party would be the victor.

**trial by ordeal**  An ancient form of justice in which the defendant in a civil or criminal case was ordered to undergo some ordeal (e.g., walking across hot ploughshares or plucking a stone from a cauldron of boiling water) in order to prove his or her innocence. The outcome of the ordeal was thought to reflect divine influence, so that the honest party would not suffer injury.

**trial by compurgation**  Also called "trial by the swearing of oaths." A historical form of justice that required the parties to a civil or criminal case to locate a specific number of compurgators (i.e., neighbors who would vouch for the truthfulness of the party's oath that she or he was guiltless). The requirement that a party secure twelve compurgators was common.

**trial court**  Conducts trials to determine the facts of a case. In trial courts, evidence is presented and testimony is given. Contrast with **appellate courts**, which hear appeals.

*trials de novo*  When a trial must be conducted again as though it had never taken place because a transcript of the proceedings was not made. Typically, a *trial de novo* occurs when a case is appealed from a **court of limited jurisdiction** to a **court of original jurisdiction**.

**triers of fact**  The jury in a jury trial, or the judge in a bench trial.

**unanimous** In complete agreement on an outcome.

**United States Supreme Court** The highest court in the United States court hierarchy; there is no higher appeal available in this country. The role of the U.S. Supreme Court is to ensure that the lower federal courts (and the state level courts) have correctly interpreted and applied the law. The U.S. Supreme Court can find state or federal laws unconstitutional. It can also order acquittals or new trials based on violations of the U.S. Constitution or federal statutes.

**unsecured bail** A type of bail that does not require defendants to deposit any money or collateral with the court. If the defendant does not return to court, however, the full bail amount is forfeited and payable on demand.

**venire** The group of potential jurors from which actual jurors are drawn. Also called the jury panel or **jury pool**.

**vertical prosecution** Each case is followed through all stages by the same prosecutor(s). Compare with **horizontal prosecution**.

**vicarious liability** Refers to the idea that an individual can be held responsible for the conduct of another person if a particular type of legal relationship exists between the two. Employers, for example, can be punished if their employees sell cigarettes or alcohol to minors.

**voir dire** French for "to speak the truth." The process of questioning jurors during jury selection in court.

**warrant** A legal document authorizing or ordering a law enforcement officer to conduct a search or make an arrest.

**weekend sentences** See **jail**.

**work release** See **jail**.

# Index